14th Conference on Computational Natural Language Learning 2010

(CoNLL 2010)

Co-Located with ACL 2010

Uppsala, Sweden
15-16 July 2010

ISBN: 978-1-61738-813-2

Printed from e-media with permission by:

Curran Associates, Inc.
57 Morehouse Lane
Red Hook, NY 12571

CURRAN ASSOCIATES INC.
proceedings.com

Some format issues inherent in the e-media version may also appear in this print version.

Printed by Curran Associates, Inc. (2010)

Association for Computational Linguistics
209 N. Eighth Street
Stroudsburg, Pennsylvania 18360

Phone: 1-570-476-8006
Fax: 1-570-476-0860

acl@aclweb.org

Additional copies of this publication are available from:

Curran Associates, Inc.
57 Morehouse Lane
Red Hook, NY 12571 USA
Phone: 845-758-0400
Fax: 845-758-2634
Email: curran@proceedings.com
Web: www.proceedings.com

Introduction

The 2010 Conference on Computational Natural Language Learning is the fourteenth in the series of annual meetings organized by SIGNLL, the ACL special interest group on natural language learning. CONLL-2010 will be held in Uppsala, Sweden, 15-16 July 2010, in conjunction with ACL.

For our special focus this year in the main session of CoNLL, we invited papers relating to grammar induction, from a machine learning, natural language engineering and cognitive perspective. We received 99 submissions on these and other relevant topics, of which 18 were eventually withdrawn. Of the remaining 81 papers, 12 were selected to appear in the conference programme as oral presentations, and 13 were chosen as posters. All accepted papers appear here in the proceedings. Following the ACL 2010 policy we allowed an extra page in the camera ready paper for authors to incorporate reviewer comments, so each accepted paper was allowed to have nine pages plus any number of pages containing only bibliographic references.

As in previous years, CoNLL-2010 has a shared task, *Learning to detect hedges and their scope in natural language text*. The Shared Task papers are collected into an accompanying volume of CoNLL-2010.

First and foremost, we would like to thank the authors who submitted their work to CoNLL-2010. We are grateful to our invited speakers, Lillian Lee and Zoubin Ghahramani, who graciously agreed to give talks at CoNLL. Special thanks to the SIGNLL board members, Lluís Màrquez and Joakim Nivre, for their valuable advice and assistance each step of the way, and Erik Tjong Kim Sang, who acted as the information officer and maintained the CoNLL-2010 web page.

We also appreciate the help we received from the ACL programme chairs, especially Stephen Clark. The help of the ACL 2010 publication chairs, Jing-Shin Chang and Philipp Koehn, technical support by Rich Gerber from softconf.com, as well as input from Priscilla Rasmussen was invaluable in producing these proceedings.

Finally, many thanks to Google for sponsoring the best paper award at CoNLL-2010.

We hope you enjoy the conference!

Mirella Lapata and Anoop Sarkar

CoNLL 2010 Conference Chairs

Program Chairs

Mirella Lapata (University of Edinburgh, United Kingdom)
Anoop Sarkar (Simon Fraser University, Canada)

Program Committee:

Steven Abney (University of Michigan, United States)
Eneko Agirre (University of the Basque Country, Spain)
Afra Alishahi (Saarland University, Germany)
Jason Baldridge (The University of Texas at Austin, United States)
Tim Baldwin (University of Melbourne, Australia)
Regina Barzilay (Massachusetts Institute of Technology, United States)
Phil Blunsom (University of Oxford, United Kingdom)
Thorsten Brants (Google Inc., United States)
Chris Brew (Ohio State University, United States)
Nicola Cancedda (Xerox Research Centre Europe, France)
Yunbo Cao (Microsoft Research Asia, China)
Xavier Carreras (Technical University of Catalonia, Spain)
Ming-Wei Chang (University of Illinois at Urbana-Champaign, United States)
Colin Cherry (National Research Council, Canada)
Massimiliano Ciaramita (Google Research, Switzerland)
Alexander Clark (Royal Holloway, University of London, United Kingdom)
James Clarke (University of Illinois at Urbana-Champaign, United States)
Walter Daelemans (University of Antwerp, Netherlands)
Vera Demberg (University of Edinburgh, United Kingdom)
Amit Dubey (University of Edinburgh, United Kingdom)
Chris Dyer (Carnegie Mellon University, United States)
Jenny Finkel (Stanford University, United States)
Radu Florian (IBM Watson Research Center, United States)
Robert Frank (Yale University, United States)
Michel Galley (Stanford University, United States)
Yoav Goldberg (Ben Gurion University of the Negev, Israel)
Cyril Goutte (National Research Council, Canada)
Gholamreza Haffari (University of British Columbia, Canada)
Keith Hall (Google Research, Switzerland)
Marti Hearst (University of California at Berkeley, United States)
James Henderson (University of Geneva, Switzerland)
Julia Hockenmaier (University of Illinois at Urbana-Champaign, United States)
Fei Huang (IBM Research, United States)
Rebecca Hwa (University of Pittsburgh, United States)
Richard Johansson (University of Trento, Italy)
Mark Johnson (Macquarie University, Australia)
Rohit Kate (The University of Texas at Austin, United States)
Frank Keller (University of Edinburgh, United Kingdom)
Philipp Koehn (University of Edinburgh, United Kingdom)
Terry Koo (Massachusetts Institute of Technology, United States)

Shankar Kumar (Google Inc., United States)
Shalom Lappin (Kings College London, United Kingdom)
Adam Lopez (University of Edinburgh, United Kingdom)
Rob Malouf (San Diego State University, United States)
Yuji Matsumoto (Nara Institute of Science and Technology, Japan)
Takuya Matsuzaki (University of Tokyo, Japan)
Ryan McDonald (Google Inc., United States)
Paola Merlo (University of Geneva, Switzerland)
Haitao Mi (Institute of Computing Technology, Chinese Academy of Sciences, China)
Yusuke Miyao (University of Tokyo, Japan)
Raymond Mooney (University of Texas at Austin, United States)
Alessandro Moschitti (University of Trento, Italy)
Gabriele Musillo (FBK-IRST, Italy)
Mark-Jan Nederhof (University of St Andrews, United Kingdom)
Hwee Tou Ng (National University of Singapore, Singapore)
Vincent Ng (University of Texas at Dallas, United States)
Grace Ngai (Hong Kong Polytechnic University, China)
Joakim Nivre (Uppsala University, Sweden)
Franz Och (Google Inc., United States)
Miles Osborne (University of Edinburgh, United Kingdom)
Christopher Parisien (University of Toronto, Canada)
Slav Petrov (Google Research, United States)
Hoifung Poon (University of Washington, United States)
David Powers (Flinders University of South Australia, Australia)
Vasin Punyakanok (BBN Technologies, United States)
Chris Quirk (Microsoft Research, United States)
Lev Ratinov (University of Illinois at Urbana-Champaign, United States)
Roi Reichart (The Hebrew University, Israel)
Sebastian Riedel (University of Massachusetts, United States)
Ellen Riloff (University of Utah, United States)
Brian Roark (Oregon Health & Science University, United States)
Dan Roth (University of Illinois at Urbana-Champaign, United States)
William Sakas (Hunter College, United States)
William Schuler (The Ohio State University, United States)
Sabine Schulte im Walde (University of Stuttgart, Germany)
Libin Shen (BBN Technologies, United States)
Benjamin Snyder (Massachusetts Institute of Technology, United States)
Richard Sproat (Oregon Health & Science University, United States)
Mark Steedman (University of Edinburgh, United Kingdom)
Jun Suzuki (NTT Communication Science Laboratories, Japan)
Hiroya Takamura (Tokyo Institute of Technology, Japan)
Ivan Titov (Saarland University, Germany)
Kristina Toutanova (Microsoft Research, United States)
Antal van den Bosch (Tilburg University, Netherlands)
Peng Xu (Google Inc., United States)
Charles Yang (University of Pennsylvania, United States)
Daniel Zeman (Charles University in Prague, Czech Republic)
Luke Zettlemoyer (University of Washington at Seattle, United States)

Invited Speakers:

Zoubin Ghahramani, University of Cambridge and Carnegie Mellon University
Lillian Lee, Cornell University

Table of Contents

Conference Program

Thursday, July 15, 2010

9:00–9:15 Opening Remarks

Session 1: Parsing (9:15–10:30)

9:15–9:40 *Improvements in Unsupervised Co-Occurrence Based Parsing*
Christian Hänig

9:40–10:05 *Viterbi Training Improves Unsupervised Dependency Parsing*
Valentin I. Spitkovsky, Hiyan Alshawi, Daniel Jurafsky and Christopher D. Manning

10:05–10:30 *Driving Semantic Parsing from the World's Response*
James Clarke, Dan Goldwasser, Ming-Wei Chang and Dan Roth

10:30–11:00 Break

Session 2: Grammar Induction (11:00–12:15)

11:00–11:25 *Efficient, Correct, Unsupervised Learning for Context-Sensitive Languages*
Alexander Clark

11:25–11:50 *Identifying Patterns for Unsupervised Grammar Induction*
Jesús Santamaría and Lourdes Araujo

11:50–12:15 *Learning Better Monolingual Models with Unannotated Bilingual Text*
David Burkett, Slav Petrov, John Blitzer and Dan Klein

12:15–14:15 Lunch

14:15–15:30 *(Invited Talk) Clueless: Explorations in Unsupervised, Knowledge-Lean Extraction of Lexical-Semantic Information*
Lillian Lee

15:30–16:00 Break

Thursday, July 15, 2010 (continued)

CoNLL 2010 Shared Task, Overview and Oral Presentations (16:00–17:30)

16:00–16:20 *The CoNLL 2010 Shared Task: Learning to Detect Hedges and their Scope in Natural Language Text*
Richárd Farkas, Veronika Vincze, György Móra, János Csirik and György Szarvas

16:20–16:30 *A Cascade Method for Detecting Hedges and their Scope in Natural Language Text*
Buzhou Tang, Xiaolong Wang, Xuan Wang, Bo Yuan and Shixi Fan

16:30–16:40 *Detecting Speculative Language using Syntactic Dependencies and Logistic Regression*
Andreas Vlachos and Mark Craven

16:40–16:50 *A Hedgehop over a Max-margin Framework using Hedge Cues*
Maria Georgescul

16:50–17:00 *Detecting Hedge Cues and their Scopes with Average Perceptron*
Feng Ji, Xipeng Qiu and Xuanjing Huang

17:00–17:10 *Memory-based Resolution of In-sentence Scopes of Hedge Cues*
Roser Morante, Vincent Van Asch and Walter Daelemans

17:10–17:20 *Resolving Speculation: MaxEnt Cue Classification and Dependency-Based Scope Rules*
Erik Velldal, Lilja Øvrelid and Stephan Oepen

17:20–17:30 *Combining Manual Rules and Supervised Learning for Hedge Cue and Scope Detection*
Marek Rei and Ted Briscoe

Shared Task Discussion Panel (17:30–18:00)

Friday, July 16, 2010

9:15–10:30 *(Invited Talk) Bayesian Hidden Markov Models and Extensions*
Zoubin Ghahramani

10:30–11:00 Break

Joint Poster Session: Main conference and shared task posters (11:00–12:30)

11:00–12:30 Main conference posters

Improved Unsupervised POS Induction Using Intrinsic Clustering Quality and a Zipfian Constraint
Roi Reichart, Raanan Fattal and Ari Rappoport

Syntactic and Semantic Structure for Opinion Expression Detection
Richard Johansson and Alessandro Moschitti

Type Level Clustering Evaluation: New Measures and a POS Induction Case Study
Roi Reichart, Omri Abend and Ari Rappoport

Recession Segmentation: Simpler Online Word Segmentation Using Limited Resources
Constantine Lignos and Charles Yang

Computing Optimal Alignments for the IBM-3 Translation Model
Thomas Schoenemann

Semi-Supervised Recognition of Sarcasm in Twitter and Amazon
Dmitry Davidov, Oren Tsur and Ari Rappoport

Learning Probabilistic Synchronous CFGs for Phrase-Based Translation
Markos Mylonakis and Khalil Sima'an

A Semi-Supervised Batch-Mode Active Learning Strategy for Improved Statistical Machine Translation
Sankaranarayanan Ananthakrishnan, Rohit Prasad, David Stallard and Prem Natarajan

Improving Word Alignment by Semi-Supervised Ensemble
Shujian Huang, Kangxi Li, Xinyu Dai and Jiajun Chen

Friday, July 16, 2010 (continued)

A Comparative Study of Bayesian Models for Unsupervised Sentiment Detection
Chenghua Lin, Yulan He and Richard Everson

A Hybrid Approach to Emotional Sentence Polarity and Intensity Classification
Jorge Carrillo de Albornoz, Laura Plaza and Pablo Gervás

Cross-Caption Coreference Resolution for Automatic Image Understanding
Micah Hodosh, Peter Young, Cyrus Rashtchian and Julia Hockenmaier

Improved Natural Language Learning via Variance-Regularization Support Vector Machines
Shane Bergsma, Dekang Lin and Dale Schuurmans

11:00–12:30 Shared Task posters: Systems for Shared Task 1 and 2

Hedge Detection using the RelHunter Approach
Eraldo Fernandes, Carlos Crestana and Ruy Milidiú

A High-Precision Approach to Detecting Hedges and Their Scopes
Halil Kilicoglu and Sabine Bergler

Exploiting Rich Features for Detecting Hedges and Their Scope
Xinxin Li, Jianping Shen, Xiang Gao and Xuan Wang

Uncertainty Detection as Approximate Max-Margin Sequence Labelling
Oscar Täckström, Sumithra Velupillai, Martin Hassel, Gunnar Eriksson, Hercules Dalianis and Jussi Karlgren

Hedge Detection and Scope Finding by Sequence Labeling with Procedural Feature Selection
Shaodian Zhang, Hai Zhao, Guodong Zhou and Bao-liang Lu

Learning to Detect Hedges and their Scope using CRF
Qi Zhao, Chengjie Sun, Bingquan Liu and Yong Cheng

Exploiting Multi-Features to Detect Hedges and Their Scope in Biomedical Texts
Huiwei Zhou, Xiaoyan Li, Degen Huang, Zezhong Li and Yuansheng Yang

Friday, July 16, 2010 (continued)

11:00–12:30 Shared Task posters: Systems for Shared Task 1

A Lucene and Maximum Entropy Model Based Hedge Detection System
Lin Chen and Barbara Di Eugenio

HedgeHunter: A System for Hedge Detection and Uncertainty Classification
David Clausen

Uncertainty Learning using SVMs and CRFs
Vinodkumar Prabhakaran

Exploiting CCG Structures with Tree Kernels for Speculation Detection
Liliana Paola Mamani Sanchez, Baoli Li and Carl Vogel

Features for Detecting Hedge Cues
Nobuyuki Shimizu and Hiroshi Nakagawa

A Simple Ensemble Method for Hedge Identification
Ferenc Szidarovszky, Illés Solt and Domonkos Tikk

A Baseline Approach for Detecting Sentences Containing Uncertainty
Erik Tjong Kim Sang

Hedge Classification with Syntactic Dependency Features based on an Ensemble Classifier
Yi Zheng, Qifeng Dai, Qiming Luo and Enhong Chen

12:30–14:00 Lunch

Session 3: Semantics and Information Extraction (14:00–15:15)

14:00–14:25 *Online Entropy-Based Model of Lexical Category Acquisition*
Grzegorz Chrupała and Afra Alishahi

14:25–14:50 *Tagging and Linking Web Forum Posts*
Su Nam Kim, Li Wang and Timothy Baldwin

14:50–15:15 *Joint Entity and Relation Extraction Using Card-Pyramid Parsing*
Rohit Kate and Raymond Mooney

15:30–16:00 Break

Friday, July 16, 2010 (continued)

Session 4: Machine learning (16:00–17:15)

16:00–16:25 *Distributed Asynchronous Online Learning for Natural Language Processing*
Kevin Gimpel, Dipanjan Das and Noah A. Smith

16:25–16:50 *On Reverse Feature Engineering of Syntactic Tree Kernels*
Daniele Pighin and Alessandro Moschitti

16:50–17:15 *Inspecting the Structural Biases of Dependency Parsing Algorithms*
Yoav Goldberg and Michael Elhadad

Closing Session (17:15–17:45)

17:15–17:45 SIGNLL Business Meeting and Best Paper Award

Improvements in unsupervised co-occurrence based parsing

Christian Hänig
Daimler AG
Research and Technology
89081 Ulm, Germany
christian.haenig@daimler.com

Abstract

This paper presents an algorithm for unsupervised co-occurrence based parsing that improves and extends existing approaches. The proposed algorithm induces a context-free grammar of the language in question in an iterative manner. The resulting structure of a sentence will be given as a hierarchical arrangement of constituents. Although this algorithm does not use any a priori knowledge about the language, it is able to detect heads, modifiers and a phrase type's different compound composition possibilities. For evaluation purposes, the algorithm is applied to manually annotated part-of-speech tags (POS tags) as well as to word classes induced by an unsupervised part-of-speech tagger.

1 Introduction

With the growing amount of textual data available in the Internet, unsupervised methods for natural language processing gain a considerable amount of interest. Due to the very special usage of language, supervised methods trained on high quality corpora (e. g. containing newspaper texts) do not achieve comparable accuracy when being applied to data from fora or blogs. Huge annotated corpora consisting of sentences extracted from the Internet barely exist until now.

Consequential a lot of effort has been put into unsupervised grammar induction during the last years and results and performance of unsupervised parsers improved steadily. Klein and Manning (2002)'s constituent context model (CCM) obtains 51.2% f-score on ATIS part-of-speech strings. The same model achieves 71.1% on Wall Street Journal corpus sentences with length of at most 10 POS tags. In (Klein and Manning, 2004) an approach combining constituency and dependency models yields 77.6% f-score. Bod (2006)'s all-subtree approach — known as Data-Oriented Parsing (DOP) — reports 82.9% for UML-DOP. Seginer (2007)'s common cover links model (CCL) does not need any prior tagging and is applied on word strings directly. The f-score for English is 75.9%, and for German (NEGRA10) 59% is achieved. Hänig et al. (2008) present a co-occurrence based constituent detection algorithm which is applied to word forms, too (unsupervised POS tags are induced using unsuPOS, see (Biemann, 2006)). An f-score of 63.4% is reported for German data.

In this paper, we want to present a new unsupervised co-occurrence based grammar induction model based on Hänig et al. (2008). In the following section, we give a short introduction to the base algorithm *unsuParse*. Afterwards, we present improvements to this algorithm. In the final section, we evaluate the proposed model against existing ones and discuss the results.

2 Co-occurrence based parsing

It has been shown in (Hänig et al., 2008) that statistical methods like calculating significant co-occurrences and context clustering are applicable to grammar induction from raw text. The underlying assumption states that each word prefers a certain position within a phrase. Two particular cases are of special interest: a word's occurrence at the beginning of a sentence and a word's occurrence at the end of a sentence. Those positions obviously are constituent borders and can be easily used to extract syntactic knowledge. One possibility is to discover constituents employing constituency tests (see (Adger, 2003)), whereby these two cases can be used to express and use one of them in a formal way: the movement test.

Three neighbourhood co-occurrences express the aforementioned observations:

Proceedings of the Fourteenth Conference on Computational Natural Language Learning, pages 1–8,
Uppsala, Sweden, 15-16 July 2010.

- Value a denotes the significance of word A standing at the last position of a sentence (where \$ is an imaginary word to mark a sentences' end).

$$a = sig\,(A, \$) \tag{1}$$

- Contrary, variable b denotes the significance of a word B being observed at the beginning of a sentence (where ˆ is an imaginary word to mark the beginning of a sentence).

$$b = sig\,(\hat{\ }, B) \tag{2}$$

- Additionally, a third value is necessary to represent the statistical significance of the neighbourhood co-occurrence containing word A and B.

$$c = sig\,(A, B) \tag{3}$$

To compute those significance values for a corpus, the log-likelihood measure (see (Dunning, 1993)) is applied using corpus size n, term frequencies n_A and n_B (for the words A and B) and frequency n_{AB} of the co-occurrence of A and B.

To detect constituent borders between two words, a separation value sep_{AB} can be defined as:

$$sep_{AB} = \frac{a}{c} \cdot \frac{b}{c} = \frac{a \cdot b}{c^2} \tag{4}$$

If word A occurs more significantly at the end of a sentence as in front of B, then $\frac{a}{c} > 1$. Additionally, b is larger than c if B is observed more significantly at the beginning of a sentence as after A and $\frac{b}{c}$ will be > 1. In this case sep_{AB} is > 1 and obviously, a constituent border would be situated between A and B.

The basic approach to create parse trees from separation values between two adjacent words is to consecutively merge the two subtrees containing the words with the smallest separation value between them — starting with each word in a separate subtree. In order to avoid data sparseness problems, co-occurrences and separation values are primarily calculated on part-of-speech tags. However, word co-occurrences will be used to preserve word form specific dependencies.

In this paper, we want to present *unsuParse+* — an extension of this co-occurrence based approach. The first extension is the distinction between endocentric and exocentric elements which introduces the detection of heads along with their modifiers (see section 2.2). Furthermore, learning of recursive constructions is facilitated. Secondly, we will consider discontiguous dependencies and present a possibility to detect rare constructions like complex noun phrases (see section 2.3). As third enhancement, we employ a simple clustering algorithm to induced phrases in order to detect constituents holding identical syntactic functions. Those phrases will be labeled the same way instead of by different phrase numbers (see section 2.4).

First, we will start with the detection of constituent candidates.

2.1 Detection of constituent borders

Instead of using sep_{AB} to detect constituent borders we use neighbourhood co-occurrence significances on account of an experiment in (Hänig et al., 2008) showing that the pure significance value c is sufficient.

Furthermore, we do not restrict the detection of phrases to bigrams and allow the detection of arbitrary n-grams. The motivation behind this is basically caused by coordinating conjunctions for which discussions on the *correct*[1] structure are raised. While Chomsky (1965) argues in favor of symmetric multiple-branching coordinating constructions (see Figure 1), recent discussions in the context of unification grammars (especially head-driven phrase structure grammar (see (Pollard and Sag, 1994)) prefer asymmetric endocentric constructions (see (Kayne, 1995) and (Sag, 2002)). The corresponding structure can be seen in Figure 2. Nevertheless, a symmetric construction containing two heads seems to be more appropriate for some languages (e. g. German, see (Lang, 2002)).

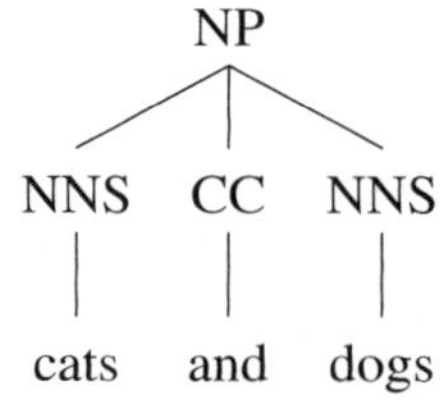

Figure 1: Symmetric coordinating conjunction

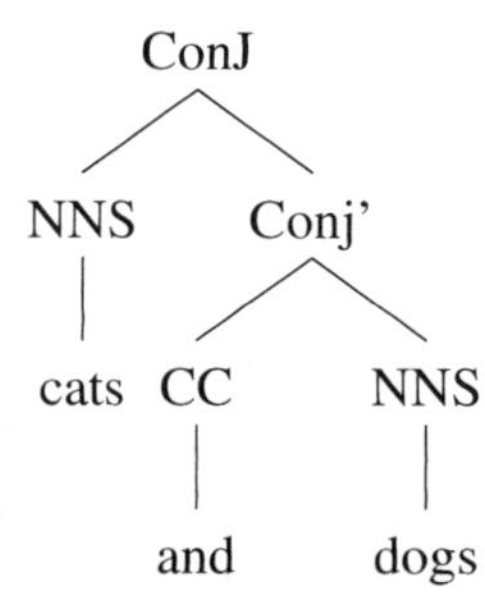

Figure 2: Asymmetric coordinating conjunction

[1]correct meaning considered to be correct

Thus, the presented algorithm is able to deal with phrases containing any number of compounds.

As in (Hänig et al., 2008), phrases will be learned in an iterative manner (see details in section 2.5). Within each iteration, the n-gram P yielding the highest significance is considered to be the best candidate for being a valid constituent.

$$P = [p_0 \ \cdots \ p_{n-1}] \tag{5}$$

The preferred position of part-of-speech tags is maintained as we define $pref\,(A)$ for every POS tag A. This value is initialized as the ratio of two particular significances as in Equ. 6:

$$pref\,(A) = \frac{sig\,(\hat{}, A)}{sig\,(A, \$)} \tag{6}$$

Analogous to sep_{AB} (see section 2) $pref\,(A)$ is > 1 if POS tag A prefers the first position within a phrase and vice versa.

Before a phrase candidate is used to create a new grammar rule, its validity has to be checked. Using the assumption that every word prefers a certain position within a constituent leads us to check the first word of a phrase candidate for preferring the first position and the last word for favoring the last one.

But there are at least two exceptions: coordinating conjunctions and compound nouns. Those constructions (e. g. *cats/NNS and/CC dogs/NNS*, *dog/NN house/NN*) usually start and end with the same phrase respectively POS tag. This would lead to wrong validation results, because NNS or NN do prefer the last position within a constituent and should not occur at the beginning. As both constructions are endocentric, they prefer the head's position within the superordinating phrase and thus, their existence does not stand in contrast to the assumption made about preferred positions.

Formally, we get the following proposition:

$$\begin{aligned} valid\,(P) \Leftrightarrow \quad & p_0 = p_{n-1} \quad \vee \\ pref\,(p_0) \geq \varphi \wedge {} & pref\,(p_{n-1}) \leq \frac{1}{\varphi} \end{aligned} \tag{7}$$

An *uncertainty* factor is introduced by φ, as some parts-of-speech tend to not appear at the borders of a sentence although they prefer a certain position within constituents. Some examples (given in Table 1) of the 5 most frequent English[2] and German[3] parts-of-speech will demonstrate this effect.

English		German	
NN	0.08	NN	0.30
IN	31.45	ART	242.48
NNP	1.39	APPR	143.62
DT	84.19	ADJA	5.06
NNS	0.31	NE	1.11

Table 1: Values of $pref\,(POS)$ for the 5 most frequent parts-of-speech of English and German

In both languages proper nouns (*NNP* resp. *NE*) occur slightly more often at the beginning of a sentence than at its end, although proper nouns prefer — like normal nouns — the last position of a phrase. To account for this effect, $pref\,(A)$ will be iteratively adapted to the observations of learned grammar rules as given in Equ. 8:

$$\begin{aligned} pref\,(p_0) &\leftarrow \frac{1}{\delta} \cdot pref\,(p_0) \\ pref\,(p_{n-1}) &\leftarrow \delta \cdot pref\,(p_{n-1}) \end{aligned} \tag{8}$$

Due to iterative learning of rules, we can use knowledge obtained during a previous iteration. Every rule contains reinforcing information about the preferred position of a part-of-speech. $pref\,(A)$ is adapted by a factor δ (with $0 < \delta < 1$) for the corresponding parts-of-speech and it will converge to its preferred position.

In later iterations, significances of phrase candidates do not differ considerably from each other and thus, the order of phrase candidates is not very reliable anymore. Consequently, parts-of-speech occur at non-preferred positions more often and trustworthy knowledge (in form of $pref\,(A)$) about the preferred positions of parts-of-speech is very helpful to avoid those phrase candidates from being validated.

We want to give one example for English: adjectives (*JJ*). Before the first iteration, $pref\,(JJ)$ is initialized with 1.046 which means that *JJ* has no preferred position. The most significant rules containing *JJ* are *JJ NN*, *JJ NNS* and *JJ NNP* — supporting a preference of the first position within a constituent. An iterative adaption of $pref\,(JJ)$ will represent this observation and disapprove constituents ending with *JJ* (like *DT JJ* or *IN JJ*) in upcoming iterations.

[2]Penn Tree Tagset, see (Marcus et al., 1993)

[3]Stuttgart-Tübingen Tagset, see (Thielen et al., 1999)

After having detected a new and valid constituent, we can use context similarity and other statistical methods to learn more about its behaviour and inner construction.

2.2 Classification into endocentric and exocentric constructions

Endocentric constructions contain a head — or more than one in symmetric coordinate constructions — which is syntactically identical to the endocentric compound. Additionally, at least one optional element subordinating to the head is contained in the construction. An exocentric construction on the other hand does not contain any head element which is syntactically identical to the whole construction.

The following example sentences will demonstrate the distinction of these two types. Sentence (a) contains a determiner phrase (DP: *a new car*) which has a noun phrase embedded (NP: *new car*). The NP can be replaced by its head as in sentence (b) and thus is regarded to be endocentric. The DP is exocentric — it can neither be replaced by the determiner (sentence (c)) nor by the NP (sentence (d)) without losing its syntactical correctness.

(a) I buy a new car.

(b) I buy a car.

(c) * I buy a.

(d) * I buy new car.

Detection of endocentric constructions yields valuable information about the language in question. It is possible to detect heads along with their modifiers without any a priori knowledge. Furthermore, detection of optional modifiers reduces the complexity of sentences and thus, facilitates learning of high precision rules.

Without classification into endocentric and exocentric constructions, two rules ($P\#1 \leftarrow JJ\ NN$ and $P\#2 \leftarrow JJ\ P\#1$ would be necessary to parse the phrase *first civil settlement* as given in Figure 3. Using knowledge about subordinating elements achieves the same result (see Figure 4) with one rule ($NN \leftarrow JJ\ NN$). Additionally, data-sparseness problems are circumvented as no rare occurrences like $JJ \ldots JJ\ NN$ need to be contained in the training corpus to eventually parse those phrases.

Following the definition of endocentricity, a phrase containing a head and an optional element

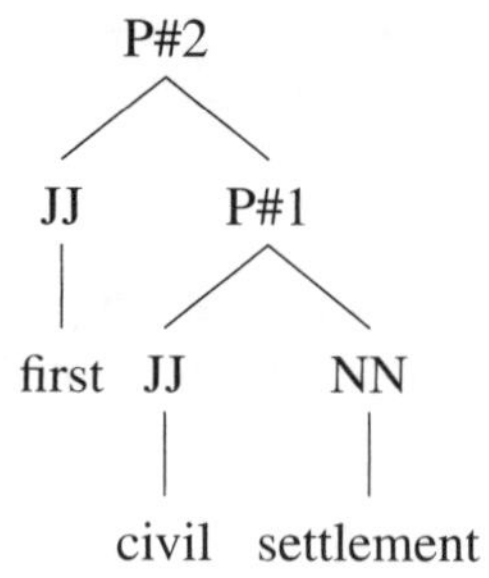

Figure 3: Structure without knowledge about endocentricity

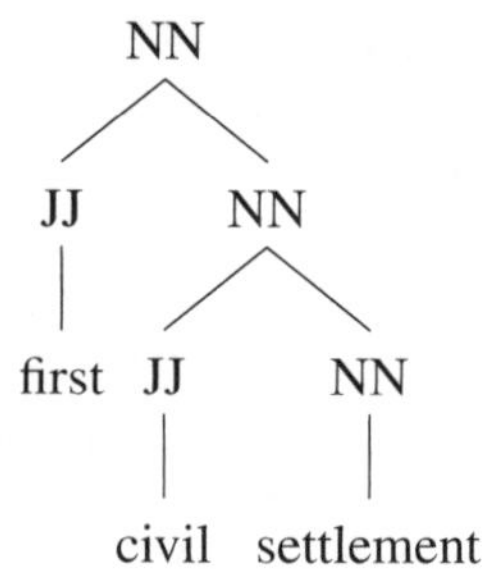

Figure 4: Structure using knowledge about endocentricity

should be equally distributed — in respect to its context – as the head. Consequentially, a phrase is considered to be endocentric, if it contains an element showing high context similarity (see Equ. 9).

$$\begin{aligned} &endocentric\,(P) \Leftrightarrow \\ &\exists i : sim\,(context\,(P)\,, context\,(p_i)) \geq \vartheta \end{aligned} \tag{9}$$

The global context $context\,(P)$ of a phrase or POS tag P is the sum of all local contexts of P within the training corpus. We use the two left and right neighbours including the aforementioned markers for the beginning and the end of a sentence if necessary. We apply the Cosine Measure to calculate the similarity between the two contexts and in case of passing a defined threshold ϑ, the phrase is considered to be endocentric. See Table 2 for some examples ($\vartheta = 0.9$).

NNS	←	JJ NNS
NN	←	JJ NN
NNP	←	NNP CC NNP
NN	←	NN CC NN
VBZ	←	RB VBZ

Table 2: Examples of endocentric constructions

2.3 Discontiguous dependencies

Additionally to endocentric constructions containing a head and a modifier, some parts-of-speech like articles and possessive pronouns do not occur without a noun or noun phrase. While those parts-of-speech are grouped together as determiners (*DT*) in the Penn Tree Tagset, for other tagsets and languages they might be distributed among multiple classes (as in the German Stuttgart–Tübingen

Tagset among *ART, PPOSAT, PIAT* ...). To detect such strong dependencies, we propose a simple test measuring the relative score of observing two words A and B together within a maximum range n.

$$dep_n(A, B) = \frac{\sum_{d=0}^{n} freq(A, B, d)}{min(freq(A), freq(B))} \tag{10}$$

Equ. 10 formally describes the relative score where $freq(A, B, d)$ denotes the frequency of A and B occurring together with exactly d other tokens between them. If $dep_n(A, B)$ passes a threshold ϑ (0.9 for our experiments), then the dependency between A and B is allowed to occur discontiguously. Including these dependencies facilitates the parsing of rare and insignificant phrases like adjectival phrases.

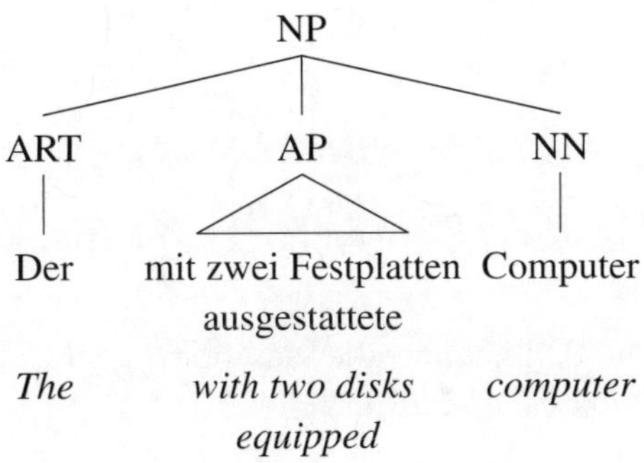

Figure 5: Adjectival Phrase

In the example given in Figure 5, the discontiguous dependency between articles (ART) and normal nouns (NN) can be applied to two possible word pairs. On the one hand, there is *Der ... Festplatten* (*The ... disks*), the other possibility is *Der ... Computer* (*The ... computer*). We choose the pair achieving the highest neighbourhood co-occurrence significance. Regarding our example, it is quite obvious that *Computer* is the noun to choose as *Der* and *Computer* show grammatical agreement while this is not the case for *Festplatten*. Consequently, the significance of *Der Computer* is much higher than the one of *Der Festplatten*. Although articles and other parts-of-speech are not unambiguous regarding gender, number and case for all languages, this approach can resolve some of those cases for certain languages.

2.4 Phrase Clustering

One objection to unsupervised parsing is the fact that phrases belonging to the same phrase type are not labeled the same way. And of course, without any prior knowledge, induced phrases will never be labeled *NP, PP* or like any other known phrase type. This complicates the application of any further algorithms relying on that knowledge. Nevertheless, it is possible to cluster syntactic identical phrases into one class.

As in section 2.2, similarity between two global contexts is calculated. If the similarity of phrase P (the one being tested) and Q (see most similar one, see Equ. 11) exceeds a threshold ϑ, then phrase P is considered to have the same phrase type as Q (see Equ. 12). In this case, P will be labeled by the label of Q and thus, is treated like Q.

$$Q = \underset{q \in phrases}{arg\ max}\ sim(context(P), context(q)) \tag{11}$$

$$Type(P) = Type(Q) \Leftrightarrow sim(P, Q) \geq \vartheta \tag{12}$$

As it can be seen in Table 3 ($\vartheta = 0.9$), clustering finds syntactic similar phrases and facilitates iterative learning as rules can be learned for each phrase type and not for each composition.

P#1	←	DT JJ NN
P#1	←	DT NN
P#1	←	PRP$ NNS
P#2	←	IN P#1
P#2	←	IN NN
P#2	←	IN NNS

Table 3: Results of phrase clustering

2.5 Iterative learning

Learning rules is realized as an iterative process. A flow chart of the proposed process is given in Figure 6.

First, an empty parser model is initialized. At the beginning of an iteration all rules are applied to transform the corpus. Resulting structures form the data which is used for the next iteration. The sentence in Figure 7 will be transformed by already induced rules.

After application of rule $NN \leftarrow JJ\ NN$, the optional element JJ is removed (see Fig. 8).

The next rule ($P\#1 \leftarrow DT\ NN$) reduces the complexity of the sentence and from now on, further rules will be created on those parts-of-speech and phrases (see Fig. 9).

Learning will be aborted after one of the following three conditions becomes true:

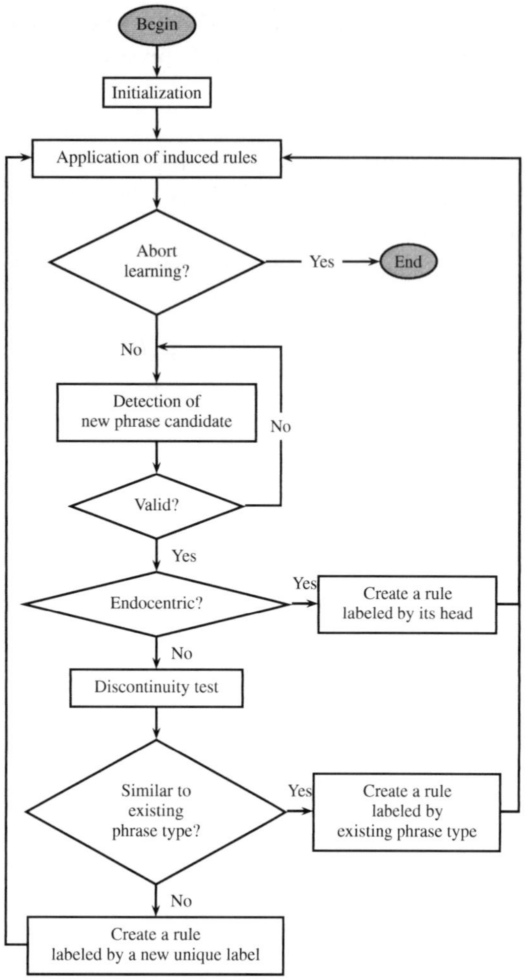

Figure 6: Flow chart
of the proposed learning process

1. The algorithm reaches the maximum number of rules.

2. The last phrase candidate is not considered to be significant enough. A threshold in relation to the highest significance can be set up.

3. All sentences contained in the training corpus are reduced to one phrase.

Afterwards, the most significant n-gram passing the validity test will be regarded as a phrase. In the following steps, the label of the new phrase will be determined. Either it is labeled by its head (in case of an endocentric construction) or by a syntactic identical phrase type that has been learned before. If neither is the case, it gets a new unique label. Afterwards, the next iteration is triggered.

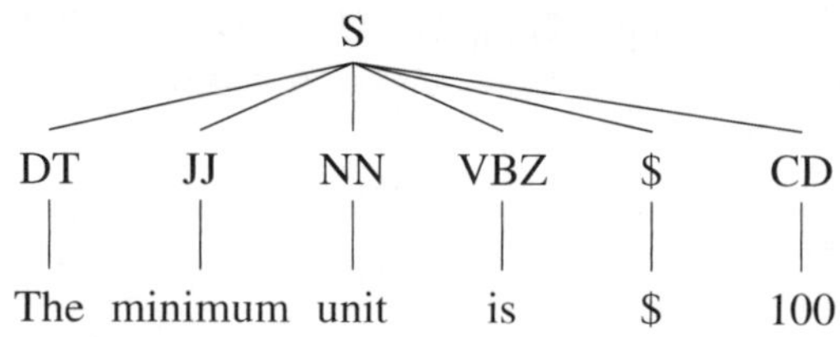

Figure 7: Example

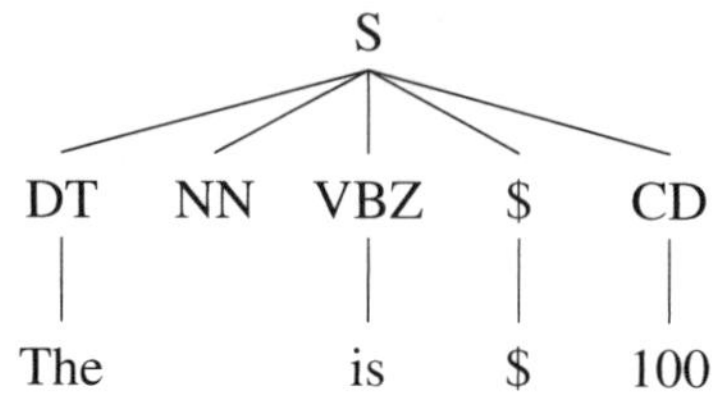

Figure 8: Example after application of rule $NN \leftarrow JJ\ NN$

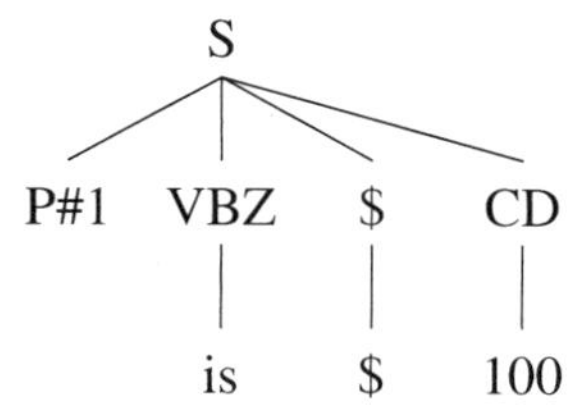

Figure 9: Example after additional application of rule $P\#1 \leftarrow DT\ NN$

3 Evaluation

To evaluate unsuParse+ against unsuParse and other unsupervised parsing algorithms, we apply the same experimental setup as in (Klein, 2005), (Bod, 2006) and (Hänig et al., 2008). For German punctuation and empty element tags are removed from the NEGRA corpus (see (Skut et al., 1998)). Afterwards, all sentences containing more than 10 elements are dismissed. The resulting corpus is referred to as NEGRA10 (2175 sentences). To take more complex sentences into account, we also prepared a corpus containing sentences to a maximum length of 40 elements (NEGRA40).

We present results for both — POS tags and word strings. As most unsupervised parsing models (except (Seginer, 2007)), we apply the hand-annotated data of the NEGRA corpus. Additionally, we used an unsupervised part-of-speech tagger (see (Biemann, 2006)) to tag the NEGRA corpus to be able to present a complete unsupervised parsing process relying on word strings only. We applied the model *de40M* which has been created on a corpus containing 40 million sentences and contains 510 word classes.

To compare the performance of different parsing algorithms, we used the Unlabeled Brackets Measure as in (Klein and Manning, 2002) and (Klein and Manning, 2004). Additionally to unlabeled precision UP and unlabeled recall UR, the unlabeled f-score UF is defined as:

$$UF = \frac{2 \cdot UP \cdot UR}{UP + UR} \quad (13)$$

The baseline algorithm is based on neighbourhood co-occurrences. First, a parse tree is initialized and all tokens of a sentence are added as leaves. Afterwards, the two adjacent nodes containing the POS tags with the highest neighbourhood co-occurrence significance are merged consecutively until a binary tree has been created.

Results for NEGRA10 are given in Table 4. *unsuParse+* improves the performance of *unsuParse* in both categories: supervised and unsupervised annotated POS tags. While recall is improved significantly for hand-annotated data, just a slight improvement is achieved for word strings. Especially clustering of phrases leads to the increased recall as rules do not need to be learned for every possible compound composition of a given phrase type as they are already covered by the phrase type itself. Models based on unsuParse achieve the highest precision among all models. This is not very surprising as most of the other models (except Common Cover Links) generate binary parses achieving a higher recall. Nevertheless, *unsuParse+* yields comparable results and obtains the highest f-score for German data.

Parsing Model	UP	UR	UF
Baseline (POS tags)	35.5	66.0	46.2
CCM	48.1	85.5	61.6
DMV + CCM	49.6	89.7	63.9
U-DOP	51.2	90.5	65.4
UML-DOP	—	—	67.0
U-DOP*	—	—	63.8
unsuParse (POS tags)	76.9	53.9	63.4
unsuParse+ (POS tags)	**71.1**	**67.9**	**69.5**
Baseline (words)	23.6	43.9	30.7
Common Cover Links	51.0	69.8	59.0
unsuParse (words)	61.2	59.1	60.2
unsuParse+ (words)	**63.1**	**60.4**	**61.7**

Table 4: UP, UR and UF for NEGRA10

Performance drops for more complex sentences (see Table 5). As for short sentences, the recall of our approach is in the same order as for the baseline. However, precision is increased by a factor of two in comparison to the baseline, which is also similar to short sentences.

Parsing Model	UP	UR	UF
Baseline (POS tags)	24.8	49.3	33.0
unsuParse+ (POS tags)	55.3	51.4	53.3

Table 5: UP, UR and UF for NEGRA40

Table 6 shows the most frequently over- and under-proposed phrases for NEGRA10. Noun and prepositional phrases are often over-proposed due to a flat representation within the NEGRA corpus. The most frequently under-proposed phrase *NE NE* is learned and classified as endocentric construction (NE $\leftarrow$ NE NE). Due to the removal of punctuation, proper nouns which naturally would be separated by e. g. commas will be represented by one flat phrase without deeper analysis of the inner structure. This includes some underpropositions which will not occur while parsing sentences containing punctuation.

Overproposed		Underproposed	
ART NN	369	NE NE	42
CARD NN	111	NN NE	35
ADV ADV	103	ART NN NE	27
ADJA NN	99	ADV ART NN	24
APPR ART NN	93	APPR PPER	23

Table 6: Most frequently over- and under-proposed constituents

4 Conclusions and further work

In this paper, we presented an improved model for co-occurrence based parsing. This model creates high accuracy parses employing a constituent detection algorithm yielding competitive results. Although no a priori knowledge about the language in question is taken into account, it is possible to detect heads, modifiers and different phrase types. Especially noun phrases and prepositional phrases are clustered into their respective classes. For further processing like relation extraction, precise results for the aforementioned phrase types are essential and provided by this algorithm in an unsupervised manner.

Our future work will include the investigation of unsupervised methods for dependency identification between verbs and their arguments. Furthermore, the inclusion of further constituency tests like substitution and deletion could provide additional certainty for constituent candidates.

References

David Adger. 2003. *Core Syntax: A Minimalist Approach*. Oxford University Press.

Chris Biemann. 2006. Unsupervised part-of-speech tagging employing efficient graph clustering. In *Proceedings of the COLING/ACL-06 Student Research Workshop*, Sydney, Australia.

Rens Bod. 2006. An all-subtrees approach to unsupervised parsing. In *ACL-44: Proceedings of the 21st International Conference on Computational Linguistics and the 44th annual meeting of the Association for Computational Linguistics*.

Noam Chomsky. 1965. *Aspects of the Theory of Syntax*. MIT Press, Cambridge, Massachusetts.

Ted Dunning. 1993. Accurate methods for the statistics of surprise and coincidence. *Computational Linguistics*, 19(1):61–74.

Christian Hänig, Stefan Bordag, and Uwe Quasthoff. 2008. Unsuparse: Unsupervised parsing with unsupervised part of speech tagging. In *Proceedings of the Sixth International Language Resources and Evaluation (LREC'08)*.

Richard S. Kayne. 1995. *The Antisymmetry of Syntax*. MIT Press.

Dan Klein and Christopher D. Manning. 2002. A generative constituent-context model for improved grammar induction. In *ACL '02: Proceedings of the 40th Annual Meeting on Association for Computational Linguistics*.

Dan Klein and Christopher D. Manning. 2004. Corpus-based induction of syntactic structure: models of dependency and constituency. In *ACL '04: Proceedings of the 42nd Annual Meeting on Association for Computational Linguistics*.

Dan Klein. 2005. *The Unsupervised Learning of Natural Language Structure*. Ph.D. thesis, Stanford University.

Ewald Lang. 2002. Die Wortart "Konjunktion". In *Lexikologie. Lexicology. Ein Internationales Handbuch zur Natur und Struktur von Wörtern und Wortschätzen*, pages 634–641. de Gruyter.

M. Marcus, B. Santorini, and M. A. Marcinkiewicz. 1993. Building a large annotated corpus of english: The penn treebank. *Computational Linguistics*, 19(2):313–330.

Carl Pollard and Ivan A. Sag. 1994. *Head-Driven Phrase Structure Grammar*. University Of Chicago Press.

Ivan Sag. 2002. Coordination and underspecification. In *roceedings of the Ninth International Conference on Head-Driven Phrase Structure Grammar*.

Yoav Seginer. 2007. Fast unsupervised incremental parsing. In *Proceedings of the 45th Annual Meeting of the Association of Computational Linguistics*.

Wojciech Skut, Thorsten Brants, Brigitte Krenn, and Hans Uszkoreit. 1998. A linguistically interpreted corpus of german newspaper text. In *ESSLLI-98 Workshop on Recent Advances in Corpus Annotation*.

C. Thielen, A. Schiller, S. Teufel, and C. Stöckert. 1999. Guidelines für das Tagging deutscher Textkorpora mit STTS. Technical report, University of Stuttgart and University of Tübingen.

Viterbi Training Improves Unsupervised Dependency Parsing

Valentin I. Spitkovsky
Computer Science Department
Stanford University and Google Inc.
valentin@cs.stanford.edu

Hiyan Alshawi
Google Inc.
Mountain View, CA, 94043, USA
hiyan@google.com

Daniel Jurafsky and **Christopher D. Manning**
Departments of Linguistics and Computer Science
Stanford University, Stanford, CA, 94305, USA
jurafsky@stanford.edu and manning@cs.stanford.edu

Abstract

We show that Viterbi (or "hard") EM is well-suited to unsupervised grammar induction. It is *more* accurate than standard inside-outside re-estimation (classic EM), significantly faster, and simpler. Our experiments with Klein and Manning's Dependency Model with Valence (DMV) attain state-of-the-art performance — 44.8% accuracy on Section 23 (all sentences) of the Wall Street Journal corpus — without clever initialization; with a good initializer, Viterbi training improves to 47.9%. This generalizes to the Brown corpus, our held-out set, where accuracy reaches 50.8% — a 7.5% gain over previous best results. We find that classic EM learns better from short sentences but cannot cope with longer ones, where Viterbi thrives. However, we explain that both algorithms optimize the wrong objectives and prove that there are fundamental disconnects between the likelihoods of sentences, best parses, and true parses, beyond the well-established discrepancies between likelihood, accuracy and extrinsic performance.

1 Introduction

Unsupervised learning is hard, often involving difficult objective functions. A typical approach is to attempt maximizing the likelihood of unlabeled data, in accordance with a probabilistic model. Sadly, such functions are riddled with local optima (Charniak, 1993, Ch. 7, *inter alia*), since their number of peaks grows exponentially with instances of hidden variables. Furthermore, a higher likelihood does not always translate into superior task-specific accuracy (Elworthy, 1994; Merialdo, 1994). Both complications are real, but we will discuss perhaps more significant shortcomings.

We prove that learning can be error-prone even in cases when likelihood *is* an appropriate measure of extrinsic performance *and* where global optimization is feasible. This is because a key challenge in unsupervised learning is that the *desired* likelihood is unknown. Its absence renders tasks like structure discovery inherently underconstrained. Search-based algorithms adopt surrogate metrics, gambling on convergence to the "right" regularities in data. Their wrong objectives create cases in which *both* efficiency *and* performance improve when expensive exact learning techniques are replaced by cheap approximations.

We propose using Viterbi training (Brown et al., 1993), instead of inside-outside re-estimation (Baker, 1979), to induce hierarchical syntactic structure from natural language text. Our experiments with Klein and Manning's (2004) Dependency Model with Valence (DMV), a popular state-of-the-art model (Headden et al., 2009; Cohen and Smith, 2009; Spitkovsky et al., 2009), beat previous benchmark accuracies by 3.8% (on Section 23 of WSJ) and 7.5% (on parsed Brown).

Since objective functions used in unsupervised grammar induction are provably wrong, advantages of exact inference may not apply. It makes sense to try the Viterbi approximation — it is also wrong, only simpler and cheaper than classic EM. As it turns out, Viterbi EM is not only faster but also more accurate, consistent with hypotheses of de Marcken (1995) and Spitkovsky et al. (2009).

We begin by reviewing the model, standard data sets and metrics, and our experimental results. After relating our contributions to prior work, we delve into proofs by construction, using the DMV.

Proceedings of the Fourteenth Conference on Computational Natural Language Learning, pages 9–17,
Uppsala, Sweden, 15-16 July 2010.

Corpus	*Sentences*	*POS Tokens*	*Corpus*	*Sentences*	*POS Tokens*
WSJ1	159	159	WSJ13	12,270	110,760
WSJ2	499	839	WSJ14	14,095	136,310
WSJ3	876	1,970	WSJ15	15,922	163,715
WSJ4	1,394	4,042	WSJ20	25,523	336,555
WSJ5	2,008	7,112	WSJ25	34,431	540,895
WSJ6	2,745	11,534	WSJ30	41,227	730,099
WSJ7	3,623	17,680	WSJ35	45,191	860,053
WSJ8	4,730	26,536	WSJ40	47,385	942,801
WSJ9	5,938	37,408	WSJ45	48,418	986,830
WSJ10	7,422	52,248	WSJ100	49,206	1,028,054
WSJ11	8,856	68,022	Section 23	2,353	48,201
WSJ12	10,500	87,750	Brown100	24,208	391,796

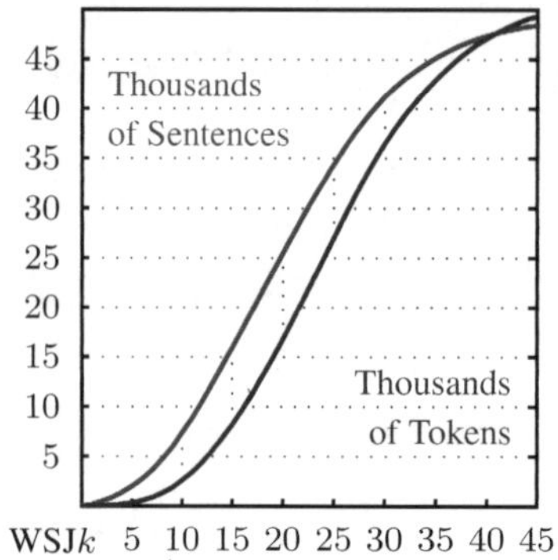

Figure 1: Sizes of WSJ$\{1, \ldots, 45, 100\}$, Section 23 of WSJ$^\infty$ and Brown100 (Spitkovsky et al., 2009).

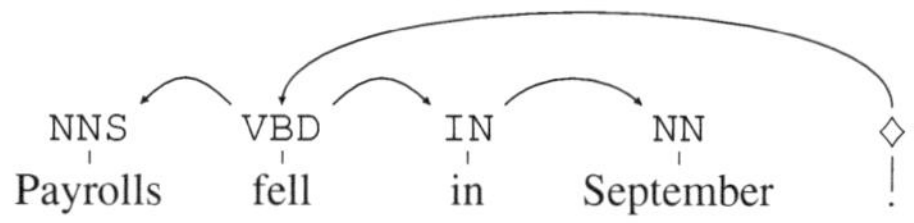

$$\begin{array}{rlcl}
\mathbb{P} = & \overbrace{(1 - \mathbb{P}_{\text{STOP}}(\diamond, \mathtt{L}, \mathtt{T}))}^{0} & \times & \mathbb{P}_{\text{ATTACH}}(\diamond, \mathtt{L}, \mathtt{VBD}) \\
\times & (1 - \mathbb{P}_{\text{STOP}}(\mathtt{VBD}, \mathtt{L}, \mathtt{T})) & \times & \mathbb{P}_{\text{ATTACH}}(\mathtt{VBD}, \mathtt{L}, \mathtt{NNS}) \\
\times & (1 - \mathbb{P}_{\text{STOP}}(\mathtt{VBD}, \mathtt{R}, \mathtt{T})) & \times & \mathbb{P}_{\text{ATTACH}}(\mathtt{VBD}, \mathtt{R}, \mathtt{IN}) \\
\times & (1 - \mathbb{P}_{\text{STOP}}(\mathtt{IN}, \mathtt{R}, \mathtt{T})) & \times & \mathbb{P}_{\text{ATTACH}}(\mathtt{IN}, \mathtt{R}, \mathtt{NN}) \\
\times & \mathbb{P}_{\text{STOP}}(\mathtt{VBD}, \mathtt{L}, \mathtt{F}) & \times & \mathbb{P}_{\text{STOP}}(\mathtt{VBD}, \mathtt{R}, \mathtt{F}) \\
\times & \mathbb{P}_{\text{STOP}}(\mathtt{NNS}, \mathtt{L}, \mathtt{T}) & \times & \mathbb{P}_{\text{STOP}}(\mathtt{NNS}, \mathtt{R}, \mathtt{T}) \\
\times & \mathbb{P}_{\text{STOP}}(\mathtt{IN}, \mathtt{L}, \mathtt{T}) & \times & \mathbb{P}_{\text{STOP}}(\mathtt{IN}, \mathtt{R}, \mathtt{F}) \\
\times & \mathbb{P}_{\text{STOP}}(\mathtt{NN}, \mathtt{L}, \mathtt{T}) & \times & \mathbb{P}_{\text{STOP}}(\mathtt{NN}, \mathtt{R}, \mathtt{T}) \\
\times & \underbrace{\mathbb{P}_{\text{STOP}}(\diamond, \mathtt{L}, \mathtt{F})}_{1} & \times & \underbrace{\mathbb{P}_{\text{STOP}}(\diamond, \mathtt{R}, \mathtt{T})}_{1}.
\end{array}$$

Figure 2: A dependency structure for a short sentence and its probability, as factored by the DMV, after summing out $\mathbb{P}_{\text{ORDER}}$ (Spitkovsky et al., 2009).

2 Dependency Model with Valence

The DMV (Klein and Manning, 2004) is a single-state head automata model (Alshawi, 1996) over lexical word classes $\{c_w\}$ — POS tags. Its generative story for a sub-tree rooted at a head (of class c_h) rests on three types of independent decisions: (i) initial direction $dir \in \{\mathtt{L}, \mathtt{R}\}$ in which to attach children, via probability $\mathbb{P}_{\text{ORDER}}(c_h)$; (ii) whether to seal dir, stopping with probability $\mathbb{P}_{\text{STOP}}(c_h, dir, adj)$, conditioned on $adj \in \{\mathtt{T}, \mathtt{F}\}$ (true iff considering dir's first, i.e., *adjacent*, child); and (iii) attachments (of class c_a), according to $\mathbb{P}_{\text{ATTACH}}(c_h, dir, c_a)$. This produces only projective trees. A root token $\diamond$ generates the head of a sentence as its left (and only) child. Figure 2 displays a simple example.

The DMV lends itself to unsupervised learning via inside-outside re-estimation (Baker, 1979). Viterbi training (Brown et al., 1993) re-estimates each next model as if supervised by the previous best parse trees. And supervised learning from reference parse trees is straight-forward, since maximum-likelihood estimation reduces to counting: $\hat{\mathbb{P}}_{\text{ATTACH}}(c_h, dir, c_a)$ is the fraction of children — those of class c_a — attached on the dir side of a head of class c_h; $\hat{\mathbb{P}}_{\text{STOP}}(c_h, dir, adj = \mathtt{T})$, the fraction of words of class c_h with no children on the dir side; and $\hat{\mathbb{P}}_{\text{STOP}}(c_h, dir, adj = \mathtt{F})$, the ratio[1] of the number of words of class c_h having a child on the dir side to their total number of such children.

3 Standard Data Sets and Evaluation

The DMV is traditionally trained and tested on customized subsets of Penn English Treebank's Wall Street Journal portion (Marcus et al., 1993). Following Klein and Manning (2004), we begin with reference constituent parses and compare against deterministically derived dependencies: after pruning out all empty sub-trees, punctuation and terminals (tagged `#` and `$`) not pronounced where they appear, we drop all sentences with more than a prescribed number of tokens remaining and use automatic "head-percolation" rules (Collins, 1999) to convert the rest, as is standard practice. We experiment with WSJk (sentences with at most k tokens), for $1 \leq k \leq 45$, and Section 23 of WSJ$^\infty$ (all sentence lengths). We also evaluate on Brown100, similarly derived from the parsed portion of the Brown corpus (Francis and Kucera, 1979), as our held-out set. Figure 1 shows these corpora's sentence and token counts.

Proposed parse trees are judged on accuracy: a *directed score* is simply the overall fraction of correctly guessed dependencies. Let S be a set of sentences, with $|s|$ the number of terminals (to-

[1]The expected number of trials needed to get one Bernoulli(p) success is $n \sim$ Geometric(p), with $n \in \mathbb{Z}^+$, $\mathbb{P}(n) = (1-p)^{n-1}p$ and $\mathbb{E}(n) = p^{-1}$; MoM and MLE agree, $\hat{p} = (\#\text{ of successes})/(\#\text{ of trials})$.

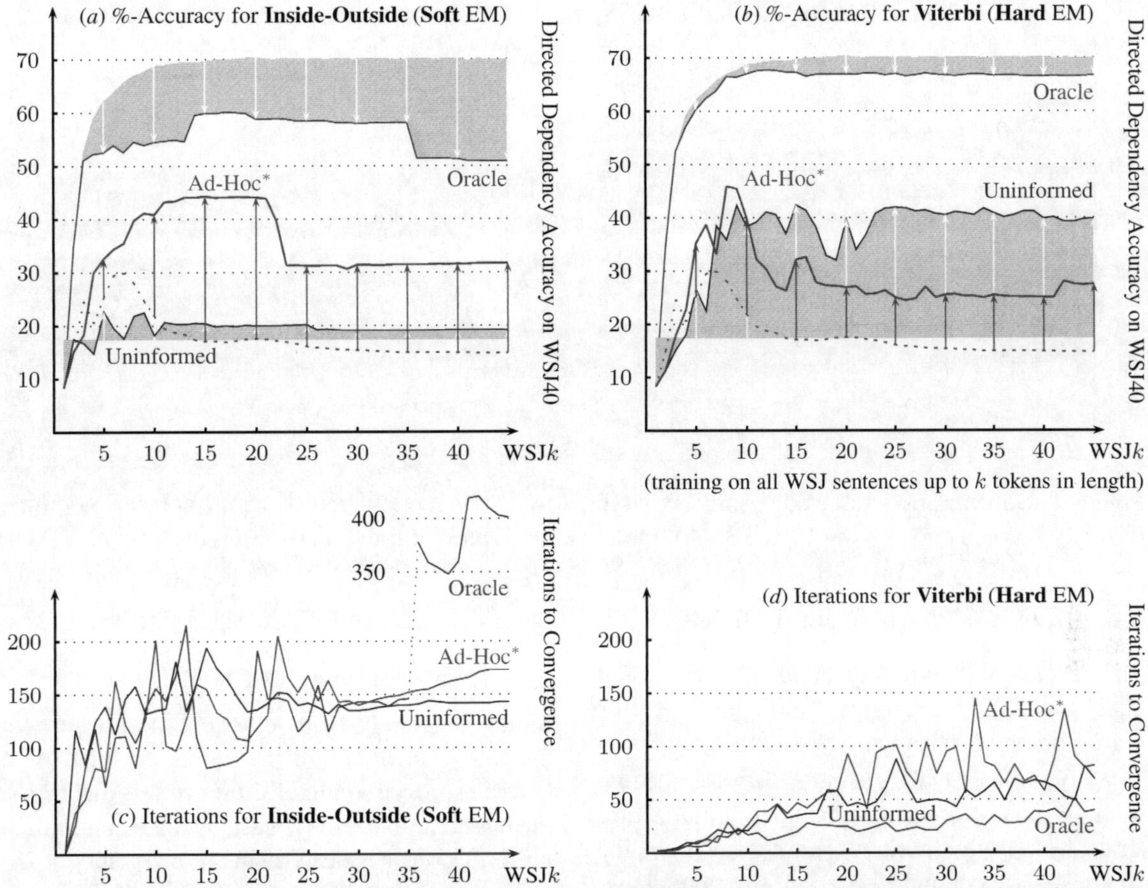

Figure 3: Directed dependency accuracies attained by the DMV, when trained on WSJk, smoothed, then tested against a fixed evaluation set, WSJ40, for three different initialization strategies (Spitkovsky et al., 2009). Red, green and blue graphs represent the supervised (maximum-likelihood oracle) initialization, a linguistically-biased initializer (Ad-Hoc*) and the uninformed (uniform) prior. Panel (b) shows results obtained with Viterbi training instead of classic EM — Panel (a), but is otherwise identical (in both, each of the 45 vertical slices captures five new experimental results and arrows connect starting performance with final accuracy, emphasizing the impact of learning). Panels (c) and (d) show the corresponding numbers of iterations until EM's convergence.

kens) for each $s \in S$. Denote by $T(s)$ the set of all dependency parse trees of s, and let $t_i(s)$ stand for the parent of token i, $1 \leq i \leq |s|$, in $t(s) \in T(s)$. Call the gold reference $t^*(s) \in T(s)$. For a given model of grammar, parameterized by θ, let $\hat{t}^\theta(s) \in T(s)$ be a (not necessarily unique) likeliest (also known as Viterbi) parse of s:

$$\hat{t}^\theta(s) \in \left\{ \arg\max_{t \in T(s)} \mathbb{P}_\theta(t) \right\};$$

then θ's directed accuracy on a reference set R is

$$100\% \cdot \frac{\sum_{s \in R} \sum_{i=1}^{|s|} 1_{\{\hat{t}_i^\theta(s) = t_i^*(s)\}}}{\sum_{s \in R} |s|}.$$

4 Experimental Setup and Results

Following Spitkovsky et al. (2009), we trained the DMV on data sets WSJ$\{1, \ldots, 45\}$ using three initialization strategies: (i) the uninformed uniform prior; (ii) a linguistically-biased initializer, Ad-Hoc*;[2] and (iii) an oracle — the supervised MLE solution. Standard training is without smoothing, iterating each run until successive changes in overall per-token cross-entropy drop below 2^{-20} bits.

We re-trained all models using Viterbi EM instead of inside-outside re-estimation, explored Laplace (add-one) smoothing during training, and experimented with hybrid initialization strategies.

[2]Ad-Hoc* is Spitkovsky et al.'s (2009) variation on Klein and Manning's (2004) "ad-hoc harmonic" completion.

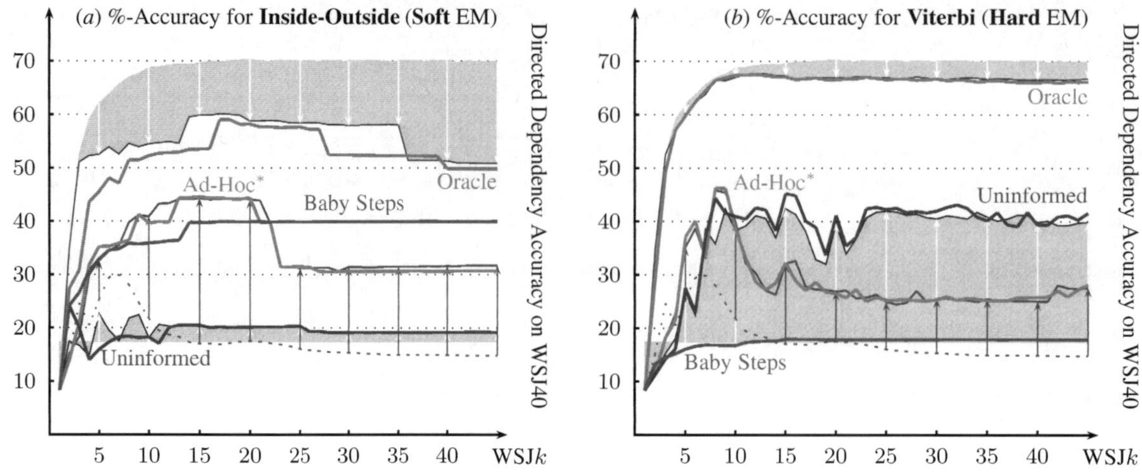

Figure 4: Superimposes directed accuracies attained by DMV models trained *with* Laplace smoothing (brightly-colored curves) over Figure 3(a,b); violet curves represent Baby Steps (Spitkovsky et al., 2009).

4.1 Result #1: Viterbi-Trained Models

The results of Spitkovsky et al. (2009), tested against WSJ40, are re-printed in Figure 3(a); our corresponding Viterbi runs appear in Figure 3(b).

We observe crucial differences between the two training modes for each of the three initialization strategies. Both algorithms walk away from the supervised maximum-likelihood solution; however, Viterbi EM loses at most a few points of accuracy (3.7% at WSJ40), whereas classic EM drops nearly twenty points (19.1% at WSJ45). In both cases, the single best unsupervised result is with good initialization, although Viterbi peaks earlier (45.9% at WSJ8) and in a narrower range (WSJ8-9) than classic EM (44.3% at WSJ15; WSJ13-20). The uniform prior never quite gets off the ground with classic EM but manages quite well under Viterbi training,[3] given sufficient data — it even beats the "clever" initializer everywhere past WSJ10. The "sweet spot" at WSJ15 — a neighborhood where both Ad-Hoc* and the oracle excel under classic EM — disappears with Viterbi. Furthermore, Viterbi does not degrade with more (complex) data, except with a biased initializer.

More than a simple efficiency hack, Viterbi EM actually improves performance. And its benefits to running times are also non-trivial: it not only skips computing the outside charts in every iteration but also converges (sometimes an order of magnitude) faster than classic EM (see Figure 3(c,d)).[4]

4.2 Result #2: Smoothed Models

Smoothing rarely helps classic EM and hurts in the case of oracle training (see Figure 4(a)). With Viterbi, supervised initialization suffers much less, the biased initializer is a wash, and the uninformed uniform prior generally gains a few points of accuracy, e.g., up 2.9% (from 42.4% to 45.2%, evaluated against WSJ40) at WSJ15 (see Figure 4(b)).

Baby Steps (Spitkovsky et al., 2009) — iterative re-training with increasingly more complex data sets, WSJ1, . . . ,WSJ45 — using smoothed Viterbi training fails miserably (see Figure 4(b)), due to Viterbi's poor initial performance at short sentences (possibly because of data sparsity and sensitivity to non-sentences — see examples in §7.3).

4.3 Result #3: State-of-the-Art Models

Simply training up smoothed Viterbi at WSJ15, using the uninformed uniform prior, yields 44.8% accuracy on Section 23 of WSJ$^{\infty}$, already beating previous state-of-the-art by 0.7% (see Table 1(*A*)).

Since both classic EM and Ad-Hoc* initializers work well with short sentences (see Figure 3(a)), it makes sense to use their pre-trained models to initialize Viterbi training, mixing the two strategies. We judged all Ad-Hoc* initializers against WSJ15 and found that the one for WSJ8 minimizes sentence-level cross-entropy (see Figure 5). This approach does not involve reference parse

[3]In a concurrently published related work, Cohen and Smith (2010) prove that the uniform-at-random initializer is a competitive starting M-step for Viterbi EM; our uninformed prior consists of uniform multinomials, seeding the E-step.

[4]For classic EM, the number of iterations to convergence appears sometimes inversely related to performance, giving credence to the notion of early termination as a regularizer.

Model	Incarnation		WSJ10	WSJ20	WSJ$^\infty$	Brown100
DMV	Bilingual Log-Normals (tie-verb-noun)	(Cohen and Smith, 2009)	62.0	48.0	42.2	
	Less is More (Ad-Hoc* @15)	(Spitkovsky et al., 2009)	56.2	48.2	44.1	43.3
A.	Smoothed Viterbi Training (@15), Initialized with the Uniform Prior		59.9	50.0	44.8	48.1
B.	A Good Initializer (Ad-Hoc*'s @8), Classically Pre-Trained (@15)		63.8	52.3	46.2	49.3
C.	Smoothed Viterbi Training (@15), Initialized with *B*		64.4	53.5	47.8	50.5
D.	Smoothed Viterbi Training (@45), Initialized with *C*		65.3	**53.8**	**47.9**	**50.8**
EVG	Smoothed (skip-head), Lexicalized	(Headden et al., 2009)	**68.8**			

Table 1: Accuracies on Section 23 of WSJ$\{10, 20, \infty\}$ and Brown100 for three recent state-of-the-art systems, our initializer, and smoothed Viterbi-trained runs that employ different initialization strategies.

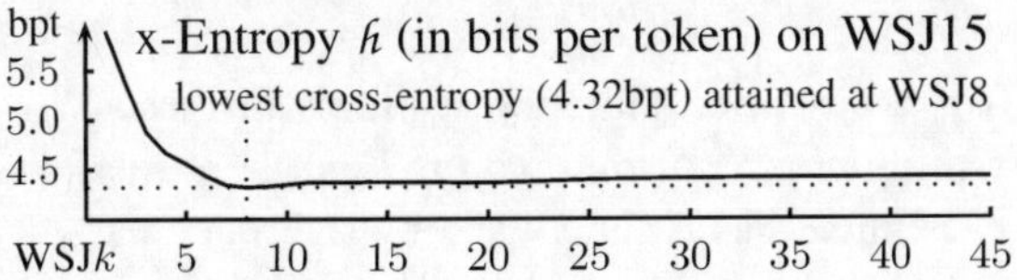

Figure 5: Sentence-level cross-entropy on WSJ15 for Ad-Hoc* initializers of WSJ$\{1, \ldots, 45\}$.

trees and is therefore still unsupervised. Using the Ad-Hoc* initializer based on WSJ8 to seed classic training at WSJ15 yields a further 1.4% gain in accuracy, scoring 46.2% on WSJ$^\infty$ (see Table 1(*B*)).

This good initializer boosts accuracy attained by smoothed Viterbi at WSJ15 to 47.8% (see Table 1(*C*)). Using its solution to re-initialize training at WSJ45 gives a tiny further improvement (0.1%) on Section 23 of WSJ$^\infty$ but bigger gains on WSJ10 (0.9%) and WSJ20 (see Table 1(*D*)).

Our results generalize. Gains due to smoothed Viterbi training and favorable initialization carry over to Brown100 — accuracy improves by 7.5% over previous published numbers (see Table 1).[5]

5 Discussion of Experimental Results

The DMV has no parameters to capture syntactic relationships beyond local trees, e.g., agreement. Spitkovsky et al. (2009) suggest that classic EM breaks down as sentences get longer precisely because the model makes unwarranted independence assumptions. They hypothesize that the DMV reserves too much probability mass for what should be unlikely productions. Since EM faithfully allocates such re-distributions across the possible parse trees, once sentences grow sufficiently long, this process begins to deplete what began as likelier structures. But medium lengths avoid a flood of exponentially-confusing longer sentences (and the sparseness of unrepresentative shorter ones).[6]

Our experiments corroborate this hypothesis. First of all, Viterbi manages to hang on to supervised solutions much better than classic EM. Second, Viterbi does not universally degrade with more (complex) training sets, except with a biased initializer. And third, Viterbi learns poorly from small data sets of short sentences (WSJk, $k < 5$).

Viterbi may be better suited to unsupervised grammar induction compared with classic EM, but neither is sufficient, by itself. Both algorithms abandon good solutions and make no guarantees with respect to extrinsic performance. Unfortunately, these two approaches share a deep flaw.

6 Related Work on Improper Objectives

It is well-known that maximizing likelihood may, in fact, degrade accuracy (Pereira and Schabes, 1992; Elworthy, 1994; Merialdo, 1994). de Marcken (1995) showed that classic EM suffers from a fatal attraction towards deterministic grammars and suggested a Viterbi training scheme as a remedy. Liang and Klein's (2008) analysis of errors in unsupervised learning began with the inappropriateness of the likelihood objective (approximation), explored problems of data sparsity (estimation) and focused on EM-specific issues related to non-convexity (identifiability and optimization).

Previous literature primarily relied on experimental evidence. de Marcken's analytical result is an exception but pertains only to EM-specific local attractors. Our analysis confirms his intuitions and moreover shows that there can be *global* preferences for deterministic grammars — problems that would persist with tractable optimization. We prove that there is a fundamental disconnect between objective functions even when likelihood is a reasonable metric and training data are infinite.

[5] In a sister paper, Spitkovsky et al. (2010) improve performance by incorporating parsing constraints harvested from the web into Viterbi training; nevertheless, results presented in this paper remain the best of models trained purely on WSJ.

[6] Klein and Manning (2004) originally trained the DMV on WSJ10 and Gillenwater et al. (2009) found it useful to discard data from WSJ3, which is mostly incomplete sentences.

7 Proofs (by Construction)

There is a subtle distinction between *three* different probability distributions that arise in parsing, each of which can be legitimately termed "likelihood" — the mass that a particular model assigns to (i) highest-scoring (Viterbi) parse trees; (ii) the correct (gold) reference trees; and (iii) the sentence strings (sums over all derivations). A classic unsupervised parser trains to optimize the third, makes actual parsing decisions according to the first, and is evaluated against the second. There are several potential disconnects here. First of all, the true generative model θ^* may not yield the largest margin separations for discriminating between gold parse trees and next best alternatives; and second, θ^* may assign sub-optimal mass to string probabilities. There is no reason why an optimal estimate $\hat{\theta}$ should make the best parser or coincide with a peak of an unsupervised objective.

7.1 The Three Likelihood Objectives

A supervised parser finds the "best" parameters $\hat{\theta}$ by maximizing the likelihood of all reference *structures* $t^*(s)$ — the product, over all sentences, of the probabilities that it assigns to each such tree:

$$\hat{\theta}_{\text{SUP}} = \arg\max_{\theta} \mathcal{L}(\theta) = \arg\max_{\theta} \prod_{s} \mathbb{P}_{\theta}(t^*(s)).$$

For the DMV, this objective function is convex — its unique peak is easy to find and should match the true distribution θ^* given enough data, barring practical problems caused by numerical instability and inappropriate independence assumptions. It is often easier to work in log-probability space:

$$\begin{aligned}\hat{\theta}_{\text{SUP}} &= \arg\max\nolimits_{\theta} \log \mathcal{L}(\theta) \\ &= \arg\max\nolimits_{\theta} \textstyle\sum_{s} \log \mathbb{P}_{\theta}(t^*(s)).\end{aligned}$$

Cross-entropy, measured in bits per token (bpt), offers an interpretable proxy for a model's quality:

$$\hbar(\theta) = -\frac{\sum_{s} \lg \mathbb{P}_{\theta}(t^*(s))}{\sum_{s} |s|}.$$

Clearly, $\arg\max_{\theta} \mathcal{L}(\theta) = \hat{\theta}_{\text{SUP}} = \arg\min_{\theta} \hbar(\theta)$.

Unsupervised parsers cannot rely on references and attempt to jointly maximize the probability of each *sentence* instead, summing over the probabilities of all possible trees, according to a model θ:

$$\hat{\theta}_{\text{UNS}} = \arg\max_{\theta} \sum_{s} \log \underbrace{\sum_{t \in T(s)} \mathbb{P}_{\theta}(t)}_{\mathbb{P}_{\theta}(s)}.$$

This objective function is not convex and in general does not have a unique peak, so in practice one usually settles for $\tilde{\theta}_{\text{UNS}}$ — a fixed point. There is no reason why $\hat{\theta}_{\text{SUP}}$ should agree with $\hat{\theta}_{\text{UNS}}$, which is in turn (often badly) approximated by $\tilde{\theta}_{\text{UNS}}$, in our case using EM. A logical alternative to maximizing the probability of sentences is to maximize the probability of the most likely parse trees instead:[7]

$$\hat{\theta}_{\text{VIT}} = \arg\max_{\theta} \sum_{s} \log \mathbb{P}_{\theta}(\hat{t}^{\theta}(s)).$$

This 1-best approximation similarly arrives at $\tilde{\theta}_{\text{VIT}}$, with no claims of optimality. Each next model is re-estimated as if supervised by reference parses.

7.2 A Warm-Up Case: Accuracy vs. $\hat{\theta}_{\text{SUP}} \neq \theta^*$

A simple way to derail accuracy is to maximize the likelihood of an incorrect model, e.g., one that makes false independence assumptions. Consider fitting the DMV to a contrived distribution — two equiprobable structures over identical three-token sentences from a unary vocabulary $\{ⓐ\}$:

(i) ⓐ ⓐ ⓐ; (ii) ⓐ ⓐ ⓐ.

There are six tokens and only two have children on any given side, so adjacent stopping MLEs are:

$$\hat{\mathbb{P}}_{\text{STOP}}(ⓐ, \text{L}, \text{T}) = \hat{\mathbb{P}}_{\text{STOP}}(ⓐ, \text{R}, \text{T}) = 1 - \frac{2}{6} = \frac{2}{3}.$$

The rest of the estimated model is deterministic:

$$\hat{\mathbb{P}}_{\text{ATTACH}}(\diamondsuit, \text{L}, ⓐ) = \hat{\mathbb{P}}_{\text{ATTACH}}(ⓐ, *, ⓐ) = 1$$

$$\text{and } \hat{\mathbb{P}}_{\text{STOP}}(ⓐ, *, \text{F}) = 1,$$

since all dependents are ⓐ and every one is an only child. But the DMV generates left- and right-attachments independently, allowing a third parse:

(iii) ⓐ ⓐ ⓐ.

It also cannot capture the fact that all structures are local (or that all dependency arcs point in the same direction), admitting two additional parse trees:

(iv) ⓐ ⓐ ⓐ; (v) ⓐ ⓐ ⓐ.

Each possible structure must make four (out of six) adjacent stops, incurring identical probabilities:

$$\hat{\mathbb{P}}_{\text{STOP}}(ⓐ, *, \text{T})^4 \times (1 - \hat{\mathbb{P}}_{\text{STOP}}(ⓐ, *, \text{T}))^2 = \frac{2^4}{3^6}.$$

[7]It is also possible to use k-best Viterbi, with $k > 1$.

Thus, the MLE model does not break symmetry and rates each of the five parse trees as equally likely. Therefore, its expected per-token accuracy is 40%. Average overlaps between structures (i-v) and answers (i,ii) are (i) 100% or 0; (ii) 0 or 100%; and (iii,iv,v) $33.\overline{3}\%$: $(3+3)/(5\times 3) = 2/5 = 0.4$.

A decoy model without left- or right-branching, i.e., $\tilde{\mathbb{P}}_{\text{STOP}}(ⓐ, \mathtt{L}, \mathtt{T}) = 1$ or $\tilde{\mathbb{P}}_{\text{STOP}}(ⓐ, \mathtt{R}, \mathtt{T}) = 1$, would assign zero probability to some of the training data. It would be forced to parse every instance of ⓐⓐⓐ either as (i) or as (ii), deterministically. Nevertheless, it would attain a higher per-token accuracy of 50%. (Judged on exact matches, at the granularity of whole trees, the decoy's guaranteed 50% accuracy clobbers the MLE's expected 20%.)

Our toy data set could be replicated n-fold without changing the analysis. This confirms that, even in the absence of estimation errors or data sparsity, there can be a fundamental disconnect between likelihood and accuracy, if the model is wrong.[8]

7.3 A Subtler Case: $\theta^* = \hat{\theta}_{\text{SUP}}$ vs. $\hat{\theta}_{\text{UNS}}$ vs. $\hat{\theta}_{\text{VIT}}$

We now prove that, even with the *right* model, mismatches between the different objective likelihoods can also handicap the truth. Our calculations are again exact, so there are no issues with numerical stability. We work with a set of parameters θ^* already factored by the DMV, so that its problems could not be blamed on invalid independence assumptions. Yet we are able to find another impostor distribution $\tilde{\theta}$ that outshines $\hat{\theta}_{\text{SUP}} = \theta^*$ on both unsupervised metrics, which proves that the true models $\hat{\theta}_{\text{SUP}}$ and θ^* are not globally optimal, as judged by the two surrogate objective functions.

This next example is organic. We began with WSJ10 and confirmed that classic EM abandons the supervised solution. We then iteratively discarded large portions of the data set, so long as the remainder maintained the (un)desired effect — EM walking away from its $\hat{\theta}_{\text{SUP}}$. This procedure isolated such behavior, arriving at a minimal set:

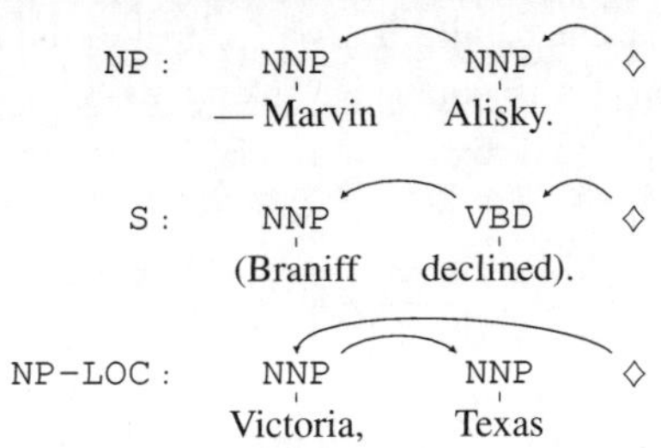

This kernel is tiny, but, as before, our analysis is invariant to n-fold replication: the problem cannot be explained away by a small training size — it persists even in infinitely large data sets. And so, we consider three reference parse trees for two-token sentences over a binary vocabulary $\{ⓐ, ⓩ\}$:

(i) ⓐ ⓐ; (ii) ⓐ ⓩ; (iii) ⓐ ⓐ.

One third of the time, ⓩ is the head; only ⓐ can be a child; and only ⓐ has right-dependents. Trees (i)-(iii) are the only two-terminal parses generated by the model and are equiprobable. Thus, these sentences are representative of a length-two restriction of everything generated by the true θ^*:

$$\mathbb{P}_{\text{ATTACH}}(\diamondsuit, \mathtt{L}, ⓐ) = \frac{2}{3} \text{ and } \mathbb{P}_{\text{STOP}}(ⓐ, *, \mathtt{T}) = \frac{4}{5},$$

since ⓐ is the head two out of three times, and since only one out of five ⓐ's attaches a child on either side. Elsewhere, the model is deterministic:

$$\mathbb{P}_{\text{STOP}}(ⓩ, \mathtt{L}, \mathtt{T}) = 0;$$

$$\mathbb{P}_{\text{STOP}}(*, *, \mathtt{F}) = \mathbb{P}_{\text{STOP}}(ⓩ, \mathtt{R}, \mathtt{T}) = 1;$$

$$\mathbb{P}_{\text{ATTACH}}(ⓐ, *, ⓐ) = \mathbb{P}_{\text{ATTACH}}(ⓩ, \mathtt{L}, ⓐ) = 1.$$

Contrast the optimal estimate $\hat{\theta}_{\text{SUP}} = \theta^*$ with the decoy *fixed point*[9] $\tilde{\theta}$ that is identical to θ^*, except

$$\tilde{\mathbb{P}}_{\text{STOP}}(ⓐ, \mathtt{L}, \mathtt{T}) = \frac{3}{5} \text{ and } \tilde{\mathbb{P}}_{\text{STOP}}(ⓐ, \mathtt{R}, \mathtt{T}) = 1.$$

The probability of stopping is now 3/5 on the left and 1 on the right, instead of 4/5 on both sides — $\tilde{\theta}$ disallows ⓐ's right-dependents but preserves its overall fertility. The probabilities of leaves ⓐ (no children), under the models $\hat{\theta}_{\text{SUP}}$ and $\tilde{\theta}$, are:

$$\hat{\mathbb{P}}(ⓐ) = \hat{\mathbb{P}}_{\text{STOP}}(ⓐ, \mathtt{L}, \mathtt{T}) \times \hat{\mathbb{P}}_{\text{STOP}}(ⓐ, \mathtt{R}, \mathtt{T}) = \left(\frac{4}{5}\right)^2$$

$$\text{and } \tilde{\mathbb{P}}(ⓐ) = \tilde{\mathbb{P}}_{\text{STOP}}(ⓐ, \mathtt{L}, \mathtt{T}) \times \tilde{\mathbb{P}}_{\text{STOP}}(ⓐ, \mathtt{R}, \mathtt{T}) = \frac{3}{5}.$$

And the probabilities of, e.g., structure ⓐ ⓩ, are:

$$\hat{\mathbb{P}}_{\text{ATTACH}}(\diamondsuit, \mathtt{L}, ⓩ) \times \hat{\mathbb{P}}_{\text{STOP}}(ⓩ, \mathtt{R}, \mathtt{T})$$
$$\times (1 - \hat{\mathbb{P}}_{\text{STOP}}(ⓩ, \mathtt{L}, \mathtt{T})) \times \hat{\mathbb{P}}_{\text{STOP}}(ⓩ, \mathtt{L}, \mathtt{F})$$
$$\times \hat{\mathbb{P}}_{\text{ATTACH}}(ⓩ, \mathtt{L}, ⓐ) \times \hat{\mathbb{P}}(ⓐ)$$

[8] And as George Box quipped, "Essentially, all models are wrong, but some are useful" (Box and Draper, 1987, p. 424).

[9] The model estimated from the parse trees induced by $\tilde{\theta}$ over the three sentences is again $\tilde{\theta}$, for both soft and hard EM.

$$= \hat{\mathbb{P}}_{\texttt{ATTACH}}(\diamondsuit, \text{L}, ⓩ) \times \hat{\mathbb{P}}(ⓐ) = \frac{1}{3} \cdot \frac{16}{25}$$

$$\text{and } \tilde{\mathbb{P}}_{\texttt{ATTACH}}(\diamondsuit, \text{L}, ⓩ) \times \tilde{\mathbb{P}}(ⓐ) = \frac{1}{3} \cdot \frac{3}{5}.$$

Similarly, the probabilities of all four possible parse trees for the two distinct sentences, ⓐⓐ and ⓐⓩ, under the two models, $\hat{\theta}_{\text{SUP}} = \theta^*$ and $\tilde{\theta}$, are:

	$\hat{\theta}_{\text{SUP}} = \theta^*$	$\tilde{\theta}$
ⓐ ↶ ⓩ	$\frac{1}{3}\left(\frac{16}{25}\right) = \frac{16}{75} = \mathbf{0.21\overline{3}}$	$\frac{1}{3}\left(\frac{3}{5}\right) = \frac{1}{5} = \mathbf{0.2}$
ⓐ ↷ ⓩ	$\mathbf{0}$	$\mathbf{0}$
ⓐ ↶ ⓐ	$\frac{2}{3}\left(\frac{4}{5}\right)\left(1 - \frac{4}{5}\right)\left(\frac{16}{25}\right) = \frac{128}{1875} = \mathbf{0.0682\overline{6}}$	$\frac{2}{3}\left(1 - \frac{3}{5}\right)\left(\frac{3}{5}\right) = \frac{4}{25} = \mathbf{0.16}$
ⓐ ↷ ⓐ	$\mathbf{0.0682\overline{6}}$	$\mathbf{0}$

To the three *true parses*, $\hat{\theta}_{\text{SUP}}$ assigns probability $\left(\frac{16}{75}\right)\left(\frac{128}{1875}\right)^2 \approx 0.0009942$ — about 1.66bpt; $\tilde{\theta}$ leaves zero mass for (iii), corresponding to a larger (infinite) cross-entropy, consistent with theory.

So far so good, but if asked for *best* (Viterbi) *parses*, $\hat{\theta}_{\text{SUP}}$ could still produce the actual trees, whereas $\tilde{\theta}$ would happily parse sentences of (iii) and (i) the same, perceiving a joint probability of $(0.2)(0.16)^2 = 0.00512$ — just 1.27bpt, appearing to outperform $\hat{\theta}_{\text{SUP}} = \theta^*$! Asked for *sentence probabilities*, $\tilde{\theta}$ would remain unchanged (it parses each sentence unambiguously), but $\hat{\theta}_{\text{SUP}}$ would aggregate to $\left(\frac{16}{75}\right)\left(2 \cdot \frac{128}{1875}\right)^2 \approx 0.003977$, improving to 1.33bpt, but still noticeably "worse" than $\tilde{\theta}$.

Despite leaving zero probability to the truth, $\tilde{\theta}$ beats θ^* on both surrogate metrics, globally. This seems like an egregious error. Judged by (extrinsic) accuracy, $\tilde{\theta}$ still holds its own: it gets four directed edges from predicting parse trees (i) and (ii) completely right, but none of (iii) — a solid 66.7%. Subject to tie-breaking, θ^* is equally likely to get (i) and/or (iii) entirely right or totally wrong (they are indistinguishable): it could earn a perfect 100%, tie $\tilde{\theta}$, or score a low 33.3%, at 1:2:1 odds, respectively — same as $\tilde{\theta}$'s deterministic 66.7% accuracy, in expectation, but with higher variance.

8 Discussion of Theoretical Results

Daumé et al. (2009) questioned the benefits of using exact models in approximate inference. In our case, the model already makes strong simplifying assumptions *and* the objective is also incorrect. It makes sense that Viterbi EM sometimes works, since an approximate wrong "solution" *could*, by chance, be better than one that is exactly wrong.

One reason why Viterbi EM may work well is that *its* score is used in selecting actual output parse trees. Wainwright (2006) provided strong theoretical and empirical arguments for using the same approximate inference method in training as in performing predictions for a learned model. He showed that if inference involves an approximation, then using the same approximate method to train the model gives even better performance guarantees than exact training methods. If our task were not parsing but language modeling, where the relevant score is the sum of the probabilities over individual derivations, perhaps classic EM would not be doing as badly, compared to Viterbi.

Viterbi training is not only faster and more accurate but also free of inside-outside's recursion constraints. It therefore invites more flexible modeling techniques, including discriminative, feature-rich approaches that target *conditional* likelihoods, essentially via (unsupervised) self-training (Clark et al., 2003; Ng and Cardie, 2003; McClosky et al., 2006a; McClosky et al., 2006b, *inter alia*).

Such "learning by doing" approaches may be relevant to understanding human language acquisition, as children frequently find themselves forced to interpret a sentence in order to interact with the world. Since most models of *human* probabilistic parsing are massively pruned (Jurafsky, 1996; Chater et al., 1998; Lewis and Vasishth, 2005, *inter alia*), the serial nature of Viterbi EM — or the very limited parallelism of k-best Viterbi — may be more appropriate in modeling this task than the fully-integrated inside-outside solution.

9 Conclusion

Without a known objective, as in unsupervised learning, correct exact optimization becomes impossible. In such cases, approximations, although liable to pass over a true optimum, may achieve faster convergence and still *improve* performance. We showed that this is the case with Viterbi training, a cheap alternative to inside-outside reestimation, for unsupervised dependency parsing.

We explained why Viterbi EM may be particularly well-suited to learning from longer sentences, in addition to any general benefits to synchronizing approximation methods across learning and inference. Our best algorithm is simpler and an order of magnitude faster than classic EM. It achieves state-of-the-art performance: 3.8% higher accuracy than previous published best results on Section 23 (all sentences) of the Wall Street Journal corpus. This improvement generalizes to the Brown corpus, our held-out evaluation set, where the same model registers a 7.5% gain.

Unfortunately, approximations alone do not bridge the real gap between objective functions. This deeper issue could be addressed by drawing parsing constraints (Pereira and Schabes, 1992) from specific applications. One example of such an approach, tied to machine translation, is synchronous grammars (Alshawi and Douglas, 2000). An alternative — observing constraints induced by hyper-text mark-up, harvested from the web — is explored in a sister paper (Spitkovsky et al., 2010), published concurrently.

Acknowledgments

Partially funded by NSF award IIS-0811974 and by the Air Force Research Laboratory (AFRL), under prime contract no. FA8750-09-C-0181; first author supported by the Fannie & John Hertz Foundation Fellowship. We thank Angel X. Chang, Mengqiu Wang and the anonymous reviewers for many helpful comments on draft versions of this paper.

References

H. Alshawi and S. Douglas. 2000. Learning dependency transduction models from unannotated examples. In *Royal Society of London Philosophical Transactions Series A*, volume 358.

H. Alshawi. 1996. Head automata for speech translation. In *Proc. of ICSLP*.

J. K. Baker. 1979. Trainable grammars for speech recognition. In *Speech Communication Papers for the 97th Meeting of the Acoustical Society of America*.

G. E. P. Box and N. R. Draper. 1987. *Empirical Model-Building and Response Surfaces*. John Wiley.

P. F. Brown, V. J. Della Pietra, S. A. Della Pietra, and R. L. Mercer. 1993. The mathematics of statistical machine translation: Parameter estimation. *Computational Linguistics*, 19.

E. Charniak. 1993. *Statistical Language Learning*. MIT Press.

N. Chater, M. J. Crocker, and M. J. Pickering. 1998. The rational analysis of inquiry: The case of parsing. In M. Oaksford and N. Chater, editors, *Rational Models of Cognition*. Oxford University Press.

S. Clark, J. Curran, and M. Osborne. 2003. Bootstrapping POS-taggers using unlabelled data. In *Proc. of CoNLL*.

S. B. Cohen and N. A. Smith. 2009. Shared logistic normal distributions for soft parameter tying in unsupervised grammar induction. In *Proc. of NAACL-HLT*.

S. B. Cohen and N. A. Smith. 2010. Viterbi training for PCFGs: Hardness results and competitiveness of uniform initialization. In *Proc. of ACL*.

M. Collins. 1999. *Head-Driven Statistical Models for Natural Language Parsing*. Ph.D. thesis, University of Pennsylvania.

H. Daumé, III, J. Langford, and D. Marcu. 2009. Search-based structured prediction. *Machine Learning*, 75(3).

C. de Marcken. 1995. Lexical heads, phrase structure and the induction of grammar. In *WVLC*.

D. Elworthy. 1994. Does Baum-Welch re-estimation help taggers? In *Proc. of ANLP*.

W. N. Francis and H. Kucera, 1979. *Manual of Information to Accompany a Standard Corpus of Present-Day Edited American English, for use with Digital Computers*. Department of Linguistic, Brown University.

J. Gillenwater, K. Ganchev, J. Graça, B. Taskar, and F. Pereira. 2009. Sparsity in grammar induction. In *NIPS: Grammar Induction, Representation of Language and Language Learning*.

W. P. Headden, III, M. Johnson, and D. McClosky. 2009. Improving unsupervised dependency parsing with richer contexts and smoothing. In *Proc. of NAACL-HLT*.

D. Jurafsky. 1996. A probabilistic model of lexical and syntactic access and disambiguation. *Cognitive Science*, 20.

D. Klein and C. D. Manning. 2004. Corpus-based induction of syntactic structure: Models of dependency and constituency. In *Proc. of ACL*.

R. L. Lewis and S. Vasishth. 2005. An activation-based model of sentence processing as skilled memory retrieval. *Cognitive Science*, 29.

P. Liang and D. Klein. 2008. Analyzing the errors of unsupervised learning. In *Proc. of HLT-ACL*.

M. P. Marcus, B. Santorini, and M. A. Marcinkiewicz. 1993. Building a large annotated corpus of English: The Penn Treebank. *Computational Linguistics*, 19(2).

D. McClosky, E. Charniak, and M. Johnson. 2006a. Effective self-training for parsing. In *Proc. of NAACL-HLT*.

D. McClosky, E. Charniak, and M. Johnson. 2006b. Reranking and self-training for parser adaptation. In *Proc. of COLING-ACL*.

B. Merialdo. 1994. Tagging English text with a probabilistic model. *Computational Linguistics*, 20(2).

V. Ng and C. Cardie. 2003. Weakly supervised natural language learning without redundant views. In *Proc. of HLT-NAACL*.

F. Pereira and Y. Schabes. 1992. Inside-outside reestimation from partially bracketed corpora. In *Proc. of ACL*.

V. I. Spitkovsky, H. Alshawi, and D. Jurafsky. 2009. Baby Steps: How "Less is More" in unsupervised dependency parsing. In *NIPS: Grammar Induction, Representation of Language and Language Learning*.

V. I. Spitkovsky, D. Jurafsky, and H. Alshawi. 2010. Profiting from mark-up: Hyper-text annotations for guided parsing. In *Proc. of ACL*.

M. J. Wainwright. 2006. Estimating the "wrong" graphical model: Benefits in the computation-limited setting. *Journal of Machine Learning Research*, 7.

Driving Semantic Parsing from the World's Response

James Clarke **Dan Goldwasser** **Ming-Wei Chang** **Dan Roth**
Department of Computer Science
University of Illinois
Urbana, IL 61820
{clarkeje,goldwas1,mchang21,danr}@illinois.edu

Abstract

Current approaches to semantic parsing, the task of converting text to a formal meaning representation, rely on annotated training data mapping sentences to logical forms. Providing this supervision is a major bottleneck in scaling semantic parsers. This paper presents a new learning paradigm aimed at alleviating the supervision burden. We develop two novel learning algorithms capable of predicting complex structures which only rely on a binary feedback signal based on the context of an external world. In addition we reformulate the semantic parsing problem to reduce the dependency of the model on syntactic patterns, thus allowing our parser to scale better using less supervision. Our results surprisingly show that without using any annotated meaning representations learning with a weak feedback signal is capable of producing a parser that is competitive with fully supervised parsers.

1 Introduction

Semantic Parsing, the process of converting text into a formal meaning representation (MR), is one of the key challenges in natural language processing. Unlike shallow approaches for semantic interpretation (e.g., semantic role labeling and information extraction) which often result in an incomplete or ambiguous interpretation of the natural language (NL) input, the output of a semantic parser is a complete meaning representation that can be executed directly by a computer program.

Semantic parsing has mainly been studied in the context of providing natural language interfaces to computer systems. In these settings the target meaning representation is defined by the semantics of the underlying task. For example, providing access to databases: a question posed in natural language is converted into a formal database query that can be executed to retrieve information. Example 1 shows a NL input query and its corresponding meaning representation.

Example 1 *Geoquery input text and output MR*
"What is the largest state that borders Texas?"
`largest(state(next_to(const(texas))))`

Previous works (Zelle and Mooney, 1996; Tang and Mooney, 2001; Zettlemoyer and Collins, 2005; Ge and Mooney, 2005; Zettlemoyer and Collins, 2007; Wong and Mooney, 2007) employ machine learning techniques to construct a semantic parser. The learning algorithm is given a set of input sentences and their corresponding meaning representations, and learns a statistical semantic parser — a set of rules mapping lexical items and syntactic patterns to their meaning representation and a score associated with each rule. Given a sentence, these rules are applied recursively to derive the most probable meaning representation. Since semantic interpretation is limited to syntactic patterns identified in the training data, the learning algorithm requires considerable amounts of annotated data to account for the syntactic variations associated with the meaning representation. Annotating sentences with their MR is a difficult, time consuming task; minimizing the supervision effort required for learning is a major challenge in scaling semantic parsers.

This paper proposes a new model and learning paradigm for semantic parsing aimed to alleviate the supervision bottleneck. Following the observation that the target meaning representation is to be executed by a computer program which in turn provides a response or outcome; we propose a *response driven learning framework* capable of exploiting feedback based on the response. The feedback can be viewed as a teacher judging whether the execution of the meaning representation produced the desired response for the input sentence.

Proceedings of the Fourteenth Conference on Computational Natural Language Learning, pages 18–27,
Uppsala, Sweden, 15-16 July 2010. ©2010 Association for Computational Linguistics

This type of supervision is very natural in many situations and requires no expertise, thus can be supplied by any user.

Continuing with Example 1, the response generated by executing a database query would be used to provide feedback. The feedback would be whether the generated response is the correct answer for the input question or not, in this case *New Mexico* is the desired response.

In response driven semantic parsing, the learner is provided with a set of natural language sentences and a feedback function that encapsulates the teacher. The feedback function informs the learner whether its interpretation of the input sentence produces the desired response. We consider scenarios where the feedback is provided as a binary signal, correct $+1$ or incorrect -1.

This weaker form of supervision poses a challenge to conventional learning methods: semantic parsing is in essence a structured prediction problem requiring supervision for a set of interdependent decisions, while the provided supervision is binary, indicating the correctness of a generated meaning representation. To bridge this difference we propose two novel learning algorithms suited to the response driven setting.

Furthermore, to account for the many syntactic variations associated with the MR, we propose a new model for semantic parsing that allows us to learn effectively and generalize better. Current semantic parsing approaches extract parsing rules mapping NL to their MR, restricting possible interpretations to previously seen syntactic patterns. We replace the rigid inference process induced by the learned parsing rules with a flexible framework. We model semantic interpretation as a sequence of interdependent decisions, mapping text spans to predicates and use syntactic information to determine how the meaning of these logical fragments should be composed. We frame this process as an Integer Linear Programming (ILP) problem, a powerful and flexible inference framework that allows us to inject relevant domain knowledge into the inference process, such as specific domain semantics that restrict the space of possible interpretations.

We evaluate our learning approach and model on the well studied Geoquery domain (Zelle and Mooney, 1996; Tang and Mooney, 2001), a database consisting of U.S. geographical information, and natural language questions. Our experimental results show that our model with response driven learning can outperform existing models trained with annotated logical forms.

The key contributions of this paper are:

Response driven learning for semantic parsing We propose a new learning paradigm for learning semantic parsers without any annotated meaning representations. The supervision for learning comes from a binary feedback signal based a response generated by executing a meaning representation. This type of supervision signal is natural to produce and can be acquired from non-expert users.

Novel training algorithms Two novel training algorithms are developed within the response driven learning paradigm. The training algorithms are applicable beyond semantic parsing and can be used in situations where it is possible to obtain binary feedback for a structured learning problem.

Flexible semantic interpretation process We propose a novel flexible semantic parsing model that can handle previously unseen syntactic variations of the meaning representation.

2 Semantic Parsing

The goal of semantic parsing is to produce a function $F : \mathcal{X} \rightarrow \mathcal{Z}$ that maps from the space natural language input sentences, $\mathcal{X}$, to the space of meaning representations, $\mathcal{Z}$. This type of task is usually cast as a structured output prediction problem, where the goal is to obtain a model that assigns the highest score to the correct meaning representation given an input sentence. However, in the task of semantic parsing, this decision relies on identifying a hidden intermediate representation (or an *alignment*) that captures the way in which fragments of the text correspond to the meaning representation. Therefore, we formulate the prediction function as follows:

$$\hat{\mathbf{z}} = F_{\mathbf{w}}(\mathbf{x}) = \arg\max_{\mathbf{y}\in\mathcal{Y},\mathbf{z}\in\mathcal{Z}} \mathbf{w}^T \Phi(\mathbf{x}, \mathbf{y}, \mathbf{z}) \quad (1)$$

Where Φ is a feature function that describes the relationships between an input sentence $\mathbf{x}$, alignment $\mathbf{y}$ and meaning representation $\mathbf{z}$. $\mathbf{w}$ is the weight vector which contains the parameters of the model. We refer to the $\arg\max$ above as the inference problem. The feature function combined with the nature of the inference problem defines the semantic parsing model. The key to producing

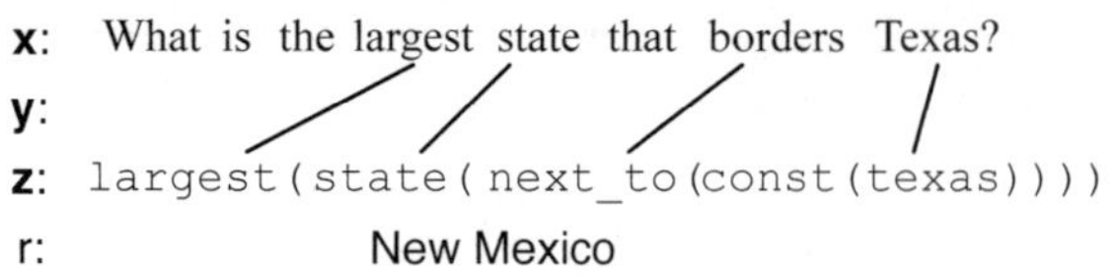

Figure 1: Example input sentence, meaning representation, alignment and answer for the Geoquery domain

a semantic parser involves defining a model and a learning algorithm to obtain $\mathbf{w}$.

In order to exemplify these concepts we consider the Geoquery domain. Geoquery contains a query language for a database of U.S. geographical facts. Figure 1 illustrates concrete examples of the terminology introduce. The input sentences $\mathbf{x}$ are natural language queries about U.S. geography. The meaning representations $\mathbf{z}$ are logical forms which can be executed on the database to obtain a response which we denote with r. The alignment $\mathbf{y}$ captures the associations between $\mathbf{x}$ and $\mathbf{z}$.

Building a semantic parser involves defining the model (feature function Φ and inference problem) and a learning strategy to obtain weights ($\mathbf{w}$) associated with the model. We defer discussion of our model until Section 4 and first focus on our learning strategy.

3 Structured Learning with Binary Feedback

Previous approaches to semantic parsing have assumed a fully supervised setting where a training set is available consisting of either: input sentences and logical forms $\{(\mathbf{x}^l, \mathbf{z}^l)\}_{l=1}^N$ (e.g., (Zettlemoyer and Collins, 2005)) or input sentences, logical forms and a mapping between their constituents $\{(\mathbf{x}^l, \mathbf{y}^l, \mathbf{z}^l)\}_{l=1}^N$ (e.g., (Ge and Mooney, 2005)). Given such training examples a weight vector $\mathbf{w}$ can be learned using structured learning methods. Obtaining, through annotation or other means, this form of training data is an expensive and difficult process which presents a major bottleneck for semantic parsing.

To reduce the burden of annotation we focus on a new learning paradigm which uses feedback from a teacher. The feedback signal is binary $(+1, -1)$ and informs the learner whether a predicted logical form $\hat{\mathbf{z}}$ when executed on the target domain produces the desired response or outcome. This is a very natural method for providing supervision in many situations and requires no expertise. For example, a user can observe the response and provide a judgement. The general form of the teacher's feedback is provided by a function $\mathit{Feedback} : \mathcal{X} \times \mathcal{Z} \rightarrow \{+1, -1\}$.

Algorithm 1 Direct Approach (Binary Learning)

Input: Sentences $\{\mathbf{x}^l\}_{l=1}^N$,
$\mathit{Feedback} : \mathcal{X} \times \mathcal{Z} \rightarrow \{+1, 1\}$,
initial weight vector $\mathbf{w}$

1: $B_l \leftarrow \{\}$ for all $l = 1, \ldots, N$
2: **repeat**
3: **for** $l = 1, \ldots, N$ **do**
4: $\hat{\mathbf{y}}, \hat{\mathbf{z}} = \arg\max_{\mathbf{y},\mathbf{z}} \mathbf{w}^T \Phi(\mathbf{x}^l, \mathbf{y}, \mathbf{z})$
5: $f = \mathit{Feedback}(\mathbf{x}^l, \hat{\mathbf{z}})$
6: add $(\Phi(\mathbf{x}^l, \hat{\mathbf{y}}, \hat{\mathbf{z}})/|\mathbf{x}^l|, f)$ to B_l
7: **end for**
8: $\mathbf{w} \leftarrow \mathit{BinaryLearn}(B)$ where $B = \cup_l B_l$
9: **until** no B_l has new unique examples
10: **return** $\mathbf{w}$

For the Geoquery domain this amounts to whether the logical form produces the correct response r for the input sentence. Geoquery has the added benefit that the teacher can be automated if we have a dataset consisting of input sentences and response pairs $\{(\mathbf{x}^l, r^l)\}_{l=1}^N$. *Feedback* evaluates whether a logical form produces a response matching r:

$$\mathit{Feedback}(\mathbf{x}^l, \mathbf{z}) = \begin{cases} +1 & \text{if } \mathit{execute}(\mathbf{z}) = r^l \\ -1 & \text{otherwise} \end{cases}$$

We are now ready to present our learning with feedback algorithms that operate in situations where input sentences, $\{\mathbf{x}^l\}_{l=1}^N$, and a teacher feedback mechanism, *Feedback*, are available. We do not assume the availability of logical forms.

3.1 Direct Approach (Binary Learning)

In general, a weight vector can be considered good if when used in the inference problem (Equation (1)) it scores the correct logical form and alignment (which may be hidden) higher than all other logical forms and alignments for a given input sentence. The intuition behind the *direct approach* is that the feedback function can be used to subsample the space of possible structures (alignments and logical forms $(\mathcal{Y} \times \mathcal{Z})$) for a given input $\mathbf{x}$. The feedback mechanism indicates whether the structure is good $(+1)$ or bad (-1). Using this intuition we can cast the problem of learning a weight vector for Equation (1) as a binary classification problem where we directly consider structures the feedback assigns $+1$ as positive examples and those assigned -1 as negative.

We represent the input to the binary classifier as the feature vector $\Phi(\mathbf{x}, \mathbf{y}, \mathbf{z})$ normalized by the size of the input sentence[1] $|\mathbf{x}|$, and the label as the result from $\mathit{Feedback}(\mathbf{x}, \mathbf{z})$.

Algorithm 1 outlines the approach in detail. The first stage of the algorithm iterates over all the training input sentences and computes the best logical form $\hat{\mathbf{z}}$ and alignment $\hat{\mathbf{y}}$ by solving the inference problem (line 4). The feedback function is queried (line 5) and a training example for the binary predictor created using the normalized feature vector from the triple containing the sentence, alignment and logical form as input and the feedback as the label. This training example is added to the working set of training examples for this input sentence (line 6). All the feedback training examples are used to train a binary classifier whose weight vector is used in the next iteration (line 8). The algorithm repeats until no new unique training examples are added to any of the working sets for any input sentence. Although the number of possible training examples is very large, in practice the algorithm is efficient and converges quickly. Note that this approach is capable of using a wide variety of linear classifiers as the base learner (line 8).

A policy is required to specify the nature of the working set of training examples (B_l) used for training the base classifier. This is pertinent in line 6 of the algorithm. Possible policies include: allowing duplicates in the working set (i.e., B_l is a multiset), disallowing duplicates (B_l is a set), or only allowing one example per input sentence ($\|B_l\| = 1$). We adopt the first approach in this paper.[2]

3.2 Aggressive Approach (Structured Learning)

There is important implicit information which the direct approach ignores. It is implicit that when the teacher indicates an input paired with an alignment and logical form is good ($+1$ feedback) that in order to repeat this behavior all other competing structures should be made suboptimal (or bad). To leverage this implicit information we adopt a structured learning strategy in which we consider the prediction as the optimal structure and all others as suboptimal. This is in contrast to the direct approach where only structures that have explicitly received negative feedback are considered subopitmal.

When a structure is found with positive feedback it is added to the training pool for a structured learner. We consider this approach *aggressive* as the structured learner implicitly considers all other structures as being suboptimal. Negative feedback indicates that the structure should not be added to the training pool as it will introduce noise into the learning process.

Algorithm 2 Aggressive Approach (Structured Learning)

Input: Sentences $\{\mathbf{x}^l\}_{l=1}^N$,
  $\mathit{Feedback} : \mathcal{X} \times \mathcal{Z} \to \{+1, 1\}$,
  initial weight vector $\mathbf{w}$
1: $S_l \leftarrow \emptyset$ for all $l = 1, \ldots, N$
2: **repeat**
3: **for** $l = 1, \ldots, N$ **do**
4: $\hat{\mathbf{y}}, \hat{\mathbf{z}} = \arg\max_{\mathbf{y},\mathbf{z}} \mathbf{w}^T \Phi(\mathbf{x}^l, \mathbf{y}, \mathbf{z})$
5: $f = \mathit{Feedback}(\mathbf{x}^l, \hat{\mathbf{z}})$
6: **if** f is $+1$ **then**
7: $S_l \leftarrow \{(\mathbf{x}^l, \hat{\mathbf{y}}, \hat{\mathbf{z}})\}$
8: **end if**
9: **end for**
10: $\mathbf{w} \leftarrow \mathit{StructLearn}(S, \Phi)$ where $S = \cup_l S_l$
11: **until** no S_l has changed
12: **return** $\mathbf{w}$

Algorithm 2 outlines the learning in more detail. As before, $\hat{\mathbf{y}}$ and $\hat{\mathbf{z}}$ are predicted using the current weight vector and feedback received (lines 4 and 5). When positive feedback is received a new training instance for a structured learner is created from the input sentence and prediction (line 7) this training instance replaces any previous instance for the input sentence. When negative feedback is received the training pool S_l is not updated. A weight vector is learned using a structured learner where the training data S contains at most one example per input sentence. In the first iteration of the outer loop the training data S will contain very few examples. In each subsequent iteration the newly learned weight vector allows the algorithm to acquire new examples. This is repeated until no

[1]Normalization is required to ensure that each sentence contributes equally to the binary learning problem regardless of the sentence's length.

[2]The working set B_l for each sentence may contain multiple positive examples with the same and differing alignments.

new examples are added or changed in S.

Like the direct approach, this learning framework is makes very few assumptions about the type of structured learner used as a base learner (line 10).[3]

4 Model

Semantic parsing is the process of converting a natural language input into a formal logic representation. This process is performed by associating lexical items and syntactic patterns with logical fragments and composing them into a complete formula. Existing approaches rely on extracting a set of *parsing rules*, mapping text constituents to a logical representation, from annotated training data and applying them recursively to obtain the meaning representation. Adapting to new data is a major limitation of these approaches as they cannot handle inputs containing syntactic patterns which were not observed in the training data. For example, assume the training data produced the following set of parsing rules:

Example 2 *Typical parsing rules*

(1) *NP* [λx.`capital(x)`] $\rightarrow$ *capital*

(2) *PP* [`const(texas)`] $\rightarrow$ *of Texas*

(3) *NNP* [`const(texas)`] $\rightarrow$ *Texas*

(4) *NP* [`capital(const(texas))`] $\rightarrow$ *NP*[λx.`capital(x)`] *PP* [`const(texas)`]

At test time the parser is given the sentences in Example 3. Despite the lexical similarity in these examples, the semantic parser will correctly parse the first sentence but fail to parse the second because the lexical items belong to different a syntactic category (i.e., the word *Texas* is not part of a preposition phrase in the second sentence).

Example 3 *Syntactic variations of the same MR*

Target logical form: `capital(const(texas))`

Sentence 1: *"What is the capital of Texas?"*

Sentence 2: *"What is Texas' capital?"*

The ability to adapt to unseen inputs is one of the key challenges in semantic parsing. Several works (Zettlemoyer and Collins, 2007; Kate, 2008) have addressed this issue explicitly by manually defining syntactic transformation rules that can help the learned parser generalize better. Unfortunately these are only partial solutions as a manually constructed rule set cannot cover the many syntactic variations.

Given the previous example, we observe that it is enough to identify that the function `capital(·)` and the constant `const(texas)` appear in the target MR, since there is only a single way to compose these entities into a single formula — `capital(const(texas))`.

Motivated by this observation we define our meaning derivation process over the rules of the MR language and use syntactic information as a way to bias the MR construction process. That is, our inference process considers the *entire* space of meaning representations irrespective of the patterns observed in the training data. This is possible as the MRs are defined by a formal language and formal grammar.[4] The syntactic information present in the natural language is used as soft evidence (features) which guides the inference process to good meaning representations.

This formulation is a major shift from existing approaches that rely on extracting parsing rules from the training data. In existing approaches the space of possible meaning representations is constrained by the patterns in the training data and syntactic structure of the natural language input. Our formulation considers the entire space of meaning representations and allows the model to adapt to previously unseen data and *always* produce a semantic interpretation by using the patterns observed in the input.

We frame our semantic interpretation process as a constrained optimization process, maximizing the objective function defined by Equation 1 which relies on extracting lexical and syntactic features instead of parsing rules. In the remainder of this section we explain the components of our inference model.

4.1 Target Meaning Representation

Following previous work, we capture the semantics of the Geoquery domain using a subset of first-order logic consisting of typed constants and functions. There are two types: entities E in the domain and numeric values N. Functions describe a functional relationship over types (e.g., `population` : $E \rightarrow N$). A complete logical form is constructed through functional composition; in our formalism this is per-

[3]Mistake driven algorithms that do not enforce margin constraints may not be able to generalize using this protocol since they will repeat the same prediction at training time and therefore will not update the model.

[4]This is true for all meaning representations designed to be executed by a computer system.

formed by the substitution operator. For example, given the function `next_to(x)` and the expression `const(texas)`, substitution replaces the occurrence of the free variable `x`, with the expression, resulting in a new logical form: `next_to(const(texas))`. Due to space limitations we refer the reader to (Zelle and Mooney, 1996) for a detailed description of the Geoquery domain.

4.2 Semantic Parsing as Constrained Optimization

Recall that the goal of semantic parsing is to produce the following function (Equation (1)):

$$F_{\mathbf{w}}(\mathbf{x}) = \arg\max_{\mathbf{y},\mathbf{z}} \mathbf{w}^T \Phi(\mathbf{x}, \mathbf{y}, \mathbf{z})$$

However, given that $\mathbf{y}$ and $\mathbf{z}$ are complex structures it is necessary to decompose the structure into a set of smaller decisions to facilitate efficient inference.

In order to define our decomposition we introduce additional notation: c is a constituent (or word span) in the input sentence $\mathbf{x}$ and $\mathcal{D}$ is the set of all function and constant symbols in the domain. The alignment $\mathbf{y}$ is defined as a set of mappings between constituents and symbols in the domain $\mathbf{y} = \{(c, s)\}$ where $s \in \mathcal{D}$.

We decompose the construction of an alignment and logical form into two types of decisions:

First-order decisions. A mapping between constituents and logical symbols (functions and constants).

Second-order decisions. Expressing how logical symbols are composed into a complete logical interpretation. For example, whether `next_to` and `state` forms `next_to(state(·))` or `state(next_to(·))`.

Note that for all possible logical forms and alignments there exists a one-to-one mapping to these decisions.

We frame the inference problem as an Integer Linear Programming (ILP) problem (Equation (2)) in which the first-order decisions are governed by α_{cs}, a binary decision variable indicating that constituent c is aligned with logical symbol `s`. And $\beta_{cs,dt}$ capture the second-order decisions indicating the symbol `t` (associated with constituent d) is an argument to function `s` (associated with constituent c).

$$F_{\mathbf{w}}(\mathbf{x}) = \arg\max_{\alpha,\beta} \sum_{c \in \mathbf{x}} \sum_{s \in D} \alpha_{cs} \cdot \mathbf{w}^T \Phi_1(\mathbf{x}, c, s) + \sum_{c,d \in \mathbf{x}} \sum_{s,t \in D} \beta_{cs,dt} \cdot \mathbf{w}^T \Phi_2(\mathbf{x}, c, s, d, t) \quad (2)$$

It is clear that there are dependencies between the α-variables and β-variables. For example, given that $\beta_{cs,dt}$ is active, the corresponding α-variables α_{cs} and α_{dt} must also be active. In order to ensure a consistent solution we introduce a set of constraints on Equation (2). In addition we add constraints which leverage the typing information inherent in the domain to eliminate logical forms that are invalid in the Geoquery domain. For example, the function `length` only accepts `river` types as input. The set of constraints are:

- A given constituent can be associated with exactly one logical symbol.
- $\beta_{cs,dt}$ is active if and only if α_{cs} and α_{dt} are active.
- If $\beta_{cs,dt}$ is active, `s` must be a function and the types of `s` and `t` should be consistent.
- Functional composition is directional and acyclic.

The flexibility of ILP has previously been advantageous in natural language processing tasks (Roth and Yih, 2007) as it allows us to easily incorporate such constraints.

4.3 Features

The inference problem defined in Equation (2) uses two feature functions: Φ_1 and Φ_2.

First-order decision features Φ_1 Determining if a logical symbol is aligned with a specific constituent depends mostly on lexical information. Following previous work (e.g., (Zettlemoyer and Collins, 2005)) we create a small lexicon, mapping logical symbols to surface forms.[5] This lexicon is small and only used as a starting point. Existing approaches rely on annotated logical forms to extend the lexicon. However, in our setting we do not have access to annotated logical forms, instead we rely on external knowledge to supply further

[5]The lexicon contains on average 1.42 words per function and 1.07 words per constant. For example the function `next_to` has the lexical entries: *borders*, *next*, *adjacent* and the constant `illinois` the lexical item *illinois*.

information. We add features which measure the lexical similarity between a constituent and a logical symbol's surface forms (as defined by the lexicon). Two metrics are used: stemmed word match and a similarity metric based on WordNet (Miller et al., 1990) which allows our model to account for words not in the lexicon. The WordNet metric measures similarity based on synonymy, hyponymy and meronymy (Do et al., 2010). In the case where the constituent is a preposition, which are notorious for being ambiguous, we add a feature that considers the current lexical context (one word to the left and right) in addition to word similarity.

Second-order decision features Φ_2 Determining how to compose two logical symbols relies on syntactic information, in our model we use the dependency tree (Klein and Manning, 2003) of the input sentence. Given a second-order decision $\beta_{cs,dt}$, the dependency feature takes the normalized distance between the head words in the constituents c and d. A set of features also indicate which logical symbols are usually composed together, without considering their alignment to text.

5 Experiments

In this section we describe our experimental setup, which includes the details of the domain, resources and parameters.

5.1 Domain and Corpus

We evaluate our system on the Geoquery domain as described previously. The domain consists of a database and Prolog query language for U.S. geographical facts. The corpus contains of 880 natural language queries paired with Prolog logical form queries ($(\mathbf{x}, \mathbf{z})$ pairs). We follow previous approaches and transform these queries into a functional representation. We randomly select 250 sentences for training and 250 sentences for testing.[6] We refer to the training set as *Response 250* (R250) indicating that each example $\mathbf{x}$ in this data set has a corresponding desired database response r. We refer the testing set as *Query 250* (Q250) where the examples only contain the natural language queries.

[6]Our inference problem is less constrained than previous approaches thus we limit the training data to 250 examples due to scalability issues. We also prune the search space by limiting the number of logical symbol candidates per word (on average 13 logical symbols per word).

Precision and recall are typically used as evaluation metrics in semantic parsing. However, as our model inherently has the ability to map any input sentence into the space of meaning representations the trade off between precision and recall does not exist. Thus, we report accuracy: the percentage of meaning representations which produce the correct response. This is equivalent to recall in previous work (Wong and Mooney, 2007; Zettlemoyer and Collins, 2005; Zettlemoyer and Collins, 2007).

5.2 Resources and Parameters

Feedback Recall that our learning framework does not require meaning representation annotations. However, we do require a *Feedback* function that informs the learner whether a predicted meaning representation when executed produces the desired response for a given input sentence. We automatically generate a set of natural language queries and response pairs $\{(\mathbf{x}, r)\}$ by executing the annotated logical forms on the database. Using this data we construct an automatic feedback function as described in Section 3.

Domain knowledge Our learning approaches require an initial weight vector as input. In order to provide an initial starting point, we initialize the weight vector using a similar procedure to the one used in (Zettlemoyer and Collins, 2007) to set weights for three features and a bias term. The weights were developed on the training set using the feedback function to guide our choices.

Underlying Learning Algorithms In the direct approach the base linear classifier we use is a linear kernel Support Vector Machine with squared-hinge loss. In the aggressive approach we define our base structured learner to be a structural Support Vector Machine with squared-hinge loss and use hamming distance as the distance function. We use a custom implementation to optimize the objective function using the Cutting-Plane method, this allows us to parrallelize the learning process by solving the inference problem for multiple training examples simultaneously.

6 Results

Our experiments are designed to answer three questions:

1. Is it possible to learn a semantic parser *without* annotated logical forms?

Algorithm	R250	Q250
NOLEARN	22.2	—
DIRECT	75.2	69.2
AGGRESSIVE	82.4	73.2
SUPERVISED	87.6	80.4

Table 1: Accuracy of learned models on R250 data and Q250 (testing) data. NOLEARN: using initialized weight vector, DIRECT: using feedback with the direct approach, AGGRESSIVE: using feedback with the aggressive approach, SUPERVISED: using gold 250 logical forms for training. Note that none of the approaches use any annotated logical forms besides the SUPERVISED approach.

Algorithm	# LF	Accuracy
AGGRESSIVE	—	73.2
SUPERVISED	250	80.4
W&M 2006	~ 310	~ 60.0
W&M 2007	~ 310	~ 75.0
Z&C 2005	600	79.29
Z&C 2007	600	86.07
W&M 2007	800	86.59

Table 2: Comparison against previously published results. Results show that with a similar number of logical forms (# LF) for training our SUPERVISED approach outperforms existing systems, while the AGGRESSIVE approach remains competitive without using any logical forms.

2. How much performance do we sacrifice by not restricting our model to parsing rules?

3. What, if any, are the differences in behaviour between the two learning with feedback approaches?

We first compare how well our model performs under four different learning regimes. NOLEARN uses a manually initialized weight vector. DIRECT and AGGRESSIVE use the two response driven learning approaches, where a feedback function but no logical forms are provided. As an upper bound we train the model using a fully SUPERVISED approach where the input sentences are paired with hand annotated logical forms.

Table 1 shows the accuracy of each setup. The model without learning (NOLEARN) gives a starting point with an accuracy of 22.2%. The response driven learning methods perform substantially better than the starting point. The DIRECT approach which uses a binary learner reaches an accuracy of 75.2% on the R250 data and 69.2% on the Q250 (testing) data. While the AGGRESSIVE approach which uses a structured learner sees a bigger improvement, reaching 82.4% and 73.2% respectively. This is only 7% below the fully SUPERVISED upper bound of the model.

To answer the second question, we compare a supervised version of our model to existing semantic parsers. The results are in Table 2. Although the numbers are not directly comparable due to different splits in the data[7], we can see that with a similar number of logical forms for training our SUPERVISED approach outperforms existing systems (Wong and Mooney, 2006; Wong and Mooney, 2007), while the AGGRESSIVE approach remains competitive without using any logical forms. Our SUPERVISED model is still very competitive with other approaches (Zettlemoyer and Collins, 2007; Wong and Mooney, 2007), which used considerably more annotated logical forms in the training phase.

In order to answer the third question, we turn our attention to the differences between the two response driven learning approaches. The DIRECT and AGGRESSIVE approaches use binary feedback to learn, however they utilize the signal differently. DIRECT uses the signal directly to learn a binary classifier capable of replicating the feedback, whereas AGGRESSIVE learns a structured predictor that can repeatedly obtain the logical forms for which positive feedback was received. Thus, although the AGGRESSIVE outperforms the DIRECT approach the concepts each approach learns may be different. Analysis over the training data shows that in 66.8% examples both approaches predict a logical form that gives the correct answer. While AGGRESSIVE correctly answers an additional 16% which DIRECT gets incorrect. In the opposite direction, DIRECT correctly answers 8.8% that AGGRESSIVE does not. Leaving only 8.4% of the examples that both approaches predict incorrect logical forms. This suggests that an approach which combines DIRECT and AGGRESSIVE may be able to improve even further.

Figure 2 shows the accuracy on the entire training data (R250) at each iteration of learning. We see that the AGGRESSIVE approach learns to cover more of the training data and at a faster rate than DIRECT. Note that the performance of the DIRECT approach drops at the first iteration. We hypothesize this is due to imbalances in the binary feedback dataset (too many negative examples) in the first iteration.

[7]It is relatively difficult to compare different approaches in the Geoquery domain given that many existing papers do not use the same data split.

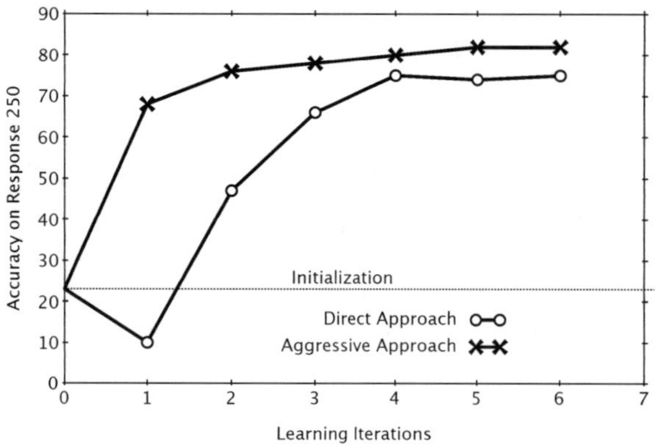

Figure 2: Accuracy on training set as number of learning iterations increases.

7 Related Work

Learning to map sentences to a meaning representation has been studied extensively in the NLP community. Early works (Zelle and Mooney, 1996; Tang and Mooney, 2000) employed inductive logic programming approaches to learn a semantic parser. More recent works apply statistical learning methods to the problem. In (Ge and Mooney, 2005; Nguyen et al., 2006), the input to the learner consists of complete syntactic derivations for the input sentences annotated with logical expressions. Other works (Wong and Mooney, 2006; Kate and Mooney, 2006; Zettlemoyer and Collins, 2005; Zettlemoyer and Collins, 2007; Zettlemoyer and Collins, 2009) try to alleviate the annotation effort by only taking sentence and logical form pairs to train the models. Learning is then defined over hidden patterns in the training data that associate logical symbols with lexical and syntactic elements.

In this work we take an additional step towards alleviating the difficulty of training semantic parsers and present a world response based training protocol. Several recent works (Chen and Mooney, 2008; Liang et al., 2009; Branavan et al., 2009) explore using an external world context as a supervision signal for semantic interpretation. These works operate in settings different to ours as they rely on an external world state that is directly referenced by the input text. Although our framework can also be applied in these settings we do not assume that the text can be grounded in a world state. In our experiments the input text consists of generalized statements which describe some information need that does not correspond directly to a grounded world state.

Our learning framework closely follows recent work on learning from indirect supervision. The direct approach resembles learning a binary classifier over a latent structure (Chang et al., 2010a); while the aggressive approach has similarities with work that uses labeled structures and a binary signal indicating the existence of good structures to improve structured prediction (Chang et al., 2010b).

8 Conclusions

In this paper we tackle one of the key bottlenecks in semantic parsing — providing sufficient supervision to train a semantic parser. Our solution is two fold, first we present a new training paradigm for semantic parsing that relies on *natural, human level supervision*. Second, we suggest a new model for semantic interpretation that does not rely on NL syntactic parsing rules, but rather uses the syntactic information to bias the interpretation process. This approach allows the model to generalize better and reduce the required amount of supervision. We demonstrate the effectiveness of our training paradigm and interpretation model over the Geoquery domain, and show that our model can outperform fully supervised systems.

Acknowledgements We are grateful to Rohit Kate and Raymond Mooney for their help with the Geoquery dataset. Thanks to Yee Seng Chan, Nick Rizzolo, Shankar Vembu and the three anonymous reviewers for their insightful comments. This material is based upon work supported by the Air Force Research Laboratory (AFRL) under prime contract no. FA8750-09-C-0181 and by DARPA under the Bootstrap Learning Program. Any opinions, findings, and conclusion or recommendations expressed in this material are those of the authors and do not necessarily reflect the views of the AFRL or DARPA.

References

S.R.K. Branavan, H. Chen, L. Zettlemoyer, and R. Barzilay. 2009. Reinforcement learning for mapping instructions to actions. In *Proc. of the Annual Meeting of the Association for Computational Linguistics (ACL)*.

M. Chang, D. Goldwasser, D. Roth, and V. Srikumar. 2010a. Discriminative learning over constrained latent representations. In *Proc. of the Annual Meeting of the North American Association of Computational Linguistics (NAACL)*.

M. Chang, D. Goldwasser, D. Roth, and V. Srikumar. 2010b. Structured output learning with indirect supervision. In *Proc. of the International Conference on Machine Learning (ICML)*.

D. Chen and R. Mooney. 2008. Learning to sportscast: a test of grounded language acquisition. In *Proc. of the International Conference on Machine Learning (ICML)*.

Q. Do, D. Roth, M. Sammons, Y. Tu, and V.G. Vydiswaran. 2010. Robust, Light-weight Approaches to compute Lexical Similarity. Computer Science Research and Technical Reports, University of Illinois. http://hdl.handle.net/2142/15462.

R. Ge and R. Mooney. 2005. A statistical semantic parser that integrates syntax and semantics. In *Proc. of the Annual Conference on Computational Natural Language Learning (CoNLL)*.

R. Kate and R. Mooney. 2006. Using string-kernels for learning semantic parsers. In *Proc. of the Annual Meeting of the Association for Computational Linguistics (ACL)*.

R. Kate. 2008. Transforming meaning representation grammars to improve semantic parsing. In *Proc. of the Annual Conference on Computational Natural Language Learning (CoNLL)*.

D. Klein and C. D. Manning. 2003. Fast exact inference with a factored model for natural language parsing. In *Proc. of the Conference on Advances in Neural Information Processing Systems (NIPS)*.

P. Liang, M. I. Jordan, and D. Klein. 2009. Learning semantic correspondences with less supervision. In *Proc. of the Annual Meeting of the Association for Computational Linguistics (ACL)*.

G. Miller, R. Beckwith, C. Fellbaum, D. Gross, and K.J. Miller. 1990. Wordnet: An on-line lexical database. *International Journal of Lexicography*.

L. Nguyen, A. Shimazu, and X. Phan. 2006. Semantic parsing with structured svm ensemble classification models. In *Proc. of the Annual Meeting of the Association for Computational Linguistics (ACL)*.

D. Roth and W. Yih. 2007. Global inference for entity and relation identification via a linear programming formulation. In Lise Getoor and Ben Taskar, editors, *Introduction to Statistical Relational Learning*.

L. Tang and R. Mooney. 2000. Automated construction of database interfaces: integrating statistical and relational learning for semantic parsing. In *Proc. of the Conference on Empirical Methods for Natural Language Processing (EMNLP)*.

L. R. Tang and R. J. Mooney. 2001. Using multiple clause constructors in inductive logic programming for semantic parsing. In *Proc. of the European Conference on Machine Learning (ECML)*.

Y.-W. Wong and R. Mooney. 2006. Learning for semantic parsing with statistical machine translation. In *Proc. of the Annual Meeting of the North American Association of Computational Linguistics (NAACL)*.

Y.-W. Wong and R. Mooney. 2007. Learning synchronous grammars for semantic parsing with lambda calculus. In *Proc. of the Annual Meeting of the Association for Computational Linguistics (ACL)*.

J. M. Zelle and R. J. Mooney. 1996. Learning to parse database queries using inductive logic proramming. In *Proc. of the National Conference on Artificial Intelligence (AAAI)*.

L. Zettlemoyer and M. Collins. 2005. Learning to map sentences to logical form: Structured classification with probabilistic categorial grammars. In *Proc. of the Annual Conference in Uncertainty in Artificial Intelligence (UAI)*.

L. Zettlemoyer and M. Collins. 2007. Online learning of relaxed CCG grammars for parsing to logical form. In *Proceedings of the 2007 Joint Conference on Empirical Methods in Natural Language Processing and on Computational Natural Language Learning (EMNLP-CoNLL)*.

L. Zettlemoyer and M. Collins. 2009. Learning context-dependent mappings from sentences to logical form. In *Proc. of the Annual Meeting of the Association for Computational Linguistics (ACL)*.

Efficient, correct, unsupervised learning of context-sensitive languages

Alexander Clark
Department of Computer Science
Royal Holloway, University of London
alexc@cs.rhul.ac.uk

Abstract

A central problem for NLP is grammar induction: the development of unsupervised learning algorithms for syntax. In this paper we present a lattice-theoretic representation for natural language syntax, called Distributional Lattice Grammars. These representations are objective or empiricist, based on a generalisation of distributional learning, and are capable of representing all regular languages, some but not all context-free languages and some non-context-free languages. We present a simple algorithm for learning these grammars together with a complete self-contained proof of the correctness and efficiency of the algorithm.

1 Introduction

Grammar induction, or unsupervised learning of syntax, no longer requires extensive justification and motivation. Both from engineering and cognitive/linguistic angles, it is a central challenge for computational linguistics. However good algorithms for this task are thin on the ground. There are numerous heuristic algorithms, some of which have had significant success in inducing constituent structure (Klein and Manning, 2004). There are algorithms with theoretical guarantees as to their correctness – such as for example Bayesian algorithms for inducing PCFGs (Johnson, 2008), but such algorithms are inefficient: an exponential search algorithm is hidden in the convergence of the MCMC samplers. The efficient algorithms that are actually used are heuristic approximations to the true posteriors. There are algorithms like the Inside-Outside algorithm (Lari and Young, 1990) which are guaranteed to converge efficiently, but not necessarily to the right answer: they converge to a local optimum that may be, and in practice nearly always is very far from the optimum. There are naive enumerative algorithms that are correct, but involve exhaustively enumerating all representations below a certain size (Horning, 1969). There are no correct *and* efficient algorithms, as there are for parsing, for example.

There is a reason for this: from a formal point of view, the problem is intractably hard for the standard representations in the Chomsky hierarchy. Abe and Warmuth (1992) showed that training stochastic regular grammars is hard; Angluin and Kharitonov (1995) showed that regular grammars cannot be learned even using queries; these results obviously apply also to PCFGs and CFGs as well as to the more complex representations built by extending CFGs, such as TAGs and so on. However, these results do not necessarily apply to other representations. Regular grammars are not learnable, but deterministic finite automata are learnable under various paradigms (Angluin, 1987). Thus it is possible to learn by changing to representations that have better properties: in particular DFAs are learnable because they are "objective"; there is a correspondence between the structure of the language, (the residual languages) and the representational primitives of the formalism (the states) which is expressed by the Myhill-Nerode theorem.

In this paper we study the learnability of a class of representations that we call distributional lattice grammars (DLGs). Lattice-based formalisms were introduced by Clark et al. (2008) and Clark (2009) as context sensitive formalisms that are potentially learnable. Clark et al. (2008) established a similar learnability result for a limited class of context free languages. In Clark (2009), the approach was extended to a significantly larger class but without an explicit learning algorithm. Most of the building blocks are however in place, though we need to make several modifications and ex-

Proceedings of the Fourteenth Conference on Computational Natural Language Learning, pages 28–37,
Uppsala, Sweden, 15-16 July 2010.

tensions to get a clean result. Most importantly, we need to replace the representation used there, which naively could be exponential, with a lazy, exemplar based model.

In this paper we present a simple algorithm for the inference of these representations and prove its correctness under the following learning paradigm: we assume that as normal there is a supply of positive examples, and additionally that the learner can query whether a string is in the language or not (an oracle for membership queries). We also prove that the algorithm is efficient in the sense that it will use a polynomial amount of computation and makes a polynomial number of queries at each step.

The contributions of this paper are as follows: after some basic discussion of distributional learning in Section 2, we define in Section 3 an exemplar-based grammatical formalism which we call Distributional Lattice Grammars. We then give a learning algorithm under a reasonable learning paradigm, together with a self contained proof in elementary terms (not presupposing any extensive knowledge of lattice theory), of the correctness of this algorithm.

2 Basic definitions

We now define our notation; we have a finite alphabet Σ; let Σ^* be the set of all strings (the free monoid) over Σ, with λ the empty string. A (formal) language is a subset of Σ^*. We can concatenate two languages A and B to get $AB = \{uv|u \in A, b \in B\}$.

A context or *environment*, as it is called in structuralist linguistics, is just an ordered pair of strings that we write (l, r) where l and r refer to left and right; l and r can be of any length. We can combine a context (l, r) with a string u with a wrapping operation that we write $\odot$: so $(l, r) \odot u$ is defined to be lur. We will sometimes write f for a context (l, r). There is a special context (λ, λ): $(\lambda, \lambda) \odot w = w$. We will extend this to sets of contexts and sets of strings in the natural way. We will write $Sub(w) = \{u|\exists(l, r) : lur = w\}$ for the set of substrings of a string, and $Con(w) = \{(l, r)|\exists u \in \Sigma^* : lur = w\}$.

For a given string w we can define the *distribution* of that string to be the set of all contexts that it can appear in: $C_L(w) = \{(l, r)|lwr \in L\}$, equivalently $\{f|f \odot w \in L\}$. Clearly $(\lambda, \lambda) \in C_L(w)$ iff $w \in L$.

Distributional learning (Harris, 1954) as a technical term refers to learning techniques which model directly or indirectly properties of the distribution of strings or words in a corpus or a language. There are a number of reasons to take distributional learning seriously: first, historically, CFGs and other PSG formalisms were intended to be learnable by distributional means. Chomsky (2006) says (p. 172, footnote 15):

> The concept of "phrase structure grammar" was explicitly designed to express the richest system that could reasonably be expected to result from the application of Harris-type procedures to a corpus.

Second, empirically we know they work well at least for lexical induction, (Schütze, 1993; Curran, 2003) and are a component of some implemented unsupervised learning systems (Klein and Manning, 2001). Linguists use them as one of the key tests for constituent structure (Carnie, 2008), and finally there is some psycholinguistic evidence that children are sensitive to distributional structure, at least in artificial grammar learning tasks (Saffran et al., 1996). These arguments together suggest that distributional learning has a somewhat privileged status.

3 Lattice grammars

Clark (2009) presents the theory of lattice based formalisms starting algebraically from the theory of residuated lattices. Here we will largely ignore this, and start from a straightforward computational treatment. We start by defining the representation.

Definition 1. *Given a non-empty finite alphabet, Σ, a distributional lattice grammar (DLG) is a 3-tuple consisting of $\langle K, D, F\rangle$, where F is a finite subset of $\Sigma^* \times \Sigma^*$, such that $(\lambda, \lambda) \in F$, K is a finite subset of Σ^* which contains λ and Σ, and D is a subset of $(F \odot KK)$.*

K here can be thought of as a finite set of exemplars, which correspond to substrings or fragments of the language. F is a set of contexts or features, that we will use to define the distributional properties of these exemplars; finally D is a set of grammatical strings, the *data*; a finite subset of the language. $F \odot KK$ using the notation above is $\{luvr|u, v \in K, (l, r) \in F\}$. This is the finite part of the language that we examine. If the language we are modeling is L, then $D = L \cap (F \odot KK)$. Since $\lambda \in K, K \subseteq KK$.

We define a concept to be an ordered pair $\langle S, C \rangle$ where $S \subseteq K$ and $C \subseteq F$, which satisfies the following two conditions: first $C \odot S \subseteq D$; that is to say every string in S can be combined with any context in C to give a grammatical string, and secondly they are maximal in that neither K nor F can be increased without violating the first condition.

We define $\mathfrak{B}(K, D, F)$ to be the set of all such concepts. We use the $\mathfrak{B}$ symbol (*Begriff*) to bring out the links to Formal Concept Analysis (Ganter and Wille, 1997; Davey and Priestley, 2002). This lattice may contain exponentially many concepts, but it is clearly finite, as the number of concepts is less than $\min(2^{|F|}, 2^{|K|})$.

There is an obvious partial order defined by $\langle S_1, C_1 \rangle \leq \langle S_2, C_2 \rangle$ iff $S_1 \subseteq S_2$, Note that $S_1 \subseteq S_2$ iff $C_2 \subseteq C_1$.

Given a set of strings S we can define a set of contexts S' to be the set of contexts that appear with every element of S.

$$S' = \{(l, r) \in F : \forall w \in S, \ \ lwr \in D\}$$

Dually we can define for a set of contexts C the set of strings C' that occur with all of the elements of C:

$$C' = \{w \in K : \forall (l, r) \in C, \ \ lwr \in D\}$$

The concepts $\langle S, C \rangle$ are just the pairs that satisfy $S' = C$ and $C' = S$; the two maps denoted by $'$ are called the polar maps. For any $S \subseteq K$, $S''' = S'$ and for any $C \subseteq F$, $C''' = C'$. Thus we can form a concept from any set of strings $S \subseteq K$ by taking $\langle S'', S' \rangle$; this is a concept as $S''' = S'$. We will write this as $\mathcal{C}(S)$, and for any $C \subseteq F$, we will write $\mathcal{C}(C) = \langle C', C'' \rangle$.

If $S \subseteq T$ then $T' \subseteq S'$, and $S'' \subseteq T''$. For any set of strings $S \subseteq K$, $S \subseteq S''$.

One crucial concept here is the concept defined by (λ, λ) or equivalently by the set $K \cap D$ which corresponds to all of the elements in the language. We will denote this concept by $\mathbf{L} = \mathcal{C}(\{(\lambda, \lambda)\}) = \mathcal{C}(K \cap D)$.

We also define a meet operation by

$$\langle S_1, C_1 \rangle \wedge \langle S_2, C_2 \rangle = \langle S_1 \cap S_2, (S_1 \cap S_2)' \rangle$$

This is the greatest lower bound of the two concepts; this is a concept since if $S_1'' = S_1$ and $S_2'' = S_2$ then $(S_1 \cap S_2)'' = (S_1 \cap S_2)$. Note that this operation is associative and commutative. We can also define a join operation dually; with these operations $\mathfrak{B}(K, D, D)$ is a complete lattice.

So far we have only used strings in $F \odot K$; we now define a concatenation operation as follows.

$$\langle S_1, C_1 \rangle \circ \langle S_2, C_2 \rangle = \langle (S_1 S_2)'', (S_1 S_2)''' \rangle$$

Since S_1 and S_2 are subsets of K, $S_1 S_2$ is a subset of KK, but not necessarily of K. $(S_1 S_2)'$ is the set of contexts shared by all elements of $S_1 S_2$ and $(S_1 S_2)''$ is the subset of K, not KK, that has all of the contexts of $(S_1 S_2)'$. $(S_1 S_2)'''$ might be larger than $(S_1 S_2)'$. We can also write this as $\mathcal{C}((S_1 S_2)')$.

Both $\wedge$ and $\circ$ are monotonic in the sense that if $X \leq Y$ then $X \circ Z \leq Y \circ Z$, $Z \circ X \leq Z \circ Y$ and $X \wedge Z \leq Y \wedge Z$. Note that all of these operations can be computed efficiently; using a perfect hash, and a naive algorithm, we can do the polar maps and $\wedge$ operations in time $\mathcal{O}(|K||F|)$, and the concatenation in time $\mathcal{O}(|K|^2|F|)$.

We now define the notion of derivation in this representation. Given a string w we recursively compute a concept for every substring of w; this concept will approximate the distribution of the string. We define ϕ_G as a function from Σ^* to $\mathfrak{B}(K, D, F)$; we define it recursively:

- If $|w| \leq 1$, then $\phi_G(w) = \langle \{w\}'', \{w\}' \rangle$
- If $|w| > 1$ then
  $\phi_G(w) = \bigwedge_{u,v \in \Sigma^+ : uv = w} \phi_G(u) \circ \phi_G(v)$

The first step is well defined because all of the strings of length at most 1 are already in K so we can look them up directly. To clarify the second step, if $w = abc$ then $\phi_G(abc) = \phi_G(a) \circ \phi_G(bc) \wedge \phi_G(ab) \circ \phi_G(c)$; we compute the string from all possible non-trivial splits of the string into a prefix and a suffix. By using a dynamic programming table that stores the values of $\phi(u)$ for all $u \in Sub(w)$ we can compute this in time $\mathcal{O}(|K|^2|F||w|^3)$; this is just an elementary variant of the CKY algorithm. We define the language defined by the DLG G to be

$$L(G) = \{w | \phi_G(w) \leq \mathcal{C}(\{(\lambda, \lambda)\})\}$$

That is to say, a string is in the language if we predict that a string has the context (λ, λ). We now consider a trivial example: the Dyck language.

Example 1. *Let L be the Dyck language (matched parenthesis language) over $\Sigma = \{a, b\}$, where a corresponds to open bracket, and b to close bracket. Define*

- $K = \{\lambda, a, b, ab\}$
- $F = \{(\lambda, \lambda), (\lambda, b), (a, \lambda)\}$.
- $D = \{\lambda, ab, abab, aabb\}$

$G = \langle K, D, F\rangle$ is a DLG. We will now write down the 5 elements of the lattice:

- $\top = \langle K, \emptyset\rangle$
- $\bot = \langle \emptyset, F\rangle$
- $\mathbf{L} = \langle\{\lambda, ab\}, \{(\lambda, \lambda)\}\rangle$
- $A = \langle\{a\}, \{(\lambda, b)\}\rangle$
- $B = \langle\{b\}, \{(a, \lambda)\}\rangle$

To compute the concatenation $A \circ B$ we first compute $\{a\}\{b\} = \{ab\}$; we then compute $\{ab\}'$ which is $\{(\lambda, \lambda)\}$, and $\{(\lambda, \lambda)\}' = \{\lambda, ab\}$, so $A \circ B = \mathbf{L}$. Similarly to compute $\mathbf{L} \circ \mathbf{L}$, we first take $\{\lambda, ab\}\{\lambda, ab\} = \{\lambda, ab, abab\}$. These all have the context (λ, λ), so the result is the concept $\mathbf{L}$. If we compute $A \circ A$ we get $\{a\}\{a\}$ which is $\{aa\}$ which has no contexts so the result is $\top$. We have $\phi_G(\lambda) = L, \phi_G(a) = A, \phi_G(b) = B$. Applying the recursive computation we can verify that $\phi_G(w) = \mathbf{L}$ iff $w \in L$ and so $L(G) = L$. We can also see that $D = L \cap (F \odot KK)$.

4 Search

In order to learn these grammars we need to find a suitable set of contexts F, a suitable set of strings K, and then work out which elements of $F \odot KK$ are grammatical. So given a choice for K and F it is easy to learn these models under a suitable regime: the details of how we collect information about D depend on the learning model.

The question is therefore whether it is easy to find suitable sets, K and F. Because of the way the formalism is designed, it transpires that the search problem is entirely tractable. In order to analyse the search space, we define two maps between the lattices as K and F are increased. We are going to augment our notation slightly; we will write $\mathfrak{B}(K, L, F)$ for $\mathfrak{B}(K, L \cap (F \odot KK), F)$ and similarly $\langle K, L, F\rangle$ for $\langle K, L \cap (F \odot KK), F\rangle$. When we use the two polar maps (such as C', S'), though we are dealing with more than one lattice, there is no ambiguity as the maps agree; we will when necessary explicitly restrict the output (e.g. $C' \cap J$) to avoid confusion.

Definition 2. *For any language L and any set of contexts $F \subseteq G$, and any sets of strings $J \subseteq K \subseteq \Sigma^*$. We define a map g from $\mathfrak{B}(J, L, F)$ to $\mathfrak{B}(K, L, F)$ (from the smaller lattice to the larger lattice) as $g(\langle S, C\rangle) = \langle C', C\rangle$.*

We also define a map f from $\mathfrak{B}(K, L, G)$ to $\mathfrak{B}(K, L, F)$, (from larger to smaller) as $f(\langle S, C\rangle) = \langle (C \cap F)', C \cap F\rangle$.

These two maps are defined in opposite directions: this is because of the duality of the lattice. By defining them in this way, as we will see, we can prove that these two maps have very similar properties. We can verify that the outputs of these maps are in fact concepts.

We now need to define two monotonicity lemmas: these lemmas are crucial to the success of the formalism. We show that as we increase K the language defined by the formalism decreases monotonically, and that as we increase F the language increases monotonically. There is some duplication in the proofs of the two lemmas; we could prove them both from more abstract properties of the maps f, g which are what are called residual maps, but we will do it directly.

Lemma 1. *Given two lattices $\mathfrak{B}(K, L, F)$ and $\mathfrak{B}(K, L, G)$ where $F \subseteq G$; For all $X, Y \in \mathfrak{B}(K, L, G)$ we have that*

1. $f(X) \circ f(Y) \geq f(X \circ Y)$
2. $f(X) \wedge f(Y) \geq f(X \wedge Y)$

Proof. The proof is elementary but difficult to read. We write $X = \langle S_X, C_X\rangle$ and similarly for Y. For part 1 of the lemma: Clearly $(S'_X \cap F) \subseteq S'_X$, so $(S'_X \cap F)' \supseteq S''_X = S_X$ and the same for S_Y. So $(S'_X \cap F)'(S'_Y \cap F)' \supseteq S_X S_Y$ (as subsets of KK). So $((S'_X \cap F)'(S'_Y \cap F)')' \subseteq (S_X S_Y)' \subseteq (S_X S_Y)'''$. Now by definition, $f(X) \circ f(Y)$ is $\mathcal{C}(Z)$ where $Z = ((S'_X \cap F)'(S'_Y \cap F)')' \cap F$ and $f(X \circ Y)$ has the set of contexts $((S_X S_Y)''' \cap F)$. Therefore $f(X \circ Y)$ has a bigger set of contexts than $f(X) \circ f(Y)$ and is thus a smaller concept. For part 2: by definition $f(X \wedge Y) = \langle (((S_X \cap S_y)' \cap F)', (S_X \cap S_y)' \cap F\rangle$ and $f(X) \wedge f(Y) = \langle (S'_X \cap F)' \cap (S'_y \cap F)', ((S'_X \cap F)' \cap (S'_y \cap F)')' \cap F\rangle$ Now $S'_X \cap F \subseteq S'_X$, so (since $S''_X = S_X$) $S_X \subseteq (S'_X \cap F)'$, and so $S_X \cap S_y \subseteq (S'_X \cap F)' \cap (S'_y \cap F)'$.

So $(S_X \cap S_y)' \supseteq ((S'_X \cap F)' \cap (S'_y \cap F)')$ which gives the result by comparing the context sets of the two sides of the inequality. □

Lemma 2. *For any language L, and two sets of contexts $F \subseteq G$, and any K, if we have two DLGs $\langle K, L, F\rangle$ with map $\phi_F : \Sigma^* \to \mathfrak{B}(K, L, F)$ and $\langle K, L, G\rangle$ with map $\phi_G : \Sigma^* \to \mathfrak{B}(K, L, G)$ then for all w, $f(\phi_G(w)) \leq \phi_F(w)$.*

Proof. By induction on the length of w; clearly if $|w| \leq 1$, $f(\phi_G(w)) = \phi_F(w)$. We now take the inductive step; by definition, (suppressing the definition of u, v in the meet)

$$f(\phi_G(w)) = f(\bigwedge_{u,v} \phi_G(u) \circ \phi_G(v))$$

By Lemma 1, part 2:

$$f(\phi_G(w)) \leq \bigwedge_{u,v} f(\phi_G(u) \circ \phi_G(v))$$

By Lemma 1, part 1:

$$f(\phi_G(w)) \leq \bigwedge_{u,v} f(\phi_G(u)) \circ f(\phi_G(v))$$

By the inductive hypothesis we have $f(\phi_G(u)) \leq \phi_F(u)$ and similarly for v and so by the monotonicity of $\wedge$ and $\circ$:

$$f(\phi_G(w)) \leq \bigwedge_{u,v} \phi_F(u) \circ \phi_F(v)$$

Since the right hand side is equal to $\phi_F(w)$, the proof is done. □

It is then immediate that

Lemma 3. *If $F \subseteq G$ then $L(\langle K, L, F\rangle) \subseteq L(\langle K, L, G\rangle)$,*

Proof. If $w \in L(\langle K, L, F\rangle)$, then $\phi_F(w) \leq \mathbf{L}$, and so $f(\phi_G(w)) \leq \mathbf{L}$ and so $\phi_G(w)$ has the context (λ, λ) and is thus in $L(\langle K, L, G\rangle)$. □

We now prove the corresponding facts about g.

Lemma 4. *For any $J \subseteq K$ and any concepts X, Y in $\mathfrak{B}(J, L, F)$, we have that*

1. $g(X) \circ g(Y) \geq g(X \circ Y)$
2. $g(X) \wedge g(Y) \geq g(X \wedge Y)$

Proof. For the first part: Write $X = \langle S_X, C_X\rangle$ as before. Note that $S_X = C'_X \cap J$. $S_X \subseteq C'_X$, so $S_X S_Y \subseteq C'_X C'_Y$, and so $(S_X S_Y)'' \subseteq (C'_X C'_Y)''$, and $((S_X S_Y)'' \cap J)' \supseteq (C'_X C'_Y)'''$. By calculation $g(X) \circ g(Y) = \langle (C'_X C'_Y)'', (C'_X C'_Y)'''\rangle$ On the other hand, $g(X \circ Y) = \langle ((S_X S_Y)'' \cap J)'', ((S_X S_Y)'' \cap J)'\rangle$ and so $g(X \circ Y)$ is smaller as it has a larger set of contexts.

For the second part: $g(X) \wedge g(Y) = \langle C'_X \cap C'_Y, (C'_X \cap C'_Y)'\rangle$ and $g(X \wedge Y) = \langle (S_X \cap S_Y)'', (S_X \cap S_Y)'\rangle$. Since $S_X = C'_X \cap J$, $S_X \subseteq C'_X$, so $(S_X \cap S_Y) \subseteq C'_X \cap C'_Y$, and therefore $(S_X \cap S_Y)'' \subseteq (C'_X \cap C'_Y)'' = C'_X \cap C'_Y$. □

We now state and prove the monotonicity lemma for g.

Lemma 5. *For all $J \subseteq K \subseteq \Sigma^* \times \Sigma^*$, and for all strings w; we have that $g(\phi_J(w)) \leq \phi_K(w)$.*

Proof. By induction on length of w. Both J and K include the basic elements of Σ and λ. First suppose $|w| \leq 1$, then $\phi_J(w) = \langle (C_L(w) \cap F)' \cap J, C_L(w) \cap F\rangle$, and $g(\phi_J(w)) = \langle (C_L(w) \cap F)', C_L(w) \cap F\rangle$ which is equal to $\phi_K(w)$.

Now suppose true for all w of length at most k, and take some w of length $k + 1$. By definition of ϕ_J:

$$g(\phi_J(w)) = g\left(\bigwedge_{u,v} \phi_J(u) \circ \phi_J(v)\right)$$

Next by Lemma 4, Part 2

$$g(\phi_J(w)) \leq \bigwedge_{u,v} g(\phi_J(u) \circ \phi_J(v))$$

By Lemma 4, Part 1

$$g(\phi_J(w)) \leq \bigwedge_{u,v} g(\phi_J(u)) \circ g(\phi_J(v))$$

By the inductive hypothesis and monotonicity of $\circ$ and $\wedge$:

$$g(\phi_J(w)) \leq \bigwedge_{u,v} \phi_K(u) \circ \phi_K(v) = \phi_K(w)$$

□

Lemma 6. *If $J \subseteq K$ then $L(\langle J, L, F\rangle) \supseteq L(\langle K, L, F\rangle)$*

Proof. Suppose $w \in L(\langle K, L, F\rangle)$. this means that $\phi_K(w) \leq L_K$. therefore $g(\phi_J(w)) \leq L_k$; which means that (λ, λ) is in the concept $g(\phi_J(w))$, which means it is in the concept $\phi_J(w)$, and therefore $w \in L(\langle J, L, F\rangle)$. □

Given these two lemmas we can make the following observations. First, if we have a fixed L and F, then as we increase K, the language will decrease until it reaches a limit, which it will attain after a finite limit.

Lemma 7. *For all L, and finite context sets F, there is a finite K such that for all K_2, $K \subset K_2$, $L(\langle K, L, F \rangle) = L(\langle K_2, L, F \rangle)$.*

Proof. We can define the lattice $\mathfrak{B}(\Sigma^*, L, F)$. Define the following equivalence relation between pairs of strings, where $(u_1, v_1) \sim (u_2, v_2)$ iff $\mathcal{C}(u_1) = \mathcal{C}(u_2)$ and $\mathcal{C}(v_1) = \mathcal{C}(v_2)$ and $\mathcal{C}(u_1 v_1) = \mathcal{C}(u_2 v_2)$. The number of equivalence classes is clearly finite. If K is sufficiently large that there is a pair of strings (u, v) in K for each equivalence class, then clearly the lattice defined by this K will be isomorphic to $\mathfrak{B}(\Sigma^*, L, F)$. Any superset of K will not change this lattice. □

Moreover this language is unique for each L, F. We will call this the limit language of L, F, and we will write it as $L(\langle \Sigma^*, L, F \rangle)$.

If $F \subseteq G$, then $L(\langle \Sigma^*, L, F \rangle) \subseteq L(\langle \Sigma^*, L, G \rangle)$. Finally, we will show that the limit languages never overgeneralise.

Lemma 8. *For any L, and for any F, $L(\langle \Sigma^*, L, F \rangle) \subseteq L$.*

Proof. Recall that $\mathcal{C}(w) = \langle \{w\}'', \{w\}' \rangle$ is the real concept. If G is a limit grammar, we can show that we always have $\phi_G(w) > \mathcal{C}(w)$, which will give us the result immediately. First note that $\mathcal{C}(u) \circ \mathcal{C}(v) \geq \mathcal{C}(uv)$, which is immediate by the definition of $\circ$. We proceed, again, by induction on the length of w. For $|w| \leq 1$, $\phi_G(w) = \mathcal{C}(w)$. For the inductive step we have $\phi_G(w) = \bigwedge_{u,v} \phi_G(u) \circ \phi_G(v)$; by inductive hypothesis we have that this must be more than $\bigwedge_{u,v} \mathcal{C}(u) \circ \mathcal{C}(v) > \bigwedge_{u,v} \mathcal{C}(uv) = \mathcal{C}(w)$ □

5 Weak generative power

First we make the following observation: if we consider an infinite variant of this, where we set $K = \Sigma^*$ and $F = \Sigma^* \times \Sigma^*$ and $D = L$, we can prove easily that, allowing infinite "representations", for any L, $L(\langle K, D, F \rangle) = L$. In this infinite data limit, $\circ$ becomes associative, and the structure of $\mathfrak{B}(K, D, F)$ becomes a residuated lattice, called the syntactic concept lattice of the language L, $\mathfrak{B}(L)$. This lattice is finite iff the language is regular. The fact that this lattice now has residuation operations suggest interesting links to the theory of categorial grammar. It is the finite case that interests us.

We will use $\mathcal{L}_{\text{DLG}}$ to refer to the class of languages that are limit languages in the sense defined above.

$$\mathcal{L}_{\text{DLG}} = \{L | \exists F, L(\langle \Sigma^*, L, F \rangle) = L\}$$

Our focus in this paper is not on the language theory: we present the following propositions. First $\mathcal{L}_{\text{DLG}}$ properly contains the class of regular languages. Secondly $\mathcal{L}_{\text{DLG}}$ contains some non-context-free languages (Clark, 2009). Thirdly it does not contain all context-free languages.

A natural question to ask is how to convert a CFG into a DLG. This is in our view the wrong question, as we are not interested in modeling CFGs but modeling natural languages, but given the status of CFGs as a default model for syntactic structure, it will help to give a few examples, and a general mechanism. Consider a non-terminal N in a CFG with start symbol S. We can define $C(N) = \{(l, r) | S \stackrel{*}{\Rightarrow} lNr\}$ and the yield $Y(N) = \{w | N \stackrel{*}{\Rightarrow} w\}$. Clearly $C(N) \odot Y(N) \subseteq L$, but these are not necessarily maximal, and thus $\langle C(N), Y(N) \rangle$ is not necessarily a concept. Nonetheless in most cases, we can construct a grammar where the non-terminals will correspond to concepts, in this way.

The basic approach is this: for each non-terminal, we identify a finite set of contexts that will pick out only the set of strings generated from that non-terminal: we find some set of contexts F_N typically a subset of $C(N)$ such that $Y(N) = \{w | \forall (l, r) \in F_N, lwr \in L\}$. We say that we can *contextually define* this non-terminal if there is such a finite set of contexts F_N. If a CFG in Chomsky normal form is such that every non-terminal can be contextually defined then the language defined by that grammar is in $\mathcal{L}_{\text{DLG}}$. If we can do that, then the rest is trivial. We take any set of features F that includes all of these F_N; probably just $F = \bigcup_N F_N$; we then pick a set of strings K that is sufficiently large to rule out all incorrect generalisations, and then define D to be $L \cap (F \odot KK)$.

Consider the language $L = \{a^n b^n c^m | n, m \geq 0\} \cup \{a^m b^n c^n | n, m \geq 0\}$. L is a classic example of an inherently ambiguous and thus non-deterministic language.

The natural CFG in CNF for L has non-terminals that generate the following sets: $\{a^n b^n | n \geq 0\}$, $\{a^{n+1} b^n | n \geq 0\}$, $\{b^n c^n | n \geq 0\}$, $\{b^n c^{n+1} | n \geq 0\}$, $\{a^*\}$ and $\{c^*\}$. We note that the six contexts $(aa, bbc), (aa, bbbc), (abb, cc)(abbb, cc), (\lambda, a)$ and (c, λ) will define exactly these sets, in the sense that the set of strings that occur in each context will be exactly the corresponding set. We can also pick out λ, a, b, c with individual contexts. Let $F = \{(\lambda, \lambda), (aaabb, bccc), (aaabbc, \lambda), (\lambda, abbccc), (aaab, bccc), (aa, bbc), (aa, bbbc), (abb, cc), (abbb, cc), (\lambda, a), (c, \lambda)\}$. If we take a sufficiently large set K, say $\lambda, a, b, c, ab, aab, bc, bcc, abc$, and set $D = L \cap F \odot KK$, then we will have a DLG for the language L. In this example, it is sufficient to have one context per non-terminal. This is not in general the case.

Consider $L = \{a^n b^n | n \geq 0\} \cup \{a^n b^{2n} | n \geq 0\}$. Here we clearly need to identify sets of strings corresponding to the two parts of this language, but it is easy to see that no one context will suffice. However, note that the first part is defined by the two contexts $(\lambda, \lambda), (a, b)$ and the second by the two contexts $(\lambda, \lambda), (a, bb)$. Thus it is sufficient to have a set F that includes these four contexts, as well as similar pairs for the other non-terminals in the grammar, and some contexts to define a and b.

We can see that we will not always be able to do this for every CFG. One fixable problem is if the CFG has two separate non-terminals, M, N such that $C(M) \supseteq C(N)$. If this is the case, then we must have that $Y(N) \supseteq Y(M)$, If we pick a set of contexts to define $Y(N)$, then clearly any string in $Y(M)$ will also be picked out by the same contexts. If this is not the case, then we can clearly try to rectify it by adding a rule $N \rightarrow M$ which will not change the language defined.

However, we cannot always pick out the non-terminals with a *finite* set of contexts. Consider the language $L = \{a^n b | n > 0\} \cup \{a^n c^m | m > n > 0\}$ defined in Clark et al. (2008). Suppose wlog that F contains no context (l, r) such that $|l| + |r| \geq k$. Then it is clear that we will not be able to pick out b without also picking out c^{k+1}, since $C_L(c^{k+1}) \cap F \supseteq C_L(b) \cap F$. Thus L, which is clearly context-free, is not in $\mathcal{L}_{\text{DLG}}$. Luckily, this example is highly artificial and does not correspond to any phenomena we are aware of in linguistics.

In terms of representing natural languages, we clearly will in many cases need more than one context to pick out syntactically relevant groups of strings. Using a very simplified example from English, if we want to identify say singular noun phrases, a context like (that is, λ) will not be sufficient since as well as noun phrases we will also have some adjective phrases. However if we include multiple contexts such as (λ, is over there) and so on, eventually we will be able to pick out exactly the relevant set of strings. One of the reasons we need to use a context sensitive representation, is so that we can consider every possible combination of contexts simultaneously: this would require an exponentially large context free grammar.

6 Learning Model

In order to prove correctness of the learning algorithm we will use a variant of Gold-style inductive inference (Gold, 1967). Our choice of this rather old-fashioned model requires justification. There are two problems with learning – the information theoretic problems studied under VC-dimension etc., and the computational complexity issues of constructing a hypothesis from the data. In our view, the latter problems are the key ones. Accordingly, we focus entirely on the efficiency issue, and allow ourself a slightly unrealistic model; see (Clark and Lappin, 2009) for arguments that this is a plausible model.

We assume that we have a sequence of positive examples, and that we can query examples for membership. Given a language L a presentation for L is an infinite sequence of strings $w_1, w_2, \ldots$ such that $\{w_i | i \in N\} = L$. An algorithm receives a sequence T and an oracle, and must produce a hypothesis H at every step, using only a polynomial number of queries to the membership oracle – polynomial in the total size of the presentation. It identifies in the limit the language L iff for every presentation T of L there is a N such that for all $n > N$ $H_n = H_N$, and $L(H_N) = L$. We say it identifies in the limit a class of languages $\mathcal{L}$ iff it identifies in the limit all L in $\mathcal{L}$. We say that it identifies the class in polynomial update time iff there is a polynomial p, such that at each step the model uses an amount of computation (and thus also a number of queries) that is less than $p(n, l)$, where n is the number of strings and l is the maximum length of a string in the observed data. We note that this is slightly too weak. It is possible to produce vacuous enumerative algorithms that can learn anything by only processing a logarithmically small prefix of the string (Pitt, 1989).

7 Learning Algorithm

We now define a simple learning algorithm, that establishes learnability under this paradigm.

There is one minor technical detail we need to deal with. We need to be able to tell when adding a string to a lazy DLG will leave the grammar unchanged. We use a slightly weaker test. Given $G_1 = \langle K, D, F\rangle$ we define as before the equivalence relation between pairs of strings of K, where $(u_1, v_1) \sim_{G_1} (u_2, v_2)$ iff $C_D(u_1) = C_D(u_2)$ and $C_D(v_1) = C_D(v_2)$ and $C_D(u_1v_1) = C_D(u_2v_2)$. Note that $C_D(u) = \{(l, r)|lur \in D\}$.

Given two grammars $G_1 = \langle K, D, F\rangle$ and $G_2 = \langle K_2, D_2, F\rangle$ where $K \subseteq K_2$ and $D \subseteq D_2$ but F is unchanged, we say that these two are *indistinguishable* iff the number of equivalence classes of $K \times K$ under $\sim_{G_1}$ is equal to the number of equivalence classes of $K_2 \times K_2$ under $\sim_{G_2}$. This can clearly be computed efficiently using a union-find algorithm, in time polynomial in $|K|$ and $|F|$. If they are indistinguishable then they define the same language.

7.1 Algorithm

Algorithm 1 presents the basic algorithm. At various points we compute sets of strings like $(F \odot KK) \cap L$; these can be computed using the membership oracle.

First we prove that the program is efficient in the sense that it runs in polynomial update time.

Lemma 9. *There is a polynomial p, such that Algorithm 1, for each w_n, runs in time bounded by $p(n, l)$ where l is the maximum length of a string in $w_1, \ldots w_n$.*

Proof. First we note that K, K_2 and F are always subsets of $Sub(E) \cup \Sigma$ and $Con(E)$, and thus both $|K|$ and $|F|$ are bounded by $nl(l+1)/2 + |\Sigma| + 1$. Computing D is efficient as $|F \odot KK|$ is bounded by $|K|^2|F|$. We can compute ϕ_G as mentioned above in time $|K|^2|F|l^3$; distinguishability is as observed earlier also polynomial. □

Before we prove the correctness of the algorithm we make some informal points. First, we are learning under a rather pessimistic model – the positive examples may be chosen to confuse us, so we cannot make any assumptions. Accordingly we have to very crudely add all substrings and all contexts, rather than using sensible heuristics to select frequent or likely ones.

Algorithm 1: DLG learning algorithm

Data: Input strings $S = \{w_1, w_2 \ldots, \}$, membership oracle $\mathcal{O}$

Result: A sequence of DLGs $G_1, G_2, \ldots$

```
K ← Σ ∪ {λ}, K2 = K ;
F ← {(λ, λ)}, E = {} ;
D = (F ⊙ KK) ∩ L ;
G = ⟨K, D, F⟩ ;
for w_i do
    E ← E ∪ {w_i} ;
    K2 ← K2 ∪ Sub(w_i) ;
    if there is some w ∈ E that is not in L(G) then
        F ← Con(E) ;
        K ← K2 ;
        D = (F ⊙ KK) ∩ L ;
        G = ⟨K, D, F⟩ ;
    end
    else
        D2 ← (F ⊙ K2K2) ∩ L ;
        if ⟨K2, D2, F⟩ not indistinguishable from ⟨K, D, F⟩ then
            K ← K2 ;
            D = (F ⊙ KK) ∩ L ;
            G = ⟨K, D, F⟩ ;
        end
    end
    Output G;
end
```

Intuitively the algorithm works as follows: if we observe a string not in our current hypothesis, then we increase the set of contexts which will increase the language defined. Since we only see positive examples, we will never explicitly find out that our hypothesis overgenerates, accordingly we always add strings to a tester set K_2 and see if this gives us a more refined model. If this seems like it might give a tighter hypothesis, then we increase K.

In what follows we will say that the hypothesis at step n, $G_n = \langle K_n, D_n, F_n\rangle$, and the language defined is L_n. We will assume that the target language is some $L \in \mathcal{L}_{\text{DLG}}$ and $w_1, \ldots$ is a presentation of L.

Lemma 10. *Then there is a point n, and a finite set of contexts F such that for all $N > n$, $F_N = F$., and $L(\langle\Sigma^*, L, F\rangle) = L$.*

Proof. Since $L \in \mathcal{L}_{\text{DLG}}$ there is some set of contexts $G \subset Con(L)$, such that $L = L(\langle \Sigma*, L, G \rangle)$. Any superset of G will define the correct limit language. Let n be the smallest n such that G is a subset of $Con(\{w_1, \ldots, w_n\})$. Consider F_n. If F_n defines the correct limit language, then we will never change F as the hypothesis will be a superset of the target. Otherwise it must define a subset of the correct language. Then either there is some $N > n$ at which it has converged to the limit language which will cause the first condition in the loop to be satisfied and F will be increased to a superset of G, or F will be increased before it converges, and thus the result holds. □

Lemma 11. *After F converges according to the previous lemma, there is some n, such that for all $N > n$, $K_N = K_n$ and $L(\langle K_n, L, F_n \rangle) = L$.*

Proof. let n_0 be the convergence point of F; for all $n > n_0$ the hypothesis will be a superset of the target language; therefore the only change that can happen is that K will increase. By definition of the limit language, it must converge after a finite number of examples. □

Theorem 1. *For every language $L \in \mathcal{L}_{\mathrm{DLG}}$, and every presentation of L, Algorithm 1 will converge to a grammar G such that $L(G) = L$.*

This result is immediate by the two preceding lemmas.

8 Conclusion

We have presented an efficient, correct learning algorithm for an interesting class of languages; this is the first such learning result for a class of languages that is potentially large enough to describe natural language.

The results presented here lack a couple of technical details to be completely convincing. In particular we would like to show that given a representation of size n, we can learn once we have seen a set of examples that is polynomially bounded by n. This will be challenging, as the size of the K we need to converge can be exponentially large in F. We can construct DFAs where the number of congruence classes of the language is an exponential function of the number of states. In order to learn languages like this, we will need to use a more efficient algorithm that can learn even with "insufficient" K: that is to say when the lattice $\mathfrak{B}(K, L, F)$ has fewer elements that $\mathfrak{B}(KK, L, F)$.

This algorithm can be implemented directly and functions as expected on synthetic examples, but would need modification to run efficiently on natural languages. In particular rather than considering whole contexts of the form (l, r) it would be natural to restrict them just to a narrow window of one or two words or tags on each side. Rather than using a membership oracle, we could probabilistically cluster the data in the table of counts of strings in $F \odot K$. In practice we will have a limited amount of data to work with and we can control over-fitting in a principled way by controlling the relative size of K and F.

This formalism represents a process of analogy from stored examples, based on distributional learning – this is very plausible in terms of what we know about cognitive processes, and is compatible with much non-Chomskyan theorizing in linguistics (Blevins and Blevins, 2009). The class of languages is a good fit to the class of natural languages; it contains, as far as we can tell, all standard examples of context free grammars, and includes non-deterministic and inherently ambiguous grammars. It is hard to say whether the class is in fact large enough to represent natural languages; but then we don't know that about any formalism, context-free or context-sensitive. All we can say is that there are no phenomena that we are aware of that don't fit. Only large scale empirical work can answer this question.

Ideologically these models are empiricist – the structure of the representation is based on the structure of the data: this has to be a good thing for computational modeling. By minimizing the amount of hidden, unobservable structure, we can improve learnability. Languages are enormously complex, and it would be simplistic to try to reduce their acquisition to a few pages of mathematics; nonetheless, we feel that the representations and grammar induction algorithms presented in this paper could be a significant piece of the puzzle.

References

N. Abe and M. K. Warmuth. 1992. On the computational complexity of approximating distributions by probabilistic automata. *Machine Learning*, 9:205–260.

D. Angluin and M. Kharitonov. 1995. When won't membership queries help? *J. Comput. Syst. Sci.*, 50:336–355.

D. Angluin. 1987. Learning regular sets from queries and counterexamples. *Information and Computation*, 75(2):87–106.

James P. Blevins and Juliette Blevins. 2009. *Analogy in grammar: Form and acquisition*. Oxford University Press.

A. Carnie. 2008. *Constituent structure*. Oxford University Press, USA.

Noam Chomsky. 2006. *Language and mind*. Cambridge University Press, 3rd edition.

Alexander Clark and Shalom Lappin. 2009. Another look at indirect negative evidence. In *Proceedings of the EACL Workshop on Cognitive Aspects of Computational Language Acquisition*, Athens, March.

Alexander Clark, Rémi Eyraud, and Amaury Habrard. 2008. A polynomial algorithm for the inference of context free languages. In *Proceedings of International Colloquium on Grammatical Inference*, pages 29–42. Springer, September.

Alexander Clark. 2009. A learnable representation for syntax using residuated lattices. In *Proceedings of the 14th Conference on Formal Grammar*, Bordeaux, France.

J.R. Curran. 2003. *From distributional to semantic similarity*. Ph.D. thesis, University of Edinburgh.

B. A. Davey and H. A. Priestley. 2002. *Introduction to Lattices and Order*. Cambridge University Press.

B. Ganter and R. Wille. 1997. *Formal Concept Analysis: Mathematical Foundations*. Springer-Verlag.

E. M. Gold. 1967. Language identification in the limit. *Information and control*, 10(5):447 – 474.

Zellig Harris. 1954. Distributional structure. *Word*, 10(2-3):146–62.

J. J. Horning. 1969. *A Study of Grammatical Inference*. Ph.D. thesis, Stanford University, Computer Science Department, California.

M. Johnson. 2008. Using adaptor grammars to identify synergies in the unsupervised acquisition of linguistic structure. In *46th Annual Meeting of the ACL*, pages 398–406.

Dan Klein and Chris Manning. 2001. Distributional phrase structure induction. In *Proceedings of CoNLL 2001*, pages 113–121.

Dan Klein and Chris Manning. 2004. Corpus-based induction of syntactic structure: Models of dependency and constituency. In *Proceedings of the 42nd Annual Meeting of the ACL*.

K. Lari and S. J. Young. 1990. The estimation of stochastic context-free grammars using the inside-outside algorithm. *Computer Speech and Language*, 4:35–56.

L. Pitt. 1989. Inductive inference, dfa's, and computational complexity. In K. P. Jantke, editor, *Analogical and Inductive Inference*, number 397 in LNAI, pages 18–44. Springer-Verglag.

J. R. Saffran, R. N. Aslin, and E. L. Newport. 1996. Statistical learning by eight month old infants. *Science*, 274:1926–1928.

Hinrich Schütze. 1993. Part of speech induction from scratch. In *Proceedings of the 31st annual meeting of the Association for Computational Linguistics*, pages 251–258.

Identifying Patterns for Unsupervised Grammar Induction

Jesús Santamaría
U. Nacional de Educación a Distancia
NLP-IR Group, Madrid, Spain.
jsant@lsi.uned.es

Lourdes Araujo
U. Nacional de Educación a Distancia
NLP-IR Group, Madrid, Spain.
lurdes@lsi.uned.es

Abstract

This paper describes a new method for unsupervised grammar induction based on the automatic extraction of certain patterns in the texts. Our starting hypothesis is that there exist some classes of words that function as separators, marking the beginning or the end of new constituents. Among these separators we distinguish those which trigger new levels in the parse tree. If we are able to detect these separators we can follow a very simple procedure to identify the constituents of a sentence by taking the classes of words between separators. This paper is devoted to describe the process that we have followed to automatically identify the set of separators from a corpus only annotated with Part-of-Speech (POS) tags. The proposed approach has allowed us to improve the results of previous proposals when parsing sentences from the Wall Street Journal corpus.

1 Introduction

Most works dealing with Grammar Induction (GI) are focused on Supervised Grammar Induction, using a corpus of syntactically annotated sentences, or treebank, as a reference to extract the grammar. The existence of a treebank for the language and for a particular type of texts from which we want to extract the grammar is a great help to GI, even taking into account the theoretical limitations of GI, such as the fact that grammars cannot be correctly identified from positive examples alone (Gold, 1967). But the manual annotation of thousands of sentences is a very expensive task and thus there are many languages for which there are not treebanks available. Even in languages for which there is a treebank, it is usually composed of a particular kind of texts (newspaper articles, for example) and may not be appropriate for other kind of texts, such as tales or poetry. These reasons have led to the appearance of several works focused on unsupervised GI.

Thanks to our knowledge of the language we know that some classes of words are particularly influential to determine the structure of a sentence. For example, let us consider the tree in Figure 1, for which the meaning of the POS tags appears in Table 1. We can observe that the tag MD (Modal) breaks the sentence into two parts. Analogously, in the tree appearing in Figure 2 the POS tag VBZ breaks the sentence. In both cases, we can see that after the breaking tag, a new level appears in the parse tree. A similar effect is observed for other POS tags, such as VB in the tree of Figure 1 and IN in the tree of Figure 2. We call these kind of POS tags *separators*. There are also other POS tags which are frequently the beginning or the end of a constituent[1]. For example in the tree in Figure 1 we can find the sequences (DT NN) and (DT JJ NN), which according to the parse tree are constituents. In the tree in Figure 2 we find the sequence (DT NNP VBG NN). In both trees we can also find sequences beginning with the tag NNP: (NNP NNP) and (NNP CD) in the tree in Figure 1 and (NNP NNP), which appears twice, in the tree in Figure 2. This suggests that there are classes of words with a trend to be the beginning or the end of constituents without giving rise to new levels in the parse tree. We call these POS tags *sub-separators*. These observations reflect some of our intuitions, such as the fact that most sentences are composed of a noun phrase and a verb phrase, being frequently the verb the beginning of the verbal phrase, which usually leads to a new level of the parse tree. We also know that determiners (DT) are frequently the beginning of the noun phrases.

[1]Constituents are language units in which we can arrange the structure of a sentence.

Proceedings of the Fourteenth Conference on Computational Natural Language Learning, pages 38–45,
Uppsala, Sweden, 15-16 July 2010.

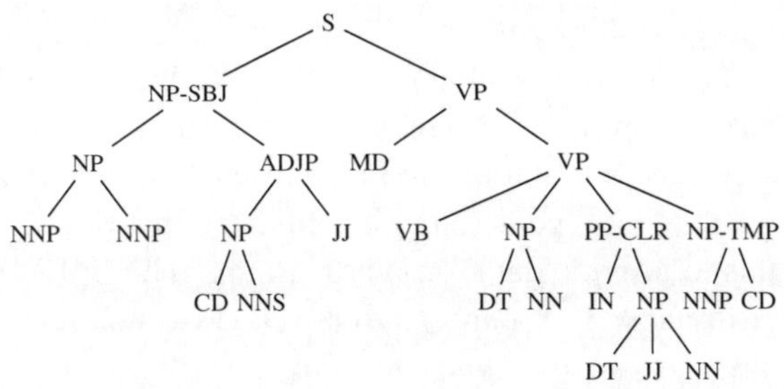

Figure 1: Parse tree for the sentence *Pierre Vinken, 61 years old, will join the board as a nonexecutive director Nov. 29.* from the Penn Treebank

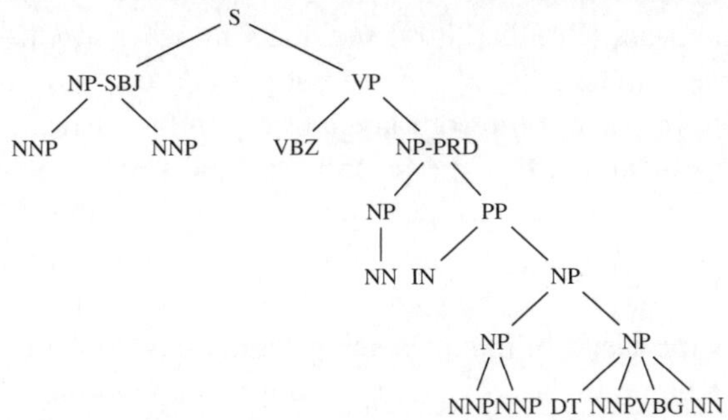

Figure 2: Parse tree for the sentence *Mr. Vinken is chairman of Elsevier N.V., the Dutch publishing group.* from the Penn Treebank

At this point we could either try to figure out what is the set of tags which work as separators, or to compute them from a parsed corpus for the considered language, provided it is available. However, because we do not want to rely on the existence of a treebank for the corresponding language and type of texts we have done something different: we have devised a statistical procedure to automatically capture the word classes which function as separators. In this way our approach can be applied to most languages, and apart from providing a tool for extracting grammars and parsing sentences, it can be useful to study the different classes of words that work as separators in different languages.

Our statistical mechanism to detect separators is applied to a corpus of sentences annotated with POS tags. This is not a strong requirement since there are very accurate POS taggers (about 97%) for many languages. The grammar that we obtain does not specify the left-hand-side of the rules, but only sequences of POS tags that are constituents.

CC	Coordinating conjunction
CD	Cardinal number
DT	Determiner
EX	Existential there
FW	Foreign word
IN	Preposition / subordinating conjunction
JJ	Adjective
JJR	Adjective, comparative
JJS	Adjective, superlative
LS	List item marker
MD	Modal
NN	Noun, singular or mass
NNS	Noun, plural
NNP	Proper noun, singular
NNPS	Proper noun, plural
PDT	Predeterminer
POS	Possessive ending
PRP	Personal pronoun
PP$	Possessive pronoun
RB	Adverb.
RBR	Adverb, comparative
RBS	Adverb., superlative
RP	Particle
SYM	Symbol (mathematical or scientific)
TO	To
UH	Interjection
VB	Verb, base form
VBD	Verb, past tense
VBG	Verb, gerund / present participle
VBN	Verb, past participle
VBP	Verb, non-3rd ps. sing. present
VBZ	Verb, 3rd ps. sing. present
WDT	wh-determiner
WP	wh-pronoun
WP$	Possessive wh-pronoun
WRB	wh-adverb

Table 1: Alphabetical list of part-of-speech tags used in the Penn Treebank, the corpus used in our experiments

At this point we have followed the Klein and Manning (2005) setting for the problem, which allows us to compare our results to theirs. As far as we know these are the best results obtained so far for unsupervised GI using a monolingual corpus. As they do, we have used the Penn treebank (Marcus et al., 1994) for our experiments, employing the syntactic annotations that it provides for evaluation purposes only. Specifically, we have used WSJ10, composed of 6842 sentences, which is the subset of the Wall Street Journal section of the Penn Treebank, containing only those sentences of 10 words or less after removing punctuation and null elements, such as $, ", etc.

The rest of the paper is organized as follows: section 2 reviews some related works; section 3 describes the details of the proposal to automatically extract the separators from a POS tagged corpus; section 4 is devoted to describe the procedure to find a parse tree using the separators; section

5 presents and discusses the experimental results, and section 6 draws the main conclusions of this work.

2 State of the Art

A growing interest in unsupervised GI has been observed recently with the appearance of several works in the topic. Some of these works have focused on finding patterns of words (Solan et al., 2005) more than syntactic structures. It has been noted that the rules produced by GI can also be interpreted semantically (David et al., 2003), where a non-terminal describes interchangeable elements which are instances of the same concepts.

Distributional approaches to unsupervised GI exploit the principle of substitutability: constituents of the same type may be exchanged with one another without affecting the syntax of the surrounding context. Distributional approaches to grammar induction fall into two categories, depending on their treatment of nested structure. The first category covers Expectation-Maximization (EM) systems (Dempster et al., 1977). These systems propose constituents based on analysis of the text, and then select a non-contradictory combination of constituents for each sentence that maximizes a given metric, usually parsing probability. One of the most successful proposals in this area is the one by Klein and Manning (2005), which, as mentioned before, starts from a corpus labelled only with POS tags. The key idea of the model proposed in this work is that constituents appear in constituent contexts. However, the EM algorithm presents some serious problems: it is very slow (Lari and Young, 1990), and is easily trapped in local maxima (Carroll and Charniak, 1992). Alignment Based Learning (ABL) (van Zaanen and Leeds, 2000) is the only EM system applied directly to raw text. However, ABL is relatively inefficient and has only been applied to small corpora. Brooks (Brooks, 2006) reverses the notion of distributional approaches: if we can identify "surrounding context" by observation, we can hypothesize that word sequences occurring in that context will be constituents of the same type. He describes a simplified model of distributional analysis (for raw test) which uses heuristics to reduce the number of candidate constituents under consideration. This is an interesting idea in spite that Brook showed that the system was only capable of learning a small subset of constituent structures in a large test corpus.

The second category is that of incremental learning systems. An incremental system analyzes a corpus in a bottom-up fashion: each time a new constituent type is found it is inserted into the corpus to provide data for later learning. The EMILE (Adriaans, 1999) and ADIOS (David et al., 2003) systems are examples for this category, not yet evaluated on large corpora.

Bilingual experiments have been also conducted with the aim to exploit information from one language to disambiguate another. Usually such a setting requires a parallel corpus or another annotated data that ties the two languages. Cohen and Smith (2009) use the English and Chinese treebanks, which are not parallel corpora, to train parsers for both languages jointly. Their results shown that the performance on English improved in the bilingual setting. Another related work (Snyder et al., 2009) uses three corpora of parallel text. Their approach is closer to the unsupervised bilingual parsing model developed by Kuhn (2004), which aims to improve monolingual performance.

The approach considered in this work follows a different direction, trying to identify certain patterns that can determine the structure of the parse trees.

3 Extracting Separators from the Corpus

To automatically extract the set of separators and sub-separators from a corpus of POS tagged sentences we start from some assumptions:

- The most frequent sequence (of any length) of POS tags in the corpus is a constituent, that we call *safe constituent* (sc). It is quite a sensible assumption, since we can expect that at least for the most frequent constituent the number of occurrences overwhelms the number of sequences appearing by chance.

- We also assume that the POS tag on the left, L_{sc}, and on the right, R_{sc}, of the safe constituent are a kind of context for other sequences that play the same role. According to this, other extended sequences with L_{sc} and R_{sc} at the ends but with other POS tags inside are also considered constituents. This assumption is somehow related to the Klein and Manning's (2005) idea underlying their unsupervised GI proposal. According to them, constituents appear in constituent contexts. Their model exploits the fact that long constituents often have short, common equivalents, which appear in similar contexts and whose constituency as a grammar rule is more easily found.

- According to the previous point, we use the tag on the left (L_{sc}) and on the right (R_{sc}) of the safe constituent as discriminant with respect to which to study the behavior of each POS tag. A POS tag E can have a bias to be inside the safe constituent, to be outside the safe constituent (separator), or not to have a bias at all (sub-separator). We define the *determining side* of a tag E, as the end tag, L_{sc} or R_{sc}, of the *sc* with the greater difference on the number of occurrences of E on both sides of the end tag. For example, if the ratio of occurrences of E on the left and on the right of L_{sc} is smaller (they are more different) than the ratio of E on the left and on the right of R_{sc}, then L_{sc} is the determining side of E, *ds(E)*[2]. Then:
  - E is considered a separator in the following cases:
    - if L_{sc} is the determining side for E and E appears a 75% more often to the left of L_{sc} than to the right (the 75% has been fixed after some estimates described below), or
    - if R_{sc} is the determining side for E and E appears a 75% more often to the right of R_{sc} than to the left.
  - E is considered a sub-separator if the following conditions hold:
    - if L_{sc} is the determining side for E and E appears a 75% less often to the left of L_{sc} than to the right (the ratios are very similar) , or
    - if R_{sc} is the determining side for E and E appears a 75% less often to the right of R_{sc} than to the left.
  - In the remaining cases E is considered to be part of a constituent (the preference is to be inside).

Let us introduce some notation to define more formally the separators and sub-separators. Let $\#(E_1, \cdots, E_n)$ be the number of occurrences of the sequence of tags $(E_1, \cdots, E_n)$. We define a predicate *sim* to denote the similarity between the number of occurrences of a sequence of two tags and the one with reverse order, as

$$sim(E_1, E_2)) =$$
$$\frac{\#(E_1, E_2)}{\#(E_2, E_1)} \geq 0.75 \text{ if } \#(E_1, E_2) \leq \#(E_2, E_1)$$
$$\frac{\#(E_2, E_1)}{\#(E_1, E_2)} \geq 0.75 \text{ if } \#(E_2, E_1) \leq \#(E_1, E_2)$$

Then a tag E is considered a separator if the following predicate is true:

$$sep(L_{sc}, E, R_{sc}) =$$
$$(sd(L_{sc}) \wedge (\#(E, L_{sc}) > \#(L_{sc}, E) \wedge$$
$$\neg sim(E, L_{sc}))) \vee$$
$$(sd(R_{sc}) \wedge (\#(R_{sc}, E) > \#(E, R_{sc}) \wedge \neg sim(E, R_{sc}))$$

A tag is considered a sub-separator when the following predicate is true:

$$subsep(L_{sc}, E, R_{sc}) =$$
$$(sd(L_{sc}) \wedge sim(E, L_{sc})) \vee$$
$$(sd(R_{sc}) \wedge sim(E, R_{sc}))$$

We have computed the number of occurrences of every sequence of POS tags in the corpus, finding that the most frequent sequence of tags is (DT,NN). This sequence, which is our safe constituent, appears 2222 times in the considered corpus WSJ10.

Applying our procedure to the corpus we have obtained the following sets of separators and sub-separators:

Separators	MD, PRP, IN, RB, RBR, CC, TO, VB, VBD, VBN, VBZ, VBP, VBG, EX, LS, RP, UH, WP, WRB, WDT
Sub-separators	DT, PDT, POS, SYM, NN, NNS, NNP, NNPS

For selecting a threshold value to discriminate the preference of a POS tag to be inside or outside of a constituent we have studied the results obtained for different threshold values greater than 50%. Table 2 shows the results. We can observe all of them are very similar for all the thresholds, as long as they are greater than 50%. Analyzing the set of POS-tags that have been classified as separators and sub-separators with each threshold we have found that the only differences are that the tag *POS* (Possessive ending), which is classified as sub-separator using a threshold between 50%

[2] If the number of occurrences of E on any side of L_{sc} or R_{sc} is zero, then we compare differences between occurrences instead of ratios.

and 75%, is classified as separator using higher thresholds, and the tag *SYM* (Symbol), which is classified as sub-separator using a threshold between 50% and 75%, is classified neither as a separator nor as a sub-separator using higher thresholds. We have adopted a threshold value of 75% because higher values can be too restrictive, and in fact provide worse results.

Similarity	F1
55%	74.55
65%	74.55
75%	74.55
85%	72.24
95%	72.24

Table 2: F-measure results obtained for different values of the threshold used to classify the set of POS-tags.

Sub-separators can be grouped to their right or to their left, depending on the case. In order to measure the bias of each of them for one direction or another we have compared the number of occurrences of the most frequent sequence composed of the sub-separator and a POS tag on the right and on the left. We choose as preference direction for a sub-separator the corresponding to the most frequent sequence. Table 3 shows the results obtained, the preference direction of each sub-separator appearing in the last column. In the case of NNP, for which the frequency of the most frequent tag to the right and to the left are the same, we have looked at the second most frequent sequence to choose the grouping direction.

sub-sep	left freq.	right freq.	D
DT	(DT, NN)(2222)	(IN,DT)(894)	L
PDT	(PDT,DT)(28)	(NN,PDT)(14)	L
POS	(POS, NN)(169)	(NNP, POS)(223)	R
SYM	(SYM, IN)(11)	(NN,SYM)(4)	L
NN	(NN, IN)(892)	(DT,NN)(2222)	R
NNS	(NNS, VBP)(591)	(JJ,NNS)(797)	R
NNP	(NNP, NNP)(2127)	(NNP,NNP)(2127)	R
NNPS	(NNPS, NNP)(42)	(NNP,NNPS)(82)	R

Table 3: Preference direction to which each sub-separator clusters. The first column corresponds to the sub-separator, the second one to the most frequent sequence composed of the sub-separator and a tag on its right, the third one to the most frequent sequence of the sub-separator and a tag on its left, and the last column to the resulting direction.

4 Identifying Constituents

Once we have the sets of separators and sub-separators the procedure to identify the constituents of each sentence is as follows:

- We identify the separators in the sentence. For example, if we consider the sentence:

  CC DT NN IN NNP NNP POS NN VBZ

  the separators are marked in boldface:

  CC DT NN **IN** NNP NNP POS NN **VBZ**

- The next step is to split the sentence according to the separators. The first separator which is a verb, if any, is used to split the sentence into two parts. Each separator can give rise to two groups: one composed of the tag sequence between the separator and the next separator, and another one which includes the separator and the POS tags up to the end of the part of the sentence in which it appears (usually sentences are divided into two parts using the first separator which is a verb). In our example, this mechanism leads to the following structure:

  [[**CC** [DT NN] [**IN** [NNP NNP POS NN]]] [**VBZ**]]

- Now it is the turn of the sub-separators (DT, PDT, POS, SYM, NN, NNS, NNP, NNPS), which are underlined in the sentence:

  [[CC [DT NN] [IN [NNP NNP POS NN]]] [VBZ]]

- Finally, each group of the sentence is split according to the sub-separators. Each sub-separator has been assigned a preference direction to form the group with the next POS tag. Looking at Table 3, which tells us the direction in which each sub-separator forms the group, we apply this step to our sentence example, obtaining:

  [[CC [DT NN] [IN [[NNP NNP POS] NN]]] [VBZ]]

The sub-separator DT is grouped with the tags on its right, while NN is grouped with the tags on its left, thus composing the group (DT NN). When two or more sub-separators appear in a sequence, they are grouped together in a unique constituent whenever they have the same grouping direction. In our sentence example this criterion leads to [NNP NNP POS] instead of [NNP[NNP[POS]]]. A constituent finishes if the next POS tag is a separator or if it is a sub-separator that makes groups towards the left. Since POS (Possessive ending) tends to be grouped with the POS tag on its left, it is the end of the constituent.

Figure 3 represents the obtained structure as a parse tree. Figure 4 represents the correct parse tree according to the Penn treebank. We can observe that both structures are very similar. The method based on separators has been able to capture most of the constituent appearing in the parse tree: (DT, NN), (NNP, NNP, POS), (NNP, NNP, POS, NN), (IN, NNP, NNP, POS, NN). The differences between both trees come from our criterion of splitting the sequence of tags into two subsequences using the first verb. This problem will be tackled in the future in a more refined model.

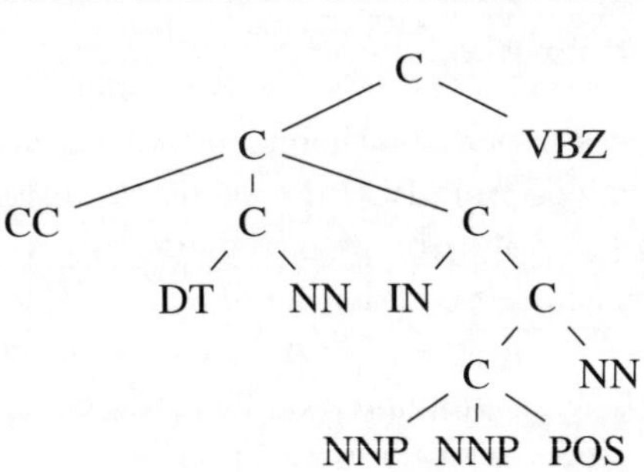

Figure 3: Parse tree for the sentence *And the nose on Mr. Courter's face grows* from the Penn treebank (WSJ), obtained with our separators method.

5 Evaluation

Our proposal has been evaluated by comparing the tree structures produced by the system to the gold-standard trees produced by linguists, which can be found in the Penn Treebank. Because we do not assign class name to our constituents, i.e. a left hand side symbol for the grammar rules, as the linguists do in treebanks, the comparison ignores the class labels, considering only groups of tags.

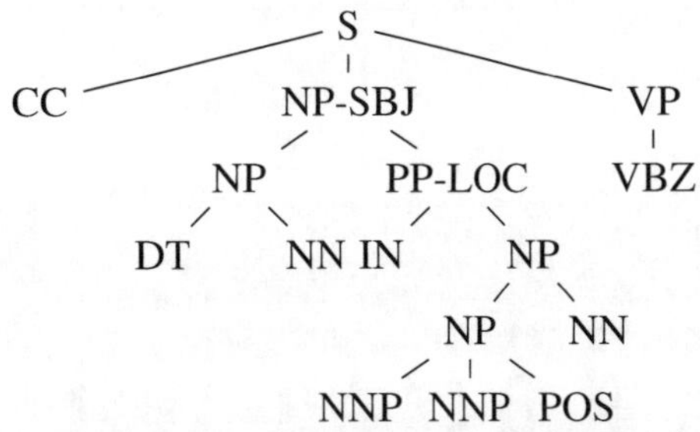

Figure 4: Parse tree appearing in the Penn treebank (WSJ) for the sentence *And the nose on Mr. Courter's face grows.*

The results presented in the work by Klein and Manning (2005) have been our reference, since as far we know they are the best ones obtained so far for unsupervised GI. For the sake of comparison, we have considered the same corpus and the same measures. Accordingly, we performed the experiments on the 6842 sentences[3] of the WSJ10 selection from the Penn treebank Wall Street Journal section.

In order to evaluate the quality of the obtained grammar we have used the most common measures for parsing and grammar induction evaluation: recall, precision, and their harmonic mean (F-measure). They are defined assuming a bracket representation of a parse tree.

Precision is given by the number of brackets in the parse to evaluate which match those in the correct tree and *recall* measures how many of the brackets in the correct tree are in the parse. These measures have counterparts for unlabeled trees, the ones considered in this work – in which the label assigned to each constituent is not checked. Constituents which could not be wrong (those of size one and those spanning the whole sentence) have not been included in the measures.

The definitions of Unlabeled Precision (UP) and Recall (UR) of a proposed corpus $P = [P_i]$ against a gold corpus $G = [G_i]$ are:

$$UP(P,G) = \frac{\sum_i |\text{brackets}(P_i) \cap \text{brackets}(G_i)|}{\sum_i |\text{brackets}(P_i)|},$$

$$UR(P,G) = \frac{\sum_i |\text{brackets}(P_i) \cap \text{brackets}(G_i)|}{\sum_i |\text{brackets}(G_i)|}.$$

Finally, UF (Unlabeled F-measure) is given by:

$$UF = \frac{2 \cdot UP(P,G) \cdot UR(P,G)}{UP(P,G) + UR(P,G)}.$$

[3]More precisely sequences of POS tags

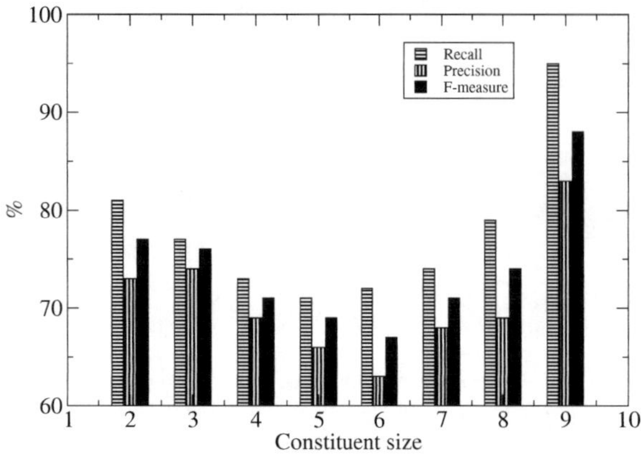

Figure 5: Results obtained per constituent size: unlabeled recall, precision, and F-measure.

Figure 5 shows the results of unlabeled recall, precision and F-measure obtained per constituent size. We can observe that recall and precision, and thus the corresponding F-measure, are quite similar for every constituent size. This is important, because obtaining a high F-measure thanks to a very high recall but with a poor precision, is not so useful. We can also observe that the best results are obtained for short and long constituents, with lower values for middle lengths, such as 5 and 6. We believe that this is because intermediate size constituents present more variability. Moreover, for intermediate sizes, the composition of the constituents is more dependent on sub-separators, for which the statistical differences are less significant than for separators.

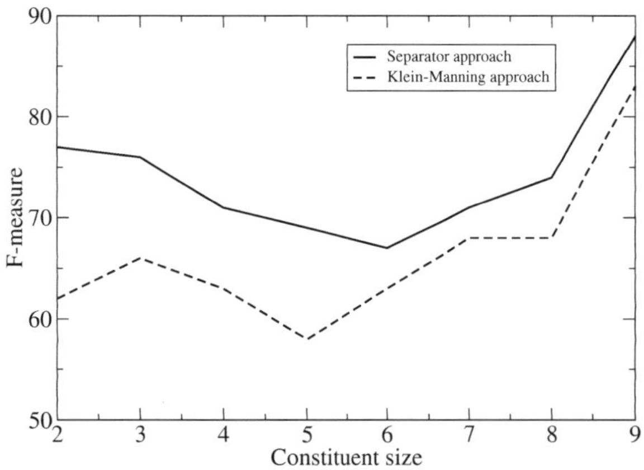

Figure 6: Comparison of the separator approach and Klein and Manning's approach per constituent size.

We have compared our results to those obtained by Klein and Manning (2005) for the same corpus. Table 4 shows the obtained results for WSJ10. We can observe that we have obtained more balanced values of recall and precision, as well as a better value for the F-measure. Thus the method proposed in this work, that we expect to refine by assigning different probabilities to separators and sub-separators, depending on the context they appear in, provides a very promising approach.

	UR	UP	UF
Separ. A.	77,63%	71,71%	74,55%
KM	80.2%	63.8%	71.1%

Table 4: Results (unlabeled recall, precision, and F-measure), obtained with the separator approach (first row) and with the Klein and Manning approach (second row) for the WSJ10 corpus.

Figure 6 compares the F-measure for the two approaches by constituents length. We can observe that the separator approach obtains better results for all the lengths. The figure also shows that the results per constituent length follow the same trend in both approaches, thus reflecting that the difficulty for middle length constituents is greater.

6 Conclusions

We have proposed a novel approach for unsupervised grammar induction which is based on identifying certain POS tags that very often divide the sentences in particular manners. These separators are obtained from POS tagged texts, thus making the model valid for many languages. The constituents corresponding to a sentence are found by means of a simple procedure based on the separators. This simple method has allowed us to improve the results of previous proposals.

We are currently working in defining a more refined statistical model which takes into account the probability of a tag to be a separator or sub-separator, depending on its context. We plan to apply a similar study to other languages, in order to study the different classes of words that function as separator in each of them.

Acknowledgements

This paper has been funded in part by the Spanish MICINN project QEAVis-Catiex (Spanish Ministerio de Educación y Ciencia - TIN2007-67581), as well as by the Regional Government of Madrid under the Research Network MA2VICMR (S2009/TIC-1542).

References

Pieter Adriaans. 1999. Learning Shallow Context-Free Languages under Simple Distributions. Technical Report, Institute for Logic, Language, and Computation, Amsterdam.

David J. Brooks. 2006. Unsupervised grammar induction by distribution and attachment. In *CoNLL-X '06: Proceedings of the Tenth Conference on Computational Natural Language Learning*, pages 117–124. Association for Computational Linguistics.

Glenn Carroll and Eugene Charniak. 1992. Two experiments on learning probabilistic dependency grammars from corpora. In *Working Notes of the Workshop Statistically-Based NLP Techniques*, pages 1–13. AAAI.

Shay B. Cohen and Noah A. Smith. 2009. Shared logistic normal distributions for soft parameter tying in unsupervised grammar induction. In *NAACL '09: Proceedings of Human Language Technologies: The 2009 Annual Conference of the North American Chapter of the Association for Computational Linguistics*, pages 74–82. Association for Computational Linguistics.

Zach Solan David, David Horn, and Shimon Edelman. 2003. Unsupervised efficient learning and representation of language structure. In *Proc. 25th Conference of the Cognitive Science Society*, pages 2577–3596. Erlbaum.

A. Dempster, N. Laird, and D. Rubin. 1977. Maximum likelihood from incomplete data via the EM algorithm. *Royal statistical Society B*, 39:1–38.

E. Mark Gold. 1967. Language identification in the limit. *Information and Control*, 10(5):447–474.

Dan Klein and Christopher D. Manning. 2005. Natural language grammar induction with a generative constituent-context model. *Pattern Recognition*, 38(9):1407–1419.

Jonas Kuhn. 2004. Experiments in parallel-text based grammar induction. In *ACL '04: Proceedings of the 42nd Annual Meeting on Association for Computational Linguistics*, page 470. Association for Computational Linguistics.

K. Lari and S. J. Young. 1990. The estimation of stochastic context-free grammars using the inside-outside algorithm. *Computer Speech and Language*, 4:35–56.

Mitchell P. Marcus, Beatrice Santorini, and Mary Ann Marcinkiewicz. 1994. Building a large annotated corpus of english: The penn treebank. *Computational Linguistics*, 19(2):313–330.

Benjamin Snyder, Tahira Naseem, and Regina Barzilay. 2009. Unsupervised multilingual grammar induction. In *ACL-IJCNLP '09: Proceedings of the Joint Conference of the 47th Annual Meeting of the ACL and the 4th International Joint Conference on Natural Language Processing of the AFNLP: Volume 1*, pages 73–81. Association for Computational Linguistics.

Zach Solan, David Horn, Eytan Ruppin, and Shimon Edelman. 2005. Unsupervised learning of natural languages. *Proceedings of the National Academy of Sciences of the United States of America*, 102(33):11629–11634.

Menno van Zaanen and Ls Jt Leeds. 2000. Learning structure using alignment based learning. In *Universities of Brighton and Sussex*, pages 75–82.

Learning Better Monolingual Models with Unannotated Bilingual Text

David Burkett[†] **Slav Petrov**[‡] **John Blitzer**[†] **Dan Klein**[†]

[†]University of California, Berkeley
{dburkett,blitzer,klein}@cs.berkeley.edu

[‡]Google Research
slav@google.com

Abstract

This work shows how to improve state-of-the-art monolingual natural language processing models using unannotated bilingual text. We build a multiview learning objective that enforces agreement between monolingual and bilingual models. In our method the first, monolingual view consists of supervised predictors learned separately for each language. The second, bilingual view consists of log-linear predictors learned over both languages on bilingual text. Our training procedure estimates the parameters of the bilingual model using the output of the monolingual model, and we show how to combine the two models to account for dependence between views. For the task of named entity recognition, using bilingual predictors increases F_1 by 16.1% absolute over a supervised monolingual model, and retraining on bilingual predictions increases *monolingual* model F_1 by 14.6%. For syntactic parsing, our bilingual predictor increases F_1 by 2.1% absolute, and retraining a monolingual model on its output gives an improvement of 2.0%.

1 Introduction

Natural language analysis in one language can be improved by exploiting translations in another language. This observation has formed the basis for important work on syntax projection across languages (Yarowsky et al., 2001; Hwa et al., 2005; Ganchev et al., 2009) and unsupervised syntax induction in multiple languages (Snyder et al., 2009), as well as other tasks, such as cross-lingual named entity recognition (Huang and Vogel, 2002; Moore, 2003) and information retrieval (Si and Callan, 2005). In all of these cases, multilingual models yield increased accuracy because different languages present different ambiguities and therefore offer complementary constraints on the shared underlying labels.

In the present work, we consider a setting where we already possess supervised monolingual models, and wish to improve these models using *unannotated* bilingual parallel text (bitext). We cast this problem in the multiple-view (multiview) learning framework (Blum and Mitchell, 1998; Collins and Singer, 1999; Balcan and Blum, 2005; Ganchev et al., 2008). Our two views are a *monolingual* view, which uses the supervised monolingual models but not bilingual information, and a *bilingual* view, which exploits features that measure agreement across languages. The parameters of the bilingual view are trained to reproduce the output of the monolingual view. We show that by introducing *weakened* monolingual models into the bilingual view, we can optimize the parameters of the bilingual model to improve monolingual models. At prediction time, we automatically account for the between-view dependence introduced by the weakened monolingual models with a simple but effective view-combination heuristic.

We demonstrate the performance of this method on two problems. The first is named entity recognition (NER). For this problem, our method automatically learns (a variation on) earlier hand-designed rule-based bilingual NER predictors (Huang and Vogel, 2002; Moore, 2003), resulting in absolute performance gains of up to 16.1% F_1. The second task we consider is statistical parsing. For this task, we follow the setup of Burkett and Klein (2008), who improved Chinese and English monolingual parsers using parallel, hand-parsed text. We achieve nearly identical improvements using a purely *unlabeled* bitext. These results carry over to machine translation, where we can achieve slightly better BLEU improvements than the *supervised* model of Burkett and Klein (2008) since we are able to train our model directly on the parallel data where we perform rule extraction.

Finally, for both of our tasks, we use our bilingual model to generate additional automatically labeled *monolingual* training data. We compare

Proceedings of the Fourteenth Conference on Computational Natural Language Learning, pages 46–54,
Uppsala, Sweden, 15-16 July 2010.

this approach to monolingual self-training and show an improvement of up to 14.4% F_1 for entity recognition. Even for parsing, where the bilingual portion of the treebank is much smaller than the monolingual, our technique still can improve over purely monolingual self-training by 0.7% F_1.

2 Prior Work on Learning from Bilingual Text

Prior work in learning monolingual models from bitexts falls roughly into three categories: Unsupervised induction, cross-lingual projection, and bilingual constraints for supervised monolingual models. Two recent, successful unsupervised induction methods are those of Blunsom et al. (2009) and Snyder et al. (2009). Both of them estimate hierarchical Bayesian models and employ bilingual data to constrain the types of models that can be derived. Projection methods, on the other hand, were among the first applications of parallel text (after machine translation) (Yarowsky et al., 2001; Yarowsky and Ngai, 2001; Hwa et al., 2005; Ganchev et al., 2009). They assume the existence of a good, monolingual model for one language but little or no information about the second language. Given a parallel sentence pair, they use the annotations for one language to heavily constrain the set of possible annotations for the other.

Our work falls into the final category: We wish to use bilingual data to improve monolingual models which are already trained on large amounts of data and effective on their own (Huang and Vogel, 2002; Smith and Smith, 2004; Snyder and Barzilay, 2008; Burkett and Klein, 2008). Procedurally, our work is most closely related to that of Burkett and Klein (2008). They used an annotated bitext to learn parse reranking models for English and Chinese, exploiting features that examine pieces of parse trees in both languages. Our method can be thought of as the semi-supervised counterpart to their supervised model. Indeed, we achieve nearly the same results, but without annotated bitexts. Smith and Smith (2004) consider a similar setting for parsing both English and Korean, but instead of learning a joint model, they consider a fixed combination of two parsers and a word aligner. Our model learns parameters for combining two monolingual models and potentially thousands of bilingual features. The result is that our model significantly improves state-of-the-art results, for both parsing and NER.

3 A Multiview Bilingual Model

Given two input sentences $x = (x_1, x_2)$ that are word-aligned translations of each other, we consider the problem of predicting (structured) labels $y = (y_1, y_2)$ by estimating conditional models on pairs of labels from both languages, $p(y_1, y_2|x_1, x_2)$. Our model consists of two views, which we will refer to as monolingual and bilingual. The monolingual view estimates the joint probability as the product of independent marginal distributions over each language, $p_M(y|x) = p_1(y_1|x_1)p_2(y_2|x_2)$. In our applications, these marginal distributions will be computed by state-of-the-art statistical taggers and parsers trained on large monolingual corpora.

This work focuses on learning parameters for the bilingual view of the data. We parameterize the bilingual view using at most one-to-one matchings between *nodes* of structured labels in each language (Burkett and Klein, 2008). In this work, we use the term *node* to indicate a particular component of a label, such as a single (multi-word) named entity or a node in a parse tree. In Figure 2(a), for example, the nodes labeled NP_1 in both the Chinese and English trees are matched. Since we don't know a priori how the components relate to one another, we treat these matchings as hidden. For each matching a and pair of labels y, we define a feature vector $\phi(y_1, a, y_2)$ which factors on edges in the matching. Our model is a conditional exponential family distribution over matchings and labels:

$$p_{\boldsymbol{\theta}}(y, a|x) = \exp\left[\boldsymbol{\theta}^\top \phi(y_1, a, y_2) - A(\boldsymbol{\theta}; x)\right] ,$$

where $\boldsymbol{\theta}$ is a parameter vector, and $A(\boldsymbol{\theta}; x)$ is the log partition function for a sentence pair x. We must approximate $A(\boldsymbol{\theta}; x)$ because summing over all at most one-to-one matchings a is #P-hard. We approximate this sum using the maximum-scoring matching (Burkett and Klein, 2008):

$$\tilde{A}(\boldsymbol{\theta}; x) = \log \sum_y \max_a \left(\exp\left[\boldsymbol{\theta}^\top \phi(y_1, a, y_2)\right]\right) .$$

In order to compute the distribution on labels y, we must marginalize over hidden alignments between nodes, which we also approximate by using the maximum-scoring matching:

$$q_{\boldsymbol{\theta}}(y|x) \stackrel{\text{def}}{=} \max_a \exp\left[\boldsymbol{\theta}^\top \phi(y_1, a, y_2) - \tilde{A}(\boldsymbol{\theta}; x)\right] .$$

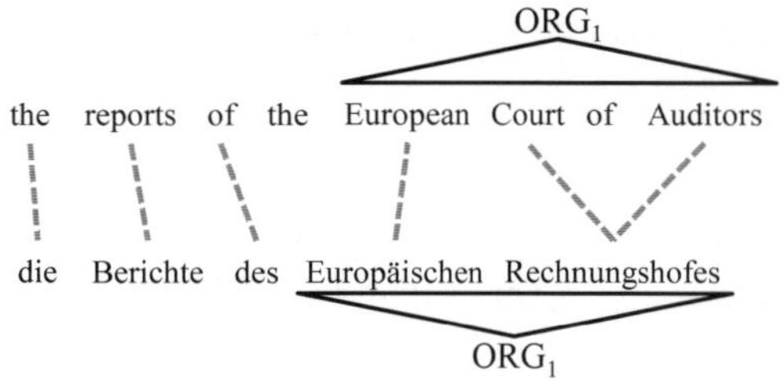

Figure 1: An example where English NER can be used to disambiguate German NER.

We further simplify inference in our model by working in a reranking setting (Collins, 2000; Charniak and Johnson, 2005), where we only consider the top k outputs from monolingual models in both languages, for a total of k^2 labels y. In practice, $k^2 \leq 10,000$ for our largest problem.

3.1 Including Weakened Models

Now that we have defined our bilingual model, we could train it to agree with the output of the monolingual model (Collins and Singer, 1999; Ganchev et al., 2008). As we will see in Section 4, however, the feature functions $\phi(y_1, a, y_2)$ make no reference to the input sentences x, other than through a fixed word alignment. With such limited monolingual information, it is impossible for the bilingual model to adequately capture all of the information necessary for NER or parsing. As a simple example, a bilingual NER model will be perfectly happy to label two aligned person names as *ORG* instead of *PER*: both labelings agree equally well. We briefly illustrate how poorly such a basic bilingual model performs in Section 10.

One way to solve this problem is to include the output of the full monolingual models as features in the bilingual view. However, we are training the bilingual view to match the output of these same models, which can be trivially achieved by putting weight on only the monolingual model scores and never recruiting any bilingual features. Therefore, we use an intermediate approach: we introduce the output of deliberately weakened monolingual models as features in the bilingual view. A weakened model is from the same class as the full monolingual models, but is intentionally crippled in some way (by removing feature templates, for example). Crucially, the weakened models will make predictions that are roughly similar to the full models, but systematically worse. Therefore, model scores from the *weakened* models provide enough power for the bilingual view to make accurate predictions, but ensure that bilingual features will be required to optimize the training objective.

Feat. types	Examples	
Algn Densty	InsideBoth=3	InEnOnly=0
Indicators	LblMatch=*true*	Bias=*true*

Table 1: Sample features used for named entity recognition for the ORG entity in Figure 1.

Let $\ell_1^W = \log p_1^W(y_1|x_1)$, $\ell_2^W = \log p_2^W(y_2|x_2)$ be the log-probability scores from the weakened models. Our final approximation to the marginal distribution over labels y is:

$$q_{\lambda_1,\lambda_2,\boldsymbol{\theta}}(y|x) \overset{def}{=} \max_a \exp\Big[\lambda_1 \ell_1^W + \lambda_2 \ell_2^W + \boldsymbol{\theta}^\top \boldsymbol{\phi}(y_1, a, y_2) - \tilde{A}(\lambda_1, \lambda_2, \boldsymbol{\theta}; x)\Big]. \quad (1)$$

Where

$$\tilde{A}(\lambda_1, \lambda_2, \boldsymbol{\theta}; x) = \log \sum_y \max_a \exp\Big[\lambda_1 \ell_1^W + \lambda_2 \ell_2^W + \boldsymbol{\theta}^\top \boldsymbol{\phi}(y_1, a, y_2)\Big]$$

is the updated approximate log partition function.

4 NER and Parsing Examples

Before formally describing our algorithm for finding the parameters $[\lambda_1, \lambda_2, \boldsymbol{\theta}]$, we first give examples of our problems of named entity recognition and syntactic parsing, together with node alignments and features for each. Figure 1 depicts a correctly-labeled sentence fragment in both English and German. In English, the capitalization of the phrase *European Court of Auditors* helps identify the span as a named entity. However, in German, all nouns are capitalized, and capitalization is therefore a less useful cue. While a monolingual German tagger is likely to miss the entity in the German text, by exploiting the parallel English text and word alignment information, we can hope to improve the German performance, and correctly tag *Europäischen Rechnungshofes*.

The monolingual features are standard features for discriminative, state-of-the-art entity recognizers, and we can produce weakened monolingual models by simply limiting the feature set. The bilingual features, $\phi(y_1, a, y_2)$, are over pairs of aligned nodes, where nodes of the labels y_1 and y_2 are simply the individual named entities. We use a small bilingual feature set consisting of two types of features. First, we use the word alignment density features from Burkett and Klein (2008), which measure how well the aligned entity pair matches up with alignments from an independent

Input:	full and weakened monolingual models: $p_1(y_1\|x_1)$, $p_2(y_2\|x_2)$, $p_1^w(y_1\|x_1)$, $p_2^w(y_2\|x_2)$ unannotated bilingual data: U
Output:	bilingual parameters: $\hat{\theta}, \hat{\lambda}_1, \hat{\lambda}_2$
1.	Label U with full monolingual models: $\forall x \in U,\ \hat{y}_M = \text{argmax}_y\, p_1(y_1\|x_1)p_2(y_2\|x_2)$.
2.	Return $\text{argmax}_{\lambda_1,\lambda_2,\theta} \prod_{x \in U} q_{\theta,\lambda_1,\lambda_2}(\hat{y}_M\|x)$, where $q_{\theta,\lambda_1,\lambda_2}$ has the form in Equation 1.

Figure 3: Bilingual training with multiple views.

word aligner. We also include two indicator features: a bias feature that allows the model to learn a general preference for matched entities, and a feature that is active whenever the pair of nodes has the same label. Figure 1 contains sample values for each of these features.

Another natural setting where bilingual constraints can be exploited is syntactic parsing. Figure 2 shows an example English prepositional phrase attachment ambiguity that can be resolved bilingually by exploiting Chinese. The English monolingual parse mistakenly attaches *to* to the verb *increased*. In Chinese, however, this ambiguity does not exist. Instead, the word 对, which aligns to *to*, has strong selectional preference for attaching to a noun on the left.

In our parsing experiments, we use the Berkeley parser (Petrov et al., 2006; Petrov and Klein, 2007), a split-merge latent variable parser, for our monolingual models. Our full model is the result of training the parser with five split-merge phases. Our weakened model uses only two. For the bilingual model, we use the same bilingual feature set as Burkett and Klein (2008). Table 2 gives some examples, but does not exhaustively enumerate those features.

5 Training Bilingual Models

Previous work in multiview learning has focused on the case of agreement regularization (Collins and Singer, 1999; Ganchev et al., 2008). If we had bilingual labeled data, together with our unlabeled data and monolingual labeled data, we could exploit these techniques. Because we do not possess bilingual labeled data, we must train the bilingual model in another way. Here we advocate training the bilingual model (consisting of the bilingual features and weakened monolingual models) to imitate the full monolingual models. In terms of agreement regularization, our procedure may be thought of as "regularizing" the bilingual model to be similar to the full monolingual models.

Input:	full and weakened monolingual models: $p_1(y_1\|x_1)$, $p_2(y_2\|x_2)$, $p_1^w(y_1\|x_1)$, $p_2^w(y_2\|x_2)$ bilingual parameters: $\hat{\theta}, \hat{\lambda}_1, \hat{\lambda}_2$ bilingual input: $x = (x_1, x_2)$
Output:	bilingual label: y^*

Bilingual w/ Weak	Bilingual w/ Full
1a. $l_1 = \log\left(p_1^w(y_1\|x_1)\right)$	**1b.** $l_1 = \log\left(p_1(y_1\|x_1)\right)$
2a. $l_2 = \log\left(p_2^w(y_2\|x_2)\right)$	**2b.** $l_2 = \log\left(p_2(y_2\|x_2)\right)$

3. Return $\text{argmax}_y \max_a \hat{\lambda}_1 l_1 + \hat{\lambda}_2 l_2 + \hat{\theta}^\top \phi(y_1, a, y_2)$

Figure 4: Prediction by combining monolingual and bilingual models.

Our training algorithm is summarized in Figure 3. For each unlabeled point $x = (x_1, x_2)$, let $\hat{y}_M$ be the joint label which has the highest score from the independent monolingual models (line 1). We then find bilingual parameters $\hat{\theta}, \hat{\lambda}_1, \hat{\lambda}_2$ that maximize $q_{\hat{\theta},\hat{\lambda}_1,\hat{\lambda}_2}(\hat{y}_x|x)$ (line 2). This max-likelihood optimization can be solved by an EM-like procedure (Burkett and Klein, 2008). This procedure iteratively updates the parameter estimates by (a) finding the optimum alignments for each candidate label pair under the current parameters and then (b) updating the parameters to maximize a modified version of Equation 1, restricted to the optimal alignments. Because we restrict alignments to the set of at most one-to-one matchings, the (a) step is tractable using the Hungarian algorithm. With the alignments fixed, the (b) step just involves maximizing likelihood under a log-linear model with no latent variables – this problem is convex and can be solved efficiently using gradient-based methods. The procedure has no guarantees, but is observed in practice to converge to a local optimum.

6 Predicting with Monolingual and Bilingual Models

Once we have learned the parameters of the bilingual model, the standard method of bilingual prediction would be to just choose the y that is most likely under $q_{\hat{\theta},\hat{\lambda}_1,\hat{\lambda}_2}$:

$$\hat{y} = \underset{y}{\text{argmax}}\, q_{\hat{\theta},\hat{\lambda}_1,\hat{\lambda}_2}(y|x)\,. \quad (2)$$

We refer to prediction under this model as "Bilingual w/ Weak," to evoke the fact that the model is making use of weakened monolingual models in its feature set.

Given that we have two views of the data, though, we should be able to leverage additional information in order to make better predictions. In

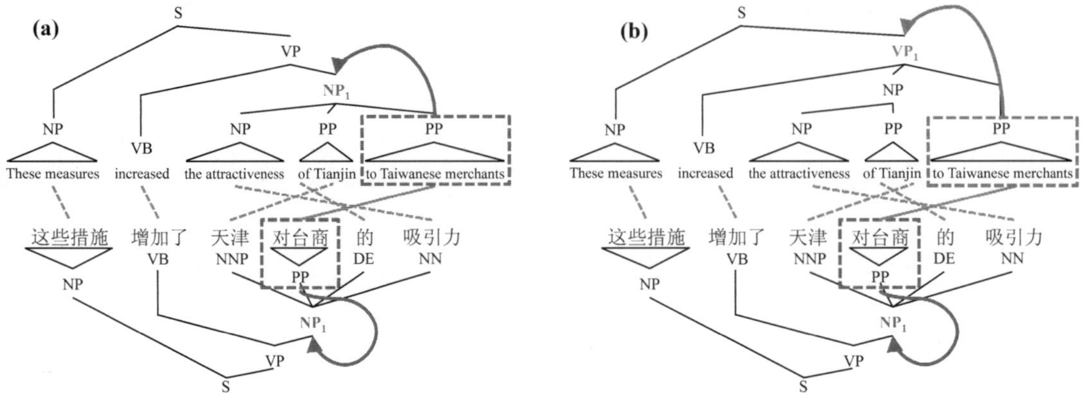

Figure 2: An example of PP attachment that is ambiguous in English, but simple in Chinese. In (a) the correct parses agree (low PP attachment), whereas in (b) the incorrect parses disagree.

Feature Types	Feature Templates	Examples	
		Correct	Incorrect
Alignment Density	INSIDEBOTH, INSIDEENONLY	INSIDEENONLY=0	INSIDEENONLY=1
Span Difference	ABSDIFFERENCE	ABSDIFFERENCE=3	ABSDIFFERENCE=4
Syntactic Indicators	LABEL⟨E,C⟩, NUMCHILDREN⟨E,C⟩	LABEL⟨NP,NP⟩=*true*	LABEL⟨VP,NP⟩=*true*

Table 2: Sample bilingual features used for parsing. The examples are features that would be extracted by aligning the parents of the PP nodes in Figure 2(a) (Correct) and Figure 2(b) (Incorrect).

particular, the monolingual view uses monolingual models that are known to be superior to the monolingual information available in the bilingual view. Thus, we would like to find some way to incorporate the full monolingual models into our prediction method. One obvious choice is to choose the labeling that maximizes the "agreement distribution" (Collins and Singer, 1999; Ganchev et al., 2008). In our setting, this amounts to choosing:

$$\hat{y} = \operatorname*{argmax}_{y} \; p_M(y|x)\; q_{\hat{\boldsymbol{\theta}},\hat{\lambda}_1\hat{\lambda}_2}(y|x)\,. \tag{3}$$

This is the correct decision rule if the views are independent and the labels y are uniformly distributed a priori,[1] but we have deliberately introduced between-view dependence in the form of the weakened monolingual models. Equation 3 implicitly double-counts monolingual information.

One way to avoid this double-counting is to simply discard the weakened monolingual models when making a joint prediction:

$$\hat{y} = \operatorname*{argmax}_{y} \; \max_{a} \; p_M(y|x) \; \exp\left[\hat{\boldsymbol{\theta}}^\top \boldsymbol{\phi}(y_1, a, y_2)\right]. \tag{4}$$

[1] See, e.g. Ando & Zhang(Ando and Zhang, 2007) for a derivation of the decision rule from Equation 3 under these assumptions.

This decision rule uniformly combines the two monolingual models and the bilingual model. Note, however, that we have already learned non-uniform weights for the weakened monolingual models. Our final decision rule uses these weights as weights for the *full* monolingual models:

$$\hat{y} = \operatorname*{argmax}_{y} \max_{a} \exp\Big[\hat{\lambda}_1 \log\big(p_1(y_1|x_1)\big) + \hat{\lambda}_2 \log\big(p_2(y_2|x_2)\big) + \hat{\boldsymbol{\theta}}^\top \boldsymbol{\phi}(y_1, a, y_2)\Big]\,. \tag{5}$$

As we will show in Section 10, this rule for combining the monolingual and bilingual views performs significantly better than the alternatives, and comes close to the optimal weighting for the bilingual and monolingual models.

We will refer to predictions made with Equation 5 as "Bilingual w/ Full", to evoke the use of the full monolingual models alongside our bilingual features. Prediction using "Bilingual w/ Weak" and "Bilingual w/ Full" is summarized in Figure 4.

7 Retraining Monolingual Models

Although bilingual models have many direct applications (e.g. in machine translation), we also wish to be able to apply our models on purely monolingual data. In this case, we can still take

Input: annotated monolingual data: L_1, L_2
unannotated bilingual data: U
monolingual models: $p_1(y_1|x_1)$, $p_2(y_2|x_2)$
bilingual parameters: $\hat{\theta}, \hat{\lambda}_1, \hat{\lambda}_2$

Output: retrained monolingual models:
$p_1^r(y_1|x_1)$, $p_2^r(y_2|x_2)$

$\forall x = (x_1, x_2) \in U$:

Self-Retrained	Bilingual-Retrained
1a. $\hat{y}_{x_1} = \text{argmax}_{y_1} p_1(y_1|x_1)$ $\hat{y}_{x_2} = \text{argmax}_{y_2} p_2(y_2|x_2)$	**1b.** Pick $\hat{y}_x$, Fig. 4 (Bilingual w/ Full)

2. Add $(x_1, \hat{y}_{x_1})$ to L_1 and add $(x_2, \hat{y}_{x_2})$ to L_2.

3. Return full monolingual models $p_1^r(y_1|x_1)$, $p_2^r(y_2|x_2)$ trained on newly enlarged L_1, L_2.

Figure 5: Retraining monolingual models.

advantage of parallel corpora by using our bilingual models to generate new training data for the monolingual models. This can be especially useful when we wish to use our monolingual models in a domain for which we lack annotated data, but for which bitexts are plentiful.[2]

Our retraining procedure is summarized in Figure 5. Once we have trained our bilingual parameters and have a "Bilingual w/ Full" predictor (using Equation 5), we can use that predictor to annotate a large corpus of parallel data (line 1b). We then retrain the full monolingual models on a concatenation of their original training data and the newly annotated data (line 3). We refer to the new *monolingual* models retrained on the output of the bilingual models as "Bilingual-Retrained," and we tested such models for both NER and parsing. For comparison, we also retrained monolingual models directly on the output of the original full monolingual models, using the same unannotated bilingual corpora for self-training (line 1a). We refer to these models as "Self-Retrained".

We evaluated our retrained monolingual models on the same test sets as our bilingual models, but using only monolingual data at test time. The texts used for retraining overlapped with the bitexts used for training the bilingual model, but both sets were disjoint from the test sets.

8 NER Experiments

We demonstrate the utility of multiview learning for named entity recognition (NER) on English/German sentence pairs. We built both our full and weakened monolingual English and German models from the CoNLL 2003 shared task training data. The bilingual model parameters were trained on 5,000 parallel sentences extracted from the Europarl corpus. For the retraining experiments, we added an additional 5,000 sentences, for 10,000 in all. For testing, we used the Europarl 2006 development set and the 2007 newswire test set. Neither of these data sets were annotated with named entities, so we manually annotated 200 sentences from each of them.

We used the Stanford NER tagger (Finkel et al., 2005) with its default configuration as our full monolingual model for each language. We weakened both the English and German models by removing several non-lexical and word-shape features. We made one more crucial change to our monolingual German model. The German entity recognizer has extremely low recall (44 %) when out of domain, so we chose $\hat{y}_x$ from Figure 3 to be the label in the top five which had the largest number of named entities.

Table 3 gives results for named entity recognition. The first two rows are the full and weakened monolingual models alone. The second two are the multiview trained bilingual models. We first note that for English, using the full bilingual model yields only slight improvements over the baseline full monolingual model, and in practice the predictions were almost identical. For this problem, the monolingual German model is much worse than the monolingual English model, and so the bilingual model doesn't offer significant improvements in English. The bilingual model does show significant German improvements, however, including a 16.1% absolute gain in F_1 over the baseline for parliamentary proceedings.

The last two rows of Table 3 give results for *monolingual* models which are trained on data that was automatically labeled using the our models. English results were again mixed, due to the relatively weak English performance of the bilingual model. For German, though, the "Bilingual-Retrained" model improves 14.4% F_1 over the "Self-Retrained" baseline.

9 Parsing Experiments

Our next set of experiments are on syntactic parsing of English and Chinese. We trained both our full and weakened monolingual English models on the Penn Wall Street Journal corpus (Marcus et al., 1993), as described in Section 4. Our full and weakened Chinese models were trained on

[2]Of course, unannotated *monolingual* data is even more plentiful, but as we will show, with the same amount of data, our method is more effective than simple monolingual self-training.

	Eng Parliament			Eng Newswire			Ger Parliament			Ger Newswire		
	Prec	Rec	F_1	Prec	Rec	F_1	Prec	Rec	F_1	Prec	Rec	F_1
Monolingual Models (Baseline)												
Weak Monolingual	52.6	65.9	58.5	67.7	83.0	74.6	71.3	36.4	48.2	80.0	51.5	62.7
Full Monolingual	65.7	71.4	68.4	80.1	88.7	84.2	69.8	44.0	54.0	73.0	56.4	63.7
Multiview Trained Bilingual Models												
Bilingual w/ Weak	56.2	70.8	62.7	71.4	86.2	78.1	70.1	66.3	68.2	76.5	76.1	**76.3**
Bilingual w/ Full	65.4	**72.4**	**68.7**	**80.6**	**88.7**	**84.4**	70.1	**70.1**	**70.1**	74.6	**77.3**	75.9
Retrained Monolingual Models												
Self-Retrained	**71.7**	**74.0**	**72.9**	79.9	87.4	83.5	70.4	44.0	54.2	79.3	58.9	67.6
Bilingual-Retrained	68.6	70.8	69.7	**80.7**	**89.3**	**84.8**	**74.5**	**63.6**	**68.6**	77.9	**69.3**	**73.4**

Table 3: NER Results. Rows are grouped by data condition. We bold all entries that are best in their group and beat the strongest monolingual baseline.

	Chinese	English
Monolingual Models (Baseline)		
Weak Monolingual	78.3	67.6
Full Monolingual	84.2	75.4
Multiview Trained Bilingual Models		
Bilingual w/ Weak	80.4	70.8
Bilingual w/ Full	**85.9**	**77.5**
Supervised Trained Bilingual Models		
Burkett and Klein (2008)	86.1	78.2
Retrained Monolingual Models		
Self-Retrained	83.6	76.7
Bilingual-Retrained	83.9	**77.4**

Table 4: Parsing results. Rows are grouped by data condition. We bold entries that are best in their group and beat the the Full Monolingual baseline.

the Penn Chinese treebank (Xue et al., 2002) (articles 400-1151), excluding the bilingual portion. The bilingual data consists of the parallel part of the Chinese treebank (articles 1-270), which also includes manually parsed English translations of each Chinese sentence (Bies et al., 2007). Only the Chinese sentences and their English translations were used to train the bilingual models – the gold trees were ignored. For retraining, we used the same data, but weighted it to match the sizes of the original monolingual treebanks. We tested on the standard Chinese treebank development set, which also includes English translations.

Table 4 gives results for syntactic parsing. For comparison, we also show results for the *supervised* bilingual model of Burkett and Klein (2008). This model uses the same features at prediction time as the multiview trained "Bilingual w/ Full" model, but it is trained on hand-annotated parses. We first examine the first four rows of Table 4. The "Bilingual w/ Full" model significantly improves performance in both English and Chinese relative to the monolingual baseline. Indeed, it performs only slightly worse than the supervised model.

Phrase-Based System	
Moses (No Parser)	18.8
Syntactic Systems	
Monolingual Parser	18.7
Supervised Bilingual (Treebank Bi-trees)	21.1
Multiview Bilingual (Treebank Bitext)	20.9
Multiview Bilingual (Domain Bitext)	**21.2**

Table 5: Machine translation results.

The last two rows of Table 4 are the results of *monolingual* parsers trained on automatically labeled data. In general, gains in English, which is out of domain relative to the Penn Treebank, are larger than those in Chinese, which is in domain. We also emphasize that, unlike our NER data, this bitext was fairly small relative to the annotated monolingual data. Therefore, while we still learn good bilingual model parameters which give a sizable agreement-based boost when doing bilingual prediction, we don't expect retraining to result in a coverage-based boost in monolingual performance.

9.1 Machine Translation Experiments

Although we don't have hand-labeled data for our largest Chinese-English parallel corpora, we can still evaluate our parsing results via our performance on a downstream machine translation (MT) task. Our experimental setup is as follows: first, we used the first 100,000 sentences of the English-Chinese bitext from Wang et al. (2007) to train Moses (Koehn et al., 2007), a phrase-based MT system that we use as a baseline. We then used the same sentences to extract tree-to-string transducer rules from target-side (English) trees (Galley et al., 2004). We compare the single-reference BLEU scores of syntactic MT systems that result from using different parsers to generate these trees.

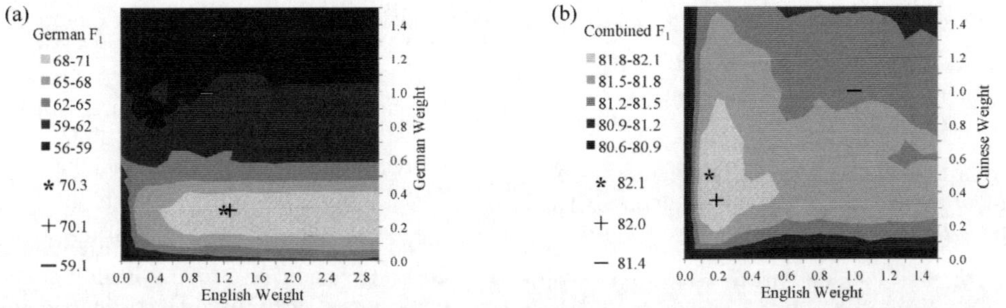

Figure 6: (a) NER and (b) parsing results for different values of λ_1 and λ_2 (see Equation 6). '*' shows optimal weights, '+' shows our learned weights, and '-' shows uniform combination weights.

For our syntactic baseline, we used the monolingual English parser. For our remaining experiments, we parsed both English and Chinese simultaneously. The supervised model and the first multiview trained model are the same Chinese treebank trained models for which we reported parsing results. We also used our multiview method to train an additional bilingual model on part of the bitext we used to extract translation rules.

The results are shown in Table 5. Once again, our multiview trained model yields comparable results to the supervised model. Furthermore, while the differences are small, our best performance comes from the model trained on in-domain data, for which no gold trees exist.

10 Analyzing Combined Prediction

In this section, we explore combinations of the full monolingual models, $p_1(y_1|x_1)$ and $p_2(y_2|x_2)$, and the bilingual model, $\max_a \hat{\boldsymbol{\theta}}^\top \phi(y_1, a, y_2)$. For parsing, the results in this section are for *combined* F_1. This simply computes F_1 over all of the sentences in both the English and Chinese test sets. For NER, we just use German F_1, since English is relatively constant across runs.

We begin by examining how poorly our model performs if we do not consider monolingual information in the bilingual view. For parsing, the combined Chinese and English F_1 for this model is 78.7%. When we combine this model uniformly with the full monolingual model, as in Equation 4, combined F_1 improves to 81.2%, but is still well below our best combined score of 82.1%. NER results for a model trained without monolingual information show an even larger decline.

Now let us consider decision rules of the form:

$$\hat{y} = \underset{y}{\operatorname{argmax}} \max_a \exp[\lambda_1 \log\left(p_1(y_1|x_1)\right) + \lambda_2 \log\left(p_2(y_2|x_2)\right) + \hat{\boldsymbol{\theta}}^\top \phi(y_1, a, y_2)] \,.$$

Note that when $\lambda_1 = \lambda_2 = 1$, this is exactly the uniform decision rule (Equation 4). When $\lambda_1 = \hat{\lambda}_1$ and $\lambda_2 = \hat{\lambda}_2$, this is the "Bilingual w/ Full" decision rule (Equation 5). Figure 6 is a contour plot of F_1 with respect to the parameters λ_1 and λ_2. Our decision rule "Bilingual w/ Full" (Equation 5, marked with a '+') is near the optimum ('*'), while the uniform decision rule ('-') performs quite poorly. This is true for both NER (Figure 6a) and parsing (Figure 6b).

There is one more decision rule which we have yet to consider: the "conditional independence" decision rule from Equation 3. While this rule cannot be shown on the plots in Figure 6 (because it uses both the full and weakened monolingual models), we note that it also performs poorly in both cases (80.7% F_1 for parsing, for example).

11 Conclusions

We show for the first time that state-of-the-art, discriminative monolingual models can be significantly improved using unannotated bilingual text. We do this by first building bilingual models that are trained to agree with pairs of independently-trained monolingual models. Then we combine the bilingual and monolingual models to account for dependence across views. By automatically annotating unlabeled bitexts with these bilingual models, we can train new *monolingual* models that do not rely on bilingual data at test time, but still perform substantially better than models trained using only monolingual resources.

Acknowledgements

This project is funded in part by NSF grants 0915265 and 0643742, an NSF graduate research fellowship, the DNI under grant HM1582-09-1-0021, and BBN under DARPA contract HR0011-06-C-0022.

References

Rie Kubota Ando and Tong Zhang. 2007. Two-view feature generation model for semi-supervised learning. In *ICML*.

Maria-Florina Balcan and Avrim Blum. 2005. A pac-style model for learning from labeled and unlabeled data. In *COLT*.

Ann Bies, Martha Palmer, Justin Mott, and Colin Warner. 2007. English chinese translation treebank v 1.0. Web download. LDC2007T02.

Avrim Blum and Tom Mitchell. 1998. Combining labeled and unlabeled data with co-training. In *COLT*.

Phil Blunsom, Trevor Cohn, and Miles Osborne. 2009. Bayesian synchronous grammar induction. In *NIPS*.

David Burkett and Dan Klein. 2008. Two languages are better than one (for syntactic parsing). In *EMNLP*.

Eugene Charniak and Mark Johnson. 2005. Coarse-to-fine n-best parsing and maxent discriminative reranking. In *ACL*.

Michael Collins and Yoram Singer. 1999. Unsupervised models for named entity classification. In *EMNLP*.

Michael Collins. 2000. Discriminative reranking for natural language parsing. In *ICML*.

Jenny Rose Finkel, Trond Grenager, and Christopher Manning. 2005. Incorporating non-local information into information extraction systems by Gibbs sampling. In *ACL*.

Michel Galley, Mark Hopkins, Kevin Knight, and Daniel Marcu. 2004. What's in a translation rule? In *HLT-NAACL*.

Kuzman Ganchev, Joao Graca, John Blitzer, and Ben Taskar. 2008. Multi-view learning over structured and non-identical outputs. In *UAI*.

Kuzman Ganchev, Jennifer Gillenwater, and Ben Taskar. 2009. Dependency grammar induction via bitext projection constraints. In *ACL*.

Fei Huang and Stephan Vogel. 2002. Improved named entity translation and bilingual named entity extraction. In *ICMI*.

Rebecca Hwa, Philip Resnik, Amy Weinberg, Clara Cabezas, and Okan Kolak. 2005. Bootstrapping parsers via syntactic projection across parallel texts. *Special Issue of the Journal of Natural Language Engineering on Parallel Texts*, 11(3):311–325.

Philipp Koehn, Hieu Hoang, Alexandra Birch, Chris Callison-Burch, Marcello Federico, Nicola Bertoldi, Brooke Cowan, Wade Shen, Christine Moran, Richard Zens, Chris Dyer, Ondrej Bojar, Alexandra Constantin, and Evan Herbst. 2007. Moses: Open source toolkit for statistical machine translation. In *ACL*.

Mitchell P. Marcus, Mary Ann Marcinkiewicz, and Beatrice Santorini. 1993. Building a large annotated corpus of english: The penn treebank. *Computational Linguistics*, 19(2):313–330.

Robert Moore. 2003. Learning translations of named-entity phrases from parallel corpora. In *EACL*.

Slav Petrov and Dan Klein. 2007. Improved inference for unlexicalized parsing. In *HLT-NAACL*.

Slav Petrov, Leon Barrett, Romain Thibaux, and Dan Klein. 2006. Learning accurate, compact, and interpretable tree annotation. In *COLING-ACL*.

Luo Si and Jamie Callan. 2005. Clef 2005: Multilingual retrieval by combining multiple multilingual ranked lists. In *CLEF*.

David A. Smith and Noah A. Smith. 2004. Bilingual parsing with factored estimation: using english to parse korean. In *EMNLP*.

Benjamin Snyder and Regina Barzilay. 2008. Cross-lingual propagation for morphological analysis. In *AAAI*.

Benjamin Snyder, Tahira Naseem, and Regina Barzilay. 2009. Unsupervised multilingual grammar induction. In *ACL*.

Wen Wang, Andreas Stolcke, and Jing Zheng. 2007. Reranking machine translation hypotheses with structured and web-based language models. In *IEEE ASRU Workshop*.

Nianwen Xue, Fu-Dong Chiou, and Martha Palmer. 2002. Building a large-scale annotated chinese corpus. In *COLING*.

David Yarowsky and Grace Ngai. 2001. Inducing multilingual pos taggers and np bracketers via robust projection across aligned corpora. In *NAACL*.

David Yarowsky, Grace Ngai, and Richard Wicentowski. 2001. Inducing multilingual text analysis tools via robust projection across aligned corpora. In *Human Language Technologies*.

Clueless: Explorations in unsupervised, knowledge-lean extraction of lexical-semantic information

Invited Talk

Lillian Lee
Department of Computer Science, Cornell University
llee@cs.cornell.edu

I will discuss two current projects on automatically extracting certain types of lexical-semantic information in settings wherein we can rely neither on annotations nor existing knowledge resources to provide us with clues. The name of the game in such settings is to find and leverage auxiliary sources of information.

Why is it that if you *know* I'll give a silly talk, it follows that you know I'll give a talk, whereas if you *doubt* I'll give a good talk, it doesn't follow that you doubt I'll give a talk? This pair of examples shows that the word "doubt" exhibits a special but prevalent kind of behavior known as downward entailingness — the licensing of reasoning from supersets to subsets, so to speak, but not vice versa. The first project I'll describe is to identify words that are downward entailing, a task that promises to enhance the performance of systems that engage in textual inference, and one that is quite challenging since it is difficult to characterize these items as a class and no corpus with downward-entailingness annotations exists. We are able to surmount these challenges by utilizing some insights from the linguistics literature regarding the relationship between downward entailing operators and what are known as negative polarity items — words such as "ever" or the idiom "have a clue" that tend to occur only in negative contexts. A cross-linguistic analysis indicates some potentially interesting connections to findings in linguistic typology.

That previous paragraph was quite a mouthful, wasn't it? Wouldn't it be nice if it were written in plain English that was easier to understand? The second project I'll talk about, which has the eventual aim to make it possible to automatically simplify text, aims to learn lexical-level simplifications, such as "work together" for "collaborate". (This represents a complement to prior work, which focused on syntactic transformations, such as passive to active voice.) We exploit edit histories in Simple English Wikipedia for this task. This isn't as simple (ahem) as it might at first seem because Simple English Wikipedia and the usual Wikipedia are far from a perfect parallel corpus and because many edits in Simple Wikipedia do not constitute simplifications. We consider both explicitly modeling different kinds of operations and various types of bootstrapping, including as clues the comments Wikipedians sometimes leave when they edit.

Joint work with Cristian Danescu-Niculescu-Mizil, Bo Pang, and Mark Yatskar.

Proceedings of the Fourteenth Conference on Computational Natural Language Learning, page 55,
Uppsala, Sweden, 15-16 July 2010.

Bayesian Hidden Markov Models and Extensions

Invited Talk

Zoubin Ghahramani
Engineering Department, University of Cambridge, Cambridge, UK
zoubin@eng.cam.ac.uk

Hidden Markov models (HMMs) are one of the cornerstones of time-series modelling. I will review HMMs, motivations for Bayesian approaches to inference in them, and our work on variational Bayesian learning. I will then focus on recent nonparametric extensions to HMMs. Traditionally, HMMs have a known structure with a fixed number of states and are trained using maximum likelihood techniques. The infinite HMM (iHMM) allows a potentially unbounded number of hidden states, letting the model use as many states as it needs for the data. The recent development of 'Beam Sampling' — an efficient inference algorithm for iHMMs based on dynamic programming — makes it possible to apply iHMMs to large problems. I will show some applications of iHMMs to unsupervised POS tagging and experiments with parallel and distributed implementations. I will also describe a factorial generalisation of the iHMM which makes it possible to have an unbounded number of binary state variables, and can be thought of as a time-series generalisation of the Indian buffet process. I will conclude with thoughts on future directions in Bayesian modelling of sequential data.

Proceedings of the Fourteenth Conference on Computational Natural Language Learning, page 56,
Uppsala, Sweden, 15-16 July 2010.

Improved Unsupervised POS Induction Using Intrinsic Clustering Quality and a Zipfian Constraint

Roi Reichart
ICNC
The Hebrew University
roiri@cs.huji.ac.il

Raanan Fattal
Institute of computer science
The Hebrew University
raananf@cs.huji.ac.il

Ari Rappoport
Institute of computer science
The Hebrew University
arir@cs.huji.ac.il

Abstract

Modern unsupervised POS taggers usually apply an optimization procedure to a non-convex function, and tend to converge to local maxima that are sensitive to starting conditions. The quality of the tagging induced by such algorithms is thus highly variable, and researchers report average results over several random initializations. Consequently, applications are not guaranteed to use an induced tagging of the quality reported for the algorithm.

In this paper we address this issue using an unsupervised test for intrinsic clustering quality. We run a base tagger with different random initializations, and select the best tagging using the quality test. As a base tagger, we modify a leading unsupervised POS tagger (Clark, 2003) to constrain the distributions of word types across clusters to be Zipfian, allowing us to utilize a perplexity-based quality test. We show that the correlation between our quality test and gold standard-based tagging quality measures is high. Our results are better in most evaluation measures than all results reported in the literature for this task, and are always better than the Clark average results.

1 Introduction

Unsupervised part-of-speech (POS) induction is of major theoretical and practical importance. It counters the arbitrary nature of manually designed tag sets, and avoids manual corpus annotation costs. The task enjoys considerable current interest in the research community (see Section 3).

Most unsupervised POS tagging algorithms apply an optimization procedure to a non-convex function, and tend to converge to local maxima that strongly depend on the algorithm's (usually random) initialization. The quality of the taggings produced by different initializations varies substantially. Figure 1 demonstrates this phenomenon for a leading POS induction algorithm (Clark, 2003). The absolute variability of the induced tagging quality is 10-15%, which is around 20% of the mean. Strong variability has also been reported by other authors (Section 3).

The common practice in the literature is to report mean results over several random initializations of the algorithm (e.g. (Clark, 2003; Smith and Eisner, 2005; Goldwater and Griffiths, 2007; Johnson, 2007)). This means that applications using the induced tagging are not guaranteed to use a tagging of the reported quality.

In this paper we address this issue using an unsupervised test for intrinsic clustering quality. We present a quality-based algorithmic family Q. Each of its concrete member algorithms Q(B) runs a base tagger B with different random initializations, and selects the best tagging according the quality test. If the test is highly positively correlated with external tagging quality measures (e.g., those based on gold standard tagging), Q(B) will produce better results than B with high probability.

We experiment with two base taggers, Clark's original tagger (CT) and *Zipf Constrained Clark (ZCC)*. ZCC is a novel algorithm of interest in its own right, which is especially suitable as a base tagger in the family Q. ZCC is a modification of Clark's algorithm in which the distribution of the number of word types in a cluster (*cluster type size*) is constrained to be Zipfian. This property holds for natural languages, hence we can expect a higher correlation between ZCC and an accepted unsupervised quality measure, perplexity.

We show that for both base taggers, the correlation between our unsupervised quality test and gold standard based tagging quality measures is high. For the English WSJ corpus, the Q(ZCC)

Proceedings of the Fourteenth Conference on Computational Natural Language Learning, pages 57–66,
Uppsala, Sweden, 15-16 July 2010.

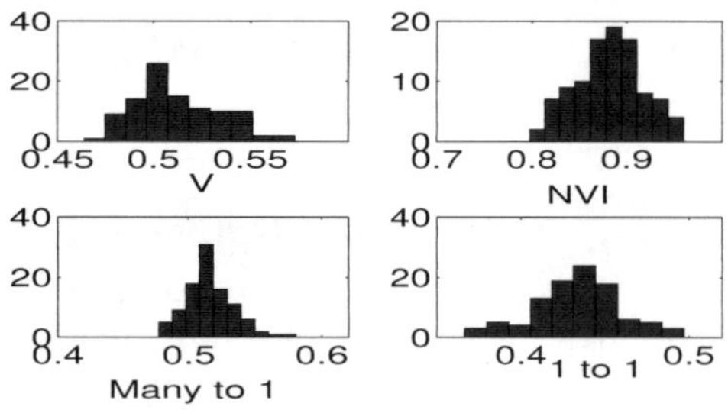

Figure 1: Distribution of the quality of the taggings produced in 100 runs of the Clark POS induction algorithm (with different random initializations) for sections 2-21 of the WSJ corpus. All graphs are 10-bin histograms presenting the number of runs (y-axis) with the corresponding quality (x-axis). Quality is evaluated with 4 clustering evaluation measures: V, NVI, greedy m-1 mapping and greedy 1-1 mapping. The quality of the induced tagging varies considerably.

algorithm gives better results than CT with probability 82-100% (depending on the external quality measure used). Q(CT) is shown to be better than the original CT algorithm as well. Our results are better in most evaluation measures than all previous results reported in the literature for this task, and are always better than Clark's average results.

Section 2 describes the ZCC algorithm and our quality measure. Section 3 discusses previous work. Section 4 presents the experimental setup and Section 5 reports our results.

2 The Q(ZCC) Algorithm

Given an N word corpus M consisting of plain text, with word types $W = \{w_1, \ldots, w_m\}$, the *unsupervised POS induction* task is to find a class membership function g from W into a set of class labels $\{c_1, \ldots, c_n\}$. In the version tackled in this paper, the number of classes n is an input of the algorithm. The membership function g can be used to tag a corpus if it is deterministic (as the function learned in this work) or if a rule for selecting a single tag for every word is provided.

Most modern unsupervised POS taggers produce taggings of variable quality that strongly depend on their initialization. Our approach towards generating a single high quality tagging is to use a family of algorithms Q. Each member Q(B) of Q utilizes a base tagger B, which is run using several random initializations. The final output is selected according to an unsupervised quality test. We focus here on Clark's tagger (Clark, 2003) (CT), probably the leading POS induction algorithm (see Table 3).

We start with a description of the original CT. We then detail ZCC, a modification of CT that constrains the clustering space by adding a Zipf-based constraint. Our perplexity-based unsupervised tagging quality test is discussed next. Finally, we provide an unsupervised technique for selecting the parameter of the Zipfian constraint.

2.1 The Original Clark Tagger (CT)

The tagger's statistical model combines distributional and morphological information with the likelihood function of the Brown algorithm (Brown et al., 1992; Ney et al., 1994; Martin et al., 1998). In the Brown algorithm a class assignment function g is selected such that the class bigram likelihood of the corpus, $p(M|g)$, is maximized. Morphological and distributional information is introduced to the Clark model through a prior $p(g)$. The prior prefers morphologically uniform clusters and skewed cluster sizes.

The probability function the algorithm tries to maximize is:

(1) $p(M, g) = p(M|g) \cdot p(g)$

(2) $p(M|g) = \prod_{i=2}^{i=N} p(g(w_i)|g(w_{i-1}))$

(3) $p(g) = \prod_{j=1}^{n} \alpha_j \prod_{g(w)=j} q_j(w)$

Where $q_j(w_i)$ is the probability of assigning $w_i \in W$ by cluster c_j according to the morphological model and α_j is the coefficient of cluster j, which equals to the number of word types assigned to that cluster divided by the total number of word types in the vocabulary W. The objective of the algorithm is formally specified by:

$$g^* = argmax_g p(M, g)$$

To find the cluster assignment g^* an iterative algorithm is applied. As initialization, the words in W are randomly assigned to clusters (clusters are thus of similar sizes). Then, for each word (words are ordered by their frequency in the corpus) the algorithm computes the effect that moving it from its current cluster to each of the other clusters would have on the probability function. The word is moved to the cluster having the highest positive effect (if there is no such cluster, the word is not moved). The last step is performed iteratively until no improvement to the probability function is possible through a single operation.

The probability function has many local maxima and the one to which the algorithm convergences strongly depends on the initial assignment of words to clusters. The quality of the clusters induced in different runs of the algorithm is highly variable (Figure 1).

2.2 The Cluster Type Size Zipf Constraint

The motivation behind using a Zipfian constraint is the following observation: when a certain statistic is known to affect the quality of the induced clustering and it is not explicitly manipulated by the algorithm, strong fluctuations in its values are likely to imply that there are uncontrolled fluctuations in the quality of the induced clusterings. Thus, introducing a constraint that we believe holds in real data increases the correlation between clustering quality and a well accepted unsupervised quality measure (perplexity).

Our ZCC algorithm searches for a class assignment function g that maximizes the probability function (1) under a constraint on the clustering space, namely constraining the cluster type size distribution induced by g to be Zipfian. This constraint holds in many languages (Mitzenmacher, 2004) and is demonstrated in Figure 3 for the English corpus with which we experiment in this paper.

Zipf's law predicts that the fraction of elements in class k is given by:

$$f(k; s; n) = \frac{1/k^s}{\sum_{i=1}^{n}(1/i^s)}$$

where s is a parameter of the distribution and n the number of clusters.

Denote the cluster type size distribution derived from the algorithm's cluster assignment function g by $T(g)$. The objective of the algorithm is

$$g^{**} = argmax_g p(M, g) \; s.t. \; T(g) \sim Zipf(s)$$

To impose the Zipfian distribution on the induced clusters size, we make two modifications to the original CT algorithm. First, at initialization, words are randomly assigned to clusters in a way that cluster sizes are distributed according to the Zipfian distribution (with a parameter s). Specifically, we randomly select words to be assigned to the first cluster until the fraction of word types in the cluster equals to the prediction given by Zipf's law. We then randomly assign words to the second cluster and so on.

Second, we change the basic operation of the algorithm from moving a word to a cluster to swapping two words between two different clusters. For each word w_i (again, words are ordered by their frequency in the corpus as in CT), the algorithm computes the effect on the probability function of moving it from its current cluster c_{curr} to each of the other clusters. We denote the cluster showing the best effect by c_{best}. Then, we search the words of c_{best} for the word w_j whose transition to c_{curr} has the best effect on the probability function. If the sum of the effects of moving w_i from c_{curr} to c_{best} and moving w_j from c_{best} to c_{curr} is positive, the swapping is performed. If swapping is not performed, we repeat the process for w_i, this time searching for c_{best} among all other clusters except of former c_{best} candidates[1].

2.3 Unsupervised Identification of High Quality Runs

Perplexity is a standard measure for language model evaluation. A language model defines the transition probabilities for every word w_i given the words that precede it. The perplexity of a language model for a given corpus having N words is defined to be

$$\sqrt[N]{\prod_{i=1}^{N} \frac{1}{p(w_i|w_1 \dots w_{i-1})}}$$

An important property of perplexity that makes it attractive as a measure for language model performance is that in some sense the best model for any corpus has the lowest perplexity for that corpus (Goodman, 2001). Thus, the lower the perplexity of the language model, the better it is.

Clark (2003) proposed a perplexity based test for the quality of his POS induction algorithm. In that test, a bigram class-based language model is trained on a training corpus (using the tagging of the unsupervised tagger) and applied to another test corpus. In such a model the transition probability from a word w_j to a word w_i is given by $p(C(w_i)|C(w_j))$ where $C(w_k)$ is the class assigned by the POS induction algorithm to w_k. In the training phase the bigram transition probabilities are computed using the training corpus, and in

[1] To make the algorithm more time efficient, for each word w_i we perform only three iterations of the searching for c_{best}, and for each c_{best} candidate we compute for at most 500 words the effect on the probability function of the removal to c_{curr}.

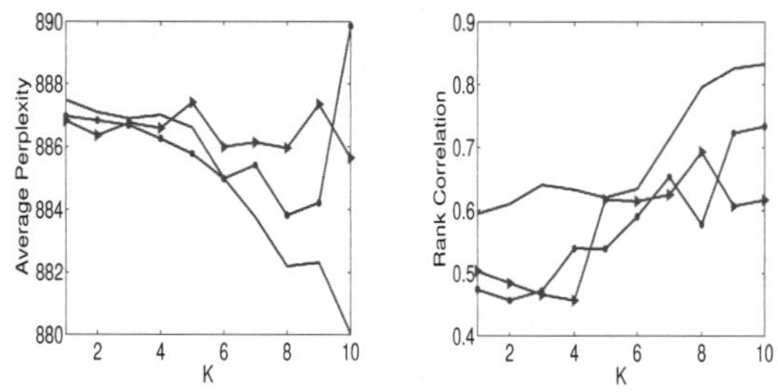

Figure 2: Left: average perplexity vs. the parameter K (tightness of the entropy outliers filter; see text for a full explanation). Right: Spearman's rank correlation between perplexity and an external (many-to-one) quality of the clustering as a function of K. The three curves are for ZCC, using different exponents (triangles: 0.9, circles: 1.3, solid: 1.1). A model whose quality improves (decreased perplexity) with K (left) demonstrates better correlation between perplexity and external quality (right). In all three graphs the x axis is in units of $5K$ (e.g., a graph x value of 2 means that 10 clusterings were removed from the top of the list and 10 from its bottom).

the test phase the perplexity of the learned model is evaluated on the test corpus. Better POS induction algorithms yield lower perplexity language models. However, Clark did not study the correlation between the perplexity measure and the gold standard tagging.

In this paper, we use Clark's perplexity based test as the unsupervised quality test used by the family Q. To provide a high quality prediction, this test should highly correlate with external clustering quality. To the best of our knowledge, such a correlation has not been explored so far.

2.4 Unsupervised Parameter Selection

The base ZCC algorithm has one input parameter, the exponent s of the Zipfian distribution. Virtually all unsupervised algorithms utilize parameters whose values affect their results. While it is methodologically valid to simply determine a value based on reasonable considerations or a development set, to keep the fully unsupervised nature of our work we now present a method for identifying the best parameter assignment. The method also casts some additional interesting light on the nature of the problem.

Like cluster type size, the distribution of cluster instance size in natural languages is also Zipfian (see Figure 3). A naive application of this constraint into the ZCC algorithm would be to allow swapping words between clusters only if they annotate the same number of word instances in the corpus. However, this constraint, either by itself or in combination with the cluster type size constraint, is too restrictive.

We utilize it for parameter selection as follows. Recall that our family of algorithms Q(B) runs a base tagger B several times. Each specific run yields a clustering C_i. The final result is selected from the set of clusterings $C = \{C_i\}$. We do not explicitly address the number of instances contained in a cluster, but we can prune from C those clusterings for which this distribution is very different. Again, imposing a constraint that is known to hold reduces quality fluctuations between different runs.

To measure the similarity between the cluster instance size distribution of two clusterings induced by two runs of the algorithm, we treat the clusters induced by a given run as samples from a random variable. The events of this variable are the induced clusters and the probability assigned to each event is equal to the number of word instances contained in the corresponding cluster, divided by the total number of word instances in the tagged corpus. The entropy of this random variable is used as a statistic for the word instance distribution. Clusterings having similar cluster instance size distributions also have similar values of this statistic.

We apply an entropy outliers filter to the set of clusterings C. In this filter, we sort the members of C (these are clusterings obtained in different runs of the base tagger) according to their cluster instance size entropy, and prune K runs from the beginning and K runs from the end of the list. The perplexity-based quality test described above is applied only to members of C that were not pruned in this step.

Figure 2 (left) shows the average perplexity of a set of clusterings as a function of the parameter K of the entropy-based filter. Results are presented for 100 runs of ZCC[2] with three different exponent values (0.9, 1.1, 1.3). These assignments yield considerably different Zipfian distributions.

While all three models have similar average perplexity over all 100 runs, only the solid line (corresponding to an exponent value of 1.1) consis-

[2]See Section 4 for the experimental setup.

tently decreases (improves) with K. The circled line (corresponding to an exponent value of 1.3) monotonically decreases with K until a certain K value, while the line with triangles (corresponding to an exponent value of 0.9) remains relatively constant.

Figure 2 (right) shows that models for which the entropy-based filter improves perplexity more drastically, exhibit better correlation between perplexity and external clustering quality[3].

Our unsupervised parameter selection method is thus based on finding a value which exhibits a consistent decrease in perplexity as a function of K, the number of clusterings pruned from the beginning and end of the entropy-sorted list. In the rest of this paper we show results where the exponent value is 1.1.

3 Previous Work

Unsupervised POS induction/tagging is a fruitful area of research. A major direction is Hidden Markov Models (HMM) (Merialdo, 1994; Banko and Moore, 2004; Wang and Schuurmans, 2005). Several recent works have tried to improve this model using Bayesian estimation (Goldwater and Griffiths, 2007; Johnson, 2007; Gao and Johnson, 2008), sophisticated initialization (Goldberg et al., 2008), induction of an initial clustering used to train an HMM (Freitag, 2004; Biemann, 2006), infinite HMM models (Van Gael et al., 2009), integration of integer linear programming into the parameter estimation process (Ravi and Knight, 2009), and biasing the model such that the number of possible tags that each word can get is small (Graça et al., 2009).

The Bayesian works integrated into the model information about the distribution of words to POS tags. For example, Johnson (2007) integrated to the EM-HMM model a prior that prefers clusterings where the distributions of hidden states to words is skewed.

Other approaches include transformation based learning (Brill, 1995), contrastive estimation for conditional random fields (Smith and Eisner, 2005), Markov random fields (Haghighi and Klein, 2006), a multilingual approach (Snyder et al., 2008; Snyder et al., 2008) and expanding a partial dictionary and use it to learn disambiguation rules (Zhao and Marcus, 2009).

These works, except (Haghighi and Klein, 2006; Johnson, 2007; Gao and Johnson, 2008) and one experiment in (Goldwater and Griffiths, 2007), used a dictionary listing the allowable tags for each word in the text. This dictionary is usually extracted from the manual tagging of the text, contradicting the unsupervised nature of the task. Clearly, the availability of such a dictionary is not always a reasonable assumption (see e.g. (Goldwater and Griffiths, 2007)).

In a different algorithmic direction, (Schuetze, 1995) applied latent semantic analysis with SVD based dimensionality reduction, and (Schuetze, 1995; Clark, 2003; Dasgupta and NG, 2007) used distributional and morphological statistics to find meaningful word types clusters. Clark (2003) is the only such work to have evaluated its algorithm as a POS tagger for large corpora, like we do in this paper.

A Zipfian constraint was utilized in (Goldwater and et al., 2006) for language modeling and morphological disambiguation.

The problem of convergence to local maxima has been discussed in (Smith and Eisner, 2005; Haghighi and Klein, 2006; Goldwater and Griffiths, 2007; Johnson, 2007; Gao and Johnson, 2008) with a detailed demonstration in (Johnson, 2007). All these authors (except Smith and Eisner (2005), see below), however, reported average results over several runs and did not try to identify the runs that produce high quality tagging.

Smith and Eisner (2005) initialized with all weights equal to zero (uninformed, deterministic initialization) and performed unsupervised model selection across smoothing parameters by evaluating the training criterion on unseen, unlabeled development data. In this paper we show that for the tagger of (Clark, 2003) such a method provides mediocre results (Table 2) even when the training criterion (likelihood or data probability for this tagger) is evaluated on the test set. Moreover, we show that our algorithm outperforms existing POS taggers for most evaluation measures (Table 3).

Identifying good solutions among many runs of a randomly-initialized algorithm is a well known problem. We discuss here the work of (Smith and Eisner, 2004) that addressed the problem in the unsupervised POS tagging context. In this work, deterministic annealing (Rose et al., 1990) was ap-

[3]The figure is for greedy many-to-one mapping and Spearman's rank correlation coefficient, explained in further Sections. Other external measures and rank correlation scores demonstrate the same pattern.

plied to an HMM model for unsupervised POS tagging with a dictionary. This method is not sensitive to its initialization, and while it is not theoretically guaranteed to converge to a better solution than the traditional EM-HMM, it was experimentally shown to achieve better results. The problem has, of course, been addressed in other contexts as well (see, e.g., (Wang et al., 2002)).

4 Experimental Setup and Evaluation

Setup. We used the English WSJ PennTreebank corpus in our experiments. We induced POS tags for sections 2-21 (43K word types, 950K word instances of which 832K (87.6%) are not punctuation marks), using Q(ZCC), Q(CT), and CT. For the unsupervised quality test, we trained the bigram class-based language model on sections 2-21 with the induced clusters, and computed its perplexity on section 23.

In Q(ZCC) and Q(CT), the base taggers were run a 100 times each, using different random initializations. In each run we induce 13 clusters, since this is the number of unique POS tags required to cover 98% of the word types in WSJ (Figure 3)[4]. Some previous work (e.g., (Smith and Eisner, 2005)) also induced 13 non-punctuation tags.

We compare the results of our algorithm to those of the original Clark algorithm[5]. The induced clusters are evaluated against two POS tag sets: one is the full set of WSJ POS tags, and the other consists of the non-punctuation tags of the first set.

Punctuation marks constitute a sizeable volume of corpus tokens and are easy to cluster correctly. Hence, evaluting against the full tag set that includes punctuation artificially increases the quality of the reported results, which is why we report results for the non-punctuation tag set. However, to be able to directly compare with previous work, we also report results for the full WSJ POS tag set. We do so by assigning a singleton cluster to each punctuation mark (in addition to the 13 clusters). This simple heuristic yields very high performance on punctuation, scoring (when all other terminals are assumed perfect tagging) 99.6% in 1-to-1 accuracy.

[4]Some words can get more than one POS tag. In the figure, for these words we increased the counters of all their possible tags.

[5]Downloaded from www.cs.rhul.ac.uk/home/alexc/RHUL/Downloads.html.

In addition to comparing the different algorithms, we compare the correlation between our tagging quality test and external clustering quality for both the original CT algorithm and our ZCC algorithm.

Clustering Quality Evaluation. The induced POS tags have arbitrary names. To evaluate them against a manually annotated corpus, a proper correspondence with the gold standard POS tags should be established. Many evaluation measures for unsupervised clustering against gold standard exist. Here we use measures from two well accepted families: mapping based and information theoretic (IT) based. For a recent discussion on this subject see (Reichart and Rappoport, 2009).

The mapping based measures are accuracy with greedy many-to-1 (M-1) and with greedy 1-to-1 (1-1) mappings of the induced to the gold labels. In the former mapping, two induced clusters can be mapped to the same gold standard cluster, while in the latter mapping each and every induced cluster is assigned a unique gold cluster.

After each induced label is mapped to a gold label, tagging accuracy is computed. Accuracy is defined to be the number of correctly tagged words in the corpus divided by the total number of words in the corpus.

The IT based measures we use are V (Rosenberg and Hirschberg, 2007) and NVI (Reichart and Rappoport, 2009). The latter is a normalization of the VI measure (Meila, 2007). VI and NVI induce the same order over clusterings but NVI values for good clusterings lie in $[0, 1]$. For V, the higher the score, the better the clustering. For NVI lower scores imply improved clustering quality. We use e as the base of the logarithm.

Evaluation of the Quality Test. To measure the correlation between the score produced by the tagging quality test and the external quality of a tagging, we use two well accepted measures: Spearman's rank correlation coefficient and Kendall Tau (Kendall and Dickinson, 1990). These measure the correlation between two sorted lists. For the computation of these measures, we rank the clusterings once according to the identification criterion and once according to the external quality measure.

The measures are given by the equations:

(6) $kendall - tau = \frac{2(n_c - n_d)}{r(r-1)}$

(7) $Spearsman = 1 - \frac{6\sum_{i=1}^{r} d_i^2}{r(r^2-1)}$

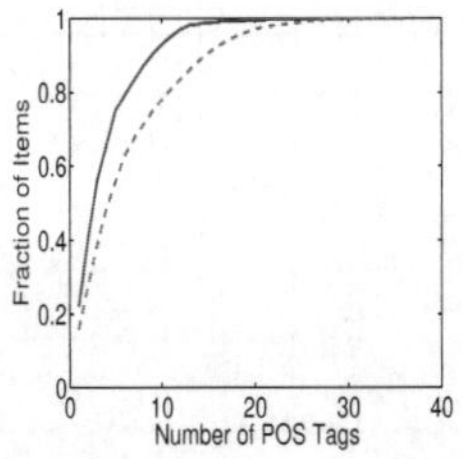

Figure 3: The fraction of word types (solid curve) and word instances (dashed curve) labeled with the k (X axis) most frequent POS tags (in types and tokens respectively) in sections 2-21 of the WSJ corpus.

where r is the number of runs (100 in our case), n_c and n_d are the numbers of concordant and discordant pairs respectively[6] and d_i is the absolute value of the difference between the ranks of item i.

The two measures have the properties that a perfect agreement between rankings results in a score of 1, a perfect disagreement results in a score of -1, completely independent rankings have the value of 0 on the average, the range of values is between -1 and 1, and increasing values imply increasing agreement between the rankings. For a discussion see (Lapata, 2006).

5 Results

Table 1 presents the results of the Q(ZCC) and Q(CT) algorithms, which are both better than those of the original Clark tagger CT. The Q algorithms provide a tagging that is better than that produced by CT in 82-100% (Q(ZCC)) and 75-100% (Q(CT)) of the cases.

The Q(ZCC) algorithm is superior when evaluated with the mapping based measures. The Q(CT) algorithm is superior when evaluated with the IT measures.

Table 3 presents reported results for all recent algorithms we are aware of that tackled the task of unsupervised POS induction from plain text [7]. The settings of the various experiments vary in terms of the exact gold annotation scheme used for evaluation (the full WSJ set was used by all authors except Goldwater and Griffiths (2007) and the GGTP-17 model which used the set of 17 coarse grained tags proposed by (Smith and Eisner, 2005)) and the size of the test set. The numbers reported for the algorithms of other works are the average performance over multiple runs, since no method for identification of high quality taggings was used.

The results of our algorithms are superior, except for the M-1 performance of some of the models of (Johnson, 2007) and of the GGTP-17 and GGTP-45 models of (Graça et al., 2009). Note that the models of (Johnson, 2007) and the GGTP-45 model induce 40-50 clusters compared to our 34 (13 non-punctuation plus the additional 21 singleton punctuation tags). Increasing the number of clusters is known to improve the M-1 measure (Reichart and Rappoport, 2009). GGTP-17 gives the best M-1 results, but its 1-1 results are much worse than those of Q(ZCC), Q(CT), and CT, and the information theoretic measures V and NVI were not reported for it.

Recall that the Q algorithms tag punctuation marks according to the scheme which assigns each of them a unique cluster (Section 4), while previous work does not distinguish punctuation marks from other tokens. To quantify the effect various punctuation schemes have on the results reported in Table 3, we evaluated the *'iHMM: PY-fixed'* model (Van Gael et al., 2009) and the Q algorithms when punctuation is excluded and when both PY-fixed and Q algorithms use the punctuation scheme described in Section 4.

For the PY-fixed, which induces 91 clusters, results are (punctuation is excluded, heuristic is used): V(0.530, 0.608), NVI (0.999, 0.823), 1-1 (0.484, 0.543), M-1 (0.591, 0.639). The results for the Q algorithms are given in Table 1 (top line: excluding punctuation, bottom line: using the heuristic). The Q algorithms are better for the V, NVI and 1-1 measures. For M-1 evaluation, PY-fixed, which induces substantially more clusters (91 compared to our 34) is better.

In what follows, we provide an analysis of the components of our algorithms. To explore the quality of our tagging component, ZCC, table 4 compares the mean, mode and standard deviation of a 100 runs of ZCC with 100 runs of the original CT algorithm[8]. The performance of the tagging

[6]A pair r, t in two lists X and Y is concordant if $sign(X_t - X_r) = sign(Y_t - Y_r)$, where X_r is the index of r in the list X.

[7]VG and GG used 2 as the base of the logarithm in IT measures, which affects VI. We converted the VI numbers reported in their papers to base e.

[8]In mode calculation we treat the 100 runs as samples of a continuous random variable. We divide the results range to 10 bins of the same size. The mode is the center of the bin having the largest number of runs. If there is more than

Alg.	V	NVI	1-1	M-1
Q(ZCC)				
no punct.	0.538 (85, 2.6)	0.849 (82, 3.2)	**0.521 (100, 4.3)**	**0.533 (84, 1.7)**
with punct.	0.637 (85, 1.8)	0.678 (82, 2.6)	**0.58 (100, 3)**	**0.591 (84, 1.18)**
Q(CT)				
no punct.	**0.545 (92, 3.3)**	**0.837 (88, 4.4)**	0.492 (99,1.4)	0.526 (75, 1)
with punct.	**0.644 (92, 2.5)**	**0.662 (88, 4.2)**	0.555 (99, 0.5)	0.585 (75, 0.58)

Table 1: Quality of the tagging produced by Q(ZCC) and Q(CT). The top (bottom) line for each algorithm presents the results when punctuation is not included (is included) in the evaluation (Section 4). The left number in the parentheses is the fraction of Clark's (CT) results that scored worse than our models (% from 100 runs). The right number in the parentheses is 100 times the difference between the score of our model and the mean score of 100 runs of Clark's (CT). Q(ZCC) is better than Q(CT) in the mappings measures, while Q(CT) is better in the IT measures. Both are better than the original Clark tagger CT.

	Data Probability				Likelihood				Perplexity			
	V		m-to-1		V		m-to-1		V		m-to-1	
Alg.	SRC	KT	SRC	KT	SRC	KT	SRC	KT	SRC	KT	SRC	KT
CT	0.2	0.143	0.071	0.045	0.338	0.23	0.22	0.148	**0.568**	**0.397**	**0.476**	**0.33**
ZCC	0.134	0.094	0.118	0.078	0.517	0.352	0.453	0.321	**0.82**	**0.62**	**0.659**	**0.484**

Table 2: Correlation of unsupervised quality measures (columns) with clustering quality of two base taggers (CT and ZCC, rows). Correlation is measured by Spearman (SRC) and Kendall Tau (KT) rank correlation coefficients. The quality measures are data probability (left part), likelihood (middle side) and perplexity (right part), and correlation is between these and two of the external evaluation measures, m-to-1 mapping and V (results for the other two clustering evaluation measures, 1-1 mapping and NVI, are very similar). Results for the perplexity quality test used by family Q are superior; data probability and likelihood provide only a mediocre indication for the quality of induced clustering. Note that the correlation values are much higher for ZCC than for CT.

components are quite similar, with a small advantage to CT in mean and to ZCC in mode.

Our quality test is based on the perplexity of a class bigram language model trained with the induced tagging. To emphasize its strength we compare it to two natural quality tests: the likelihood and value of the probability function to which the tagging algorithm converges (equations (2) and (1) in Section 2.1). The results are shown in Table 2 First, we see that our perplexity quality test is much better correlated with the quality of the tagging induced by both ZCC and CT. Second, the correlation is indeed much higher for ZCC than for CT.

The power of Q(ZCC) lies in the combination between the perplexity-based quality test and the tagging component ZCC. The performance of the tagging component ZCC does not provide a definite improvement over the original Clark tagger. ZCC compromises mean tagging results for an improved correlation between Q's quality measure and gold standard-based tagging evaluation.

one such bin, we average their centers. We use this technique since it is rare to see two different runs of either algorithm with the exact same quality.

6 Conclusion

In this paper we addressed unsupervised POS tagging as a task where the quality of a single tagging is to be reported, rather than the average performance of a tagging algorithm over many runs. We introduced a family of algorithms Q(B) based on an unsupervised test for tagging quality that is used to select a high quality tagging from the output of multiple runs of a POS tagger B.

We introduced the ZCC tagger which modifies the original Clark tagger by constraining the clustering space using a cluster type size Zipfian constraint, conforming with a known property of natural languages.

We showed that the tagging produced by our Q(ZCC) algorithm is better than that of the Clark algorithm with a probability of 82-100%, depending on the measure used. Moreover, our tagging outperforms in most evaluation measures the results reported in all recent works that addressed the task.

In future work, we intend to try to improve

Alg.	V	VI	M-1	1-1
Q(ZCC)	0.637	2.06	0.591	**0.58**
Q(CT)	**0.644**	**2.01**	0.585	0.555
CT	0.619	2.14	0.576	0.543
HK	–	–	–	0.413
J	–	4.23 - 5.74	0.43 - 0.62	0.37 – 0.47
GG	–	2.8	–	–
G-J	–	4.03 – 4.47	–	0.4 – 0.499
VG	0.54 - 0.59	2.49 – 2.91	–	–
GGTP-45	—	—	0.654	0.445
GGTP-17	—	—	**0.702**	0.495

Table 3: Comparison of our algorithms with the recent fully unsupervised POS taggers for which results are reported. HK: (Haghighi and Klein, 2006), trained and evaluated with a corpus of 193K tokens and 45 induced tags. GG: (Goldwater and Griffiths, 2007), trained and evaluated with a corpus of 24K tokens and 17 induced tags. J : (Johnson, 2007) inducing 25-50 tags (the results that are higher than Q in the M-1 measure are for 40-50 tags). GJ: (Gao and Johnson, 2008), inducing 50 tags. VG: (Van Gael et al., 2009), inducing 47-192 tags. GGTP-45: (Graça et al., 2009), inducing 45 tags. GGTP-17: (Graça et al., 2009), inducing 17 tags. All five were trained and evaluated with the full WSJ PTB (1.17M words). Lower VI values indicates better clustering.

Statistic	V	NVI	M-1	1-1
CT				
Mean	0.512	0.881	0.516	0.478
Mode	0.502	0.886	0.514	0.465
Std	0.022	0.035	0.018	0.028
ZCC				
Mean	0.503	0.908	0.512	0.478
Mode	0.509	0.907	0.518	0.47
Std	0.021	0.036	0.018	0.0295

Table 4: Average performance of ZCC compared with CT (results presented without punctuation). Presented are mean, mode (see text for its calculation), and standard deviation (std). CT mean results are slightly better, and both algorithms have about the same standard deviation. ZCC sacrifices a small amount of mean quality for a good correlation with our quality test, which allows Q(ZCC) to be much better than the mean of CT and most of its runs.

our quality measure, experiment with additional languages, and apply the 'family of algorithms' paradigm to additional relevant NLP tasks.

References

Michele Banko and Robert C. Moore, 2003. Part of Speech Tagging in Context. *COLING '04.*

Chris Biemann, 2006. *Unsupervised Part-of-Speech Tagging Employing Efficient Graph Clustering.* COLING-ACL '06 Student Research Workshop.

Thorsten Brants, 1997. The NEGRA Export Format. *CLAUS Report, Saarland University.*

Eric Brill, 1995. Unsupervised Learning if Disambiguation Rules for Part of Speech Tagging. *3rd Workshop on Very Large Corpora.*

Peter F. Brown, Vincent J. Della Pietra, Peter V. de Souze, Jenifer C. Lai and Robert Mercer, 1992. Class-Based N-Gram Models of Natural Language. *Computational Linguistics*, 18:467-479.

Alexander Clark, 2003. Combining Distributional and Morphological Information for Part of Speech Induction. *EACL '03.*

Sajib Dasgupta and Vincent Ng, 2007. Unsupervised Part-of-Speech Acquisition for Resource-Scarce Languages. *EMNLP '07.*

Steven Finch, Nick Chater and Martin Redington, 1995. Acquiring syntactic information from distributional statistics. *Connectionist models of memory and language.* UCL Press, London.

Dayne Freitag, 2004. *Toward Unsupervised Whole-Corpus Tagging.* COLING '04.

Jianfeng Gao and Mark Johnson, 2008. A comparison of Bayesian estimators for unsupervised Hidden Markov Model POS taggers. *EMNLP '08.*

Yoav Goldberg, Meni Adler and Michael Elhadad, 2008. EM Can Find Pretty Good HMM POS-Taggers (When Given a Good Start). *ACL '08*

Sharon Goldwater, Tom Griffiths, and Mark Johnson, 2006. Interpolating between types and tokens by estimating power-law generators. *NIPS '06.*

Sharon Goldwater and Tom Griffiths, 2007. A fully Bayesian approach to unsupervised part-of-speech tagging. *ACL '07.*

Joshua Goodman, 2001. A Bit of Progress in Language Modeling, Extended Version. *Microsoft Research Technical Report MSR-TR-2001-72.*

João Graça, Kuzman Ganchev, Ben Taskar and Frenando Pereira, 2009. Posterior vs. Parameter Sparsity in Latent Variable Models. *NIPS '09.*

Maurice Kendall and Jean Dickinson, 1990. Rank Correlation methods. Oxford University Press, New York.

Aria Haghighi and Dan Klein, 2006. Prototype-driven Learning for Sequence Labeling. *HLT-NAACL '06.*

Mark Johnson, 2007. Why Doesnt EM Find Good HMM POS-Taggers? *EMNLP-CoNLL '07.*

Harold W. Kuhn, 1955. The Hungarian method for the assignment problem. *Naval Research Logistics Quarterly*, 2:83-97.

Mirella Lapata, 2006. Automatic Evaluation of Information Ordering: Kendall's Tau. *Computational Linguistics*, 4:471-484.

Sven Martin, Jorg Liermann, and Hermann Ney, 1998. Algorithms for bigram and trigram word clustering. *Speech Communication*, 24:19-37.

Marina Meila, 2007. Comparing Clustering - an Information Based Distance. *Journal of Multivariate Analysis*, 98:873-895.

Bernard Merialdo, 1994. Tagging English Text with a Probabilistic Model. *Computational Linguistics*, 20(2):155-172.

Michael Mitzenmacher , 2004. A Brief History of Generative Models for Power Law and Lognormal Distributions. *Internet Mathematics*, 1(2):226-251.

James Munkres, 1957. Algorithms for the Assignment and Transportation Problems. *Journal of the SIAM*, 5(1):32-38.

Hermann Ney, Ute Essen, and Reinhard Kneser, 1994. On structuring probabilistic dependencies in stochastic language modelling. *Computer Speech and Language*, 8:1-38.

Sujith Ravi and Kevin Knight, 2009. Minimized Models for Unsupervised Part-of-Speech Tagging. *ACL '09.*

Roi Reichart and Ari Rappoport, 2009. The NVI Clustering Evaluation Measure. *CoNLL '09.*

Kenneth Rose, Eitan Gurewitz, and Geoffrey C. Fox, 1990. Statistical Mechanics and Phase Transitions in Clustering. *Physical Review Letters*, 65(8):945-948.

Andrew Rosenberg and Julia Hirschberg, 2007. V-Measure: A Conditional Entropy-Based External Cluster Evaluation Measure. *EMNLP '07.*

Hinrich Schuetze, 1995. Distributional part-of-speech tagging. *EACL '95.*

Noah A. Smith and Jason Eisner, 2004. Annealing Techniques for Unsupervised Statistical Language Learning. *ACL '04.*

Noah A. Smith and Jason Eisner, 2005. Contrastive Estimation: Training Log-Linear Models on Unlabeled Data. *ACL '05.*

Benjamin Snyder, Tahira Naseem, Jacob Eisenstein, and Regina Barzilay, 2009. Adding More Languages Improves Unsupervised Multilingual Part-of-Speech Tagging: A Bayesian Non-Parametric Approach. *NAACL '09.*

Benjamin Snyder, Tahira Naseem, Jacob Eisenstein, and Regina Barzilay, 2008. Unsupervised Multilingual Learning for POS Tagging. *EMNLP '08.*

Jurgen Van Gael, Andreas Vlachos and Zoubin Ghahramani, 2009. *The Infinite HMM for Unsupervised POS Tagging.* EMNLP '09.

Qin Iris Wang and Dale Schuurmans, 2005. Improved Estimation for Unsupervised Part-of-Speech Tagging. *IEEE NLP-KE '05.*

Shaojun Wang, Dale Schuurmans and Yunxin Zhao, 2002. The Latent Maximum Entropy Principle. *ISIT '02.*

Qiuye Zhao and Mitch Marcus, 2009. *A Simple Unsupervised Learner for POS Disambiguation Rules Given Only a Minimal Lexicon.* EMNLP '09.

Syntactic and Semantic Structure for Opinion Expression Detection

Richard Johansson and **Alessandro Moschitti**
DISI, University of Trento
Via Sommarive 14 Povo, 38123 Trento (TN), Italy
{johansson, moschitti}@disi.unitn.it

Abstract

We demonstrate that *relational features* derived from dependency-syntactic and semantic role structures are useful for the task of detecting opinionated expressions in natural-language text, significantly improving over conventional models based on sequence labeling with local features. These features allow us to model the way opinionated expressions *interact* in a sentence over arbitrary distances.

While the relational features make the prediction task more computationally expensive, we show that it can be tackled effectively by using a reranker. We evaluate a number of machine learning approaches for the reranker, and the best model results in a 10-point absolute improvement in soft recall on the MPQA corpus, while decreasing precision only slightly.

1 Introduction

The automatic detection and analysis of opinionated text – *subjectivity analysis* – is potentially useful for a number of natural language processing tasks. Examples include retrieval systems answering queries about how a particular person feels about a product or political question, and various types of market analysis tools such as review mining systems.

A primary task in subjectivity analysis is to mark up the *opinionated expressions*, i.e. the text snippets signaling the subjective content of the text. This is necessary for further analysis, such as the determination of opinion holder and the polarity of the opinion. The MPQA corpus (Wiebe et al., 2005), a widely used corpus annotated with subjectivity information, defines two types of subjective expressions: *direct subjective expressions* (DSEs), which are explicit mentions of opinion, and *expressive subjective elements* (ESEs), which signal the attitude of the speaker by the choice of words. DSEs are often verbs of statement and categorization, where the opinion and its holder tend to be direct semantic arguments of the verb. ESEs, on the other hand, are less easy to categorize syntactically; prototypical examples would include value-expressing adjectives such as *beautiful*, *biased*, etc. In addition to DSEs and ESEs, the MPQA corpus also contains annotation for non-subjective statements, which are referred to as *objective speech events* (OSEs). Examples (1) and (2) show two sentences from the MPQA corpus where DSEs and ESEs have been manually annotated.

(1) For instance, he [denounced]$_{DSE}$ as a [human rights violation]$_{ESE}$ the banning and seizure of satellite dishes in Iran.

(2) This [is viewed]$_{DSE}$ as the [main impediment]$_{ESE}$ to the establishment of political order in the country .

The task of marking up these expressions has usually been approached using straightforward sequence labeling techniques using simple features in a small contextual window (Choi et al., 2006; Breck et al., 2007). However, due to the simplicity of the feature sets, this approach fails to take into account the fact that the semantic and pragmatic interpretation of sentences is not only determined by words but also by syntactic and shallow-semantic *relations*. Crucially, taking grammatical relations into account allows us to model how expressions *interact* in various ways that influence their interpretation as subjective or not. Consider, for instance, the word *said* in examples (3) and (4) below, where the interpretation as a DSE or an OSE is influenced by the subjective content of the enclosed statement.

Proceedings of the Fourteenth Conference on Computational Natural Language Learning, pages 67–76,
Uppsala, Sweden, 15-16 July 2010.

(3) "We will identify the [culprits]$_{ESE}$ of these clashes and [punish]$_{ESE}$ them," he [said]$_{DSE}$.
(4) On Monday, 80 Libyan soldiers disembarked from an Antonov transport plane carrying military equipment, an African diplomat [said]$_{OSE}$.

In this paper, we demonstrate how syntactic and semantic structural information can be used to improve opinion detection. While this feature model makes it impossible to use the standard sequence labeling method, we show that with a simple strategy based on reranking, incorporating structural features results in a significant improvement. We investigate two different reranking strategies: the Preference Kernel approach (Shen and Joshi, 2003) and an approach based on structure learning (Collins, 2002). In an evaluation on the MPQA corpus, the best system we evaluated, a structure learning-based reranker using the Passive–Aggressive learning algorithm, achieved a 10-point absolute improvement in soft recall, and a 5-point improvement in F-measure, over the baseline sequence labeler .

2 Motivation and Related Work

Most approaches to analysing the sentiment of natural-language text have relied fundamentally on purely lexical information (see (Pang et al., 2002; Yu and Hatzivassiloglou, 2003), *inter alia*) or low-level grammatical information such as part-of-speech tags and functional words (Wiebe et al., 1999). This is in line with the general consensus in the information retrieval community that very little can be gained by complex linguistic processing for tasks such as text categorization and search (Moschitti and Basili, 2004).

However, it has been suggested that subjectivity analysis is inherently more subtle than categorization and that *structural* linguistic information should therefore be given more attention in this context. For instance, Karlgren et al. (2010) argued from a Construction Grammar viewpoint (Croft, 2005) that *grammatical constructions* not only connect words, but can also be viewed as lexical items in their own right. Starting from this intuition, they showed that incorporating construction items into a bag-of-words feature representation resulted in improved results on a number of coarse-grained opinion analysis tasks. These constructional features were domain-independent and were manually extracted from dependency parse trees. They found that the most prominent constructional feature for subjectivity analysis was the Tense Shift construction.

While the position by Karlgren et al. (2010) – that constructional features *signal* opinion – originates from a particular theoretical framework and may be controversial, syntactic and shallow-semantic relations have repeatedly proven useful for subtasks of subjectivity analysis that are inherently *relational*, above all for determining the holder or topic of a given opinion. Works using syntactic features to extract topics and holders of opinions are numerous (Bethard et al., 2005; Kobayashi et al., 2007; Joshi and Penstein-Rosé, 2009; Wu et al., 2009). Semantic role analysis has also proven useful: Kim and Hovy (2006) used a FrameNet-based semantic role labeler to determine holder and topic of opinions. Similarly, Choi et al. (2006) successfully used a PropBank-based semantic role labeler for opinion holder extraction, and Wiegand and Klakow (2010) recently applied tree kernel learning methods on a combination of syntactic and semantic role trees for the same task. Ruppenhofer et al. (2008) argued that semantic role techniques are useful but not completely sufficient for holder and topic identification, and that other linguistic phenomena must be studied as well. One such linguistic pheonomenon is the *discourse* structure, which has recently attracted some attention in the opinion analysis community (Somasundaran et al., 2009).

3 Opinion Expression Detection Using Syntactic and Semantic Structures

Previous systems for opinionated expression markup have typically used simple feature sets which have allowed the use of efficient off-the-shelf sequence labeling methods based on Viterbi search (Choi et al., 2006; Breck et al., 2007). This is not possible in our case since we would like to extract structural, relational features that involve *pairs* of opinionated expressions and may apply over an arbitrarily long distance in the sentence.

While it is possible that search algorithms for exact or approximate inference can be constructured for the $\arg\max$ problem in this model, we sidestepped this issue by using a *reranking* decomposition of the problem: We first apply a standard Viterbi-based sequence labeler using no structural features and generate a small candidate set of size k. Then, a second and more complex model picks the top candidate from this set without having to search the whole candidate space.

The advantages of a reranking approach compared to more complex approaches requiring advanced search techniques are mainly simplicity and efficiency: this approach is conceptually simple and fairly easy to implement provided that k-best output can be generated efficiently, and features can be arbitrarily complex – we don't have to think about how the features affect the algorithmic complexity of the inference step. A common objection to reranking is that the candidate set may not be diverse enough to allow for much improvement unless it is very large; the candidates may be trivial variations that are all very similar to the top-scoring candidate (Huang, 2008).

3.1 Syntactic and Semantic Structures

We used the syntactic–semantic parser by Johansson and Nugues (2008a) to annotate the sentences with dependency syntax (Mel'čuk, 1988) and shallow semantic structures in the PropBank (Palmer et al., 2005) and NomBank (Meyers et al., 2004) frameworks. Figure 1 shows an example of the annotation: The sentence *they called him a liar*, where *called* is a DSE and *liar* is an ESE, has been annotated with dependency syntax (above the text) and PropBank-based semantic role structure (below the text). The predicate *called*, which is an instance of the PropBank frame `call.01`, has three semantic arguments: the Agent (A0), the Theme (A1), and the Predicate (A2), which are realized on the surface-syntactic level as a subject, a direct object, and an object predicative complement, respectively.

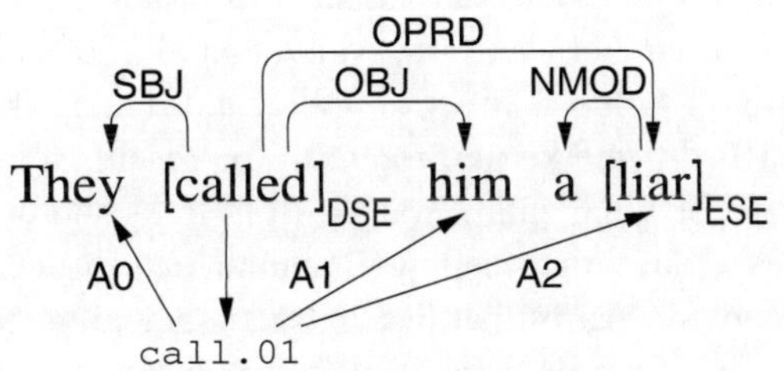

Figure 1: Syntactic and shallow semantic structure.

3.2 Sequence Labeler

We implemented a standard sequence labeler following the approach of Collins (2002), while training the model using the Passive–Aggressive algorithm (Crammer et al., 2006) instead of the perceptron. We encoded the opinionated expression brackets using the IOB2 encoding scheme (Tjong Kim Sang and Veenstra, 1999). Figure 2 shows an example of a sentence with a DSE and an ESE and how they are encoded in the IOB2 encoding.

This	O
is	O
viewed	B-DSE
as	O
the	O
main	B-ESE
impediment	I-ESE

Figure 2: Sequence labeling example.

The sequence labeler used word, POS tag, and lemma features in a window of size 3. In addition, we used prior polarity and intensity features derived from the lexicon created by Wilson et al. (2005). In the example, *viewed* is listed as having strong prior subjectivity but no polarity, and *impediment* has strong prior subjectivity and negative polarity. Note that prior subjectivity does not always imply subjectivity in a particular context; this is why contextual features are essential for this task.

This sequence labeler is used to generate the candidate set for the reranker; the Viterbi algorithm is easily modified to give k-best output. To generate training data for the reranker, we carried out a 5-fold cross-validation procedure: We split the training set into 5 pieces, trained a sequence labeler on pieces 1 to 4, applied it to piece 5 and so on.

3.3 Reranker Features

The rerankers use two types of structural features: syntactic features extracted from the dependency tree, and semantic features extracted from the predicate–argument (semantic role) graph.

The syntactic features are based on paths through the dependency tree. This creates a small complication for multiword opinionated expressions; we select the shortest possible path in such cases. For instance, in Example (1), the path will be computed between *denounced* and *violation*, and in Example (2) between *viewed* and *impediment*.

We used the following syntactic features:

Syntactic Path. Given a pair of opinion expressions, we use a feature representing the labels of the two expressions and the path between them through the syntactic tree. For instance, for the DSE *called* and the ESE *liar* in Figure 1, we represent the syntactic configuration using the feature `DSE:OPRD↓:ESE`, meaning that the path from the DSE to the ESE consists of a single link, where the dependency edge label is `OPRD` (object predicative complement).

Lexicalized Path. Same as above, but with lexical information attached: `DSE/called:OPRD↓:ESE/liar`.

Dominance. In addition to the features based on syntactic paths, we created a more generic feature template describing dominance relations between expressions. For instance, from the graph in Figure 1, we extract the feature `DSE/called→ESE/liar`, meaning that a DSE with the word *called* dominates an ESE with the word *liar*.

The semantic features were the following:

Predicate Sense Label. For every predicate found inside an opinion expression, we add a feature consisting of the expression label and the predicate sense identifier. For instance, the verb *call* which is also a DSE is represented with the feature `DSE/call.01`.

Predicate and Argument Label. For every argument of a predicate inside an opinion expression, we create a feature representing the predicate–argument pair: `DSE/call.01:A0`.

Connecting Argument Label. When a predicate inside some opinion expression is connected to some argument inside another opinion expression, we use a feature consisting of the two expression labels and the argument label. For instance, the ESE *liar* is connected to the DSE *call* via an A2 label, and we represent this using a feature `DSE:A2:ESE`.

Apart from the syntactic and semantic features, we also used the score output from the base sequence labeler as a feature. We normalized the scores over the k candidates so that their exponentials summed to 1.

3.4 Preference Kernel Approach

The first reranking strategy we investigated was the Preference Kernel approach (Shen and Joshi, 2003). In this method, the reranking problem – learning to select the correct candidate h^1 from a candidate set $\{h^1, \ldots, h^k\}$ – is reduced to a binary classification problem by creating *pairs*: positive training instances $\langle h^1, h^2 \rangle, \ldots, \langle h^1, h^k \rangle$ and negative instances $\langle h^2, h^1 \rangle, \ldots, \langle h^k, h^1 \rangle$. This approach has the advantage that the abundant tools for binary machine learning can be exploited.

It is also easy to show (Shen and Joshi, 2003) that if we have a kernel K over the candidate space T, we can construct a valid kernel P_K over the space of pairs $T \times T$ as follows:

$$
\begin{aligned}
P_K(h_1, h_2) \quad = & \quad K(h_1^1, h_2^1) + K(h_1^2, h_2^2) \\
- & \quad K(h_1^1, h_2^2) - K(h_1^2, h_2^1),
\end{aligned}
$$

where h_i are the pairs of hypotheses $\langle h_i^1, h_i^2 \rangle$ generated by the base model. This makes it possible to use kernel methods to train the reranker. We tried two types of kernels: linear kernels and tree kernels.

3.4.1 Linear Kernel

We created feature vectors extracted from the candidate sequences using the features described in Section 3.3. We then trained linear SVMs using the LIBLINEAR software (Fan et al., 2008), using L1 loss and L2 regularization.

3.4.2 Tree Kernel

Tree kernels have been successful for a number of structure extraction tasks, such as relation extraction (Zhang et al., 2006; Nguyen et al., 2009) and opinion holder extraction (Wiegand and Klakow, 2010). A tree kernel implicitly represents a large space of fragments extracted from trees and could thus reduce the need for manual feature design. Since the paths that we extract manually (Section 3.3) can be expressed as tree fragments, this method could be an interesting alternative to the manually extracted features used with the linear kernel.

We therefore implemented a reranker using the Partial Tree Kernel (Moschitti, 2006), and we trained it using the SVMLight-TK software[1], which is a modification of SVMLight (Joachims,

[1]Available at `http://dit.unitn.it/~moschitt`

1999)[2]. It is still an open question how dependency trees should be represented for use with tree kernels (Suzuki et al., 2003; Nguyen et al., 2009); we used the representation shown in Figure 3. Note that we have concatenated the opinion expression labels to the POS tag nodes. We did not use any of the features from Section 3.3 except for the base sequence labeler score.

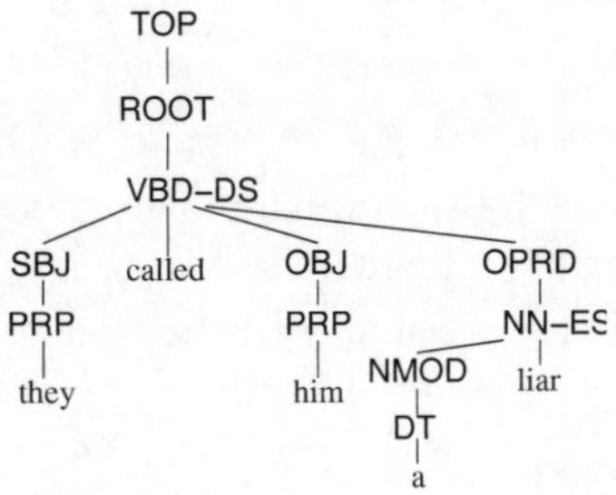

Figure 3: Representation of a dependency tree with opinion expressions for tree kernels.

3.5 Structure Learning Approach

The Preference Kernel approach reduces the reranking problem to a binary classification task on pairs, after which a standard SVM optimizer is used to train the reranker. A problem with this method is that the optimization problem solved by the SVM – maximizing the classification accuracy on a set of independent pairs – is not directly related to the performance of the reranker. Instead, the method employed by many rerankers following Collins and Duffy (2002) directly learn a scoring function that is trained to maximize performance on the reranking task. We will refer to this approach as the *structure learning* method.

While there are batch learning algorithms that work in this setting (Tsochantaridis et al., 2005), online learning methods have been more popular for efficiency reasons. We investigated two online learning algorithms: the popular *structured perceptron* Collins and Duffy (2002) and the Passive–Aggressive (PA) algorithm (Crammer et al., 2006). To increase robustness, we averaged the weight vectors seen during training as in the Voted Perceptron (Freund and Schapire, 1999).

The difference between the two algorithms is the way the weight vector is incremented in each step. In the perceptron, for a given input x, we update based on the difference between the correct output y and the predicted output $\hat{y}$, where Φ is the feature representation function:

$$\begin{aligned} \hat{y} &\leftarrow \arg\max_h w \cdot \Phi(x,h) \\ w &\leftarrow w + \Phi(x,y) - \Phi(x,\hat{y}) \end{aligned}$$

In the PA algorithm, which is based on the theory of large-margin learning, we instead find the $\hat{y}$ that violates the margin constraints maximally. The update step length τ is computed based on the margin; this update is bounded by a regularization constant C:

$$\begin{aligned} \hat{y} &\leftarrow \arg\max_h w \cdot \Phi(x,h) + \sqrt{\rho(y,h)} \\ \tau &\leftarrow \min\left(C, \frac{w(\Phi(x,\hat{y})-\Phi(x,y))+\sqrt{\rho(y,\hat{y})}}{\|\Phi(x,\hat{y})-\Phi(x,y)\|^2}\right) \\ w &\leftarrow w + \tau(\Phi(x,y) - \Phi(x,\hat{y})) \end{aligned}$$

The algorithm uses a cost function ρ. We used the function $\rho(y,\hat{y}) = 1 - F(y,\hat{y})$, where F is the soft F-measure described in Section 4.1. With this approach, the learning algorithm thus directly optimizes the measure we are interested in, i.e. the F-measure.

4 Experiments

We carried out the experiments on version 2 of the MPQA corpus (Wiebe et al., 2005), which we split into a test set (150 documents, 3,743 sentences) and a training set (541 documents, 12,010 sentences).

4.1 Evaluation Metrics

Since expression boundaries are hard to define exactly in annotation guidelines (Wiebe et al., 2005), we used soft precision and recall measures to score the quality of the system output. To derive the soft precision and recall, we first define the *span coverage* c of a span s with respect to another span s', which measures how well s' is covered by s:

$$c(s,s') = \frac{|s \cap s'|}{|s'|}$$

In this formula, the operator $|\cdot|$ counts tokens, and the intersection $\cap$ gives the set of tokens that two spans have in common. Since our evaluation takes span labels (DSE, ESE, OSE) into account, we set $c(s,s')$ to zero if the labels associated with s and s' are different.

Using the span coverage, we define the *span set coverage* C of a set of spans $\boldsymbol{S}$ with respect to a set $\boldsymbol{S'}$:

$$C(\boldsymbol{S},\boldsymbol{S'}) = \sum_{s_j \in \boldsymbol{S}} \sum_{s'_k \in \boldsymbol{S'}} c(s_j, s'_k)$$

[2] `http://svmlight.joachims.org`

We now define the soft precision P and recall R of a proposed set of spans $\hat{\boldsymbol{S}}$ with respect to a gold standard set $\boldsymbol{S}$ as follows:

$$P(\boldsymbol{S}, \hat{\boldsymbol{S}}) = \frac{C(\boldsymbol{S}, \hat{\boldsymbol{S}})}{|\hat{\boldsymbol{S}}|} \quad R(\boldsymbol{S}, \hat{\boldsymbol{S}}) = \frac{C(\hat{\boldsymbol{S}}, \boldsymbol{S})}{|\boldsymbol{S}|}$$

Note that the operator $|\cdot|$ counts spans in this formula.

Conventionally, when measuring the quality of a system for an information extraction task, a predicted entity is counted as correct if it exactly matches the boundaries of a corresponding entity in the gold standard; there is thus no reward for close matches. However, since the boundaries of the spans annotated in the MPQA corpus are not strictly defined in the annotation guidelines (Wiebe et al., 2005), measuring precision and recall using exact boundary scoring will result in figures that are too low to be indicative of the usefulness of the system. Therefore, most work using this corpus instead use overlap-based precision and recall measures, where a span is counted as correctly detected if it *overlaps* with a span in the gold standard (Choi et al., 2006; Breck et al., 2007). As pointed out by Breck et al. (2007), this is problematic since it will tend to reward long spans – for instance, a span covering the whole sentence will always be counted as correct if the gold standard contains any span for that sentence.

The precision and recall measures proposed here correct the problem with overlap-based measures: If the system proposes a span covering the whole sentence, the span coverage will be low and result in a low soft precision. Note that our measures are bounded below by the exact measures and above by the overlap-based measures.

4.2 Reranking Approaches

We compared the reranking architectures and the machine learning methods described in Section 3. In these experiments, we used a candidate set size k of 8. Table 1 shows the results of the evaluations using the precision and recall measures described above. The baseline is the result of taking the top-scoring output from the sequence labeler without applying any reranking.

The results show that the rerankers using manual feature extraction outperform the tree-kernel-based reranker, which obtains a score just above the baseline. It should be noted that the massive training time of kernel-based machine learning precluded a detailed tuning of parameters and

System	P	R	F
Baseline	63.36	46.77	53.82
Pref-linear	64.60	50.17	56.48
Pref-TK	63.97	46.94	54.15
Struct-Perc	62.84	48.13	54.51
Struct-PA	63.50	51.79	57.04

Table 1: Evaluation of reranking architectures and learning methods.

representation – on the other hand, we did not need to spend much time on parameter tuning and feature design for the other rerankers.

In addition, we note that the best performance was obtained using the PA algorithm and the structure learning architecture. The PA algorithm is a simple online learning method and still outperforms the SVM used in the preference-kernel reranker. This suggests that the structure learning approach is superior for this task. It is possible that a batch learning method such as SVM^{struct} (Tsochantaridis et al., 2005) could improve the results even further.

4.3 Candidate Set Size

In any method based on reranking, it is important to study the influence of the candidate set size on the quality of the reranked output. In addition, an interesting question is what the upper bound on reranker performance is – the *oracle* performance. Table 2 shows the result of an experiment that investigates these questions. We used the reranker based on the Passive–Aggressive method in this experiment since this reranker gave the best results in the previous experiment.

	Reranked			Oracle		
k	P	R	F	P	R	F
1	63.36	46.77	53.82	63.36	46.77	53.82
2	63.70	48.17	54.86	72.66	55.18	62.72
4	63.57	49.78	55.84	79.12	62.24	69.68
8	63.50	51.79	57.04	83.72	68.14	75.13
16	63.00	52.94	57.54	86.92	72.79	79.23
32	62.15	54.50	58.07	89.18	76.76	82.51
64	61.02	55.67	58.22	91.08	80.19	85.28
128	60.22	56.45	58.27	92.63	83.00	87.55
256	59.87	57.22	58.51	94.01	85.27	89.43

Table 2: Oracle and reranker performance as a function of candidate set size.

As is common in reranking tasks, the reranker can exploit only a fraction of the potential improvement – the reduction of the F-measure error is between 10 and 15 percent of the oracle error reduction for all candidate set sizes.

The most visible effect of the reranker is that the recall is greatly improved. However, this does not seem to have an adverse effect on the precision until the candidate set size goes above 8 – in fact, the precision actually improves over the baseline for small candidate set sizes. After the size goes above 8, the recall (and the F-measure) still rises, but at the cost of decreased precision.

4.4 Impact of Features

We studied the impact of syntactic and semantic structural features on the performance of the reranker. Table 3 shows the result of the investigation for syntactic features. Using all the syntactic features (and no semantic features) gives an F-measure roughly 4 points above the baseline, using the PA reranker with a k of 64. We then measured the F-measure obtained when each one of the three syntactic features had been removed. It is clear that the unlexicalized syntactic path is the most important syntactic feature; the effect of the two lexicalized features seems to be negligible.

System	P	R	F
Baseline	63.36	46.77	53.82
All syntactic	62.45	53.19	57.45
No SYN PATH	64.40	48.69	55.46
No LEX PATH	62.62	53.19	57.52
No DOMINANCE	62.32	52.92	57.24

Table 3: Effect of syntactic features.

A similar result was obtained when studying the semantic features (Table 4). Removing the CONNECTING ARGUMENT LABEL feature, which is unlexicalized, has a greater effect than removing the other two semantic features, which are lexicalized.

System	P	R	F
Baseline	63.36	46.77	53.82
All semantic	61.26	53.85	57.31
No PREDICATE SL	61.28	53.81	57.30
No PRED+ARGLBL	60.96	53.61	57.05
No CONN ARGLBL	60.73	50.47	55.12

Table 4: Effect of semantic features.

Since our most effective structural features combine a pair of opinion expression labels with a tree fragment, it is interesting to study whether the expression labels alone would be enough. If this were the case, we could conclude that the improvement is caused not by the structural features, but just by learning which combinations of labels are common in the training set, such as that DSE+ESE would be more common than OSE+ESE. We thus carried out an experiment comparing a reranker using label pair features against rerankers based on syntactic features only, semantic features only, and the full feature set. Table 5 shows the results. We see that the reranker using label pairs indeed achieves a performance well above the baseline. However, its performance is below that of any reranker using structural features. In addition, we see no improvement when adding label pair features to the structural feature set; this is to be expected since the label pair information is subsumed by the structural features.

System	P	R	F
Baseline	63.36	46.77	53.82
Label pairs	62.05	52.68	56.98
All syntactic	62.45	53.19	57.45
All semantic	61.26	53.85	57.31
Syn + sem	61.02	55.67	58.22
Syn + sem + pairs	61.61	54.78	57.99

Table 5: Structural features compared to label pairs.

4.5 Comparison with Breck et al. (2007)

Comparison of systems in opinion expression detection is often nontrivial since evaluation settings have differed widely. Since our problem setting – marking up and labeling opinion expressions in the MPQA corpus – is most similar to that described by Breck et al. (2007), we carried out an evaluation using the setting used in their experiment.

For compatibility with their experimental setup, this experiment differed from the ones described in the previous sections in the following ways:

- The system did not need to distinguish DSEs and ESEs and did not have to detect the OSEs.
- The results were measured using the overlap-based precision and recall, although this is problematic as pointed out in Section 4.1.

- Instead of the training/test split we used in the previous evaluations, the systems were evaluated using a 10-fold cross-validation over the same set of 400 documents as used in Breck's experiment.

Again, our reranker uses the PA method with a k of 64. Table 6 shows the results.

System	P	R	F
Breck et al. (2007)	71.64	74.70	73.05
Baseline	80.85	64.38	71.68
Reranked	76.40	78.23	77.30

Table 6: Results using the Breck et al. (2007) evaluation setting.

We see that the performance of our system is clearly higher – in both precision and recall – than that reported by Breck et al. (2007). This shows again that the structural features are effective for the task of finding opinionated expressions.

We note that the performance of our baseline sequence labeler is lower than theirs; this is to be expected since they used a more complex batch learning algorithm (conditional random fields) while we used an online learner, and they spent more effort on feature design. This indicates that we should be able to achieve even higher performance using a stronger base model.

5 Conclusion

We have shown that features derived from grammatical and semantic role structure can be used to improve the detection of opinionated expressions in subjectivity analysis. Most significantly, the recall is drastically increased (10 points) while the precision decreases only slightly (3 points). This result compares favorably with previously published results, which have been biased towards precision and scored low on recall.

The long-distance structural features gives us a model that has predictive power as well as being of theoretical interest: this model takes into account the *interactions* between opinion expressions in a sentence. While these structural features give us a powerful model, they come at a computational cost; prediction is more complex than in a standard sequence labeler based on purely local features. However, we have shown that a prediction strategy based on reranking suffices for this task.

We analyzed the impact of the syntactic and semantic features and saw that the best model includes both types of features. The most effective features we have found are purely structural, i.e. based on tree fragments in a syntactic or semantic tree. Features involving words did not seem to have the same impact. We also showed that the improvement is not explainable by mere correlations between opinion expression labels.

We investigated a number of implementation strategies for the reranker and concluded that the structural learning framework seemed to give the best performance. We were not able to achieve the same performance using tree kernels as with manually extracted features. It is possible that this could be improved with a better strategy for representing dependency structure for tree kernels, or if the tree kernels could be incorporated into the structural learning framework.

The flexible architecture we have presented enables interesting future research: (i) a straightforward improvement is the use of lexical similarity to reduce data sparseness, e.g. (Basili et al., 2005; Basili et al., 2006; Bloehdorn et al., 2006). However, the similarity between subjective words, which have multiple senses against other words may negatively impact the system accuracy. Therefore, the use of the syntactic/semantic kernels, i.e. (Bloehdorn and Moschitti, 2007a; Bloehdorn and Moschitti, 2007b), to syntactically contextualize word similarities may improve the reranker accuracy. (ii) The latter can be further boosted by studying complex structural kernels, e.g. (Moschitti, 2008; Nguyen et al., 2009; Dinarelli et al., 2009). (iii) More specific predicate argument structures such those proposed in FrameNet, e.g. (Baker et al., 1998; Giuglea and Moschitti, 2004; Giuglea and Moschitti, 2006; Johansson and Nugues, 2008b) may be useful to characterize the opinion holder and the sentence semantic context.

Finally, while the strategy based on reranking resulted in a significant performance boost, it remains to be seen whether a higher accuracy can be achieved by developing a more sophisticated inference algorithm based on dynamic programming. However, while the development of such an algorithm is an interesting problem, it will not necessarily result in a more usable system – when using a reranker, it is easy to trade accuracy for efficiency.

Acknowledgements

The research leading to these results has received funding from the European Community's Seventh Framework Programme (FP7/2007-2013) under grant agreement 231126: LivingKnowledge – Facts, Opinions and Bias in Time, and from Trustworthy Eternal Systems via Evolving Software, Data and Knowledge (EternalS, project number FP7 247758). In addition, we would like to thank Eric Breck for clarifying his results and experimental setup.

References

Collin F. Baker, Charles J. Fillmore, and John B. Lowe. 1998. The Berkeley FrameNet Project. In *Proceedings of COLING/ACL-1998*.

Roberto Basili, Marco Cammisa, and Alessandro Moschitti. 2005. Effective use of WordNet semantics via kernel-based learning. In *Proceedings of CoNLL-2005*, pages 1–8, Ann Arbor, Michigan.

Roberto Basili, Marco Cammisa, and Alessandro Moschitti. 2006. A semantic kernel to classify texts with very few training examples. In *in Informatica, an international journal of Computing and Informatics*.

Steven Bethard, Hong Yu, Ashley Thornton, Vasileios Hatzivassiloglou, and Dan Jurafsky. 2005. Extracting opinion propositions and opinion holders using syntactic and lexical cues. In James G. Shanahan, Yan Qu, and Janyce Wiebe, editors, *Computing Attitude and Affect in Text: Theory and Applications*.

Stephan Bloehdorn and Alessandro Moschitti. 2007a. Combined syntactic and semantic kernels for text classification. In *Proceedings of ECIR 2007*, Rome, Italy.

Stephan Bloehdorn and Alessandro Moschitti. 2007b. Structure and semantics for expressive text kernels. In *In Proceedings of CIKM '07*.

Stephan Bloehdorn, Roberto Basili, Marco Cammisa, and Alessandro Moschitti. 2006. Semantic kernels for text classification based on topological measures of feature similarity. In *Proceedings of ICDM 06*, Hong Kong, 2006.

Eric Breck, Yejin Choi, and Claire Cardie. 2007. Identifying expressions of opinion in context. In *Proceedings of IJCAI-2007*, Hyderabad, India.

Yejin Choi, Eric Breck, and Claire Cardie. 2006. Joint extraction of entities and relations for opinion recognition. In *Proceedings of EMNLP 2006*.

Michael Collins and Nigel Duffy. 2002. New ranking algorithms for parsing and tagging: Kernels over discrete structures, and the voted perceptron. In *Proceedings of ACL'02*.

Michael Collins. 2002. Discriminative training methods for hidden Markov models: Theory and experiments with perceptron algorithms. In *Proceedings of the 2002 Conference on Empirical Methods in Natural Language Processing (EMNLP 2002)*, pages 1–8.

Koby Crammer, Ofer Dekel, Joseph Keshet, Shai Shalev-Schwartz, and Yoram Singer. 2006. Online passive-aggressive algorithms. *Journal of Machine Learning Research*, 2006(7):551–585.

William Croft. 2005. Radical and typological arguments for radical construction grammar. In J.-O. Östman and M. Fried, editors, *Construction Grammars: Cognitive grounding and theoretical extensions*.

Marco Dinarelli, Alessandro Moschitti, and Giuseppe Riccardi. 2009. Re-ranking models based-on small training data for spoken language understanding. In *Proceedings of the 2009 Conference on Empirical Methods in Natural Language Processing*, pages 1076–1085, Singapore, August.

Rong-En Fan, Kai-Wei Chang, Cho-Jui Hsieh, Xiang-Rui Wang, and Chih-Jen Lin. 2008. LIBLINEAR: A library for large linear classification. *Journal of Machine Learning Research*, 9:1871–1874.

Yoav Freund and Robert E. Schapire. 1999. Large margin classification using the perceptron algorithm. *Machine Learning*, 37(3):277–296.

Ana-Maria Giuglea and Alessandro Moschitti. 2004. Knowledge Discovering using FrameNet, VerbNet and PropBank. In *In Proceedings of the Workshop on Ontology and Knowledge Discovering at ECML 2004*, Pisa, Italy.

Ana-Maria Giuglea and Alessandro Moschitti. 2006. Semantic role labeling via FrameNet, VerbNet and PropBank. In *Proceedings of the 21st International Conference on Computational Linguistics and 44th Annual Meeting of the Association for Computational Linguistics*, pages 929–936, Sydney, Australia, July.

Liang Huang. 2008. Forest reranking: Discriminative parsing with non-local features. In *Proceedings of ACL-08: HLT*, pages 586–594, Columbus, United States.

Thorsten Joachims. 1999. Making large-scale SVM learning practical. *Advances in Kernel Methods – Support Vector Learning*, 13.

Richard Johansson and Pierre Nugues. 2008a. Dependency-based syntactic–semantic analysis with PropBank and NomBank. In *CoNLL 2008: Proceedings of the Twelfth Conference on Natural Language Learning*, pages 183–187, Manchester, United Kingdom.

Richard Johansson and Pierre Nugues. 2008b. The effect of syntactic representation on semantic role labeling. In *Proceedings of the 22nd International Conference on Computational Linguistics (Coling 2008)*, pages 393–400, Manchester, UK.

Mahesh Joshi and Carolyn Penstein-Rosé. 2009. Generalizing dependency features for opinion mining. In *Proceedings of ACL/IJCNLP 2009, Short Papers Track.*

Jussi Karlgren, Gunnar Eriksson, Magnus Sahlgren, and Oscar Täckström. 2010. Between bags and trees – constructional patterns in text used for attitude identification. In *Proceedings of ECIR 2010, 32nd European Conference on Information Retrieval*, Milton Keynes, United Kingdom.

Soo-Min Kim and Eduard Hovy. 2006. Extracting opinions, opinion holders, and topics expressed in online news media text. In *Proceedings of ACL/COLING Workshop on Sentiment and Subjectivity in Text.*

Nozomi Kobayashi, Kentaro Inui, and Yuji Matsumoto. 2007. Extracting aspect-evaluation and aspect-of relations in opinion mining. In *Proceedings of Conference on Empirical Methods in Natural Language Processing (EMNLP-CoNLL-2007).*

Igor A. Mel'čuk. 1988. *Dependency Syntax: Theory and Practice.* State University Press of New York, Albany.

Adam Meyers, Ruth Reeves, Catherine Macleod, Rachel Szekely, Veronika Zielinska, Brian Young, and Ralph Grishman. 2004. The NomBank project: An interim report. In *HLT-NAACL 2004 Workshop: Frontiers in Corpus Annotation*, pages 24–31, Boston, United States.

Alessandro Moschitti and Roberto Basili. 2004. Complex linguistic features for text classification: A comprehensive study. In *Proceedings of ECIR.*

Alessandro Moschitti. 2006. Making tree kernels practical for natural language learning. In *Proccedings of EACL'06.*

Alessandro Moschitti. 2008. Kernel methods, syntax and semantics for relational text categorization. In *Proceeding of CIKM '08*, NY, USA.

Truc-Vien T. Nguyen, Alessandro Moschitti, and Giuseppe Riccardi. 2009. Convolution kernels on constituent, dependency and sequential structures for relation extraction. In *Proceedings of EMNLP.*

Martha Palmer, Dan Gildea, and Paul Kingsbury. 2005. The proposition bank: An annotated corpus of semantic roles. *Computational Linguistics*, 31(1):71–105.

Bo Pang, Lillian Lee, and Shivakumar Vaithyanathan. 2002. Thumbs up? Sentiment classification using machine learning techniques. In *Proceedings of EMNLP.*

Josef Ruppenhofer, Swapna Somasundaran, and Janyce Wiebe. 2008. Finding the sources and targets of subjective expressions. In *Proceedings of LREC.*

Libin Shen and Aravind Joshi. 2003. An SVM based voting algorithm with application to parse reranking. In *Proceedings of the CoNLL.*

Swapna Somasundaran, Galileo Namata, Janyce Wiebe, and Lise Getoor. 2009. Supervised and unsupervised methods in employing discourse relations for improving opinion polarity classification. In *Proceedings of EMNLP 2009: conference on Empirical Methods in Natural Language Processing.*

Jun Suzuki, Tsutomu Hirao, Yutaka Sasaki, and Eisaku Maeda. 2003. Hierarchical directed acyclic graph kernel: Methods for structured natural language data. In *Proceedings of the 41th Annual Meeting of Association for Computational Linguistics (ACL).*

Erik F. Tjong Kim Sang and Jorn Veenstra. 1999. Representing text chunks. In *Proceedings of EACL99*, pages 173–179, Bergen, Norway.

Iannis Tsochantaridis, Thorsten Joachims, Thomas Hofmann, and Yasemin Altun. 2005. Large margin methods for structured and interdependent output variables. *Journal of Machine Learning Research*, 6(Sep):1453–1484.

Janyce Wiebe, Rebecca Bruce, and Thomas O'Hara. 1999. Development and use of a gold standard data set for subjectivity classifications. In *Proceedings of the 37th Annual Meeting of the Association for Computational Linguistics.*

Janyce Wiebe, Theresa Wilson, and Claire Cardie. 2005. Annotating expressions of opinions and emotions in language. *Language Resources and Evaluation*, 39(2-3):165–210.

Michael Wiegand and Dietrich Klakow. 2010. Convolution kernels for opinion holder extraction. In *Proceedings of HLT-NAACL 2010.* To appear.

Theresa Wilson, Janyce Wiebe, and Paul Hoffmann. 2005. Recognizing contextual polarity in phrase-level sentiment analysis. In *Proceedings of HLT/EMNLP 2005.*

Yuanbin Wu, Qi Zhang, Xuanjing Huang, and Lide Wu. 2009. Phrase dependency parsing for opinion mining. In *Proceedings of EMNLP.*

Hong Yu and Vasileios Hatzivassiloglou. 2003. Towards answering opinion questions: Separating facts from opinions and identifying the polarity of opinion sentences. In *Proceedings of the Conference on Empirical Methods in Natural Language Processing (EMNLP-2003)*, pages 129–136, Sapporo, Japan.

Min Zhang, Jie Zhang, and Jian Su. 2006. Exploring Syntactic Features for Relation Extraction using a Convolution tree kernel. In *Proceedings of NAACL.*

Type Level Clustering Evaluation: New Measures and a POS Induction Case Study

Roi Reichart[1*] **Omri Abend**[2*†] **Ari Rappoport**[2]

[1]ICNC [2]Institute of Computer Science
Hebrew University of Jerusalem
{roiri|omria01|arir}@cs.huji.ac.il

Abstract

Clustering is a central technique in NLP. Consequently, clustering evaluation is of great importance. Many clustering algorithms are evaluated by their success in tagging corpus tokens. In this paper we discuss *type level* evaluation, which reflects class membership only and is independent of the token statistics of a particular reference corpus. Type level evaluation casts light on the merits of algorithms, and for some applications is a more natural measure of the algorithm's quality.

We propose new type level evaluation measures that, contrary to existing measures, are applicable when items are polysemous, the common case in NLP. We demonstrate the benefits of our measures using a detailed case study, POS induction. We experiment with seven leading algorithms, obtaining useful insights and showing that token and type level measures can weakly or even negatively correlate, which underscores the fact that these two approaches reveal different aspects of clustering quality.

1 Introduction

Clustering is a central machine learning technique. In NLP, clustering has been used for virtually every semi- and unsupervised task, including POS tagging (Clark, 2003), labeled parse tree induction (Reichart and Rappoport, 2008), verb-type classification (Schulte im Walde, 2006), lexical acquisition (Davidov and Rappoport, 2006; Davidov and Rappoport, 2008), multilingual document clustering (Montavlo et al., 2006), coreference resolution (Nicolae and Nicolae, 2006) and named entity recognition (Elsner et al., 2009). Consequently, the methodology of clustering evaluation is of great importance. In this paper we focus on external clustering evaluation, i.e., evaluation against manually annotated gold standards, which exist for almost all such NLP tasks. External evaluation is the dominant form of clustering evaluation in NLP, although other methods have been proposed (see e.g. (Frank et al., 2009)).

In this paper we discuss *type level* evaluation, which evaluates the set membership structure created by the clustering, independently of the token statistics of the gold standard corpus. Many clustering algorithms are evaluated by their success in tagging corpus tokens (Clark, 2003; Nicolae and Nicolae, 2006; Goldwater and Griffiths, 2007; Gao and Johnson, 2008; Elsner et al., 2009). However, in many cases a type level evaluation is the natural one. This is the case, for example, when a POS induction algorithm is used to compute a tag dictionary (the set of tags that each word can take), or when a lexical acquisition algorithm is used for constructing a lexicon containing the set of frames that a verb can participate in, or when a sense induction algorithm computes the set of possible senses of each word. In addition, even when the goal is corpus tagging, a type level evaluation is highly valuable, since it may cast light on the relative or absolute merits of different algorithms (as we show in this paper).

Clustering evaluation has been extensively investigated (Section 3). However, the discussion centers around the monosemous case, where each item belongs to exactly one cluster, although polysemy is the common case in NLP.

The contribution of the present paper is as follows. First, we discuss the issue of type level evaluation and explain why even in the monosemous case a token level evaluation presents a skewed

[*] Both authors equally contributed to this paper.

[†] Omri Abend is grateful to the Azrieli Foundation for the award of an Azrieli Fellowship.

Proceedings of the Fourteenth Conference on Computational Natural Language Learning, pages 77–87,
Uppsala, Sweden, 15-16 July 2010.

picture (Section 2). Second, we show for the common polysemous case why adapting existing information-theoretic measures to type level evaluation is not natural (Section 3). Third, we propose new mapping-based measures and algorithms to compute them (Section 4). Finally, we perform a detailed case study with part-of-speech (POS) induction (Section 5). We compare seven leading algorithms, showing that token and type level measures can weakly or even negatively correlate. This shows that type level evaluation indeed reveals aspects of a clustering solution that are not revealed by the common tagging-based evaluation.

Clustering is a vast research area. As far as we know, this is the first NLP paper to propose type level measures for the polysemous case.

2 Type Level Clustering Evaluation

This section motivates why both type and token level external evaluations should be done, even in the monosemous case.

Clustering algorithms compute a set of *induced clusters* (a *clustering*). Some algorithms directly compute a clustering, while some others produce a tagging of corpus tokens from which a clustering can be easily derived. A clustering is *monosemous* if each item is allowed to belong to a single cluster only, and *polysemous* otherwise. An *external* evaluation is one which is based on a comparison of an algorithm's result to a gold standard. In this paper we focus solely on external evaluation, which is the most common evaluation approach in NLP.

Token and type level evaluations reflect different aspects of a clustering. External token level evaluation assesses clustering quality according to the clustering's accuracy on a given manually annotated corpus. This is certainly a useful evaluation measure, e.g. when the purpose of the clustering algorithm is to annotate a corpus to serve as input to another application.

External type level evaluation views the computed clustering as a set membership structure and evalutes it independently of the token statistics in the gold standard corpus. There are two main cases in which this is useful. First, a type level evaluation can be the natural one in light of the problem itself. For example, if the purpose of the clustering algorithm is to automatically build a lexicon (e.g., VerbNet (Kipper et al., 2000)), then the lexicon structure itself should be evaluated. Second, it may be valuable to decouple corpus statistics from the induced clustering when the latter is to be used for annotating corpora that exhibit different statistics. In other words, if we evaluate an algorithm that will be invoked on a diverse set of corpora having different token statistics, a type level evaluation might provide a better picture (or at least a complementary one) on the quality of the clustering algorithm.

To motivate type level evaluation, consider POS induction, which exemplifies both cases above. Clearly, a word form may belong to several parts of speech (e.g., 'contrast' is both a noun and a verb, 'fast' is both an adjective and an adverb, 'that' can be a determiner, conjunction and adverb, etc.). As an evaluation of a POS induction algorithm, it is natural to evaluate the lexicon it generates, even if the main goal is to annotate a corpus. The lexicon lists the possible POS tags for each word, and thus its evaluation is a polysemous type level one.

Even if we ignore polysemy, type level evaluation is useful for a POS induction algorithm used to tag a corpus. There are POS classes whose members are very frequent, e.g., determiners and prepositions. Here, a very small number of word types usually accounts for a large portion of corpus tokens. For example, in the WSJ Penn Treebank (Marcus et al., 1993), there are 43,740 word types and over 1M word tokens. Of the types, 88 are tagged as prepositions. These types account for only 0.2% of the types, but for as many as 11.9% of the tokens. An algorithm which is accurate only on prepositions would do much better in a token level evaluation than in a type level one.

This phenomenon is not restricted to prepositions or English. In the WSJ corpus, determiners account for 0.05% of the types but for 9.8% of the tokens. In the German NEGRA corpus (Brants, 1997), the article class (both definite and indefinite) accounts for 0.04% of the word types and for 12.5% of the word tokens, and the coordinating conjunctions class accounts for 0.05% of the word types but for 3% of the tokens.

The type and token behavior differences result from the Zipfian distribution of word tokens to word types (Mitzenmacher, 2004). Since the word frequency distribution is Zipfian, any clustering algorithm that is accurate only on a small number of frequent words (not necessarily members of a particular class) would perform well in a token level evaluation but not in a type one. For example, the most frequent 100 word types (regardless of POS class) in WSJ (NEGRA) account for 43.9% (41.3%) of the tokens in the corpus. These words appear in 32 out of the 34 non-punctuation POS classes in WSJ and in 38 out of the 51 classes in NEGRA.

Other natural language entities also demonstrate Zipfian distribution of tokens to types. For example, the distribution of syntactic categories in parse tree constituents is Zipfian, as shown in (Reichart and Rappoport, 2008) for English, German and Chinese corpora. Thus, the distinction between token and type level evaluation is important also for grammar induction algorithms.

It may be argued that a token level evaluation is sufficient since it already reflects type information. In this paper we demonstrate that this is not the case, by showing that they correlate weakly or even negatively in an important NLP task.

3 Existing Clustering Evaluation Measures

Clustering evaluation is challenging. Many measures have been proposed in the past decades (Pfitzner et al., 2008). In this section, we briefly survey the three main types: mapping based, counting pairs, and information theoretic measures, and motivate our decision to focus on the first in this paper.

Mapping based measures are based on a post-processing step in which each induced cluster is mapped to a gold class (or vice versa). The standard mappings are greedy many-to-one (M-1) and greedy one-to-one (1-1). Several measures which rely on these mappings were proposed. The most common and perhaps the simplest one is accuracy, which computes the fraction of items correctly clustered under the mapping. Other measures include: L (Larsen, 1999), D (Van Dongen, 2000), misclassification index (MI) (Zeng et al., 2002), H (Meila and Heckerman, 2001), clustering F-measure (Fung et al., 2003) and micro-averaged precision and recall (Dhillon et al., 2003). In Section 4 we show why existing mapping-based measures cannot be applied to the polysemous type case and present new mapping-based measures for this case.

Counting pairs measures are based on a combinatorial approach which examines the number of data element pairs that are clustered similarly in the reference and proposed clustering. Among these are Rand Index (Rand, 1971), Adjusted Rand Index (Hubert and Arabie, 1985), Γ statistic (Hubert and Schultz, 1976), Jaccard (Milligan et al., 1983), Fowlkes-Mallows (Fowlkes and Mallows, 1983) and Mirkin (Mirkin, 1996). Schulte im Walde (2006) used such a measure for type level evaluation of monosemous verb type clustering.

Meila (2007) described a few problems with such measures. A serious one is that their values are unbounded, making it hard to interpret their results. This can be solved by adjusting their values to lie in $[0, 1]$, but even adjusted measures suffer from severe distributional problems, limiting their usability in practice. We thus do not address counting pairs measures in this paper.

Information-theoretic (IT) measures. IT measures assume that the items in the dataset are taken from a known distribution (usually the uniform distribution), and thus the gold and induced clusters can be treated as random variables. These measures utilize a co-occurrence matrix I between the gold and induced clusters. We denote the induced clustering by K and the gold clustering by C. I_{ij} contains the number of items in the intersection of the i-th gold class and the j-th induced cluster. When assuming the uniform distribution, the probability of an event (a gold class c or an induced cluster k) is its relative size, so $p(c) = \sum_{k=1}^{|K|} \frac{I_{ck}}{N}$ and $p(k) = \sum_{c=1}^{|C|} \frac{I_{ck}}{N}$ (N is the total number of clustered items).

Under this assumption we define the entropies and the conditional entropies:

$$H(C) = -\sum_{c=1}^{|C|} \frac{\sum_{k=1}^{|K|} I_{ck}}{N} log \frac{\sum_{k=1}^{|K|} I_{ck}}{N}$$

$$H(C|K) = -\sum_{k=1}^{|K|} \sum_{c=1}^{|C|} \frac{I_{ck}}{N} log \frac{I_{ck}}{\sum_{c=1}^{|C|} I_{ck}}$$

$H(K)$ and $H(K|C)$ are defined similarly.

In Section 5 we use two IT measures for token level evaluation, V (Rosenberg and Hirschberg, 2007) and NVI (Reichart and Rappoport, 2009) (a normalized version of VI (Meila, 2007)). The appealing properties of these measures have been extensively discussed in these references; see also (Pfitzner et al., 2008). V and NVI are defined as follows:

$$h = \begin{cases} 1 & H(C) = 0 \\ 1 - \frac{H(C|K)}{H(C)} & H(C) \neq 0 \end{cases}$$

$$c = \begin{cases} 1 & H(K) = 0 \\ 1 - \frac{H(K|C)}{H(K)} & H(K) \neq 0 \end{cases}$$

$$V = \frac{2hc}{h+c}$$

$$NVI(C,K) = \begin{cases} \frac{H(C|K)+H(K|C)}{H(C)} & H(C) \neq 0 \\ H(K) & H(C) = 0 \end{cases}$$

In the monosemous case (type or token), the application of the measures described in this section to type level evaluation is straightforward. In the polysemous case, however, they suffer from serious shortcomings.

Consider a case in which each item is assigned exactly r gold clusters and each gold cluster has the exact same number of items (i.e., each has a size of $\frac{l \cdot r}{|C|}$, where l is the number of items). Now, consider an induced clustering where there are $|C|$ induced clusters ($|K| = |C|$) and each item is assigned to all induced clusters. The co-occurrence matrix in this case should have identical values in all its entries. Even if we allow the weight each item contributes to the matrix to depend on its gold and induced entry sizes, the situation will remain the same. This is because all items have the exact same entry size and both gold and induced clusterings have uniform cluster sizes.

In this case, the random variables defined by the induced and gold clustering assignments are independent (this easily follows from the definition of independent events, since the joint probability is the multiplication of the marginals). Hence, $H(K|C) = H(K)$ and $H(C|K) = H(C)$, and both V and NVI obtain their worst possible values[1]. However, the score should surely depend on r (the size of each word's gold entry). Specifically, when $r = |C|$ we get that the induced and gold clusterings are identical. This case should not get the worst score, and it should definitely score higher than the case in which $r = 1$, where K is dramatically different from C.

The problem can in theory be solved by providing the number of clusters per item as an input to the algorithm. However, in NLP this is unrealistic (even if the total number of clusters can be provided) and the number should be determined by the algorithm. We therefore do not consider IT-based measures in this paper, deferring them to future work.

4 Mapping Based Measures for Polysemous Type Evaluation

In this section we present new type level evaluation measures for the polysemous case. As we show below, these measures do not suffer from the problems discussed for IT measures in Section 3.

All measures are mapping-based: first, a mapping between the induced and gold clusters is performed, and then a measure E is computed. As is common in the clustering evaluation literature (Section 3), we use M-1 and 1-1 greedy mappings, defined to be those that maximize the corresponding measure E.

Let $C = \{c_1, ..., c_n\}$ be the set of gold classes and $K = \{k_1, ..., k_m\}$ be the set of induced clusters. Denote the number of words types by l. Let $A_i \subset C, B_i \subset K, i = 1...l$ be the set of gold classes and set of induced clusters for each word. The polysemous nature of task is reflected by the fact that A_i and B_i are subsets, rather than members, of C and K respectively.

Our measures address quality from two persectives, that of the individual items clustered (Section 4.1) and that of the clusters (Section 4.2). Item-based measures especially suit evaluation of clustering quality for the purpose of lexicon induction, and have no counterpart in the monosemous case. Cluster-based measures are a direct generalization of existing mapping based measures to the polysemous case.

The difficulty in designing item-based and cluster-based measures is that the number of clusters assigned to each item is determined by the clustering algorithm. Below we show how to overcome this.

4.1 Item-Based Evaluation

For a given mapping $h : K \rightarrow C$, denote $h(B_i) = \{h(x) : x \in B_i\}$. A fundamental quantity for item-based evaluation is the number of correct clusters for each item (word type) under this mapping, denoted by IM_i (IM stands for 'item match'):

$$IM_i = |A_i \cap h(B_i)|$$

The total item match IM is defined to be:

$$IM = \sum_{i=1}^{l} IM_i = \sum_{i=1}^{l} |A_i \cap h(B_i)|$$

In the monosemous case, IM is normalized by the number of items, yielding an accuracy score. Applying a similar definition in the polysemous case, normalizing instead by the total number of gold clusters assigned to the items, can be easily manipulated. Even a clustering which has the correct number of induced clusters (equal to the number of gold classes) but which assigns each item to

[1] V values are in $[0, 1]$, 0 being the worst. NVI obtains its highest and worst possible value, $1 + \frac{log(|K|)}{H(C)}$.

all induced clusters, receives a perfect score under both greedy M-1 and 1-1 mappings. This holds for any induced clustering for which $\forall i, A_i \subset h(B_i)$. Note that using a mapping from C to K (or a combination of both directions) would exhibit the same problem.

To overcome the problem, we use the harmonic average of two normalized terms (F-score). We use two average variants, micro and macro. Macro average computes the total number of matches over all words and normalizes in the end. Recall (R), Precision (P) and their harmonic average (F-score) are accordingly defined:

$$R = \frac{IM}{\sum_{i=1}^{l} |A_i|} \qquad P = \frac{IM}{\sum_{i=1}^{l} |h(B_i)|}$$

$$MacroI = \frac{2RP}{R+P} =$$

$$= \frac{2IM}{\sum_{i=1}^{l} |A_i| + \sum_{i=1}^{l} |h(B_i)|} = F(h) \cdot \sum_{i=1}^{l} IM_i$$

$F(h)$ is a constant depending on h. As all items are equally weighted, those with larger gold and induced entries have more impact on the measure.

The micro average, aiming to give all items an equal status, first computes an F-score for each item and then averages over them. Hence, each item contributes at most 1 to the measure. This *MicroI* measure is given by:

$$R_i = \frac{IM_i}{|A_i|} \quad P_i = \frac{IM_i}{|h(B_i)|} \quad F_i = \frac{2R_iP_i}{R_i+P_i} = \frac{2IM_i}{|A_i|+|h(B_i)|}$$

$$MicroI = \frac{1}{l}\sum_{i=1}^{l} F_i = \frac{1}{l}\sum_{i=1}^{l} \frac{2IM_i}{|A_i| + |h(B_i)|} =$$

$$= \frac{1}{l}\sum_{i=1}^{l} w_i(h) \cdot IM_i$$

Where $w_i(h)$ is a weight depending on h but also on i.

For both measures, the maximum score is 1. It is obtained if and only if $A_i = h(B_i)$ for every i.

In 1-1 mapping, when the number of induced clusters is larger than the number of gold clusters, some of the induced clusters are not mapped. To preserve the nature of 1-1 mapping that punishes for excessive clusters[2], we define $|h(B_i)|$ to be equal to $|B_i|$ even for these unmapped clusters.

Recall that any induced clustering in which $\forall i, A_i \subset h(B_i)$ gets the best score under a greedy mapping with the accuracy measure. In MacroI and MicroI the obtained recalls are perfect, but the precision terms reflect deviation from the correct solution.

[2]And to allow us to compute it accurately, see below.

In the example in Section 3 showing an unreasonable behavior of IT-based measures, the score depends on r for both MacroI and MicroI. With our new measures, recall is always 1, but precision is $\frac{r}{n}$. This is true both for 1-1 and M-1 mappings. Hence, the new measures show reasonable behavior in this example for all r values.

MicroI was used in (Dasgupta and Ng, 2007) with a manually compiled mapping. Their mapping was not based on a well-defined scheme but on a heuristic. Moreover, providing a manual mapping might be impractical when the number of clusters is large, and can be inaccurate, especially when the clustering is not of very high quality.

In the following we discuss how to compute the 1-1 and M-1 greedy mappings for each measure.

1-1 Mapping. We compute h by finding the maximal weighted matching in a bipartite graph. In this graph one side represents the induced clusters, the other represents the gold classes and the matchings correspond to 1-1 mappings. The problem can be efficiently solved by the Kuhn-Munkres algorithm (Kuhn, 1955; Munkres, 1957).

To be able to use this technique, edge weights must not depend upon h. In 1-1 mapping, $|h(B_i)| = |B_i|$, and therefore $F(h) = F$ and $w_i(h) = w_i$. That is, both quantities are independent of h[3]. For MacroI, the weight on the edge between the s-th gold class and the j-th induced cluster is: $W(e_{sj}) = \sum_{i=1}^{l} F \cdot I_{s \in A_i} I_{j \in B_i}$. For MicroI it is: $W(e_{sj}) = \sum_{i=1}^{l} w_i \cdot I_{s \in A_i} I_{j \in B_i}$. $I_{s \in A_i}$ is 1 if $s \in A_i$ and 0 otherwise.

M-1 Mapping. There are two problems in applying the bipartite graph technique to finding an M-1 mapping. First, under such mapping $w_i(h)$ and $F(h)$ do depend on h. The problem may be solved by selecting some constant weighting scheme. However, a more serious problem also arises.

Consider a case in which an item x has a gold entry $\{C_1\}$ and an induced entry $\{K_1, K_2\}$. Say the chosen mapping mapped both K_1 and K_2 to C_1. By summing over the graph's edges selected by the mapping, we add weight ($F(h)$ for MacroI and $w_i(h)$ for MicroI) both to the edge between K_1 and C_1 and to the edge between K_2 and C_1. However, the item's IM_i is only 1. This prohibits

[3]Consequently, the increase in MacroI and MicroI following an increase of 1 in an item's gold/induced intersection size (IM_i) is independent of h.

the use of the bipartite graph method for the M-1 case.

Since we are not aware of any exact method for solving this problem, we use a hill-climbing algorithm. We start with a random mapping and a random order on the induced clusters. Then we iterate over the induced clusters and map each of them to the gold class which maximizes the measure given that the rest of the mapping remains constant. We repeat the process until no improvement to the measure can be obtained by changing the assignment of a single induced cluster. Since the score depends on the initial random mapping and random order, we repeat this process several times and choose the maximum between the obtained scores.

4.2 Cluster-Based Evaluation

The cluster-based evaluation measures we propose are a direct generalization of existing monosemous mapping based measures to the polysemous type case.

For a given mapping $h : K \rightarrow C$, we define $\bar{h} : K^h \rightarrow C$. K^h is defined to be a clustering which is obtained by performing set union between every two clusters in K that are mapped to the same gold cluster. The resulting $\bar{h}$ is always 1-1. We denote $|K^h| = m^h$.

Our motivation for using $\bar{h}$ in the definition of the measures instead of h is to stay as close as possible to accuracy, the most common mapping-based measure in the monosemous case. M-1 (monosemous) accuracy does not punish for splitting classes. For instance, in a case where there is a gold cluster c_i and two induced clusters k_1 and k_2 such that $c_i = k_1 \cup k_2$, the M-1 accuracy is the same as in the case where there is one cluster k_1 such that $c_i = k_1$. M-1 accuracy, despite its indifference to splitting, was shown to reflect better than 1-1 accuracy the clustering's applicability for subsequent applications (at least in some contexts) (Headden III et al., 2008).

Recall that in item-based evaluation, IM_i measures the intersection between the induced and gold entries of each item. Therefore, the set union operation is not needed for that case, since when an item appears in two induced clusters that are mapped to the same gold cluster, its IM_i is increased only by 1.

A fundamental quantity for cluster-based evaluation is the intersection between each induced cluster and the gold class to which it is mapped. We denote this value by CM_j (CM stands for 'cluster match'):

$$CM_j = |k_j \cap \bar{h}(k_j)|$$

The total intersection (CM) is accordingly defined to be:

$$CM = \sum_{j=1}^{m^h} CM_j = \sum_{j=1}^{m^h} |k_j \cap \bar{h}(k_j)|$$

As with the item-based evaluation (Section 4.1), using CM or a derived accuracy as a measure is problematic. A clustering that assigns n induced classes to each word (n is the number of gold classes) will get the highest possible score under every greedy mapping (1-1 or M-1), as will any clustering in which $\forall i, A_i \subset h(B_i)$.

As in the item-based evaluation, a possible solution is based on defining recall, precision and F-score measures, computed either in the micro or in the macro level. The macro cluster-based measure turns out to be identical to the macro item-based measure MacroI[4].

The following derivation shows the equivalence for the 1-1 case. The M-1 case is similar. We note that $h = \bar{h}$ in the 1-1 case and we therefore exchange them in the definition of CM. It is enough to show that $CM = IM$, since the denominator is the same in both cases:

$$\begin{aligned} CM &= \sum_{j=1}^{m} |k_j \cap h(k_j)| = \\ &= \sum_{j=1}^{m} \sum_{i=1}^{l} I_{i \in k_j} I_{i \in h(k_j)} = \\ &= \sum_{i=1}^{l} \sum_{j=1}^{m} I_{i \in k_j} I_{i \in h(k_j)} = \\ &= \sum_{i=1}^{l} |A_i \cap h(B_i)| = IM \end{aligned}$$

The micro cluster-based measures are defined:

$$R_j = \frac{CM_j}{|\bar{h}(k_j)|} \quad P_j = \frac{CM_j}{|k_j|} \quad F_j = \frac{2R_jP_j}{R_j+P_j}$$

The micro cluster measure MicroC is obtained by taking a weighted average over the F_j's:

$$MicroC = \sum_{k \in K^h} \frac{|k|}{N^*} F_k$$

Where $N^* = \sum_{z \in K^h} |z|$ is the number of clustered items after performing the set union and including repetitions. If, in the 1-1 case where $m > n$, an induced cluster is not mapped, we define $F_k = 0$. A definition of the measure using a reverse mapping (i.e., from C to K) would have used a weighted average with weights proportional to the gold classes' sizes.

[4]Hence, we have six type level measures: MacroI (which is equal to MacroC), MicroI, and MicroC, each of which in two versions, M-1 and 1-1.

The definition of $\bar{h}$ causes a similar computational difficulty as in the M-1 item-based measures. Consequently, we apply a hill climbing algorithm similar to the one described in Section 4.1.

The 1-1 mapping is computed using the same bipartite graph method described in Section 4.1. The graph's vertices correspond to gold and induced clusters and an edge's weight is the F-score between the class and cluster corresponding to its vertices times the cluster's weight ($|k|/N^*$).

5 Evaluation of POS Induction Models

As a detailed case study for the ideas presented in this paper, we apply the various measures for the POS induction task, using seven leading POS induction algorithms.

5.1 Experimental Setup

POS Induction Algorithms. We experimented with the following models: ARR10 (Abend et al., 2010), Clark03 (Clark, 2003), GG07 (Goldwater and Griffiths, 2007), GJ08 (Gao and Johnson, 2008), and GVG09 (Van Gael et al., 2009) (three models). Additional recent good results for various variants of the POS induction problem are described in e.g., (Smith and Eisner, 2004; Graça et al., 2009).

Clark03 and ARR10 are monosemous algorithms, allowing a single cluster for each word type. The other algorithms are polysemous. They perform sequence labeling where each token is tagged in its context, and different tokens (instances) of the same type (word form) may receive different tags.

Data Set. All models were tested on sections 2-21 of the PTB-WSJ, which consists of 39832 sentences, 950028 tokens and 39546 unique types. Of the tokens, 832629 (87.6%) are not punctuation marks.

Evaluation Measures. Type level evaluation used the measures MacroI (which is equal to MacroC), MicroI and MicroC both with greedy 1-1 and M-1 mappings as described in Section 4. The type level gold (induced) entry is defined to be the set of all gold (induced) clusters with which it appears.

For the token level evaluation, six measures are used (see Section 3): accuracy with M-1 and 1-1 mappings, NVI, V, H(C|K) and H(K|C), using e as the logarithm's base. We use the full WSJ POS tags set excluding punctuation[5].

Punctuation. Punctuation marks occupy a large volume of the corpus tokens (12.4% in our experimental corpus), and are easy to cluster. Clustering punctuation marks thus greatly inflates token level results. To study the relationship between type and token level evaluations in a focused manner, we excluded punctuation from the evaluation (they are still used during training, so algorithms that rely on them are not harmed).

Number of Induced Clusters. The number of gold POS tags in WSJ is 45, of which 11 are punctuation marks. Therefore, for the ARR10 and Clark03 models, 34 clusters were induced. For GJ08 we received the output with 45 clusters. The iHMM models of GVG09 determine the number of clusters automatically (resulting in 47, 91 and 192 clusters, see below). For GG07, our computing resources did not enable us to induce 45 clusters and we therefore used 17[6]. Our focus in this paper is to study the type vs. token distinction rather than to provide a full scope comparison between algorithms, for which more clustering sizes would need to be examined.

Configurations. We ran the ARR10 tagger with the configuration detailed in (Abend et al., 2010). For Clark03, we ran his *neyessenmorph* model[7] 10 times (using an unknown words threshold of 5) and report the average score for each measure. The models of GVG09 were run in the three configurations reported in their paper: one with a Dirichlet process prior and fixed parameters, another with a Pittman-Yore prior with fixed parameters, and a third with a Dirichlet process prior with parameters learnt from the data. All five models were run in an optimal configuration.

We obtained the code of Goldwater and Griffiths' BHMM model and ran it for 10K iterations with an annealing technique for parameter estimation. That was the best parameter estimation technique available to us. This is the first time that this model is evaluated on such a large experimental corpus, and it performed well under these conditions.

The output of the model of GJ08 was sent to us by the authors. The model was run on sec-

[5]We use all WSJ tokens in the training stage, but omit punctuation marks during evaluation.

[6]The 17 most frequent tags cover 94% of the word instances and more than 99% of the word types in the WSJ gold standard tagging.

[7]www.cs.rhul.ac.uk/home/alexc/RHUL/Downloads.html

tions 2-21 of the WSJ-PTB using significantly inferior computing resources compared to those used for producing the results reported in their paper. While this model cannot be compared to the aforementioned six models due to the suboptimal configuration, we evaluate its output using our measures to get a broader variety of experimental results[8].

5.2 Results and Discussion

Table 1 presents the scores of the compared models under all evaluation measures (six token level, six type level). What is important here to note are the differences between type and token level evaluations for the algorithms. We are mainly interested in two things: (1) seeing how relative rankings change in the two evaluation types, thus showing that the two types are not highly correlated and are both useful; and (2) insights gained by using a type level evaluation in addition to the usual token level one.

Note that the table should not be used to deduce which algorithm is the 'best' for the task, even according to a single evaluation type. This is because, as explained above, the algorithms do not induce the same number of clusters and this affects their results.

Results indicate that type level evaluation reveals aspects of the clustering quality that are not expressed in the token level. For the Clark03 model the disparity is most apparent. While in the token level it performs very well (better than the polysemous algorithms for the 1-1, V and NVI token level measures), in the type level it is the second worst in the item-based 1-1 scores and the worst in the M-1 scores.

Here we have a clear demonstration of the value of type level evaluation. The Clark03 algorithm is assessed as excellent using token level evaluation (second only to ARR10 in M-1, 1-1, V and NVI), and only a type level one shows its relatively poor type performance. Although readers may think that this is natural due to the algorithm's monosemous nature, this is not the case, since the monosemous ARR10 generally ranked first in the type level measures (more on this below).

The disparity is also observed for polysemous algorithms. The GG07 model's token level scores are mediocre, while in the type level MicroC 1-1 measure this model is the best and in the type level MicroI and MacroI 1-1 measures it is the second best.

Monosemous vs. polysemous algorithms. The table shows that the ARR10 model achieves the best results in most type and token level evaluation measures. The fact that this monosemous algorithm outperforms the polysemous ones, even in a type level evaluation, may seem strange at first sight but can be explained as follows. Polysemous tokens account for almost 60% of the corpus (565K out of 950K), so we could expect that a monosemous algorithm should do badly in a token-level evaluation. However, for most of the polysemous tokens the polysemy is only weakly present in the corpus[9], so it is hard to detect even for polysemous algorithms. Regarding types, polysemous types constitute only 16.6% of the corpus types, so a monosemous algorithm which is quite good in assigning types to clusters has a good chance of beating polysemous algorithms in a type level evaluation.

Hence, monosemous POS induction algorithms are not at such a great disadvantage relative to polysemous ones. This observation, which was fully motivated by our type level case study, might be used to guide future work on POS induction, and it thus serves as another demonstration for the utility of type level evaluation.

Hill climbing algorithm. For the type level measures with greedy M-1 mapping, we used the hill-climbing algorithm described in Section 4. Recall that the mapping to which our algorithm converges depends on its random initialization. We therefore ran the algorithm with 10 different random initializations and report the obtained maximum for MacroI, MicroI and MicroC in Table 1. The different initializations caused very little fluctuation: not more than 1% in the 9 (7) best runs for the item-based (MicroC) measures. We take this result as an indication that the obtained maximum is a good approximation of the global maximum.

We tried to improve the algorithm by selecting an intelligent initialization heuristic. We used the M-1 mapping obtained by mapping each induced cluster to the gold class with which it has the high-

[8]We would like to thank all authors for sending us the data.

[9]Only about 27% of the tokens are instances of words that are polysemous but not weakly polysemous (we call a word *weakly polysemous* if more than 95% of its instances (tokens) are tagged by the same tag).

	Token Level Evaluation						Type Level Evaluation					
							MacroI		MicroI		MicroC	
	M-1	1-1	NVI	V	H(C|K)	H(K|C)	M-1	1-1	M-1	1-1	M-1	1-1
ARR10	**0.675**	**0.588**	**0.809**	**0.608**	1.041	**1.22**	0.579	**0.444**	**0.596**	**0.455**	**0.624**	0.403
Clark03	0.65	0.484	0.887	0.586	1.04	1.441	0.396	0.301	0.384	0.288	0.463	0.347
GG07	0.5	0.415	0.989	0.479	1.523	1.241	0.497	0.405	0.461	0.398	0.563	**0.445**
GVG09(1)	0.51	0.444	1.033	0.477	1.471	1.409	0.513	0.354	0.436	0.352	0.486	0.33
GVG09(2)	0.591	0.484	0.998	0.529	1.221	1.564	0.637	0.369	0.52	0.373	0.548	0.32
GVG09(3)	0.668	0.368	1.132	0.534	**0.978**	2.18	**0.736**	0.280	0.558	0.276	0.565	0.199
GJ08*	0.605	0.383	1.09	0.506	1.231	1.818	0.467	0.298	0.446	0.311	0.561	0.291

Table 1: Token level (left columns) and type level (right columns) results for seven POS induction algorithms (rows) (see text for details). Token and type level performance are weakly correlated and complement each other as evaluation measures. ARR10, a monosemous algorithm, yields the best results in most measures. (GJ08* results are different from those reported in the original paper because it was run with weaker computing resources than those used there.)

est weight edge in the bipartite graph. Recall from Section 4.1 that this is a reasonable approximation of the greedy M-1 mapping. Again, we ran it for the three type level measures for 10 times with a random update order on the induced clusters. This had only a minor effect on the final scores.

Number of clusters. Previous work (Reichart and Rappoport, 2009) demonstrated that in data sets where a relatively small fraction of the gold classes covers most of the items, it is reasonable to choose this number to be the number of induced clusters. In our experimental data set, this number (the 'prominent cluster number') is around 17 (see Section 5.1). Up to this number, increasing the number of clusters is likely to have a positive effect on token level M-1, 1-1, H(C|K), and H(K|C) scores. Inducing a larger number of clusters, however, is likely to positively affect M-1 and H(C|K) but to have a negative effect on 1-1 and H(K|C).

This tendency is reflected in Table 1. For the GG07 model the number of induced clusters, 17, approximates the number of prominent clusters and is lower than the number of induced clusters of the other models. This is reflected by its low token level M-1 and H(C|K) performance and its high quality H(K|C) and NVI token level scores. The GVG (1)-(3) models induced 47, 91 and 192 clusters respectively. This might explain the high token level M-1 and H(C|K) performance of GVG(3), as well as its high M-1 type level performance, compared to its mediocre scores in other measures.

The item based measures. The table indicates that there is no substantial difference between the two item based type level scores with 1-1 mapping. The definitions of MacroI and MicroI imply that if $|A_i| + |h(B_i)|$ (which equals $|A_i| + |B_i|$ under a 1-1 mapping) is constant for all word types, then a clustering will score equally on both 1-1 type measures. Indeed, in our experimental corpus 83.4% of the word types have one POS tag, 12.5% have 2, 3.1% have 3 and only 1% of the words have more. Therefore, $|A_i|$ is roughly constant. The ARR10 and Clark03 models assign a word type to a single cluster. For the other models, the number of clusters per word type is generally similar to that of the gold standard. Consequently, $|B_i|$ is roughly constant as well, which explains the similar behavior of the two measures.

Note that for other clustering tasks $|A_i|$ may not necessarily be constant, so the MacroI and MicroI scores are not likely to be as similar under the 1-1 mapping.

6 Summary

We discussed type level evaluation for polysemous clustering, presented new mapping-based evaluation measures, and applied them to the evaluation of POS induction algorithms, demonstrating that type level measures provide value beyond the common token level ones.

We hope that type level evaluation in general and the proposed measures in particular will be used in the future for evaluating clustering performance in NLP tasks.

References

Omri Abend, Roi Reichart and Ari Rappoport, 2010. Improved Unsupervised POS Induction through Prototype Discovery. *ACL '10.*

Thorsten Brants, 1997. The NEGRA Export Format. *CLAUS Report, Saarland University.*

Alexander Clark, 2003. Combining Distributional and Morphological Information for Part of Speech Induction. *EACL '03.*

Sajib Dasgupta and Vincent Ng, 2007. Unsupervised Part-of-Speech Acquisition for Resource-Scarce Languages. *EMNLP-CoNLL '07.*

Dmitry Davidov, Ari Rappoport, 2006. Efficient Unsupervised Discovery of Word Categories using Symmetric Patterns and High Frequency Words. *COLING-ACL '06.*

Dmitry Davidov, Ari Rappoport. 2008. Unsupervised Discovery of Generic Relationships Using Pattern Clusters and its Evaluation by Automatically Generated SAT Analogy Questions. *ACL '08*

I. S. Dhillon, S. Mallela, and D. S. Modha, 2003. Information Theoretic Co-clustering. *KDD '03*

Micha Elsner, Eugene Charniak, and Mark Johnson, 2009. Structured Generative Models for Unsupervised Named-Entity Clustering. *NAACL '09.*

Stella Frank, Sharon Goldwater, and Frank Keller, 2009. Evaluating Models of Syntactic Category Acquisition without Using a Gold Standard. *Proc. 31st Annual Conf. of the Cognitive Science Society,* 2576–2581.

E.B Fowlkes and C.L. Mallows, 1983. A Method for Comparing Two Hierarchical Clusterings. *Journal of American statistical Association,*78:553-569.

Benjamin C. M. Fung, Ke Wang, and Martin Ester, 2003. Hierarchical Document Clustering using Frequent Itemsets. *SIAM International Conference on Data Mining '03.*

Jianfeng Gao and Mark Johnson, 2008. *A Comparison of Bayesian Estimators for Unsupervised Hidden Markov Model POS Taggers. EMNLP '08.*

Sharon Goldwater and Tom Griffiths, 2007. Fully Bayesian Approach to Unsupervised Part-of-Speech Tagging. *ACL '07.*

João Graça, Kuzman Ganchev, Ben Taskar and Frenando Pereira, 2009. Posterior vs. Parameter Sparsity in Latent Variable Models. *NIPS '09.*

William P. Headden III, David McClosky and Eugene Charniak, 2008. *Evaluating Unsupervised Part-of-Speech Tagging for Grammar Induction.* COLING '08.

L. Hubert and J. Schultz, 1976. Quadratic Assignment as a General Data Analysis Strategy. *British Journal of Mathematical and Statistical Psychology*, 29:190-241.

L. Hubert and P. Arabie, 1985. Comparing Partitions. *Journal of Classification*, 2:193-218.

Maurice Kandall and Jean Dickinson, 1990. Rank Correlation Methods. *Oxford University Press, New York.*

Karin Kipper, Hoa Trang Dang and Martha Palmer, 2000. Class-Based Construction of a Verb Lexicon. AAAI '00.

Harold W. Kuhn, 1955. The Hungarian Method for the Assignment Problem. *Naval Research Logistics Quarterly, 2:83-97.*

Bjornar Larsen and Chinatsu Aone, 1999. Fast and effective text mining using linear-time document clustering. *KDD '99.*

Marcus, Mitchell P., Beatrice Santorini, and Mary Ann Marcinkiewicz. 1993. Building a large annotated corpus of english: The penn treebank. *Computational Linguistics*, 19(2):313-330.

Marina Meila and David Heckerman, 2001. An Experimental Comparison of Model-based Clustering Methods. *Machine Learning*, 42(1/2):9-29.

Marina Meila, 2007. Comparing Clustering – an Information Based Distance. *Journal of Multivariate Analysis*, 98:873-895.

C.W Milligan, S.C Soon and L.M Sokol, 1983. The Effect of Cluster Size, Dimensionality and the Number of Clusters on Recovery of True Cluster Structure. *IEEE transactions on Pattern Analysis and Machine Intelligence*, 5:40-47.

Boris G. Mirkin, 1996. Mathematical Classification and Clustering. *Kluwer Academic Press.*

Michael Mitzenmacher , 2004. A Brief History of Generative Models for Power Law and Lognormal Distributions . *Internet Mathematics*, 1(2):226-251.

Soto Montalvo, Raquel Martnez, Arantza Casillas, and Vctor Fresno, 2006. Multilingual Document Clustering: an Heuristic Approach Based on Cognate Named Entities. *ACL '06.*

James Munkres, 1957. Algorithms for the Assignment and Transportation Problems. *Journal of the SIAM, 5(1):32-38.*

Cristina Nicolae and Gabriel Nicolae, 2006. BESTCUT: A Graph Algorithm for Coreference Resolution. *EMNLP '06.*

Darius M. Pfitzner, Richard E. Leibbrandt and David M.W Powers, 2008. Characterization and Evaluation of Similarity Measures for Pairs of Clusterings. *Knowledge and Information Systems: An International Journal*, DOI 10.1007/s10115-008-0150-6.

William Rand, 1971. Objective Criteria for the Evaluation of Clustering Methods. *Journal of the American Statstical Association*, 66(336):846-850.

Roi Reichart and Ari Rappoport, 2008. Unsupervised Induction of Labeled Parse Trees by Clustering with Syntactic Features. *COLING '08*.

Roi Reichart and Ari Rappoport, 2009. The NVI Clustering Evaluation Measure. *CoNLL '09*.

Andrew Rosenberg and Julia Hirschberg, 2007. V-Measure: A Conditional Entropy-based External Cluster Evaluation Measure. *EMNLP '07*.

Sabine Schulte im Walde, 2006. Experiments on the Automatic Induction of German Semantic Verb Classes. *Computational Linguistics*, 32(2):159-194.

Noah A. Smith and Jason Eisner, 2004. Annealing Techniques for Unsupervised Statistical Language Learning. *ACL '04*.

Stijn Van Dongen, 2000. Performance Criteria for Graph Clustering and Markov Cluster Experiments. *Technical report CWI, Amsterdam*

Jurgen Van Gael, Andreas Vlachos and Zoubin Ghahramani, 2009. The Infinite HMM for Unsupervised POS Tagging. *EMNLP '09*.

Yujing Zeng, Jianshan Tang, Javier Garcia-Frias, and Guang R. Gao, 2002. An Adaptive Meta-clustering Approach: Combining the Information from Different Clustering Results . *CSB* 00:276

Recession Segmentation: Simpler Online Word Segmentation Using Limited Resources*

Constantine Lignos, Charles Yang
Dept. of Computer and Information Science, Dept. of Linguistics
University of Pennsylvania
lignos@cis.upenn.edu, charles.yang@ling.upenn.edu

Abstract

In this paper we present a cognitively plausible approach to word segmentation that segments in an online fashion using only local information and a lexicon of previously segmented words. Unlike popular statistical optimization techniques, the learner uses structural information of the input syllables rather than distributional cues to segment words. We develop a memory model for the learner that like a child learner does not recall previously hypothesized words perfectly. The learner attains an F-score of 86.69% in ideal conditions and 85.05% when word recall is unreliable and stress in the input is reduced. These results demonstrate the power that a simple learner can have when paired with appropriate structural constraints on its hypotheses.

1 Introduction

The problem of word segmentation presents an important challenge in language acquisition. The child learner must segment a continuous stream of sounds into words without knowing what the individual words are until the stream has been segmented. Computational models present an opportunity to test the potentially innate constraints, structures, and algorithms that a child may be using to guide her acquisition. In this work we develop a segmentation model from the constraints suggested by Yang (2004) and evaluate it in idealized conditions and conditions that better approximate the environment of a child learner. We seek to determine how these limitations in the learner's input and memory affect the learner's performance and to demonstrate that the presented learner is robust even under non-ideal conditions.

*Portions of this work were adapted from an earlier manuscript, *Word Segmentation: Quick But Not Dirty*.

2 Related Work

Most recent work in word segmentation of child-directed speech has operated within statistical optimization frameworks, particularly Bayesian approaches (Goldwater et al., 2009; Johnson and Goldwater, 2009). These models have established the state-of-the-art for the task of selecting appropriate word boundaries from a stream of unstructured phonemes. But while these models deliver excellent performance, it is not clear how they inform the *process* of acquisition.

Trying to find cognitive insight from these types of models is difficult because of the inherent mismatch in the quality and types of hypotheses they maintain during learning. Children are incremental learners (Brown, 1973), and learners relying on statistical optimization are generally not. A child's competence grows gradually as she hears and produces more and more utterances, going through predictable changes to her working grammar (Marcus et al., 1992) that statistical optimization techniques typically do not go through and do not intend to replicate.

Statistical models provide excellent information about the features, distributional cues, and priors that can be used in learning, but provide little information about *how* a child learner can use this information and how her knowledge of language develops as the learning process evolves. Previous simulations in word segmentation using the same type of distributional information as many statistical optimization-based learners but without an optimization model suggest that statistics alone are not sufficient for learning to succeed in a computationally efficient online manner; further constraints on the search space are needed (Yang, 2004).

Previous computational models have demanded tremendous memory and computational capacity from human learners. For example, the algorithm

Proceedings of the Fourteenth Conference on Computational Natural Language Learning, pages 88–97,
Uppsala, Sweden, 15-16 July 2010. ©2010 Association for Computational Linguistics

of Brent & Cartwright (1996) produces a set of possible lexicons that describe the learning corpus, each of which is evaluated as the learner iterates until no further improvement is possible. It is unlikely that an algorithm of this type is something a human learner is capable of using given the requirement to remember at the very least a long history of recent utterances encountered and constantly reanalyze them to find a optimal segmentation. Work in this tradition makes no claims, however, that these methods are actually the ones used by human learners.

On the other hand, previous computational models often underestimate the human learner's knowledge of linguistic representations. Most of these models are "synthetic" in the sense of Brent (1999): the raw material for segmentation is a stream of segments, which are then successively grouped into larger units and eventually, conjectured words. This assumption may make the child learner's job unnecessarily hard; since syllables are hierarchical structures consisting of segments, treating the linguistic data as unstructured segment sequences makes the problem harder than it actually is. For a given utterance, there are fewer syllables than segments, and hence fewer segmentation possibilities.

Modeling the corpus using hierarchical grammars that can model the input at varying levels (word collocations, words, syllables, onsets, etc.) provide the learner the most flexibility, allowing the learner to build structure from the individual phonemes and apply distributions at each level of abstraction (Johnson and Goldwater, 2009). While this results in state-of-the-art performance for segmentation performed at the phoneme level, this approach requires significant computational resources as each additional level of representation increases the complexity of learning. In addition, it is not clear that some of the intermediate levels in such an approach, such as word level collocations which are not syntactic constituents, would have any linguistic or psychological reality to a human learner.

A number of psychologically-motivated models of word segmentation rely on the use of syllabic transitional probabilities (TPs), basing the use of TPs on experimental work in artificial language learning (Saffran et al., 1996a; Saffran et al., 1996b) and in corpus studies (Swingley, 2005). The identification of the syllable as the basic unit of segmentation is supported research in experimental psychology using infants as young as 4-days-old (Bijeljac-Babic et al., 1993), but when syllable transitional probabilities are evaluated in online learning procedures that only use local information (Yang, 2004), the results are surprisingly poor, even under the assumption that the learner has already syllabified the input perfectly. Precision is 41.6%, and recall is 23.3%, which we will show is worse than a simple baseline of assuming every syllable is a word. The below-baseline performance is unsurprising given that in order for this type of model to posit a word boundary, a transitional probability between syllables must be lower than its neighbors. This condition cannot be met if the input is a sequence of monosyllabic words for which a boundary must be postulated for every syllable; it is impossible to treat every boundary as a local minimum.

While the pseudo-words used in infant studies measuring the ability to use transitional probability information are uniformly three-syllables long, much of child-directed English consists of sequences of monosyllabic words. Corpus statistics reveal that on average a monosyllabic word is followed by another monosyllabic word 85% of time (Yang, 2004), and thus learners that use only local transitional probabilities without any global optimization are unlikely to succeed. This problem does not affect online approaches that use global information, such as computing the maximum likelihood of the corpus incrementally (Venkataraman, 2001). Since these approaches do not require each boundary be a local minimum, they are able to correctly handle a sequence of monosyllable words.

We believe that the computational modeling of psychological processes, with special attention to concrete mechanisms and quantitative evaluations, can play an important role in identifying the constraints and structures relevant to children's acquisition of language. Rather than using a prior which guides the learner to a desired distribution, we examine learning with respect to a model in which the hypothesis space is constrained by structural requirements.

In this paper we take a different approach than statistical optimization approaches by exploring how well a learner can perform while processing a corpus in an online fashion with only local information and a lexicon of previously segmented words. We present a simple, efficient approach to word segmentation that uses structural information rather than distributional cues in the input to segment words. We seek to demonstrate that even in the face of impoverished input and limited resources, a simple learner can succeed when it operates with the appropriate constraints.

3 Constraining the Learning Space

Modern machine learning research (Gold, 1967; Valiant, 1984; Vapnik, 2000) suggests that constraints on the learning space and the learning algorithm are essential for realistically efficient learning. If a domain-neutral learning model fails on a specific task where children succeed, it is likely that children are equipped with knowledge and constraints specific to the task at hand. It is important to identify such constraints to see to what extent they complement, or even replace, domain neutral learning mechanisms.

A particularly useful constraint for word segmentation, introduced to the problem of word segmentation by Yang (2004) but previously discussed by Halle and Vergnaud (1987), is as follows:

Unique Stress Constraint (USC): A word can bear at most one primary stress.

A simple example of how adult learners might use the USC is upon hearing novel names or words. Taking *Star Wars* characters as an example, it is clear that *chew***b***acca* is one word but *d***a***rthv***a***der* cannot be as the latter bears two primary stresses.

The USC could give the learner many isolated words for free. If the learner hears an utterance that contains exactly one primary stress, it is likely it is a single word. Moreover, the segmentation for a multiple word utterance can be equally straightforward under USC. Consider a sequence $W_1S_1S_2S_3W_2$, where W stands for a weak syllable and S stands for a strong syllable. A learner equipped with USC will immediately know that the sequence consists of three words: specifically, W_1S_1, S_2, and S_2W_2.

The USC can also constrain the use of other learning techniques. For example, the syllable consequence $S_1W_1W_2W_3S_2$ cannot be segmented by USC alone, but it may still provide cues that facilitate the application of other segmentation strategies. For instance, the learner knows that the sequence consists of at least two words, as indicated by two strong syllables. Moreover, it also knows that in the window between S_1 and S_2 there must be one or more word boundaries.

Yang (2004) evaluates the effectiveness of the USC in conjunction with a simple approach to using transitional probabilities. The performance of the approach presented there improves dramatically if the learner is equipped with the assumption that each word can have only one primary stress. If the learner knows this, then it may limit the search for local minima to only the window between two syllables that both bear primary stress, e.g., between the two **a**'s in the sequence *l***a***nguage***a***cquisition*. This assumption is plausible given that 7.5-month-old infants are sensitive to strong/weak prosodic distinctions (Jusczyk, 1999). Yang's stress-delimited algorithm achieves the precision of 73.5% and recall of 71.2%, a significant improvement over using TPs alone, but still below the baseline presented in our results.

The improvement of the transitional probability-based approach when provided with a simple linguistic constraint suggests that structural constraints can be powerful in narrowing the hypothesis space so that even sparse, local information can prove useful and simple segmentation strategies can become more effective.

It should be noted that the classification of every syllable as "weak" or "strong" is a significant simplification. Stress is better organized into hierarchical patterns constructed on top of syllables that vary in relative prominence based on the domain of each level of the hierarchy, and generally languages avoid adjacent strong syllables (Liberman and Prince, 1977). We later discuss a manipulation of the corpus used by Yang (2004) to address this concern.

Additionally, there are significant challenges in reconstructing stress from an acoustic signal (Van Kuijk and Boves, 1999). For a child learner to use the algorithm presented here, she would need to have mechanisms for detecting stress in the speech signal and categorizing the gradient stress in utterances into a discrete level for each syllable. These mechanisms are not addressed in this work; our focus is on an algorithm that can succeed given discrete stress information for each syllable. Given the evidence that infants can distinguish weak and strong syllables and use that information to detect word boundaries (Jusczyk et al., 1999), we believe that it is reasonable to assume that identifying syllabic stress is a task an infant learner can perform at the developmental stage of word segmentation.

4 A Simple Algorithm for Word Segmentation

We now present a simple algebraic approach to word segmentation based on the constraints suggested by Yang (2004). The learner we present is algebraic in that it has a lexicon which stores previously segmented words and identifies the input as a combination of words already in the lexicon and novel words. No transitional probabilities or any distributional data are calculated from the input. The learner operates in an online fashion, segmenting each utterance in a primarily left-to-right fashion and updating its lexicon as it segments.

The USC is used in two ways by the learner. First, if the current syllable has primary stress and the next syllable also has primary stress, a word boundary is placed between the current and next syllable. Second, whenever the algorithm is faced with the choice of accepting a novel word into the lexicon and outputting it as a word, the learner "abstains" from doing so if the word violates USC, that is if it contains more than one primary stress. Since not all words are stressed, if a word contains no primary stresses it is considered an acceptable word; only a word with *more that one* primary stress is prohibited. If a sequence of syllables has more than one primary stress and cannot be segmented further, the learner does not include that sequence in its segmentation of the utterance and does not add it to the lexicon as it cannot be a valid word.

The algorithm is as follows, with each step explained in further detail in the following paragraphs.

For each utterance in the corpus, do the following:

1. As each syllable is encountered, use *Initial Subtraction* and *USC Segmentation* to segment words from the beginning of the utterance if possible.

2. If unsegmented syllables still remain, apply *Final Subtraction*, segmenting words iteratively from the end of the utterance if possible.

3. If unsegmented syllables still remain, if those syllables constitute a valid word under the USC, segment them as a single word and add them to the lexicon. Otherwise, abstain, and do not include these syllables in the segmentation of the sentence and do not add them to the lexicon.

Initial Subtraction. If the syllables of the utterance from the last segmentation (or the start of the utterance) up to this point matches a word in the lexicon but adding one more syllable would result in it not being a known word, segment off the recognized word and increase its frequency. This iteratively segments the longest prefix word from the utterance.

USC Segmentation. If the current and next syllables have primary stress, place a word boundary after the current syllable, treating all syllables from the last segmentation point up to and and including the current syllable as a potential word. If these syllables form a valid word under the USC, segment them as a word and add them to the lexicon. Otherwise, abstain, not including these syllables in the segmentation of the sentence and not adding them to the lexicon.

Final Subtraction. After initial subtraction and USC Segmentation have been maximally applied to the utterance, the learner is often left with a sequence of syllables that is not prefixed by any known word and does not have any adjacent primary stresses. In this situation the learner works from right to left on the remaining utterance, iteratively removing words from the end of the utterance if possible. Similar to the approach used in Initial Subtraction, the longest word that is a suffix word of the remaining syllables is segmented off, and this is repeated until the entire utterance is segmented or syllables remain that are not suffixed by any known word.

The ability to abstain is a significant difference between this learner and most recent work on this task. Because the learner has a structural description for a word, the USC, it is able to reject any hypothesized words that do not meet the description. This improves the learner's precision and recall because it reduces the number of incorrect predictions the learner makes. The USC also allows the learner keep impossible words out of its lexicon.

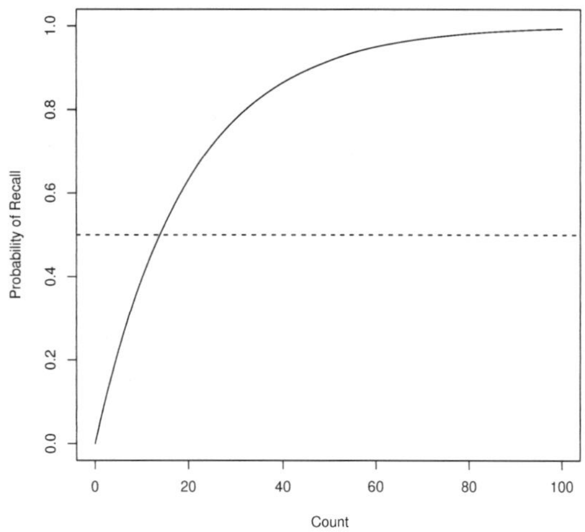

Figure 1: The selected probabilistic memory function for $\alpha = 0.05$. The dashed line at 0.05 represents the threshold above which a word is more likely than not to be recalled, occurring at a count of approximately 14.

5 A Probabilistic Lexicon

To simulate the imperfect memory of a child learner, we use a simple exponential function to generate the probability with which a word is retrieved from the lexicon:

$$p_r(word) = 1.0 - e^{-\alpha c(word)}$$

$p_r(word)$ is the probability of a $word$ being retrieved, α is a constant, and $c(word)$ is the number of times the word has been identified in segmentations thus far. This type of memory function is a simplified representation of models of humans' memory recall capabilities (Anderson et al., 1998; Gillund and Shiffrin, 1984). This memory function for the value of $\alpha = 0.05$, the value used in our experiments, is given in Figure 1. We later show that the choice of α has little impact on the learner's segmentation performance, and thus the more or less arbitrary selection of a value for α is of little consequence.

When the algorithm attempts to subtract words from the beginning or end of an utterance, it may miss words in the lexicon due to this probabilistic retrieval. The learner only has one opportunity to recall a word in a given utterance. For example, in the utterance *P.EH1.N S.AH0.L* (*pencil*), if the learner has *P.EH1.N* and *P.EH1.N S.AH0.L* in its lexicon but *P.EH1.N* is more frequent, it may fail to recall *P.EH1.N S.AH0.L* when examining the second syllable but succeed in recognizing *P.EH1.N* in the first. Thus it will break off *P.EH1.N* instead of *P.EH1.N S.AH0.L.* This means the learner may fail to reliably break off the longest words, instead breaking off the longest word that is successfully recalled.

While probabilistic memory means that the learner will fail to recognize words it has seen before, potentially decreasing recall, it also provides the learner the benefit of probabilistically failing to repeat previous mistakes if they occur rarely.

Probabilistic word recall results in a "rich get richer" phenomenon as the learner segments; words that are used more often in segmentations are more likely to be reused in later segmentations. While recent work from Bayesian approaches has used a Dirichlet Process to generate these distributions (Goldwater et al., 2006), in this learner the reuse of frequent items in learning is a result of the memory model rather than an explicit process of reusing old outcomes or generating new ones. This growth is an inherent property of the cognitive model of memory used here rather than an externally imposed computational technique.

6 Evaluation

Our computational model is designed to process child-directed speech. The corpus we use to evaluate it is the same corpus used by Yang (2004). Adult utterances were extracted from the Brown (1973) data in the CHILDES corpus (MacWhinney, 2000), consisting of three children's data: Adam, Eve, and Sarah. We obtained the phonetic transcriptions of words from the Carnegie Mellon Pronouncing Dictionary (CMUdict) Version 0.6 (Weide, 1998), using the first pronunciation of each word. In CMUdict, lexical stress information is preserved by numbers: 0 for unstressed, 1 for primary stress, 2 for secondary stress. For instance, *cat* is represented as *K.AE1.T, catalog* is *K.AE1.T.AH0.L.AO0.G,* and *catapult* is *K.AE1.T.AH0.P.AH2.L.T.* We treat primary stress as "strong" and secondary or unstressed syllables as "weak."

For each word, the phonetic segments were grouped into syllables. This process is straightforward by the use of the principle "Maximize Onset," which maximizes the length of the onset as long as it is valid consonant cluster of English, i.e., it conforms to the phonotactic constraints of English. For example, *Einstein* is *AY1.N.S.T.AY0.N* as segments and parsed into *AY1.N S.T.AY0.N* as syllables: this is because */st/* is the longest valid onset for the second syllable containing *AY0* while */nst/* is longer but violates English phonotactics. While we performed syllabification as a preprocessing step outside of learning, a child learner would presumably learn the required phonotactics as a part of learning to segment words. 9-month old infants are believed to have learned some phonotactic constraints of their native language (Mattys and Jusczyk, 2001), and learning these constraints can be done with only minimal exposure (Onishi et al., 2002).

Finally, spaces and punctuation between words were removed, but the boundaries between utterances–as indicated by line breaks in CHILDES–are retained. Altogether, there are 226,178 words, consisting of 263,660 syllables. The learning material is a list of unsegmented syllable sequences grouped into utterances, and the learner's task is to find word boundaries that group substrings of syllables together, building a lexicon of words as it segments.

We evaluated the learner's performance to address these questions:

- How does probabilistic memory affect learner performance?
- How much does degrading stress information relied on by USC segmentation reduce performance?
- What is the interaction between the probabilistic lexicon and non-idealized stress information?

To evaluate the learner, we tested configurations that used a probabilistic lexicon and ones with perfect memory in two scenarios: Dictionary Stress, and Reduced Stress. We create the Reduced Stress condition in order to simulate that stress is often reduced in casual speech, and that language-specific stress rules may cause reductions or shifts in stress that prevent two strong syllables from occurring in sequence. The difference between the scenarios is defined as follows:

Dictionary Stress. The stress information is given to the learner as it was looked up in CMUdict. For example, the first utterance from the Adam corpus would be *B.IH1.G D.R.AH1.M* (*big drum*), an utterance with two stressed monosyllables (SS). In most languages, however, conditions where two stressed syllables are in sequence are handled by reducing the stress of one syllable. This is simulated in the reduced stress condition.

Reduced Stress. The stress information obtained from CMUdict is post-processed in the context of each utterance. For any two adjacent primary stressed syllables, the first syllable is reduced from a strong syllable to a weak one. This is applied iteratively from left to right, so for any sequence of n adjacent primary-stress syllables, only the nth syllable retains primary stress; all others are reduced. This removes the most valuable clue as to where utterances can be segmented, as USC segmentation no longer applies. This simulates the stress retraction effect found in real speech, which tries to avoid adjacent primary stresses.

Learners that use probabilistic memory were allowed to iterate over the input two times with access to the lexicon developed over previous iterations but no access to previous segmentations. This simulates a child hearing many of the same words and utterances again, and reduces the effect of the small corpus size used on the learning process. Because the probabilistic memory reduces the algorithm's ability to build a lexicon, performance in a single iteration is lower than perfect memory conditions. In all other conditions, the learner is allowed only a single pass over the corpus.

The precision and recall metrics are calculated for the segmentation that the learner outputs and the lexicon itself. For an utterance, each word in the learner's segmentation that also appears in the gold standard segmentation is counted as correct, and each word in the learner's segmentation not present in the gold standard segmentation is a false alarm. F-score is computed using equally balanced precision and recall (F_0). The correct words, false words, and number of words in the gold standard are summed over the output in each iteration to produce performance measures for that iteration.

Precision, recall, and F-score are similarly computed for the lexicon; every word in the learner's lexicon present in the gold standard is counted as correct, and every word in the learner's lexicon not present in the gold standard is a false alarm. These computations are performed over word types in the lexicon, thus all words in the lexicon are of equal weight in computing performance regardless of their frequency. In the probabilistic memory conditions, however, the memory function defines the probability of each word being recalled (and thus being considered a part of the lexicon) at evaluation time.

In addition to evaluating the learner, we also implemented three baseline approaches to compare the learner against. The *Utterance* baseline segmenter assumes every utterance is a single word. The *Monosyllabic* baseline segmenter assumes every syllable is a single word. The *USC* segmenter inserts word boundaries between all adjacent syllables with primary stress in the corpus.

6.1 Results

The performance of the learner and baseline segmenters is given in Table 1. While the Utterance segmenter provides expectedly poor performance, the Monosyllabic segmenter sets a relatively high baseline for the task. Because of the impoverished morphology of English and the short words that tend to be used in child-directed speech, assuming each syllable is a word proves to be an excellent heuristic. It is unlikely that this heuristic will perform as well in other languages. Because the USC segmenter only creates segmentation points where there are words of adjacent primary stress, it is prone to attaching unstressed monosyllabic function words to content words, causing very low lexicon precision (13.56%).

With both perfect memory and dictionary stress information, the learner attains an F-score of 86.69%, with precision (83.78%) lower than recall (89.81%). First, we consider the effects of probabilistic memory on the learner. In the Dictionary Stress condition, using probabilistic memory decreases F_o by 1.15%, a relatively small impact given that with the setting of $\alpha = 0.05$ the learner must use a word approximately 14 times before it can retrieve it with 50% reliability and 45 times before it can retrieve it with 90% reliability. In the first iteration over the data set, 17.87% of lexicon lookups for words that have been hypothesized before fail. The impact on F_0 is caused by a drop in recall, as would be expected for a such a memory model.

To examine the effect of the α parameter for probabilistic memory on learner performance, we plot the utterance and lexicon F_0 after the learner iterates over the corpus once in the Probabilistic

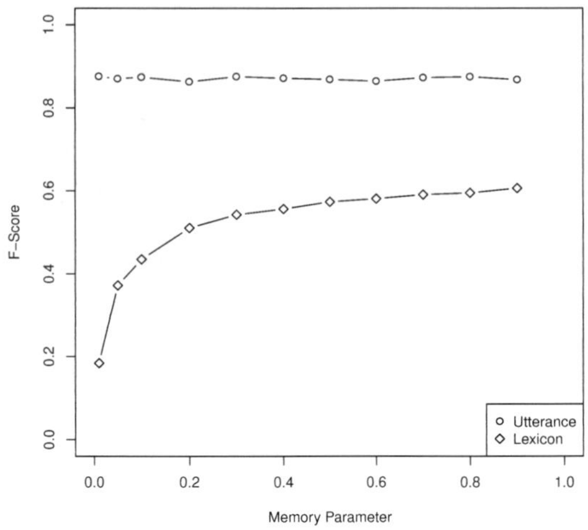

Figure 2: Learner utterance and lexicon F-scores after two iterations when α is varied in the Probabilistic Memory, Dictionary Stress condition

	Perfect Memory, Dictionary Stress	Perfect Memory, Reduced Stress
USC Seg.	114,333	0
Initial Sub.	65,800	164,989
Final Sub.	5,690	14,813
Total	185,823	179,802

Table 2: Number of segmentations performed by each operation: USC Segmentation, Initial Subtraction, and Final Subtraction.

Memory, Dictionary Stress condition. As Figure 2 shows, the choice of α has little effect on the utterance F_0 through most of a broad range from 0.01 to 0.9. Because the setting of α determines the number of times a word must be hypothesized before it can reliably be recalled, it expectedly has a significant effect on lexicon F_0. The selection of $\alpha = 0.05$ for our experiments is thus unlikely to have had any significant bearing on the utterance segmentation performance, although for lower values of α precision is favored while for larger values recall is favored. Larger values of α imply the learner is able to recall items after fewer exposures. While a larger value of α would have yielded higher performance in lexicon performance, it also assumes much more about the learner's memory capabilities.

The Reduced Stress condition also has only a

	Utterances			Lexicon		
Segmenter	Precision	Recall	F_0	Precision	Recall	F_0
Utterance	18.61%	4.67%	7.47%	3.57%	30.35%	6.39%
Monosyllabic	73.29%	85.44%	78.90%	55.41%	43.88%	48.97%
USC	81.06%	61.52%	69.95%	13.56%	66.97%	22.55%
Perfect Memory, Dictionary Stress	83.78%	89.81%	86.69%	67.72%	58.60%	62.83%
Perfect Memory, Reduced Stress	82.32%	85.81%	84.03%	39.18%	50.08%	43.97%
Prob. Memory, Dictionary Stress	84.05%	87.07%	85.54%	72.34%	30.01%	42.42%
Prob. Memory, Reduced Stress	84.85%	85.24%	85.05%	41.13%	22.91%	29.43%

Table 1: Baseline and Learner Performance. Performance is reported after two iterations over the corpus for probabilistic memory learners and after a single iteration for all other learners.

small impact on utterance segmentation performance. This suggests that the USC's primary value to the learner is in constraining the contents of the lexicon and identifying words in isolation as good candidates for the lexicon. In the Reduced Stress condition where the USC is not directly responsible for any segmentations as there are no adjacent primary-stressed syllables, the learner relies much more heavily on subtractive techniques. Table 2 gives the number of segmentations performed using each segmentation operation. The total number of segmentations is very similar between the Dictionary and Reduced Stress conditions, but because USC Segmentation is not effective on Reduced Stress input, Initial and Final Subtraction are used much more heavily.

7 Discussion

The design of the segmenter presented here suggests that both the quality of memory and the structural purity of the input would be critical factors in the learner's success. Our results suggest, however, that using probabilistic memory and a less idealized version of stress in natural language have little impact on the performance of the presented learner. They do cause the learner to learn much more slowly, causing the learner to need to be presented with more material and resulting in worse performance in the lexicon evaluation. But this slower learning is unlikely to be a concern for a child learner who would be exposed to much larger amounts of data than the corpora here provide.

Cognitive literature suggests that limited memory during learning may be essential to a learner in its early stages (Elman, 1993). But we do not see any notable improvement as a result of the probabilistic memory model used in our experiments, although the learner does do better in the Reduced Stress condition with Probabilistic Memory than Perfect Memory. This should not be interpreted as a negative result as we only analyze a single learner and memory model. Adding decay to the model such that among words of equal frequency those that have not been used in segmentation recently are less likely to be remembered may be sufficient to create the desired effect.

The success of this learner suggests that the type of "bootstrapping" approaches can succeed in word segmentation. The learner presented uses USC to identify utterances that are likely to be lone words, seeding the lexicon with initial information. Even if these first items in the lexicon are of relatively low purity, often combining function words and content words into one, the learner is able to expand its lexicon by using these hypothesized words to segment new input. As the learner segments more, these hypotheses become more reliable, allowing the learner to build a lexicon of good quality.

The subtraction approaches presented in this work provide a basic algorithm for to handling segmentation of incoming data in an online fashion. The subtractive heuristics used here are of course not guaranteed to result in a perfect segmentation even with a perfect lexicon; they are presented to show how a simple model of processing incoming data can be paired with structural constraints on the hypothesis space to learn word segmentation in a computationally efficient and cognitively plausible online fashion.

8 Conclusions

The learner's strong performance using minimal computational resources and unreliable memory suggest that simple learners can succeed in unsupervised tasks as long as they take advantage of domain-specific knowledge to constrain the hypothesis space. Our results show that, even in adversarial conditions, structural constraints remain powerful tools for simple learning algorithms in difficult tasks.

Future work in this area should focus on learners that can take advantage of the benefits of a probabilistic lexicon and memory models suited to them. Also, a more complex model of the type of stress variation present in natural speech would help better determine a learner that uses USC's ability to handle realistic variation in the input. Our model of stress reduction is a worst-case scenario for USC segmentation but is unlikely to be an accurate model of real speech. Future work should adopt a more naturalistic model to determine whether the robustness found in our results holds true in more realistic stress permutations.

Acknowledgements

We thank Kyle Gorman, Josef Fruehwald, and Dan Swingley for their helpful discussions regarding this work. We are grateful to and Mitch Marcus and Jana Beck for their feedback on earlier versions of this paper.

References

J.R. Anderson, D. Bothell, C. Lebiere, and M. Matessa. 1998. An integrated theory of list memory. *Journal of Memory and Language*, 38(4):341–380.

R. Bijeljac-Babic, J. Bertoncini, and J. Mehler. 1993. How do 4-day-old infants categorize multisyllabic utterances? *Developmental Psychology*, 29:711–711.

M.R. Brent and T.A. Cartwright. 1996. Distributional regularity and phonotactic constraints are useful for segmentation. *Cognition*, 61(1-2):93–125.

M.R. Brent. 1999. An efficient, probabilistically sound algorithm for segmentation and word discovery. *Machine Learning*, 34(1):71–105.

R. Brown. 1973. *A First Language: The Early Stages.* Harvard Univ. Press, Cambridge, Massachusetts 02138.

J.L. Elman. 1993. Learning and development in neural networks: The importance of starting small. *Cognition*, 48(1):71–99.

G. Gillund and R.M. Shiffrin. 1984. A retrieval model for both recognition and recall. *Psychological Review*, 91(1):1–67.

E.M. Gold. 1967. Language identification in the limit. *Information and control*, 10(5):447–474.

S. Goldwater, T. Griffiths, and M. Johnson. 2006. Interpolating between types and tokens by estimating power-law generators. *Advances in Neural Information Processing Systems*, 18:459.

S. Goldwater, T.L. Griffiths, and M. Johnson. 2009. A Bayesian framework for word segmentation: Exploring the effects of context. *Cognition.*

M. Halle and J.R. Vergnaud. 1987. *An essay on stress.* MIT Press.

M. Johnson and S. Goldwater. 2009. Improving nonparameteric Bayesian inference: experiments on unsupervised word segmentation with adaptor grammars. In *Proceedings of Human Language Technologies: The 2009 Annual Conference of the North American Chapter of the Association for Computational Linguistics*, pages 317–325. Association for Computational Linguistics.

P.W. Jusczyk, D.M. Houston, and M. Newsome. 1999. The Beginnings of Word Segmentation in English-Learning Infants. *Cognitive Psychology*, 39(3-4):159–207.

P.W. Jusczyk. 1999. How infants begin to extract words from speech. *Trends in Cognitive Sciences*, 3(9):323–328.

M. Liberman and A. Prince. 1977. On stress and linguistic rhythm. *Linguistic Inquiry*, 8(2):249–336.

B. MacWhinney. 2000. *The CHILDES Project: Tools for Analyzing Talk.* Lawrence Erlbaum Associates.

G.F. Marcus, S. Pinker, M. Ullman, M. Hollander, T.J. Rosen, F. Xu, and H. Clahsen. 1992. Overregularization in language acquisition. *Monographs of the Society for Research in Child Development*, 57(4).

S.L. Mattys and P.W. Jusczyk. 2001. Phonotactic cues for segmentation of fluent speech by infants. *Cognition*, 78(2):91–121.

K.H. Onishi, K.E. Chambers, and C. Fisher. 2002. Learning phonotactic constraints from brief auditory experience. *Cognition*, 83(1):B13–B23.

J.R. Saffran, R.N. Aslin, and E.L. Newport. 1996a. Statistical Learning by 8-month-old Infants. *Science*, 274(5294):1926.

J.R. Saffran, E.L. Newport, and R.N. Aslin. 1996b. Word Segmentation: The Role of Distributional Cues. *Journal of Memory and Language*, 35(4):606–621.

D. Swingley. 2005. Statistical clustering and the contents of the infant vocabulary. *Cognitive Psychology*, 50(1):86–132.

LG Valiant. 1984. A theory of the learnable. *Communications of the ACM*, 27(11):1142.

D. Van Kuijk and L. Boves. 1999. Acoustic characteristics of lexical stress in continuous telephone speech. *Speech Communication*, 27(2):95–111.

V.N. Vapnik. 2000. *The nature of statistical learning theory*. Springer.

A. Venkataraman. 2001. A statistical model for word discovery in transcribed speech. *Computational Linguistics*, 27(3):351–372.

R.L. Weide. 1998. The Carnegie Mellon Pronouncing Dictionary [cmudict. 0.6].

C.D. Yang. 2004. Universal Grammar, statistics or both? *Trends in Cognitive Sciences*, 8(10):451–456.

Computing Optimal Alignments for the IBM-3 Translation Model

Thomas Schoenemann
Centre for Mathematical Sciences
Lund University, Sweden

Abstract

Prior work on training the IBM-3 translation model is based on suboptimal methods for computing Viterbi alignments. In this paper, we present the first method guaranteed to produce globally optimal alignments. This not only results in improved alignments, it also gives us the opportunity to evaluate the quality of standard hillclimbing methods. Indeed, hillclimbing works reasonably well in practice but still fails to find the global optimum for between 2% and 12% of all sentence pairs and the probabilities can be several tens of orders of magnitude away from the Viterbi alignment.

By reformulating the alignment problem as an Integer Linear Program, we can use standard machinery from global optimization theory to compute the solutions. We use the well-known branch-and-cut method, but also show how it can be customized to the specific problem discussed in this paper. In fact, a large number of alignments can be excluded from the start without losing global optimality.

1 Introduction

Brown et al. (1993) proposed to approach the problem of automatic natural language translation from a statistical viewpoint and introduced five probability models, known as IBM 1-5. Their models were *single word based*, where each source word could produce at most one target word.

State-of-the-art statistical translation systems follow the *phrase based* approach, e.g. (Och and Ney, 2000; Marcu and Wong, 2002; Koehn, 2004; Chiang, 2007; Hoang et al., 2007), and hence allow more general alignments. Yet, single word based models (Brown et al., 1993; Brown et al., 1995; Vogel et al., 1996) are still highly relevant: many phrase based systems extract phrases from the alignments found by training the single word based models, and those that train phrases directly usually underperform these systems (DeNero et al., 2006).

Single word based models can be divided into two classes. On the one hand, models like IBM-1, IBM-2 and the HMM are computationally easy to handle: both marginals and Viterbi alignments can be computed by dynamic programming or even simpler techniques.

On the other hand there are fertility based models, including IBM 3-5 and Model 6. These models have been shown to be of higher practical relevance than the members of the first class (Och and Ney, 2003) since they usually produce better alignments. At the same time, computing Viterbi alignments for these methods has been shown to be NP-hard (Udupa and Maji, 2006), and computing marginals is no easier.

The standard way to handle these models – as implemented in GIZA++ (Al-Onaizan et al., 1999; Och and Ney, 2003) – is to use a hillclimbing algorithm. Recently Udupa and Maji (2005) proposed an interesting approximation based on solving sequences of exponentially large subproblems by means of dynamic programming and also addressed the decoding problem. In both cases there is no way to tell how far away the result is from the Viterbi alignment.

In this paper we solve the problem of finding IBM-3 Viterbi alignments by means of Integer Linear Programming (Schrijver, 1986). While there is no polynomial run-time guarantee, in practice the applied branch-and-cut framework is fast enough to find optimal solutions even for the large Canadian Hansards task (restricted to sentences with at most 75 words), with a training time of 6 hours on a 2.4 GHz Core 2 Duo (single threaded).

Proceedings of the Fourteenth Conference on Computational Natural Language Learning, pages 98–106,
Uppsala, Sweden, 15-16 July 2010.

Integer Linear Programming in the context of machine translation first appeared in the work of Germann et al. (2004), who addressed the *translation* problem (often called *decoding*) in terms of a travelings-salesman like formulation. Recently, DeNero and Klein (2008) addressed the training problem for phrase-based models by means of integer linear programming, and proved that the problem is NP-hard. The main difference to our work is that they allow only consecutive words in the phrases. In their formulation, allowing arbitrary phrases would require an exponential number of variables. In contrast, our approach handles the classical single word based model where any kind of "phrases" in the source sentence are aligned to one-word phrases in the target sentence.

Lacoste-Julien et al. (2006) propose an integer linear program for a symmetrized word-level alignment model. Their approach also allows to take the alignments of neighboring words into account. In contrast to our work, they only have a very crude fertility model and they are considering a substantially different model. It should be noted, however, that a subclass of their problems can be solved in polynomial time - the problem is closely related to bipartite graph matching. Less general approaches based on matching have been proposed in (Matusov et al., 2004) and (Taskar et al., 2005).

Recently Bodrumlu et al. (2009) proposed a very innovative cost function for jointly optimizing dictionary entries and alignments, which they minimize using integer linear programming. They also include a mechanism to derive N-best lists. However, they mention rather long computation times for rather small corpora. It is not clear if the large Hansards tasks could be addressed by their method.

An overview of integer linear programming approaches for natural language processing can be found on `http://ilpnlp.wikidot.com/`. To facilitate further research in this area, the source code will be made publicly available.

Contribution The key contribution of our work is a method to handle exact fertility models as arising in the IBM-3 model in a global optimization framework. This is done by a linear number of linear consistency constraints. Unlike all previous works on integer linear programming for machine translation, we do not solely use binary coefficients in the constraint matrix, hence showing that the full potential of the method has so far not been explored.

At the same time, our method allows us to give a detailed analysis of the quality of hillclimbing approaches. Moreover, we give a more detailed description of how to obtain a fast problem-tailored integer solver than in previous publications, and include a mechanism to a priori exclude some variables without losing optimality.

2 The IBM-3 Translation Model

Given a source sentence f_1^J, the statistical approach to machine translation is to assign each possible target sentence e_1^I a probability to be an accurate translation. For convenience in the translation process, this probability is usually rewritten as

$$P(e_1^I|f_1^J) = \frac{1}{p(f_1^J)} \cdot p(e_1^I) \cdot p(f_1^J|e_1^I) ,$$

and the training problem is to derive suitable parameters for the latter term from a bilingual corpus. Here, the probability is expressed by summing over hidden variables called *alignments*. The common assumption in single word based models is that each source position j produces a single target position $a_j \in \{0, \ldots, I\}$, where an artificial 0-position has been introduced to mark words without a correspondence in the target sentence. The alignment of a source sentence is then a vector a_1^J, and the probability can now be written as

$$p(f_1^J|e_1^I) = \sum_{a_1^J} p(f_1^J, a_1^J|e_1^I) .$$

We will focus on training the IBM-3 model which is based on the concept of *fertilities*: given an alignment a_1^J, the fertility $\Phi_i(a_1^J) = \sum_{j:a_j=i} 1$ of target word i expresses the number of source words aligned to it. Omitting the dependence on a_1^J (and defining $p(j|0) = 1$), the probability is expressed as

$$\begin{aligned} p(f_1^J, a_1^J|e_1^I) &= p(\Phi_0|J) \cdot \prod_{i=1}^{I} \left[\Phi_i!\, p(\Phi_i|e_i)\right] \\ &\cdot \prod_j \left[p(f_j|e_{a_j}) \cdot p(j|a_j)\right] . \end{aligned} \tag{1}$$

For the probability $p(\Phi_0|J)$ of the fertility of the empty word, we use the modification introduced in (Och and Ney, 2003), see there for details. In summary, the model comprises a single word based translation model, an inverted zero-order alignment model and a fertility model. We now discuss how to find the optimal alignment for given probabilities, i.e. to solve the problem

$$\arg\max_{a_1^J} \; p(f_1^J, a_1^J | e_1^I) \tag{2}$$

for each bilingual sentence pair in the training set. This is a desirable step in the approximate EM-algorithm that is commonly used to train the model.

3 Finding IBM-3 Viterbi Alignments via Integer Linear Programming

Instead of solving (2) directly we consider the equivalent task of minimizing the negative logarithm of the probability function. A significant part of the arising cost function is already linear in terms of the alignment variables, a first step for the integer linear program (ILP) we will derive.

To model the problem as an ILP, we introduce two sets of variables. Firstly, for any source position $j \in \{1, \ldots, J\}$ and any target position $i \in \{0, \ldots, I\}$ we introduce an integer variable $x_{ij} \in \{0, 1\}$ which we want to be 1 exactly if $a_j = i$ and 0 otherwise. Since each source position must be aligned to exactly one target position, we arrive at the set of linear constraints

$$\sum_i x_{ij} = 1 \quad , j = 1, \ldots, J \; . \tag{3}$$

The negative logarithm of the bottom row of (1) is now easily written as a linear function in terms of the variables x_{ij}:

$$\sum_{i,j} c_{ij}^x \cdot x_{ij} \quad ,$$

$$c_{ij}^x = -\log \Big[p(f_j | e_i) \cdot p(j|i) \Big] \; .$$

For the part of the cost depending on the fertilities, we introduce another set of integer variables $y_{if} \in \{0, 1\}$. Here $i \in \{0, \ldots, I\}$ and f ranges from 0 to some pre-specified limit on the maximal fertility, which we set to $\max(15, J/2)$ in our experiments (fertilities $> J$ need not be considered). We want y_{if} to be 1 if the fertility of i is f, 0 otherwise. Hence, again these variables must sum to 1:

$$\sum_f y_{if} = 1 \quad , i = 0, \ldots, I \; . \tag{4}$$

The associated part of the cost function is written as

$$\sum_{i,f} c_{if}^y \cdot y_{if} \quad ,$$

$$c_{if}^y = -\log \Big[f! \, p(f | e_i) \Big] \quad , i = 1, \ldots, I$$

$$c_{0f}^y = -\log \Big[p(\Phi_0 = f | J) \Big] \; .$$

It remains to ensure that the variables y_{if} expressing the fertilities are consistent with the fertilities induced by the alignment variables x_{ij}. This is done via the following set of linear constraints:

$$\sum_j x_{ij} = \sum_f f \cdot y_{if} \quad , i = 0, \ldots, I \; . \tag{5}$$

Problem (2) is now reduced to solving the integer linear program

$$\arg\min_{\{x_{ij}\}, \{y_{if}\}} \; \sum_{i,j} c_{ij}^x \, x_{ij} + \sum_{i,f} c_{if}^y \, y_{if}$$

$$\text{subject to (3), (4), (5)}$$

$$x_{ij} \in \{0, 1\}, \;\; y_{if} \in \{0, 1\} \; , \tag{6}$$

with roughly $2\,I\,J$ variables and roughly $J + 2I$ constraints.

4 Solving the Integer Linear Program

To solve the arising integer linear programming problem, we first relax the integrality constraints on the variables to continuous ones:

$$x_{ij} \in [0, 1], \;\; y_{if} \in [0, 1] \; ,$$

and obtain a lower bound on the problems by solving the arising linear programming relaxation via the dual simplex method.

While in practice this can be done in a matter of milli-seconds even for sentences with $I, J > 50$, the result is frequently a fractional solution. Here the alignment variables are usually integral but the fertility variables are not.

In case the LP-relaxation does not produce an integer solution, the found solution is used as the initialization of a branch-and-cut framework. Here one first tries to strengthen the LP-relaxation by deriving additional inequalities that must be valid for all integral solutions see e.g. (Schrijver, 1986; Wolter, 2006) and `www.coin-or.org`. These inequalities are commonly called *cuts*. Then one applies a branch-and-bound scheme on the integer variables. In each step of this scheme, additional inequalities are derived. The process is further sped-up by introducing a heuristic to derive an upper bound on the cost function. Such bounds are generally given by feasible integral solutions. We use our own heuristic as a plug-in to the solver. It generates solutions by thresholding the alignment variables (winner-take-all) and deriving the induced fertility variables. An initial upper bound is furthermore given by the alignment found by hillclimbing.

We suspect that further speed-ups are possible by using so-called follow-up nodes: e.g. if in the branch-and-bound an alignment variable x_{ij} is set to 1, one can conclude that the fertility variable y_{i0} must be 0. Also, sets of binary variables that must sum to 1 as in (3) and (4) are known as *special ordered sets of type I* and there are variants of branch-and-cut that can exploit these properties. However, in our context they did not result in speed-ups.

Our code is currently based on the open source COIN-OR project[1] and involves the linear programming solver CLP, the integer programming solver CBC, and the cut generator library CGL. We have also tested two commercial solvers. For the problem described in this paper, CBC performed best. Tests on other integer programming tasks showed however that the Gurobi solver outperforms CBC on quite a number of problems.

5 Speed-ups by Deriving Bounds

It turns out that, depending on the cost function, some variables may a priori be excluded from the optimization problem without losing global optimality. That is, they can be excluded even *before* the first LP-relaxation is solved.

The affected variables have relatively high cost coefficients and they are identified by considering lower bounds and an upper bound on the cost function. Starting from the lower bounds, one can then identify variables that when included in a solution would raise the cost beyond the upper bound.

An upper bound u on the problem is given by any alignment. We use the one found by hillclimbing. If during the branch-and-cut process tighter upper bounds become available, the process could be reapplied (as a so-called *column cut generator*).

For the lower bounds we use different ones to exclude alignment variables and to exclude fertility variables.

[1] `www.coin-or.org`

5.1 Excluding Alignment Variables

To derive a lower bound for the alignment variables, we first observe that the cost c^x_{ij} for the alignment variables are all positive, whereas the cost c^y_{if} for the fertilities are frequently negative, due to the factorial of f. A rather tight lower bound on the fertility cost can be derived by solving the problem

$$l_{F,1} = \min_{\{\Phi_i\}} \sum_{i=0}^{I} c^y_{i\Phi_i} \quad \text{s.t. } \textstyle\sum_i \Phi_i = J \quad , \tag{7}$$

which is easily solved by dynamic programming proceeding along i. A lower bound on the alignment cost is given by

$$l_A = \textstyle\sum_j l_{A,j} \ ,$$

$$\text{where} \quad l_{A,j} = \min_{i=0,\dots,I} c^x_{ij} \ .$$

The lower bound is then given by $l_1 = l_{F,1} + l_A$, and we can be certain that source word j will not be aligned to target word i if

$$c^x_{ij} > l_{A,j} + (u - l_1) \ .$$

5.2 Excluding Fertility Variables

Excluding fertility variables is more difficult as cost can be negative and we have used a constraint to derive $l_{F,1}$ above.

At present we are using a two ways to generate a lower bound and apply the exclusion process with each of them sequentially. Both bounds are looser than l_1, but they immensely help to get the computation times to an acceptable level.

The first bound builds upon l_1 as derived above, but using a looser bound $l_{F,2}$ for the fertility cost:

$$l_{F,2} = \sum_i \min_{\Phi_i} c^y_{i\Phi_i} \ .$$

This results in a bound $l_2 = l_{F,2} + l_A$, and fertility variables can now be excluded in a similar manner as above.

Our second bound is usually much tighter and purely based on the fertility variables:

$$l_3 = \sum_i \min_{\Phi_i} \left[c^y_{i\Phi_i} + \min_{\mathcal{J} \subseteq \{1,\dots,J\} : |\mathcal{J} = \Phi_i|} c^x_i(\mathcal{J}) \right] ,$$

$$\text{with } c^x_i(\mathcal{J}) = \sum_{j \in \mathcal{J}} c^x_{ij} \ ,$$

and where the cost of the empty set is defined as 0. Although this expression looks rather involved, it is actually quite easy to compute by simply sorting the respective cost entries. A fertility variable y_{if} can now be excluded if the difference between c^y_{if} and the contribution of i to l_3 exceeds $u - l_3$.

We consider it likely that more variables can be excluded by deriving bounds in the spirit of (7), but with the additional constraint that $\Phi_i = f$ for some i and f. We leave this for future work.

6 Experiments

We have tested our method on three different tasks involving a total of three different languages and each in both directions. The first task is the well-known Canadian Hansards[2] task (senate debates) for French and English. Because of the large dataset we are currently only considering sentence pairs where both sentences have at most 75 words. Longer sentences are usually not useful to derive model parameters.

The other two datasets are released by the European Corpus Initiative[3]. We choose the Union Bank of Switzerland (UBS) corpus for English and German and the Avalanche Bulletins, originally released by SFISAR, for French and German. For the latter task we have annotated alignments for 150 of the training sentences, where one annotator specified sure and possible alignments. For details, also on the alignment error rate, see (Och and Ney, 2003).

All corpora have been preprocessed with language-specific rules; their statistics are given in Table 1. We have integrated our method into the standard toolkit GIZA++[4] and are using the training scheme $1^5H^53^54^5$ for all tasks. While we focus on the IBM-3 stage, we also discuss the quality of the resulting IBM-4 parameters and alignments.

Experiments were run on a 2.4 GHz Core 2 Duo with 4 GB memory. For most sentence pairs, the memory consumption of our method is only marginally more than in standard GIZA++ (600 MB). In the first iteration on the large Hansards task, however, there are a few very difficult sentence pairs where the solver needs up to 90 minutes and 1.5 GB . We observed this in both translation directions.

[2]www.isi.edu/natural-language/download/hansard/

[3]The entire CD with many more corpora is available for currently 50 Euros.

[4]available at code.google.com/p/giza-pp/ .

Avalanche Bulletin		
	French	German
# sentences	2989	
max. sentence length	88	57
total words	64825	45629
vocabulary size	1707	2113

UBS		
	English	German
# sentences	2689	
max. sentence length	92	91
total words	62617	53417
vocabulary size	5785	9127

Canadian Hansards (max. 75)		
	French	English
# sentences	180706	
max. sentence length	75	75
total words	3730570	3329022
vocabulary size	48065	37633

Table 1: **Corpus statistics** for all employed (training) corpora, after preprocessing.

6.1 Evaluating Hillclimbing

In our first set of experiments, we compute Viterbi alignments merely to evaluate the quality of the standard training process. That is, the model parameters are updated based on the alignments found by hillclimbing. Table 2 reveals that, as expected, hillclimbing does not always find the global optimum: depending on the task and iteration number, between 2 and 12 percent of all hillclimbing alignments are suboptimal. For short sentences (i.e. $I, J \leq 20$) hillclimbing usually finds the global optimum.

Somewhat more surprisingly, even when a good and hence quite focused initialization of the IBM-3 model parameters is given (by training HMMs first), the probability of the Viterbi alignment can be up to a factor of 10^{37} away from the optimum. This factor occurred on the Hansards task for a sentence pair with 46 source and 46 target words and the fertility of the empty word changed from 9 (for hillclimbing) to 5.

6.2 Hillclimbing vs. Viterbi Alignments

We now turn to a training scheme where the Viterbi alignments are used to actually update the model parameters, and compare it to the standard training scheme (based on hillclimbing).

	Candian Hansards (max 75)				
	French → English				
Iteration #	1	2	3	4	5
# suboptimal alignments in hillclimbing	10.7%	10.7%	10.8%	11.1%	11.4%
Maximal factor to Viterbi alignment	$1.9 \cdot 10^{37}$	$9.1 \cdot 10^{17}$	$7.3 \cdot 10^{14}$	$3.3 \cdot 10^{12}$	$8.1 \cdot 10^{14}$
	English → French				
Iteration #	1	2	3	4	5
# suboptimal alignments in hillclimbing	7.3%	7.5%	7.4%	7.4%	7.5%
Maximal factor to Viterbi alignment	$5.6 \cdot 10^{38}$	$6.6 \cdot 10^{20}$	$7.6 \cdot 10^{11}$	$4.3 \cdot 10^{10}$	$8.3 \cdot 10^{11}$

	Avalanche Bulletins				
	French → German				
Iteration #	1	2	3	4	5
# suboptimal alignments in hillclimbing	7.5%	5.6%	4.9%	4.9%	4.4%
Maximal factor to Viterbi alignment	$6.1 \cdot 10^{5}$	877	368	$2.5 \cdot 10^{4}$	429
	German → French				
Iteration #	1	2	3	4	5
# suboptimal alignments in hillclimbing	4.2%	2.7%	2.5%	2.3%	2.1%
Maximal factor to Viterbi alignment	40	302	44	$3.3 \cdot 10^{4}$	$9.2 \cdot 10^{4}$

	Union Bank of Switzerland (UBS)				
	English → German				
Iteration #	1	2	3	4	5
# suboptimal alignments in hillclimbing	5.0%	4.0%	3.5%	3.3%	3.2%
Maximal factor to Viterbi alignment	677	22	53	40	32
	German → English				
Iteration #	1	2	3	4	5
# suboptimal alignments in hillclimbing	5.5%	3.3%	2.5%	2.2%	2.3%
Maximal factor to Viterbi alignment	$1.4 \cdot 10^{7}$	808	33	33	$1.8 \cdot 10^{4}$

Table 2: **Analysis of Hillclimbing on all considered tasks.** All numbers are for the IBM-3 translation model. Iteration 1 is the first iteration after the transfer from HMM, the final iteration is the transfer to IBM4. The factors are w.r.t. the original formulation, not the negative logarithm of it and are defined as the maximal ratio between the Viterbi probability and the hillclimbing probability.

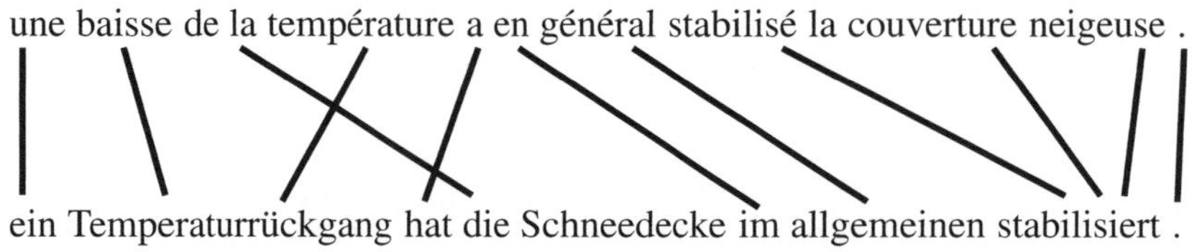

Standard training (hillclimbing).

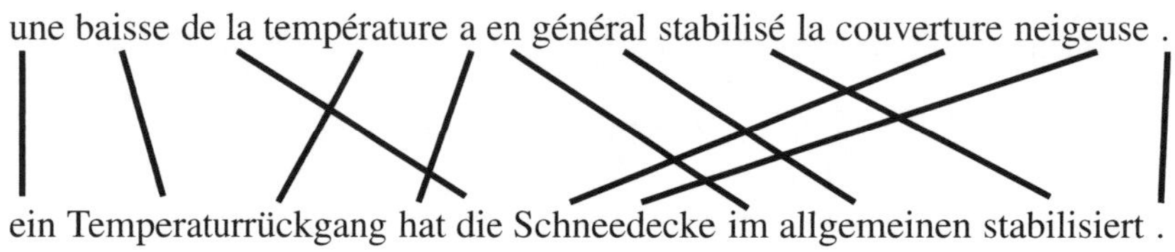

Proposed training (Viterbi alignments).

Figure 1: **Comparison of training schemes.** Shown are the alignments of the final IBM-3 iteration.

Indeed Table 3 demonstrates that with the new training scheme, the perplexities of the final IBM-3 iteration are consistently lower. Yet, this effect does not carry over to IBM-4 training, where the perplexities are consistently higher. Either this is due to overfitting or it is better to use the same method for alignment computation for both IBM-3 and IBM-4. After all, both start from the HMM Viterbi alignments.

Interestingly, the maximal factor between the hillclimbing alignment and the Viterbi alignment is now consistently higher on all tasks and in all iterations. The extreme cases are a factor of 10^{76} for the Canadian Hansards English $\rightarrow$ French task and 10^{30} for the Bulletin French $\rightarrow$ German task.

Table 4 demonstrates that the alignment error rates of both schemes are comparable. Indeed, a manual evaluation of the alignments showed that most of the changes affect words like articles or prepositions that are generally hard to translate. In many cases neither the heuristic nor the Viterbi alignment could be considered correct. An interesting case where the proposed scheme produced the better alignment is shown in Figure 1.

In summary, our results give a thorough justification for the commonly used heuristics. A test with the original non-deficient empty word model of the IBM-3 furthermore confirmed the impression of (Och and Ney, 2003) that overly many words are aligned to the empty word: the tendency is even stronger in the Viterbi alignments.

6.3 Optimizing Running Time

The possibilities to influence the run-times of the branch-and-cut framework are vast: there are nu-

	Union Bank (UBS) E $\rightarrow$ G	
	Final IBM-3	Final IBM-4
Standard train.	49.21	35.73
Proposed train.	49.00	35.76

	Union Bank (UBS) G $\rightarrow$ E	
	Final IBM-3	Final IBM-4
Standard train.	62.38	47.39
Proposed train.	62.08	47.43

	Avalanche F $\rightarrow$ G	
	Final IBM-3	Final IBM-4
Standard train.	35.44	21.99
Proposed train.	35.23	22.04

	Avalanche G $\rightarrow$ F	
	Final IBM-3	Final IBM-4
Standard train.	34.60	22.78
Proposed train.	34.48	22.76

	Canadian Hansards F $\rightarrow$ E	
	Final IBM-3	Final IBM-4
Standard train.	105.28	55.22
Proposed train.	92.09	55.35

	Canadian Hansards E $\rightarrow$ F	
	Final IBM-3	Final IBM-4
Standard train.	70.58	37.64
Proposed train.	70.03	37.73

Table 3: **Analysis of the perplexities in training.**

	French → German	
	Final IBM-3	Final IBM-4
Standard train.	24.31%	23.01%
Proposed train.	24.31%	23.24%

	German → French	
	Final IBM-3	Final IBM-4
Standard train.	33.03%	33.44%
Proposed train.	33.00%	33.27%

Table 4: **Alignment error rates** on the Avalanche bulletin task.

merous ways to generate cuts and several of them can be used simultaneously. The CBC-package also allows to specify how many rounds of cuts to derive at each node. Then there is the question of whether to use the bounds derived in Section 5 to a priori exclude variables. Finally, branch-and-cut need not be done on all variables: since solving LP-relaxations typically results in integral alignments, it suffices to do branch-and-cut on the fertility variables and only add the alignment variables in case non-integral values arise (this never happened in our experiments[5]).

We could not possibly test all combinations of the listed possibilities, and our primary focus was to achieve acceptable run-times for the large Hansards task. Still, in the end we have a quite uniform picture: the lowest run-times are achieved by using Gomory Cuts only. Moreover, including all variables for branching was between 1.5 and 2 times faster than only including fertility variables. Only by exploiting the bounds derived in Section 5 the run-times for the Hansards task in direction from English to French became acceptable. We believe that further speed-ups are possible by deriving tighter bounds, and are planning to investigate this in the future.

We end up with roughly 6 hours for the Hansards task, roughly 3 minutes for the UBS task, and about 2.5 minutes for the Avalanche task. In all cases the run-times are much higher than in the standard GIZA++ training. However, we are now getting optimality guarantees where previously one could not even tell how far away one is from the optimum. And the Viterbi alignments of several sentence pairs can of course be computed in parallel.

Lastly, we mention the possibility of setting a limit on the branch-and-cut process, either on the running time or on the number of nodes. There is then no longer a guarantee for global optimality, but at least one is getting a bound on the gap to the optimum and one can be certain that the training time will be sufficiently low.

[5]In fact, when fixing the fertility variables, the problem reduces to the polynomial time solvable assignment problem.

7 Conclusion

We present the first method to compute IBM-3 Viterbi alignments with a guarantee of optimality. In contrast to other works on integer linear programming for machine translation, our formulation is able to include a precise and very general fertility model. The resulting integer linear program can be solved sufficiently fast in practice, and we have given many comments on how problem-specific knowledge can be incorporated into standard solvers.

The proposed method allows for the first time to analyze the quality of hillclimbing approaches for IBM-3 training. It was shown that they can be very far from the optimum. At the same time, this seems to happen mostly for difficult sentences that are not suitable to derive good model parameters.

In future work we want to derive tighter bounds to a priori exclude variables, combine the method with the N-best list generation of (Bodrumlu et al., 2009) and evaluate on a larger set of corpora. Finally we are planning to test other integer programming solvers.

Acknowledgments We thank Fredrik Kahl for helpful comments and an anonymous reviewer for pointing out freely available software packages. This research was funded by the European Research Council (GlobalVision grant no. 209480).

References

Y. Al-Onaizan, J. Curin, M. Jahr, K. Knight, J. Lafferty, I. D. Melamed, F. J. Och, D. Purdy, N. A. Smith, and D. Yarowsky. 1999. Statistical machine translation, Final report, JHU workshop. `http://www.clsp.jhu.edu/ws99/`.

Tugba Bodrumlu, Kevin Knight, and Sujith Ravi. 2009. A new objective function for word alignment. In *Proceedings of the Workshop on Integer Linear Programming for Natural Langauge Processing (ILP)*, Boulder, Colorado, June.

P.F. Brown, S.A. Della Pietra, V.J. Della Pietra, and R.L. Mercer. 1993. The mathematics of statistical machine translation: Parameter estimation. *Computational Linguistics*, 19(2):263–311, June.

P.F. Brown, J. Cocke, S.A. Della Pietra, V.J. Della Pietra, F. Jelinek, J. Lai, and R.L. Mercer. 1995. Method and system for natural language translation. U.S. patent #5.477.451.

David Chiang. 2007. Hierarchical phrase-based translation. *Computational Linguistics*, 33(2):201–228.

J. DeNero and D. Klein. 2008. The complexity of phrase alignment problems. In *Annual Meeting of the Association for Computational Linguistics (ACL)*, Columbus, Ohio, June.

John DeNero, Dan Gillick, James Zhang, and Dan Klein. 2006. Why generative phrase models underperform surface heuristics. In *StatMT '06: Proceedings of the Workshop on Statistical Machine Translation*, pages 31–38, Morristown, NJ, USA, June.

U. Germann, M. Jahr, K. Knight, D. Marcu, and K. Yamada. 2004. Fast decoding and optimal decoding for machine translation. *Artificial Intelligence*, 154(1–2), April.

H. Hoang, A. Birch, C. Callison-Burch, R. Zens, A. Constantin, M. Federico, N. Bertoldi, C. Dyer, B. Cowan, W. Shen, C. Moran, and O. Bojar. 2007. Moses: Open source toolkit for statistical machine translation. In *Annual Meeting of the Association for Computational Linguistics (ACL)*, pages 177–180, Prague, Czech Republic, June.

P. Koehn. 2004. Pharaoh: A beam search decoder for phrase-based statistical machine translation models. In *Conference of the Association for Machine Translation in the Americas (AMTA)*, pages 115–124, Washington, D.C., October.

S. Lacoste-Julien, B. Taskar, D. Klein, and M. Jordan. 2006. Word alignment via quadratic assignment. In *Human Language Technology Conference of the North American Chapter of the Association of Computational Linguistics*, New York, New York, June.

D. Marcu and W. Wong. 2002. A phrase-based, joint probability model for statistical machine translation. In *Conference on Empirical Methods in Natural Language Processing (EMNLP)*, Philadelphia, Pennsylvania, July.

E. Matusov, R. Zens, and H. Ney. 2004. Symmetric word alignments for statistical machine translation. In *International Conference on Computational Linguistics (COLING)*, Geneva, Switzerland, August.

Franz Josef Och and Hermann Ney. 2000. Improved statistical alignment models. In *Annual Meeting of the Association for Computational Linguistics (ACL)*, pages 440–447, Hongkong, China, October.

F.J. Och and H. Ney. 2003. A systematic comparison of various statistical alignment models. *Computational Linguistics*, 29(1):19–51.

A. Schrijver. 1986. *Theory of Linear and Integer Programming*. Wiley-Interscience Series in Discrete Mathematics and Optimization. John Wiley & Sons.

B. Taskar, S. Lacoste-Julien, and D. Klein. 2005. A discriminative matching approach to word alignment. In *Conference on Empirical Methods in Natural Language Processing (EMNLP)*, Vancouver, Canada, October.

R. Udupa and H.K. Maji. 2005. Theory of alignment generators and applications to statistical machine translation. In *The International Joint Conferences on Artificial Intelligence*, Edinburgh, Scotland, August.

R. Udupa and H.K. Maji. 2006. Computational complexity of statistical machine translation. In *Conference of the European Chapter of the Association for Computational Linguistics (EACL)*, Trento, Italy, April.

S. Vogel, H. Ney, and C. Tillmann. 1996. HMM-based word alignment in statistical translation. In *International Conference on Computational Linguistics (COLING)*, pages 836–841, Copenhagen, Denmark, August.

K. Wolter. 2006. Implementation of Cutting Plane Separators for Mixed Integer Programs. Master's thesis, Technische Universität Berlin, Germany.

Semi-Supervised Recognition of Sarcastic Sentences in Twitter and Amazon

Dmitry Davidov
ICNC
The Hebrew University
Jerusalem, Israel
dmitry@alice.nc.huji.ac.il

Oren Tsur
Institute of Computer Science
The Hebrew University
Jerusalem, Israel
oren@cs.huji.ac.il

Ari Rappoport
Institute of Computer Science
The Hebrew University
Jerusalem, Israel
arir@cs.huji.ac.il

Abstract

Sarcasm is a form of speech act in which the speakers convey their message in an implicit way. The inherently ambiguous nature of sarcasm sometimes makes it hard even for humans to decide whether an utterance is sarcastic or not. Recognition of sarcasm can benefit many sentiment analysis NLP applications, such as review summarization, dialogue systems and review ranking systems.

In this paper we experiment with semi-supervised sarcasm identification on two very different data sets: a collection of 5.9 million tweets collected from Twitter, and a collection of 66000 product reviews from Amazon. Using the Mechanical Turk we created a gold standard sample in which each sentence was tagged by 3 annotators, obtaining F-scores of 0.78 on the product reviews dataset and 0.83 on the Twitter dataset. We discuss the differences between the datasets and how the algorithm uses them (e.g., for the Amazon dataset the algorithm makes use of structured information). We also discuss the utility of Twitter #sarcasm hashtags for the task.

1 Introduction

Sarcasm (also known as *verbal irony*) is a sophisticated form of speech act in which the speakers convey their message in an implicit way. One inherent characteristic of the sarcastic speech act is that it is sometimes hard to recognize. The difficulty in recognition of sarcasm causes misunderstanding in everyday communication and poses problems to many NLP systems such as online review summarization systems, dialogue systems or brand monitoring systems due to the failure of state of the art sentiment analysis systems to detect sarcastic comments. In this paper we experiment with a semi-supervised framework for automatic identification of sarcastic sentences.

One definition for sarcasm is: *the activity of saying or writing the opposite of what you mean, or of speaking in a way intended to make someone else feel stupid or show them that you are angry* (Macmillan English Dictionary (2007)). Using the former definition, sarcastic utterances appear in many forms (Brown, 1980; Gibbs and O'Brien, 1991). It is best to present a number of examples which show different facets of the phenomenon, followed by a brief review of different aspects of the sarcastic use. The sentences are all taken from our experimental data sets:

1. *"thank you Janet Jackson for yet another year of Super Bowl classic rock!"* (Twitter)
2. *"He's with his other woman: XBox 360. It's 4:30 fool. Sure I can sleep through the gunfire"* (Twitter)
3. *"Wow GPRS data speeds are blazing fast."* (Twitter)
4. *"[I] Love The Cover"* (book, amazon)
5. *"Defective by design"* (music player, amazon)

Example (1) refers to the supposedly lame music performance in super bowl 2010 and attributes it to the aftermath of the scandalous performance of Janet Jackson in the previous year. Note that the previous year is not mentioned and the reader has to guess the context (use universal knowledge). The words *yet* and *another* might hint at sarcasm.

Proceedings of the Fourteenth Conference on Computational Natural Language Learning, pages 107–116,
Uppsala, Sweden, 15-16 July 2010.

Example (2) is composed of three short sentences, each of them sarcastic on its own. However, combining them in one tweet brings the sarcasm to its extreme. Example (3) is a factual statement without explicit opinion. However, having a fast connection is a positive thing. A possible sarcasm emerges from the over exaggeration ('wow', '*blazing*-fast').

Example (4) from Amazon, might be a genuine compliment if it appears in the body of the review. However, recalling the expression 'don't judge a book by its cover', choosing it as the title of the review reveals its sarcastic nature. Although the negative sentiment is very explicit in the iPod review (5), the sarcastic effect emerges from the pun that assumes the knowledge that the design is one of the most celebrated features of Apple's products. (None of the above reasoning was directly introduced to our algorithm.)

Modeling the underlying patterns of sarcastic utterances is interesting from the psychological and cognitive perspectives and can benefit various NLP systems such as review summarization (Popescu and Etzioni, 2005; Pang and Lee, 2004; Wiebe et al., 2004; Hu and Liu, 2004) and dialogue systems. Following the 'brilliant-but-cruel' hypothesis (Danescu-Niculescu-Mizil et al., 2009), it can help improve ranking and recommendation systems (Tsur and Rappoport, 2009). All systems currently fail to correctly classify the sentiment of sarcastic sentences.

In this paper we utilize the semi-supervised sarcasm identification algorithm (SASI) of (Tsur et al., 2010). The algorithm employs two modules: semi supervised pattern acquisition for identifying sarcastic patterns that serve as features for a classifier, and a classification stage that classifies each sentence to a sarcastic class. We experiment with two radically different datasets: 5.9 million tweets collected from Twitter, and 66000 Amazon product reviews. Although for the Amazon dataset the algorithm utilizes structured information, results for the Twitter dataset are higher. We discuss the possible reasons for this, and also the utility of Twitter #sarcasm hashtags for the task. Our algorithm performed well in both domains, substantially outperforming a strong baseline based on semantic gap and user annotations. To further test its robustness we also trained the algorithm in a cross domain manner, achieving good results.

2 Data

The datasets we used are interesting in their own right for many applications. In addition, our algorithm utilizes some aspects that are unique to these datasets. Hence, before describing the algorithm, we describe the datasets in detail.

Twitter Dataset. Since Twitter is a relatively new service, a somewhat lengthy description of the medium and the data is appropriate.

Twitter is a very popular microblogging service. It allows users to publish and read short messages called *tweets* (also used as a verb: to tweet: the act of publishing on Twitter). The tweet length is restricted to 140 characters. A user who publishes a tweet is referred to as a *tweeter* and the readers are casual readers or *followers* if they are registered to get all tweets by this tweeter.

Apart from simple text, tweets may contain references to url addresses, references to other Twitter users (these appear as @<user>) or a content tag (called *hashtags*) assigned by the tweeter (#<tag>). An example of a tweet is: *"listening to Andrew Ridgley by Black Box Recorder on @Grooveshark: http://tinysong.com/cO6i #goodmusic"*, where 'grooveshark' is a Twitter user name and #goodmusic is a tag that allows to search for tweets with the same tag. Though frequently used, these types of meta tags are optional. In order to ignore specific references we substituted such occurrences with special tags: [LINK], [USER] and [HASHTAG] thus we have *"listening to Andrew Ridgley by Black Box Recorder on [USER]: [LINK] [HASHTAG]"*. It is important to mention that hashtags are not formal and each tweeter can define and use new tags as s/he likes.

The number of special tags in a tweet is only subject to the 140 characters constraint. There is no specific grammar that enforces the location of special tags within a tweet.

The informal nature of the medium and the 140 characters length constraint encourages massive use of slang, shortened lingo, ascii emoticons and other tokens absent from formal lexicons.

These characteristics make Twitter a fascinating domain for NLP applications, although posing great challenges due to the length constraint, the complete freedom of style and the out of discourse nature of tweets.

We used 5.9 million unique tweets in our dataset: the average number of words is 14.2

words per tweet, 18.7% contain a url, 35.3% contain reference to another tweeter and 6.9% contain at least one hashtag[1].

The #sarcasm hashtag One of the hashtags used by Twitter users is dedicated to indicate sarcastic tweets. An example of the use of the tag is: *'I guess you should expect a WONDERFUL video tomorrow. #sarcasm'*. The sarcastic hashtag is added by the *tweeter*. This hashtag is used infrequently as most users are not aware of it, hence, the majority of sarcastic tweets are not explicitly tagged by the tweeters. We use tagged tweets as a secondary gold standard. We discuss the use of this tag in Section 5.

Amazon dataset. We used the same dataset used by (Tsur et al., 2010), containing 66000 reviews for 120 products from Amazon.com. The corpus contained reviews for books from different genres and various electronic products. Amazon reviews are much longer than tweets (some reach 2000 words, average length is 953 characters), they are more structured and grammatical (good reviews are very structured) and they come in a known context of a specific product. Reviews are semi-structured as besides the body of the review they all have the following fields: writer, date, star rating (the overall satisfaction of the review writer) and a one line summary.

Reviews refer to a specific product and rarely address each other. Each review sentence is, therefore, part of a context – the specific product, the star rating, the summary and other sentences in that review. In that sense, sentences in the Amazon dataset differ radically from the contextless tweets. It is worth mentioning that the majority of reviews are on the very positive side (star rating average of 4.2 stars).

3 Classification Algorithm

Our algorithm is semi-supervised. The input is a relatively small seed of labeled sentences. The seed is annotated in a discrete range of $1 \ldots 5$ where 5 indicates a clearly sarcastic sentence and 1 indicates a clear absence of sarcasm. A $1 \ldots 5$ scale was used in order to allow some subjectivity and since some instances of sarcasm are more explicit than others.

[1]The Twitter data was generously provided to us by Brendan O'Connor.

Given the labeled sentences, we extracted a set of features to be used in feature vectors. Two basic feature types are utilized: syntactic and pattern-based features. We constructed feature vectors for each of the labeled examples in the training set and used them to build a classifier model and assign scores to unlabeled examples. We next provide a description of the algorithmic framework of (Tsur et al., 2010).

Data preprocessing A sarcastic utterance usually has a *target*. In the Amazon dataset these targets can be exploited by a computational algorithm, since each review targets a product, its manufacturer or one of its features, and these are explicitly represented or easily recognized. The Twitter dataset is totally unstructured and lacks textual context, so we did not attempt to identify targets.

Our algorithmic methodology is based on patterns. We could use patterns that include the targets identified in the Amazon dataset. However, in order to use less specific patterns, we automatically replace each appearance of a product, author, company, book name (Amazon) and user, url and hashtag (Twitter) with the corresponding generalized meta tags '[PRODUCT]','[COMPANY]','[TITLE]' and '[AUTHOR]' tags[2] and '[USER]','[LINK]' and '[HASHTAG]'. We also removed all HTML tags and special symbols from the review text.

Pattern extraction Our main feature type is based on surface patterns. In order to extract such patterns automatically, we followed the algorithm given in (Davidov and Rappoport, 2006). We classified words into high-frequency words (HFWs) and content words (CWs). A word whose corpus frequency is more (less) than F_H (F_C) is considered to be a HFW (CW). Unlike in (Davidov and Rappoport, 2006), we consider all punctuation characters as HFWs. We also consider [product], [company], [title], [author] tags as HFWs for pattern extraction. We define a pattern as an ordered sequence of high frequency words and slots for content words. The F_H and F_C thresholds were set to 1000 words per million (upper bound for F_C) and 100 words per million (lower bound for F_H)[3].

[2]Appropriate names are provided with each review so this replacement can be done automatically.

[3]Note that F_H and F_C set bounds that allow overlap between some HFWs and CWs.

The patterns allow 2-6 HFWs and 1-6 slots for CWs. For each sentence it is possible to generate dozens of patterns that may overlap. For example, given a sentence "Garmin apparently does not care much about product quality or customer support", we have generated several patterns including "[COMPANY] CW does not CW much", "does not CW much about CW CW or", "not CW much" and "about CW CW or CW CW.". Note that "[COMPANY]" and "." are treated as high frequency words.

Pattern selection The pattern extraction stage provides us with hundreds of patterns. However, some of them are either too general or too specific. In order to reduce the feature space, we have used two criteria to select useful patterns.

First, we removed all patterns which appear only in sentences originating from a single product/book (Amazon). Such patterns are usually product-specific. Next we removed all patterns which appear in the seed both in some example labeled 5 (clearly sarcastic) and in some other example labeled 1 (obviously not sarcastic). This filters out frequent generic and uninformative patterns. Pattern selection was performed only on the Amazon dataset as it exploits review's meta data.

Pattern matching Once patterns are selected, we have used each pattern to construct a single entry in the feature vectors. For each sentence we calculated a feature value for each pattern as follows:

$$\begin{cases} 1: & \text{Exact match – all the pattern components appear in the sentence in correct order without any additional words.} \\ \alpha: & \text{Sparse match – same as exact match but additional non-matching words can be inserted between pattern components.} \\ \gamma * n/N: & \text{Incomplete match – only } n > 1 \text{ of } N \text{ pattern components appear in the sentence, while some non-matching words can be inserted in-between. At least one of the appearing components should be a HFW.} \\ 0: & \text{No match – nothing or only a single pattern component appears in the sentence.} \end{cases}$$

$0 \leq \alpha \leq 1$ and $0 \leq \gamma \leq 1$ are parameters we use to assign reduced scores for imperfect matches. Since the patterns we use are relatively long, exact matches are uncommon, and taking advantage of partial matches allows us to significantly reduce the sparsity of the feature vectors. We used

$\alpha \backslash \gamma$	0.05	0.1	0.2
0.05	0.48	0.45	0.39
0.1	0.50	0.51	0.40
0.2	0.40	0.42	0.33

Table 1: Results (F-Score for "no enrichment" mode) of cross validation with various values for α and γ on Twitter+Amazon data

$\alpha = \gamma = 0.1$ in all experiments. Table 1 demonstrates the results obtained with different values for α and γ.

Thus, for the sentence "Garmin apparently does not care much about product quality or customer support", the value for "[company] CW does not" would be 1 (exact match); for "[company] CW not" would be 0.1 (sparse match due to insertion of 'does'); and for "[company] CW CW does not" would be $0.1 * 4/5 = 0.08$ (incomplete match since the second CW is missing).

Punctuation-based features In addition to pattern-based features we used the following generic features: (1) Sentence length in words, (2) Number of "!" characters in the sentence, (3) Number of "?" characters in the sentence, (4) Number of quotes in the sentence, and (5) Number of capitalized/all capitals words in the sentence. All these features were normalized by dividing them by the (maximal observed value · averaged maximal value of the other feature groups), thus the maximal weight of each of these features is equal to the averaged weight of a single pattern/word/n-gram feature.

Data enrichment Since we start with only a small annotated seed for training (particularly, the number of clearly sarcastic sentences in the seed is modest) and since annotation is noisy and expensive, we would like to find more training examples without requiring additional annotation effort.

To achieve this, we posited that sarcastic sentences frequently co-appear in texts with other sarcastic sentences (i.e. example (2) in Section 1). We performed an automated web search using the Yahoo! BOSS API[4], where for each sentence s in the training set (seed), we composed a search engine query q_s containing this sentence[5]. We collected up to 50 search engine snippets for each example and added the sentences found in these snippets to the training set. The label (level of sar-

[4]http://developer.yahoo.com/search/boss.

[5]If the sentence contained more than 6 words, only the first 6 words were included in the search engine query.

casm) $Label(s_q)$ of a newly extracted sentence s_q is similar to the label $Label(s)$ of the seed sentence s that was used for the query that acquired it. The seed sentences together with newly acquired sentences constitute the (enriched) training set.

Data enrichment was performed only for the Amazon dataset where we have a manually tagged seed and the sentence structure is closer to standard English grammar. We refer the reader to (Tsur et al., 2010) for more details about the enrichment process and for a short discussion about the usefulness of web-based data enrichment in the scope of sarcasm recognition.

Classification In order to assign a score to new examples in the test set we use a k-nearest neighbors (kNN)-like strategy. We construct feature vectors for each example in the training and test sets. We would like to calculate the score for each example in the test set. For each feature vector v in the test set, we compute the Euclidean distance to each of the matching vectors in the extended training set, where matching vectors share at least one pattern feature with v.

Let $t_i, i = 1..k$ be the k vectors with lowest Euclidean distance to v[6]. Then v is classified with a label l as follows:

$$Count(l) = \text{Fraction of training vectors with label } l$$

$$Label(v) = \left[\frac{1}{k}\sum_i \frac{Count(Label(t_i)) \cdot Label(t_i)}{\sum_j Count(label(t_j))}\right]$$

Thus the score is a weighted average of the k closest training set vectors. If there are less than k matching vectors for the given example then fewer vectors are used in the computation. If there are no matching vectors found for v, we assigned the default value $Label(v) = 1$, since sarcastic sentences are fewer in number than non-sarcastic ones (this is a 'most common tag' strategy).

4 Evaluation Setup

Seed and extended training sets (Amazon). As described in the previous section, SASI is semi supervised, hence requires a small seed of annotated data. We used the same seed of 80 positive (sarcastic) examples and 505 negative examples described at (Tsur et al., 2010).

After automatically expanding the training set, our training data now contains 471 positive examples and 5020 negative examples. These ratios are to be expected, since non-sarcastic sentences outnumber sarcastic ones, definitely when most online reviews are positive (Liu et al., 2007). This generally positive tendency is also reflected in our data – the average number of stars is 4.12.

Seed training set with #sarcasm (Twitter). We used a sample of 1500 tweets marked with the #sarcasm hashtag as a positive set that represents sarcasm styles special to Twitter. However, this set is very noisy (see discussion in Section 5).

Seed training set (cross domain). Results obtained by training on the 1500 #sarcasm hashtagged tweets were not promising. Examination of the #sarcasm tagged tweets shows that the annotation is biased and noisy as we discuss in length in Section 5. A better annotated set was needed in order to properly train the algorithm. Sarcastic tweets are sparse and hard to find and annotate manually. In order to overcome sparsity we used the positive seed annotated on the Amazon dataset. The training set was completed by manually selected negative example from the Twitter dataset. Note that in this setting our training set is thus of mixed domains.

4.1 Star-sentiment baseline

Many studies on sarcasm suggest that sarcasm emerges from the gap between the expected utterance and the actual utterance (see echoic mention, allusion and pretense theories in Related Work Section(6)). We implemented a baseline designed to capture the notion of sarcasm as reflected by these models, trying to meet the definition "saying the opposite of what you mean in a way intended to make someone else feel stupid or show you are angry".

We exploit the meta-data provided by Amazon, namely the star rating each reviewer is obliged to provide, in order to identify unhappy reviewers. From this set of negative reviews, our baseline classifies as sarcastic those sentences that exhibit strong positive sentiment. The list of positive sentiment words is predefined and captures words typically found in reviews (for example, 'great', 'excellent', 'best', 'top', 'exciting', etc).

4.2 Evaluation procedure

We used two experimental frameworks to test SASI's accuracy. In the first experiment we evaluated the pattern acquisition process, how consistent it is and to what extent it contributes to correct

[6]We used $k = 5$ for all experiments.

classification. We did that by 5-fold cross validation over the seed data.

In the second experiment we evaluated SASI on a test set of unseen sentences, comparing its output to a gold standard annotated by a large number of human annotators (using the Mechanical Turk). This way we verify that there is no over-fitting and that the algorithm is not biased by the notion of sarcasm of a single seed annotator.

5-fold cross validation (Amazon). In this experimental setting, the seed data was divided to 5 parts and a 5-fold cross validation test is executed. Each time, we use 4 parts of the seed as the training data and only this part is used for the feature selection and data enrichment. This 5-fold process was repeated ten times. This procedure was repeated with different sets of optional features.

We used 5-fold cross validation and not the standard 10-fold since the number of seed examples (especially positive) is relatively small hence 10-fold is too sensitive to the broad range of possible sarcastic patterns (see the examples in Section 1).

Classifying new sentences (Amazon & Twitter). Evaluation of sarcasm is a hard task due to the elusive nature of sarcasm, as discussed in Section 1. In order to evaluate the quality of our algorithm, we used SASI to classify *all* sentences in both corpora (besides the small seed that was pre-annotated and was used for the evaluation in the 5-fold cross validation experiment). Since it is impossible to created a gold standard classification of each and every sentence in the corpus, we created a small test set by sampling 90 sentences which were classified as sarcastic (labels 3-5) and 90 sentences classified as not sarcastic (labels 1,2). The sampling was performed on the whole corpus leaving out only the seed data.

Again, the meta data available in the Amazon dataset allows us a stricter evaluation. In order to make the evaluation harder for our algorithm and more relevant, we introduced two constraints to the sampling process: *i)* we sampled only sentences containing a named-entity or a reference to a named entity. This constraint was introduced in order to keep the evaluation set relevant, since sentences that refer to the named entity (the target of the review) are more likely to contain an explicit or implicit sentiment. *ii)* we restricted the non-sarcastic sentences to belong to negative reviews (1-3 stars) so that all sentences in the evaluation set are drawn from the same population, increasing the chances they convey various levels of direct or indirect *negative* sentiment[7].

Experimenting with the Twitter dataset, we simply classified each tweet into one of 5 classes (class 1: not sarcastic, class 5: clearly sarcastic) according to the label given by the algorithm. Just like the evaluation of the algorithm on the Amazon dataset, we created a small evaluation set by sampling 90 sentences which were classified as sarcastic (labels 3-5) and 90 sentences classified as not sarcastic (labels 1,2).

Procedure Each evaluation set was randomly divided to 5 batches. Each batch contained 36 sentences from the evaluation set and 4 anchor sentences: two with sarcasm and two sheer neutral. The anchor sentences were not part of the test set and were the same in all five batches. The purpose of the anchor sentences is to control the evaluation procedure and verify that annotation is reasonable. We ignored the anchor sentences when assessing the algorithm's accuracy.

We used Amazon's Mechanical Turk[8] service in order to create a gold standard for the evaluation. We employed 15 annotators for each evaluation set. We used a relatively large number of annotators in order to overcome the possible bias induced by subjectivity (Muecke, 1982). Each annotator was asked to assess the level of sarcasm of each sentence of a set of 40 sentences on a scale of 1-5. In total, each sentence was annotated by three different annotators.

Inter Annotator Agreement. To simplify the assessment of inter-annotator agreement, the scaling was reduced to a binary classification where 1 and 2 were marked as non-sarcastic and 3-5 as sarcastic (recall that 3 indicates a hint of sarcasm and 5 indicates 'clearly sarcastic'). We checked the Fleiss' κ statistic to measure agreement between multiple annotators. The inter-annotator agreement statistic was $\kappa = 0.34$ on the Amazon dataset and $\kappa = 0.41$ on the Twitter dataset.

These agreement statistics indicates a fair agreement. Given the fuzzy nature of the task at

[7]Note that the second constraint makes the problem less easy. If taken from all reviews, many of the sentences would be positive sentences which are clearly non-sarcastic. Doing this would bias selection to positive vs. negative samples instead of sarcastic-nonsarcastic samples.

[8]https://www.mturk.com/mturk/welcome

	Prec.	Recall	Accuracy	F-score
punctuation	0.256	0.312	0.821	0.281
patterns	0.743	**0.788**	0.943	0.765
pat+punct	0.868	0.763	0.945	0.812
enrich punct	0.4	0.390	0.832	0.395
enrich pat	0.762	0.777	0.937	0.769
all: SASI	**0.912**	0.756	**0.947**	**0.827**

Table 2: 5-fold cross validation results on the Amazon gold standard using various feature types. *punctuation*: punctuation mark;, *patterns*: patterns; *enrich*: after data enrichment; *enrich punct*: data enrichment based on punctuation only; *enrich pat*: data enrichment based on patterns only; SASI: all features combined.

hand, this κ value is certainly satisfactory. We attribute the better agreement on the twitter data to the fact that in twitter each sentence (tweet) is context free, hence the sentiment in the sentence is expressed in a way that can be perceived more easily. Sentences from product reviews come as part of a full review, hence the the sarcasm sometimes relies on other sentences in the review. In our evaluation scheme, our annotators were presented with individual sentences, making the agreement lower for those sentences taken out of their original context. The agreement on the control set (anchor sentences) had $\kappa = 0.53$.

Using Twitter #sarcasm hashtag. In addition to the gold standard annotated using the Mechanical Turk, we collected 1500 tweets that were tagged #sarcastic by their tweeters. We call this sample the *hash*-gold standard. It was used to further evaluate recall. This set (along with the negative sample) was used for a 5-fold cross validation in the same manner describe for Amazon.

5 Results and discussion

5-fold cross validation (Amazon). Results are analyzed and discussed in detail in (Tsur et al., 2010), however, we summarize it here (Table 2) in order to facilitate comparison with the results obtained on the Twitter dataset. SASI, including all components, exhibits the best overall performances with 91.2% precision and with F-Score of 0.827. Interestingly, although data enrichment brings SASI to the best performance in both precision and F-score, patterns+punctuations achieves almost comparable results.

Newly introduced sentences (Amazon). In the second experiment we evaluated SASI based on a gold standard annotation created by 15 annotators. Table 3 presents the results of our algorithm as well as results of the heuristic baseline that makes

	Prec.	Recall	**FalsePos**	**FalseNeg**	**F Score**
Star-sent.	0.5	0.16	0.05	0.44	0.242
SASI (AM)	0.766	0.813	0.11	0.12	0.788
SASI (TW)	0.794	0.863	0.094	0.15	0.827

Table 3: Evaluation on the Amazon (AM) and the Twitter (TW) evaluation sets obtained by averaging on 3 human annotations per sentence. TW results were obtained with cross-domain training.

	Prec.	Recall	Accuracy	F-score
punctuation	0.259	0.26	0.788	0.259
patterns	0.765	0.326	0.889	0.457
enrich punct	0.18	0.316	0.76	0.236
enrich pat	0.685	0.356	0.885	0.47
all no enrich	**0.798**	0.37	**0.906**	0.505
all SASI:	0.727	**0.436**	0.896	**0.545**

Table 4: 5-fold cross validation results on the Twitter *hash*-gold standard using various feature types. *punctuation*: punctuation marks; *patterns*: patterns; *enrich*: after data enrichment; *enrich punct*: data enrichment based on punctuation only; *enrich pat*: data enrichment based on patterns only; SASI: all features combined.

use of meta-data, designed to capture the gap between an explicit negative sentiment (reflected by the review's star rating) and explicit positive sentiment words used in the review. Precision of SASI is 0.766, a significant improvement over the baseline with precision of 0.5.

The F-score shows more impressive improvement as the baseline shows decent precision but a very limited recall since it is incapable of recognizing subtle sarcastic sentences. These results fit the works of (Brown, 1980; Gibbs and O'Brien, 1991) claiming many sarcastic utterances do not conform to the popular definition of "saying or writing the opposite of what you mean". Table 3 also presents the false positive and false negative ratios. The low false negative ratio of the baseline confirms that while recognizing a common type of sarcasm, the naive definition of sarcasm cannot capture many other types sarcasm.

Newly introduced sentences (Twitter). Results on the Twitter dataset are even better than those obtained on the Amazon dataset, with accuracy of 0.947 (see Table 3 for precision and recall).

Tweets are less structured and are context free, hence one would expect SASI to perform poorly on tweets. Moreover, the positive part of the seed is taken from the Amazon corpus hence might seem tailored to sarcasm type targeted at products and part of a harsh review. On top of that, the positive seed introduces some patterns with tags that never occur in the Twitter test set ([product/company/title/author]).

Our explanation of the excellent results is threefold: *i*) SASI's robustness is achieved by the sparse match (α) and incomplete match (γ) that tolerate imperfect pattern matching and enable the use of variations of the patterns in the learned feature vector. α and γ allow the introduction of patterns with components that are absent from the positive seed, and can perform even with patterns that contain special tags that are not part of the test set. *ii*) SASI learns a model which spans a feature space with more than 300 dimensions. Only part of the patterns consist of meta tags that are special to product reviews, the rest are strong enough to capture the structure of general sarcastic sentences and not product-specific sarcastic sentences only. *iii*) Finally, in many cases, it might be that the contextless nature of Twitter forces tweeters to express sarcasm in a way that is easy to understand from individual sentence. Amazon sentences co-appear with other sentences (in the same review) thus the sarcastic meaning emerges from the context. Our evaluation scheme presents the annotators with single sentences therefore Amazon sentences might be harder to agree on.

***hash* gold standard (Twitter).** In order to further test out algorithm we built a model consisting of the positive sample of the Amazon training, the #sarcasm hash-tagged tweets and a sample of non sarcastic tweets as the negative training set. We evaluated it in a 5-fold cross validation manner (only against the *hash*-gold standard). While precision is still high with 0.727, recall drops to 0.436 and the F-Score is 0.545.

Looking at the *hash*-gold standard set, we observed three main uses for the #sarcasm hashtag. Differences between the various uses can explain the relatively low recall. *i*) The tag is used as a search anchor. Tweeters add the hashtag to tweets in order to make them retrievable when searching for the tag. *ii*) The tag is often abused and added to non sarcastic tweets, typically to clarify that a previous tweet should have been read sarcastically, e.g.: *"@wrightfan05 it was #Sarcasm "*. *iii*) The tag serves as a sarcasm marker in cases of a very subtle sarcasm where the lack of context, the 140 length constraint and the sentence structure make it impossible to get the sarcasm without the explicit marker. Typical examples are: *"#sarcasm not at all."* or *"can't wait to get home tonite #sarcasm."*, which cannot be decided sarcastic without the full context or the #sarcasm marker.

These three observations suggest that the hash-gold standard is noisy (containing non-sarcastic tweets) and is biased toward the hardest (inseparable) forms of sarcasm where even humans get it wrong without an explicit indication. Given the noise and the bias, the recall is not as bad as the raw numbers suggest and is actually in synch with the results obtained on the Mechanical Turk human-annotated gold standard. Table 4 presents detailed results and the contribution of each type of feature to the classification.

We note that the relative sparseness of sarcastic utterances in everyday communication as well as in these two datasets make it hard to accurately estimate the recall value over these huge unannotated data sets. Our experiment, however, indicates that we achieve reasonable recall rates.

Punctuation Surprisingly, punctuation marks serve as the weakest predictors, in contrast to Teppermann et al. (2006). An exception is three consecutive dots, which when combine with other features constitute a strong predictor. Interestingly though, while in the cross validation experiments SASI performance varies greatly (due to the problematic use of the *#sarcasm* hashtag, described previously), performance based only on punctuation are similar (Table 2 and Table 4).

Tsur et al. (2010) presents some additional examples for the contribution of each type of feature and their combinations.

6 Related Work

While the use of irony and sarcasm is well studied from its linguistic and psychologic aspects (Muecke, 1982; Stingfellow, 1994; Gibbs and Colston, 2007), automatic recognition of sarcasm is a novel task, addressed only by few works. In the context of opinion mining, sarcasm is mentioned briefly as a hard nut that is yet to be cracked, see comprehensive overview by (Pang and Lee, 2008).

Tepperman et al. (2006) identify sarcasm in spoken dialogue systems, their work is restricted to sarcastic utterances that contain the expression 'yeah-right' and it depends heavily on cues in the spoken dialogue such as laughter, pauses within the speech stream, the gender (recognized by voice) of the speaker and prosodic features.

Burfoot and Baldwin (2009) use SVM to determine whether newswire articles are true or satirical. They introduce the notion of *validity* which models absurdity via a measure somewhat close to

PMI. Validity is relatively lower when a sentence includes a made-up entity or when a sentence contains unusual combinations of named entities such as, for example, those in the satirical article beginning "Missing Brazilian balloonist Padre spotted straddling Pink Floyd flying pig". We note that while sarcasm can be based on exaggeration or unusual collocations, this model covers only a limited subset of the sarcastic utterances.

Tsur et al. (2010) propose a semi supervised framework for recognition of sarcasm. The proposed algorithm utilizes some features specific to (Amazon) product reviews. This paper continues this line, proposing SASI a robust algorithm that successfully captures sarcastic sentences in other, radically different, domains such as twitter.

Utsumi (1996; 2000) introduces the *implicit display* theory, a cognitive computational framework that models the *ironic environment*. The complex axiomatic system depends heavily on complex formalism representing world knowledge. While comprehensive, it is currently impractical to implement on a large scale or for an open domain.

Mihalcea and Strapparava (2005) and Mihalcea and Pulman (2007) present a system that identifies humorous one-liners. They classify sentences using naive Bayes and SVM. They conclude that the most frequently observed semantic features are negative polarity and human-centeredness. These features are also observed in some sarcastic utterances.

Some philosophical, psychological and linguistic theories of irony and sarcasm are worth referencing as a theoretical framework: the *constraints satisfaction* theory (Utsumi, 1996; Katz, 2005), the *role playing* theory (Clark and Gerrig, 1984), the *echoic mention* framework (Wilson and Sperber, 1992) and the *pretence* framework (Gibbs, 1986). These are all based on violation of the maxims proposed by Grice (1975).

7 Conclusion

We used SASI, the first robust algorithm for recognition of sarcasm, to experiment with a novel Twitter dataset and compare performance with an Amazon product reviews dataset. Evaluating in various ways and with different parameters configurations, we achieved high precision, recall and F-Score on both datasets even for cross-domain training and with no need for domain adaptation.

In the future we will test the contribution of sarcasm recognition for review ranking and summarization systems and for brand monitoring systems.

References

R. L. Brown. 1980. The pragmatics of verbal irony. In R. W. Shuy and A. Snukal, editors, *Language use and the uses of language*, pages 111–127. Georgetown University Press.

Clint Burfoot and Timothy Baldwin. 2009. Automatic satire detection: Are you having a laugh? In *Proceedings of the ACL-IJCNLP 2009 Conference Short Papers*, pages 161–164, Suntec, Singapore, August. Association for Computational Linguistics.

H. Clark and R. Gerrig. 1984. On the pretence theory of irony. *Journal of Experimental Psychology: General*, 113:121–126.

Cristian Danescu-Niculescu-Mizil, Gueorgi Kossinets, Jon Kleinberg, and Lillian Lee. 2009. How opinions are received by online communities: A case study on amazon.com helpfulness votes. Jun.

D. Davidov and A. Rappoport. 2006. Efficient unsupervised discovery of word categories using symmetric patterns and high frequency words. In *COLING-ACL*.

Macmillan English Dictionary. 2007. *Macmillan English Dictionary*. Macmillan Education, 2 edition.

Raymond W Gibbs and Herbert L. Colston, editors. 2007. *Irony in Language and Thought*. Routledge (Taylor and Francis), New York.

R. W. Gibbs and J. E. O'Brien. 1991. Psychological aspects of irony understanding. *Journal of Pragmatics*, 16:523–530.

R. Gibbs. 1986. On the psycholinguistics of sarcasm. *Journal of Experimental Psychology: General*, 105:3–15.

H. P. Grice. 1975. Logic and conversation. In Peter Cole and Jerry L. Morgan, editors, *Syntax and semantics*, volume 3. New York: Academic Press.

Minqing Hu and Bing Liu. 2004. Mining and summarizing customer reviews. In *KDD '04: Proceedings of the tenth ACM SIGKDD international conference on Knowledge discovery and data mining*, pages 168–177, New York, NY, USA. ACM.

A. Katz. 2005. Discourse and social-cultural factors in understanding non literal language. In Colston H. and Katz A., editors, *Figurative language comprehension: Social and cultural influences*, pages 183–208. Lawrence Erlbaum Associates.

Jingjing Liu, Yunbo Cao, Chin-Yew Lin, Yalou Huang, and Ming Zhou. 2007. Low-quality product review detection in opinion summarization. In *Proceedings of the 2007 Joint Conference on Empirical Methods in Natural Language Processing and Computational Natural Language Learning (EMNLP-CoNLL)*, pages 334–342.

Rada Mihalcea and Stephen G. Pulman. 2007. Characterizing humour: An exploration of features in humorous texts. In *CICLing*, pages 337–347.

Rada Mihalcea and Carlo Strapparava. 2005. Making computers laugh: Investigations in automatic humor recognition. pages 531–538, Vancouver, Canada.

D.C. Muecke. 1982. *Irony and the ironic*. Methuen, London, New York.

Bo Pang and Lillian Lee. 2004. A sentimental education: Sentiment analysis using subjectivity summarization based on minimum cuts. In *Proceedings of the ACL*, pages 271–278.

Bo Pang and Lillian Lee. 2008. *Opinion Mining and Sentiment Analysis*. Now Publishers Inc, July.

Ana-Maria Popescu and Oren Etzioni. 2005. Extracting product features and opinions from reviews. In *HLT '05: Proceedings of the conference on Human Language Technology and Empirical Methods in Natural Language Processing*, pages 339–346, Morristown, NJ, USA. Association for Computational Linguistics.

Frank Jr. Stingfellow. 1994. *The Meaning of Irony*. State University of NY, New York.

J. Tepperman, D. Traum, and S. Narayanan. 2006. Yeah right: Sarcasm recognition for spoken dialogue systems. In *InterSpeech ICSLP*, Pittsburgh, PA.

Oren Tsur and Ari Rappoport. 2009. Revrank: A fully unsupervised algorithm for selecting the most helpful book reviews. In *International AAAI Conference on Weblogs and Social Media*.

Oren Tsur, Dmitry Davidiv, and Ari Rappoport. 2010. Icwsm – a great catchy name: Semi-supervised recognition of sarcastic sentences in product reviews. In *International AAAI Conference on Weblogs and Social Media*.

Akira Utsumi. 1996. A unified theory of irony and its computational formalization. In *COLING*, pages 962–967.

Akira Utsumi. 2000. Verbal irony as implicit display of ironic environment: Distinguishing ironic utterances from nonirony. *Journal of Pragmatics*, 32(12):1777–1806.

Janyce Wiebe, Theresa Wilson, Rebecca Bruce, Matthew Bell, and Melanie Martin. 2004. Learning subjective language. *Computational Linguistics*, 30(3):277– 308, January.

D. Wilson and D. Sperber. 1992. On verbal irony. *Lingua*, 87:53–76.

Learning Probabilistic Synchronous CFGs for Phrase-based Translation

Markos Mylonakis
ILLC
University of Amsterdam
m.mylonakis@uva.nl

Khalil Sima'an
ILLC
University of Amsterdam
k.simaan@uva.nl

Abstract

Probabilistic phrase-based synchronous grammars are now considered promising devices for statistical machine translation because they can express reordering phenomena between pairs of languages. Learning these hierarchical, probabilistic devices from parallel corpora constitutes a major challenge, because of multiple latent model variables as well as the risk of data overfitting. This paper presents an effective method for learning a family of particular interest to MT, binary Synchronous Context-Free Grammars with inverted/monotone orientation (a.k.a. Binary ITG). A second contribution concerns devising a lexicalized phrase reordering mechanism that has complimentary strengths to Chiang's model. The latter conditions reordering decisions on the surrounding lexical context of phrases, whereas our mechanism works with the lexical content of phrase pairs (akin to standard phrase-based systems). Surprisingly, our experiments on French-English data show that our learning method applied to far simpler models exhibits performance indistinguishable from the Hiero system.

1 Introduction

A fundamental problem in phrase-based machine translation concerns the learning of a probabilistic synchronous context-free grammar (SCFG) over phrase pairs from an input parallel corpus. Chiang's Hiero system (Chiang, 2007) exemplifies the gains to be had by combining phrase-based translation (Och and Ney, 2004) with the hierarchical reordering capabilities of SCFGs, particularly originating from Binary Inversion Transduction Grammars (BITG) (Wu, 1997). Yet, existing empirical work is largely based on successful heuristic techniques, and the learning of Hiero-like BITG/SCFG remains an unsolved problem,

The difficulty of this problem stems from the need for simultaneously learning of two kinds of preferences (see Fig.1) (1) lexical translation probabilities ($P(\langle e, f\rangle \mid X)$) of source ($f$) and target ($e$) phrase pairs, and (2) phrase reordering preferences of a target string relative to a source string, expressed in synchronous productions probabilities (for monotone or switching productions). Theoretically speaking, both kinds of preferences may involve latent structure relative to the parallel corpus. The mapping between source-target sentence pairs can be expressed in terms of latent phrase segmentations and latent word/phrase-alignments, and the hierarchical phrase reordering can be expressed in terms of latent binary synchronous hierarchical structures (cf. Fig. 1). But each of these three kinds of latent structures may be made explicit using external resources: word-alignment could be considered solved using Giza++ (Och and Ney, 2003)), phrase pairs can be obtained from these word-alignments (Och and Ney, 2004), and the hierarchical synchronous structure can be grown over source/target linguistic syntactic trees output by an existing parser.

The Joint Phrase Translation Model (Marcu and Wong, 2002) constitutes a specific case, albeit without the hierarchical, synchronous reordering

Start	$S \rightarrow X_{\boxed{1}} \; / \; X_{\boxed{1}}$	(1)
Monotone	$X \rightarrow X_{\boxed{1}} \, X_{\boxed{2}} \, / X_{\boxed{1}} \, X_{\boxed{2}}$	(2)
Switching	$X \rightarrow X_{\boxed{1}} \, X_{\boxed{2}} \, / X_{\boxed{2}} \, X_{\boxed{1}}$	(3)
Emission	$X \rightarrow e \; / \; f$	(4)

Figure 1: A phrase-pair SCFG (BITG)

Proceedings of the Fourteenth Conference on Computational Natural Language Learning, pages 117–125,
Uppsala, Sweden, 15-16 July 2010.

component. Other existing work, e.g. (Chiang, 2007), assumes the word-alignments are given in the parallel corpus, but the problem of learning phrase translation probabilities is usually avoided by using surface counts of phrase pairs (Koehn et al., 2003). The problem of learning the hierarchical, synchronous grammar reordering rules is oftentimes addressed as a learning problem in its own right assuming all the rest is given (Blunsom et al., 2008b).

A small number of efforts has been dedicated to the simultaneous learning of the probabilities of phrase translation pairs as well as hierarchical reordering, e.g., (DeNero et al., 2008; Zhang et al., 2008; Blunsom et al., 2009). Of these, some concentrate on evaluating word-alignment, directly such as (Zhang et al., 2008) or indirectly by evaluating a heuristically trained hierarchical translation system from sampled phrasal alignments (Blunsom et al., 2009). However, very few evaluate on actual translation performance of induced synchronous grammars (DeNero et al., 2008). In the majority of cases, the Hiero system, which constitutes the yardstick by which hierarchical systems are measured, remains superior in translation performance, see e.g. (DeNero et al., 2008).

This paper tackles the problem of learning *generative BITG models* as translation models assuming latent segmentation and latent reordering: this is the most similar setting to the training of Hiero. Unlike all other work that heuristically selects a subset of phrase pairs, we start out from an SCFG that works with *all* phrase pairs in the training set and concentrate on the aspects of learning. This learning problem is fraught with the risks of overfitting and can easily result in inadequate reordering preferences (see e.g. (DeNero et al., 2006)).

Almost instantly, we find that the translation performance of all-phrase probabilistic SCFGs learned in this setting crucially depends on the interplay between two aspects of learning:

- Defining a more constrained parameter space, where the reordering productions are phrase-lexicalised and made sensitive to neighbouring reorderings, and
- Defining an objective function that effectively smoothes the maximum-likelihood criterion.

One contribution of this paper is in devising an effective, data-driven smoothed Maximum-Likelihood that can cope with a model working with *all* phrase pair SCFGs. This builds upon our previous work on estimating parameters of a "bag-of-phrases" model for Machine Translation (Mylonakis and Sima'an, 2008). However, learning SCFGs poses significant novel challenges, the core of which lies on the hierarchical nature of a stochastic SCFG translation model and the relevant additional layer of latent structure. We address these issues in this work. Another important contribution is in defining a lexicalised reordering component within BITG that captures order divergences orthogonal to Chiang's model (Chiang, 2007) but somewhat akin to Phrase-Based Statistical Machine Translation reordering models (Koehn et al., 2003).

Our analysis shows that the learning difficulties can be attributed to a rather weak generative model. Yet, our best system exhibits Hiero-level performance on French-English Europarl data using an SCFG-based decoder (Li et al., 2009). Our findings should be insightful for others attempting to make the leap from shallow phrase-based systems to hierarchical SCFG-based translation models using learning methods, as opposed to heuristics.

The rest of the paper is structured as follows. Section 2 briefly introduces the SCFG formalism and discusses its adoption in the context of Statistical Machine Translation (SMT). In section 3, we consider some of the pitfalls of stochastic SCFG grammar learning and address them by introducing a novel learning objective and algorithm. In the section that follows we browse through latent translation structure choices, while in section 5 we present our empirical experiments on evaluating the induced stochastic SCFGs on a translation task and compare their performance with a hierarchical translation baseline. We close with a comparison of related work and a final discussion including future research directions.

2 Synchronous Grammars for Machine Translation

Synchronous Context Free Grammars (SCFGs) provide an appealing formalism to describe the translation process, which explains the generation of parallel strings recursively and allows capturing long-range reordering phenomena. Formally, an SCFG **G** is defined as the tuple (N, E, F, R, S), where N is the finite set of non-terminals with $S \in N$ the start symbol, F and E are finite sets of words for the source and target language and R is a finite set of rewrite rules. Every rule expands a left-hand side non-terminal to a right-hand side pair of strings, a source language string over the vocabulary $F \cup N$ and a target language string over $E \cup N$. The number of non-terminals in the two strings is equal and the rule is complemented with a mapping between them.

String pairs in the language of the SCFG are those with a valid derivation, consisting of a sequence of rule applications, starting from S and recursively expanding the linked non-terminals at the right-hand side of rules. *Stochastic* SCFGs augment every rule in R with a probability, under the constraint that probabilities of rules with the same left-hand side sum up to one. The probability of each derived string pair is then the product of the probabilities of rules used in the derivation. Unless otherwise stated, for the rest of the paper when we refer to SCFGs we will be pointing to their stochastic extension.

The *rank* of an SCFG is defined as the maximum number of non-terminals in a grammar's rule right-hand side. Contrary to monolingual Context Free Grammars, there does not always exist a conversion of an SCFG of a higher rank to one of a lower rank with the same language of string pairs. For this, most machine translation applications focus on SCFGs of rank two (binary SCFGs), or *binarisable* ones witch can be converted to a binary SCFG, given that these seem to cover most of the translation phenomena encountered in language pairs (Wu, 1997) and the related processing algorithms are less demanding computationally.

Although SCFGS were initially introduced for machine translation as a stochastic *word-based* translation process in the form of the Inversion-Transduction Grammar (Wu, 1997), they were actually able to offer state-of-the-art performance in their latter *phrase-based* implementation by Chiang (Chiang, 2005). Chiang's Hiero hierarchical translation system is based on a synchronous grammar with a single non-terminal X covering all learned phrase-pairs. Beginning from the start symbol S, an initial phrase-span structure is constructed monotonically using a simple 'glue grammar':

$$S \rightarrow S_{\boxed{1}}\, X_{\boxed{2}} \;/\; S_{\boxed{1}}\, X_{\boxed{2}}$$
$$S \rightarrow X_{\boxed{1}} \;/\; X_{\boxed{1}}$$

The true power of the system lies in expanding these initial phrase-spans with a set of hierarchical translation rules, which allow conditioning reordering decisions based on lexical context. For the French to English language pair, some examples would be:

$$S \rightarrow \quad X_{\boxed{1}}\ \textit{économiques} \;/\; \textit{financial}\ X_{\boxed{1}}$$
$$S \rightarrow \quad \textit{cette}\ X_{\boxed{1}}\ \textit{de}\ X_{\boxed{2}} \;/\; \textit{this}\ X_{\boxed{1}}\ X_{\boxed{2}}$$
$$S \rightarrow \quad \textit{politique}\ X_{\boxed{1}}\ \textit{commune de}\ X_{\boxed{2}} \;/\; X_{\boxed{2}}\,'\,\textit{s common}\ X_{\boxed{1}}\ \textit{policy}$$

Further work builds on the Hiero grammar to expand it with constituency syntax motivated non-terminals (Zollmann and Venugopal, 2006).

3 Synchronous Grammar Learning

The learning of phrase-based stochastic SCFGs with a Maximum Likelihood objective is exposed to overfitting as other *all-fragment models* such as Phrase-Based SMT (PBSMT) (Marcu and Wong, 2002; DeNero et al., 2006) and Data-Oriented Parsing (DOP) (Bod et al., 2003; Zollmann and Sima'an, 2006). Maximum Likelihood Estimation (MLE) returns degenerate grammar estimates that memorise well the parallel training corpus but generalise poorly to unseen data.

The bias-variance decomposition of the generalisation error Err sheds light on this learning problem. For an estimator $\hat{p}$ with training data $\mathcal{D}$, Err can be expressed as the expected Kullback-Leibler (KL) divergence between the target distribution q and that the estimate $\hat{p}$. This error decomposes into bias and variance terms (Heskes, 1998):

$$Err = \overbrace{KL(q, \bar{p})}^{bias} + \overbrace{E_{\mathcal{D}} KL(\bar{p}, \hat{p})}^{variance} \tag{5}$$

Bias is the KL-divergence between q and the mean estimate over all training data $\bar{p} - E_{\mathcal{D}}\hat{p}(\mathcal{D})$. Variance is the expected divergence between the average estimate and the estimator's actual choice. MLE estimators for all-fragment models are *zero-biased* with zero divergence between the average estimate and the true data distribution. In contrast, their variance is unboundedly large, leading to unbounded generalisation error on unseen cases.

3.1 Cross Validated MLE

A well-known method for estimating generalisation error is k-fold *Cross-Validation* (CV) (Hastie et al., 2001). By partitioning the training data $\mathcal{D}$ into k parts H_1^k, we estimate Err as the expected error over all $1 \leq i \leq k$, when testing on H_i with a model trained by MLE on the rest of the data $D^{-i} = \cup_{j \neq i} H_j$.

Here we use CV to leverage the bias-variance trade-off for learning stochastic all-phrase SCFGs. Given an input all-phrase SCFG grammar with phrase-pairs extracted from the training data, we maximise training data likelihood (MLE) subject to CV smoothing: for each data part H_i ($1 \leq i \leq k$), we consider only derivations which employ grammar rules extracted from the rest of the data $\mathcal{D}^{-i}$. Other work (Mylonakis and Sima'an, 2008) has also explored MLE under CV for a "bag-of-phrases model" that does not deal with reordering preferences, does not employ latent hierarchical structure and works with a non-hierarchical decoder, and partially considers the sparsity issues that arise within CV training. The present paper deals with these issues.

Because of the latent segmentation and hierarchical variables, CV-smoothed MLE cannot be solved analytically and we devise a CV instance of the Expectation-Maximization (EM) algorithm, with an implementation based on a synchronous version of the Inside-Outside algorithm (see Fig. 2). For each word-aligned sentence pair in a partition H_i, the set of eligible derivations (denoted $\mathbf{D}^{-i}$) are those that can be built using only phrase-pairs and productions found in $\mathcal{D}^{-i}$. An essential part of the learning process involves defining the grammar extractor $G(\mathcal{D})$, a function from data to an all-phrase SCFG. We will discuss various extractors in section 4.

Our CV-EM algorithm is an EM instance, guaranteeing convergence and a non-decreasing CV-smoothed data likelihood after each iteration. The running time remains $O(n^6)$, where n is input length, but by considering only derivation spans which do not cross word-alignment points, this runs in reasonable times for relatively large corpora.

3.2 Bayesian Aspects of CV-MLE

Beside being an estimator, the CV-MLE learning algorithm has the added value of being a grammar learner focusing on reducing generalisation error,

INPUT: Word-aligned parallel training data $\mathcal{D}$
Grammar extractor G
The number of parts k to partition $\mathcal{D}$
OUTPUT: SCFG $\mathbf{G}$ with rule probabilities $\hat{p}$

Partition training data $\mathcal{D}$ into parts $H_1, \ldots, H_k$.
For $1 \leq i \leq k$ **do**
Extract grammar rules set $\mathbf{G}_i = G(H_i)$
Initialise $\mathbf{G} = \cup_i \mathbf{G}_i$, $\hat{p}_0$ uniform
Let $j = 0$
Repeat
Let $j = j + 1$
E-step:
For $1 \leq i \leq k$ **do**
Calculate expected counts given $\mathbf{G}$, $\hat{p}_{j-1}$,
for derivations $\mathbf{D}^{-i}$ of H_i
using rules from $\cup_{k \neq i} G(k)$
M-step: set $\hat{p}_j$ to ML estimate given
expected counts
Until convergence

Figure 2: The CV Expectation Maximization algorithm

in the sense that probabilities of grammar productions should reflect the frequency with which these productions are expected to be used for translating future data. Additionally, since the CV criterion prohibits for every data point derivations that use rules only extracted from the same data part, such rules are assigned zero probabilities in the final estimate and are effectively excluded from the grammar. In this way, the algorithm 'shapes' the input grammar, concentrating probability mass on productions that are likely to be used with future data.

One view point of CV-MLE is that each partition $\mathcal{D}^{-i}$ and H_i induces a prior probability $Prior(\pi; \mathcal{D}^{-i})$ on every parameter assignment π, obtained from $\mathcal{D}^{-i}$. This prior assigns zero probability to all π parameter sets with non-zero probabilities for rules not in $G(\mathcal{D}^{-i})$, and uniformly distributes probability to the rest of the parameter sets. In light of this, the CV-MLE objective can be written as follows:

$$\arg\max_{\pi} \prod_i Prior(\pi; \mathcal{D}^{-i}) \times P(H_i \mid \pi) \quad (6)$$

This *data-driven* prior aims to directly favour parameter sets which are expected to better generalise according to the CV criterion, without relying on arbitrary constraints such as limiting the length of phrase pairs in the right-hand side of grammar rules. Furthermore, other frequently employed priors such as the Dirichlet distribution and the Dirichlet Process promote better generalising rule probability distributions based on externally set hyperparameter values, whose selection is frequently sensitive in terms of language pairs, or even the training corpus itself. In contrast, the CV-MLE prior aims for a data-driven Bayesian model, focusing on getting information from the data, instead of imposing external human knowledge on them (see also (Mackay and Petoy, 1995)).

3.3 Smoothing the Model

One remaining wrinkle in the CV-EM scheme is the treatment of boundary cases. There will often be sentence-pairs in H_i, that cannot be fully derived by the grammar extracted from the rest of the data $\mathcal{D}^{-i}$ either because of (1) 'unknown' words (i.e. not appearing in other parts of the CV partition) or (2) complicated combinations of adjacent word-alignments. We employ external smoothing of the grammar, *prior* to learning.

Our solution is to extend the SCFG extracted from $\mathcal{D}^{-i}$ with new emission productions deriving the 'unknown' phrase-pairs (i.e., found in H_i but not in $\mathcal{D}^{-i}$). Crucially, the probabilities of these productions are drawn from a fixed smoothing distribution, i.e., they remain constant throughout estimation. Our smoothing distribution of phrase-pairs for all pre-terminals considers source-target phrase lengths drawn from a Poisson distribution with unit mean, drawing subsequently the words of each of the phrases uniformly from the vocabulary of each language, similar to (Blunsom et al., 2009).

$$p_{smooth}(f/e) = \frac{p_{poisson}(|f|;1)\ p_{poisson}(|e|;1)}{V_f^{|f|}\ V_e^{|e|}}$$

Since the smoothing distribution puts stronger preference on shorter phrase-pairs and avoids competing with the 'known' phrase-pairs, it leads the learner to prefer using as little as possible such smoothing rules, covering only the phrase-pairs required to complete full derivations.

4 Parameter Spaces and Grammar Extractors

A *Grammar Extractor* (GE) plays a major role in our probabilistic SCFG learning pipeline. A GE is a function from a word-aligned parallel corpus to a probabilistic SCFG model. Together with the constraints that render a proper probabilistic SCFG[1], this defines the parameter space.

The extractors used in this paper create SCFGs productions of two different kinds: (a) hierarchical synchronous productions that define the space of possible derivations up to the level of the SCFG pre-terminals, and (2) the phrase-pair emission rules that expand the pre-terminals to phrase-pairs of varying lengths. Given the word-alignments, the set of phrase-pairs extracted is the set of *all* translational equivalents (without length upper-bound) under the word-alignment as defined in (Och and Ney, 2004; Koehn et al., 2003).

Below we focus on the two grammar extractors employed in our experiments. We start out from the most generic, BITG-like formulation, and aim at incremental refinement of the hierarchical productions in order to capture relevant, content-based phrase-pair reordering preferences in the training data.

Single non-terminal SCFG This is a phrase-based binary SCFG grammar employing a single non-terminal X covering each extracted phrase-pair. The other productions consist of monotone and switching expansions of phrase-pair spans covered by X. Finally, the whole sentence-pair is considered to be covered by X. We will call this 'plain SCFG' extractor. See Fig. 1.

Lexicalised Reordering SCFG One weakness of the plain SCFG is that the reordering decisions in the derivations are made without reference to lexical content of the phrases; this is because all phrase-pairs are covered by the same non-terminal. As a refinement, we propose a grammar extractor that aims at modelling the reordering behaviour of phrase-pairs by taking their content into account. This time, the X non-terminal is reserved for phrase-pairs and spans which will take part in monotonic productions only. Two fresh non-terminals, XSL and XSR, are used for covering phrase-pairs that participate in order switching with other, adjacent phrase-pairs. The non-terminal XSL covers phrase-pairs which appear first in the source language order, and the latter those which follow them. The grammar rules produced by this GE, dubbed 'switch grammar', are listed in Fig. 3.

[1] The sum of productions that have the same left-hand label must be one.

Start $S \rightarrow X_{\boxed{1}} / X_{\boxed{1}}$

Monotone Expansion

$X \rightarrow X_{\boxed{1}}\, X_{\boxed{2}} / X_{\boxed{1}}\, X_{\boxed{2}}$
$XSL \rightarrow X_{\boxed{1}}\, X_{\boxed{2}} / X_{\boxed{1}}\, X_{\boxed{2}}$
$XSR \rightarrow X_{\boxed{1}}\, X_{\boxed{2}} / X_{\boxed{1}}\, X_{\boxed{2}}$

Switching Expansion

$X \rightarrow XSL_{\boxed{1}}\, XSR_{\boxed{2}} / XSR_{\boxed{2}}\, XSL_{\boxed{1}}$
$XSL \rightarrow XSL_{\boxed{1}}\, XSR_{\boxed{2}} / XSR_{\boxed{2}}\, XSL_{\boxed{1}}$
$XSR \rightarrow XSL_{\boxed{1}}\, XSR_{\boxed{2}} / XSR_{\boxed{2}}\, XSL_{\boxed{1}}$

Phrase-Pair Emission

$X \rightarrow e/f$
$XSL \rightarrow e\ /\ f$
$XSR \rightarrow e\ /\ f$

Figure 3: Lexicalised-Reordering SCFG

The reordering information captured by the switch grammar is in a sense orthogonal to that of Hiero-like systems utilising rules such as those listed in section 2. Hiero rules encode hierarchical reordering patterns based on surrounding context. In contrast, the switch grammar models the reordering preferences of the phrase-pairs themselves, similarly to the monotone-swap-discontinuous reordering models of Phrase-based SMT models (Koehn et al., 2003). Furthermore, it strives to match pairs of such preferences, combining together phrase-pairs with compatible reordering preferences.

5 Experiments

In this section we proceed to integrate our estimates within an SCFG-based decoder. We subsequently evaluate our performance in relation to a state-of-the-art Hiero baseline on a French to English translation task.

5.1 Decoding

The joint model of bilingual string derivations provided by the learned SCFG grammar can be used for translation given a input source sentence, since $\arg\max_e p(e|f) = \arg\max_e p(e, f)$. We use our learned stochastic SCFG grammar with the decoding component of the Joshua SCFG toolkit (Li et al., 2009). The full translation model interpolates log-linearly the probability of a grammar derivation together with the language model probability of the target string. The model is further smoothed, similarly to phrase-based models and the Hiero system, with smoothing features ϕ_i such as the lexical translation scores of the phrase-pairs involved and rule usage penalties. As usual with statistical translation, we aim for retrieving the target sentence e corresponding to the most probable derivation $D \overset{*}{\Rightarrow} (f, e)$ with rules r, with:

$$p(D) \propto p(e)^{\lambda_{lm}} p_{scfg}(e, f)^{\lambda_{scfg}} \prod_i \prod_{r \in D} \phi_i(r)^{\lambda_i}$$

The interpolation weights are tuned using Minimum Error Rate Training (Och, 2003).

5.2 Results

We test empirically the learner's output grammars for translating from French to English, using $k = 5$ for the Cross Validation data partitioning. The training material is a GIZA++ word-aligned corpus of 200K sentence-pairs from the Europarl corpus (Koehn, 2005), with our development and test parallel corpora of 2K sentence-pairs stemming from the same source. Training the grammar parameters until convergence demands around 6 hours on an 8-core 2.26 GHz Intel Xeon system. Decoding employs a 4-gram language model, trained on English Europarl data of 19.5M words, smoothed using modified Kneser-Ney discounting (Chen and Goodman, 1998), and lexical translation smoothing features based on the GIZA++ alignments.

In a sense, the real baseline to which we might compare against should be a system employing the MLE estimate for the grammar extracted from the whole training corpus. However, as we have already discussed, this assigns zero probability to all sentence-pairs outside of the training data and is subsequently bound to perform extremely poorly, as decoding would then completely rely on the smoothing features. Instead, we opt to compare against a hierarchical translation baseline provided by the Joshua toolkit, trained and tuned on the same data as our learning algorithm. The grammar used by the baseline is much richer than the ones learned by our algorithm, also employing rules which translate with context, as shown in section 2. Nevertheless, since it is not clear how the reordering rules probabilities of a grammar similar to the ones we use could be trained heuristically, we choose to relate the performance of our learned stochastic SCFG grammars to the particular, state-of-the-art in SCFG-based translation, system.

Table 1 presents the translation performance results of our systems and the baseline. On first

System	Lexical Smoothing	BLEU
joshua-baseline	No	27.79
plain scfg	No	28.04
switch scfg	No	28.48
joshua-baseline	Yes	29.96
plain scfg	Yes	29.75
switch scfg	Yes	29.88

Table 1: Empirical results, with and without additional lexical translation smoothing features during decoding

observation, it is evident that our learning algorithm outputs stochastic SCFGs which manage to generalise, avoiding the degenerate behaviour of plain MLE training for these models. Given the notoriety of the estimation process, this is noteworthy on its own. Having a learning algorithm at hand which realises in a reasonable extent the potential of each stochastic grammar design (as implemented in the relevant grammar extractors), we can now compare between the two grammar extractors used in our experiments. The results table highlights the importance of conditioning the reordering process on lexical grounds. The plain grammar with the single phrase-pair non-terminal cannot accomplish this and achieves a lower BLEU score. On the other hand, the switch SCFG allows such conditioning. The learner takes advantage of this feature to output a grammar which performs better in taking reordering decisions, something that is reflected in both the actual translations as well as the BLEU score achieved.

Furthermore, our results highlight the importance of the smoothing decoding features. The unsmoothed baseline system itself scores considerably less when employing solely the heuristic translation score. Our unsmoothed switch grammar decoding setup improves on the baseline by a considerable difference of 0.7 BLEU. Subsequently, when adding the smoothing lexical translation features, both systems record a significant increase in performance, reaching comparable levels of performance.

The degenerate behaviour of MLE for SCFGs can be greatly limited by constraining ourselves to grammars employing *minimal* phrase-pairs ; phrase-pairs which cannot be further broken down into smaller ones according to the word-alignment. One could argue that it is enough to perform plain MLE with such minimal phrase-pair SCFGs, instead of using our more elaborate learning algorithm with phrase-pairs of all lengths. To investigate this, for our final experiment we used a plain MLE estimate of the switch grammar to translate, limiting the grammar's phrase-pair emission rules to only those which involve minimal phrase-pairs. The very low score of 17.82 BLEU (without lexical smoothing) not only highlights the performance gains of using longer phrase-pairs in hierarchical translation models, but most importantly provides a strong incentive to address the overfitting behaviour of MLE estimators for such models, instead of avoiding it.

6 Related work

Most learning of phrase-based models, e.g., (Marcu and Wong, 2002; DeNero et al., 2006; Mylonakis and Sima'an, 2008), works without hierarchical components (i.e., not based on the explicit learning of an SCFG/BITG). These learning problems pose other kinds of learning challenges than the ones posed by explicit learning of SCFGs. Chiang's original work (Chiang, 2007) is also related. Yet, the learning problem is not expressed in terms of an explicit objective function because surface heuristic counts are used. It has been very difficult to match the performance of Chiang's model without use of these heuristic counts.

A somewhat related work, (Blunsom et al., 2008b), attempts learning new non-terminal labels for synchronous productions in order to improve translation. This work differs substantially from our work because it employs a heuristic estimate for the phrase pair probabilities, thereby concentrating on a different learning problem: that of refining the grammar symbols. Our approach might also benefit from such a refinement but we do not attempt this problem here. In contrast, (Blunsom et al., 2008a) works with the expanded phrase pair set of (Chiang, 2005), formulating an exponential model and concentrating on marginalising out the latent segmentation variables. Again, the learning problem is rather different from ours. Similarly, the work in (Zhang et al., 2008) reports on a multi-stage model, *without* a latent segmentation variable, but with a strong prior preferring sparse estimates embedded in a Variational Bayes (VB) estimator. This work concentrates the efforts on pruning both the space of phrase pairs and the space of (ITG) analyses.

To the best of our knowledge, this work is the first to attempt learning probabilistic phrase-based BITGs as translation models in a setting where both a phrase segmentation component and a hierarchical reordering component are assumed latent variables. Like this work, (Mylonakis and Sima'an, 2008; DeNero et al., 2008) also employ an all-phrases model. Our paper shows that it is possible to train such huge grammars under iterative schemes like CV-EM, without need for sampling or pruning. At the surface of it, our CV-EM estimator is also a kind of Bayesian learner, but in reality it is a more specific form of regularisation, similar to smoothing techniques used in language modelling (Chen and Goodman, 1998; Mackay and Petoy, 1995).

7 Discussion and Future Research

Phrase-based stochastic SCFGs provide a rich formalism to express translation phenomena, which has been shown to offer competitive performance in practice. Since learning SCFGs for machine translation has proven notoriously difficult, most successful SCFG models for SMT rely on rules extracted from word-alignment patterns and heuristically computed rule scores, with the impact and the limits imposed by these choices yet unknown.

Some of the reasons behind the challenges of SCFG learning can be traced back to the introduction of latent variables at different, competing levels: word and phrase-alignment as well as hierarchical reordering structure, with larger phrase-pairs reducing the need for extensive reordering structure and vice versa. While imposing priors such as the often used Dirichlet distribution or the Dirichlet Process provides a method to overcome these pitfalls, we believe that the data-driven regularisation employed in this work provides an effective alternative to them, focusing more on the data instead of importing generic external human knowledge.

We believe that this work makes a significant step towards learning synchronous grammars for SMT. This is an objective not only worthy because of promises of increased performance, but, most importantly, also by increasing the depth of our understanding on SCFGs as vehicles of latent translation structures. Our usage of the induced grammars directly for translation, instead of an intermediate task such as phrase-alignment, aims exactly at this.

While the latent structures that we explored in this paper were relatively simple in comparison with Hiero-like SCFGs, they take a different, content-driven approach on learning reordering preferences than the context-driven approach of Hiero. We believe that these approaches are not merely orthogonal, but could also prove complementary. Taking advantage of the possible synergies between content and context-driven reordering learning is an appealing direction of future research. This is particularly promising for other language pairs, such as Chinese to English, where Hiero-like grammars have been shown to perform particularly well.

Acknowledgments: Both authors are supported by a VIDI grant (nr. 639.022.604) from The Netherlands Organization for Scientific Research (NWO).

References

P. Blunsom, T. Cohn, and M. Osborne. 2008a. A discriminative latent variable model for statistical machine translation. In *Proceedings of ACL-08: HLT*, pages 200–208. Association for Computational Linguistics.

Phil Blunsom, Trevor Cohn, and Miles Osborne. 2008b. Bayesian synchronous grammar induction. In *Advances in Neural Information Processing Systems 21*, Vancouver, Canada, December.

Phil Blunsom, Trevor Cohn, Chris Dyer, and Miles Osborne. 2009. A gibbs sampler for phrasal synchronous grammar induction. In *Proceedings of the 47th Annual Meeting of the Association of Computational Linguistics*, Singapore, August. Association for Computational Linguistics.

R. Bod, R. Scha, and K. Sima'an, editors. 2003. *Data Oriented Parsing*. CSLI Publications, Stanford University, Stanford, California, USA.

S. Chen and J. Goodman. 1998. *An empirical study of smoothing techniques for language modeling*. Technical Report TR-10-98, Harvard University, August.

D. Chiang. 2005. A hierarchical phrase-based model for statistical machine translation. In *Proceedings of ACL 2005*, pages 263–270.

David Chiang. 2007. Hierarchical phrase-based translation. *Computational Linguistics*, 33.

J. DeNero, D. Gillick, J. Zhang, and D. Klein. 2006. Why generative phrase models underperform surface heuristics. In *Proceedings on the Workshop on Statistical Machine Translation*, pages 31–38, New York City. Association for Computational Linguistics.

John DeNero, Alexandre Bouchard-Côté, and Dan Klein. 2008. Sampling alignment structure under a Bayesian translation model. In *Proceedings of the 2008 Conference on Empirical Methods in Natural Language Processing*, pages 314–323, Honolulu, Hawaii, October. Association for Computational Linguistics.

T. Hastie, R. Tibshirani, and J. H. Friedman. 2001. *The Elements of Statistical Learning*. Springer.

Tom Heskes. 1998. Bias/variance decompositions for likelihood-based estimators. *Neural Computation*, 10:1425–1433.

P. Koehn, F. J. Och, and D. Marcu. 2003. Statistical phrase-based translation. In *HLT-NAACL 2003*.

P. Koehn. 2005. Europarl: A Parallel Corpus for Statistical Machine Translation. In *MT Summit 2005*.

Zhifei Li, Chris Callison-Burch, Chris Dyer, Sanjeev Khudanpur, Lane Schwartz, Wren Thornton, Jonathan Weese, and Omar Zaidan. 2009. Joshua: An open source toolkit for parsing-based machine translation. In *Proceedings of the Fourth Workshop on Statistical Machine Translation*, pages 135–139, Athens, Greece, March. Association for Computational Linguistics.

David J. C. Mackay and Linda C. Bauman Petoy. 1995. A hierarchical dirichlet language model. *Natural Language Engineering*, 1:1–19.

D. Marcu and W. Wong. 2002. A phrase-based, joint probability model for statistical machine translation. In *Proceedings of Empirical methods in natural language processing*, pages 133–139. Association for Computational Linguistics.

Markos Mylonakis and Khalil Sima'an. 2008. Phrase translation probabilities with itg priors and smoothing as learning objective. In *Proceedings of the 2008 Conference on Empirical Methods in Natural Language Processing*, pages 630–639, Honolulu, USA, October.

F. J. Och and H. Ney. 2003. A systematic comparison of various statistical alignment models. *Computational Linguistics*, 29(1):19–51.

F. J. Och and H. Ney. 2004. The alignment template approach to statistical machine translation. *Computational Linguistics*, 30(4):417–449.

Franz Josef Och. 2003. Minimum error rate training in statistical machine translation. In *Proceedings of the 41st Annual Meeting of the Association for Computational Linguistics*, pages 160–167, Sapporo, Japan, July. Association for Computational Linguistics.

D. Wu. 1997. Stochastic inversion transduction grammars and bilingual parsing of parallel corpora. *Computational Linguistics*, 23(3):377–403.

H. Zhang, Ch. Quirk, R. C. Moore, and D. Gildea. 2008. Bayesian learning of non-compositional phrases with synchronous parsing. In *Proceedings of ACL-08: HLT*, pages 97–105, Columbus, Ohio, June. Association for Computational Linguistics.

A. Zollmann and K. Sima'an. 2006. An efficient and consistent estimator for data-oriented parsing. *Journal of Automata, Languages and Combinatorics (JALC)*, 10 (2005) Number 2/3:367–388.

Andreas Zollmann and Ashish Venugopal. 2006. Syntax augmented machine translation via chart parsing. In *Proceedings on the Workshop on Statistical Machine Translation*, pages 138–141, New York City, June. Association for Computational Linguistics.

A Semi-Supervised Batch-Mode Active Learning Strategy for Improved Statistical Machine Translation

Sankaranarayanan Ananthakrishnan, Rohit Prasad, David Stallard and Prem Natarajan
BBN Technologies
10 Moulton Street
Cambridge, MA, U.S.A.
{sanantha,rprasad,stallard,prem}@bbn.com

Abstract

The availability of substantial, in-domain parallel corpora is critical for the development of high-performance statistical machine translation (SMT) systems. Such corpora, however, are expensive to produce due to the labor intensive nature of manual translation. We propose to alleviate this problem with a novel, semi-supervised, batch-mode *active learning* strategy that attempts to maximize in-domain coverage by selecting sentences, which represent a balance between domain match, translation difficulty, and batch diversity. Simulation experiments on an English-to-Pashto translation task show that the proposed strategy not only outperforms the random selection baseline, but also traditional active learning techniques based on dissimilarity to existing training data. Our approach achieves a relative improvement of 45.9% in BLEU over the seed baseline, while the closest competitor gained only 24.8% with the same number of selected sentences.

1 Introduction

Rapid development of statistical machine translation (SMT) systems for resource-poor language pairs is a problem of significant interest to the research community in academia, industry, and government. Tight turn-around schedules, budget restrictions, and scarcity of human translators preclude the production of large parallel corpora, which form the backbone of SMT systems.

Given these constraints, the focus is on making the best possible use of available resources. This usually involves some form of prioritized data collection. In other words, one would like to construct the smallest possible parallel training corpus that achieves a desired level of performance on unseen test data.

Within an *active learning* framework, this can be cast as a data selection problem. The goal is to choose, for manual translation, the most informative instances from a large *pool* of source language sentences. The resulting sentence pairs, in combination with any existing in-domain *seed* parallel corpus, are expected to provide a significantly higher performance gain than a naïve random selection strategy. This process is repeated until a certain level of performance is attained.

Previous work on active learning for SMT has focused on unsupervised dissimilarity measures for sentence selection. Eck et al. (2005) describe a selection strategy that attempts to maximize coverage by choosing sentences with the highest proportion of previously unseen n-grams. However, if the pool is not completely in-domain, this strategy may select irrelevant sentences, whose translations are unlikely to improve performance on an in-domain test set. They also propose a technique, based on TF-IDF, to de-emphasize sentences similar to those that have already been selected. However, this strategy is bootstrapped by random initial choices that do not necessarily favor sentences that are difficult to translate. Finally, they work exclusively with the source language and do not use any SMT-derived features to guide selection.

Haffari et al. (2009) propose a number of features, such as similarity to the seed corpus, translation probability, relative frequencies of n-grams and "phrases" in the seed vs. pool data, etc., for active learning. While many of their experiments use the above features independently to compare their relative efficacy, one of their experiments attempts to predict a rank, as a linear combination of these features, for each candidate sentence. The top-ranked sentences are chosen for manual translation. The latter strategy is particularly relevant to this paper, because the goal of our active

Proceedings of the Fourteenth Conference on Computational Natural Language Learning, pages 126–134,
Uppsala, Sweden, 15-16 July 2010.

learning strategy is not to compare features, but to learn the trade-off between various characteristics of the candidate sentences that potentially maximizes translation improvement.

The parameters of the linear ranking model proposed by Haffari et al. (2009) are trained using two held-out development sets $\mathbf{D_1}$ and $\mathbf{D_2}$ - the model attempts to learn the ordering of $\mathbf{D_1}$ that incrementally maximizes translation performance on $\mathbf{D_2}$. Besides the need for multiple parallel corpora and the computationally intensive nature of incrementally retraining an SMT system, their approach suffers from another major deficiency. It requires that the pool have the same distributional characteristics as the development sets used to train the ranking model. Additionally, they select all sentences that constitute a batch in a single operation following the ranking procedure. Since similar or identical sentences in the pool will typically meet the selection criteria simultaneously, this can have the undesired effect of choosing redundant batches with low diversity. This results in under-utilization of human translation resources.

In this paper, we propose a novel batch-mode active learning strategy that ameliorates the above issues. Our semi-supervised learning approach combines a parallel ranking strategy with several features, including domain representativeness, translation confidence, and batch diversity. The proposed approach includes a greedy, incremental batch selection strategy, which encourages diversity and reduces redundancy. The following sections detail our active learning approach, including the experimental setup and simulation results that clearly demonstrate its effectiveness.

2 Active Learning Paradigm

Active learning has been studied extensively in the context of multi-class labeling problems, and theoretically optimal selection strategies have been identified for simple classification tasks with metric features (Freund et al., 1997). However, natural language applications such as SMT present a significantly higher level of complexity. For instance, SMT model parameters (translation rules, language model n-grams, etc.) are not fixed in number or type, and vary depending on the training instances. This gives rise to the concept of *domain*. Even large quantities of out-of-domain training data usually do not improve translation performance. As we will see, this causes simple active selection techniques based on dissimilarity or translation difficulty to be ineffective, because they tend to favor out-of-domain sentences.

Our proposed active learning strategy is motivated by the idea that the chosen sentences should maximize coverage, and by extension, translation performance on an unseen test set. It should pick sentences that represent the target domain, while simultaneously enriching the training data with hitherto unseen, difficult-to-translate constructs that are likely to improve performance on a test set. We refer to the former as *representativeness* and to the latter as *difficulty*.

Since it is computationally prohibitive to retrain an SMT system for individual translation pairs, a batch of sentences is usually selected at each iteration. We desire that each batch be sufficiently *diverse*; this increases the number of concepts (phrase pairs, translation rules, etc.) that can be learned from manual translations of a selected batch. Thus, our active learning strategy attempts, at each iteration, to select a batch of mutually diverse source sentences, which, while introducing new concepts, shares at least some commonality with the target domain. This is done in a completely statistical, data-driven fashion.

In designing this active learning paradigm, we make the following assumptions.

- A small seed parallel corpus $\mathbf{S}$ is available for training an initial SMT system. This may range from a few hundred to a few thousand sentence pairs.
- Sentences must be selected from a large pool $\mathbf{P}$. This may be an arbitrary collection of in- and out-of-domain source language sentences. Some measure of redundancy is permitted and expected, i.e. some sentences may be identical or very similar to others.
- A development set $\mathbf{D}$ is available to tune the SMT system and train the selection algorithm. An unseen test set $\mathbf{T}$ is used to evaluate it.
- The seed, development, and test sets are derived from the target domain distribution.

To re-iterate, we do not assume or require the pool to have the same domain distribution as the seed, development, and test sets. This reflects a real-world scenario, where the pool may be drawn from multiple sources (e.g. targeted collections, newswire text, web, etc.). This is a key departure from existing work on active learning for SMT.

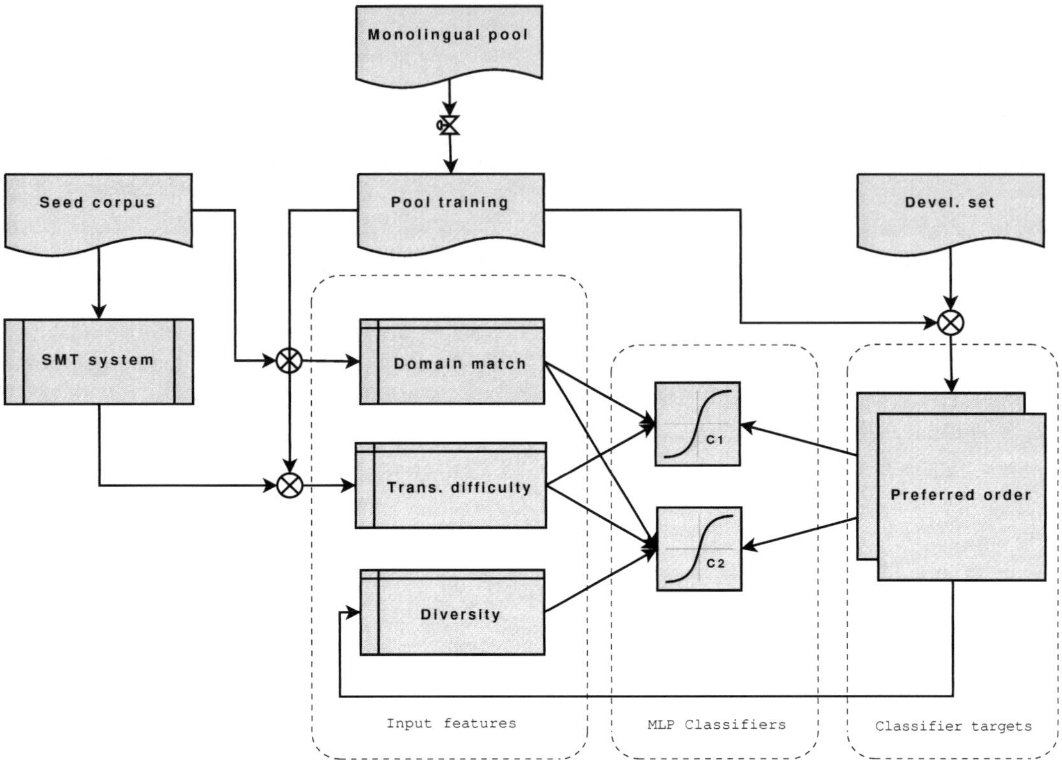

Figure 1: Flow-diagram of the active learner.

3 Active Learning Architecture

Figure 1 illustrates the proposed active learning architecture in the form of a high-level flow-diagram. We begin by randomly sampling a small fraction of the large monolingual pool $\mathbf{P}$ to create a *pool training set* $\mathbf{P_T}$, which is used to train the learner. The remainder, which we call the *pool evaluation set* $\mathbf{P_E}$, is set aside for active selection. We also train an initial phrase-based SMT system (Koehn et al., 2003) with the available seed corpus. The pool training set $\mathbf{P_T}$, in conjunction with the seed corpus $\mathbf{S}$, initial SMT system, and held-out development set $\mathbf{D}$, is used to derive a number of input features as well as target labels for training two parallel classifiers.

3.1 Preferred Ordering

The learner must be able to map input features to an ordering of the pool sentences that attempts to maximize coverage on an unseen test set. We teach it to do this by providing it with an ordering of $\mathbf{P_T}$ that incrementally maximizes source coverage on $\mathbf{D}$. This *preferred ordering* algorithm incrementally maps sentences in $\mathbf{P_T}$ to a ordered set $\mathbf{O_T}$ by picking, at each iteration, the sentence with the highest *coverage criterion* with respect to $\mathbf{D}$, and inserting it at the current position within $\mathbf{O_T}$. The coverage criterion is based on content-word n-gram overlap with $\mathbf{D}$, discounted by constructs already observed in $\mathbf{S}$ and higher-ranked sentences in $\mathbf{O_T}$, as illustrated in Algorithm 1. Our hypothesis is that sentences, which maximally improve coverage, likely lead to bigger gains in translation performance as well.

The $O(|\mathbf{P_T}|^2)$ complexity of this algorithm is one reason we restrict $\mathbf{P_T}$ to a few thousand sentences. Another reason not to order the entire pool and simply select the top-ranked sentences, is that batches thus constructed would overfit the development set on which the ordering is based, and not generalize well to an unseen test set.

3.2 Ranker Features

Each candidate sentence in the pool is represented by a vector of features, which fall under one of the three categories, viz. representativeness, difficulty, and diversity. We refer to the first two as *context-independent*, because they can be computed independently for each sentence. Diversity is a *context-dependent* feature and must be evaluated in the context of an ordering of sentences.

Algorithm 1 Preferred ordering

$\mathbf{O_T} \leftarrow ()$
$S_g \leftarrow \text{count}(g) \quad \forall g \in \text{ngr}(\mathbf{S})$
$D_g \leftarrow \text{count}(g) \quad \forall g \in \text{ngr}(\mathbf{D})$
for $k = 1$ to $|\mathbf{P_T}|$ **do**
  $\mathbf{P_U} \leftarrow \mathbf{P_T} - \mathbf{O_T}$
  $y^* \leftarrow \arg\max_{y \in \mathbf{P_U}} \sum_{g \in \text{ngr}(y)} \frac{y_g \times D_g \times n}{S_g + 1}$
  $O_T(k) \leftarrow y^*$
  $S_g \leftarrow S_g + y^*_g \quad \forall g \in \text{ngr}(y^*)$
end for
return $\mathbf{O_T}$

3.2.1 Domain Representativeness

Domain representativeness features gauge the degree of similarity between a candidate pool sentence and the seed training data. We quantify this using an n-gram overlap measure between candidate sentence x and the seed corpus $\mathbf{S}$ defined by Equation 1.

$$sim(x, \mathbf{S}) = \frac{\sum_{g \in \text{ngr}(x)} x_g \times \frac{min(S_g^n, C_n)}{C_n}}{\sum_{g \in \text{ngr}(x)} x_g} \quad (1)$$

x_g is the number of times n-gram g occurs in x, S_g the number of times it occurs in the seed corpus, n its length in words, and C_n the count of n-grams of length n in $\mathbf{S}$. Longer n-grams that occur frequently in the seed receive high similarity scores, and vice-versa. In evaluating this feature, we only consider n-grams up to length five that contain least one content word.

Another simple domain similarity feature we use is sentence length. Sentences in conversational domains are typically short, while those in web and newswire domains run longer.

3.2.2 Translation Difficulty

All else being equal, the selection strategy should favor sentences that the existing SMT system finds difficult to translate. To this end, we estimate a confidence score for each SMT hypothesis, using a discriminative classification framework reminiscent of Blatz et al. (2004). Confidence estimation is treated as a binary classification problem, where each hypothesized word is labeled "*correct*" or "*incorrect*". Word-level reference labels for training the classifier are obtained from Translation Edit Rate (TER) analysis, which produces the lowest-cost alignment between the hypotheses and the gold-standard references (Snover et al., 2006). A hypothesized word is "*correct*" if it aligns to itself in this alignment, and "*incorrect*" otherwise.

We derive features for confidence estimation from the phrase derivations used by the decoder in generating the hypotheses. For each target word, we look up the corresponding source phrase that produced it, and use this information to compute a number of features from the translation phrase table and target language model (LM). These include the in-context LM probability of the target word, the forward and reverse phrase translation probabilities, the maximum forward and reverse word-level lexical translation probabilities, number of competing target phrases in which the target word occurs, etc. In all, we use 11 word-level features (independent of the active learning features) to train the classifier in conjunction with the abovementioned binary reference labels.

A logistic regression model is used to directly estimate the posterior probability of the binary word label. Thus, our confidence score is essentially the probability of the word being "*incorrect*". Sentence-level confidence is computed as the geometric average of word-level posteriors. Confidence estimation models are trained on the held-out development set.

We employ two additional measures of translation difficulty for active learning: (a) the number of "unknown" words in target hypotheses caused by untranslatable source words, and (b) the average length of source phrases in the 1-best SMT decoder derivations.

3.2.3 Batch Diversity

Batch diversity is evaluated in the context of an explicit ordering of the candidate sentences. In general, sentences that are substantially similar to those above them in a ranked list have low diversity, and vice-versa. We use content-word n-gram overlap to measure similarity with previous sentences, per Equation 2.

$$d(b \mid \mathbf{B}) = 1.0 - \frac{\sum_{g \in \text{ngr}(b)} n \times B_g}{\sum_{g \in \text{ngr}(b)} n \times max(B_g, 1.0)} \quad (2)$$

$\mathbf{B}$ represents the set of sentences ranked higher than the candidate b, for which we wish to evaluate diversity. B_g is the number of times n-gram g

occurs in $\mathbf{B}$. Longer, previously unseen n-grams serve to boost diversity. The first sentence in a given ordering is always assigned unit diversity. The coverage criterion used by the preferred ordering algorithm in Section 3.1 ensures good correspondence between the rank of a sentence and its diversity, i.e. higher-ranked in-domain sentences have higher diversity, and vice-versa.

3.3 Training the Learner

The active learner is trained on the pool training set $\mathbf{P_T}$. The seed training corpus $\mathbf{S}$ serves as the basis for extracting domain similarity features for each sentence in this set. Translation difficulty features are evaluated by decoding sentences in $\mathbf{P_T}$ with the seed SMT system. Finally, we compute diversity for each sentence in $\mathbf{P_T}$ based on its preferred order $\mathbf{O_T}$ according to Equation 2. Learning is *semi-supervised* as it does not require translation references for either $\mathbf{P_T}$ or $\mathbf{D}$.

Traditional ranking algorithms such as `PRank` (Crammer and Singer, 2001) work best when the number of ranks is much smaller than the sample size; more than one sample can be assigned the same rank. In the active learning problem, however, each sample is associated with a unique rank. Moreover, the dynamic range of ranks in $\mathbf{O_T}$ is significantly smaller than that in $\mathbf{P_E}$, to which the ranking model is applied, resulting in a mismatch between training and evaluation conditions.

We overcome these issues by re-casting the ranking problem as a binary classification task. The top 10% sentences in $\mathbf{O_T}$ are assigned a "*select*" label, while the remaining are assigned a contrary "*do-not-select*" label. The input features are mapped to class posterior probabilities using multi-layer perceptron (MLP) classifiers. The use of posteriors allows us to assign a unique rank to each candidate sentence. The best candidate sentence is the one to which the classifier assigns the highest posterior probability for the "*select*" label. We use one hidden layer with eight sigmoid-activated nodes in this implementation.

Note that we actually train two MLP classifiers with different sets of input features as shown in Figure 1. Classifier $\mathcal{C}_1$ is trained using only the context-independent features, whereas $\mathcal{C}_2$ is trained with the full set of features including batch diversity. These classifiers are used to implement an incremental, greedy selection algorithm with parallel ranking, as explained below.

Algorithm 2 Incremental greedy selection

> $\mathbf{B} \leftarrow ()$
> **for** $k = 1$ to N **do**
> $\quad \mathbf{P_{ci}} \leftarrow \{x \in \mathbf{P_E} \mid d(x \mid \mathbf{B}) = 1.0\}$
> $\quad \mathbf{P_{cd}} \leftarrow \{x \in \mathbf{P_E} \mid d(x \mid \mathbf{B}) < 1.0\}$
> $\quad \mathbf{C} \leftarrow \mathcal{C}_1(f_{ci}(\mathbf{P_{ci}})) \cup \mathcal{C}_2(f_{cd}(\mathbf{P_{cd}}, \mathbf{B}))$
> $\quad b_k \leftarrow \arg\max_{x \in \mathbf{P_E}} \mathbf{C}(x)$
> $\quad \mathbf{P_E} \leftarrow \mathbf{P_E} - \{b_k\}$
> **end for**
> **return** $\mathbf{B}$

4 Incremental Greedy Selection

Traditional rank-and-select batch construction approaches choose constituent sentences independently, and therefore cannot ensure that the chosen sentences are sufficiently diverse. Our strategy implements a greedy selection algorithm that constructs each batch iteratively; the decision b_k (the sentence to fill the kth position in a batch) depends on all previous decisions $b_1, \cdots, b_{k-1}$. This allows de-emphasizing sentences similar to those that have already been placed in the batch, while favoring samples containing previously unseen constructs.

4.1 Parallel Ranking

We begin with an empty batch $\mathbf{B}$, to which sentences from the pool evaluation set $\mathbf{P_E}$ must be added. We then partition the sentences in $\mathbf{P_E}$ in two mutually-exclusive groups $\mathbf{P_{cd}}$ and $\mathbf{P_{ci}}$. The former contains candidates that share at least one content-word n-gram with any existing sentences in $\mathbf{B}$, while the latter consists of sentences that do not share any overlap with them. Note that $\mathbf{B}$ is empty to start with; thus, $\mathbf{P_{cd}}$ is empty and $\mathbf{P_{ci}} = \mathbf{P_E}$ at the beginning of the first iteration of selection. The diversity feature is computed for each sentence in $\mathbf{P_{cd}}$ based on existing selections in $\mathbf{B}$, while the context-independent features are evaluated for sentences in both partitions.

Next, we apply $\mathcal{C}_1$ to $\mathbf{P_{ci}}$ and $\mathcal{C}_2$ to $\mathbf{P_{cd}}$ and independently obtain posterior probabilities for the "*select*" label for both partitions. We take the union of class posteriors from both partitions and select the sentence with the highest probability of the "*select*" label to fill the next slot b_k, corresponding to iteration k, in the batch. The selected sentence is subsequently removed from $\mathbf{P_E}$.

The above *parallel ranking* technique (Algorithm 2) is applied iteratively until the batch reaches a pre-determined size N. At iteration k, the remaining sentences in $\mathbf{P_E}$ are partitioned based on overlap with previous selections $b_1, \cdots, b_{k-1}$ and ranked based on the union of posterior probabilities generated by the corresponding classifiers. This ensures that sentences substantially similar to those that have already been selected receive a low diversity score, and are suitably de-emphasized. Depending on the characteristics of the pool, batches constructed by this algorithm are likely more diverse than a simple rank-and-select approach.

5 Experimental Setup and Results

We demonstrate the effectiveness of the proposed sentence selection algorithm by performing a set of simulation experiments in the context of an English-to-Pashto (E2P) translation task. We simulate a low-resource condition by using a very small number of training sentence pairs, sampled from the collection, to bootstrap a phrase-based SMT system. The remainder of this parallel corpus is set aside as the pool.

At each iteration, the selection algorithm picks a fixed-size batch of source sentences from the pool. The seed training data are augmented with the chosen source sentences and their translations. A new set of translation models is then estimated and used to decode the test set. We track SMT performance across several iterations and compare the proposed algorithm to a random selection baseline as well as other common selection strategies.

5.1 Data Configuration

Our English-Pashto data originates from a two-way collection of spoken dialogues, and thus consists of two parallel sub-corpora: a directional E2P corpus and a directional Pashto-to-English (P2E) corpus. Each sub-corpus has its own independent training, development, and test partitions. The directional E2P training, development, and test sets consist of 33.9k, 2.4k, and 1.1k sentence pairs, respectively. The directional P2E training set consists of 76.5k sentence pairs.

We obtain a seed training corpus for the simulation experiments by randomly sampling 1,000 sentence pairs from the directional E2P training partition. The remainder of this set, and the entire reversed directional P2E training partition are combined to create the pool (109.4k sentence pairs). In the past, we have observed that the reversed directional P2E data gives very little performance gain in the E2P direction even though its vocabulary is similar, and can be considered "out-of-domain" as far as the E2P translation task is concerned. Thus, our pool consists of 30% in-domain and 70% out-of-domain sentence pairs, making for a challenging active learning problem. A pool training set of 10k source sentences is sampled from this collection, leaving us with 99.4k candidate sentences.

5.2 Selection Strategies

We implement the following strategies for sentence selection. In all cases, we use a fixed-size batch of 200 sentences per iteration.

- *Random selection*, in which source sentences are uniformly sampled from $\mathbf{P_E}$.
- *Similarity selection*, where we choose sentences that exhibit the highest content-word n-gram overlap with $\mathbf{S}$.
- *Dissimilarity selection*, which selects sentences having the lowest degree of content-word n-gram overlap with $\mathbf{S}$.
- *Active learning* with greedy incremental selection, using a learner to maximize coverage by combining various input features.

We simulate a total of 30 iterations, with the original 1,000 sample seed corpus growing to 7,000 sentence pairs.

5.3 Simulation Results

We track SMT performance at each iteration in two ways. The first and most effective method is to simply use an objective measure of translation quality, such as BLEU (Papineni et al., 2001). Figure 2(a) illustrates the variation in BLEU scores across iterations for each selection strategy. We note that the proposed active learning strategy performs significantly better at every iteration than random, similarity, and dissimilarity-based selection. At the end of 30 iterations, the BLEU score gained 2.46 points, a relative improvement of 45.9%. By contrast, the nearest competitor was the random selection baseline, whose performance gained only 1.33 points in BLEU, a 24.8% improvement. Note that we tune the phrase-based SMT feature weights using MERT (Och, 2003) once in the beginning, and use the same weights across all iterations. This allowed us to compare selection methods without variations introduced by fluctuation of the weights.

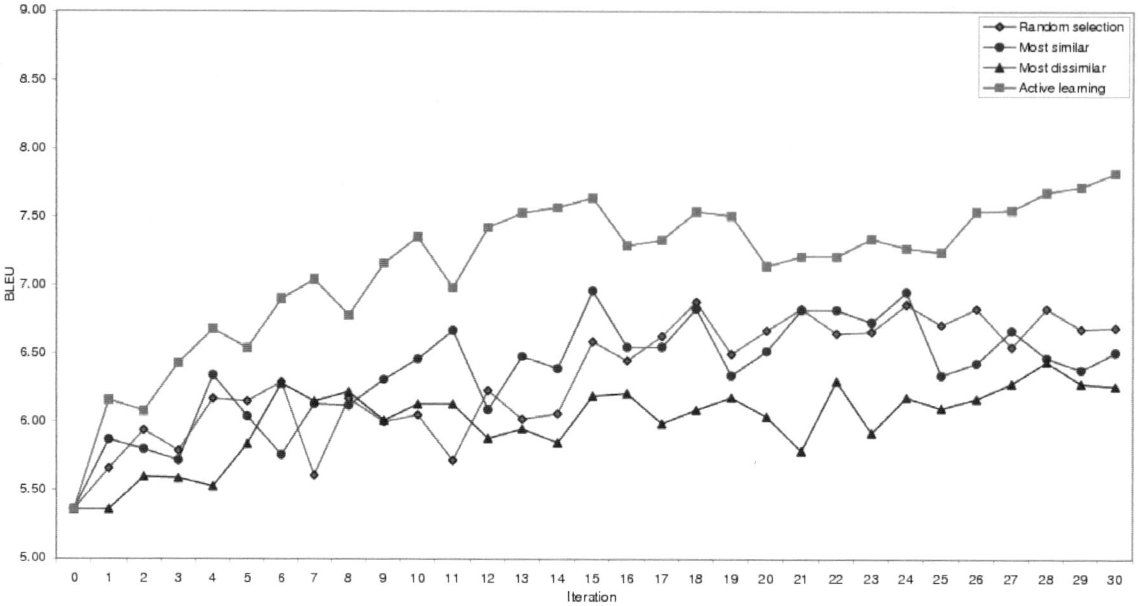

(a) Trajectory of BLEU

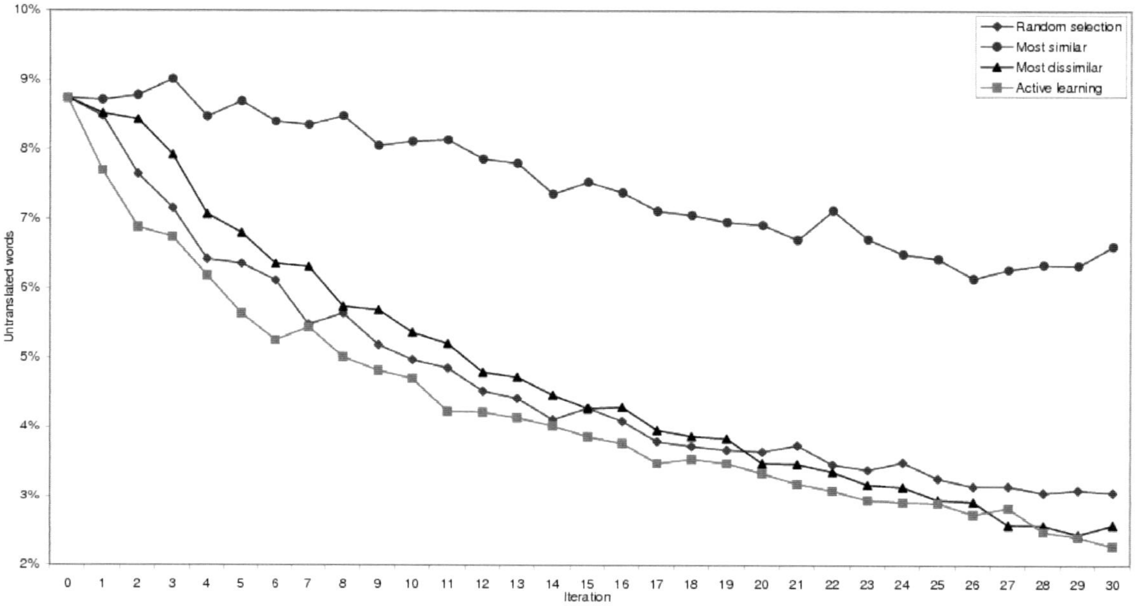

(b) Trajectory of untranslated word ratio

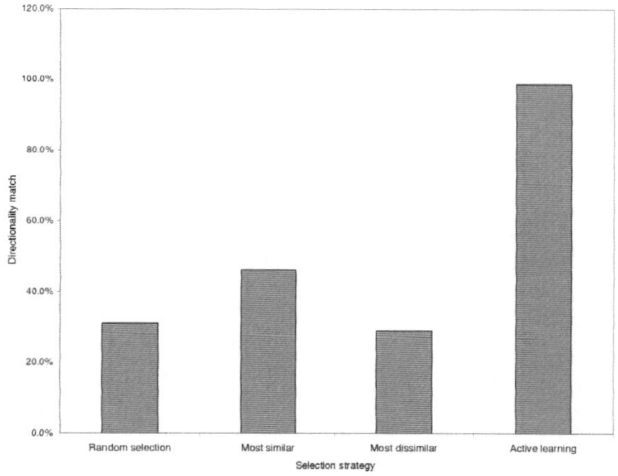

(c) Directionality match

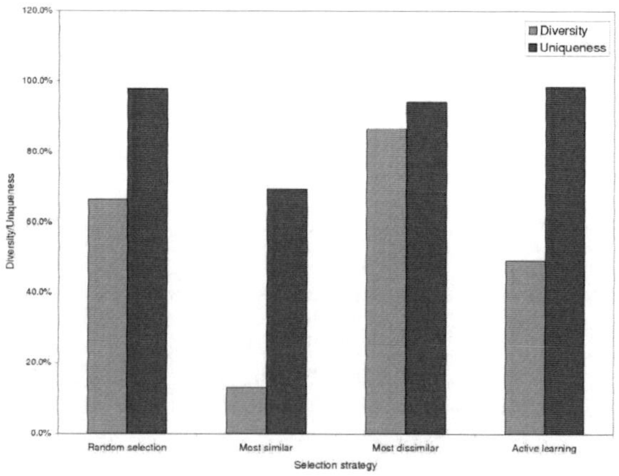

(d) Diversity/Uniqueness

Figure 2: Simulation results for data selection. Batch size at each iteration is 200 sentences.

The second method measures test set coverage in terms of the proportion of untranslated words in the SMT hypotheses, which arise due to the absence of appropriate in-context phrase pairs in the training data. Figure 2(b) shows the variation in this measure for the four selection techniques. Again, the proposed active learning algorithm outperforms its competitors across nearly all iterations, with very large improvements in the initial stages. Overall, the proportion of untranslated words dropped from 8.74% to 2.28% after 30 iterations, while the closest competitor (dissimilarity selection) dropped to 2.59%.

It is also instructive to compare the distribution of the 6,000 sentences selected by each strategy at the end of the simulation to determine whether they came from the "in-domain" E2P set or the "out-of-domain" P2E collection. Figure 2(c) demonstrates that only 1.3% of sentences were selected from the reversed P2E set by the proposed active learning strategy. On the other hand, 70.9% of the sentences selected by the dissimilarity-based technique came from the P2E collection, explaining its low BLEU scores on the E2P test set. Surprisingly, similarity selection also chose a large fraction of sentences from the P2E collection; this was traced to a uniform distribution of very common sentences (e.g. "*thank you*", "*okay*", etc.) across the E2P and P2E sets.

Figure 2(d) compares the uniqueness and overall n-gram diversity of the 6,000 sentences chosen by each strategy. The similarity selector received the lowest score on this scale, explaining the lack of improvement in coverage as measured by the proportion of untranslated words in the SMT hypotheses. Again, the proposed approach exhibits the highest degree of uniqueness, underscoring its value in lowering batch redundancy.

It is interesting to note that dissimilarity selection is closest to the proposed active learning strategy in terms of coverage, and yet exhibits the worst BLEU scores. This confirms that, while there is overlap in their vocabularies, the E2P and P2E sets differ significantly in terms of longer-span constructs that influence SMT performance.

These results clearly demonstrate the power of the proposed strategy in choosing diverse, in-domain sentences that not only provide superior performance in terms of BLEU, but also improve coverage, leading to fewer untranslated concepts in the SMT hypotheses.

6 Conclusion and Future Directions

Rapid development of SMT systems for resource-poor language pairs requires judicious use of human translation capital. We described a novel active learning strategy that automatically learns to pick, from a large monolingual pool, sentences that maximize in-domain coverage. In conjunction with their translations, they are expected to improve SMT performance at a significantly faster rate than existing selection techniques.

We introduced two key ideas that distinguish our approach from previous work. First, we utilize a sample of the candidate pool, rather than an additional in-domain development set, to learn the mapping between the features and the sentences that maximize coverage. This removes the restriction that the pool be derived from the target domain distribution; it can be an arbitrary collection of in- and out-of-domain sentences.

Second, we construct batches using an incremental, greedy selection strategy with parallel ranking, instead of a traditional batch rank-and-select approach. This reduces redundancy, allowing more concepts to be covered in a given batch, and making better use of available resources.

We showed through simulation experiments that the proposed strategy selects diverse batches of high-impact, in-domain sentences that result in a much more rapid improvement in translation performance than random and dissimilarity-based selection. This is reflected in objective indicators of translation quality (BLEU), and in terms of coverage as measured by the proportion of untranslated words in SMT hypotheses. We plan to evaluate the scalability of our approach by running simulations on a number of additional language pairs, domains, and corpus sizes.

An issue with iterative active learning in general is the cost of re-training the SMT system for each batch. Small batches provide for smooth performance trajectories and better error recovery at an increased computational cost. We are currently investigating incremental approaches that allow SMT models to be updated online with minimal performance loss compared to full re-training.

Finally, there is no inherent limitation in the proposed framework that ties it to a phrase-based SMT system. With suitable modifications to the input feature set, it can be adapted to work with various SMT architectures, including hierarchical and syntax-based systems.

References

John Blatz, Erin Fitzgerald, George Foster, Simona Gandrabur, Cyril Goutte, Alex Kulesza, Alberto Sanchis, and Nicola Ueffing. 2004. Confidence estimation for machine translation. In *COLING '04: Proceedings of the 20th international conference on Computational Linguistics*, page 315, Morristown, NJ, USA. Association for Computational Linguistics.

Koby Crammer and Yoram Singer. 2001. Pranking with ranking. In *Advances in Neural Information Processing Systems 14*, pages 641–647. MIT Press.

Matthias Eck, Stephan Vogel, and Alex Waibel. 2005. Low cost portability for statistical machine translation based in N-gram frequency and TF-IDF. In *Proceedings of IWSLT*, Pittsburgh, PA, October.

Yoav Freund, H. Sebastian Seung, Eli Shamir, and Naftali Tishby. 1997. Selective sampling using the query by committee algorithm. *Machine Learning*, 28(2-3):133–168.

Gholamreza Haffari, Maxim Roy, and Anoop Sarkar. 2009. Active learning for statistical phrase-based machine translation. In *NAACL '09: Proceedings of Human Language Technologies: The 2009 Annual Conference of the North American Chapter of the Association for Computational Linguistics*, pages 415–423, Morristown, NJ, USA. Association for Computational Linguistics.

Philipp Koehn, Franz Josef Och, and Daniel Marcu. 2003. Statistical phrase-based translation. In *NAACL '03: Proceedings of the 2003 Conference of the North American Chapter of the Association for Computational Linguistics on Human Language Technology*, pages 48–54, Morristown, NJ, USA. Association for Computational Linguistics.

Franz Josef Och. 2003. Minimum error rate training in statistical machine translation. In *ACL '03: Proceedings of the 41st Annual Meeting on Association for Computational Linguistics*, pages 160–167, Morristown, NJ, USA. Association for Computational Linguistics.

Kishore Papineni, Salim Roukos, Todd Ward, and Wei-Jing Zhu. 2001. BLEU: A method for automatic evaluation of machine translation. In *ACL '02: Proceedings of the 40th Annual Meeting on Association for Computational Linguistics*, pages 311–318, Morristown, NJ, USA. Association for Computational Linguistics.

Matthew Snover, Bonnie Dorr, Richard Schwartz, Linnea Micciulla, and John Makhoul. 2006. A study of translation edit rate with targeted human annotation. In *Proceedings AMTA*, pages 223–231, August.

Improving Word Alignment by Semi-supervised Ensemble

Shujian Huang[1], **Kangxi Li**[2], **Xinyu Dai**[1], **Jiajun Chen**[1]
[1]State Key Laboratory for Novel Software Technology at Nanjing University
Nanjing 210093, P.R.China
{huangsj,daixy,chenjj}@nlp.nju.edu.cn
[2]School of Foreign Studies, Nanjing University
Nanjing 210093, P.R.China
richardlkx@126.com

Abstract

Supervised learning has been recently used to improve the performance of word alignment. However, due to the limited amount of labeled data, the performance of "pure" supervised learning, which only used labeled data, is limited. As a result, many existing methods employ features learnt from a large amount of unlabeled data to assist the task. In this paper, we propose a semi-supervised ensemble method to better incorporate both labeled and unlabeled data during learning. Firstly, we employ an ensemble learning framework, which effectively uses alignment results from different unsupervised alignment models. We then propose to use a semi-supervised learning method, namely Tri-training, to train classifiers using both labeled and unlabeled data collaboratively and further improve the result. Experimental results show that our methods can substantially improve the quality of word alignment. The final translation quality of a phrase-based translation system is slightly improved, as well.

1 Introduction

Word alignment is the process of learning bilingual word correspondences. Conventional word alignment process is treated as an unsupervised learning task, which automatically learns the correspondences between bilingual words using an EM style algorithm (Brown et al., 1993; Vogel et al., 1996; Och and Ney, 2003). Recently, supervised learning methods have been used to improve the performance. They firstly re-formalize word alignment as some kind of classification task. Then the labeled data is used to train the classification model, which is finally used to classify unseen test data (Liu et al., 2005; Taskar et al., 2005; Moore, 2005; Cherry and Lin, 2006; Haghighi et al., 2009).

It is well understood that the performance of supervised learning relies heavily on the feature set. As more and more features are added into the model, more data is needed for training. However, due to the expensive cost of labeling, we usually cannot get as much labeled word alignment data as we want. This may limit the performance of supervised methods (Wu et al., 2006). One possible alternative is to use features learnt in some unsupervised manner to help the task. For example, Moore (2005) uses statistics like log-likelihood-ratio and conditional-likelihood-probability to measure word associations; Liu et al. (2005) and Taskar et al. (2005) use results from IBM Model 3 and Model 4, respectively.

Ayan and Dorr (2006) propose another way of incorporating unlabeled data. They first train some existing alignment models, e.g. IBM Model4 and Hidden Markov Model, using unlabeled data. The results of these models are then combined using a maximum entropy classifier, which is trained using labeled data. This method is highly efficient in training because it only makes decisions on alignment links from existing models and avoids searching the entire alignment space.

In this paper, we follow Ayan and Dorr (2006)'s idea of combining multiple alignment results. And we use more features, such as bi-lexical features, which help capture more information from unlabeled data. To further improve the decision making during combination, we propose to use a semi-supervised strategy, namely Tri-training (Zhou and Li, 2005), which ensembles three classifiers using both labeled and unlabeled data. More specifically, Tri-training iteratively trains three classifiers and labels all the unlabeled instances. It then uses some instances among the unlabeled ones to expand the labeled training set of each in-

Proceedings of the Fourteenth Conference on Computational Natural Language Learning, pages 135–143,
Uppsala, Sweden, 15-16 July 2010.

dividual classifier. As word alignment task usually faces a huge parallel corpus, which contains millions of unlabeled instances, we develop specific algorithms to adapt Tri-training for this large scale task.

The next section introduces the supervised alignment combination framework; Section 3 presents our semi-supervised learning algorithm. We show the experiments and results in Section 4; briefly overview related work in Section 5 and conclude in the last section.

2 Word Alignment as a Classification Task

2.1 Modeling

Given a sentence pair $(\mathbf{e}, \mathbf{f})$, where $\mathbf{e} = e_1, e_2, \ldots, e_I$ and $\mathbf{f} = f_1, f_2, \ldots, f_J$, an alignment link $a_{i,j}$ indicates the translation correspondence between words e_i and f_j. Word alignment is to learn the correct alignment A between $\mathbf{e}$ and $\mathbf{f}$, which is a set of such alignment links.

As the number of possible alignment links grows exponentially with the length of $\mathbf{e}$ and $\mathbf{f}$, we restrict the candidate set using results from several existing alignment models. Note that, all the models we employ are unsupervised models. We will refer to them as sub-models in the rest of this paper.

Let $\mathcal{A} = \{A_1, A_2, \ldots, A_n\}$ be a set of alignment results from sub-models; A_I and A_U be the intersection and union of these results, respectively. We define our learning task as: for each alignment link $a_{i,j}$ in the candidate set $A_C = A_U - A_I$, deciding whether $a_{i,j}$ should be included in the alignment result. We use a random variable $y_{i,j}$ (or simply y) to indicate whether an alignment link $a_{i,j} \in A_C$ is correct. A Maximum Entropy model is employed to directly model the distribution of y. The probability of y is defined in Formula 1, where $h_m(y, \mathbf{e}, \mathbf{f}, \mathcal{A}, i, j)$ is the mth feature function, and λ_m is the corresponding weight.

$$p(y|\mathbf{e}, \mathbf{f}, \mathcal{A}, i, j) = \frac{exp\sum_{m=1}^{M} \lambda_m h_m(y, \mathbf{e}, \mathbf{f}, \mathcal{A}, i, j)}{\sum_{\hat{y}\in\{0,1\}} exp\sum_{m=1}^{M} \lambda_m h_m(\hat{y}, \mathbf{e}, \mathbf{f}, \mathcal{A}, i, j)} \tag{1}$$

While Ayan and Dorr (Ayan and Dorr, 2006) make decisions on each alignment link in A_U, we take a different strategy by assuming that all the alignment links in A_I are correct, which means alignment links in A_I are always included in the combination result. One reason for using this strategy is that it makes no sense to exclude an alignment link, which all the sub-models vote for including. Also, links in A_I usually have a good quality (In our experiment, A_I can always achieve an accuracy higher than 96%). On the other hand, because A_I is decided before the supervised learning starts, it will be able to provide evidence for making decisions on candidate links.

Also note that, Formula 1 is based on the assumption that given A_I, the decision on each y is independent of each other. This is the crucial point that saves us from searching the whole alignment space. We take this assumption so that the Tri-training strategy can be easily applied.

2.2 Features

For ensemble, the most important features are the decisions of sub-models. We also use some other features, such as POS tags, neighborhood information, etc. Details of the features for a given link $a_{i,j}$ are listed below.

Decision of sub-models: Whether $a_{i,j}$ exists in the result of kth sub-model A_k. Besides individual features for each model, we also include features describing the combination of sub-models' decisions. For example, if we have 3 sub-models, there will be 8 features indicating the decisions of all the sub-models as 000, 001, 010, ..., 111.

Part of speech tags: POS tags of previous, current and next words in both languages. We also include features describing the POS tag pairs of previous, current and next word pairs in the two languages.

Neighborhood: Whether each neighbor link exists in the intersection A_I. Neighbor links refer to links in a 3*3 window with (i, j) in the center.

Fertilities: The number of words that e_i (or f_j) is aligned to in A_I.

Relative distance: The relative distance between e_i and f_j, which is calculated as $abs(i/I - j/J)$.

Conditional Link Probability (CLP) : The conditional link probability (Moore, 2005) of e_i

and f_j. CLP of word e and f is estimated on an aligned parallel corpus using Formula 2,

$$CLP_d(e, f) = \frac{link(e, f) - d}{cooc(e, f)} \quad (2)$$

where $link(e, f)$ is the number of times e and f are linked in the aligned corpus; $cooc(e, f)$ is the number of times e and f appear in the same sentence pair; d is a discounting constant which is set to 0.4 following Moore (2005). We estimate these counts on our set of unlabeled data, with the union of all sub-model results A_U as the alignment. Union is used in order to get a better link coverage. Probabilities are computed only for those words that occur at least twice in the parallel corpus.

bi-lexical features: The lexical word pair e_i-f_j.

Lexical features have been proved to be useful in tasks such as parsing and name entity recognition. Taskar et al. (2005) also employ similar bi-lexical features of the top 5 non-punctuation words for word alignment. Using bi-lexicons for arbitrary word pairs will capture more evidence from the data; although it results in a huge feature set which may suffer from data sparseness. In the next section, we introduce a semi-supervised strategy will may alleviate this problem and further improve the learning procedure.

3 Semi-supervised methods

Semi-supervised methods aim at using unlabeled instances to assist the supervised learning. One of the prominent achievements in this area is the Co-training paradigm proposed by Blum and Mitchell (1998). Co-training applies when the features of an instance can be naturally divided into two sufficient and redundant subsets. Two weak classifiers can be trained using each subset of features and strengthened using unlabeled data. Blum and Mitchell (1998) prove the effectiveness of this algorithm, under the assumption that features in one set is conditionally independent of features in the other set. Intuitively speaking, if this conditional independence assumption holds, the most confident instance of one classifier will act as a random instance for the other classifier. Thus it can be safely used to expand the training set of the other classifier.

The standard Co-training algorithm requires a naturally splitting in the feature set, which is hard to meet in most scenarios, including the task of word alignment. Variations include using random split feature sets or two different classification algorithms. In this paper, we use the other Co-training style algorithm called Tri-training, which requires neither sufficient and redundant views nor different classification algorithms.

3.1 Tri-training

Similar with Co-training, the basic idea of Tri-training (Zhou and Li, 2005) is to iteratively expand the labeled training set for the next-round training based on the decisions of the current classifiers. However, Tri-training employs three classifiers instead of two. To get diverse initial classifiers, the training set of each classifier is initially generated via bootstrap sampling from the original labeled training set and updated separately. In each round, these three classifiers are used to classify all the unlabeled instances. An unlabeled instance is added to the training set of any classifier if the other two classifiers agree on the labeling of this example. So there is no need to explicitly measure the confidence of any individual classifier, which might be a problem for some learning algorithms. Zhou and Li (2005) also give a terminate criterion derived from PAC analysis. As the algorithm goes, the number of labeled instances increases, which may bring in more bi-lexical features and alleviate the problem of data sparseness.

3.2 Tri-training for Word Alignment

One crucial problem for word alignment is the huge amount of unlabeled instances. Typical parallel corpus for word alignment contains at least hundreds of thousands of sentence pairs, with each sentence pair containing tens of instances. That makes a large set of millions of instances. Therefore, we develop a modified version of Tri-training algorithm using sampling techniques, which can work well with such large scale data. A sketch of our algorithm is shown in Figure 1.

The algorithm takes original labeled instance set L, unlabeled sentence set S_U, sub-model results $\mathcal{A}_s$ for each s in S_U and a sampling ratio r as input. F_k represents the kth classifier. Variables with superscript i represent their values during the ith iteration.

Line 2 initializes candidate instance set $A_{C,s}$ of each sentence s to be the difference set between

Input: L, S_U, $\mathcal{A}_s$ for each s and sampling ratio r.
1: **for all** sentence s in S_U **do**
2: $A^0_{C,s} \leftarrow A_{U,s} - A_{I,s}$ //initializing candidate set
3: **end for**
4: **for all** $l \in \{1, 2, 3\}$ **do**
5: $L^0_l \leftarrow Subsample(L, 0.33)$
6: $F^0_l \leftarrow Train(L^0_l)$
7: **end for**
8: **repeat**
9: **for all** $l \in \{1, 2, 3\}$ **do**
10: Let $m, n \in \{1, 2, 3\}$ and $m \neq n \neq l$; $L^i_l = \emptyset$
11: **for all** sentence s in S_U **do**
12: **for all** instance a in $A^{i-1}_{C,s}$ **do**
13: **if** $F^{i-1}_m(a) = F^{i-1}_n(a)$ **then**
14: $A^{i-1}_{C,s} \leftarrow A^{i-1}_{C,s} - \{(a, F^{i-1}_m(a))\}$
15: $L^i_l \leftarrow L^i_l \cup \{(a, F^{i-1}_m(a))\}$
16: **end if**
17: **end for**
18: **end for**
19: **end for**
20: **for all** $l \in \{1, 2, 3\}$ **do**
21: $L^i_l \leftarrow Subsampling(L^i_l, r) \cup L^{i-1}_l$
22: $F^i_l \leftarrow Train(L^i_l)$
23: $A^i_{C,s} \leftarrow A^{i-1}_{C,s}$
24: **end for**
25: **until** all $A^i_{C,s}$ are unchanged or empty
Output: $F(x) \leftarrow arg\max_{y\in\{0,1\}} \sum_{l:F_l(x)=y} 1$

Figure 1: Modified Tri-training Algorithm

$A_{U,s}$ and $A_{I,s}$. In line 5-6, sub-samplings are performed on the original labeled set L and the initial classifier F^0_l is trained using the sampling results. In each iteration, the algorithm labels each instance in the candidate set $A^i_{C,s}$ for each classifier with the other two classifiers trained in last iteration. Instances are removed from the candidate set and added to the labeled training set (L^i_l) of classifier l, if they are given the same label by the other two classifiers (line 13-16).

A sub-sampling is performed before the labeled training set is used for training (line 21), which means all the instances in L^i_l are accepted as correct, but only part of them are added into the training set. The sampling rate is controlled by a parameter r, which we empirically set to 0.01 in all our experiments. The classifier is then re-trained using the augmented training set L^i_l (line 22). The algorithm iterates until all instances in the candidate sets get labeled or the candidate sets do not change since the last iteration (line 25). The resulting classifiers can be used to label new instances via majority voting.

Our algorithm differs from Zhou and Li (2005) in the following three aspects. First of all, comparing to the original bootstrap sampling initialization, we use a more aggressive strategy, which actually divides the original labeled set into three parts. This strategy ensures that initial classifiers are trained using different sets of instances and maximizes the diversity between classifiers. We will compare these two initializations in the experiments section. Secondly, we introduce sampling techniques for the huge number of unlabeled instances. Sampling is essential for maintaining a reasonable growing speed of training data and keeping the computation physically feasible. Thirdly, because the original terminate criterion requires an error estimation process in each iteration, we adapt the much simpler terminate criterion of standard Co-training into our algorithm, which iterates until all the unlabeled data are finally labeled or the candidate sets do not change since the last iteration. In other words, our algorithm inherits both the benefits of using three classifiers and the simplicity of using Co-training style termination criterion. Parallel computing techniques are also used during the processing of unlabeled data to speed up the computation.

Source	Usage	Sent. Pairs	Cand. Links
LDC	Train	288111	8.8M
NIST'02	Train	200	5,849
NIST'02	Eval	291	7,797

Table 1: Data used in the experiment

4 Experiments and Results

4.1 Data and Evaluation Methodology

All our experiments are conducted on the language pair of Chinese and English. For training alignment systems, a parallel corpus coming from LDC2005T10 and LDC2005T14 is used as unlabeled training data. Labeled data comes from NIST Open MT Eval'02, which has 491 labeled sentence pairs. The first 200 labeled sentence pairs are used as labeled training data and the rest are used for evaluation (Table 1). The number of candidate alignment links in each data set is also listed in Table 1. These candidate alignment links are generated using the three sub-models described in Section 4.2.

The quality of word alignment is evaluated in terms of alignment error rate (AER) (Och and Ney, 2003), classifier's accuracy and recall of correct decisions. Formula 3 shows the definition of AER, where P and S refer to the set of possible and sure alignment links, respectively. In our experiments,

ModelName	AER_Dev	AER_Test	Accuracy	Recall	F_1
Model4C2E	0.4269	0.4196	0.4898	0.3114	0.3808
Model4E2C	0.3715	0.3592	0.5642	0.5368	0.5502
BerkeleyAl.	0.3075	0.2939	0.7064	0.6377	0.6703
Model4GDF	0.3328	0.3336	0.6059	0.6184	0.6121
Supervised	**0.2291**	**0.2430**	**0.8124**	**0.7027**	**0.7536**

Table 2: Experiments of Sub-models

ModelName	AER_Dev	AER_Test	Accuracy	Recall	F_1
Supervised	0.2291	**0.2430**	**0.8124**	0.7027	0.7536
BerkeleyAl.	0.3075	0.2939	0.7064	0.6377	0.6703
Tri-Bootstrap^0	0.2301	0.2488	0.8030	0.6858	0.7398
Tri-Divide^0	0.2458	0.2525	0.8002	0.6630	0.7251
Tri-Bootstrap	**0.2264**	0.2468	0.7934	0.7449	0.7684
Tri-Divide	0.2416	0.2494	0.7832	**0.7605**	**0.7717**

Table 3: Experiments of Semi-supervised Models

we treat all alignment links as sure links.

$$AER = 1 - \frac{|A \cap P| + |A \cap S|}{|A| + |S|} \quad (3)$$

We also define a F_1 score to be the harmonic mean of classifier's accuracy and recall of correct decisions (Formula 4).

$$F_1 = \frac{2 * accuracy * recall}{accuracy + recall} \quad (4)$$

We also evaluate the machine translation quality using unlabeled data (in Table 1) and these alignment results as aligned training data. We use multi-references data sets from NIST Open MT Evaluation as development and test data. The English side of the parallel corpus is trained into a language model using SRILM (Stolcke, 2002). Moses (Koehn et al., 2003) is used for decoding. Translation quality is measured by BLEU4 score ignoring the case.

4.2 Experiments of Sub-models

We use the following three sub-models: bidirectional results of Giza++ (Och and Ney, 2003) Model4, namely *Model4C2E* and *Model4E2C*, and the joint training result of BerkeleyAligner (Liang et al., 2006) (*BerkeleyAl.*). To evaluate AER, all three data sets listed in Table 1 are combined and used for the unsupervised training of each sub-model.

Table 2 presents the alignment quality of those sub-models, as well as a supervised ensemble of them, as described in Section 2.1. We use the symmetrized IBM Model4 results by the grow-diag-final-and heuristic as our baseline (*Model4GDF*). Scores in Table 2 show the great improvement of supervised learning, which reduce the alignment error rate significantly (more than 5% AER points from the best sub-model, i.e. BerkeleyAligner). This result is consistent with Ayan and Dorr (2006)'s experiments. It is quite reasonable that supervised model achieves a much higher classification accuracy of 0.8124 than any unsupervised sub-model. Besides, it also achieves the highest recall of correct alignment links (0.7027).

4.3 Experiments of Semi-supervised Models

We present our experiment results on semi-supervised models in Table 3. The two strategies of generating initial classifiers are compared. *Tri-Bootstrap* is the model using the original bootstrap sampling initialization; and *Tri-Divide* is the model using the dividing initialization as described in Section 3.2. Items with superscripts 0 indicate models before the first iteration, i.e. initial models. The scores of BerkeleyAligner and the supervised model are also included for comparison.

In general, all supervised and semi-supervised models achieve better results than the best sub-model, which proves the effectiveness of labeled training data. It is also reasonable that initial models are not as good as the supervised model, because they only use part of the labeled data for training. After the iterative training, both the two

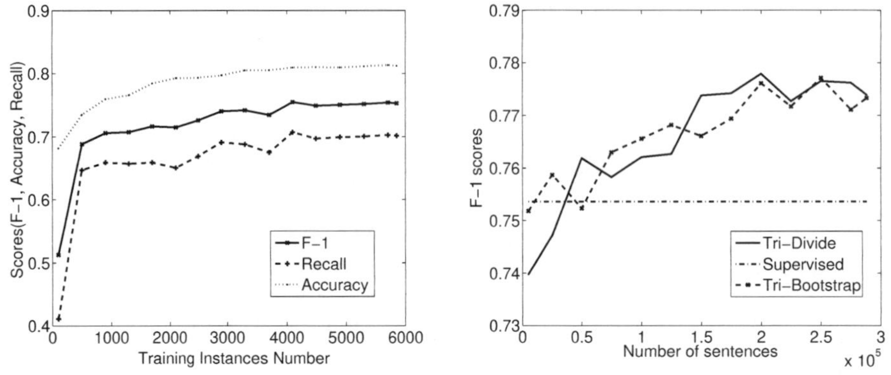

(a) (b)

Figure 2: (a) Experiments on the Size of Labeled Training Data in Supervised Training; (b) Experiments on the Size of Unlabeled Data in Tri-training

Tri-training models get a significant increase in recall. We attribute this to the use of bi-lexical features described in Section 2.2. Analysis of the resulting model shows that the number of bi-lexical features increases from around 300 to nearly 7,800 after Tri-training. It demonstrates that semi-supervised algorithms are able to learn more bi-lexical features automatically from the unlabeled data, which may help recognize more translation equivalences. However, we also notice that the accuracy drops a little after Tri-training. This might also be caused by the large set of bi-lexical features, which may contain some noises.

In the comparison of initialization strategies, the dividing strategy achieves a much higher recall of 0.7605, which is also the highest among all models. It also achieves the best F_1 score of 0.7717, higher than the bootstrap sampling strategy (0.7684). This result confirms that diversity of initial classifiers is important for Co-training style algorithms.

4.4 Experiments on the Size of Data

4.4.1 Size of Labeled Data

We design this experiment to see how the size of labeled data affects the supervised training procedure. Our labeled training set contains 5,800 training instances. We randomly sample different sets of instances from the whole set and perform the supervised training.

The alignment results are plotted in Figure 2a. Basically, both accuracy and recall increase with the size of labeled data. However, we also find that the increase of all the scores gets slower when the number of training instances exceeds 3,000. One possible explanation for this is that the training set itself is too small and contains redundant instances, which may prevent further improvement. We can see in the Section 4.4.2 that the scores can be largely improved when more data is added.

4.4.2 Size of Unlabeled Data

For better understanding the effect of unlabeled data, we run the Tri-training algorithm on unlabeled corpus of different sizes. The original unlabeled corpus contains about 288 thousand sentence pairs. We create 12 sub-corpus of it with different sizes by selecting certain amounts of sentences from the beginning. Our smallest sub-corpus consists of the first 5,000 sentence pairs of the original corpus; while the largest sub-corpus contains the first 275 thousand sentence pairs. The alignment results on these different sub-corpus are evaluated (See Figure 2b).

The result shows that as the size of unlabeled data grows, the F_1 score of *Tri-Divide* increases from around 0.74 to 0.772. The F_1 score of *Tri-Bootstrap* also gets a similar increase. This proves that adding unlabeled data does help the learning process. The result also suggests that when the size of unlabeled data is small, both *Tri-Bootstrap* and *Tri-Divide* get lower scores than the supervised model. This is because the Tri-training models only use part of the labeled data for the training of each individual classifier, while the supervised model use the whole set. We can see that when there are more than 50 thousand unlabeled sentence pairs, both Tri-training models outperform the supervised model significantly.

ModelName	Dev04	Test05	Test06	Test08
Model4C2E	24.54	17.10	17.52	14.59
Model4E2C	26.54	19.00	20.18	16.56
BerkeleyAl.	26.19	20.08	19.65	16.70
Model4GDF	26.75	20.67	20.58	17.05
Supervised	**27.07**	20.00	19.47	16.13
Tri-Bootstrap	26.88	20.49	20.76	**17.31**
Tri-Divide	27.04	**20.96**	**20.79**	17.18

Table 4: Experiments on machine translation (BLEU4 scores in percentage)

Note that, both experiments on data size show some unsteadiness during the learning process. We attribute this mainly to the random sampling we use in the algorithm. As there are, in all, about 8.8 million instances , it is highly possible that some of these instances are redundant or noisy. And because our random sampling does not distinguish different instances, the quality of resulting model may get affected if these redundant or noisy instances are selected and added to the training set.

4.5 Experiments on Machine Translation

We compare the machine translation results of each sub-models, supervised models and semi-supervised models in Table 4. Among sub-models, BerkeleyAligner gets better BLEU4 scores in almost all the data sets except TEST06, which agrees with its highest F_1 score among all sub-models. The supervised method gets the highest BLEU score of 27.07 on the dev set. However, its performance on the test sets is a bit lower than that of BerkeleyAligner.

As we expect, our two semi-supervised models achieve highest scores on almost all the data sets, which are also higher than the commonly used grow-diag-final-and symmetrization of IBM Model 4. More specifically, *Tri-Divide* is the best of all systems. It gets a dev score of 27.04, which is comparable with the highest one (27.07). *Tri-Divide* also gets the highest BLEU scores on Test05 and Test06 (20.96 and 20.79, respectively), which are nearly 1 point higher than all sub-models. The other Tri-training model, *Tri-Bootstrap*, gets the highest score on Test08, which is also significantly better than those sub-models.

Despite the large improvement in F_1 score, our two Tri-training models only get slightly better score than the well-known *Model4GDF*. This kind of inconsistence between AER or F_1 scores and BLEU scores is a known issue in machine translation community (Fraser and Marcu, 2007). One possible explanation is that both AER or F_1 are 0-1 loss functions, which means missing one link and adding one redundant link will get the same penalty. And more importantly, every wrong link receives the same penalty under these metrics. However, these different errors may have different effects on the machine translation quality. Thus, improving alignment quality according to AER or F_1 may not directly lead to an increase of BLEU scores. The relationship among these metrics are still under investigation.

5 Related work

Previous work mainly focuses on supervised learning of word alignment. Liu et al. (2005) propose a log-linear model for the alignment between two sentences, in which different features can be used to describe the alignment quality. Moore (2005) proposes a similar framework, but with more features and a different search method. Other models such as SVM and CRF are also used (Taskar et al., 2005; Cherry and Lin, 2006; Haghighi et al., 2009). For alignment ensemble, Wu and Wang (2005) introduce a boosting approach, in which the labeled data is used to calculate the weight of each sub-model.

These researches all focus on the modeling of alignment structure and employ some strategy to search for the optimal alignment. Our main contribution here is the use Co-training style semi-supervised methods to assist the ensemble learning framework of Ayan and Dorr (2006). Although we use a maximum entropy model in our experiment, other models like SVM and CRF can also be incorporated into our learning framework.

In the area of semi-supervised learning of word alignment, Callison-Burch et al. (2004) compare the results of interpolating statistical machine translation models learnt from labeled and unlabeled data, respectively. Wu et al. (2006) propose a modified boosting algorithm, where two different models are also trained using labeled and unlabeled data respectively and interpolated. Fraser and Marcu (2006) propose an EMD algorithm, where labeled data is used for discriminative reranking. It should be pointed out that these pieces of work all use two separate processes for learning with labeled and unlabeled data. They either train and interpolate two separate models or rerank previously learnt models with labeled data only. Our proposed semi-supervised strategy is able to incorporate both labeled and unlabeled data in the same process, which is in a different line of thinking.

6 Conclusions and Future Work

Semi-supervised techniques are useful when there is a large amount of unlabeled data. In this paper, we introduce a semi-supervised learning method, called Tri-training, to improve the word alignment combination task. Although experiments have proved the effectiveness of our methods, there is one defect that should be mentioned. As we previously assume that all the decisions on alignment links are independent of each other (in Section 2.1), our model are only able to capture link level evidence like bi-lexical features. Some global features, such as final word fertility, cannot be integrated into the current framework. In the future, we plan to apply our semi-supervised strategy in more complicated learning frameworks, which are able to capture those global features.

Currently we use a random sampling to handle the 8.8 million instances. We will also explore better and more aggressive sampling techniques, which may lead to more stable training results and also enable us to process larger corpus.

Acknowledgments

The authors would like to thank Dr. Ming Li, Mr. Junming Xu and the anonymous reviewers for their valuable comments. This work is supported by the National Fundamental Research Program of China(2010CB327903) and the Scientific Research Foundation of Graduate School of Nanjing University(2008CL08).

References

Necip Fazil Ayan and Bonnie J. Dorr. 2006. A maximum entropy approach to combining word alignments. In *Proceedings of the main conference on Human Language Technology Conference of the North American Chapter of the Association of Computational Linguistics*, pages 96–103, Morristown, NJ, USA. Association for Computational Linguistics.

Avrim Blum and Tom Mitchell. 1998. Combining labeled and unlabeled data with co-training. In *Proceedings of the 11th Annual Conference on Computational Learning Theory*, pages 92–100. Morgan Kaufmann Publishers.

Peter F. Brown, Stephen Della Pietra, Vincent J. Della Pietra, and Robert L. Mercer. 1993. The mathematic of statistical machine translation: Parameter estimation. *Computational Linguistics*, 19(2):263–311.

Chris Callison-Burch, David Talbot, and Miles Osborne. 2004. Statistical machine translation with word- and sentence-aligned parallel corpora. In *ACL '04: Proceedings of the 42nd Annual Meeting on Association for Computational Linguistics*, page 175, Morristown, NJ, USA. Association for Computational Linguistics.

Colin Cherry and Dekang Lin. 2006. Soft syntactic constraints for word alignment through discriminative training. In *Proceedings of the COLING/ACL on Main conference poster sessions*, pages 105–112, Morristown, NJ, USA. Association for Computational Linguistics.

Alexander Fraser and Daniel Marcu. 2006. Semi-supervised training for statistical word alignment. In *ACL-44: Proceedings of the 21st International Conference on Computational Linguistics and the 44th annual meeting of the Association for Computational Linguistics*, pages 769–776, Morristown, NJ, USA. Association for Computational Linguistics.

Alexander Fraser and Daniel Marcu. 2007. Measuring word alignment quality for statistical machine translation. *Comput. Linguist.*, 33(3):293–303.

Aria Haghighi, John Blitzer, and Dan Klein. 2009. Better word alignments with supervised itg models. In *Association for Computational Linguistics*, Singapore.

Philipp Koehn, Franz Josef Och, and Daniel Marcu. 2003. Statistical phrase-based translation. In *HLT-NAACL*.

Percy Liang, Benjamin Taskar, and Dan Klein. 2006. Alignment by agreement. In Robert C. Moore, Jeff A. Bilmes, Jennifer Chu-Carroll, and Mark Sanderson, editors, *HLT-NAACL*. The Association for Computational Linguistics.

Yang Liu, Qun Liu, and Shouxun Lin. 2005. Log-linear models for word alignment. In *ACL '05: Proceedings of the 43rd Annual Meeting on Association for Computational Linguistics*, pages 459–466, Morristown, NJ, USA. Association for Computational Linguistics.

Robert C. Moore. 2005. A discriminative framework for bilingual word alignment. In *HLT '05: Proceedings of the conference on Human Language Technology and Empirical Methods in Natural Language Processing*, pages 81–88, Morristown, NJ, USA. Association for Computational Linguistics.

Franz Josef Och and Hermann Ney. 2003. A systematic comparison of various statistical alignment models. *Comput. Linguist.*, 29(1):19–51.

A. Stolcke. 2002. Srilm - an extensible language modeling toolkit. In *Proceedings of International Conference on Spoken Language Processing*, page 901 904.

Ben Taskar, Simon Lacoste-Julien, and Dan Klein. 2005. A discriminative matching approach to word alignment. In *HLT '05: Proceedings of the conference on Human Language Technology and Empirical Methods in Natural Language Processing*, pages 73–80, Morristown, NJ, USA. Association for Computational Linguistics.

Stephan Vogel, Hermann Ney, and Christoph Tillmann. 1996. Hmm-based word alignment in statistical translation. In *Proceedings of the 16th International Conference on Computational Linguistics*, pages 836–841.

Hua Wu and Haifeng Wang. 2005. Boosting statistical word alignment. In *Proceedings of MT SUMMIT X*, pages 364–371, Phuket Island, Thailand, September.

Hua Wu, Haifeng Wang, and Zhanyi Liu. 2006. Boosting statistical word alignment using labeled and unlabeled data. In *Proceedings of the COLING/ACL 2006 Main Conference Poster Sessions*, pages 913–920, Sydney, Australia, July. Association for Computational Linguistics.

Zhi-Hua Zhou and Ming Li. 2005. Tri-training: Exploiting unlabeled data using three classifiers. volume 17, pages 1529–1541, Piscataway, NJ, USA. IEEE Educational Activities Department.

A Comparative Study of Bayesian Models for Unsupervised Sentiment Detection

Chenghua Lin
School of Engineering,
Computing and Mathematics
University of Exeter
Exeter, EX4 4QF, UK.
cl322@exeter.ac.uk

Yulan He
Knowledge Media Institute
The Open University
Milton Keynes
MK7 6AA, UK
Y.He@open.ac.uk

Richard Everson
School of Engineering,
Computing and Mathematics
University of Exeter
Exeter, EX4 4QF, UK.
R.E.Everson@exeter.ac.uk

Abstract

This paper presents a comparative study of three closely related Bayesian models for unsupervised document level sentiment classification, namely, the latent sentiment model (LSM), the joint sentiment-topic (JST) model, and the Reverse-JST model. Extensive experiments have been conducted on two corpora, the movie review dataset and the multi-domain sentiment dataset. It has been found that while all the three models achieve either better or comparable performance on these two corpora when compared to the existing unsupervised sentiment classification approaches, both JST and Reverse-JST are able to extract sentiment-oriented topics. In addition, Reverse-JST always performs worse than JST suggesting that the JST model is more appropriate for joint sentiment topic detection.

1 Introduction

With the explosion of web 2.0, various types of social media such as blogs, discussion forums and peer-to-peer networks present a wealth of information that can be very helpful in assessing the general public's sentiments and opinions towards products and services. Recent surveys have revealed that opinion-rich resources like online reviews are having greater economic impact on both consumers and companies compared to the traditional media (Pang and Lee, 2008). Driven by the demand of gleaning insights of such great amounts of user-generated data, work on new methodologies for automated sentiment analysis has bloomed splendidly.

Compared to the traditional topic-based text classification, sentiment classification is deemed to be more challenging as sentiment is often embodied in subtle linguistic mechanisms such as the use of sarcasm or incorporated with highly domain-specific information. Although the task of identifying the overall sentiment polarity of a document has been well studied, most of the work is highly domain dependent and favoured in supervised learning (Pang et al., 2002; Pang and Lee, 2004; Whitelaw et al., 2005; Kennedy and Inkpen, 2006; McDonald et al., 2007), requiring annotated corpora for every possible domain of interest, which is impractical for real applications. Also, it is well-known that sentiment classifiers trained on one domain often fail to produce satisfactory results when shifted to another domain, since sentiment expression can be quite different in different domains (Aue and Gamon, 2005). Moreover, aside from the diversity of genres and large-scale size of Web corpora, user-generated contents evolve rapidly over time, which demands much more efficient algorithms for sentiment analysis than the current approaches can offer. These observations have thus motivated the problem of using unsupervised approaches for domain-independent joint sentiment topic detection.

Some recent research efforts have been made to adapt sentiment classifiers trained on one domain to another domain (Aue and Gamon, 2005; Blitzer et al., 2007; Li and Zong, 2008; Andreevskaia and Bergler, 2008). However, the adaption performance of these lines of work pretty much depends on the distribution similarity between the source and target domain, and considerable effort is still required to obtain labelled data for training.

Intuitively, sentiment polarities are dependent on contextual information, such as topics or domains. In this regard, some recent work (Mei et al., 2007; Titov and McDonald, 2008a) has tried to model both sentiment and topics. However, these two models either require postprocessing to calculate the positive/negative coverage in a document for polarity identification (Mei et al., 2007) or re-

Proceedings of the Fourteenth Conference on Computational Natural Language Learning, pages 144–152,
Uppsala, Sweden, 15-16 July 2010.

quire some kind of supervised setting in which review text should contain ratings for aspects of interest (Titov and McDonald, 2008a). More recently, Dasgupta and Ng (2009) proposed an unsupervised sentiment classification algorithm by integrating user feedbacks into a spectral clustering algorithm. Features induced for each dimension of spectral clustering can be considered as sentiment-oriented topics. Nevertheless, human judgement of identifying the most important dimensions during spectral clustering is required.

Lin and He (2009) proposed a joint sentiment-topic (JST) model for unsupervised joint sentiment topic detection. They assumed that topics are generated dependent on sentiment distributions and then words are generated conditioned on sentiment-topic pairs. While this is a reasonable design choice, one may argue that the reverse is also true that sentiments may vary according to topics. Thus in this paper, we studied the reverse dependence of the JST model called Reverse-JST, in which sentiments are generated dependent on topic distributions in the modelling process. We also note that, when the topic number is set to 1, both JST and reversed-JST essentially become a simple latent Dirichlet allocation (LDA) model with only S (number of sentiment label) topics, each of which corresponds to a sentiment label. We called it latent sentiment model (LSM) in this paper. Extensive experiments have been conducted on the movie review (MR)[1] (Pang et al., 2002) and multi-domain sentiment (MDS)[2] (Blitzer et al., 2007) datasets to compare the performance of LSM, JST and Reverse-JST. Results show that all these three models are able to give either better or comparable performance compared to the existing unsupervised sentiment classification approaches. In addition, both JST and reverse-JST are able to extract sentiment-oriented topics. Furthermore, the fact that reverse-JST always performs worse than JST suggests that the JST model is more appropriate for joint sentiment topic detection.

The rest of the paper is organized as follows. Section 2 presents related work. Section 3 describes the LSM, JST and Reserver-JST models. Experimental setup and results on the MR and MDS datasets are discussed in Section 4 and 5 respectively. Finally, Section 6 concludes the paper and outlines the future work.

[1] http://www.cs.cornell.edu/people/pabo/movie-review-data

[2] http://www.cs.jhu.edu/~mdredze/datasets/sentiment/index2.html

2 Related Work

As opposed to the work (Pang et al., 2002; Pang and Lee, 2004; Whitelaw et al., 2005; Kennedy and Inkpen, 2006) that only focused on sentiment classification in one particular domain, recent research attempts have been made to address the problem of sentiment classification across domains. Aue and Gamon (2005) explored various strategies for customizing sentiment classifiers to new domains, where the training is based on a small number of labelled examples and large amounts of unlabelled in-domain data. However, their experiments achieved only limited success, with most of the classification accuracy below 80%. In the same vein, some more recent work focused on domain adaption for sentiment classifiers. Blitzer et al. (2007) used the structural correspondence learning (SCL) algorithm with mutual information. Li and Zong (2008) combined multiple single classifiers trained on individual domains using SVMs. However, the adaption performance in (Blitzer et al., 2007) depends on the selection of pivot features that used to link the source and target domains; whereas the approach of Li and Zong (2008) heavily relies on labelled data from all the domains to train the integrated classifier and thus lack the flexibility to adapt the trained classifier to domains where label information is not available.

Recent years have also seen increasing interests in modelling both sentiment and topics simultaneously. The topic-sentiment mixture (TSM) model (Mei et al., 2007) can jointly model sentiment and topics by constructing an extra background component and two additional sentiment subtopics on top of the probabilistic latent semantic indexing (pLSI) (Hofmann, 1999). However, TSM may suffer from the problem of overfitting the data which is known as a deficiency of pLSI, and post-processing is also required in order to calculate the sentiment prediction for a document. The multi-aspect sentiment (MAS) model (Titov and McDonald, 2008a), which is extended from the multi-grain latent Dirichlet allocation (MG-LDA) model (Titov and McDonald, 2008b), allows sentiment text aggregation for sentiment summary of each rating aspect extracted from MG-LDA. One drawback of MAS is that it requires that every aspect is rated at least in some documents, which is practically infeasible. More recently, Dasgupta and Ng (2009) proposed an unsupervised sentiment classification algorithm where user feedbacks are provided on the spectral clustering process in an interactive manner to ensure that text are clustered along the sentiment dimension. Features induced for each dimension of spectral clustering can be considered as sentiment-oriented topics. Nevertheless, human judgement of identifying the most important dimensions during spectral clustering is required.

Among various efforts for improving sentiment detection accuracy, one direction is to incorporate prior information or subjectivity lexicon (i.e., words bearing positive or negative sentiment) into the sentiment model. Such sentiment lexicons can be acquired from domain-independent sources in many different ways, from manually built appraisal groups (Whitelaw et al., 2005), to semi-automatically (Abbasi et al., 2008) and fully automatically (Kaji and Kitsuregawa, 2006) constructed lexicons. When incorporating lexical knowledge as prior information into a sentiment-topic model, Andreevskaia and Bergler (2008) integrated the lexicon-based and corpus-based approaches for sentence-level sentiment annotation across different domains; Li et al. (2009) employed lexical prior knowledge for semi-supervised sentiment classification based on non-negative matrix tri-factorization, where the domain-independent prior knowledge was incorporated in conjunction with domain-dependent unlabelled data and a few labelled documents. However, this approach performed worse than the JST model on the movie review data even with 40% labelled documents as will be shown in Section 5.

3 Latent Sentiment-Topic Models

This section describes three closely related Bayesian models for unsupervised sentiment classification, the latent sentiment model (LSM), the joint sentiment-topic (JST) model, and the joint topic sentiment model by reversing the generative process of sentiment and topics in the JST model, called Reverse-JST.

3.1 Latent Sentiment Model (LSM)

The LSM model, as shown in Figure 1(a), can be treated as a special case of LDA where a mixture of only three sentiment labels are modelled, i.e. positive, negative and neutral.

Assuming that we have a total number of S sentiment labels[3]; a corpus with a collection of D documents is denoted by $C = \{d_1, d_2, ..., d_D\}$; each document in the corpus is a sequence of N_d words denoted by $d = (w_1, w_2, ..., w_{N_d})$, and each word in the document is an item from a vocabulary index with V distinct terms denoted by $\{1, 2, ..., V\}$. The procedure of generating a word in LSM starts by firstly choosing a distribution over three sentiment labels for a document. Following that, one picks up a sentiment label from the sentiment label distribution and finally draws a word according to the sentiment label-word distribution.

The joint probability of words and sentiment label assignment in LSM can be factored into two terms:

$$P(\mathbf{w}, \mathbf{l}) = P(\mathbf{w}|\mathbf{l})P(\mathbf{l}|d). \quad (1)$$

Letting the superscript $-t$ denote a quantity that excludes data from the tth position, the conditional posterior for l_t by marginalizing out the random variables φ and π is

$$P(l_t = k|\mathbf{w}, \mathbf{l}^{-\mathbf{t}}, \beta, \gamma) \propto \frac{N_{w_t,k}^{-t} + \beta}{N_k^{-t} + V\beta} \cdot \frac{N_{k,d}^{-t} + \gamma_k}{N_d^{-t} + \sum_k \gamma_k}, \quad (2)$$

where $N_{w_t,k}$ is the number of times word w_t has associated with sentiment label k; N_k is the the number of times words in the corpus assigned to sentiment label k; $N_{k,d}$ is the number of times sentiment label k has been assigned to some word tokens in document d; N_d is the total number of words in the document collection.

Gibbs sampling is used to estimate the posterior distribution of LSM, as well as the JST and Reverse-JST models that will be discussed in the following two sections.

3.2 Joint Sentiment-Topic Model (JST)

In contrast to LSM that only models document sentiment, the JST model (Lin and He, 2009) can detect sentiment and topic simultaneously, by modelling each document with S (number of sentiment labels) topic-document distributions. It should be noted that when the topic number is set to 1, JST effectively becomes the LSM model with only three topics corresponding to each of the

[3]For all the three models, i.e., LSM, JST and Reverse-JST, we set the sentiment label number S to 3 representing the positive, negative and neutral polarities, respectively.

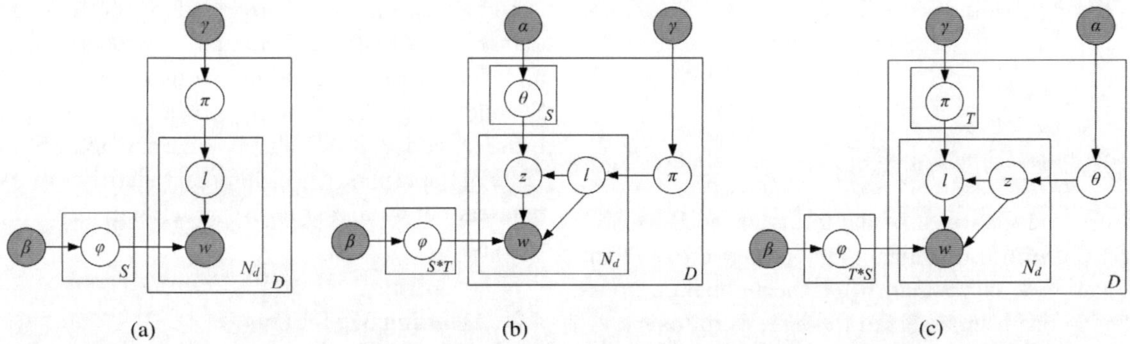

Figure 1: (a) LSM model; (b) JST model; (c) Reverse-JST model.

three sentiment labels. Let T be the total number of topics, the procedure of generating a word w_i according to the graphical model shown in Figure 1(b) is:

- For each document d, choose a distribution $\pi_d \sim \text{Dir}(\gamma)$.
- For each sentiment label l of document d, choose a distribution $\theta_{d,l} \sim \text{Dir}(\alpha)$.
- For each word w_i in document d
  - choose a sentiment label $l_i \sim \text{Multinomial}(\pi_d)$,
  - choose a topic $z_i \sim \text{Multinomial}(\theta_{d,l_i})$,
  - choose a word w_i from $\varphi^{l_i}_{z_i}$, a Multinomial distribution over words conditioned on topic z_i and sentiment label l_i.

In JST, the joint probability of words and topic-sentiment label assignments can be factored into three terms:

$$P(\mathbf{w}, \mathbf{z}, \mathbf{l}) = P(\mathbf{w}|\mathbf{z}, \mathbf{l})P(\mathbf{z}|\mathbf{l}, d)P(\mathbf{l}|d). \quad (3)$$

The conditional posterior for z_t and l_t can be obtained by marginalizing out the random variables φ, θ, and π:

$$P(z_t = j, l_t = k|\mathbf{w}, \mathbf{z}^{-\mathbf{t}}, \mathbf{l}^{-\mathbf{t}}, \alpha, \beta, \gamma) \propto$$
$$\frac{N^{-t}_{w_t,j,k} + \beta}{N^{-t}_{j,k} + V\beta} \cdot \frac{N^{-t}_{j,k,d} + \alpha}{N^{-t}_{k,d} + T\alpha} \cdot \frac{N^{-t}_{k,d} + \gamma_k}{N^{-t}_d + \sum_k \gamma_k}, \quad (4)$$

where $N_{w_t,j,k}$ is the number of times word w_t appeared in topic j and with sentiment label k; $N_{j,k}$ is the number of times words assigned to topic j and sentiment label k, $N_{k,j,d}$ is the number of times a word from document d has been associated with topic j and sentiment label k; $N_{k,d}$ is the number of times sentiment label k has been assigned to some word tokens in document d.

3.3 Reverse Joint Sentiment-Topic Model (Reverse-JST)

We also studied a variant of the JST model, called Reverse-JST. As opposed to JST in which topic generation is conditioned on sentiment labels, sentiment label generation in Reverse-JST is dependent on topics. As shown in Figure 1(c), Reverse-JST is effectively a four-layer hierarchical Bayesian model, where topics are associated with documents, under which sentiment labels are associated with topics and words are associated with both topics and sentiment labels.

The procedure of generating a word w_i in Reverse-JST is shown below:

- For each document d, choose a distribution $\theta_d \sim \text{Dir}(\alpha)$.
- For each topic z of document d, choose a distribution $\pi_{d,z} \sim \text{Dir}(\gamma)$.
- For each word w_i in document d
  - choose a topic $z_i \sim \text{Multinomial}(\theta_d)$,
  - choose a sentiment label $l_i \sim \text{Multinomial}(\pi_{d,z_i})$,
  - choose a word w_i from $\varphi^{l_i}_{z_i}$, a multinomial distribution over words conditioned on the topic z_i and sentiment label l_i.

Analogy to JST, in Reverse-JST the joint probability of words and the topic-sentiment label assignments can be factored into the following three terms:

$$P(\mathbf{w}, \mathbf{l}, \mathbf{z}) = P(\mathbf{w}|\mathbf{l}, \mathbf{z})P(\mathbf{l}|\mathbf{z}, d)P(\mathbf{z}|d), \quad (5)$$

and the conditional posterior for z_t and l_t can be derived by integrating out the random variables φ,

θ, and π, yielding

$$P(z_t = j, l_t = k | \mathbf{w}, \mathbf{z}_{-t}, \mathbf{l}_{-t}, \alpha, \beta, \gamma) \propto$$
$$\frac{N^{-t}_{w_t,j,k} + \beta}{N^{-t}_{j,k} + V\beta} \cdot \frac{N^{-t}_{k,j,d} + \gamma_k}{N^{-t}_{j,d} + \sum_k \gamma_k} \cdot \frac{N^{-t}_{j,d} + \alpha}{N^{-t}_{d} + T\alpha}. \quad (6)$$

It it noted that most of the terms in the Reverse-JST posterior is identical to the posterior of JST in Equation 4, except that $N_{j,d}$ is the number of times topic j has been assigned to some word tokens in document d.

As we do not have a direct sentiment label-document distribution in Reverse-JST, a distribution over sentiment label for document $P(\mathbf{l}|d)$ is calculated as $P(\mathbf{l}|d) = \sum_z P(\mathbf{l}|z, d)P(z|d)$. For all the three models, the probability $P(\mathbf{l}|d)$ will be used to determine document sentiment polarity. We define that a document d is classified as a positive-sentiment document if its probability of positive sentiment label given document $P(\mathbf{l_{pos}}|d)$, is greater than its probability of negative sentiment label given document $P(\mathbf{l_{neg}}|d)$, and vice versa.

4 Experimental Setup

4.1 Dataset Description

Two publicly available datasets, the MR and MDS datasets, were used in our experiments. The MR dataset (also known as the polarity dataset) has become a benchmark for many studies since the work of Pang et al. (2002). The version 2.0 used in our experiment consists of 1000 positive and 1000 negative movie reviews drawn from the IMDB movie archive, with an average of 30 sentences in each document. We also experimented with another dataset, namely *subjective MR*, by removing the sentences that do not bear opinion information from the MR dataset, following the approach of Pang and Lee (2004). The resulting dataset still contains 2000 documents with a total of 334,336 words and 18,013 distinct terms, about half the size of the original MR dataset without performing subjectivity detection.

First used by Blitzer et al. (2007), the MDS dataset contains 4 different types of product reviews taken from Amazon.com including books, DVDs, electronics and kitchen appliances, with 1000 positive and 1000 negative examples for each domain[4].

Preprocessing was performed on both of the datasets. Firstly, punctuation, numbers, non-alphabet characters and stop words were removed. Secondly, standard stemming was performed in order to reduce the vocabulary size and address the issue of data sparseness. Summary statistics of the datasets before and after preprocessing are shown in Table 1.

4.2 Defining Model Priors

In the experiments, two subjectivity lexicons, namely the MPQA[5] and the appraisal lexicon[6], were combined and incorporated as prior information into the model learning. These two lexicons contain lexical words whose polarity orientation have been fully specified. We extracted the words with strong positive and negative orientation and performed stemming in the preprocessing. In addition, words whose polarity changed after stemming were removed automatically, resulting in 1584 positive and 2612 negative words, respectively. It is worth noting that the lexicons used here are fully domain-independent and do not bear any supervised information specifically to the MR, subjMR and MDS datasets. Finally, the prior information was produced by retaining all words in the MPQA and appraisal lexicons that occurred in the experimental datasets. The prior information statistics for each dataset is listed in the last row of Table 1.

In contrast to Lin and He (2009) that only utilized prior information during the initialization of the posterior distributions, we use the prior information in the Gibbs sampling inference step and argue that this is a more appropriate experimental setting. For the Gibbs sampling step of JST and Reverse-JST, if the currently observed word token matches a word in the sentiment lexicon, a corresponding sentiment label will be assigned and only a new topic will be sampled. Otherwise, a new sentiment-topic pair will be sampled for that word token. For LSM, if the current word token matches a word in the sentiment lexicon, a corresponding sentiment label will be assigned and skip the Gibbs sampling procedure. Otherwise, a new sentiment label will be sampled.

[4]We did not perform subjectivity detection on the MDS dataset since its average document length is much shorter than that of the MR dataset, with some documents even having one sentence only.

[5]`http://www.cs.pitt.edu/mpqa/`

[6]`http://lingcog.iit.edu/arc/appraisal_lexicon_2007b.tar.gz`

Table 1: Dataset and sentiment lexicon statistics. (Note:†denotes before preprocessing and * denotes after preprocessing.)

Dataset	# of words					
	MR	subjMR	MDS			
			Book	DVD	Electronic	Kitchen
Corpus size†	1,331,252	812,250	352,020	341,234	221,331	186,122
Corpus size*	627,317	334,336	157,441	153,422	95,441	79,654
Vocabulary†	38,906	34,559	22,028	21,424	10,669	9,525
Vocabulary*	25,166	18,013	14,459	14,806	7,063	6,252
# of lexicon (pos./neg.)*	1248/1877	1150/1667	1000/1352	979/1307	574/552	582/504

Table 2: LSM sentiment classification results.

	Aaccuracy (%)						
			MDS				
	MR	subjMR	Book	DVD	Electronic	Kitchen	MDS overall
LSM (without prior info.)	61.7	57.9	51.6	53.5	58.4	56.8	55.1
LSM (with prior info.)	74.1	76.1	64.2	66.3	72.5	74.1	69.3
Dasgupta and Ng (2009)	70.9	N/A	69.5	70.8	65.8	69.7	68.9
Li et al.(2009) with 10% doc. label	60	N/A	N/A				62
Li et al.(2009) with 40% doc. label	73.5	N/A					73

5 Experimental Results

5.1 LSM Sentiment Classification Results

In this section, we discuss the sentiment classification results of LSM at document level by incorporating prior information extracted from the MPQA and appraisal lexicon. The symmetry Dirichlet prior β was set to 0.01, and the asymmetric Dirichlet sentiment prior γ was set to 0.01 and 0.9 for the positive and negative sentiment label, respectively. Classification accuracies were averaged over 5 runs for each dataset with 2000 Gibbs sampling iterations.

As can be observed from Table 2, the performance of LSM is only mediocre for all the 6 datasets when no prior information was incorporated. A significant improvement, with an average of more than 13%, is observed after incorporating prior information, especially notable for subjMR and kitchen with 18.2% and 17.3% improvement, respectively. It is also noted that LSM with subjMR dataset achieved 2% improvement over the original MR dataset, implying that the subjMR dataset has better representation of subjective information than the original dataset by filtering out the objective contents. For the MDS dataset, LSM achieved 72.5% and 74.1% accuracy on electronic and kitchen domain respectively, which is much better than the book and DVD domain with only around 65% accuracy. Manually analysing the MDS dataset reveals that the book and DVD reviews often contain a lot of descriptions of book contents or movie plots, which make the reviews from these two domains difficult to classify; whereas in the electronic and kitchen domain, comments on the product are often expressed in a straightforward manner.

When compared to the recently proposed unsupervised approach based on a spectral clustering algorithm (Dasgupta and Ng, 2009), except for the book and DVD domain, LSM achieved better performance in all the other domains with more than 5% overall improvement. Nevertheless, the approach proposed by Dasgupta and Ng (2009) requires users to specify which dimensions (defined by the eigenvectors in spectral clustering) are most closely related to sentiment by inspecting a set of features derived from the reviews for each dimension, and clustering is performed again on the data to derive the final results. In all the Bayesian models studied here, no human judgement is required. Another recently proposed non-negative matrix tri-factorization approach (Li et al., 2009) also employed lexical prior knowledge for semi-supervised sentiment classification. However, when incorporating 10% of labelled documents for training, the non-negative matrix tri-factorization approach performed much worse than LSM, with only around 60% accuracy achieved for all the datasets. Even with 40% labelled documents, it still performs worse than LSM on the MR dataset and slightly outperforms LSM on the MDS dataset. It is worth noting that no labelled documents were used in the LSM results reported here.

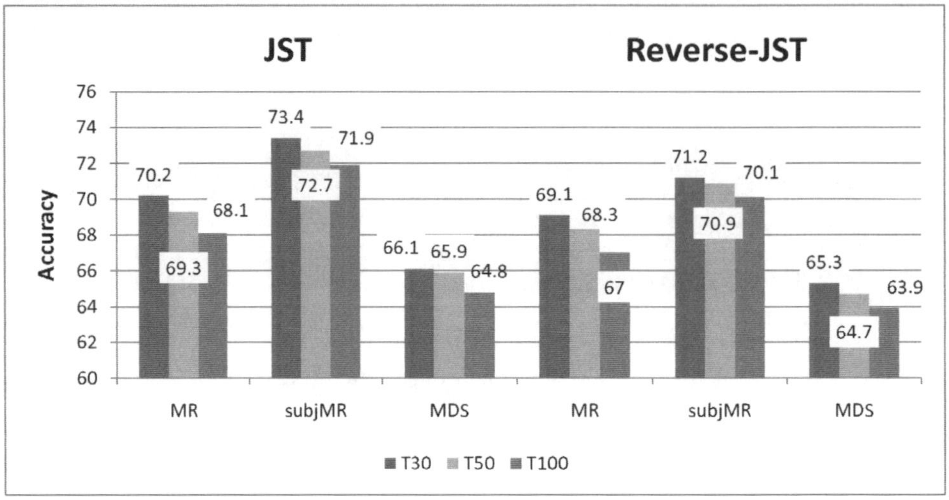

Figure 2: JST and Reverse-JST sentiment classification results with multiple topics.

5.2 JST and Reverse-JST Results with Multiple Topics

As both JST and Reverse-JST model document level sentiment and mixture of topic simultaneously, it is worth to explore how the sentiment classification and topic extraction tasks affect/benifit each other. With this in mind, we conducted a set of experiments on both JST and Reverse-JST, with topic number varying from 30, 50 to 100. The symmetry Dirichlet prior α and β were set to $50/T$ and 0.01 respectively for both models. The asymmetry sentiment prior γ was empirically set to (0.01, 1.8) for JST and (0.01, 0.012) for Reverse-JST, corresponding to positive and negative sentiment prior, respectively. Results were averaged over 5 runs with 2000 Gibbs sampling iterations.

As can be seen from Figure 2 that, for both models, the sentiment classification accuracy based on the subjMR dataset still outperformed the results based on the original MR dataset, where an overall improvement of 3% is observed for JST and about 2% for Reverse-JST. When comparing JST and Reverse-JST, it can be observed that Reverse-JST performed slightly worse than JST for all sets of experiments with about 1% to 2% drop in accuracy. By closely examining the posterior of JST and Reverse-JST (c.f. Equation 4 and 6), we noticed that the count $N_{j,d}$ (number of times topic j associated with some word tokens in document d) in the Reverse-JST posterior would be relatively small due to the factor of large topic number setting. On the contrary, the count $N_{k,d}$ (number of times sentiment label k assigned to some word tokens in document d) in the JST posterior would be relatively large as k is only defined over 3 different sentiment labels. This essentially makes JST less sensitive to the data sparseness problem and the perturbation of hyperparameter setting. In addition, JST encodes an assumption that there is approximately a single sentiment for the entire document, i.e. the documents are usually either mostly positive or mostly negative. This assumption is important as it allows the model to cluster different terms which share similar sentiment. In Reverse-JST, this assumption is not enforced unless only one topic for each sentiment is defined. Therefore, JST appears to be a more appropriate model design for joint sentiment topic detection.

In addition, it is observed that the sentiment classification accuracy of both JST and Reverse-JST drops slightly when the topic number increases from 30 to 100, with the changes of 2% (MR) and 1.5% (subjMR and MDS overall result) being observed for both models. This is likely due to the fact that when the topic number increases, the probability mass attracted under a sentiment-topic pair would become smaller, which essentially creates data sparseness problem. When comparing with LSM, we notice that the difference in sentiment classification accuracy is only marginal by additionally modelling a mixture of topics. But both JST and Reverse-JST are able to extract sentiment-oriented topics apart from document level sentiment detection.

Table 3: Topic examples extracted by JST under different sentiment labels.

Book		DVD		Electronic		Kitchen	
pos.	neg.	pos.	neg.	pos.	neg.	pos.	neg.
recip	war	action	murder	mous	drive	color	fan
food	militari	good	killer	hand	fail	beauti	room
cook	armi	fight	crime	logitech	data	plate	cool
cookbook	soldier	right	cop	comfort	complet	durabl	air
beauti	govern	scene	crime	scroll	manufactur	qualiti	loud
simpl	thing	chase	case	wheel	failur	fiestawar	nois
eat	evid	hit	prison	smooth	lose	blue	live
famili	led	art	detect	feel	backup	finger	annoi
ic	iraq	martial	investig	accur	poorli	white	blow
kitchen	polici	stunt	mysteri	track	error	dinnerwar	vornado
varieti	destruct	chan	commit	touch	storag	bright	bedroom
good	critic	brilliant	thriller	click	gb	purpl	inferior
pictur	inspect	hero	attornei	conveni	flash	scarlet	window
tast	invas	style	suspect	month	disast	dark	vibrat
cream	court	chines	shock	mice	recogn	eleg	power

5.3 Topic Extraction

We also evaluated the effectiveness of topic sentiment captured. In contrast to LDA in which a word is drawn from the topic-word distribution, in JST or Reverse-JST, a word is drawn from the distribution over words conditioned on both topic and sentiment label. As an illustration, Table 3 shows eight topic examples extracted from the MDS dataset by JST, where each topic was drawn from a particular product domain under positive or negative sentiment label.

As can be seen from Table 3, the eight extracted topics are quite informative and coherent, and each of the topics represents a certain product review from the corresponding domain. For example, the positive book topic probably discusses a good cookbook; the positive DVD topic is apparently about a popular action movie by Jackie Chan; the negative electronic topic is likely to be complains regarding data lose due to the flash drive failure, and the negative kitchen topic is probably the dissatisfaction of the high noise level of the *Vornado* brand fan. In terms of topic sentiment, by examining through the topics in the table, it is evident that topics under the positive and negative sentiment label indeed bear positive and negative sentiment respectively. The above analysis reveals the effectiveness of JST in extracting topics and capturing topic sentiment from text.

6 Conclusions and Future Work

In this paper, we studied three closed related Bayesian models for unsupervised sentiment detection, namely LSM, JST and Reverse-JST. As opposing to most of the existing approaches to sentiment classification which favour in supervised learning, these three models detect sentiment in a fully unsupervised manner. While all the three models gives either better or comparable performance compared to the existing approaches on unsupervised sentiment classification on the MR and MDS datasets, JST and Reverse-JST can also model a mixture of topics and the sentiment associated with each topic. Moreover, extensive experiments conducted on the datasets from different domains reveal that JST always outperformed Reverse-JST, suggesting JST being a more appropriate model design for joint sentiment topic detection.

There are several directions we plan to investigate in the future. One is incremental learning of the JST parameters when facing with new data. Another one is semi-supervised learning of the JST model with some supervised information being incorporating into the model parameter estimation procedure such as some known topic knowledge for certain product reviews or the document labels derived automatically from the user-supplied review ratings.

References

Ahmed Abbasi, Hsinchun Chen, and Arab Salem. 2008. Sentiment analysis in multiple languages: Feature selection for opinion classification in web forums. *ACM Trans. Inf. Syst.*, 26(3):1–34.

Alina Andreevskaia and Sabine Bergler. 2008. When specialists and generalists work together: Overcoming domain dependence in sentiment tagging. In *Proceedings of (ACL-HLT)*, pages 290–298.

A. Aue and M. Gamon. 2005. Customizing sentiment

classifiers to new domains: a case study. In *Proceedings of Recent Advances in Natural Language Processing (RANLP)*.

John Blitzer, Mark Dredze, and Fernando Pereira. 2007. Biographies, bollywood, boom-boxes and blenders: Domain adaptation for sentiment classification. In *Proceedings of the Association for Computational Linguistics (ACL)*, pages 440–447.

S. Dasgupta and V. Ng. 2009. Topic-wise, Sentiment-wise, or Otherwise? Identifying the Hidden Dimension for Unsupervised Text Classification. In *Proceedings of the 2009 Conference on Empirical Methods in Natural Language Processing*, pages 580–589.

Thomas Hofmann. 1999. Probabilistic latent semantic indexing. In *Proceedings of the ACM Special Interest Group on Information Retrieval (SIGIR)*, pages 50–57.

Nobuhiro Kaji and Masaru Kitsuregawa. 2006. Automatic construction of polarity-tagged corpus from html documents. In *Proceedings of the COLING/ACL on Main conference poster sessions*, pages 452–459.

A. Kennedy and D. Inkpen. 2006. Sentiment classification of movie reviews using contextual valence shifters. *Computational Intelligence*, 22(2):110–125.

Shoushan Li and Chengqing Zong. 2008. Multi-domain sentiment classification. In *Proceedings of the Association for Computational Linguistics and the Human Language Technology Conference (ACL-HLT), Short Papers*, pages 257–260.

Tao Li, Yi Zhang, and Vikas Sindhwani. 2009. A non-negative matrix tri-factorization approach to sentiment classification with lexical prior knowledge. In *Proceedings of (ACL-IJCNLP)*, pages 244–252.

Chenghua Lin and Yulan He. 2009. Joint sentiment/topic model for sentiment analysis. In *Proceedings of the ACM international conference on Information and knowledge management (CIKM)*.

Ryan McDonald, Kerry Hannan, Tyler Neylon, Mike Wells, and Jeff Reynar. 2007. Structured models for fine-to-coarse sentiment analysis. In *Proceedings of the Annual Meeting of the Association of Computational Linguistics (ACL)*, pages 432–439.

Qiaozhu Mei, Xu Ling, Matthew Wondra, Hang Su, and ChengXiang Zhai. 2007. Topic sentiment mixture: modeling facets and opinions in weblogs. In *Proceedings of the conference on World Wide Web (WWW)*, pages 171–180.

Bo Pang and Lillian Lee. 2004. A sentimental education: sentiment analysis using subjectivity summarization based on minimum cuts. In *Proceedings of the Annual Meeting on Association for Computational Linguistics (ACL)*, page 271.

Bo Pang and Lillian Lee. 2008. Opinion mining and sentiment analysis. *Found. Trends Inf. Retr.*, 2(1-2):1–135.

Bo Pang, Lillian Lee, and Shivakumar Vaithyanathan. 2002. Thumbs up?: sentiment classification using machine learning techniques. In *Proceedings of the Conference on Empirical Methods in Natural Language Processing (EMNLP)*, pages 79–86.

Ivan Titov and Ryan McDonald. 2008a. A joint model of text and aspect ratings for sentiment summarization. In *Proceedings of the Aunal Meeting on Association for Computational Linguistics and the Human Language Technology Conference (ACL-HLT)*, pages 308–316.

Ivan Titov and Ryan McDonald. 2008b. Modeling online reviews with multi-grain topic models. In *Proceeding of the International Conference on World Wide Web (WWW 08')*, pages 111–120.

Casey Whitelaw, Navendu Garg, and Shlomo Argamon. 2005. Using appraisal groups for sentiment analysis. In *Proceedings of the ACM international conference on Information and Knowledge Management (CIKM)*, pages 625–631.

A Hybrid Approach to Emotional Sentence Polarity and Intensity Classification

Jorge Carrillo de Albornoz, Laura Plaza, Pablo Gervás
Universidad Complutense de Madrid
Madrid, Spain
{jcalbornoz,lplazam}@fdi.ucm.es, pgervas@sip.ucm.es

Abstract

In this paper, the authors present a new approach to sentence level sentiment analysis. The aim is to determine whether a sentence expresses a positive, negative or neutral sentiment, as well as its intensity. The method performs WSD over the words in the sentence in order to work with concepts rather than terms, and makes use of the knowledge in an affective lexicon to label these concepts with emotional categories. It also deals with the effect of negations and quantifiers on polarity and intensity analysis. An extensive evaluation in two different domains is performed in order to determine how the method behaves in 2-classes (*positive* and *negative*), 3-classes (*positive, negative* and *neutral*) and 5-classes (*strongly negative*, *weakly negative*, *neutral*, *weakly positive* and *strongly positive*) classification tasks. The results obtained compare favorably with those achieved by other systems addressing similar evaluations.

1 Introduction

Sentiment analysis has gained much attention from the research community in recent years. It is concerned with the problem of discovering emotional meanings in text, and most common tasks usually include emotion labeling (assigning a text its main emotion), polarity recognition (classifying a statement into positive or negative) and subjectivity identification (determining whether a text is subjective or objective). The growing research interest is mainly due to the practical applications of sentiment analysis. Companies and organizations are interested in finding out costumer sentiments and opinions, while individuals are interested in others' opinions when purchasing a product or deciding whether or not watching a movie.

Many approaches have dealt with sentiment analysis as the problem of classifying product or service reviews (Pang et al., 2002; Turney, 2002), while others have attempted to classify news items (Devitt and Ahmad, 2007). The task is usually addressed as a 2-classes classification problem (*positive* vs. *negative*). Recent works have included the *neutral* class, trying to detect not only the polarity but also the absence of emotional meaning (Wilson et al., 2005; Esuli and Sebastiani, 2006). However, few approaches try to face a more fine-grained prediction of the intensity (e.g. classifying the polarity into *strongly negative*, *weakly negative*, *neutral*, *weakly positive* and *strongly positive*).

Another important problem of most of these approximations is that they usually work with terms, and so disregard the contextual meaning of those terms in the sentence (Martineau and Finin, 2009; Moilanen and Pulman, 2007). The use of word disambiguation is not usual in this task, due to the fact that most approaches use lexical resources created to work with terms. However, it is essential to correctly capture the meaning of these terms within the text.

In this paper, we present a hybrid approach based on machine learning techniques and lexical rules to classify sentences according to their polarity and intensity. Thus, given an input text, the method is able to determine the polarity of each sentence (i.e. if it is negative or positive), as well as its intensity. The system tackles the effect of negations and quantifiers in sentiment analysis, and addresses the problem of word ambiguity, taken into account the contextual meaning of the terms in the text by using a word sense disambiguation algorithm.

The paper is organized as follows. Section 2 exposes some background and related work on sentiment analysis. Section 3 presents the lexical resources and corpora used by the system. Sec-

Proceedings of the Fourteenth Conference on Computational Natural Language Learning, pages 153–161,
Uppsala, Sweden, 15-16 July 2010.

tion 4 describes the method proposed for polarity and intensity classification. Section 5 presents the evaluation framework and discusses the experimental results. Finally, section 6 provides concluding remarks and future lines of work.

2 Related work

The sentiment analysis discipline in computational linguistic is mainly focused on identifying/classifying different emotional contents within a phrase, sentence or document. This field usually encloses tasks such as emotion identification, subjectivity classification and polarity recognition. Sentiment analysis has obtained great popularity in the last years mostly due to its successful application to different business domains, such as the evaluation of products and services, where the goal is to discern whether the opinion expressed by a user about a product or service is favorable or unfavorable.

Focusing on polarity recognition, the aim of this task is the classification of texts into positive or negative according to their emotional meaning. Most of the approaches rely on machine learning techniques or rule based methods. Statistical approaches based on term frequencies and bags of words are frequently used in machine learning approximations. Pang et al. (2002) present a comparison between three different machine learning algorithms trained with bags of features computed over term frequencies, and conclude that SVM classifiers can be efficiently used in polarity identification. Martineau and Finin (2009) use a similar approach where the words are scored using a Delta TF-IDF function before classifying the documents. On the other hand, Meena and Prabhakar (2007) study the effect of conjuncts in polarity recognition using rule based methods over the syntax tree of the sentence. Whitelaw et al. (2005) introduce the concept of "appraisal groups" which are combined with bags of word features to automatically classify movie reviews. To this aim, they use a semi-automated method to generate a lexicon of appraising adjectives and modifiers.

During the past few years, the problem of polarity recognition has been usually faced as a step beyond the identification of the subjectivity or objectivity of texts (Wiebe et al., 1999). Different approximations have been proposed to deal with this problem. Pang and Lee (2004) propose a graph-based method which finds minimum cuts in a document graph to classify the sentences into subjective or objective. After that, they use a bag of words approximation to classify the subjective sentences into positive or negative. Kim and Hovy (2004) also introduce a previous step to identify the subjectivity of sentences regarding a certain topic, and later classify these sentences into positives or negatives.

Most recent approaches do not only deal with the 2-classes classification problem, but also introduce a new class representing neutrality. Thus, the aim of these works is to classify the text into positive, negative or neutral. Wilson et al. (2005) present a double subjectivity classifier based on features such as syntactic classes and sentence position, and more semantic features such as adjective graduation. The first classifier determines the subjectivity or neutrality of the phrases in the text, while the second determines its polarity (including neutrality). Esuli and Sebastiani (2006) also address this problem testing three different variants of a semi-supervised method, and classify the input into positive, negative or neutral. The method proposed yields good results in the 2-classes polarity classification, while the results decrease when dealing with 3-classes. A more ambitious classification task is proposed by Brooke (2009), where the goal is to measure the intensity of polarity. To this aim, the author classifies the input into 3-classes (*strongly-negative, ambivalent,* and *strongly-positive*), 4 classes (*strongly-negative, weakly-negative, weakly-positive* and *strongly-positive*) and 5-classes (*strongly-negative, weakly-negative, ambivalent, weakly-positive* and *strongly-positive*). The results decrease considerably with the number of classes, from 62% of accuracy for 3-classes to 38% of accuracy for 5-classes.

3 Corpora and resources

The evaluation of the system has been carried out using two corpora from two very distinct domains: the Sentence Polarity Movie Review Dataset[1] and the one used in the SemEval 2007 Affective Text task[2]. The first one consists of 10.662 sentences selected from different movie review websites. These sentences are labeled as positive or negative depending on whether they express a positive or negative opinion within the movie review. The second one consists of a training set and a test set of 250 and 1000 news headlines respectively, extracted from different news sites. Each sentence is labeled with a value

[1] http://www.cs.cornell.edu/People/pabo/movie-review-data/

[2] http://www.cse.unt.edu/~rada/affectivetext/

between -100 and 100, where -100 means highly negative emotional intensity, 100 means highly positive and 0 means neutral. To the purpose of this work, the test set from the SemEval corpus and 1000 sentences randomly extracted from the Sentence Polarity Movie Review corpus (500 positive and 500 negative) were used as evaluation datasets.

In order to identify the emotional categories associated to the concepts in the sentences, an affective lexical database based on semantic senses, instead of terms, is needed. To this aim, the authors have tested different resources and finally selected the WordNet Affect affective database (Strapparava and Valitutti, 2004). This affective lexicon has the particularity of assigning emotional categories to synsets of the WordNet lexical database (Miller et al., 1990), allowing the system to correctly disambiguate the terms using one of the many WordNet-based word sense disambiguation algorithms. The emotional categories in WordNet Affect are organized hierarchically, and its first level distinguishes between *positive-emotion*, *negative-emotion*, *neutral-emotion* and *ambiguous-emotion*. The second level encloses the emotional categories themselves, and consists of a set of 32 categories. For this work, a subset of 16 emotional categories from this level has been selected, since the hierarchy proposed in WordNet Affect is considerably broader than those commonly used in sentiment analysis. On the other hand, the first level of emotional categories may be useful to predict the polarity, but it is clearly not enough to predict the intensity of this polarity. To be precise, the subset of emotional categories used in this work is: *{joy, love, liking, calmness, positive-expectation, hope, fear, sadness, dislike, shame, compassion, despair, anxiety, surprise, ambiguous-agitation* and *ambiguous-expectation}*. The authors consider this subset to be a good representation of the human feeling.

Since the WordNet Affect hierarchy does not provide an antonym relationship, the authors has created that relation for the previous set of emotional categories. Only relationships between emotional categories with a strongly opposite meaning are created, such as *liking-disliking* and *joy-sadness*. The purpose of this antonym relationship is twofold: first, it contributes to handle negation forms; and second, it can be used to automatically expand the affective lexicon. Both issues are discussed in detail later in the document.

On the other hand, since a good amount of words with a highly emotional meaning, such as *dead*, *cancer* and *violent*, are not labeled in WordNet Affect, these words have been manually labeled by the authors and have been later extended with their *synonyms*, *antonyms* and *derived adjectives* using the corresponding semantic and lexical relations in WordNet. This process has been done in two steps in order to measure the effect of the number of synsets labeled on the classification accuracy, as described in section 5.

The WordNet Affect 1.1 lexicon consists of a set of 911 synsets. However, the authors have detected that a good number of these synsets have been labeled more than once, and with different emotional categories (e.g. the synset "a#00117872 {angered, enraged, furious, infuriated, maddened}" is labeled with three different categories: *anger*, *fury* and *infuriation*). Thus, after removing these synsets and those labeled with an emotional category not included in the 16-categories subset used in this work, the affective lexicon presents 798 synsets. After the first step of semi-automatic labeling, the affective lexicon increased the number of synsets in 372, of which 100 synsets were manually labeled, and 272 were automatically derived throughout the WordNet relations. The second and last step of semi-automatic labeling added 603 synsets to the lexicon, of which 200 synsets were manually labeled, and 403 were automatically derived. The final lexicon presents 1773 synsets and 4521 words labeled with an emotional category. Table 1 shows the distribution of the affective lexicon in grammatical categories.

Grammatical Category	WNAffect	WNAffect + 1st step	WNAffect + 2nd step
Nouns	280	440	699
Verbs	122	200	309
Adjectives	273	394	600
Adverbs	123	136	165

Table 1: Distribution in grammatical categories of the synsets in the affective lexicon.

4 The method

In this section, the method for automatically labeling sentences with an emotional intensity and polarity is presented. The problem is faced as a text classification task, which is accomplishes throughout four steps. Each step is explained in detail in the following subsections.

4.1 Pre-processing: POS tagging and concept identification

In order to determine the appropriate emotional category for each word in its context, a pre-processing step is accomplished to translate each term in the sentence to its adequate sense in WordNet. To this aim, the system analyzes the text, splits it into sentences and tags the tokens with their part of speech. The Gate architecture[3] and the Stanford Parser[4] were selected to carry out this process. In particular the *Annie English Tokeniser*, *Hash Gazetter*, *RegEx Sentence Splitter* and the *Stanford Parser* modules in Gate are used to analyze the input. In this step also the syntax tree and dependencies are retrieved from the Stanford Parser. These features will be used in the post-processing step in order to identify the negations and the quantifiers, as well as their scope.

Once the sentences have been split and tagged, the method maps each word of each sentence into its sense in WordNet according to its context. To this end, the *lesk* WSD algorithm implemented in the WordNet Sense-Relate perl package is used (Patwardhan et al., 2005). The disambiguation is carried out only over the words belonging to the grammatical categories *noun*, *verb*, *adjective* and *adverb*, as only these categories can present an emotional meaning. As a result, we get the stem and sense in WordNet of each word, and this information is used to retrieve its synset.

A good example of the importance of performing word disambiguation can be shown in the sentence "*Test to predict breast cancer relapse is approved*" from the SemEval news corpus. The noun *cancer* has five possible entries in WordNet and only one refers to a "*malignant growth or tumor*", while the others are related with "*astrology*" and the "*cancer zodiacal constellation*". Obviously, without a WSD algorithm, the wrong synset will be considered, and a wrong emotion will be assigned to the concept.

Besides, to enrich the emotion identification step, the hypernyms of each concept are also retrieved from WordNet.

4.2 Emotion identification

The aim of the emotion identification step is to map the WordNet concepts previously identified to those present in the affective lexicon, as well as to retrieve from this lexicon the corresponding emotional category of each concept.

We hypothesize that the hypernyms of a concept entail the same emotions than the concept itself, but the intensity of such emotions decreases as we move up the hierarchy (i.e. the more general the hypernym becomes, the less its emotional intensity is). Following this hypothesis, when no entry is found in the affective lexicon for a given concept, the emotional category associated to its nearest hypernym, if any, is used to label the concept. However, only a certain level of hypernymy is accepted, since an excessive generalization introduces some noise in the emotion identification. This parameter has been empirically set to *3* (Carrillo de Albornoz et al., 2010). Previous experiments have shown that, upper this level, the working hypothesis becomes unreliable.

The sentence "*Siesta cuts risk of heart disease death study finds*" clearly illustrates the process described above. In this sentence, the concepts *risk*, *death* and *disease* are labeled with an emotional category: in particular, the categories assigned to them are *fear, fear* and *dislike* respectively. However, while the two firsts are retrieved from the affective lexicon by their own synsets, the last one is labeled through its hypernym: since no matching is found for *disease* in the lexicon, the analysis over its hypernyms detects the category *dislike* assigned to the synset of its first hypernym, which contains words such as *illness* and *sickness*, and the same emotion *(dislike)* is assigned to *disease*.

It must be noted that, to perform this analysis, a previous mapping between 2.1 and 1.6 WordNet versions was needed, since the method and the affective lexicon work on different versions of the database.

4.3 Post-processing: Negation and quantifiers detection

Once the concepts of the sentence have been labeled with their emotional categories, the next step aims to detect and solve the effect of the negations and the quantifiers on the emotional categories identified in the previous step.

The effect of negation has been broadly studied in NLP (Morante and Daelemans, 2009) and sentiment analysis (Jia et al., 2009). Two main considerations must be taken into account when dealing with negation. First, the negation scope may affect only a word (***no reason***), a proposition (*Beckham* ***does not want to play again for Real***) or even a subject (***No one*** *would like to do*

[3] http://gate.ac.uk/

[4] http://nlp.stanford.edu/software/lex-parser.shtml

this). Different approximations have been proposed to delimit the scope of negation. Some assume the scope to be those words between the negation token and the first punctuation mark (Pang et al., 2002), others consider a fixed number of words after the negation token (Hu and Liu, 2004). Second, the impact of negation is usually neutralized by reversing the polarity of the sentence (Polanyi and Zaenen, 2006) or using contextual valence shifters which increase or dismiss the final value of negativity or positivity of the sentence (Kennedy and Inkpen, 2006).

In this work, the negation scope is detected using the syntax tree and dependencies generated by the Stanford Parser. The dependency *neg* allows us to easily determine the presence of several simple types of negation, such as those preceded by *don't*, *didn't*, *not*, *never*, etc. Other words not identified with this dependency, but also with a negation meaning, such as *no*, *none*, *nor* or *nobody,* are identified using a negation token list. To determine the negation scope, we find in the syntax tree the first common ancestor that encloses the negation token and the word immediately after it, and assume all descendant leaf nodes to be affected by the negation.

For each concept in the sentence that falls into the scope of a negation, the system retrieves its antonym emotional category, if any, and assigns this category to the concept. If no antonym emotion is obtained, the concept is labeled with no emotion, according to the premise that the negation may change or neutralize the emotional polarity. An example of this process can be shown in the sentence "*Children and adults enamored of all things pokemon won't be disappointed*". In this sentence, the Stanford Parser discovers a negation and the system, through the syntax tree, determines that the scope of the negation encloses the words "*won't be disappointed*". As the synset of "*disappointed*" has been labeled with the emotional category *despair,* its antonym is retrieved, and the emotional category of the antonym, *hope,* is used to label the concept.

On the other hand, the quantifiers are words considered in sentiment analysis as *amplifiers* or *downtoners* (Quirk et al., 1985). That is to say, the word *very* in the sentence "*That is a very good idea*" amplifies the intensity of the emotional meaning and the positivity of the sentence, while the word *less* in the sentence "*It is less handsome than I was expecting*" dismisses its intensity and polarity. The most common approach to identify quantifiers is the use of lists of words which play specific grammatical roles in the sentence. These lists normally contain a fixed value for all positive words and another value for all negative words (Polanyi and Zaenen, 2006). By contrast, Brooke (2009) proposes a novel approach where each quantifier is assigned its own polarity and weight.

The quantifiers are usually represented as sentence modifiers, assuming their scope to be the whole sentence and modifying its overall polarity. However, when dealing with sentences like "*The house is really nice and the neighborhood is not bad*", these approaches assume that the quantifier *really* amplifies the intensity of both conjunctives, when it only should amplify the intensity of the first one. By contrast, our approach determines the scope of the quantifiers by the syntax tree and the dependencies over them. Thus, when a quantifier is detected in a sentence, the dependencies are checked and only those that play certain roles, such as adverbial or adjectival modifiers, are considered. All concepts affected by a quantifier are marked with the weight corresponding to that quantifier, which will serve to amplify/dismiss the emotions of these concepts in the classification step. The quantifier list used here is the one proposed in Brooke (2009).

The sentence "*Stale first act, scrooge story, blatant product placement, some very good comedic songs*" illustrates the analysis of the quantifiers. The system detects two tokens which are in the quantifier list and play the appropriate grammatical roles. The first quantifier *some* affects to the words "*very good comedic songs*", while the second quantifier *very* only affects to "*good*". So these concepts are marked with the specific weight of each quantifier. Note that the concept "*good*" is marked twice.

4.4 Sentence classification

Up to this point, the sentence has been labeled with a set of emotional categories, negations and their scope have been detected and the quantifiers and the concepts affected by them have been identified. In this step, this information is used to translate the sentence into a *Vector of Emotional Occurrences (VEO)*, which will be the input to the machine learning classification algorithm. Thus, each sentence is represented as a vector of 16 values, each of one representing an emotional category. The VEO vector is generated as follows:

- If the concept has been labeled with an emotional category, the position of the vector for this category is increased in *1*.

- If no emotional category has been found for the concept, then the category of its first hypernym labeled is used. As the hypernym generalizes the meaning of the concept, the value assigned to the position of the emotional category in the VEO is weighted as follows:

$$VEO[i] = VEO[i] + \frac{1}{Hyper.Depth + 1}$$

- If a negation scope encloses the concept, then the antonym emotion is used, as described in the previous step. The emotional category position of this antonym in the VEO is increased in *0.9*. Different tests have been carried out to set this parameter, and the *0.9* value got the best results. The reason for using a lower value for the emotional categories derived from negations is that the authors consider that a negation changes the emotional meaning of a concept but usually in a lower percentage. For example, the sentence "*The neighborhood is not bad*" does not necessarily mean that it is a good neighborhood, but it is a quite acceptable one.
- If a concept is affected by a quantifier, then the weight of that quantifier is added to the position in the VEO of the emotional category assigned to the concept.

Thus, a sentence like "*This movie.... isn't worth the energy it takes to describe how really bad it is*" will be represented by the VEO [1.0, 0, 0.0, 0, 0, 0.0, 0, 0, 2.95, 0, 0, 0, 0, 0, 0, 0]. In this sentence, the concept *movie* is labeled with the emotional category *joy,* the concept *worth* is labeled with *positive-expectation*, the concept *energy* is labeled with *liking,* and the concept *bad* is labeled with *dislike.* Since the concepts *worth* and *energy* fall into the negation scope, they both change their emotional category to *dislike.* Besides, since the concept *bad* is amplified by the quantifier *really*, the weight of this concept in the VEO is increased in *0.15*.

5 Evaluation framework and results

In this work, two different corpora have been used for evaluation (see Section 3): a movie review corpus containing 1000 sentences labeled with either a positive or negative polarity; and a news headlines corpus composed of 1000 sentences labeled with an emotional intensity value between -100 and 100.

To determine the best machine learning algorithm for the task, 20 classifiers currently implemented in Weka[5] were compared. We only show the results of the best performance classifiers: a logistic regression model *(Logistic)*, a C4.5 decision tree *(J48Graph)* and a support vector machine *(LibSVM)*. The best outcomes for the three algorithms were reported when using their default parameters, except for J48Graph, where the confidence factor was set to *0.2*. The evaluation is accomplishes using 10-fold cross validation. Therefore, 100 instances of each dataset are held back for testing in each fold, and the additional 900 instances are used for training.

5.1 Evaluating polarity classification

We first analyze the effect of expanding the coverage of the emotional lexicon by semi-automatically adding to WordNet Affect more synsets labeled with emotional categories, as explained in Section 3. To this end, we compare the results of the method using three different affective lexical databases: WordNet Affect and WordNet Affect extended with 372 and 603 synsets, respectively. For the sake of comparing the results in both corpora, the news dataset has been mapped to a -100/100 classification (-100 = [-100, 0), 100 = [0,100]).

Table 2 shows the results as average precision and accuracy of these experiments. Note that, as the weight of mislabeling for both classes is the same and the classes are balanced, accuracy is equal to recall in all cases. Labeling 975 new synsets significantly improves the performance of our system in both datasets and for all ML techniques. In particular, the best improvement is achieved by the Logistic classifier: from 52.7% to 72.4% of accuracy in the news dataset, and from 50.5% to 61.5% of accuracy in the movies dataset.

Emotional Lexicon	Method	News Corpus		Movie Reviews	
		Pr.	*Ac.*	*Pr.*	*Ac.*
WNAffect	*Logistic*	52.8	52.7	51.3	50.5
	J48Graph	27.7	52.6	50	50
	LibSVM	27.7	52.6	53.2	50.6
WNAffect + 372 synsets	*Logistic*	69.9	65.2	53.9	53.8
	J48Graph	70.1	64.8	55.3	55.1
	LibSVM	68.9	63.9	52	51.8
WNAffect + 603 synsets	*Logistic*	73.8	72.4	61.6	61.5
	J48Graph	73.6	70.9	60.9	60.9
	LibSVM	71.6	70.3	62.5	59.4

Table 2: Precision and accuracy percentages achieved by our system using different affective databases.

[5] http://www.cs.waikato.ac.nz/ml/weka/

We have observed that, especially in the news dataset, an important number of sentences that are labeled with a low positive or negative emotional intensity could be perfectly considered as neutral. The intensity of these sentences highly depends on the previous knowledge and particular interpretation of the reader. For instance, the sentence "*Looking beyond the iPhone*" does not express any emotion itself, unless you are fan or detractor of Apple. However, this sentence is labeled in the corpus with a *15* intensity value. It is likely that these kinds of sentences introduce noise into the dataset. In order to estimate the influence of such sentences in the experimental results, we conducted a test removing from the news dataset those instances with an intensity value in the range [-25, 25]. As expected, the accuracy of the method increases substantially, i.e. from 72.4% to 76.3% for logistic regression.

The second group of experiments is directed to evaluate if dealing with negations and quantifiers improves the performance of the method. To this end, the approach described in Section 4.3 was applied to both datasets. Table 3 shows that processing negations consistently improves the accuracy of all algorithms in both datasets; while the effect of the quantifiers is not straightforward. Even if we expected that using quantifiers would lead to better results, the performance in both datasets decreases in 2 out of the 3 ML algorithms. However, combining both features improves the results in both datasets. The reason seems to be that, when no previous negation detection is performed, if the emotional category assigned to certain concepts are wrong (because these concepts are affected by negations), the quantifiers will be weighting the wrong emotions.

Features	Method	News Corpus		Movie Reviews	
		Pr.	Ac.	Pr.	Ac.
Negations	*Logistic*	74.2	72.5	61.7	61.6
	J48Graph	74.1	71.2	62.8	62.6
	LibSVM	72.7	71.1	62.4	60.1
Quantifiers	*Logistic*	73.7	72.2	61.9	61.9
	J48Graph	73.6	70.9	59.5	59.5
	LibSVM	72.1	70.6	61.1	59
Negations + Quantifiers	*Logistic*	74.4	72.7	62.4	62.4
	J48Graph	74.1	71.2	62.5	62.1
	LibSVM	72.8	71.2	62.6	60.5

Table 3: Precision and accuracy of the system improved with negation and quantifier detection.

The comparison with related work is difficult due to the different datasets and methods used in the evaluations. For instance, Pang et al. (2002) use the Movie Review Polarity Dataset, achieving an accuracy of 82.9% training a SVM over a bag of words. However, their aim was to determine the polarity of documents (i.e. the whole movie reviews) instead of sentences. When working at the sentence level, the information from the context is missed, and the results are expected to be considerably lower. As a matter of fact, it happens that many sentences in the Sentence Polarity Movie Review Dataset are labeled as positive or negative, but do not express any polarity when taken out of the context of the overall movie review. This conclusion is also drawn by Meena and Prabhakar (2007), who achieve an accuracy of 39% over a movie review corpus (not specified) working at the sentence level, using a rule based method to analyze the effect of conjuncts. This accuracy is well below that of our method (62.6%).

Molianen and Pulman (2007) present a sentiment composition model where the polarity of a sentence is calculated as a complex function of the polarity of its parts. They evaluate their system over the SemEval 2007 news corpus, and achieve an accuracy of 65.6%, under our same experimental conditions, which is also significantly lower than the accuracy obtained by our method.

5.2 Evaluating intensity classification

Apart from identifying of polarity, we also want to examine the ability of our system to determine the emotional intensity in the sentences. To this aim, we define two intensity distributions: the 3-classes and the 5-classes distribution. For the first distribution, we map the news dataset to 3-classes: negative [-100, -50), neutral [-50, 50) and positive [50, 100]. For the second distribution, we map the dataset to 5-classes: strongly negative [-100, -60), negative [-60, -20), neutral [-20, 20), positive [20, 60) and strongly positive [60, 100]. We can see in Table 4 that, as the number of intensity classes increases, the results are progressively worse, since the task is progressively more difficult.

Intensity classes	Method	News Corpus	
		Pr.	Ac.
2-classes	*Logistic*	74.4	72.7
	J48Graph	74.1	71.2
	LibSVM	72.8	71.2
3-classes	*Logistic*	60.2	63.8
	J48Graph	66	64.8
	LibSVM	54.8	64.6
5-classes	*Logistic*	48.3	55.4
	J48Graph	47.3	54.8
	LibSVM	43.1	53.1

Table 4: Precision and accuracy in three different intensity classification tasks.

The 3-classes distribution coincides exactly with that used in one of the SemEval 2007 Affective task, so that we can easily compare our results with those of the systems that participated in the task. The CLaC and CLaC-NB systems (Andreevskaia and Bergler, 2007) achieved, respectively, the best precision and recall. CLaC reported a precision of 61.42 % and a recall of 9.20%; while CLaC-NB reported a precision of 31.18% and a recall of 66.38%. Our method clearly outperforms both systems in precision, while provides a recall (which is equal to the accuracy) near to that of the best system. Besides, our results for both metrics are well-balanced, which does not occur in the other systems.

Regarding the 5-classes distribution evaluation, to the authors' knowledge no other work has been evaluated under these conditions. However, our system reports promising results: using 5 classes it achieves better results than other participant in the SemEval task using just 3 classes (Chaumartin, 2007; Katz et al., 2007).

5.3 Evaluating the effect of word ambiguity on sentiment analysis

A further test has been conducted to examine the effect of word ambiguity on the classification results. To this aim, we repeated the experiments above without using WSD. First, we simply assigned to each word its first sense in WordNet. Second, we selected these senses randomly. The results are presented in Table 5. We only show those of the best algorithm for each intensity distribution.

Intensity classes	Method	News Corpus Pr.	News Corpus Ac.
2-classes (Logistic)	*WSD*	74.4	72.6
	1st Sense	71.6	69.3
	Random Sense	69.1	64.1
3-classes (J48Graph)	*WSD*	66	64.8
	1st Sense	59	62.9
	Random Sense	50.8	61
5-classes (Logistic)	*WSD*	48.3	55.4
	1st Sense	43.7	53.8
	Random Sense	46.8	51.6

Table 5: Precision and accuracy for three different word disambiguation strategies.

It can be observed that, even though the use of word disambiguation improves the classification precision and accuracy, the improvement with respect to the first sense heuristic is less than expected. This may be due to the fact that the senses of the words in WordNet are ranked according to their frequency, and so the first sense of a word is also the most frequent one. Besides, the Most Frequent Sense (MFS) heuristic in WSD is usually regarded as a difficult competitor. On the contrary, the improvement with respect to the random sense heuristic is quite remarkable.

6 Conclusions and future work

In this paper, a novel approach to sentence level sentiment analysis has been described. The system has resulted in a good method for sentence polarity classification, as well as for intensity identification. The results obtained outperform those achieved by other systems which aim to solve the same task.

Nonetheless, some considerations must be noted. Even with the extended affective lexicon, around 1 in 4 sentences of each corpus has not been assigned any emotional category, sometimes because their concepts are not labeled in the lexicon, but mostly because their concepts do not have any emotional meaning *per se*. A test on the news corpus removing those sentences not labeled with any emotional meaning has been performed for the 2-classes classification problem, allowing the method to obtain an accuracy of 81.7%. However, to correctly classify these sentences, it would be necessary to have additional information about their contexts (i.e. the body of the news item, its section in the newspaper, etc.).

Finally, the authors plan to extend the method to deal with modal and conditional operators, which will allow us to distinguish among situations that have happened, situations that are happening, situations that *could, might* or *possibly* happen or will happen, situations that are wished to happen, etc.

Acknowledgments

This research is funded by the Spanish Ministry of Science and Innovation (TIN2009-14659-C03-01), the Comunidad Autonoma de Madrid and the European Social Fund through the IV PRICIT program, and the Spanish Ministry of Education through the FPU program.

References

Julian Brooke. 2009. A Semantic Approach to Automated Text Sentiment Analysis. Simon Fraser University. Ph. D. Thesis.

Jorge Carrillo de Albornoz, Laura Plaza and Pablo Gervás. 2010. Improving Emotional Intensity Classification using Word Sense Disambiguation. *Research in Computing Science 46* :131-142.

François-Régis Chaumartin. 2007. UPAR7: A Knowledge-based System for Headline Sentiment Tagging. In *Proceedings of the 4th Workshop on Semantic Evaluations (SemEval 2007)*, pages 422-425.

Ann Devitt and Khurshid Ahmad. 2007. Sentiment Polarity Identification in Financial News: A Cohesion-based Approach. In *Proceedings of the 45th Annual Meeting of the ACL,* pages 984-991.

Andrea Esuli and Fabrizio Sebastiani. 2006. Determining Term Subjectivity and Term Orientation for Opinion Mining. In *Proceedings of the 11th Conference of the EACL,* pages 193-200.

Minging Hu and Bing Liu. 2004. Mining and Summarizing Customer Reviews. In *Proceedings of the 10th ACM SIGKDD Conference on Knowledge Discovery and Data Mining*, pages 168-177.

Lifeng Jia, Clement Yu and Weiji Meng. 2009. The Effect of Negation on Sentiment Analysis and Retrieval Effectiveness. In *Proceeding of the 18th ACM Conference on Information and Knowledge Management*, pages 1827-1830.

Phil Katz, Matthew Singleton and Richard Wicentowski. 2007. SWAT-MP: the SemEval-2007 Systems for Task 5 and Task 14. In *Proceedings of the 4th Workshop on Semantic Evaluations (SemEval 2007)*, pages 308-313.

Alistair Kennedy and Diana Inkpen. 2006. Sentiment Classification of Movie Reviews Using Contextual Valence Shifters. *Computational Intelligence 22(2):* 110-125.

Soo-Min Kim and Eduard Hovy. 2004. Determining the Sentiment of Opinions. In *Proceedings of COLING 2004,* pages 1367-1373.

Justin Martineau and Tim Finin. 2009. Delta TFIDF: An Improved Feature Space for Sentiment Analysis. In *Proceedings of the 3rd AAAI International Conference on Weblogs and Social Media.*

Arun Meena and T.V. Prabhakar. 2007. Sentence Level Sentiment Analysis in the Presence of Conjuncts Using Linguistic Analysis. In *Proceedings of ECIR 2007*, pages 573-580.

George A. Miller, Richard Beckwith, Christiane Fellbaum Derek Gross and Katherine Miller. 1990. Introduction to WordNet: An On-Line Lexical Database. *International Journal of Lexicography 3(4)*:235-244.

Karo Moilanen and Stephen Pulman. 2007. Sentiment Composition. In *Proceedings of RANLP 2007,* pages 378-382.

Roser Morante and Walter Daelemans. 2009. A Metalearning Approach to Processing the Scope of Negation. In *Proceedings of the CONLL 2009*, pages 21-29.

Bo Pang, Lillian Lee and Shivakumar Vaithyanathan. 2002. Thumbs up? Sentiment Classification using Machine Learning Techniques. In *Proceedings of CoRR 2002.*

Bo Pang and Lillian Lee. 2004. A Sentimental Education: Sentiment Analysis using Subjectivity Summarization based on Minimum Cuts. In *Proceedings of the 42nd Annual Meeting of the ACL,* pages 271-278.

Siddharth Patwardhan, Satanjeev Banerjee and Ted Pedersen. 2005. SenseRelate::TargetWord - A Generalized Framework for Word Sense Disambiguation. In *Proceedings of the ACL 2005 on Interactive Poster and Demonstration Sessions,* pages 73-76.

Livia Polanyi and Annie Zaenen. 2006. Contextual Valence Shifters. Computing Attitude and Affect in Text: Theory and Applications. In *The Information Retrieval Series 20,* pages 1-10.

Randolph Quirk, Sidney Greenbaum, Geoffrey Leech and Jan Svartvik. 1985. A Comprehensive Grammar of the English Language. Longman.

Carlo Strapparava and Alessandro Valitutti. 2004. Wordnet-Affect: an Affective Extension of WordNet. In *Proceedings of the LREC 2004*, pages 1083-1086.

Peter D. Turney. 2002. Thumbs up or Thumbs down?: Semantic Orientation applied to Unsupervised Classification of Reviews. In *Proceedings of the 40th Annual Meeting of the ACL,* pages 417-424.

Casey Whitelaw, Navendu Garg and Shlomo Argamon. 2005. Using Appraisal Groups for Sentiment Analysis. In *Proceedings of the 14th ACM Conference on Information and Knowledge Management,* pages 625-631.

Janyce M. Wiebe, Rebecca F. Bruce and Thomas P. O'Hara. 1999. Development and Use of a Gold-standard Data Set for Subjectivity Classification. In *Proceedings of the 37th Annual Meeting of the ACL,* pages 246-253.

Theresa Wilson, Janyce Wiebe and Paul Hoffman. 2005. Recognizing Contextual Polarity in Phrase-level Sentiment Analysis. In *Proceedings of the HLT-EMNLP 2005,* pages 347-354.

Cross-caption coreference resolution for automatic image understanding

Micah Hodosh **Peter Young** **Cyrus Rashtchian** **Julia Hockenmaier**
Department of Computer Science
University of Illinois at Urbana-Champaign
{mhodosh2, pyoung2, crashtc2, juliahmr}@illinois.edu

Abstract

Recent work in computer vision has aimed to associate image regions with keywords describing the depicted entities, but actual image 'understanding' would also require identifying their attributes, relations and activities. Since this information cannot be conveyed by simple keywords, we have collected a corpus of "action" photos each associated with five descriptive captions. In order to obtain a consistent semantic representation for each image, we need to first identify which NPs refer to the same entities. We present three hierarchical Bayesian models for cross-caption coreference resolution. We have also created a simple ontology of entity classes that appear in images and evaluate how well these can be recovered.

1 Introduction

Many photos capture a moment in time, telling a brief story of people, animals and objects, their attributes, and their relationship to each other. Although different people may give different interpretations to the same picture, people can readily interpret photos and describe the entities and events they perceive in complex sentences. This level of image understanding still remains an elusive goal for computer vision: although current methods may be able to identify the overall scene (Quattoni and Torralba, 2009) or some specific classes of entities (Felzenszwalb et al., 2008), they are only starting to be able to identify attributes of entities (Farhadi et al., 2009), and are far from recovering a complete semantic interpretation of the depicted situation. Like natural language processing, computer vision requires suitable training data, and there are currently no publicly available data sets that would enable the development of such systems.

Photo sharing sites such as Flickr allow users to annotate images with keywords and other descriptions, and vision researchers have access to large collections of images annotated with keywords (e.g. the Corel collection). A lot of recent work in computer vision has been aimed at predicting these keywords (Blei et al., 2003; Barnard et al., 2003; Feng and Lapata, 2008; Deschacht and Moens, 2007; Jeon et al., 2003). But keywords alone are not expressive enough to capture relations between entities. Some research has used the text that surrounds an image in a news article as a proxy (Feng and Lapata, 2008; Deschacht and Moens, 2007). However, in many cases, the surrounding text or a user-provided caption does not simply describe what is depicted in the image (since this is usually obvious to the human reader for which this text is intended), but provides additional information. We have collected a corpus of 8108 images associated with several simple descriptive captions. In contrast to the text near an image on the web, the captions in our corpus provide direct, if partial and slightly noisy, descriptions of the image content. Our data set differs from paraphrase corpora (Barzilay and McKeown, 2001; Dolan et al., 2004) in that the different captions of an image are produced independently by different writers. There are many ways of describing the same image, because it is often possible to focus on different aspects of the depicted situation, and because certain aspects of the situation may be unclear to the human viewer.

One of our goals is to use these captions to obtain a semantic representation of each image that is consistent with all of its captions. In order to obtain such a representation, it is necessary to identify the entities that appear in the image, and to perform cross-caption coreference resolution, i.e. to identify all mentions of the same entity in the five captions associated with an image. In this paper, we compare different meth-

Proceedings of the Fourteenth Conference on Computational Natural Language Learning, pages 162–171,
Uppsala, Sweden, 15-16 July 2010.

Figure 1: An image with five captions from our corpus. Coreference chains and ontological classes are indicated in color.

ods of cross-caption coreference resolution on our corpus. In order to facilitate further computer vision research, we have also defined a set of coarse-grained ontological classes that we use to automatically categorize the entities in our data set.

2 A corpus of action images and captions

Image collection and sentence annotation We have constructed a corpus consisting of 8108 photographs from Flickr.com, each paired with five one-sentence descriptive captions written by Amazon's Mechanical Turk[1] workers. We downloaded a few thousand images from each of six selected Flickr groups[2]. To facilitate future computer vision research on our data, we filtered out images in black-and-white or sepia, as well as images with watermarks, signatures, borders or other obvious editing. Since our collection focuses on images depicting actions, we then filtered out images of scenery, portraits, and mood photography. This was done independently by two members of our group and adjudicated by a third.

We paid Turk workers $0.10 to write one descriptive sentence for each of five distinct and randomly chosen images that were displayed one at a time. We required a small qualification test that examined the workers' English grammar and spelling and we restricted the task to U.S. workers (see Rashtchian et al. (2010) for more details). Our final corpus contains five sentences for each of our 8108 images, totaling 478,317 word tokens, and an average sentence length of 11.8 words. We first spell-checked[3] these sentences, and used OpenNLP[4] to POS-tag them. We identified NPs using OpenNLP's chunker, followed by a semi-automatic procedure to correct for a number of systematic chunking errors that could easily be corrected. We randomly selected 200 images for further manual annotation, to be used as test and development data in our experiments.

Gold standard coreference annotation We manually annotated NP chunks, ontological classes, and cross-caption coreference chains for each of the 200 images in our test and development data. Each image was annotated independently by two annotators and adjudicated by a third.[5] The development set contains 1604 mentions. On average, each caption has 3.2 mentions, and each image has 5.9 coreference chains (distinct entities).

Ontological annotation of entities In order to understand the role entities mentioned in the sentences play in the image, we have defined a simple ontology of entity classes (Table 1). We distinguish entities that constitute the background of an image from those that appear in the foreground. These entities can be animate (people or animals) or inanimate. For inanimate objects, we distinguish static objects from "movable" objects. We also distinguish man-made from natural objects and backgrounds, since this matters for computer vision algorithms. We have labeled the entity mentions in our test and development data with classes from this ontology. Again, two of us annotated each image's mentions, and adjudication was performed by a single person. Our ontology is similar to, but smaller than the one proposed by Hollink and Worring (2005) for video retrieval, which in turn is based on Hoogs et al. (2003) and Hunter (2001).

3 Predicting image entities from captions

Figure 1 shows an image from our corpus. Different captions use different words to refer to the

[1]https://www.mturk.com

[2]The groups:"strangers!", "Wild-Child (Kids in Action)", "Dogs in Action (Read the Rules)", "Outdoor Activities", "Action Photography", "Flickr-Social (two or more people in the photo)".

[3]We used Unix's `aspell` to generate possible corrections and chose between them based on corpus frequencies.

[4]http://opennlp.sourceforge.net

[5]We used MMAX2 (Müller and Strube, 2006) both for annotation and adjudication.

Ontological Class	Examples
animal	*dog, horse, cow*
background_man-made	*street, pool, carpet*
background_natural	*ocean, field, air*
body_part	*hair, mouth, arms*
clothing	*shirt, hat, sunglasses*
event	*trick, sunset, game*
fixed_object_man-made	*furniture, statue, ramp*
fixed_object_natural	*rock, puddle, bush*
image_attribute	*camera, picture, closeup*
material_man-made	*paint, frosting*
material_natural	*water, snow, dirt*
movable_man-made	*ball, toy, bowl*
movable_natural	*leaves, snowball*
nondepictable	*something, Batman*
orientation	*front, top, [the] distance*
part_of	*edge, side, top, tires*
person	*family, skateboarder*
property_of	*shadow, shade, theme*
vehicle	*surfboard, bike, boat*
writing	*graffiti, map*

Table 1: Our ontology for entities in images.

same entity, or even seemingly contradictory modifiers (*"orange"* vs. *"brown"* dog). In order to predict what entities appear in an image from its captions, we need to identify how many entities each sentence describes, and what role these entities play in the image (e.g. person, animal, background). Because we have five sentences associated with each image, we also need to identify which noun phrases in the different captions of the same image refer to the same entity. Because the captions were generated independently, there are no discourse cues such as anaphora to identify coreference. This creates problems for standard coreference resolution systems trained on regular text. Our data also differs from standard coreference data sets in that entities are rarely referred to by proper nouns.

Our first task is to identify which noun phrases may refer to the same entity. We do this by identifying the set of entity types that each NP may refer to. We use WordNet (Fellbaum, 1998) to identify the possible entity types (WordNet synsets) of each head noun. Since the salient entities in each image are likely to be mentioned by more than one caption writer, we then aim to restrict those types to those that may be shared by some head nouns in the other captions of the same image. This gives us an inventory of entity types for each mention, which we use to identify coreferences, restricted by the constraint that all coreferent mentions refer to an entity of the same type.

4 Using WordNet to identify entity types

WordNet (Fellbaum, 1998) provides a rich ontology of entity types that facilitates our coreference task.[6] We use WordNet to obtain a lexicon of possible entity types for each mention (based on their lexical heads, assumed to be the last word with a nominal POS tag[7]). We first generate a set of candidate synsets based solely on the lexical heads, and then generate lexicon entries based on relations between the candidates.

WordNet synsets provide us with synonyms, and hypernym/hyponym relations. For each mention, we generate a list of candidate synsets. We require that the candidates are one of the first four synsets reported and that their frequency is to be at least one-tenth of the most frequent synset. We limit candidates to ones with "physical_entity#n#1", "event#n#1", or "visual_property#n#1" as a hypernym, in order to ensure that the synset describes something that is depictable. To avoid word senses that refer to a person in a metaphorical fashion, (e.g. *pig* meaning slovenly person or *red* meaning communist), we ignore synsets that refer to people if the word has a synset that is an animal or color.[8]

In general, we would like for mentions to be able to take on more specific word senses. For example, we would like to be able to identify that *"woman"* and *"person"* may refer to the same entity, whereas *"man"* and *"woman"* typically would not. However, we also do not want a type inventory that is too large or too fine-grained.

Once the candidate synsets are generated, we consider all pairs of nouns (n_1, n_2) that occur in different captions of the same image and examine all corresponding pairs of candidate synsets (s_1, s_2). If s_2 is a synonym or hypernym of s_1, it is possible that two captions have different words describing the same entity, so we add s_1 and s_2[9] to the lexicon of n_1. Adding s_2 to n_1's lexicon allows it to act as an umbrella sense covering other nouns describing the same entity.[10] We add s_2 to

[6] For the prediction of ontological classes, we use our own ontology because WordNet is too fine-grained for this purpose.

[7] If there are two NP chunks that form a "[NP ... group] of [NP...]" construction, we only use the second NP chunk.

[8] An exception list handles cases (*diver, blonde*), where the human sense is more likely than the animal or color sense.

[9] We don't add s_2 if it is "object#n#1" or "clothing#n#1".

[10] This is needed when captions use different aspects of the entity to describe it (for example, *"skier"* and *"a skiing man"*).

the lexicon of n_2 (since if n_1 is using the sense s_1, then n_2 must be using the sense s_2) and if n_1 occurs at least five times in the corpus, we add s_1 to the lexicon of n_2.

5 A heuristic coreference algorithm

Based on WordNet candidate synsets, we define a heuristic algorithm that finds the optimal entity assignment for the mentions associated with each image. This algorithm is based on the principles driving our generative model described below, and on the observation that salient entities will be mentioned in many captions and that captions tend to use similar words to describe the same entity.

Simple heuristic algorithm:

1. For each noun, choose the synset that appears in the most number of captions of an image, and break ties by choosing the synset that covers the fewest distinct lemmatized nouns.

2. Group all of the noun phrase chunks that share a synset into a single coreference chain.

6 Bayesian coreference models

Since we cannot afford to manually annotate our entire data set with coreference information, we follow Haghighi and Klein (2007)'s work on unsupervised coreference resolution, and develop a series of generative Bayesian models for our task.

6.1 Model 0: Simple Mixture Model

In our first model, based on Haghighi and Klein's baseline Dirichlet Process model, each image i corresponds to the set of observed mentions $\mathbf{w}^i$ from across its captions. Image i has a hidden global topic T_i, drawn from a distribution with a GEM prior with hyperparameter γ as explained by Teh et al. (2006). In a Dirichlet process, the GEM distribution is an infinite analog of the Dirichlet distribution, allowing for a potentially infinite number of mixture components. $P(T_i = t)$ is proportional to γ if t is a new component, or to the number of times t has been drawn before otherwise. Given a topic choice $T_i = t$, entity type assignments Z_j for all mentions w_j in image i are in turn drawn from a topic-specific multinomial θ_t over all possible entity types $\mathbf{E}$ that was drawn from a Dirichlet prior with hyperparameter β. Similarly, given an entity type $Z_i = z$, each corresponding (observed) head word w_j is drawn from an entity type-specific multinomial ϕ_z over all possible words $\mathbf{V}$, drawn from a finite Dirichlet prior with hyperparameter α. The set of all images belonging to the same topic is analogous to an individual document in Haghighi and Klein's baseline model.[11] All headwords of the same entity type are assumed to be coreferent, similar to Haghighi and Klein's model. As described in section 4, we use WordNet to identify the subset of types that can actually produce the given words. Therefore, similar to the way Andrzejewski and Zhu (2009) handled a priori knowledge of topics, we will define an indicator variable δ_{ij} that is 1 iff the WordNet information allows word i to be produced from entity set j and 0 otherwise.

6.1.1 Sampling Model 0

We find $arg\,max_{\mathbf{Z},\mathbf{T}} P(\mathbf{Z}, \mathbf{T}|\mathbf{X})$ with Gibbs sampling. Here, $\mathbf{Z}$ and $\mathbf{T}$ are the collection of type and topic assignments, with $\mathbf{Z}^{-j} = \mathbf{Z} - \{Z_j\}$ and $\mathbf{T}^{-i} = \mathbf{T} - \{T_i\}$. This style of notation will be extended analogously to other variables. Let $n_{e,x}$ represent the number of times word x is produced from entity e across all topics and let p_j be the number of images assigned to topic j. Let $m_{t,e}$ represent the number of times entity type e is generated by topic t. Each iteration consists of two steps: first, each Z_i is resampled, fixing $\mathbf{T}$; and then each T_i is resampled based on $\mathbf{Z}$[12].

1. Sampling Z_j:

$$P(Z_j = e | w_j \in \mathbf{w}^i, \mathbf{Z}^{-j}, \mathbf{T}) \propto P(w_j | Z_j = e) P(Z_j = e | T_i)$$

$$P(w_j = x | Z_j = e) \propto \left(\frac{n_{e,x}^{-j} + \alpha}{\sum_{x'} n_{e,x'}^{-j} + \alpha} \right) \delta_{xe}$$

$$P(Z_j = e | T_i = t) = \frac{m_{t,e}^{-j} + \beta}{\sum_{e'} m_{t,e'}^{-j} + \beta}$$

2. Sampling T_i:

$$\begin{aligned} P(T_i = j | \mathbf{w}, \mathbf{Z}, \mathbf{T}^{-i}) &\propto P(T_i = j | \mathbf{T}^{-i}) P(\mathbf{Z} | T_i = j, \mathbf{T}^{-i}) \\ &\propto P(T_i = j | \mathbf{T}^{-i}) \prod_{k \in \mathbf{w}^i} P(Z_k | T_i = j) \\ &= P(T_i = j | \mathbf{T}^{-i}) \prod_{k \in \mathbf{w}^i} \frac{m_{j,Z_k}^{-i} + \beta}{\sum_{e'} m_{j,e'}^{-i} + \beta} \end{aligned}$$

$$P(T_i = j | \mathbf{T}^{-i}) \propto \begin{cases} \gamma, & \text{If its a new topic} \\ p_j & \text{Otherwise} \end{cases}$$

[11] Since we do not have multiple images of the same well-known people or places, referred to by their names, we do not perform any cross-image coreference

[12] Sampling on the exponentiated posterior to find the mode as Haghighi and Klein (2007) did was found to not significantly affect results on our tasks

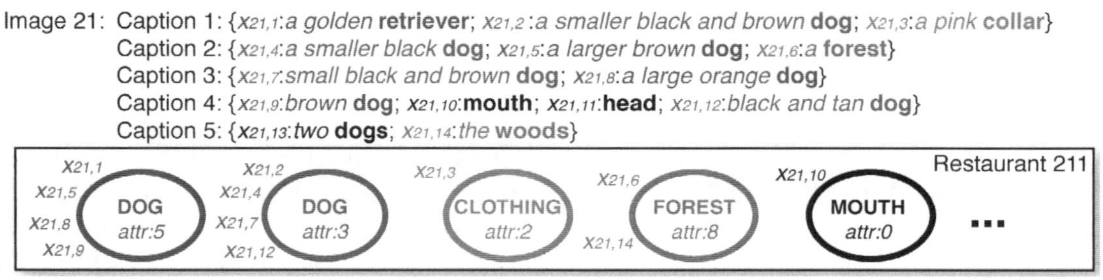

Figure 2: Models 1 and 2 as Chinese restaurant franchises: each image topic is a franchise, each image is a restaurant, each entity is a table, each mention is a customer. Model 2 adds attributes (in italics).

6.2 Model 1: Explicit Entities

Model 0 does not have an explicit representation of entities beyond their type and thus cannot distinguish multiple entities of the same type in an image. Although Model 1 also represents mentions only by their head words (and thus cannot distinguish *black dog* from *brown dog*), it creates explicit entities based on the Chinese restaurant franchise interpretation of the hierarchical Dirichlet Process model (Teh et al., 2006). Figure 2 (ignoring the modifiers / attributes for now) illustrates the Chinese restaurant franchise interpretation of our model. Using this metaphor, there are a series of restaurants (= images), each consisting of a potentially infinite number of tables (= entities), that are frequented by customers (= entity mentions) who will be seated at the tables. Restaurants belong to franchises (= image topics). Each table is served one dish (= entity type, e.g. DOG, CLOTHING) shared by all the customers. The head word of a mention $x_{i,j}$ is generated in the following manner: customer j enters restaurant i (belonging to franchise T_i) and sits down at one of the existing tables with probability proportional to the number of other customers there, or sits at a new table with probability proportional to a constant. A dish e^i_a (DOG) from a potentially infinite menu is served to each new table a, with probability proportional to the total number of tables it is served at in the franchise T_i (or to a constant if it is a new dish). The (observed) head word of the mention $x_{j,i}$ (*dog, retriever*) is then drawn from the multinomial distribution over words defined by the entity type (DOG) at the table. The menu (set of dishes) available to each restaurant and table is restricted by our lexicon of WordNet synsets for each mention. More formally, each image topic t defines a distribution over entities drawn from a global GEM prior with hyperparameter κ. Therefore, the probability of an entity a is proportional to the number of its existing mentions in images of the same topic, or to κ, if it is previoulsy unmentioned. The type of each entity, e_a, is drawn from a topic-dependent multinomial with global Dirichlet prior. The head words of mentions are generated by their entity type as in Model 0. Mentions assigned to the same entity are considered to be coreferent. Based on the nature of our corpus, we again assume that two words cannot be coreferent within a sentence, restrict the distribution to not allow inter-sentence coreference and renormalize the values accordingly.

6.2.1 Sampling Model 1

There are three parts to our resampling procedure: resampling the entity assignment for each word, resampling the entity type for each entity, and resampling the topic of each image. The kth word of image i, sentence j, will now be $w^i_{j,k}$; e^i_a is the entity type of entity a in image i; $a^i_{j,k}$ is the entity that word k of sentence j is produced from in image i, and $Z^i_{j,k}$ represents that entity's type. $\mathbf{a}$ is the set of all current entity assignments and $\mathbf{e}$ are the type assignments for entities. m is now defined as the number of entities of a certain type being drawn for an image, n is defined as before and $c_{i,a}$ is the number of times entity a is expressed in image i. Topics are resampled as in Model 0.

Entity Assignment Resampling Entity assignments for words are resampled one sentence at a time in the order the headwords appear in the sentence. For each word in the sentence, entity assignments are defined by the distribution of Figure 3. The headword is assigned to an existing entity with probability proportional to the number of entities already assigned to that entity and the probability that the entity emits that word. The word is assigned to a new entity with a newly

Model 1:

$$P(e^i_a = e|\mathbf{a}, \mathbf{w}, T_i = t, \mathbf{e}^{-\mathbf{i},\mathbf{a}}) \propto (m^{-\mathbf{e}^{\mathbf{i},\mathbf{a}}}_{t,e} + \beta) \prod_{\{w^i_{j,k}=x|a^i_{j,k}=a\}} \frac{n^{-\mathbf{e}^{\mathbf{i},\mathbf{a}}}_{e,x} + \alpha}{\sum_y (n^{-\mathbf{e}^{\mathbf{i},\mathbf{a}}}_{e,y} + \alpha)} \delta_{x,e}$$

$$P(a^i_{j,k} = a|\mathbf{a}^{-(i,j,k'|k' \geq k)}, \mathbf{e}, \mathbf{T}) \propto \begin{cases} c^{-j,k'}_{i,a} P(w^i_{j,k}|Z^i_{j,k} = e^i_a, \mathbf{a}^{-(i,j,k'|k' \geq k)}) \rho^i_{j,a}, \text{ if } a \text{ is not new} \\ \kappa P(e^i_a|\mathbf{e}^{-\mathbf{i},\mathbf{a}}, T_i) P(w^i_{j,k}|Z^i_{j,k} = e^i_a, \mathbf{a}^{-(i,j,k'|k' \geq k)}), \text{o/w} \end{cases}$$

With:

$$P(w^i_{j,k} = x|Z^i_{j,k} = e, \mathbf{a}^{-(i,j,k'|k' \geq k)}) \propto \frac{n^{-(i,j,k'|k' \geq k)}_{e,x} + \alpha}{\sum_y (n^{-(i,j,k'|k' \geq k)}_{e,y} + \alpha)} \delta_{x,e}$$

$$P(e^i_a = e|\mathbf{e}^{-\mathbf{i},\mathbf{a}}, T_i = t) \propto \frac{m^{-\mathbf{e}^{\mathbf{i},\mathbf{a}}}_{t,e} + \beta}{\sum_{e'} (m^{-\mathbf{e}^{\mathbf{i},\mathbf{a}}}_{t,e'} + \beta)}$$

Model 2:

$$P(a^i_{j,k} = a|\mathbf{a}^{-(i,j,k'|k' \geq k)}, \mathbf{e}, \mathbf{T}, \mathbf{b}) \propto \begin{cases} c^{-j,k'}_{i,a} P(w^i_{j,k}|Z^i_{j,k} = e^i_a, \mathbf{a}^{-(i,j,k'|k' \geq k)}) \rho^i_{j,a} P(\mathbf{d}^i_{j,k}|b^i_a), \text{ if } a \text{ is not new} \\ \kappa P(e^i_a|\mathbf{e}^{-\mathbf{i},\mathbf{a}}, T_i) P(w^i_{j,k}|Z^i_{j,k} = e^i_a, \mathbf{a}^{-(i,j,k'|k' \geq k)}) P(b^i_a) P(\mathbf{d}^i_a|b^i_a), \text{o/w} \end{cases}$$

$$P(b^i_a = b|\mathbf{D}^i_a, \mathbf{b}^{-\mathbf{i},\mathbf{a}}) \propto P(b^i_a = b|\mathbf{b}^{-i,a}) \prod_{d \in \mathbf{D}^i_a} \frac{(s^{-i,a}_{b,d} + \zeta)}{\sum_{d'} (s^{-i,a}_{b,d'} + \zeta)}$$

Figure 3: Sampling equations for Models 1 and 2

drawn entity type with probability proportional κ, the probability that the entity type is for an image of the given topic (normalized over WordNet's possible entities for the word), and the probability the drawn type produces the word. $\rho^i_{j,a} = 1$ iff entity a of image i does not appear in sentence j and $\rho^i_{j,a} = 0$ otherwise. $\mathbf{a}^{-(i,j,k'|k' \geq k)}$ represents removing the kth or later words in sentence j of image i

Entity Type Resampling Fixing the assignments, the type of each entity is redrawn based on the distribution in Figure 3. It is proportional to the probability that a certain entity type is in an image of a given topic and, independently for each of the words, the probability that the given word expresses the type. $n^{-\mathbf{e}^{\mathbf{i},\mathbf{a}}}_{e,x}$ is the number of times entity type e is expressed as word x not counting the words attached to the currently entity being resampled and $m^{-\mathbf{e}^{\mathbf{i},\mathbf{a}}}_{t,e}$ is the number of times an entity of type e appears in an image of topic t not counting the current entity being resampled. The probability of a given image belonging to a topic is proportional the number of images already in the topic (or γ) followed by the probability that each of the entities in the image were drawn from that topic.

6.3 Model 2: Explicit Entities and Modifiers

Certain entities cannot be distinguished simply by head word alone, such in the example in Figure 2. Model 2 augments Model 1 with the ability to generate modifiers. In addition to an entity type, each entity draws an attribute from a global distribution drawn from a GEM distribution with hyperparameter η. An attribute is a multinomial distribution, on possible modifier words, drawn from a Dirichlet prior with parameter ζ. From the attribute, each modifier word is drawn independently. Therefore given an attribute b and a set of modifiers $\mathbf{d}$: $P(\mathbf{d}|b) \propto \prod_{d \in \mathbf{d}} (s_d + \zeta)$ where s_d is number of times modifier d is produced by attribute b. In addition, the probability of a certain attribute b given all other assignments is given by:

$$P(b^i_a = b|\mathbf{b}^{-i,a}) \propto \begin{cases} \eta, & \text{If its a new attribute} \\ r_b, & \text{Otherwise} \end{cases}$$

where r_b is the number of entities with attribute b. As in Model 1, mentions assigned to the same entity are considered coreferent. Consider the *"smaller black dog"* mention in Figure 2. When the mention is being resampled, the attribute choice for each table will bias the probability distribution towards the table whose attribute is more likely to produce *"smaller"* and *"black"*. Therefore, the model can now better distinguish the two dogs in the image.

6.3.1 Sampling Model 2

The addition of modifiers only directly effects the distribution when resampling entity assignments since attributes are independent of entity types, image topics, and headwords of noun phrases. The sampling distribution are again shown in Figure 3. In a separate sampling step, it is now necessary to resample the attribute assigned to each entity: The probability of drawing a certain attribute is illustrated in Figure 3 with $\mathbf{D}^i_a$ as the set of all the modifiers of all the noun phrases currently assigned to entity a of image i, and $s_{b,d}^{-i,a}$ as the number of times attribute b produces modifier d without the current assignment of entity a of image i.

6.4 Implementation

The topic assignments for each image are initialized to correspond to the Flickr groups the images were taken from. Each mention was initialized as its own entity with type and attribute sampled from a uniform distribution.

As our training is unsupervised, each of the models were ran on the entire dataset. For Model 0, after burn-in, 20 samples of Z were taken spaced 200 iterations apart, while for Model 1 samples were taken spaced 100 apart, and 25 apart for Model 2. The implementation of Model 2 ran too slow to effectively judge when burn in occurred, impacting the results.

The values of parameters α, β, γ, κ, η, ζ, and the number of initial attributes were hand-tuned based on the average performance on our annotated development subset of 100 images.[13]

7 Evaluation of coreference resolution

We evaluate each of the generative models and the heuristic coreference algorithm on the annotated test subset of our corpus consisting of 100 images with both the OpenNLP chunking and the gold standard chunking. We report our scores based on the MUC evaluation metric. The results are reported in Table 2 as the average scores across all the samples of two independent runs of each model. We also present results on Model 0 without using WordNet where every word can be an expression of one of 200 fake entity sets. The same table also shows the performance of a baseline model and the upper bound on performance imposed by WordNet.

A baseline model: In our baseline model, two noun phrases in captions of the same image are coreferent if they share the same head noun.

Upper bound on performance: Although WordNet synsets provide a good indication of whether two mentions can refer to the same entity or not, they may also be overly restrictive in other cases. We measure the upper bound on performance that our reliance on WordNet imposes by finding the best-scoring coreference assignment that is consistent with our lexicon. This achieves an F-score of 90.2 on the test data with gold chunks.

Performance increases in each subsequent model. The heuristic beats each of the models, but in some sense it is an extreme version of Model 1. Both it and Model 1 attempt to produce entity sets that cover as many captions as possible, while minimizing the number of distinct words involved. The heuristic locally forces this case, at the expense of no longer being a generative model.

8 Ontological Class Prediction

As a further step towards understanding the semantics of images, we develop a model that labels each entity with one of the ontological classes defined in section 2. The immediate difficulty of this task is that our ontology includes not only semantic distinctions, but also spatial and visual ones. While it may be easy to tell which words are animals and which are people, there is only a fine distinction at the language level whether an object is movable, fixed, or part of the background.[14]

8.1 Model and Features

We define our task as a classification problem, where each entity must be assigned to one of twenty classes defined by our ontology. We use a Maximum Entropy classifier, implemented in the MALLET toolkit (McCallum, 2002), and define the following text features:

NP Chunk: We include all the words in the NP chunk, unfiltered.

WordNet Synsets and Hypernyms: The most likely synset is either the first one that appears in WordNet or one of the ones predicted by our coreference system. For each of these possibilities, we include all of that synset's hypernyms.

Syntactic Role: We parsed our captions with the C&C parser (Clark and Curran, 2007), and record whether the word appears as a direct object of a verb, as the object of a preposition, as the subject of the sentence, or as a modifier. If it is a modifier, we also add the head word of the phrase being modified.

[13] $(0.1, 0.1, 100, 0.001875, 100, 0.0002, 20)$ respectively.

[14] For example, we deem bowls and silverware to be movable objects; furniture, fixed; and carpets, background. Moreover, in all three cases, we must correctly distinguish that these objects are man-made and not found in nature.

Model	OpenNLP chunks			Gold chunks		
	Rec.	Prec.	F1	Rec.	Prec.	F1
Baseline	57.3	89.5	69.9	64.1	96.2	77.0
Upper bound				82.1	100	90.2
WN Heuristic	70.6	84.8	77.0	80.4	90.6	85.2
Model 0 w/o WN	79.7	59.8	68.4	85.1	62.7	72.2
Model 0	66.8	83.1	74.1	75.9	90.3	82.5
Model 1	69.6	83.8	76.0	78.0	90.8	83.9
Model 2	69.2	84.4	76.1	77.9	91.5	84.1

Table 2: Coreference resolution results (MUC scores; Models 0-2 are averaged over all samples)

8.2 Experiments

We use two baselines. The naive baseline categorizes words by selecting the most frequent class of the word. If no instances of the word have occurred, it uses the overall most frequent class. The WordNet baseline works by finding the most frequent class amongst the most relevant synsets for a word. It calculates the class frequency for each synset by assuming each word has the sense of its first synset and incrementing the frequency of the first synset and its hypernyms. When categorizing a word, it finds the set of closest hypernyms of the word that have a non-zero frequency, and chooses the class with the greatest sum of frequency counts amongst those hypernyms.

We train the MaxEnt classifier using semi-supervised learning. Initially, we train a classifier using the 500 sentence gold standard development set. For each class, we use the top 5%[15] of the labels to label the unlabeled data and provide additional training data. We then retrain the classifier on the newly labeled examples and the development set, and run it on the test set. For each coreference chain in the test set, we relabel all of the mentions in the chain to use the majority class, if a clear majority exists. If no such majority exists, we leave the labels as is. The MaxEnt classifier experiments were conducted by varying the source of the synset assigned to each word. For each of our coreference systems, we report two scores (Table 3). The first is the average accuracy when using the output from two runs of each model with about 20 samples per run, and the second uses the output that performs best on the coreference task when scored on the development data.

Discussion Although we use WordNet to classify our entity mentions, we designed our ontology by considering only the images and their captions, with no particular mapping to WordNet in mind.

[15]This was tuned using 10-fold cross-validation of the development set.

Classifier (synset prediction)	Accuracy (gold chunks)		
Naive Baseline	72.0		
WordNet Baseline	81.0		
MaxEnt (1st-synset)	84.4		
MaxEnt (WN heuristic)	82.7		
	Avg.	σ	**Best-Coref**
MaxEnt (Model 1)	83.9	0.5	84.5
MaxEnt (Model 2)	84.1	0.4	85.3

Table 3: Prediction of ontological classes

Therefore, these experiments provide of a proof of concept for the semi-supervised labeling of a corpus using any semantic/visual ontology.

Overall, Model 2 had the best performance for this task. This demonstrates that the additional features of Model 2 force synset selections that are consistent across the entire corpus, and are sensitive to the modifiers appearing with them. The WordNet heuristic selects synsets in a fairly arbitrary manner - all other things being equal, the synsets are chosen without reference to what other synsets are chosen by similar clusters of nouns.

9 Evaluating entity prediction

Together, the coreference resolution algorithm and ontology classification model provide us with a set of distinct, ontologically-categorized entities appearing in each image. We perform a final experiment to evaluate how well our models can recover the mentioned entities and their ontological types for each image. We now represent each entity as a tuple (L, c), where L is its coreference chain, and c is the ontological class of these mentions. [16]

We compute the precision and recall between the predicted and gold standard tuples for each image. We consider a tuple (L', c') correctly predicted only when a copy of (L', c') occurs both in the set of predicted tuples and the set of gold standard tuples.[17] Then, as usual, for precision we

[16]Note that for each image, the tuples of all entities correspond to a partition of the set of the head-word mentions in an image.

[17]We assign no partial credit because incorrect typing or

Model	Recall	Precision	F-score
Baseline	28.4	20.6	23.9
WordNet Heuristic	48.3	43.9	46.0
Model 1 (avg)	51.7	42.8	46.8
Model 1 (best-coref)	50.9	45.4	48.0
Model 2 (avg)	52.2	42.7	47.0
Model 2 (best-coref)	52.3	46.0	49.0

Table 4: Overall entity recovery. We measure how many entities we identify correctly (requiring complete recovery of their coreference chains and correct prediction of their ontological class.

normalize the number of overlapping tuples by the number of predicted tuples, and for recall, by the number of gold standard tuples. We report average precision and recall over all images in our test set.

We report scores for four different pairs of ontological class and coreference chain predictions. As a baseline, we use the ontological classes predicted by the our naive baseline and the chains predicted by the "same-words-are-coreferent" coreference resolution baseline.

We also report results using the classes and chains predicted by Model 1, Model 2, and the WordNet Heuristic Algorithm. The influence of the different coreference algorithms comes from the entity types that are used to determine coreference chains, and that also correspond to WordNet candidate synsets. In other words, although the final coreference chain may be predicted by two different models, the synsets they use to do so may differ, affecting the synset and hypernym features used for ontological prediction. We present results in Table 4 for these four different set-ups.

The synsets chosen by the different coreference algorithms clearly have different applicability when it comes to ontological class prediction. Although Model 2 performs comparably to Model 1 and does worse than the WordNet heuristic algorithm for coreference chain prediction, it certainly does better on this task. Since our end goal is creating a unified semantic representation, this final task judges the effectiveness of our models to capture the most detailed entity information. The success of Model 2 means that the incorporation of adjectives informs the proper choice of synsets that are useful in predicting ontological classes.

10 Conclusion

As a first step towards automatic image understanding, we have collected a corpus of images associated with several simple descriptive captions, which provide more detailed information about the image than simple keywords. We plan to make this data set available for further research in computer vision and natural language processing. In order to enable the creation of a semantic representation of the image content that is consistent with the captions in our data set, we use WordNet and a series of Bayesian models to perform cross-caption coreference resolution. Similar to Haghighi and Klein (2009), who find that linguistic heuristics can provide very strong baselines for standard coreference resultion, relatively simple heuristics based on WordNet alone perform surprisingly well on our task, although they are outperformed by our Bayesian models for overall entity prediction. Since our generative models are based on Dirichlet Process priors, they are designed to favor a small number of unique entities per image. In the heuristic algorithm, this bias is built in explicitly, resulting in slightly higher performance on the coreference resolution task. However, while the generative models can use global information to learn what entity type each word is likely to represent, the heuristic is unable to capture any non-local information about the entities, and thus provides less useful input for the prediction of ontological classes.

Future work will aim to improve on these results by overcoming the upper bound on performance imposed by WordNet, and through a more sophisticated model of modifiers. We will also investigate how image features can be incorporated into our model to improve performance on entity detection. Ultimately, identifying the depicted entities from multiple image captions will require novel ways to correctly handle the semantics of plural NPs (i.e. that one caption's *"two dogs"* consist of another's *"golden retreiver"* and *"smaller black dog"*). We foresee similar challenges when dealing with verbs and events.

The creation of an actual semantic representation of the image content is a challenging problem in itself, since the different captions often focus on different aspects of the depicted situation, or provide different interpretation of ambiguous situations. We believe that this poses many interesting challenges for natural language processing, and will ultimately require ways to integrate the information conveyed in the caption with visual features extracted from the image.

incomplete coreference chaining both completely change the semantics of an image.

Acknowledgements

This research was funded by NSF grant IIS 08-03603 INT2-Medium: Understanding the Meaning of Images. We are grateful for David Forsyth and Dan Roth's advice, and for Alex Sorokins support with MTurk.

References

David Andrzejewski and Xiaojin Zhu. 2009. Latent Dirichlet allocation with topic-in-set knowledge. In *NAACL HLT 2009 Workshop on Semi-Supervised Learning for Natural Language Processing*, pages 43–48.

Kobus Barnard, Pinar Duygulu, David Forsyth, Nando De Freitas, David M. Blei, and Michael I. Jordan. 2003. Matching words and pictures. *Journal of Machine Learning Research*, 3:1107–1135.

Regina Barzilay and Kathleen R. McKeown. 2001. Extracting paraphrases from a parallel corpus. In *Proceedings of the 39th annual meeting of the Association for Computational Linguistics*, pages 50–57, Toulouse, France, July.

David M. Blei, Michael I, David M. Blei, and Michael I. 2003. Modeling annotated data. In *Proceedings of the 26th International ACM SIGIR Conference*, pages 127–134.

Stephen Clark and James R. Curran. 2007. Wide-coverage efficient statistical parsing with CCG and log-linear models. *Computational Linguistics*, 33(4):493–552.

Koen Deschacht and Marie-Francine Moens. 2007. Text analysis for automatic image annotation. In *Proceedings of the 45th Annual Meeting of the Association of Computational Linguistics*.

Bill Dolan, Chris Quirk, and Chris Brockett. 2004. Unsupervised construction of large paraphrase corpora: Exploiting massively parallel news sources. In *Proceedings of Coling 2004*, pages 350–356, Geneva, Switzerland, August. COLING.

A. Farhadi, I. Endres, D. Hoiem, and D. Forsyth. 2009. Describing objects by their attributes. In *IEEE Conference on Computer Vision and Pattern Recognition*, pages 1778–1785, June.

Christiane Fellbaum, editor. 1998. *WordNet An Electronic Lexical Database*. The MIT Press, Cambridge, MA ; London, May.

P. Felzenszwalb, D. McAllester, and D. Ramanan. 2008. A discriminatively trained, multiscale, deformable part model. In *IEEE Conference on Computer Vision and Pattern Recognition*, pages 1–8, June.

Yansong Feng and Mirella Lapata. 2008. Automatic image annotation using auxiliary text information. In *Proceedings of ACL-08: HLT*, pages 272–280, Columbus, Ohio, June.

Aria Haghighi and Dan Klein. 2007. Unsupervised coreference resolution in a nonparametric Bayesian model. In *Proceedings of the 45th Annual Meeting of the Association of Computational Linguistics*, pages 848–855, Prague, Czech Republic.

Aria Haghighi and Dan Klein. 2009. Simple coreference resolution with rich syntactic and semantic features. In *Proceedings of the 2009 Conference on Empirical Methods in Natural Language Processing*, pages 1152–1161, Singapore, August. Association for Computational Linguistics.

L. Hollink and M. Worring. 2005. Building a visual ontology for video retrieval. In *MULTIMEDIA '05: Proceedings of the 13th annual ACM international conference on Multimedia*, pages 479–482, New York, NY, USA. ACM.

A. Hoogs, J. Rittscher, G. Stein, and J. Schmiederer. 2003. Video content annotation using visual analysis and a large semantic knowledgebase. In *IEEE Computer Society Conference on Computer Vision and Pattern Recognition*, volume 2, pages II–327 – II–334 vol.2, June.

Jane Hunter. 2001. Adding multimedia to the semantic web - building an mpeg-7 ontology. In *In International Semantic Web Working Symposium (SWWS*, pages 261–281.

Lavrenko Manmatha Jeon, V. Lavrenko, R. Manmatha, and J. Jeon. 2003. A model for learning the semantics of pictures. In *Seventeenth Annual Conference on Neural Information Processing Systems (NIPS)*. MIT Press.

Andrew Kachites McCallum. 2002. Mallet: A machine learning for language toolkit. http://mallet.cs.umass.edu.

Christoph Müller and Michael Strube. 2006. Multi-level annotation of linguistic data with MMAX2. In Sabine Braun et al, editor, *Corpus Technology and Language Pedagogy*, pages 197–214. Peter Lang, Frankfurt a.M., Germany.

Ariadna Quattoni and Antonio B. Torralba. 2009. Recognizing indoor scenes. In *IEEE Conference on Computer Vision and Pattern Recognition*, pages 413–420. IEEE.

Cyrus Rashtchian, Peter Young, Micah Hodosh, and Julia Hockenmaier. 2010. Collecting image annotations using amazons mechanical turk. In *NAACL Workshop Creating Speech and Language Data With Amazons Mechanical Turk*.

Yee Whye Teh, Michael I Jordan, Matthew J Beal, and David M Blei. 2006. Hierarchical dirichlet processes. *Journal of the American Statistical Association*, 101(476):1566–1581.

Improved Natural Language Learning via Variance-Regularization Support Vector Machines

Shane Bergsma
University of Alberta
sbergsma@ualberta.ca

Dekang Lin
Google, Inc.
lindek@google.com

Dale Schuurmans
University of Alberta
dale@cs.ualberta.ca

Abstract

We present a simple technique for learning better SVMs using fewer training examples. Rather than using the standard SVM regularization, we regularize toward low weight-variance. Our new SVM objective remains a convex quadratic function of the weights, and is therefore computationally no harder to optimize than a standard SVM. Variance regularization is shown to enable dramatic improvements in the learning rates of SVMs on three lexical disambiguation tasks.

1 Introduction

Discriminative training is commonly used in NLP and speech to scale the contribution of different models or systems in a combined predictor. For example, discriminative training can be used to scale the contribution of the language model and translation model in machine translation (Och and Ney, 2002). Without training data, it is often reasonable to weight the different models equally. We propose a simple technique that exploits this intuition for better learning with fewer training examples. We regularize the feature weights in a Support Vector Machine (Cortes and Vapnik, 1995) toward a low-variance solution. Since the new SVM quadratic program is convex, it is no harder to optimize than the standard SVM objective.

When training data is generated through human effort, faster learning saves time and money. When examples are labeled automatically, through user feedback (Joachims, 2002) or from textual pseudo-examples (Smith and Eisner, 2005; Okanohara and Tsujii, 2007), faster learning can reduce the lag before a new system is useful.

We demonstrate faster learning on lexical disambiguation tasks. For these tasks, a system predicts a label for a word in text, based on the word's context. Possible labels include part-of-speech tags, named-entity types, and word senses. A number of disambiguation systems make predictions with the help of N-gram counts from a web-scale auxiliary corpus, typically via a search-engine (Lapata and Keller, 2005) or N-gram corpus (Bergsma et al., 2009). When discriminative training is used to weigh the counts for classification, many of the learned feature weights have similar values. Good weights have low variance.

For example, consider the task of preposition selection. A system selects the most likely preposition given the context, and flags a possible error if it disagrees with the user's choice:

- I worked in Russia **from** 1997 to 2001.
- I worked in Russia ***during** 1997 to 2001.

Bergsma et al. (2009) use a variety of web counts to predict the correct preposition. They have features for COUNT(*in Russia* from), COUNT(*Russia* from *1997*), COUNT(from *1997 to*), etc. If these are high, **from** is predicted. Similarly, they have features for COUNT(*in Russia* during), COUNT(*Russia* during *1997*), COUNT(during *1997 to*). These features predict **during**. All counts are in the log domain. The task has thirty-four different prepositions to choose from. A 34-way classifier is trained on examples of correct preposition usage; it learns which context positions and sizes are most reliable and assigns feature weights accordingly.

A very strong unsupervised baseline, however, is to simply weight all the count features equally. In fact, in Bergsma et al. (2009), the supervised approach requires over 30,000 training examples before it outperforms this baseline. In contrast, we show that by regularizing a classifier toward equal weights, a supervised predictor outperforms the unsupervised approach after only ten examples, and does as well with 1000 examples as the standard classifier does with 100,000.

Proceedings of the Fourteenth Conference on Computational Natural Language Learning, pages 172–181,
Uppsala, Sweden, 15-16 July 2010.

Section 2 first describes a general multi-class SVM. We call the base vector of information used by the SVM the *attributes*. A standard multi-class SVM creates features for the cross-product of attributes and classes. E.g., the attribute COUNT(*Russia* during *1997*) is not only a feature for predicting the preposition **during**, but also for predicting the 33 other prepositions. The SVM must therefore learn to disregard many irrelevant features. We observe that this is not necessary, and develop an SVM that only uses the relevant attributes in the score for each class. Building on this efficient framework, we incorporate variance regularization into the SVM's quadratic program.

We apply our algorithms to three tasks: preposition selection, context-sensitive spelling correction, and non-referential pronoun detection (Section 4). We reproduce Bergsma et al. (2009)'s results using a multi-class SVM. Our new models achieve much better accuracy with fewer training examples. We also exceed the accuracy of a reasonable alternative technique for increasing the learning rate: including the output of the unsupervised system as a feature in the SVM.

Variance regularization is an elegant addition to the suite of methods in NLP that improve performance when access to labeled data is limited. Section 5 discusses some related approaches. While we motivate our algorithm as a way to learn better weights when the features are counts from an auxiliary corpus, there are other potential uses of our method. We outline some of these in Section 6, and note other directions for future research.

2 Three Multi-Class SVM Models

We describe three max-margin multi-class classifiers and their corresponding quadratic programs. Although we describe linear SVMs, they can be extended to nonlinear cases in the standard way by writing the optimal function as a linear combination of kernel functions over the input examples.

In each case, after providing the general technique, we relate the approach to our motivating application: learning weights for count features in a discriminative web-scale N-gram model.

2.1 Standard Multi-Class SVM

We define a K-class SVM following Crammer and Singer (2001). This is a generalization of binary SVMs (Cortes and Vapnik, 1995). We have a set $\{(\bar{x}^1, y^1), ..., (\bar{x}^M, y^M)\}$ of M training examples. Each $\bar{x}$ is an N-dimensional attribute vector, and $y \in \{1, ..., K\}$ are classes. A classifier, H, maps an attribute vector, $\bar{x}$, to a class, y. H is parameterized by a K-by-N matrix of weights, $\mathbf{W}$:

$$H_{\mathbf{W}}(\bar{x}) = \operatorname*{argmax}_{r=1}^{K} \{\bar{W}_r \cdot \bar{x}\} \quad (1)$$

where $\bar{W}_r$ is the rth row of $\mathbf{W}$. That is, the predicted label is the index of the row of $\mathbf{W}$ that has the highest inner-product with the attributes, $\bar{x}$.

We seek weights such that the classifier makes few errors on training data and generalizes well to unseen data. There are KN weights to learn, for the cross-product of attributes and classes. The most common approach is to train K separate one-versus-all binary SVMs, one for each class. The weights learned for the rth SVM provide the weights $\bar{W}_r$ in (1). We call this approach **OVA-SVM**. Note in some settings various one-versus-one strategies may be more effective than one-versus-all (Hsu and Lin, 2002).

The weights can also be found using a single constrained optimization (Vapnik, 1998; Weston and Watkins, 1998). Following the soft-margin version in Crammer and Singer (2001):

$$\begin{aligned} &\min_{\mathbf{W}, \xi^1, \ldots, \xi^M} && \frac{1}{2} \sum_{i=1}^{K} ||\bar{W}_i||^2 + C \sum_{i=1}^{m} \xi^i \\ &\text{subject to :} && \xi^i \geq 0 \\ &\forall r \neq y^i, && \bar{W}_{y^i} \cdot \bar{x}^i - \bar{W}_r \cdot \bar{x}^i \geq 1 - \xi^i \quad (2) \end{aligned}$$

The constraints require the correct class to be scored higher than other classes by a certain margin, with slack for non-separable cases. Minimizing the weights is a form of regularization. Tuning the C-parameter controls the emphasis on regularization versus separation of training examples.

We call this the **K-SVM**. The K-SVM outperformed the OVA-SVM in Crammer and Singer (2001), but see Rifkin and Klautau (2004). The popularity of K-SVM is partly due to convenience; it is included in popular SVM software like SVM-*multiclass*[1] and LIBLINEAR (Fan et al., 2008).

Note that with two classes, K-SVM is less efficient than a standard binary SVM. A binary classifier outputs class 1 if $(\bar{w} \cdot \bar{x} > 0)$ and class 2 otherwise. The K-SVM encodes a binary classifier using $\bar{W}_1 = \bar{w}$ and $\bar{W}_2 = -\bar{w}$, therefore requiring twice the memory of a binary SVM. However, both binary and 2-class formulations have the same solution (Weston and Watkins, 1998).

[1] http://svmlight.joachims.org/svm_multiclass.html

2.1.1 Web-Scale N-gram K-SVM

K-SVM was used with N-gram models in Bergsma et al. (2009). For preposition selection, attributes were web counts of patterns filled with 34 prepositions, corresponding to the 34 classes. Each preposition serves as the *filler* of each *context pattern*. Fourteen patterns were used for each filler: all five 5-grams, four 4-grams, three 3-grams, and two 2-grams spanning the position to be predicted. There are $N = 14*34 = 476$ total attributes, and therefore $KN = 476 * 34 = 16184$ weights in **W**.

This K-SVM classifier can potentially exploit very subtle information. Let $\bar{W}_{in}$ and $\bar{W}_{before}$ be weights for the classes **in** and **before**. Notice some of the attributes weighted in the inner products $\bar{W}_{before} \cdot \bar{x}$ and $\bar{W}_{in} \cdot \bar{x}$ will be for counts of the preposition *after*. Relatively high counts for a context with *after* should deter us from choosing **in** more than from choosing **before**. These correlations can be encoded in the classifier via the corresponding weights on *after*-counts in $\bar{W}_{in}$ and $\bar{W}_{before}$. How useful are these correlations and how much training data is needed before they can be learned and exploited effectively?

We next develop a model that, for each class, only scores those attributes deemed to be directly relevant to the class. Our experiments thus empirically address these questions for different tasks.

2.2 SVM with Class-Specific Attributes

Suppose we can partition our attribute vectors into sub-vectors that only include attributes that we declare as relevant to the corresponding class: $\bar{x} = (\bar{x}_1, ..., \bar{x}_K)$. We develop a classifier that only uses the class-specific attributes in the score for each class. The classifier uses an N-dimensional weight vector, $\bar{w}$, which follows the attribute partition, $\bar{w} = (\bar{w}_1, ..., \bar{w}_K)$. The classifier is:

$$H_{\bar{w}}(\bar{x}) = \operatorname*{argmax}_{r=1}^{K} \{\bar{w}_r \cdot \bar{x}_r\} \quad (3)$$

We call this classifier the **CS-SVM** (an SVM with **C**lass-**S**pecific attributes).

The weights can be determined using the follow (soft-margin) optimization:

$$\begin{aligned} &\min_{\bar{w}, \xi^1, \ldots, \xi^m} && \frac{1}{2}\bar{w}^T\bar{w} + C\sum_{i=1}^{m}\xi^i \\ &\text{subject to :} && \xi^i \geq 0 \\ &\forall r \neq y^i, && \bar{w}_{y^i} \cdot \bar{x}^i_{y^i} - \bar{w}_r \cdot \bar{x}^i_r \geq 1 - \xi^i \quad (4) \end{aligned}$$

There are several advantages to this formulation. Foremost, rather than having KN weights, it can have only N. For linear classifiers, the number of examples needed to reach optimum performance is at most linear in the number of weights (Vapnik, 1998; Ng and Jordan, 2002). In fact, both the total number and number of *active* features per example decrease by K. Thus this reduction saves far more memory than what could be obtained by an equal reduction in dimensionality via pruning infrequent attributes.

Also, note that unlike the K-SVM (Section 2.1), in the binary case the CS-SVM is completely equivalent (thus equally efficient) to a standard SVM.

We will not always *a priori* know the class associated with each attribute. Also, some attributes may be predictive of multiple classes. In such cases, we can include ambiguous attributes in every sub-vector (needing N+$D(K$-1) total weights if D attributes are duplicated). In the degenerate case where every attribute is duplicated, CS-SVM is equivalent to K-SVM; both have KN weights.

2.2.1 Optimization as a Binary SVM

We could solve the optimization problem in (4) directly using a quadratic programming solver. However, through an equivalent transformation into a binary SVM, we can take advantage of efficient, custom SVM optimization algorithms.

We follow Har-Peled et al. (2003) in transforming a multi-class example into a set of binary examples, each specifying a constraint from (4). We extend the attribute sub-vector corresponding to each class to be N-dimensional. We do this by substituting zero-vectors for all the other sub-vectors in the partition. The attribute vector for the rth class is then $\bar{z}_r = (\bar{0}, ..., \bar{0}, \bar{x}_r, \bar{0}, ..., \bar{0})$. This is known as Kesler's Construction and has a long history in classification (Duda and Hart, 1973; Crammer and Singer, 2003). We then create binary rank constraints for a ranking SVM (Joachims, 2002) (ranking SVMs reduce to standard binary SVMs). We create K instances for each multi-class example $(\bar{x}^i, y^i)$, with the transformed vector of the true class, $\bar{z}_{y^i}$, assigned a higher-rank than all the other, equally-ranked classes, $\bar{z}_{\{r \neq y^i\}}$. Training a ranking SVM using these constraints gives the same weights as solving (4), but allows us to use efficient, custom SVM software.[2] Note the K-SVM

[2]One subtlety is whether to use a single slack, ξ^i, for all K-1 constraints per example i (Crammer and Singer, 2001), or a different slack for each constraint (Joachims, 2002). Us-

can also be trained this way, by including every attribute in every sub-vector, as described earlier.

2.2.2 Web-Scale N-gram CS-SVM

Returning to our preposition selection example, an obvious attribute partition for the CS-SVM is to include as attributes for predicting preposition r only those counts for patterns filled with preposition r. Thus $\bar{x}_{in}$ will only include counts for context patterns filled with *in* and $\bar{x}_{before}$ will only include counts for context patterns filled with *before*. With 34 sub-vectors and 14 attributes in each, there are only $14 * 34 = 476$ total weights. In contrast, K-SVM had 16184 weights to learn.

It is instructive to compare the CS-SVM in (3) to the unsupervised SUMLM approach in Bergsma et al. (2009). That approach can be written as:

$$H(\bar{x}) = \underset{r=1}{\overset{K}{\operatorname{argmax}}}\{\bar{1} \cdot \bar{x}_r\} \qquad (5)$$

where $\bar{1}$ is an N-dimensional vector of ones. This is CS-SVM with all weights set to unity. The counts for each preposition are simply summed, and whichever one scores the highest is taken as the output (actually only a subset of the counts are used, see Section 4.1). As mentioned earlier, this system performs remarkably well on several tasks.

2.3 Variance Regularization SVMs

Suppose we choose our attribute partition well and train the CS-SVM on a sufficient number of examples to achieve good performance. It is a reasonable hypothesis that the learned weights will be predominantly positive. This is because each sub-vector $\bar{x}_r$ was chosen to only include attributes that are predictive of class r. Unlike the classifier in (1) which weighs positive and negative evidence together for each class, in CS-SVM, negative evidence only plays a roll as it contributes to the score of competing classes.

If all the attributes are equally important, the weights should be equal, as in the unsupervised approach in (5). If some are more important than others, the training examples should reflect this and the learner can adjust the weights accordingly.[3] In the absence of this training evidence, it is reasonable to bias the classifier toward an equal-weight solution.

ing the former may be better as it results in a tighter bound on empirical risk (Tsochantaridis et al., 2005).

[3]E.g., the true preposition might be better predicted by the counts of patterns that tend to include the preposition's grammatical object, i.e., patterns that include more right-context.

Rather than the standard SVM regularization that minimizes the norm of the weights as in (4), we therefore regularize toward weights that have low variance. More formally, we can regard the set of weights, $w_1, ..., w_N$, as the distribution of a discrete random variable, W. We can calculate the mean and variance of this variable from its distribution. We seek a variable that has low variance.

We begin with a more general objective and then explain how a specific choice of covariance matrix, $\mathbf{C}$, minimizes the variance of the weights. We propose the regularizer:

$$\begin{aligned} &\min_{\bar{w},\xi^1,\ldots,\xi^m} && \frac{1}{2}\bar{w}^T\mathbf{C}\bar{w} + C\sum_{i=1}^{m}\xi^i \\ &\text{subject to :} && \xi^i \geq 0 \\ &\forall r \neq y^i, && \bar{w}_{y^i}\cdot\bar{x}^i_{y^i} - \bar{w}_r\cdot\bar{x}^i_r \geq 1-\xi^i \end{aligned} \qquad (6)$$

where $\mathbf{C}$ is a normalized covariance matrix such that $\sum_{i,j} C_{i,j} = 0$. This ensures uniform weight vectors receive zero regularization penalty. Since all covariance matrices are positive semi-definite, the quadratic program (QP) remains convex in $\bar{w}$, and thus amenable to general purpose QP-solvers.

Since the unsupervised system in (5) has zero weight variance, the SVM learned in (6) should do as least as well as (5) as we tune the C-parameter on development data. That is, as C approaches zero, variance minimization becomes the sole objective of (6), and uniform weights are produced.

We use covariance matrices of the form:

$$\mathbf{C} = \operatorname{diag}(\bar{p}) - \bar{p}\bar{p}^T \qquad (7)$$

where $\operatorname{diag}(\bar{p})$ is the matrix constructed by putting $\bar{p}$ on the main diagonal. Here, $\bar{p}$ is an arbitrary N-dimensional weighting vector, such that $p \geq 0$ and $\sum_i p_i = 1$. $\bar{p}$ dictates the contribution of each w_i to the mean and variance of the weights in $\bar{w}$. It is easy to see that $\sum_{i,j} C_{i,j} = \sum_i p_i - \sum_i \sum_j p_i p_j = 0$.

We now show that $\bar{w}^T(\operatorname{diag}(\bar{p}) - \bar{p}\bar{p}^T)\bar{w}$ expresses the variance of the weights in $\bar{w}$ with respect to the probability weighting $\bar{p}$. The variance of a random variable with mean $E[W] = \mu$ is:

$$\operatorname{Var}[W] = E[(W-\mu)^2] = E[W^2] - E[W]^2$$

The mean of the weights using probability weighting $\bar{p}$ is $E[W] = \bar{w}^T\bar{p} = \bar{p}\bar{w}$. Also, $E[W^2] = \bar{w}^T \operatorname{diag}(\bar{p})\bar{w}$. Thus:

$$\begin{aligned} \operatorname{Var}[W] &= \bar{w}^T \operatorname{diag}(\bar{p})\bar{w} - (\bar{w}^T\bar{p})(\bar{p}\bar{w}) \\ &= \bar{w}^T(\operatorname{diag}(\bar{p}) - \bar{p}\bar{p})\bar{w} \end{aligned}$$

In our experiments, we deem each weight to be equally important to the variance calculation, and set $p_i = \frac{1}{N}, \forall i = 1, \ldots, N$.

The goal of the regularization in (6) using $\mathbf{C}$ from (7) can be regarded as directing the SVM toward a good unsupervised system, regardless of the constraints (training examples). In some unsupervised systems, however, only a subset of the attributes are used. In other cases, distinct subsets of weights should have low variance, rather than minimizing the variance across all weights. There are examples of these situations in Section 4.

We can account for these cases in our QP. We provide separate terms in our quadratic function for the subsets of $\bar{w}$ that should have low variance. Suppose we create L subsets of $\bar{w}$: $\tilde{\omega}_1, \ldots \tilde{\omega}_L$, where $\tilde{\omega}_j$ is $\bar{w}$ with elements set to zero that are not in subset j. We then minimize $\frac{1}{2}(\tilde{\omega}_1^T \mathbf{C}_1 \tilde{\omega}_1 + \ldots + \tilde{\omega}_L^T \mathbf{C}_L \tilde{\omega}_L)$. If the terms in subset j have low variance, $\mathbf{C}_j = \mathbf{C}$ from (7) is used. If the subset corresponds to attributes that are not *a priori* known to be useful, an identity matrix can instead be used, $\mathbf{C}_j = \mathbf{I}$, and these weights will be regularized toward zero as in a standard SVM.[4]

Variance regularization therefore exploits extra knowledge by the system designer. The designer decides which weights should have similar values, and the SVM is biased to prefer this solution.

One consequence of being able to regularize different subsets of weights is that we can also apply variance regularization to the standard multi-class SVM (Section 2.1). We can use an identity $\mathbf{C}_i$ matrix for all *irrelevant* weights, i.e., weights that correspond to class-attribute pairs where the attribute is not directly relevant to the class. In our experiments, however, we apply variance regularization to the more efficient CS-SVM.

We refer to a CS-SVM trained using the variance minimization quadratic program as the **VAR-SVM**.

2.3.1 Web-Scale N-gram VAR-SVM

If variance regularization is applied to all weights, attributes COUNT(*in Russia* during), COUNT(*Russia* during *1997*), and COUNT(during *1997 to*) will be encouraged to have similar weights in the score for class **during**. Furthermore, these will be weighted similarly to other patterns, filled with other prepositions, used in the scores for other classes.

[4]Weights must appear in $\geq$1 subsets (possibly only in the $\mathbf{C}_j = \mathbf{I}$ subset). Each occurs in at most one in our experiments. Note it is straightforward to express this as a single covariance matrix regularizer over $\bar{w}$; we omit the details.

Alternatively, we could minimize the variance separately over all 5-gram patterns, then over all 4-gram patterns, etc., or over all patterns with a filler in the same position. In our experiments, we took a very simple approach: we minimized the variance of all attributes that are weighted equally in the unsupervised baselines. If a feature is not included in a baseline, it is regularized toward zero.

3 Experimental Details

We use the data sets from Bergsma et al. (2009). These are the three tasks where web-scale N-gram counts were previously used as features in a standard K-SVM. In each case a classifier makes a decision for a particular word based on the word's surrounding context. The attributes of the classifier are the log counts of different fillers occurring in the context patterns. We retrieve counts from the web-scale Google Web 5-gram Corpus (Brants and Franz, 2006), which includes N-grams of length one to five. We apply add-one smoothing to all counts. Every classifier also has bias features (for every class). We simply include, where appropriate, attributes that are always unity.

We use LIBLINEAR (Fan et al., 2008) to train K-SVM and OVA-SVM, and SVM^{rank} (Joachims, 2006) to train CS-SVM. For VAR-SVM, we solve the primal form of the quadratic program directly in CPLEX (2005), a general optimization package.

We vary the number of training examples for each classifier. The C-parameters of all SVMs are tuned on development data. We evaluate using **accuracy**: the percentage of test examples that are classified correctly. We also provide the accuracy of the majority-class baseline and best unsupervised system, as defined in Bergsma et al. (2009).

As an alternative way to increase the learning rate, we augment a classifier's features using the output of the unsupervised system: For each class, we include one feature for the sum of all counts (in the unsupervised system) that predict that class. We denote these augmented systems with a $+$ as in K-SVM^+ and CS-SVM^+.

4 Applications

4.1 Preposition Selection

Preposition errors are common among new English speakers (Chodorow et al., 2007). Systems that can reliably identify these errors are needed in word processing and educational software.

System	Training Examples 10	100	1K	10K	100K
OvA-SVM	16.0	50.6	66.1	71.1	73.5
K-SVM	13.7	50.0	65.8	72.0	74.7
K-SVM$^+$	22.2	56.8	70.5	73.7	**75.2**
CS-SVM	27.1	58.8	69.0	73.5	74.2
CS-SVM$^+$	39.6	64.8	71.5	74.0	74.4
VAR-SVM	**73.8**	**74.2**	**74.7**	**74.9**	74.9

Table 1: Accuracy (%) of preposition-selection SVMs. Unsupervised accuracy is 73.7%.

In our experiments, a classifier must choose the correct preposition among 34 candidates, using counts for filled 2-to-5-gram patterns. We use 100K training, 10K development, and 10K test examples. The unsupervised approach sums the counts of all 3-to-5-gram patterns for each preposition. We therefore regularize the variance of the 3-to-5-gram weights in VAR-SVM, and simultaneously minimize the norm of the 2-gram weights.

4.1.1 Results

The majority-class is the preposition **of**; it occurs in 20.3% of test examples. The unsupervised system scores 73.7%. For further perspective on these results, note Chodorow et al. (2007) achieved 69% with 7M training examples, while Tetreault and Chodorow (2008) found the human performance was around 75%. However, these results are not directly comparable as they are on different data.

Table 1 gives the accuracy for different amounts of training data. Here, as in the other tasks, K-SVM mirrors the learning rate in Bergsma et al. (2009). There are several distinct phases among the relative ranking of the systems. For smaller amounts of training data ($\leq$1000 examples) K-SVM performs worst, while VAR-SVM is statistically significantly better than all other systems, and always exceeds the performance of the unsupervised approach.[5] Augmenting the attributes with sum counts (the + systems) strongly helps with fewer examples, especially in conjunction with the more efficient CS-SVM. However, VAR-SVM clearly helps more. We noted earlier that VAR-SVM is guaranteed to do as well as the unsupervised system on the development data, but here we confirm that it can also exploit even small amounts of training data to further improve accuracy.

CS-SVM outperforms K-SVM except with 100K examples, while OvA-SVM is better than K-SVM for small amounts of data.[6] K-SVM performs best with all the data; it uses the most expressive representation, but needs 100K examples to make use of it. On the other hand, feature augmentation and variance regularization provide diminishing returns as the amount of training data increases.

System	Training Examples 10	100	1K	10K	100K
CS-SVM	86.0	93.5	95.1	**95.7**	95.7
CS-SVM$^+$	91.0	94.9	95.3	**95.7**	95.7
VAR-SVM	**94.9**	**95.3**	**95.6**	**95.7**	**95.8**

Table 2: Accuracy (%) of spell-correction SVMs. Unsupervised accuracy is 94.8%.

4.2 Context-Sensitive Spelling Correction

Context-sensitive spelling correction, or real-word error/malapropism detection (Golding and Roth, 1999; Hirst and Budanitsky, 2005), is the task of identifying errors when a misspelling results in a real word in the lexicon, e.g., using *site* when *sight* or *cite* was intended. Contextual spell checkers are among the most widely-used NLP technology, as they are included in commercial word processing software (Church et al., 2007).

For every occurrence of a word in a pre-defined confusion set (e.g. {*cite, sight, cite*}), the classifier selects the most likely word from the set. We use the five confusion sets from Bergsma et al. (2009); four are binary and one is a 3-way classification. We use 100K training, 10K development, and 10K test examples for each, and average accuracy across the sets. All 2-to-5 gram counts are used in the unsupervised system, so the variance of all weights is regularized in VAR-SVM.

4.2.1 Results

On this task, the majority-class baseline is much higher, 66.9%, and so is the accuracy of the top unsupervised system: 94.8%. Since four of the five sets are binary classifications, where K-SVM and CS-SVM are equivalent, we only give the accuracy of the CS-SVM (it does perform better on the one 3-way set). VAR-SVM again exceeds the unsupervised accuracy for all training sizes, and generally

[5]Significance is calculated using a χ^2 test over the test set correct/incorrect contingency table.

[6]Rifkin and Klautau (2004) argue OvA-SVM is as good as K-SVM, but this is "predicated on the assumption that the classes are 'independent'," i.e., that examples from class 0 are no closer to class 1 than to class 2. This is not true of this task (e.g. $\bar{x}_{before}$ is closer to $\bar{x}_{after}$ than $\bar{x}_{in}$, etc.).

System	Training Examples 10	100	1K
CS-SVM	59.0	71.0	84.3
CS-SVM$^+$	59.4	74.9	**84.5**
VAR-SVM	**70.2**	76.2	**84.5**
VAR-SVM+FreeB	64.2	**80.3**	**84.5**

Table 3: Accuracy (%) of non-referential detection SVMs. Unsupervised accuracy is 80.1%.

performs as well as the augmented CS-SVM$^+$ using an order of magnitude less training data (Table 2). Differences from ≤1K are significant.

4.3 Non-Referential Pronoun Detection

Non-referential detection predicts whether the English pronoun *it* refers to a preceding noun ("*it* lost money") or is used as a grammatical placeholder ("*it* is important to..."). This binary classification is a necessary but often neglected step for noun phrase coreference resolution (Paice and Husk, 1987; Bergsma et al., 2008; Ng, 2009).

Bergsma et al. (2008) use features for the counts of various fillers in the pronoun's context patterns. If *it* is the most common filler, the pronoun is likely non-referential. If other fillers are common (like *they* or *he*), it is likely a referential instance. For example, "*he* lost money" is common on the web, but "*he* is important to" is not. We use the same fillers as in previous work, and preprocess the N-gram corpus in the same way.

The unsupervised system picks non-referential if the difference between the summed count of *it* fillers and the summed count of *they* fillers is above a threshold (note this no longer fits (5), with consequences discussed below). We thus separately minimize the variance of the *it* pattern weights and the *they* pattern weights. We use 1K training, 533 development, and 534 test examples.

4.3.1 Results

The most common class is **referential**, occurring in 59.4% of test examples. The unsupervised system again does much better, at 80.1%.

Annotated training examples are much harder to obtain for this task and we experiment with a smaller range of training sizes (Table 3). The performance of VAR-SVM exceeds the performance of K-SVM across all training sizes (bold accuracies are significantly better than either CS-SVM for ≤100 examples). However, the gains were not as large as we had hoped, and accuracy remains worse than the unsupervised system when not using all the training data. When using all the data, a fairly large C-parameter performs best on development data, so regularization plays less of a role.

After development experiments, we speculated that the poor performance relative to the unsupervised approach was related to class bias. In the other tasks, the unsupervised system chooses the highest summed score. Here, the difference in *it* and *they* counts is compared to a *threshold*. Since the bias feature is regularized toward zero, then, unlike the other tasks, using a low C-parameter does not produce the unsupervised system, so performance can begin below the unsupervised level.

Since we wanted the system to learn this threshold, even when highly regularized, we removed the regularization penalty from the bias weight, letting the optimization freely set the weight to minimize training error. With more freedom, the new classifier (VAR-SVM+FreeB) performs worse with 10 examples, but exceeds the unsupervised approach with 100 training points. Although this was somewhat successful, developing better strategies for bias remains useful future work.

5 Related Work

There is a large body of work on regularization in machine learning, including work that uses positive semi-definite matrices in the SVM quadratic program. The graph Laplacian has been used to encourage geometrically-similar feature vectors to be classified similarly (Belkin et al., 2006). An appealing property of these approaches is that they incorporate information from unlabeled examples. Wang et al. (2006) use Laplacian regularization for the task of dependency parsing. They regularize such that features for distributionally-similar words have similar weights. Rather than penalize pairwise differences proportional to a similarity function, we simply penalize weight variance.

In the field of computer vision, Tefas et al. (2001) (binary) and Kotsia et al. (2009) (multiclass) also regularize weights with respect to a covariance matrix. They use labeled data to find the sum of the sample covariance matrices from each class, similar to linear discriminant analysis. We propose the idea in general, and instantiate with a different $\mathbf{C}$ matrix: a variance regularizer over $\bar{w}$. Most importantly, our instantiated covariance matrix does not require labeled data to generate.

In a Bayesian setting, Raina et al. (2006) model

feature correlations in a logistic regression classifier. They propose a method to construct a covariance matrix for a multivariate Gaussian prior on the classifier's weights. Labeled data for other, related tasks is used to infer potentially correlated features on the target task. Like in our results, they found that the gains from modeling dependencies diminish as more training data is available.

We also mention two related online learning approaches. Similar to our goal of regularizing toward a good unsupervised system, Crammer et al. (2006) regularize $\bar{w}$ toward a (different) target vector at each update, rather than strictly minimizing $||\bar{w}||^2$. The target vector is the vector learned from the cumulative effect of previous updates. Dredze et al. (2008) maintain the variance of each weight and use this to guide the online updates. However, covariance between weights is not considered.

We believe new SVM regularizations in general, and variance regularization in particular, will increasingly be used in combination with related NLP strategies that learn better when labeled data is scarce. These may include: using more-general features, e.g. ones generated from raw text (Miller et al., 2004; Koo et al., 2008), leveraging out-of-domain examples to improve in-domain classification (Blitzer et al., 2007; Daumé III, 2007), active learning (Cohn et al., 1994; Tong and Koller, 2002), and approaches that treat unlabeled data as labeled, such as bootstrapping (Yarowsky, 1995), co-training (Blum and Mitchell, 1998), and self-training (McClosky et al., 2006).

6 Future Work

The primary direction of future research will be to apply the VAR-SVM to new problems and tasks. There are many situations where a system designer has an intuition about the role a feature will play in prediction; the feature was perhaps added with this role in mind. By biasing the SVM to use features as intended, VAR-SVM may learn better with fewer training examples. The relationship between attributes and classes may be explicit when, e.g., a rule-based system is optimized via discriminative learning, or annotators justify their decisions by indicating the relevant attributes (Zaidan et al., 2007). Also, if features are *a priori* thought to have different predictive worth, the attribute *values* could be scaled such that variance regularization, as we formulated it, has the desired effect.

Other avenues of future work will be to extend the VAR-SVM in three directions: efficiency, representational power, and problem domain.

While we optimized the VAR-SVM objective in CPLEX, general purpose QP-solvers "do not exploit the special structure of [the SVM optimization] problem," and consequently often train in time super-linear with the number of training examples (Joachims et al., 2009). It would be useful to fit our optimization problem to efficient SVM training methods, especially for linear classifiers.

VAR-SVM's representational power could be extended by using non-linear SVMs. Kernels can be used with a covariance regularizer (Kotsia et al., 2009). Since $\mathbf{C}$ is positive semi-definite, the square root of its inverse is defined. We can therefore map the input examples using $(\mathbf{C}^{-\frac{1}{2}}\bar{x})$, and write an equivalent objective function in terms of kernel functions over the transformed examples.

Also, since structured-prediction SVMs build on the multi-class framework (Tsochantaridis et al., 2005), variance regularization can be incorporated naturally into more complex prediction tasks, such as parsers, taggers, and aligners.

VAR-SVM may also help in new domains where annotated data is lacking. VAR-SVM should be stronger cross-domain than K-SVM; regularization with domain-neutral prior-knowledge can offset domain-specific biases. Learned weight vectors from other domains may also provide cross-domain regularization guidance.

7 Conclusion

We presented variance-regularization SVMs, an approach to learning that creates better classifiers using fewer training examples. Variance regularization incorporates a bias for known good weights into the SVM's quadratic program. The VAR-SVM can therefore exploit extra knowledge by the system designer. Since the objective remains a convex quadratic function of the weights, the program is computationally no harder to optimize than a standard SVM. We also demonstrated how to design multi-class SVMs using only class-specific attributes, and compared the performance of this approach to standard multi-class SVMs on the task of preposition selection.

While variance regularization is most helpful on tasks with many classes and features, like preposition selection, it achieved gains on all our tasks when training with smaller sample sizes. It should be useful on a variety of other NLP problems.

References

Mikhail Belkin, Partha Niyogi, and Vikas Sindhwani. 2006. Manifold regularization: A geometric framework for learning from labeled and unlabeled examples. *JMLR*, 7:2399–2434.

Shane Bergsma, Dekang Lin, and Randy Goebel. 2008. Distributional identification of non-referential pronouns. In *ACL-08: HLT*.

Shane Bergsma, Dekang Lin, and Randy Goebel. 2009. Web-scale N-gram models for lexical disambiguation. In *IJCAI*.

John Blitzer, Mark Dredze, and Fernando Pereira. 2007. Biographies, bollywood, boom-boxes and blenders: Domain adaptation for sentiment classification. In *ACL*.

Avrim Blum and Tom Mitchell. 1998. Combining labeled and unlabeled data with co-training. In *COLT*.

Thorsten Brants and Alex Franz. 2006. The Google Web 1T 5-gram Corpus Version 1.1. LDC2006T13.

Martin Chodorow, Joel R. Tetreault, and Na-Rae Han. 2007. Detection of grammatical errors involving prepositions. In *ACL-SIGSEM Workshop on Prepositions*.

Kenneth Church, Ted Hart, and Jianfeng Gao. 2007. Compressing trigram language models with Golomb coding. In *EMNLP-CoNLL*.

David Cohn, Les Atlas, and Richard Ladner. 1994. Improving generalization with active learning. *Mach. Learn.*, 15(2):201–221.

Corinna Cortes and Vladimir Vapnik. 1995. Support-vector networks. *Mach. Learn.*, 20(3):273–297.

CPLEX. 2005. IBM ILOG CPLEX 9.1. `www.ilog.com/products/cplex/`.

Koby Crammer and Yoram Singer. 2001. On the algorithmic implementation of multiclass kernel-based vector machines. *JMLR*, 2:265–292.

Koby Crammer and Yoram Singer. 2003. Ultraconservative online algorithms for multiclass problems. *JMLR*, 3:951–991.

Koby Crammer, Ofer Dekel, Joseph Keshet, Shai Shalev-Shwartz, and Yoram Singer. 2006. Online passive-aggressive algorithms. *JMLR*, 7:551–585.

Hal Daumé III. 2007. Frustratingly easy domain adaptation. In *ACL*.

Mark Dredze, Koby Crammer, and Fernando Pereira. 2008. Confidence-weighted linear classification. In *ICML*.

Richard O. Duda and Peter E. Hart. 1973. *Pattern Classification and Scene Analysis*. John Wiley & Sons.

Rong-En Fan, Kai-Wei Chang, Cho-Jui Hsieh, Xiang-Rui Wang, and Chih-Jen Lin. 2008. LIBLINEAR: A library for large linear classification. *JMLR*, 9:1871–1874.

Andrew R. Golding and Dan Roth. 1999. A Winnow-based approach to context-sensitive spelling correction. *Mach. Learn.*, 34(1-3):107–130.

Sariel Har-Peled, Dan Roth, and Dav Zimak. 2003. Constraint classification for multiclass classification and ranking. In *NIPS*.

Graeme Hirst and Alexander Budanitsky. 2005. Correcting real-word spelling errors by restoring lexical cohesion. *Nat. Lang. Eng.*, 11(1):87–111.

Chih-Wei Hsu and Chih-Jen Lin. 2002. A comparison of methods for multiclass support vector machines. *IEEE Trans. Neur. Networks*, 13(2):415–425.

Thorsten Joachims, Thomas Finley, and Chun-Nam John Yu. 2009. Cutting-plane training of structural SVMs. *Mach. Learn.*, 77(1):27–59.

Thorsten Joachims. 2002. Optimizing search engines using clickthrough data. In *KDD*.

Thorsten Joachims. 2006. Training linear SVMs in linear time. In *KDD*.

Terry Koo, Xavier Carreras, and Michael Collins. 2008. Simple semi-supervised dependency parsing. In *ACL-08: HLT*.

Irene Kotsia, Stefanos Zafeiriou, and Ioannis Pitas. 2009. Novel multiclass classifiers based on the minimization of the within-class variance. *IEEE Trans. Neur. Networks*, 20(1):14–34.

Mirella Lapata and Frank Keller. 2005. Web-based models for natural language processing. *ACM Trans. Speech and Language Processing*, 2(1):1–31.

David McClosky, Eugene Charniak, and Mark Johnson. 2006. Effective self-training for parsing. In *HLT-NAACL*.

Scott Miller, Jethran Guinness, and Alex Zamanian. 2004. Name tagging with word clusters and discriminative training. In *HLT-NAACL*.

Andrew Y. Ng and Michael I. Jordan. 2002. Discriminative vs. generative classifiers: A comparison of logistic regression and naive bayes. In *NIPS*.

Vincent Ng. 2009. Graph-cut-based anaphoricity determination for coreference resolution. In *NAACL-HLT*.

Franz J. Och and Hermann Ney. 2002. Discriminative training and maximum entropy models for statistical machine translation. In *ACL*.

Daisuke Okanohara and Jun'ichi Tsujii. 2007. A discriminative language model with pseudo-negative samples. In *ACL*.

Chris D. Paice and Gareth D. Husk. 1987. Towards the automatic recognition of anaphoric features in English text: the impersonal pronoun "it". *Computer Speech and Language*, 2:109–132.

Rajat Raina, Andrew Y. Ng, and Daphne Koller. 2006. Constructing informative priors using transfer learning. In *ICML*.

Ryan Rifkin and Aldebaro Klautau. 2004. In defense of one-vs-all classification. *JMLR*, 5:101–141.

Noah A. Smith and Jason Eisner. 2005. Contrastive estimation: training log-linear models on unlabeled data. In *ACL*.

Anastasios Tefas, Constantine Kotropoulos, and Ioannis Pitas. 2001. Using support vector machines to enhance the performance of elastic graph matching for frontal face authentication. *IEEE Trans. Pattern Anal. Machine Intell.*, 23:735–746.

Joel R. Tetreault and Martin Chodorow. 2008. The ups and downs of preposition error detection in ESL writing. In *COLING*.

Simon Tong and Daphne Koller. 2002. Support vector machine active learning with applications to text classification. *JMLR*, 2:45–66.

Ioannis Tsochantaridis, Thorsten Joachims, Thomas Hofmann, and Yasemin Altun. 2005. Large margin methods for structured and interdependent output variables. *JMLR*, 6:1453–1484.

Vladimir N. Vapnik. 1998. *Statistical Learning Theory*. John Wiley & Sons.

Qin Iris Wang, Colin Cherry, Dan Lizotte, and Dale Schuurmans. 2006. Improved large margin dependency parsing via local constraints and Laplacian regularization. In *CoNLL*.

Jason Weston and Chris Watkins. 1998. Multi-class support vector machines. Technical Report CSD-TR-98-04, Department of Computer Science, Royal Holloway, University of London.

David Yarowsky. 1995. Unsupervised word sense disambiguation rivaling supervised methods. In *ACL*.

Omar Zaidan, Jason Eisner, and Christine Piatko. 2007. Using "annotator rationales" to improve machine learning for text categorization. In *NAACL-HLT*.

Online Entropy-based Model of Lexical Category Acquisition

Grzegorz Chrupała
Saarland University
gchrupala@lsv.uni-saarland.de

Afra Alishahi
Saarland University
afra@coli.uni-saarland.de

Abstract

Children learn a robust representation of lexical categories at a young age. We propose an incremental model of this process which efficiently groups words into lexical categories based on their local context using an information-theoretic criterion. We train our model on a corpus of child-directed speech from CHILDES and show that the model learns a fine-grained set of intuitive word categories. Furthermore, we propose a novel evaluation approach by comparing the efficiency of our induced categories against other category sets (including traditional part of speech tags) in a variety of language tasks. We show the categories induced by our model typically outperform the other category sets.

1 The Acquisition of Lexical Categories

Psycholinguistic studies suggest that early on children acquire robust knowledge of the abstract lexical categories such as nouns, verbs and determiners (e.g., Gelman & Taylor, 1984; Kemp et al., 2005). Children's grouping of words into categories might be based on various cues, including phonological and morphological properties of a word, the distributional information about its surrounding context, and its semantic features. Among these, the distributional properties of the local context of a word have been thoroughly studied. It has been shown that child-directed speech provides informative co-occurrence cues, which can be reliably used to form lexical categories (Redington et al., 1998; Mintz, 2003).

The process of learning lexical categories by children is necessarily incremental. Human language acquisition is bounded by memory and processing limitations, and it is implausible that humans process large volumes of text at once and induce an optimum set of categories. Efficient online computational models are needed to investigate whether distributional information is equally useful in an online process of word categorization. However, the few incremental models of category acquisition which have been proposed so far are generally inefficient and over-sensitive to the properties of the input data (Cartwright & Brent, 1997; Parisien et al., 2008). Moreover, the unsupervised nature of these models makes their assessment a challenge, and the evaluation techniques proposed in the literature are limited.

The main contributions of our research are twofold. First, we propose an incremental entropy model for efficiently clustering words into categories given their local context. We train our model on a corpus of child-directed speech from CHILDES (MacWhinney, 2000) and show that the model learns a fine-grained set of intuitive word categories. Second, we propose a novel evaluation approach by comparing the efficiency of our induced categories against other category sets, including the traditional part of speech tags, in a variety of language tasks. We evaluate our model on word prediction (where a missing word is guessed based on its sentential context), semantic inference (where the semantic properties of a novel word are predicted based on the context), and grammaticality judgment (where the syntactic well-formedness of a sentence is assessed based on the category labels assigned to its words). The results show that the categories induced by our model can be successfully used in a variety of tasks and typically perform better than other category sets.

1.1 Unsupervised Models of Category Induction

Several computational models have used distributional information for categorizing words (e.g. Brown et al., 1992; Redington et al., 1998; Clark, 2000; Mintz, 2002). The majority of these mod-

Proceedings of the Fourteenth Conference on Computational Natural Language Learning, pages 182–191,
Uppsala, Sweden, 15-16 July 2010.

els partition the vocabulary into a set of optimum clusters (e.g., Brown et al., 1992; Clark, 2000). The generated clusters are intuitive, and can be used in different tasks such as word prediction and parsing. Moreover, these models confirm the learnability of abstract word categories, and show that distributional cues are a useful source of information for this purpose. However, (i) they categorize word types rather than word tokens, and as such provide no account of words belonging to more than one category, and (ii) the batch algorithms used by these systems make them implausible for modeling human category induction. Unsupervised models of PoS tagging such as Goldwater & Griffiths (2007) do assign labels to word-tokens, but they still typically use batch processing, and what is even more problematic, they hard-wire important aspects of the model, such as the final number of categories.

Only few previously proposed models process data incrementally, categorize word-tokens and do not pre-specify a fixed category set. The model of Cartwright & Brent (1997) uses an algorithm which incrementally merges word clusters so that a Minimum Description Length criterion for a template grammar is optimized. The model treats whole sentences as contextual units, which sacrifices a degree of incrementality, as well as making it less robust to noise in the input.

Parisien et al. (2008) propose a Bayesian clustering model which copes with ambiguity and exhibits the developmental trends observed in children (e.g. the order of acquisition of different categories). However, their model is overly sensitive to context variability, which results in the creation of sparse categories. To remedy this issue they introduce a "bootstrapping" component where the categories assigned to context words are use to determine the category of the current target word. They also perform periodical cluster reorganization. These mechanisms improve the overall performance of the model when trained on large amounts of training data, but they complicate the model with ad-hoc extensions and add to the (already considerable) computational load.

What is lacking is an incremental model of lexical category which can efficiently process naturalistic input data and gradually build robust categories with little training data.

1.2 Evaluation of the Induced Categories

There is no standard and straightforward method for evaluating the unsupervised models of category learning (see Clark, 2003, for discussion). Many unsupervised models of lexical category acquisition treat the traditional part of speech (PoS) tags as the gold standard, and measure the accuracy and completeness of their induced categories based on how closely they resemble the PoS categories (e.g. Redington et al., 1998; Mintz, 2003; Parisien et al., 2008). However, it is not at all clear whether humans form the same types of categories. In fact, many language tasks might benefit from finer-grained categories than the traditional PoS tags used for corpus annotation.

Frank et al. (2009) propose a different, automatically generated set of gold standard categories for evaluating an unsupervised categorization model. The gold-standard categories are formed according to "substitutability": if one word can be replaced by another and the resulting sentence is still grammatical, then there is a good chance that the two words belong to the same category. They extract 3-word frames from the training data, and form the gold standard categories based on the words that appear in the same frame. They emphasize that in order to provide some degree of generalization, different data sets must be used for forming the gold-standard categories and performing the evaluation. However, the resulting categories are bound to be incomplete, and using them as gold standard inevitably favors categorization models which use a similar frame-based principle.

All in all, using any set of gold standard categories for evaluating an unsupervised categorization model has the disadvantage of favoring one set of principles and intuitions over another; that is, assuming that there is a *correct* set of categories which the model should converge to. Alternatively, automatically induced categories can be evaluated based on how *useful* they are in performing different tasks. This approach is taken by Clark (2000), where the perplexity of a finite-state model is used to compare different category sets.

We build on this idea and propose a more general usage-based approach to evaluating the automatically induced categories from a data set, emphasizing that the ultimate goal of a category induction model is to form categories that can be efficiently used in a variety of language tasks. We argue that for such tasks, a finer-grained set of categories might be more appropriate than the coarse-grained PoS categories. Therefore, we propose a number of tasks for which we compare the performance based on various category sets, including those induced by our model.

2 An Incremental Entropy-based Model of Category Induction

A model of human category acquisition should possess two key features:

- It should process input as it arrives, and incrementally update the current set of clusters.
- The set of clusters should not be fixed in advance, but rather determined by the characteristics of the input data.

We propose a simple algorithm which fulfills those two conditions.

Our goal is to categorize word usages based on the similarity of their form (the content) and their surrounding words (the context). While grouping word usages into categories, we attempt to trade off two conflicting criteria. First, the categories should be informative about the properties of their members. Second, the number and distribution of the categories should be parsimonious. An appropriate tool for formalizing both informativeness and parsimony is information-theoretic entropy.

The parsimony criterion can be formalized as the entropy of the random variable (Y) representing the cluster assignments:

$$H(Y) = -\sum_{i=1}^{N} P(Y = y_i)\log_2(P(Y = y_i)) \quad (1)$$

where N is the number of clusters and $P(Y = y_i)$ stands for the relative size of the ith cluster.

The informativeness criterion can be formalized as the conditional entropy of training examples (X) given the cluster assignments:

$$H(X|Y) = \sum_{i=1}^{N} P(Y = y_i)H(X|Y = y_i) \quad (2)$$

and $H(X|Y = y_i)$ is calculated as

$$H(X|Y = y_i) = -\sum_{j=1}^{T} [P(X = x_j|Y = y_i) \times \log_2(P(X = x_j|Y = y_i)] \quad (3)$$

where T is the number of word usages in the training set.

The two criteria presented by Equations 1 and 2 can be combined together as the joint entropy of the two random variables X and Y:

$$H(X,Y) = H(X|Y) + H(Y) \quad (4)$$

For a random variable X corresponding to a single feature, minimizing the joint entropy $H(X,Y)$ will trade off our two desired criteria.

The joint entropy will be minimal if each distinct value of variable X is assigned the same category (i.e. same value of Y). There are many assignments which satisfy this condition. They range from putting all values of X in a single category, to having a unique category for each unique value of X. We favor the latter solution algorithmically by creating a new category in case of ties.

Finally, since our training examples contain a bundle of categorical features, we minimize the joint entropy simultaneously for all the features. We consider our training examples to be vectors of random variables $(X_j)_{j=1}^{M}$, where each random variable corresponds to one feature. For an incoming example we will choose the cluster assignment which leads to the least increase in the joint entropy $H(X_j, Y)$, summed over all the features j:

$$\sum_{j=1}^{M} H(X_j,Y) = \sum_{j=1}^{M} [H(X_j|Y) + H(Y)] = \sum_{j=1}^{M} [H(X_j|Y)] + M \times H(Y) \quad (5)$$

In the next section, we present an incremental algorithm which uses this criterion for inducing categories from a sequence of input data.

The Incremental Algorithm. For each word usage that the model processes at time t, we need to find the best category among the ones that have been formed so far, as well as a potential new category. The decision is made based on the change in the function $\sum_{j=1}^{M} H(X_j, Y)$ (Equation 5) from point $t-1$ to point t, as a result of assigning the current input x^t to a category y:

$$\Delta H_y^t = \sum_{j=1}^{M} [H_y^t(X_j,Y) - H^{t-1}(X_j,Y)] \quad (6)$$

where $H_y^t(X,Y)$ is the joint entropy of the assignment Y for the input $X = \{x^1, \ldots, x^t\}$, *after* the last input item x^t is assigned to the category y. The winning category $\hat{y}$ is the one that leads to the smallest increase. Ties are broken by preferring a new category.

$$\hat{y} = \begin{cases} \text{argmin}_{y \in \{y\}_{i=1}^{N}} \Delta H_y^t & \text{if } \exists y_n [\Delta H_{y_n}^t < \Delta H_{y_{N+1}}^t] \\ y_{N+1} & \text{otherwise} \end{cases} \quad (7)$$

where N is the number of categories created up to point t, and y_{N+1} represents a new category.

Efficiency. We maintain the relative size $P^t(y)$ and the entropy $H(X_j|Y = y)$ for each category y over time. When performing an assignment of x^t to a category y_i, we only need to update the conditional entropies $H(X_j|Y = y_i)$ for all features X_j for this particular category, since other categories have not changed. For a feature X_j at point t, the change in the conditional entropy for the selected category y_i is given by:

$$\begin{aligned}\Delta H^t_{y_i}(X_j|Y) &= H^t_{y_i}(X_j|Y) - H^{t-1}(X_j|Y) \\ &= \sum_{y_k \neq y_i} [P(Y = y_k)H^{t-1}(X_j|Y = y_i)] \\ &\quad - P^{t-1}(Y = y_i)H^{t-1}(X|Y = y_i) \\ &\quad - P^t(Y = y_i)H^t(X_j|Y = y_i)\end{aligned}$$

where only the last term depends on the current time index t. Therefore, the entropy $H(X_j|Y)$ at each step can be efficiently updated by calculating this term for the modified category at that step.

A number of previous studies have considered entropy-based criteria for clustering (e.g. Barbará et al., 2002; Li et al., 2004). The main contribution of our proposed model is the emphasis on rarely explored combination of the two characteristics we consider crucial for modeling human category acquisition, incrementality and an open set of clusters.

3 Experimental Setup

We evaluate the categories formed by our model through three different tasks. The first task is word prediction, where a target word is predicted based on the sentential context it appears in. The second task is to infer the semantic properties of a novel word based on its context. The third task is to assess the grammaticality of a sentence tagged with category labels. We run our model on a corpus of child-directed speech, and use the categories that it induces from that corpus in the above-mentioned tasks. For each task, we compare the performance using our induced categories against the performance using other category sets. In the following sections, we describe the properties of the data sets used for training and testing the model, and the formation of other category sets against which we compare our model.

Data Set	Sessions	#Sentences	#Words
Training	26–28	22,491	125,339
Development	29–30	15,193	85,361
Test	32–33	14,940	84,130

Table 1: Experimental data

3.1 Input Data

We use the Manchester corpus (Theakston et al., 2001) from CHILDES database (MacWhinney, 2000) as experimental data. The Manchester corpus consists of conversations with 12 children between the ages of eighteen months to three years old. The corpus is manually tagged using 60 PoS labels. We use the mother's speech from transcripts of 6 children, remove punctuation, and concatenate the corresponding sessions.

We used data from three sessions as the training set, two sessions as the development set, and two sessions as the test set. We discarded all one-word sentences from the data sets, as they do not provide any context for our evaluation tasks. Table 1 summarizes the properties of each data set.

3.2 Category Sets

We define each word usage in the training or test data set as a vector of three categorical features: the content feature (i.e., the focus word in a usage), and two context features (i.e. the preceding and following bigrams). We ran our clustering algorithm on the training set, which resulted in a set of 944 categories (of which 442 have only one member). Table 3 shows two sample categories from the training set, and Figure 1 shows the size distribution of the categories.

For each evaluation task, we use the following category sets to label the test set:

ΔH. The categories induced by our entropy-based model from the training set, as described above.

PoS. The part-of-speech tags the Manchester corpus is annotated with.

Words. The set of all the word types in the data set (i.e. assuming that all the usages of the same word form are grouped together).

Parisien. The induced categories by the model of Parisien et al. (2008) from the training set.

	Gold PoS	Words	Parisien	ΔH
VI	(0.000)	5.294	5.983	**4.806**
ARI	(1.000)	0.139	0.099	**0.168**

Table 2: Comparison against gold PoS tags using Variation of Information (VI) and Adjusted Rand Index (ARI).

Sample Cluster 1	
going	(928)
doing	(190)
back	(150)
coming	(80)
looking	(76)
making	(64)
playing	(55)
taking	(45)
...	

Sample Cluster 2	
than	(45)
more	(20)
silly	(10)
bigger	(9)
frightened	(5)
dark	(4)
harder	(4)
funny	(3)
...	

Table 3: Sample categories induced from the training data. The frequency of each word in the category is shown in parentheses.

For the first two tasks (word prediction and semantic inference), we do not use the content feature in labeling the test set, since the assumption underlying both tasks is that we do not have access to the form of the target word. Therefore, we do not measure the performance of these tasks on the **Words** category set. However, we do use the content feature in labeling the test examples in grammaticality judgment.

For completeness, in Table 2 we report the results of evaluation against Gold PoS tags using two metrics, Variation of Information (Meila, 2003) and Adjusted Rand Index (Hubert & Arabie, 1985).

4 Word Prediction

Humans can predict a word based on the context it is used in with remarkable accuracy (e.g. Lesher et al., 2002). Different versions of this task such as Cloze Test (Taylor, 1953) are used for the assessment of native and second language learning.

We simulate this task, where a missing word is predicted based on its context. We use each of the category sets introduced in Section 3.2 to label a word usage in the test set, without using the word form itself as a feature. That is, we assume that the target word is unknown, and find the best category for it based only on its surrounding context.

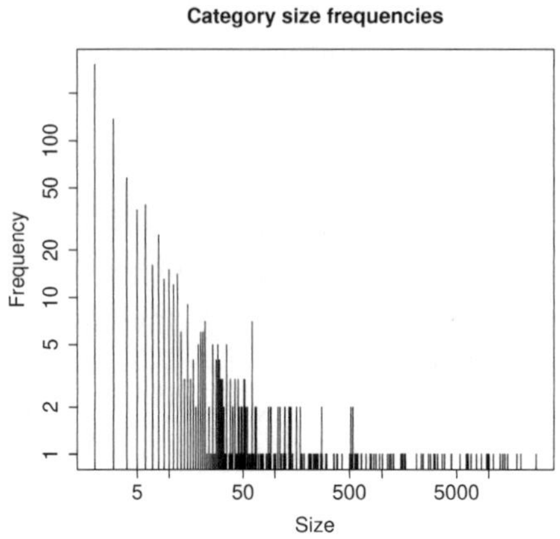

Figure 1: The distribution of the induced categories based on their size

We then output a ranked list of the content feature values of the selected category as the prediction of the model for the target word. To evaluate this prediction, we use the reciprocal rank of the target word in the predicted list.

The third row of Table 4 shows the Mean Reciprocal Rank (MRR) over all the word usages in the test data across different category sets. The results show that the category labels predicted by our model (ΔH) perform much better than those of Parisien, but still not as good as the gold-standard part of speech categories. The fact that PoS tags are better here does not necessarily mean that the PoS category set is better for word prediction as such, since they are manually assigned and thus noise-free, unlike the automatic category labels predicted by the two models. In the second set of experiments described below we try to factor in the uncertainty about category assignment inherent in automatic labeling.

Using only the best category output by the model to produce word predictions is simple and neutral; however, it discards part of the information learned by the model. We can predict words more accurately by combining information from the whole ranked list of category labels.

We use the ΔH model to rank the values of the content feature in the following fashion: for the current test usage, we rank each cluster assignment y by the change in the $\Delta H^t_{y_i}$ function that it causes. For each of the assignments, we compute the relative frequencies $P(w|y_i)$ of each possible focus word. The final rank of the word w in context h is determined by the sum of the cluster-

	Gold PoS	Words	Parisien	ΔH
Word Prediction (MRR)	**0.354**	-	0.212	0.309
Semantic Inference (MAP)	0.351	-	0.213	**0.366**
Grammaticality Judgment (Accuracy)	**0.728**	0.685	0.683	0.715

Table 4: The performance in each of the three tasks using different category sets.

dependent relative frequencies weighted by the normalized reciprocal ranks of the clusters:

$$P(w|h) = \sum_{i=1}^{N} P(w|y_i) \frac{\mathrm{R}(y_i|h)^{-1}}{\sum_{i=1}^{N} \mathrm{R}(y_i|h)^{-1}} \quad (8)$$

where $\mathrm{R}(y_i|h)^{-1}$ is the reciprocal rank of cluster y_i for context h according to the model.

We compare the performance of the ΔH model with this word-prediction method to that of an n-gram language model, which is an established technique for assigning probabilities to words based on their context. For the language model we use several n-gram orders ($n = 1 \ldots 5$), and smooth the n-gram counts using absolute discounting (Zhai & Lafferty, 2004). The probability of the word w given the context h is given by the following model of order n:

$$P_n(w|h) = \max\left(0, \frac{\mathrm{c}(h,w) - d}{\mathrm{c}(h)}\right) + \alpha(h) P_{n-1}(w|h) \quad (9)$$

where d is the discount parameter, $\mathrm{c}(\cdot)$ is the frequency count function, P_{n-1} is the lower-order back-off distribution, and α is the normalization factor:

$$\alpha(h) = \begin{cases} 1 & \text{if } \mathrm{r}(h) = 0 \\ d\mathrm{r}(h)\frac{1}{\mathrm{c}(h)} & \text{otherwise} \end{cases} \quad (10)$$

and $\mathrm{r}(h)$ is the number of distinct words that follow context h in the training corpus.

In addition to the ΔH model and the n-gram language models, we also report how well words can be predicted from their manually assigned PoS tags from CHILDES: for each token we predict the most likely word given the token's true PoS tag based on frequencies in the training data.

Table 4 summarizes the evaluation results. The ΔH model can predict missing words better than any of the n-gram language models, and even slightly better than the true POS tags. Given the simplicity of our clustering model, this is a very encouraging result. Simple n-gram language models are known for providing quite a strong baseline for word prediction; for example, Brown et al. (1992)'s class-based language model failed to improve test-set perplexity over a word-based trigram model.

Model	MRR
LM $n = 1$	0.1253
LM $n = 2$	0.2884
LM $n = 3$	0.3278
LM $n = 4$	0.3305
LM $n = 5$	0.3297
ΔH	**0.3591**
Gold POS	0.3540

Table 5: Mean reciprocal rank on the word prediction task on the test set

5 Semantic Inference

Several experimental studies have shown that children and adults can infer (some aspects of) the semantic properties of a novel word based on the context it appears in (e.g. Landau & Gleitman, 1985; Gleitman, 1990; Naigles & Hoff-Ginsberg, 1995). For example, in an experimental study by Fisher et al. (2006), two-year-olds watched as a hand placed a duck on a box, and pointed to it as a new word was uttered. Half of the children heard the word presented as a noun (*This is a corp!*), while half heard it as a preposition (*This is acorp my box!*). After training, children heard a test sentence (*What else is acorp (my box)?*) while watching two test events: one showed another duck beside the box, and the other showed a different object on the box. Looking-preferences revealed effects of sentence context: subjects in the preposition condition interpreted the novel word as a location, whereas those in the noun condition interpreted it as an object.

To study a similar effect in our model, we associate each word with a set of semantic features. For nouns, we extract the semantic features from WordNet 3.0 (Fellbaum, 1998) as follows: We take all the hypernyms of the first sense of the word, and the first word in the synset of each hypernym to the set of the semantic features of

ball
→ GAME EQUIPMENT#1
→ EQUIPMENT#1
→ INSTRUMENTALITY#3, INSTRUMENTATION#1
→ ARTIFACT#1, ARTEFACT#1
→ WHOLE#2, UNIT#6
→ OBJECT#1, PHYSICAL OBJECT#1
→ PHYSICAL ENTITY#1
→ ENTITY#1

ball: { GAME EQUIPMENT#1,EQUIPMENT#1, INSTRUMENTALITY#3,ARTIFACT#1, ... }

Figure 2: Semantic features of *ball*, as extracted from WordNet.

the target word (see Figure 2 for an example). For verbs, we additionally extract features from a verb-specific resource, VerbNet 2.3 (Schuler, 2005). Due to lack of proper resources for other lexical categories, we limit our evaluation to nouns and verbs.

The semantic features of words are not used in the formation of lexical categories. However, at each point of time in learning, we can associate a *semantic profile* to a category as the aggregated set of the semantic features of its members: each feature in the set is assigned a count that indicates the number of the category members which have that semantic property. This is done for each of the category sets described in Section 3.2.

As in the word-prediction task, we use different category sets to label each word usage in a test set based only on the context features of the word. When the model encounters a novel word, it can use the semantic profile of the word's labeled category as a prediction of the semantic properties of that word. We can evaluate the quality of this prediction by comparing the *true* meaning representation of the target word (i.e., its set of semantic features according to the lexicon) against the semantic profile of the selected category. We use the Mean Average Precision (MAP) (Manning et al., 2008) for comparing the ranked list of semantic features predicted by the model with the flat set of semantic features extracted from WordNet and VerbNet. Average Precision for a ranked list F with respect to a set R of correct features is:

$$\mathrm{AP}_R(F) = \frac{1}{|R|}\sum_{r=1}^{|F|} P(r) \times \mathbf{1}_R(F_r) \qquad (11)$$

where $P(r)$ is precision at rank r and $\mathbf{1}_R$ is the indicator function of set R.

The middle row of Table 4 shows the MAP scores over all the noun or verb usages in the test set, based on four different category sets. As can be seen, the categories induced by our model (ΔH) outperform all the other category sets. The word-type categories are particularly unsuitable for this task, since they provide the least degree of generalization over the semantic properties of a group of words. The categories of Parisien et al. (2008) result in a better performance than word types, but they are still too sparse for this task. However, the average score gained by part of speech tags is also lower than the one by our categories. This suggests that too broad categories are also unsuitable for this task, since they can only provide predictions about the most general semantic properties, such as ENTITY for nouns, and ACTION for verbs. These findings again confirm our hypothesis that a finer-grained set of categories that are extracted directly from the input data provide the highest predictive power in a naturalistic language task such as semantic inference.

6 Grammaticality Judgment

Speakers of a natural language have a general agreement on the *grammaticality* of different sentences. Grammaticality judgment has been viewed as one of the main criteria for measuring how well a language is learned by a human learner. Experimental studies have shown that children as young as five years old can judge the grammaticality of the sentences that they hear, and that both children's and adults' grammaticality judgments are influenced by the distributional properties of words and their context (e.g., Theakston, 2004).

Several methods have been proposed for automatically distinguishing between grammatical and ungrammatical usages (e.g., Wagner et al., 2007). The 'shallow' methods are mainly based on n-gram frequencies of words or categories in a corpus, whereas the 'deep' methods treat a parsing failure as an indication of a grammatical error. Since our focus is on evaluating our category set, we use trigram probabilities as a measure of grammaticality, using Equation 9 with $n = 3$.

As before, we label each test sentence using different category sets, and calculate the probability for each trigram in that sentence. We define the overall grammaticality score of a sentence as the minimum of the probabilities of all the trigrams in that sentence. Note that, unlike the previous tasks, here we do use the content word as a feature in labeling a test word usage. The actual word form affects the grammaticality of its usage, and this information is available to the human subjects who evaluate the grammaticality of a sentence.

Since we know of no publicly available corpus of ungrammatical sentences, we artificially construct one: for each sentence in our test data set, we randomly move one word to another position.[1] We define the accuracy of this task as the proportion of the test usages for which the model calculates a higher grammaticality score for the original sentence than for its ungrammatical version.

The last row of Table 4 shows the accuracy of the grammaticality judgment task across different category sets. As can be seen, the highest accuracy in choosing the grammatical sentence over the ungrammatical one is achieved by using the PoS categories (0.728), followed by the categories induced by our model (0.715). These levels of accuracy are rather good considering that some of the automatically generated errors are also grammatical (e.g., *there you are* vs. *you are there*, or *can you reach it* vs. *you can reach it*). The results by the other two category sets are lower and very close to each other.

These results suggest that, unlike the semantic inference task, the grammaticality judgment task might require a coarser-grained set of categories which provide a higher level of abstraction. However, taking into account that the PoS categories are manually assigned to the test usages, the difference in their performance might be due to lack of noise in the labeling procedure. We plan to investigate this matter in future by improving our categorization model (as discussed in Section 7). Also, we intend to implement more accurate ways of estimating grammaticality, using an approach similar to that described for word prediction task in Section 4.

7 Discussion

We have proposed an incremental model of lexical category acquisition based on the distributional properties of words. Our model uses an information theoretic clustering algorithm which attempts to optimize the category assignments of the incoming word usages at each point in time. The model can efficiently process the training data, and induce an intuitive set of categories from child-directed speech. However, due to the incremental nature of the clustering algorithm, it does not revise its previous decisions according to the data that it later receives. A potential remedy would be to consider merging the clusters that have recently been updated, in order to allow for recovery from early mistakes the model has made.

We used the categories induced by our model in word prediction, inferring the semantic properties of novel words, and grammaticality judgment. Our experimental results show that the performance in these tasks using our categories is comparable or better than the performance based on the manually assigned part of speech tags in our experimental data. Furthermore, in all these tasks the performance using our categories improves over a previous incremental categorization model (Parisien et al., 2008). However, the model of Parisien employs a number of cluster reorganization techniques which improve the overall quality of the clusters after processing a substantial amount of input data. In future we plan to increase the size of our training data, and perform a more extensive comparison with the model of Parisien et al. (2008).

The promising results of our experiments suggest that an information-theoretic approach is a plausible one for modeling the induction of lexical categories from distributional data. Our results imply that in many language tasks, a fine-grained set of categories which are formed in response to the properties of the input are more appropriate than the coarser-grained part of speech categories. Therefore, the ubiquitous approach of using PoS categories as the gold standard in evaluating unsupervised category induction models needs to be reevaluated. To further investigate this claim, in future we plan to collect experimental data from human subjects performing our suggested tasks, and measure the correlation between their performance and that of our model.

Acknowledgments

We would like to thank Nicolas Stroppa for insightful comments on our paper, and Chris Parisien for sharing the implementation of his model. Grzegorz Chrupała was funded by the BMBF project NL-Search under contract number 01IS08020B. Afra Alishahi was funded by IRTG 715 "Language Technology and Cognitive Systems" provided by the German Research Foundation (DFG).

[1] We used the software of Foster & Andersen (2009).

References

Barbará, D., Li, Y., & Couto, J. (2002). COOLCAT: an entropy-based algorithm for categorical clustering. In *Proceedings of the Eleventh International Conference on Information and Knowledge Management* (pp. 582–589).

Brown, P., Mercer, R., Della Pietra, V., & Lai, J. (1992). Class-based n-gram models of natural language. *Computational linguistics*, *18*(4), 467–479.

Cartwright, T., & Brent, M. (1997). Syntactic categorization in early language acquisition: Formalizing the role of distributional analysis. *Cognition*, *63*(2), 121–170.

Clark, A. (2000). Inducing syntactic categories by context distribution clustering. In *Proceedings of the 2nd workshop on Learning Language in Logic and the 4th conference on Computational Natural Language Learning* (pp. 91–94).

Clark, A. (2003). Combining distributional and morphological information for part of speech induction. In *Proceedings of the 10th Conference of the European Chapter of the Association for Computational Linguistics* (pp. 59–66).

Fellbaum, C. (Ed.). (1998). *WordNet, an electronic lexical database*. MIT Press.

Fisher, C., Klingler, S., & Song, H. (2006). What does syntax say about space? 2-year-olds use sentence structure to learn new prepositions. *Cognition*, *101*(1), 19–29.

Foster, J., & Andersen, Ø. (2009). GenERRate: generating errors for use in grammatical error detection. In *Proceedings of the fourth workshop on innovative use of nlp for building educational applications* (pp. 82–90).

Frank, S., Goldwater, S., & Keller, F. (2009). Evaluating models of syntactic category acquisition without using a gold standard. In *Proceedings of the 31st Annual Meeting of the Cognitive Science Society*.

Gelman, S., & Taylor, M. (1984). How two-year-old children interpret proper and common names for unfamiliar objects. *Child Development*, 1535–1540.

Gleitman, L. (1990). The structural sources of verb meanings. *Language acquisition*, *1*(1), 3–55.

Goldwater, S., & Griffiths, T. (2007). A fully Bayesian approach to unsupervised part-of-speech tagging. In *Proceedings of the 45th Annual Meeting of the Association for Computational Linguistics* (Vol. 45, p. 744).

Hubert, L., & Arabie, P. (1985). Comparing partitions. *Journal of classification*, *2*(1), 193–218.

Kemp, N., Lieven, E., & Tomasello, M. (2005). Young Children's Knowledge of the" Determiner" and" Adjective" Categories. *Journal of Speech, Language and Hearing Research*, *48*(3), 592–609.

Landau, B., & Gleitman, L. (1985). *Language and experience: Evidence from the blind child*. Harvard University Press Cambridge, Mass.

Lesher, G., Moulton, B., Higginbotham, D., & Alsofrom, B. (2002). Limits of human word prediction performance. *Proceedings of the CSUN 2002*.

Li, T., Ma, S., & Ogihara, M. (2004). Entropy-based criterion in categorical clustering. In *Proceedings of the 21st International Conference on Machine Learning* (p. 68).

MacWhinney, B. (2000). *The CHILDES project: Tools for analyzing talk*. Lawrence Erlbaum Associates Inc, US.

Manning, C., Raghavan, P., & Schtze, H. (2008). *Introduction to Information Retrieval*. Cambridge University Press New York, NY, USA.

Meila, M. (2003). Comparing Clusterings by the Variation of Information. In *Learning theory and kernel machines* (pp. 173–187). Springer.

Mintz, T. (2002). Category induction from distributional cues in an artificial language. *Memory and Cognition*, *30*(5), 678–686.

Mintz, T. (2003). Frequent frames as a cue for grammatical categories in child directed speech. *Cognition*, *90*(1), 91–117.

Naigles, L., & Hoff-Ginsberg, E. (1995). Input to Verb Learning: Evidence for the Plausibility of Syntactic Bootstrapping. *Developmental Psychology*, *31*(5), 827–37.

Parisien, C., Fazly, A., & Stevenson, S. (2008). An incremental bayesian model for learning syntactic categories. In *Proceedings of the Twelfth Conference on Computational Natural Language Learning*.

Redington, M., Crater, N., & Finch, S. (1998). Distributional information: A powerful cue for acquiring syntactic categories. *Cognitive Science: A Multidisciplinary Journal*, *22*(4), 425–469.

Schuler, K. (2005). *VerbNet: A broad-coverage, comprehensive verb lexicon*. Unpublished doctoral dissertation, University of Pennsylvania.

Taylor, W. (1953). Cloze procedure: A new tool for measuring readability. *Journalism Quarterly*, *30*(4), 415–433.

Theakston, A. (2004). The role of entrenchment in childrens and adults performance on grammaticality judgment tasks. *Cognitive Development*, *19*(1), 15–34.

Theakston, A., Lieven, E., Pine, J., & Rowland, C. (2001). The role of performance limitations in the acquisition of verb-argument structure: An alternative account. *Journal of Child Language*, *28*(01), 127–152.

Wagner, J., Foster, J., & van Genabith, J. (2007). A comparative evaluation of deep and shallow approaches to the automatic detection of common grammatical errors. *Proceedings of EMNLP-CoNLL-2007*.

Zhai, C., & Lafferty, J. (2004). A study of smoothing methods for language models applied to information retrieval. *ACM Transactions on Information Systems (TOIS)*, *22*(2), 214.

Tagging and Linking Web Forum Posts

Su Nam Kim, Li Wang and **Timothy Baldwin**
Dept of Computer Science and Software Engineering
University of Melbourne, Australia
sunamkim@gmail.com, li.wang.d@gmail.com, tb@ldwin.net

Abstract

We propose a method for annotating post-to-post discourse structure in online user forum data, in the hopes of improving troubleshooting-oriented information access. We introduce the tasks of: (1) post classification, based on a novel dialogue act tag set; and (2) link classification. We also introduce three feature sets (structural features, post context features and semantic features) and experiment with three discriminative learners (maximum entropy, SVM-HMM and CRF). We achieve above-baseline results for both dialogue act and link classification, with interesting divergences in which feature sets perform well over the two sub-tasks, and go on to perform preliminary investigation of the interaction between post tagging and linking.

1 Introduction

With the advent of Web 2.0, there has been an explosion of web authorship from individuals of all walks of life. Notably, social networks, blogs and web user forums have entered the mainstream of modern-day society, creating both new opportunities and challenges for organisations seeking to engage with clients or users of any description. One area of particular interest is web-based user support, e.g. to aid a user in purchasing a gift for a friend, or advising a customer on how to configure a newly-acquired wireless router. While such interactions traditionally took place on an individual basis, leading to considerable redundancy for frequently-arising requests or problems, user forums support near-real-time user interaction in the form of a targeted thread made up of individual user posts. Additionally, they have the potential for perpetual logging to allow other users to benefit from them. This in turn facilitates "support sharing"—i.e. the ability for users to look over the logs of past support interactions to determine whether there is a documented, immediately-applicable solution to their current problem—on a scale previously unimaginable. This research is targeted at this task of enhanced support sharing, in the form of text mining over troubleshooting-oriented web user forum data (Baldwin et al., to appear).

One facet of our proposed strategy for enhancing information access to troubleshooting-oriented web user forum data is to preprocess threads to uncover the "content structure" of the thread, in the form of its post-to-post discourse structure. Specifically, we identify which earlier post(s) a given post responds to (linking) and in what manner (tagging), in an amalgam of dialogue act tagging (Stolcke et al., 2000) and coherence-based discourse analysis (Carlson et al., 2001; Wolf and Gibson, 2005). The reason we do this is gauge the relative role/import of individual posts, to index and weight component terms accordingly, ultimately in an attempt to enhance information access. Evidence to suggest that this structure can enhance information retrieval effectiveness comes from Xi et al. (2004) and Seo et al. (2009) (see Section 2).

To illustrate the task, consider the thread from the CNET forum shown in Figure 1, made up of 5 posts (*Post 1, ..., Post 5*) with 4 distinct participants (*A, B, C, D*). In the first post, *A* initiates the thread by requesting assistance in creating a web form. In response, *B* proposes a Javascript-based solution (i.e. responds to the first post with a proposed solution), and *C* proposes an independent solution based on .NET (i.e. also responds to the first post with a proposed solution). Next, *A* responds to *C*'s post asking for details of how to include this in a web page (i.e. responds to the third post asking for clarification), and in the final post, *D* proposes a different solution again (i.e. responds to the first post with a different solution again).

Proceedings of the Fourteenth Conference on Computational Natural Language Learning, pages 192–202,
Uppsala, Sweden, 15-16 July 2010. ©2010 Association for Computational Linguistics

HTML Input Code - CNET Coding & scripting Forums

User *A* Post 1	**HTML Input Code** ... Please can someone tell me how to create an input box that asks the user to enter their ID, and then allows them to press go. It will then redirect to the page ...
User *B* Post 2	**Re: html input code** Part 1: create a form with a text field. See ... Part 2: give it a Javascript action ...
User *C* Post 3	**asp.net c# video** Ive prepared for you video.link click ...
User *A* Post 4	**Thank You!** Thanks a lot for that ... I have Microsoft Visual Studio 6, what program should I do this in? Lastly, how do I actually include this in my site?...
User *D* Post 5	**A little more help** ... You would simply do it this way: ... You could also just ... An example of this is:...

Figure 1: Snippeted posts in a CNET thread

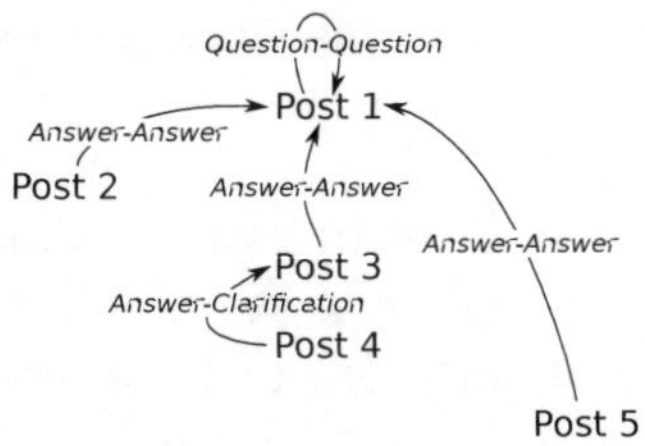

Figure 2: Post links and dialogue act labels for the example thread in Figure 1

In this, we therefore end up with a tree-based dependency link structure, with each post (other than the initial post) relating back to a unique preceding post via a range of link types, as indicated in Figure 2. Note, however, that more generally, it is possible for a post to link to multiple preceding posts (e.g. refuting one proposed solution, and proposing a different solution to the problem in the initial post).

Our primary contributions in this paper are: (1) a novel post label set for post structure in web forum data, and associated dataset; and (2) a series of results for post dependency linking and labelling, which achieve strong results for the respective tasks.

2 Related Work

Related work exists in the broad fields of dialogue processing, discourse analysis and information retrieval, and can be broken down into the following tasks: (1) dialogue act tagging; (2) discourse "disentanglement"; (3) community question answering; and (4) newsgroup/user forum search.

Dialogue act (DA) tagging is a means of capturing the function of a given utterance relative to an encompassing discourse, and has been proposed variously as a means of enhancing dialogue summarisation (Murray et al., 2006), and tracking commitments and promises in email (Cohen et al., 2004; Lampert et al., 2008), as well as being shown to improve speech recognition accuracy (Stolcke et al., 2000). A wide range of DA tag sets have been proposed, usually customised to a particular medium such as speech dialogue (Stolcke et al., 2000; Shriberg et al., 2004), task-focused email (Cohen et al., 2004; Wang et al., 2007; Lampert et al., 2008) or instant messaging (Ivanovic, 2008). The most immediately relevant DA-based work we are aware of is that of Xi et al. (2004), who proposed a 5-way classification for newsgroup data (including QUESTION and AGREEMENT/AMMENDMENT), but did not present any results based on the tagset.

A range of supervised models have been applied to DA classification, including graphical models (Ji and Bilmes, 2005), kernel methods (Wang et al., 2007), dependency networks (Carvalho and Cohen, 2005), transformation-based learning (Samuel et al., 1998), maxent models (Ang et al., 2005) and HMMs (Ivanovic, 2008). There is some contention about the import of context in DA classification, with the prevailing view being that context aids classification (Carvalho and Cohen, 2005; Ang et al., 2005; Ji and Bilmes, 2005), but also evidence to suggest that strictly local modelling is superior (Ries, 1999; Serafin and Di Eugenio, 2004).

In this work, we draw on existing work (esp. Xi et al. (2004)) in proposing a novel DA tag set customised to the analysis of troubleshooting-oriented web user forums (Section 3), and compare a range of text classification and structured classification methods for post-level DA classification.

Discourse disentanglement is the process of automatically identifying coherent sub-discourses in a single thread (in the context of user forums/mailing lists), chat session (in the context of IRC chat data: Elsner and Charniak (2008)), system interaction (in the context of HCI: Lemon et al. (2002)) or document (Wolf and Gibson, 2005). The exact definition of what constitutes a sub-discourse varies across domains, but for our purposes, entails an attempt to resolve the information need of the initiator by a particular approach; if there are competing approaches proposed in a single thread, multiple sub-discourses will necessarily arise. The data structure used to represent the disentangled discourse varies from a simple connected sub-graph (Elsner and Charniak, 2008), to a stack/tree (Grosz and Sidner, 1986; Lemon et al., 2002; Seo et al., 2009), to a full directed acyclic graph (DAG: Rosé et al. (1995), Wolf and Gibson (2005), Schuth et al. (2007)). Disentanglement has been carried out via analysis of direct citation/user name references (Schuth et al., 2007; Seo et al., 2009), topic modelling (Lin et al., 2009), and clustering over content-based features for pairs of posts, optionally incorporating various constraints on post recency (Elsner and Charniak, 2008; Wang et al., 2008; Seo et al., 2009).

In this work, we follow Rosé et al. (1995) and Wolf and Gibson (2005) in adopting a DAG representation of discourse structure, and draw on the wide set of features used in discourse entanglement to model coherence.

Community question answering (cQA) is the task of identifying question–answer pairs in a given thread, e.g. for the purposes of thread summarisation (Shrestha and McKeown, 2004) or automated compilation of resources akin to Yahoo! Answers. cQA has been applied to both mailing list and user forum threads, conventionally based on question classification, followed by ranking of candidate answers relative to each question (Shrestha and McKeown, 2004; Ding et al., 2008; Cong et al., 2008; Cao et al., 2009). The task is somewhat peripheral to our work, but relevant in that it involves the implicit tagging of certain posts as containing questions/answers, as well as linking the posts together. Once again, we draw on the features used in cQA in this research.

There has been a spike of recent interest in **newsgroup/user forum search**. Xi et al. (2004) proposed a structured information retrieval (IR) model for newsgroup search, based on author features, thread structure (based on the tree defined by the reply-to structure), thread "topology" features and content-based features, and used a supervised ranking method to improve over a baseline IR system. Elsas and Carbonell (2009) — building on earlier work on blog search (Elsas et al., 2008) — proposed a probabilistic IR approach which ranks user forum threads relative to selected posts in the overall thread, and again demonstrated the superiority of this method over a model which ignores thread structure. Finally, Seo et al. (2009) automatically derived thread structure from user forum threads, and demonstrated that the IR effectiveness over the "threaded" structure was superior to that using a monolithic document representation.

The observations and results of Xi et al. (2004) and Seo et al. (2009) that threading information (or in our case "disentangled" DAG structure) enhances IR effectiveness is a core motivator for this research.

3 Post Label Set

Our post label set contains 12 categories, intended to capture the typical interactions that take place in troubleshooting-oriented threads on technical forums. There are 2 super-categories (QUESTION, ANSWER) and 3 singleton classes (RESOLUTION, REPRODUCTION, and OTHER). QUESTION, in turn, contains 4 sub-classes (QUESTION, ADD, CONFIRMATION, CORRECTION), while ANSWER contains 5 sub-classes (ANSWER, ADD, CONFIRMATION, CORRECTION, and OBJECTION), partially mirroring the sub-structure of QUESTION. We represent the amalgam of a super- and subclass as QUESTION-ADD, for example.

All tags other than QUESTION-QUESTION and OTHER are relational, i.e. relate a given post to a unique earlier post. A given post can potentially be labelled with multiple tags (e.g. confirm details of a proposed solution, in addition to providing extra details of the problem), although, based on the strictly chronological ordering of posts in threads, a post can only link to posts earlier in the thread (and can also not cross thread boundaries). Additionally, the link structure is assumed to be transitive, in that if post A links to post B and post B to post C, post A is implicitly linked to post C. As such, an explicit link from post A to post C should exist only in the case that the link between them is not inferrable transitively.

Detailed definitions of each post tag are given below. Note that **initiator** refers to the user who started the thread with the first post.

QUESTION-QUESTION (Q-Q): the post contains a new question, independent of the thread context that precedes it. In general, QUESTION-QUESTION is reserved for the first post in a given thread.

QUESTION-ADD (Q-ADD): the post supplements a question by providing additional information, or asking a follow-up question.

QUESTION-CONFIRMATION (Q-CONF): the post points out error(s) in a question without correcting them, or confirms details of the question.

QUESTION-CORRECTION (Q-CORR): the post corrects error(s) in a question.

ANSWER-ANSWER (A-A): the post proposes an answer to a question.

ANSWER-ADD (A-ADD): the post supplements an answer by providing additional information.

ANSWER-CONFIRMATION (A-CONF): the post points out error(s) in an answer without correcting them, or confirms details of the answer.

ANSWER-CORRECTION (A-CORR): the post corrects error(s) in an answer.

ANSWER-OBJECTION (A-OBJ): the post objects to an answer on experiential or theoretical grounds (e.g. *It won't work.*).

RESOLUTION (RES): the post confirms that an answer works, on the basis of implementing it.

REPRODUCTION (REP): the post either: (1) confirms that the same problem is being experienced (by a non-initiator, e.g. *I'm seeing the same thing.*); or (2) confirms that the answer should work.

OTHER (OTHER): the post does not belong to any of the above classes.

4 Feature Description

In this section, we describe our post feature representation, in the form of four feature types.

4.1 Lexical features

As our first feature type, we use simple lexical features, in the form of unigram and bigram tokens contained within a given post (without stopping). We also POS tagged and lemmatised the posts, postfixing the lemmatised token with its POS tag (using Lingua::EN::Tagger and `morpha` (Minnen et al., 2001)). Finally, we bin together the counts for each token, and represent it via its raw frequency.

4.2 Structural features

The identity of the post author, and position of the post within the thread, can be indicators of the post/link structure of a given post. We represent the post author as a simple binary feature indicating whether s/he is the thread initiator, and the post position via its relative position in the thread (as a ratio, relative to the total number of posts).

4.3 Post context features

As mentioned in Section 2, post context has generally (but not always) been shown to enhance the classification accuracy of DA tagging tasks, in the form of Markov features providing predicted post labels for previous posts, or more simply, post-to-post similarity. We experiment with a range of post context features, all of which are compatible with features both from the same label set as that being classified (e.g. link features for link classification), as well as features from a second label set (e.g. DA label features for link classification).

Previous Post: There is a strong prior for posts to link to their immediately preceding post (as observed for 79.9% of the data in our dataset), and also strong sequentiality in our post label set (e.g. a post following a Q-Q is most likely to be an A-A). As such, we represent the predicted post label of the immediately preceding post, as a first-order Markov feature, as well as a binary feature to indicate whether the author of the previous post also authored the current post.

Previous Post from Same Author: A given user tends to author posts of the same basic type (e.g. QUESTION or ANSWER) in a given thread, and pairings such as A-A and A-CONF from a given author are very rare. To capture this observation, we look to see if the author of the current post has posted earlier in the thread, and if so, include the label and relative location (in posts) of their most recent previous post.

Full History: As a final option, we include the predictions for all posts $P_1, ..., P_{i-1}$ preceding the current post P_i.

4.4 Semantic features

We tested four semantic features based on post content and title.

Title Similarity: For forums such as CNET which include titles for individual posts (as represented in Figure 1), a post having the same or similar title as a previous post is often a strong indicator that it responds to that post. This both provides a strong indicator of which post a given post responds (links) to, and can aid in DA tagging. We use simple cosine similarity to find the post with the most-similar title, and represent its relative location to the current post.

Post Similarity: Posts of the same general type tend to have similar content and be linked. For example, A-A and A-ADD posts tend to share content. We capture this by identifying the post with most-similar content based on cosine similarity, and represent its relative location to the current post.

Post Characteristics: We separately represent the number of question marks, exclamation marks and URLs in the current post. In general, question marks occur in QUESTION and CONFIRMATION posts, exclamation marks occur in RES and OBJECTION posts, and URLs occur in A-A and A-ADD posts.

User Profile: Some authors tend to answer questions more, while others tend to ask more questions. We capture the class priors for the author of the current post by the distribution of post labels in their posts in the training data.

5 Experimental Setup

As our dataset, we collected 320 threads containing a total of 1,332 posts from the Operating System, Software, Hardware, and Web Development sub-forums of CNET.[1]

The annotation of post labels and links was carried by two annotators in a custom-built web interface which supported multiple labels and links for a given post. For posts with multilabels, we used a modified version of Cohen's Kappa, which returned κ values of 0.59 and 0.78 for the post label and link annotations, respectively. Any disagreements in labelling were resolved through adjudication.

Of the 1332 posts, 65 posts have multiple labels (which possibly link to a common post) and 22 posts link to two different links. The majority post label in the dataset is A-A (40.30%).

We built machine learners using a conventional Maximum Entropy (ME) learner,[2] as well as two structural learners, namely: (1) SVM-HMMs (Joachims et al., 2009), as implemented in SVM-struct[3], with a linear kernel; and (2) conditional random fields (CRFs) using CRF++.[4] SVM-HMMs and CRFs have been successfully applied to a range of sequential tagging tasks such as syllabification (Bartlett et al., 2009), chunk parsing (Sha and Pereira, 2003) and word segmentation (Zhao et al., 2006). Both are discriminative models which capture structural dependencies, which is highly desirable in terms of modelling sequential preferences between post labels (e.g. A-CONF typically following a A-A). SVM-HMM has the additional advantage of scaling to large numbers of features (namely the lexical features). As such, we only experiment with lexical features for SVM-HMM and ME.

All of our evaluation is based on stratified 10-fold cross-validation, stratifying at the thread level to ensure that if a given post is contained in the test data for a given iteration, all other posts in that same thread are also in the test data (or more pertinently, not in the training data). We evaluate using micro-averaged precision, recall and F-score ($\beta = 1$). We test the statistical significance of all above-baseline results using randomised estimation ($p < 0.05$; Yeh (2000)), and present all such results in bold in our results tables.

In our experiments, we first look at the post classification task in isolation (i.e. we predict which labels to associate with each post, underspecifying which posts those labels relate to). We then move on to look at the link classification task, again in isolation (i.e. we predict which previous posts each post links to, underspecifying the nature of the link). Finally, we perform preliminary investigation of the joint task of DA and link classification, by incorporating DA class features into the link classification task.

6 DA Classification Results

Our first experiment is based on post-level dialogue act (DA) classification, ignoring link structure in the first instance. That is, we predict the labels on edges emanating from each post in the DAG representation of the post structure, without

[1] http://forums.cnet.com/?tag=TOCleftColumn.0

[2] http://maxent.sourceforge.net/

[3] http://www.cs.cornell.edu/People/tj/svm_light/svm_hmm.html

[4] http://crfpp.sourceforge.net/

Features	CRF	SVM-HMM	ME
Lexical	—	.566	.410
Structural	**.742**	.638	**.723**

Table 1: DA classification F-score with lexical and structural features (above-baseline results in **bold**)

specifying the edge destination. Returning to our example in Figure 2, e.g., the gold-standard classification for Post 1 would be Q-Q, Post 2 would be A-A, etc.

As a baseline for DA classification, simple majority voting attains an F-score of 0.403, based on the A-A class. A more realistic baseline, however, is a position-conditioned variant, where the first post is always classified as Q-Q, and all subsequent posts are classified as A-A, achieving an F-score of 0.641.

6.1 Lexical and structural features

First, we experiment with lexical and structural features (recalling that we are unable to scale the CRF model to full lexical features). Lexical features produce below-baseline performance, while simple structural features immediately lead to an improvement over the baseline for CRF and ME.

The reason for the poor performance with lexical features is that our dataset contains only around 1300 posts, each of which is less than 100 words in length on average. The models are simply unable to generalise over this small amount of data, and in the case of SVM-HMM, the presence of lexical features, if anything, appears to obscure the structured nature of the labelling task (i.e. the classifier is unable to learn the simple heuristic used by the modified majority class baseline).

The success of the structural features, on the other hand, points to the presence of predictable sequences of post labels in the data. That SVM-HMM is unable to achieve baseline performance with structural features is slightly troubling.

6.2 Post context features

Next, we test the two post context features: *Previous Post* (P) and *Previous Post from Same Author* (A). Given the success of structural features, we retain these in our experiments. Note that the labels used in the post context are those which are interactively learned by that model for the previous posts.

Table 2 presents the results for structural features combined with DA-based post context; we do not present any combinations of Previous Post and Full History, as Full History includes the Previous Post.

Features	CRF	SVM-HMM	ME
Struct+R	**.740**	.640	.632
Struct+A	**.742**	**.676**	**.693**
Struct+F	**.744**	.641	.577
Struct+RA	.397	.636	**.665**
Struct+AF	.405	.642	.586

Table 2: DA classification F-score with structural and DA-based post context features (R = "Previous Post", A = "Previous Post from Same Author", and F = "Full History"; above-baseline results in **bold**)

Comparing back to the original results using only the structural results, we can observe that Previous Post from Same Author and Full History (A and F, resp., in the table) lead to a slight increment in F-score for both CRF and SVM-HMM, but degrade the performance of ME. Previous Post leads to either a marginal improvement, or a drop in results, most noticeably for ME. It is slightly surprising that the CRF should benefit from context features at all, given that it is optimising over the full tag sequence, but the impact is relatively localised, and when all sets of context features are used, the combined weight of noisy features appears to swamp the learner, leading to a sharp degradation in F-score.

6.3 Semantic features

We next investigate the relative impact of the semantic features, once again including structural features in all experiments. Table 3 presents the F-score using the different combinations of semantic features.

Similarly to the post context features, the semantic features produced slight increments over the structural features in isolation, especially for CRF and ME. For the first time, SVM-HMM achieved above-baseline results, when incorporating title similarity and post characteristics. Of the individual semantic features, title and post similarity appear to be the best performers. Slightly disappointingly, the combination of semantic features generally led to a degradation in F-score, almost certainly due to data sparseness. The best overall result was achieved with CRF, incorporat-

Features	CRF	SVM-HMM	ME
Struct+T	**.751**	.636	**.660**
Struct+P	**.747**	.636	**.662**
Struct+C	**.738**	.587	.630
Struct+U	**.722**	.564	.620
Struct+TP	**.740**	.627	**.720**
Struct+TC	**.744**	**.646**	.589
Struct+TU	**.738**	.600	.609
Struct+PC	**.745**	.630	.583
Struct+PU	**.736**	.626	.605
Struct+CU	**.730**	.599	.619
Struct+TPC	**.739**	.622	.580
Struct+TPU	**.729**	.613	.6120
Struct+TCU	**.750**	.611	.6120
Struct+PCU	**.738**	.616	.614
Struct+TPCU	**.737**	.619	.605

Table 3: DA classification F-score with semantic features (T = "Title Similarity", P = "Post Similarity", C = "Post Characteristics", and U = "User Profile"; above-baseline results in **bold**)

Features	R	A	RA
Struct+T	**.649**	**.649**	**.649**
Struct+P	**.737**	**.736**	**.742**
Struct+C	**.741**	**.741**	**.742**
Struct+U	**.745**	**.742**	**.737**
Struct+TP	**.645**	**.656**	**.658**
Struct+TC	.383	.402	.408
Struct+TU	**.650**	**.652**	**.652**
Struct+PC	**.730**	**.743**	**.753**
Struct+PU	.232	.232	.286
Struct+CU	**.719**	.471	**.710**
Struct+TPC	.498	.469	.579
Struct+TPU	.248	.232	.248
Struct+TCU	.388	.377	.380
Struct+PCU	.231	.231	.261
Struct+TPCU	.231	.231	.231

Table 4: DA classification F-score for CRF with different combinations of post context features and semantic features (R = "Previous Post", and A = "Previous Post from Same Author"; T = "Title Similarity", P = "Post Similarity", C = "Post Characteristics", and U = "User Profile"; above-baseline results in **bold**)

ing structural features and title similarity, at an F-score of 0.751.

To further explore the interaction between post context and semantic features, we built CRF classifiers for different combinations of post context and semantic features, and present the results in Table 4.[5] We achieved moderate gains in F-score, with all post context features, in combination with structural features, post similarity and post characteristics achieving an F-score of 0.753, slightly higher than the best result achieved for just structural and post context features.

It is important to refer back to the results for lexical features (comparable to what would have been achieved with a standard text categorisation approach to the task), and observe that we have achieved far higher F-scores using features customised to user forum data. It is also important to reflect that post context (in terms of the features and the structured classification results of CRF) appears to markedly improve our results, contrasting with the results of Ries (1999) and Serafin and Di Eugenio (2004).

[5]We omit the results for Full History post context for reasons of space, but there is relatively little deviation from the numbers presented.

7 Link Classification Results

Our second experiment is based on link classification in isolation. Here, we predict unlabelled edges, e.g. in Figure 2, the gold-standard classification for Post 1 would be NULL, Post 2 would be Post 1, Post 3 would be Post 1, etc.

Note that the initial post cannot link to any other post, and also that the second post always links to the first post. As this is a hard constraint on the data, and these posts simply act to inflate the overall numbers, we exclude all first and second posts from our evaluation of link classification.

We experimented with a range of baselines as presented in Table 5, but found that the best performer by far was the simple heuristic of linking each post (except for the initial post) to its immediately preceding post. This leads to an F-score of 0.631, comparable to that for the post classification task.

7.1 Lexical and structural features

Once again, we started by exploring the effectiveness of lexical and structural features using the three learners, as detailed in Table 6.

Similarly to the results for post classification,

Baseline	Prec	Rec	F-score
Previous post	.641	.622	**.631**
First post	.278	.269	.274
Title similarity	.311	.301	.306
Post similarity	.255	.247	.251

Table 5: Baselines for link classification

Features	CRF	SVM-HMM	ME
Lexical	—	.154	.274
Structural	.446	.220	.478

Table 6: Link classification F-score with lexical and structural features (above-baseline results in **bold**)

structural features are more effective than lexical features for link classification, but this time, neither feature set approaches the baseline F-score for any of the learners. Once again, the results for SVM-HMM are well below those for the other two learners.

7.2 Post context features

Next, we experiment with link-based post context features, in combination with the structural features, as the results were found to be consistently better when combined with the structural features (despite the below-baseline performance of the structural features in this case). The link-based post context features in all cases are generated using the CRF with structural features from Table 6. As before, we do not present any combinations of Previous Post and Full History, as Full History includes the Previous Post

As seen in Table 9, here, for the first time, we achieve an above-baseline result for link classification, for SVM and ME based on Previous Post from Same Author in isolation, and also sometimes in combination with the other feature sets. The results for CRF also improve, but not to a level of statistical significance over the baseline. Similarly to the results for DA classification, the results for CRF drop appreciably when we combine feature sets.

7.3 Semantic features

Finally, we experiment with semantic features, once again in combination with structural features. The results are presented in Table 8.

The results for semantic features largely mirror those for post classification: small improvements are observed for title similarity with CRF, but otherwise, the results degrade across the board, and the combination of different feature sets compounds this effect.

Features	CRF	SVM-HMM	ME
Struct+R	.234	.605	.618
Struct+A	.365	**.665**	**.665**
Struct+F	.624	**.648**	.615
Struct+RA	.230	.615	**.661**
Struct+AF	.359	**.663**	.621

Table 7: Link classification F-score with structural and link-based post context features (R = "Previous Post", A = "Previous Post from Same Author", and F = "Full History"; above-baseline results in **bold**)

Features	CRF	SVM-HMM	ME
Struct+T	.464	.223	.477
Struct+P	.433	.198	.453
Struct+C	.438	.213	.419
Struct+U	.407	.160	.376
Struct+TP	.459	.194	.491
Struct+TC	.449	.229	.404
Struct+TU	.456	.174	.353
Struct+PC	.422	.152	.387
Struct+PU	.439	.166	.349
Struct+CU	.397	.178	.366
Struct+TPC	.449	.185	.418
Struct+TPU	.449	.160	.365
Struct+TCU	.459	.185	.358
Struct+PCU	.439	.161	.358
Struct+TPCU	.443	.163	.365

Table 8: Link classification F-score with semantic features (T = "Title Similarity", P = "Post Similarity", C = "Post Characteristics", and U = "User Profile"; above-baseline results in **bold**)

The best overall result achieved for link classification is thus the 0.743 for CRF with the structural and post context features.

We additionally experimented with combinations of features as for post classification, but were unable to improve on this result.

7.4 Link Classification using DA Features

Ultimately, we require both DA and link classification of each post, which is possible by combining the outputs of the component classifiers described

Features	CRF	SVM-HMM	ME
Struct+R	.586	.352	.430
Struct+A	.591	.278	.568
Struct+F	**.704**	.477	.546
Struct+RA	.637	.384	.551
Struct+AF	**.743**	.527	.603

Table 9: Link classification F-score with structural and post-based post context features (R = "Previous Post", A = "Previous Post from Same Author", and F = "Full History"; above-baseline results in **bold**)

above, by rolling the two tasks into a single classification task, or alternatively by looking to joint modelling methods. As a preliminary step in this direction, and means of exploring the interaction between the two tasks, we repeat the experiment based on post context features from above (see Section 7.2), but rather than using link-based post context, we use DA-based post context.

As can be seen in Table 9, the results for SVM-HMM and ME drop appreciably as compared to the results using link-based post context in Table 9, while the results for CRF jump to the highest level achieved for the task for all three learners. The effect can be ascribed to the ability of CRF to natively model the (bidirectional) link classification history in the process of performing structured learning, and the newly-introduced post features complementing the link classification task.

8 Discussion and Future Work

Ultimately, we require both DA and link classification of each post, which is possible in (at least) the following three ways: (1) by combining the outputs of the component classifiers described above; (2) by rolling the two tasks into a single classification task; or (3) by looking to joint modelling methods. Our results in Section 7.4 are suggestive of the empirical potential of performing the two tasks jointly, which we hope to explore in future work.

One puzzling effect observed in our experiments was the generally poor results for SVM. Error analysis indicates that the classifier was heavily biased towards the high-frequency classes, e.g. classifying all posts as either Q-Q or A-A for DA classification. The classifications for the other two learners were much more evenly spread across the different classes.

CRF was limited in that it was unable to capture lexical features, but ultimately, lexical features were found to be considerably less effective than structural and post context features for both tasks, and the ability of the CRF to optimise the post labelling over the full sequence of posts in a thread more than compensated for this shortcoming. Having said this, there is more work to be done exploring synergies between the different feature sets, especially for DA classification where all feature sets were found to produce above-baseline results.

Another possible direction for future research is to explore the impact of inter-post time on link structure, based on the observation that follow-up posts from the initiator tend to be temporally adjacent to posts they respond to with relatively short time intervals, while posts from non-initiators which are well spaced out tend not to respond to one another. Combining this with profiling of the cross-thread behaviour of individual forum participants (Weimer et al., 2007; Lui and Baldwin, 2009), and formal modelling of "forum behaviour" is also a promising line of research, taking the lead from the work of Götz et al. (2009), inter alia.

9 Conclusion

In this work, we have proposed a method for analysing post-to-post discourse structure in online user forum data, in the form of post linking and dialogue act tagging. We introduced three feature sets: structural features, post context features and semantic features. We experimented with three learners (maximum entropy, SVM-HMM and CRF), and established that CRF is the superior approach to the task, achieving above-baseline results for both post and link classification. We also demonstrated the complementarity of the proposed feature sets, especially for the post classification task, and carried out a preliminary exploration of the interaction between the linking and dialogue act tagging tasks.

Acknowledgements

This research was supported in part by funding from Microsoft Research Asia.

References

Jeremy Ang, Yang Liu, and Elizabeth Shriberg. 2005. Automatic dialog act segmentation and classification in multiparty meetings. In *Proceedings of the 2005 IEEE International Conference on Acoustics, Speech, and Signal Processing (ICASSP 2005)*, pages 1061–1064, Philadelphia, USA.

Timothy Baldwin, David Martinez, Richard Penman, Su Nam Kim, Marco Lui, Li Wang, and Andrew MacKinlay. to appear. Intelligent Linux information access by data mining: the ILIAD project. In *Proceedings of the NAACL 2010 Workshop on Computational Linguistics in a World of Social Media: #SocialMedia*, Los Angeles, USA.

Susan Bartlett, Grzegorz Kondrak, and Colin Cherry. 2009. On the syllabification of phonemes. In *Proceedings of the North American Chapter of the Association for Computational Linguistics – Human Language Technologies 2009 (NAACL HLT 2009)*, pages 308–316, Boulder, USA.

Xin Cao, Gao Cong, Bin Cui, Christian S. Jensen, and Ce Zhang. 2009. The use of categorization information in language models for question retrieval. In *Proceedings of the 18th ACM Conference on Information and Knowledge Management (CIKM 2009)*, pages 265–274, Hong Kong, China.

Lynn Carlson, Daniel Marcu, and Mary Ellen Okurowski. 2001. Building a discourse-tagged corpus in the framework of rhetorical structure theory. In *Proceedings of the Second SIGdial Workshop on Discourse and Dialogue*, pages 1–10, Aalborg, Denmark. Association for Computational Linguistics Morristown, NJ, USA.

Vitor R. Carvalho and William W. Cohen. 2005. On the collective classification of email "speech acts". In *Proceedings of 28th International ACM-SIGIR Conference on Research and Development in Information Retrieval (SIGIR 2005)*, pages 345–352.

William W. Cohen, Vitor R. Carvalho, and Tom M. Mitchell. 2004. Learning to classify email into "speech acts". In *Proceedings of the 2004 Conference on Empirical Methods in Natural Language Processing (EMNLP 2004)*, pages 309–316, Barcelona, Spain.

Gao Cong, Long Wang, Chin-Yew Lin, Young-In Song, and Yueheng Sun. 2008. Finding question-answer pairs from online forums. In *Proceedings of 31st International ACM-SIGIR Conference on Research and Development in Information Retrieval (SIGIR'08)*, pages 467–474, Singapore.

Shilin Ding, Gao Cong, Chin-Yew Lin, and Xiaoyan Zhu. 2008. Using conditional random fields to extract context and answers of questions from online forums. In *Proceedings of the 46th Annual Meeting of the ACL: HLT (ACL 2008)*, pages 710–718, Columbus, USA.

Jonathan L. Elsas and Jaime G. Carbonell. 2009. It pays to be picky: An evaluation of thread retrieval in online forums. In *Proceedings of 32nd International ACM-SIGIR Conference on Research and Development in Information Retrieval (SIGIR'09)*, pages 714–715, Boston, USA.

Jonathan L. Elsas, Jaime Arguello, Jamie Callan, and Jaime G. Carbonell. 2008. Retrieval and feedback models for blog feed search. In *Proceedings of 31st International ACM-SIGIR Conference on Research and Development in Information Retrieval (SIGIR'08)*, pages 347–354, Singapore.

Micha Elsner and Eugene Charniak. 2008. You talking to me? a corpus and algorithm for conversation disentanglement. In *Proceedings of the 46th Annual Meeting of the ACL: HLT (ACL 2008)*, pages 834–842, Columbus, USA.

Michaela Götz, Jure Leskovec, Mary McGlohon, and Christos Faloutsos. 2009. Modeling blog dynamics. In *Proceedings of the Third International Conference on Weblogs and Social Media (ICWSM 2009)*, pages 26–33, San Jose, USA.

Barbara J. Grosz and Candace L. Sidner. 1986. Attention, intention and the structure of discourse. *Computational Linguistics*, 12(3):175–204.

Edward Ivanovic. 2008. Automatic instant messaging dialogue using statistical models and dialogue acts. Master's thesis, University of Melbourne.

Gang Ji and Jeff Bilmes. 2005. Dialog act tagging using graphical models. In *Proceedings of the 2005 IEEE International Conference on Acoustics, Speech, and Signal Processing (ICASSP 2005)*, pages 33–36, Philadelphia, USA.

Thorsten Joachims, Thomas Finley, and Chun-Nam John Yu. 2009. Cutting-plane training of structural SVMs. *Machine Learning*, 77(1):27–59.

Andrew Lampert, Robert Dale, and Cécile Paris. 2008. The nature of requests and commitments in email messages. In *Proceedings of the AAAI 2008 Workshop on Enhanced Messaging*, pages 42–47, Chicago, USA.

Oliver Lemon, Alex Gruenstein, and Stanley Peters. 2002. Collaborative activities and multi-tasking in dialogue systems. *Traitement Automatique des Langues (TAL), Special Issue on Dialogue*, 43(2):131–154.

Chen Lin, Jiang-Ming Yang, Rui Cai, Xin-Jing Wang, Wei Wang, and Lei Zhang. 2009. Modeling semantics and structure of discussion threads. In *Proceedings of the 18th International Conference on the World Wide Web (WWW 2009)*, pages 1103–1104, Madrid, Spain.

Marco Lui and Timothy Baldwin. 2009. You are what you post: User-level features in threaded discourse. In *Proceedings of the Fourteenth Australasian Document Computing Symposium (ADCS 2009)*, Sydney, Australia.

Guido Minnen, John Carroll, and Darren Pearce. 2001. Applied morphological processing of English. *Natural Language Engineering*, 7(3):207–223.

Gabriel Murray, Steve Renals, Jean Carletta, and Johanna Moore. 2006. Incorporating speaker and discourse features into speech summarization. In *Proceedings of the Main Conference on Human Language Technology Conference of the North American Chapter of the Association of Computational Linguistics*, pages 367–374.

Klaus Ries. 1999. HMM and neural network based speech act detection. In *Proceedings of the 1999 IEEE International Conference on Acoustics, Speech, and Signal Processing (ICASSP-99)*, pages 497–500, Phoenix, USA.

Carolyn Penstein Rosé, Barbara Di Eugenio, Lori S. Levin, and Carol Van Ess-Dykema. 1995. Discourse processing of dialogues with multiple threads. In *Proceedings of the 33rd Annual Meeting of the Association for Computational Linguistics*, pages 31–38, Cambridge, USA.

Ken Samuel, Carbeery Sandra Carberry, and K. Vijay-Shanker. 1998. Dialogue act tagging with transformation-based learning. In *Proceedings of the 36th Annual Meeting of the ACL and 17th International Conference on Computational Linguistics (COLING/ACL-98)*, pages 1150–1156, Montreal, Canada.

Anne Schuth, Maarten Marx, and Maarten de Rijke. 2007. Extracting the discussion structure in comments on news-articles. In *Proceedings of the 9th Annual ACM International Workshop on Web Information and Data Management*, pages 97–104, Lisboa, Portugal.

Jangwon Seo, W. Bruce Croft, and David A. Smith. 2009. Online community search using thread structure. In *Proceedings of the 18th ACM Conference on Information and Knowledge Management (CIKM 2009)*, pages 1907–1910, Hong Kong, China.

Riccardo Serafin and Barbara Di Eugenio. 2004. FLSA: Extending latent semantic analysis with features for dialogue act classification. In *Proceedings of the 42nd Annual Meeting of the Association for Computational Linguistics (ACL 2004)*, pages 692–699, Barcelona, Spain.

Fei Sha and Fernando Pereira. 2003. Shallow parsing with conditional random fields. In *Proceedings of the 3rd International Conference on Human Language Technology Research and 4th Annual Meeting of the NAACL (HLT-NAACL 2003)*, pages 213–220, Edmonton, Canada.

Lokesh Shrestha and Kathleen McKeown. 2004. Detection of question-answer pairs in email conversations. In *Proceedings of the 20th International Conference on Computational Linguistics (COLING 2004)*, pages 889–895, Geneva, Switzerland.

Elinzabeth Shriberg, Raj Dhillon, Sonali Bhagat, Jeremy Ang, and Hannah Carvey. 2004. The ICSI meeting recorder dialog act (MRDA) corpus. In *Proceedings of the 5th SIGdial Workshop on Discourse and Dialogue*, pages 97–100, Cambridge, USA.

Andreas Stolcke, Klaus Ries, Noah Coccaro, Elizabeth Shriberg, Rebecca Bates, Daniel Jurafsky, Pail Taylor, Rachel Martin, Carol Van Ess-Dykema, and Marie Meteer. 2000. Dialogue Act Modeling for Automatic Tagging and Recognition of Conversational Speech. *Computational Linguistics*, 26(3):339–373.

Yi-Chia Wang, Mahesh Joshi, and Carolyn Rosé. 2007. A feature based approach to leveraging context for classifying newsgroup style discussion segments. In *Proceedings of the 45th Annual Meeting of the Association for Computational Linguistics Companion Volume Proceedings of the Demo and Poster Sessions (ACL 2007)*, pages 73–76, Prague, Czech Republic.

Yi-Chia Wang, Mahesh Joshi, William W. Cohen, and Carolyn Rosé. 2008. Recovering implicit thread structure in newsgroup style conversations. In *Proceedings of the Second International Conference on Weblogs and Social Media (ICWSM 2008)*, pages 152–160, Seattle, USA.

Markus Weimer, Iryna Gurevych, and Max Mühlhäuser. 2007. Automatically assessing the post quality in online discussions on software. In *Proceedings of the 45th Annual Meeting of the ACL: Interactive Poster and Demonstration Sessions*, pages 125–128, Prague, Czech Republic.

Florian Wolf and Edward Gibson. 2005. Representing discourse coherence: A corpus-based study. *Computational Linguistics*, 31(2):249–287.

Wensi Xi, Jesper Lind, and Eric Brill. 2004. Learning effective ranking functions for newsgroup search. In *Proceedings of 27th International ACM-SIGIR Conference on Research and Development in Information Retrieval (SIGIR 2004)*, pages 394–401. Sheffield, UK.

Alexander Yeh. 2000. More accurate tests for the statistical significance of result differences. In *Proceedings of the 18th International Conference on Computational Linguistics (COLING 2000)*, pages 947–953, Saarbrücken, Germany.

Hai Zhao, Chang-Ning Huang, and Mu Li. 2006. An improved Chinese word segmentation system with conditional random field. In *Proceedings of the Fifth SIGHAN Workshop on Chinese Language Processing*, pages 162–165. Sydney, Australia.

Joint Entity and Relation Extraction using Card-Pyramid Parsing

Rohit J. Kate and Raymond J. Mooney
Department of Computer Science
The University of Texas at Austin
1 University Station C0500
Austin, TX 78712-0233, USA
{rjkate,mooney}@cs.utexas.edu

Abstract

Both entity and relation extraction can benefit from being performed jointly, allowing each task to correct the errors of the other. We present a new method for joint entity and relation extraction using a graph we call a "card-pyramid." This graph compactly encodes all possible entities and relations in a sentence, reducing the task of their joint extraction to jointly labeling its nodes. We give an efficient labeling algorithm that is analogous to parsing using dynamic programming. Experimental results show improved results for our joint extraction method compared to a pipelined approach.

1 Introduction

Information extraction (IE) is the task of extracting structured information from text. The two most common sub-tasks of IE are extracting entities (like *Person*, *Location* and *Organization*) and extracting relations between them (like *Work_For* which relates a *Person* and an *Organization*, *Org-Based_In* which relates an *Organization* and a *Location* etc.). Figure 1 shows a sample sentence annotated with entities and relations. The application domain and requirements of the downstream tasks usually dictate the type of entities and relations that an IE system needs to extract.

Most work in IE has concentrated on entity extraction alone (Tjong Kim Sang, 2002; Sang and Meulder, 2003) or on relation extraction assuming entities are either given or previously extracted (Bunescu et al., 2005; Zhang et al., 2006; Giuliano et al., 2007; Qian et al., 2008). However, these tasks are very closely inter-related. While identifying correct entities is essential for identifying relations between them, identifying correct relations can in turn improve identification of entities. For example, if the relation *Work_For* is identified with high confidence by a relation extractor, then it can enforce identifying its arguments as *Person* and *Organization*, about which the entity extractor might not have been confident.

A brute force algorithm for finding the most probable joint extraction will soon become intractable as the number of entities in a sentence grows. If there are n entities in a sentence, then there are $O(n^2)$ possible relations between them and if each relation can take l labels then there are $O(l^{n^2})$ total possibilities, which is intractable even for small l and n. Hence, an efficient inference mechanism is needed for joint entity and relation extraction.

The only work we are aware of for jointly extracting entities and relations is by Roth & Yih (2004; 2007). Their method first identifies the possible entities and relations in a sentence using separate classifiers which are applied independently and then computes a most probable consistent global set of entities and relations using linear programming. In this paper, we present a different approach to joint extraction using a "card-pyramid" graph. The labeled nodes in this graph compactly encode the possible entities and relations in a sentence. The task of joint extraction then reduces to finding the most probable joint assignment to the nodes in the card-pyramid. We give an efficient dynamic-programming algorithm for this task which resembles CYK parsing for context-free grammars (Jurafsky and Martin, 2008). The algorithm does a beam search and gives an approximate solution for a finite beam size. A natural advantage of this approach is that extraction from a part of the sentence is influenced by extraction from its subparts and vice-versa, thus leading to a joint extraction. During extraction from a part of the sentence it also allows use of features based on the extraction from its sub-parts, thus leading to a more integrated extraction. We use Roth & Yih's

Proceedings of the Fourteenth Conference on Computational Natural Language Learning, pages 203–212,
Uppsala, Sweden, 15-16 July 2010.

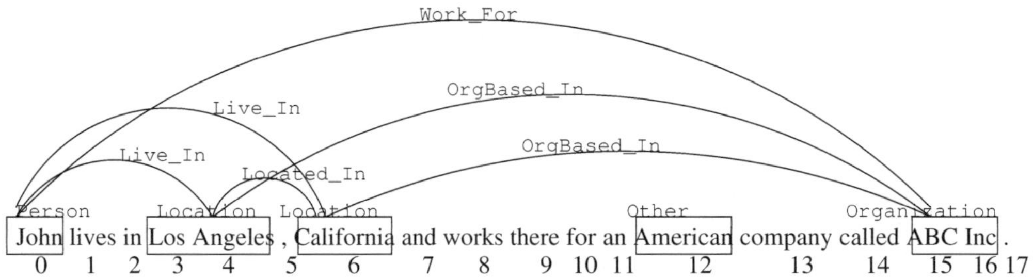

Figure 1: A sentence shown with entities and relations.

Figure 2: A pyramid built out of playing-cards.

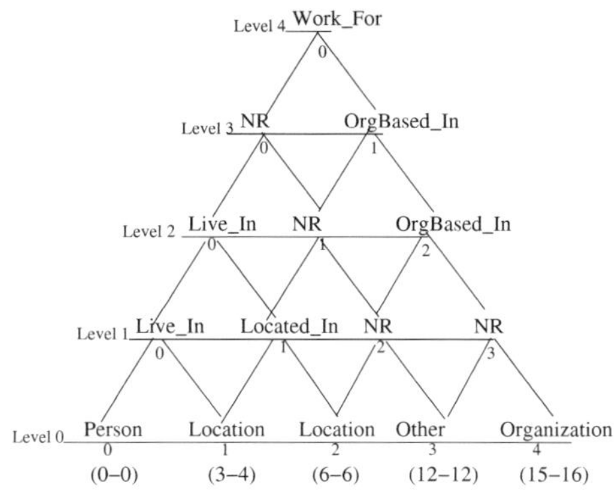

Figure 3: The card-pyramid for the sentence shown in Figure 1. Levels are shown by the horizontal lines under which the positions of its nodes are indicated.

(2004; 2007) dataset in our experiments and show that card-pyramid parsing improves accuracy over both their approach and a pipelined extractor.

2 Card-Pyramid Parsing for Joint Extraction

In this section, we first introduce the card-pyramid structure and describe how it represents entities and their relations in a sentence. We then describe an efficient algorithm for doing joint extraction using this structure.

2.1 Card-Pyramid Structure

We define a binary directed graph we call a *card-pyramid* because it looks like a pyramid built out of playing-cards as shown in Figure 2. A card-pyramid is a "tree-like" graph with one root, internal nodes, and leaves, such that if there are n leaves, then there are exactly n levels with a decreasing number of nodes from bottom to top, leaves are at the lowest level (0) and the root is at the highest level $(n-1)$ (see Figure 3 for an example). In addition, every non-leaf node at position i in level l is the parent of exactly two nodes at positions i and $i+1$ at level $l-1$. Note that a card-pyramid is not a tree because many of its nodes have two parents. A useful property of a card-pyramid is that a non-leaf node at position i in level l is always the lowest common ancestor of the leaves at positions i and $l+i$.

We now describe how entities and relations in a sentence are easily represented in a card-pyramid. We assume that in addition to the given entity types, there is an extra type, *Other*, indicating that the entity is of none of the given types. Similarly, there is an extra relation type, *NR*, indicating that its two entity arguments are not related.

Figure 3 shows the card-pyramid corresponding to the annotated sentence shown in figure 1. To obtain it, first, all entities present in the sentence are made leaves of the card-pyramid in the same order as they appear in the sentence. The label of a leaf is the type of the corresponding entity. The leaf also stores the range of the indices of its entity's words in the sentence. Note that although there is no overlap between entities in the given example (nor in the dataset we used for our experiments), overlapping entities do not pose a problem. Overlapping entities can still be ordered and supplied as the leaves of the card-pyramid. Next, the relation between every two entities (leaves) is encoded as the label of their lowest common ancestor. If two entities are not related, then the label of their lowest common ancestor is *NR*. This way, every non-leaf node relates exactly two entities: the left-most and right-most leaves beneath it.

2.2 Card-Pyramid Parsing

The task of jointly extracting entities and relations from a sentence reduces to jointly labeling the nodes of a card-pyramid which has all the candidate entities (i.e. entity boundaries) of the sentence as its leaves. We call this process card-pyramid parsing. We assume that all candidate entities are given up-front. If needed, candidate entities can be either obtained automatically (Punyakanok and Roth, 2001) or generated using a simple heuristic, like including all noun-phrase chunks as candidate entities. Or, in the worst case, each substring of words in the sentence can be given as a candidate entity. Liberally including candidate entities is possible since they can simply be given the label *Other* if they are none of the given types.

In this section we describe our card-pyramid parsing algorithm whose pseudo-code is shown in Figure 4. While the process is analogous to context-free grammar (CFG) parsing, particularly CYK bottom-up parsing, there are several major differences. Firstly, in card-pyramid parsing the structure is already known and the only task is labeling the nodes, whereas in CFG parsing the structure is not known in advance. This fact simplifies some aspects of card-pyramid parsing. Secondly, in CFG parsing the subtrees under a node do not overlap which simplifies parsing. However, in card-pyramid parsing there is significant overlap between the two sub-card-pyramids under a given node and this overlap needs to be consistently labeled. This could have potentially complicated parsing, but there turns out to be a simple constant-time method for checking consistency of the overlap. Thirdly, while CFG parsing parses the words in a sentence, here we are parsing candidate entities. Finally, as described below, in card-pyramid parsing, a production at a non-leaf node relates the left-most and right-most leaves beneath it, while in CFG parsing a production at a non-leaf node relates its immediate children which could be other non-leaf nodes.

Parsing requires specifying a grammar for the card-pyramid. The productions in this grammar are of two types. For leaf nodes, the productions are of the form *entityLabel* $\rightarrow$ *ce* where *ce*, which stands for candidate entity, is the only terminal symbol in the grammar. We call these productions *entity productions*. For non-leaf nodes, the productions are of the form *relationLabel* $\rightarrow$ *entityLabel1 entityLabel2*. We call these productions *relation productions*. Note that their right-hand-side (RHS) non-terminals are entity labels and not other relation labels. From a training set of labeled sentences, the corresponding card-pyramids can be constructed using the procedure described in the previous section. From these card-pyramids, the entity productions are obtained by simply reading off the labels of the leaves. A relation productions is obtained from each non-leaf node by making the node's label the production's left-hand-side (LHS) non-terminal and making the labels of its left-most and right-most leaves the production's RHS non-terminals. For the example shown in Figure 3, some of the productions are *Work_For* $\rightarrow$ *Person Organization*, *NR* $\rightarrow$ *Person Other*, *OrgBased_In* $\rightarrow$ *Loc Org*, *Person* $\rightarrow$ *ce*, *Location* $\rightarrow$ *ce* etc. Note that there could be two separate productions like *Work_For* $\rightarrow$ *Person Organization* and *Work_For* $\rightarrow$ *Organization Person* based on the order in which the entities are found in a sentence. For the relations which take arguments of the same type, like *Kill(Person,Person)*, two productions are used with different LHS non-terminals (*Kill* and *Kill_reverse*) to distinguish between the argument order of the entities.

The parsing algorithm needs a classifier for every entity production which gives the probability of a candidate entity being of the type given in the production's LHS. In the pseudo-code, this classifier is given by the function: *entity-classifier(production, sentence, range)*. The function *range(r)* represents the boundaries or the range of the word indices for the rth candidate entity. Similarly, we assume that a classifier is given for every relation production which gives the probability that its two RHS entities are related by its LHS relation. In the pseudo-code it is the function: *relation-classifier(production, sentence, range1, range2, sub-card-pyramid1, sub-card-pyramid2)*, where *range1* and *range2* are the ranges of the word indices of the two entities and *sub-card-pyramid1* and *sub-card-pyramid2* are the sub-card-pyramids rooted at its two children. Thus, along with the two entities and the words in the sentence, information from these sub-card-pyramids is also used in deciding the relation at a node. In the next section, we further specify these entity and relation classifiers and explain how they are trained. We note that this use of multiple classifiers to determine the most probable parse is similar to the method used in the KRISP semantic parser (Kate and Mooney, 2006).

Given the candidate entities in a sentence, the grammar, and the entity and relation classifiers, the card-pyramid parsing algorithm tries to find the most probable joint-labeling of all of its nodes, and thus jointly extracts entities and their relations. The parsing algorithm does a beam search and maintains a *beam* at each node of the card-pyramid. A node is represented by $l[i][j]$ in the pseudo-code which stands for the node in the jth position in the ith level. Note that at level i, the nodes range from $l[i][0]$ to $l[i][n-i-1]$, where n is the number of leaves. The beam at each node is a queue of items we call *beam elements*. At leaf nodes, a beam element simply stores a possible entity label with its corresponding probability. At non-leaf nodes, a beam element contains a possible joint assignment of labels to all the nodes in the sub-card-pyramid rooted at that node with its probability. This is efficiently maintained through indices to the beam elements of its children nodes.

The parsing proceeds as follows. First, the entity classifiers are used to fill the beams at the leaf nodes. The *add(beam, beam-element)* function adds the beam element to the beam while maintaining its maximum beam-width size and sorted order based on the probabilities. Next, the beams of the non-leaf nodes are filled in a bottom-up manner. At any node, the beams of its children nodes are considered and every combination of their beam elements are tried. To be considered further, the two possible sub-card-pyramids encoded by the two beam elements must have a consistent overlap. This is easily enforced by checking that its left child's right child's beam element is same as its right child's left child's beam element. If this condition is satisfied, then those relation productions are considered which have the left-most leaf of the left child and right-most leaf of the right child as its RHS non-terminals.[1] For every such production in the grammar, [2] the probability of the relation is determined using the relation classifier. This probability is then multiplied by the probabilities of the children sub-card-pyramids. But, because of the overlap between the two children, a probability mass gets multiplied twice. Hence the probability of the overlap sub-card-pyramid is then suitably divided. Finally, the estimated most-probable labeling is obtained from the top beam element of the root node.

We note that this algorithm may not find the optimal solution but only an approximate solution owing to a limited beam size, this is unlike probabilistic CFG parsing algorithms in which the optimal solution is found. A limitless beam size will find the optimal solution but will reduce the algorithm to a computationally intractable brute force search. The parsing algorithm with a finite beam size keeps the search computationally tractable while allowing a joint labelling.

3 Classifiers for Entity and Relation Extraction

The card-pyramid parsing described in the previous section requires classifiers for each of the entity and relation productions. In this section, we describe the classifiers we used in our experiments and how they were trained.

We use a support vector machine (SVM) (Cristianini and Shawe-Taylor, 2000) classifier for each of the entity productions in the grammar. An entity classifier gets as input a sentence and a candidate entity indicated by the range of the indices of its words. It outputs the probability that the candidate entity is of the respective entity type. Probabilities for the SVM outputs are computed using the method by Platt (1999). We use all possible word subsequences of the candidate entity words as implicit features using a word-subsequence kernel (Lodhi et al., 2002). In addition, we use the following standard entity extraction features: the part-of-speech (POS) tag sequence of the candidate entity words, two words before and after the candidate entity and their POS tags, whether any or all candidate entity words are capitalized,

[1]These are stored in the beam elements.

[2]Note that this step enforces the consistency constraint of Roth and Yih (Roth and Yih, 2004; Roth and Yih, 2007) that a relation can only be between the entities of specific types. The grammar in our approach inherently enforces this constraint.

```
function Card-Pyramid-Parsing(Sentence,Grammar,entity-classifiers,relation-classifiers)
n = number of candidate entities in S
// Let range(r) represent the range of the indices of the words for the rth candidate entity.
// Let l[i][j] represent the jth node at ith level in the card-pyramid.

// For leaves
// A beam element at a leaf node is (label,probability).
for j = 0 to n // for every leaf
 for each entityLabel → candidate_entity ∈ Grammar
    prob = entity-classifier(entityLabel → candidate_entity, S, range(j))
    add(l[0][j].beam, (entityLabel,prob))

// For non-leaf nodes
// A beam element at a non-leaf node is (label,probability,leftIndex,rightIndex,leftMostLeaf,rightMostLeaf)
// where leftIndex and rightIndex are the indices in the beams of the left and right children respectively.
for i = 1 to n // for every level above the leaves
 for j = 0 to n − i − 1 // for every position at a level
  // for each combination of beam elements of the two children
  for each f ∈ l[i − 1][j].beam and g ∈ l[i − 1][j + 1].beam
    // the overlapped part must be same (overlap happens for i > 1)
    if (i == 1||f.rightIndex == g.leftIndex)
     for each relationLabel → f.leftMostLeaf g.rightMostLeaf ∈ Grammar
       // probability of that relation between the left-most and right-most leaf under the node
       prob = relation-classifier(relationLabel → f.leftMostLeaf g.rightMostLeaf, S, range(i), range(i + j), f, g);
       prob *= f.probability ∗ g.probability // multiply probabilities of the children sub-card-pyramids
       // divide by the common probability that got multiplied twice
       if (i > 1) prob /= l[i − 2][j + 1].beam[f.rightIndex].probability
       add(l[i][j].beam, (relationLabel, prob, index of f, index of g, f.leftMostLeaf, g.rightMostLeaf)

return the labels starting from the first beam element of the root i.e. l[n][0].beam[0]
```

Figure 4: Card-Pyramid Parsing Algorithm.

whether any or all words are found in a list of entity names, whether any word has sufffix "ment" or "ing", and finally the alphanumeric pattern of characters (Collins, 2002) of the last candidate entity word obtained by replacing each character by its character type (lowercase, uppercase or numeric) and collapsing any consecutive repetition (for example, the alphanumeric pattern for CoNLL2010 will be AaA0). The full kernel is computed by adding the word-subsequence kernel and the dot-product of all these features, exploiting the convolution property of kernels.

We also use an SVM classifier for each of the relation productions in the grammar which outputs the probability that the relation holds between the two entities. A relation classifier is applied at an internal node of a card-pyramid. It takes the input in two parts. The first part is the sentence and the range of the word indices of its two entities l and r which are the left-most and the right-most leaves under it respectively. The second part consists of the sub-card-pyramids rooted at the node's two children which represent a possible entity and relation labeling for all the nodes underneath. In general, any information from the sub-card-pyramids could be used in the classifier. We use the following information: pairs of relations that exist between l and b and between b and r for every entity (leaf) b that exists between the two entities l and r. For example, in figure 3, the relation classifier at the root node which relates *Person(0-0)* and *Organization (15-16)* will take three pairs of relations as the information from the two sub-card-pyramids of its children: "*Live_In—OrgBased_In*" (with *Location(3-4)* as the in-between entity), "*Live_In—OrgBased_In*" (with *Location(6-6)* as the in-between entity) and "*NR—NR*" (with *Other(12-12)* as the in-between entity). This information tells how the two entities are related to the entities present in between them. This can affect the relation between the two entities, for example, if the sentence mentions that a person lives at a location and also mentions that an organization is based at that location then that person is likely to work at that organization. Note that this information can not be incorporated in a pipelined approach in which each relation is determined independently. It is also not possible to incorporate this in the linear programming method presented in (Roth and Yih, 2004; Roth and Yih, 2007) because that method computes the probabilities of all the relations independently before finding the optimal solution through linear programming. It would also not help to add hard constraints to their linear program relating the relations because they need not always hold.

We add the kernels for each part of the input to compute the final kernel for the SVM classifiers. The kernel for the second part of the input is computed by simply counting the number of common pairs of relations between two examples thus implicitly considering every pair of relation (as described in the last paragraph) as a feature. For the first part of the input, we use word-subsequence kernels which have shown to be effective for relation extraction (Bunescu and Mooney, 2005b). We compute the kernel as the sum of the word-subsequence kernels between: the words between the two entities (*between pattern*), k (a parameter) words before the first entity (*before pattern*), k words after the second entity (*after pattern*) and the words from the beginning of the first entity to the end of the second entity (*between-and-entity pattern*). The *before*, *between* and *after* patterns have been found useful in previous work (Bunescu and Mooney, 2005b; Giuliano et al., 2007). Sometimes the words of the entities can indicate the relations they are in, hence we also use the *between-and-entity* pattern. When a relation classifier is used at a node, the labels of the leaves beneath it are already known, so we replace candidate entity words that are in the *between* and *between-and-entity*[3] patterns by their entity labels. This provides useful information to the relation classifier and also makes these patterns less sparse for training.

Given training data of sentences annotated with entities and relations, the positive and negative examples for training the entity and relation classifiers are collected in the following way. First, the corresponding card-pyramids are obtained for each of the training sentences as described in section 2.1. For every entity production in a card-pyramid, a positive example is collected for its corresponding classifier as the sentence and the range of the entity's word indices. Similarly, for every relation production in a card-pyramid, a positive example is collected for its corresponding classifier as the sentence, the ranges of the two entities' word indices and the sub-card-pyramids rooted at its two children. The positive examples of a production become the negative examples for all those productions which have the same right-hand-sides but different left-hand-sides. We found that for NR productions, training separate classifiers is harmful because it has the unwanted side-effect of preferring one label assignment of entities over another due to the fact that these productions gave different probabilities for the "not-related" relation between the entities. To avoid this, we found that it suffices if all these classifiers for NR productions always return 0.5 as the probability. This ensures that a real relation will be preferred over NR if and only if its probability is greater than 0.5, otherwise nothing will change.

[3]Except for the two entities at the ends

4 Experiments

We conducted experiments to compare our card-pyramid parsing approach for joint entity and relation extraction to a pipelined approach.

4.1 Methodology

We used the dataset[4] created by Roth & Yih (2004; 2007) that was also used by Giuliano et el. (2007). The sentences in this data were taken from the TREC corpus and annotated with entities and relations. As in the previous work with this dataset, in order to observe the interaction between entities and relations, our experiments used only the 1437 sentences that include at least one relation. The boundaries of the entities are already supplied by this dataset. There are three types of entities: *Person* (1685), *Location* (1968) and *Organization* (978), in addition there is a fourth type *Other* (705), which indicates that the candidate entity is none of the three types. There are five types of relations: *Located_In* (406) indicates that one *Location* is located inside another *Location*, *Work_For* (394) indicates that a *Person* works for an *Organization*, *OrgBased_In* (451) indicates that an *Organization* is based in a *Location*, *Live_In* (521) indicates that a *Person* lives at a *Location* and *Kill* (268) indicates that a *Person* killed another *Person*. There are 17007 pairs of entities that are not related by any of the five relations and hence have the *NR* relation between them which thus significantly outnumbers other relations.

Our implementation uses the LIBSVM[5] software for SVM classifiers. We kept the noise penalty parameter of SVM very high (100) assuming there is little noise in our data. For the word-subsequence kernel, we set 5 as the maximum length of a subsequence and 0.25 as the penalty parameter for subsequence gaps (Lodhi et al., 2002). We used $k = 5$ words for *before* and *after* patterns for the relation classifiers. These parameter values were determined through pilot experiments on a subset of the data. We used a beam

[4]Available at: http://l2r.cs.uiuc.edu/~cogcomp/Data/ER/conll04.corp

[5]http://www.csie.ntu.edu.tw/~cjlin/libsvm/

Entity	*Person*			*Location*			*Organization*		
Approach	Rec	Pre	F	Rec	Pre	F	Rec	Pre	F
Pipeline	93.6	92.0	92.8	94.0	90.3	92.1	87.9	90.6	89.2
Card-pyramid	94.2	92.1	93.2	94.2	90.8	**92.4**†	88.7	90.5	89.5
RY07 Pipeline	89.1	88.7	88.6	88.1	89.8	88.9	71.4	89.3	78.7
RY07 Joint	89.5	89.1	**89.0**	88.7	89.7	**89.1**	72.0	89.5	79.2

Relation	*Located_In*			*Work_For*			*OrgBased_In*			*Live_In*			*Kill*		
Approach	Rec	Pre	F	Rec	Pre	F	Rec	Pre	F	Rec	Pre	F	Rec	Pre	F
Pipeline	57.0	71.5	62.3	66.0	74.1	69.7	60.2	70.6	64.6	56.6	68.1	61.7	61.2	91.1	73.1
Card-pyramid	56.7	67.5	58.3	68.3	73.5	70.7	64.1	66.2	64.7	60.1	66.4	**62.9**†	64.1	91.6	**75.2**
RY07 Pipeline	56.4	52.5	50.7	44.4	60.8	51.2	42.1	77.8	54.3	50.0	58.9	53.5	81.5	73.0	76.5
RY07 Joint	55.7	53.9	51.3	42.3	72.0	**53.1**	41.6	79.8	54.3	49.0	59.1	53.0	81.5	77.5	**79.0**†

Table 1: Results of five-fold cross-validation for entity and relation extraction using pipelined and joint extraction. Boldface indicates statistical significance ($p < 0.1$ using paired t-test) when compared to the corresponding value in the other row grouped with it. Symbol † indicates statistical significance with $p < 0.05$. Only statistical significance for F-measures are indicated. RY07 stands for the "E ↔ R" model in (Roth and Yih, 2007).

size of 5 in our card-pyramid parsing algorithm at which the performance plateaus.

We note that by using a beam size of 1 and by not using the second part of input for relation classifiers as described in section 3 (i.e. by ignoring the relations at the lower levels), the card-parsing algorithm reduces to the traditional pipelined approach because then only the best entity label for each candidate entity is considered for relation extraction. Hence, in our experiments we simply use this setting as our pipelined approach.

We performed a 5-fold cross-validation to compare with the previous work with this dataset by Roth & Yih (2007), however, our folds are not same as their folds which were not available. We also note that our entity and relation classifiers are different from theirs. They experimented with several models to see the effect of joint inference on them, we compare with the results they obtained with their most sophisticated model which they denote by "E ↔ R". For every entity type and relation type, we measured *Precision* (percentage of output labels correct), *Recall* (percentage of gold-standard labels correctly identified) and *F-measure* (the harmonic mean of *Precision* and *Recall*).

4.2 Results and Discussion

Table 1 shows the results of entity and relation extraction. The statistical significance is shown only for F-measures. We first note that except for the *Kill* relation, all the results of our pipelined approach are far better than the pipelined approach of (Roth and Yih, 2007), for both entities and relations. This shows that the entity and relation classifiers we used are better that the ones they used. These strong baselines also set a higher ceiling for our joint extraction method to improve upon.

The entity extraction results show that on all the entities the card-pyramid parsing approach for joint extraction obtains a better performance than the pipelined approach. This shows that entity extraction benefits when it is jointly done with relation extraction. Joint extraction using card-pyramid parsing also gave improvement in performance on all the relations except the *Located_In* relation.[6]

The results thus show that entity and relation extraction correct some of each other's errors when jointly performed. Roth & Yih (2004; 2007) report that 5% to 25% of the relation predictions of their pipeline models were *incoherent*, meaning that the types of the entities related by the relations are not of the required types. Their joint inference method corrects these mistakes, hence a part of the improvement their joint model obtains over their pipeline model is due to the fact that their pipeline model can output incoherent relations. Since the types of the entities a relation's arguments should

[6]Through error analysis we found that the drop in the performance for this relation was mainly because of an unusual sentence in the data which had twenty *Location* entities in it separated by commas. After incorrectly extracting *Located_In* relation between the *Location* entities at the lower levels, these erroneous extractions would be taken into account at higher levels in the card-pyramid, leading to extracting many more incorrect instances of this relation while doing joint extraction. Since this is the only such sentence in the data, when it is present in the test set during cross-validation, the joint method never gets a chance to learn not to make these mistakes. The drop occurs in only that one fold and hence the overall drop is not found as statistically significant despite being relatively large.

take are known, we believe that filtering out the incoherent relation predictions of their pipeline model can improve its precision without hurting the recall. On the other hand our pipelined approach never outputs incoherent relations because the grammar of relation productions enforce that the relations are always between entities of the required types. Thus the improvement obtained by our joint extraction method over our pipelined approach is always non-trivial.

5 Related Work

To our knowledge, Roth & Yih (2004; 2007) have done the only other work on joint entity and relation extraction. Their method employs independent entity and relation classifiers whose outputs are used to compute a most probable consistent global set of entities and relations using linear programming. One key advantage of our card-pyramid method over their method is that the classifiers can take the output of other classifiers under its node as input features during parsing. This is not possible in their approach because all classifier outputs are determined before they are passed to the linear program solver. Thus our approach is more integrated and allows greater interaction between dependent extraction decisions.

Miller et al. (2000) adapt a probabilistic context-free parser for information extraction by augmenting syntactic labels with entity and relation labels. They thus do a joint syntactic parsing and information extraction using a fixed template. However, as designed, such a CFG approach cannot handle the cases when an entity is involved in multiple relations and when the relations criss-cross each other in the sentence, as in Figure 1. These cases occur frequently in the dataset we used in our experiments and many other relation-extraction tasks.

Giuliano et al. (2007) thoroughly evaluate the effect of entity extraction on relation extraction using the dataset used in our experiments. However, they employ a pipeline architecture and did not investigate joint relation and entity extraction. Carlson et al. (2009) present a method to simultaneously do semi-supervised training of entity and relation classifiers. However, their coupling method is meant to take advantage of the available unsupervised data and does not do joint inference.

Riedel et al. (2009) present an approach for extracting bio-molecular events and their arguments using Markov Logic. Such an approach could also be adapted for jointly extracting entities and their relations, however, this would restrict entity and relation extraction to the same machine learning method that is used with Markov Logic. For example, one would not be able to use kernel-based SVM for relation extraction, which has been very successful at this task, because Markov Logic does not support kernel-based machine learning. In contrast, our joint approach is independent of the individual machine learning methods for entity and relation extraction, and hence allows use of the best machine learning methods available for each of them.

6 Future Work

There are several possible directions for extending the current approach. The card-pyramid structure could be used to perform other language-processing tasks jointly with entity and relation extraction. For example, co-reference resolution between two entities within a sentence can be easily incorporated in card-pyramid parsing by introducing a production like $coref \rightarrow Person\ Person$, indicating that the two person entities are the same.

In this work, and in most previous work, relations are always considered between two entities. However, there could be relations between more than two entities. In that case, it should be possible to binarize those relations and then use card-pyramid parsing. If the relations are between relations instead of between entities, then card-pyramid parsing can handle it by considering the labels of the immediate children as RHS non-terminals instead of the labels of the left-most and the right-most leaves beneath it. Thus, it would be interesting to apply card-pyramid parsing to extract higher-order relations (such as causal or temporal relations).

Given the regular graph structure of the card-pyramid, it would be interesting to investigate whether it can be modeled using a probabilistic graphical model (Koller and Friedman, 2009). In that case, instead of using multiple probabilistic classifiers, one could employ a single jointly-trained probabilistic model, which is theoretically more appealing and might give better results.

Finally, we note that a better relation classifier could be used in the current approach which makes more use of linguistic information. For example, by using dependency-based kernels (Bunescu and Mooney, 2005a; Kate, 2008) or syntactic kernels (Qian et al., 2008; Moschitti, 2009) or by including the word categories and their POS tags in the subsequences. Also, it will be interesting to see if a kernel that computes the similarity between sub-card-pyramids could be developed and used for relation classification.

7 Conclusions

We introduced a card-pyramid graph structure and presented a new method for jointly extracting entities and their relations from a sentence using it. A card-pyramid compactly encodes the entities and relations in a sentence thus reducing the joint extraction task to jointly labeling its nodes. We presented an efficient parsing algorithm for jointly labeling a card-pyramid using dynamic programming and beam search. The experiments demonstrated the benefit of our joint extraction method over a pipelined approach.

Acknowledgments

This research was funded by Air Force Contract FA8750-09-C-0172 under the DARPA Machine Reading Program.

References

Razvan C. Bunescu and Raymond J. Mooney. 2005a. A shortest path dependency kernel for relation extraction. In *Proc. of the Human Language Technology Conf. and Conf. on Empirical Methods in Natural Language Processing (HLT/EMNLP-05)*, pages 724–731, Vancouver, BC, October.

Razvan C. Bunescu and Raymond J. Mooney. 2005b. Subsequence kernels for relation extraction. In Y. Weiss, B. Schölkopf, and J. Platt, editors, *Advances in Neural Information Processing Systems 18*, Vancouver, BC.

Razvan Bunescu, Ruifang Ge, Rohit J. Kate, Edward M. Marcotte, Raymond J. Mooney, Arun Kumar Ramani, and Yuk Wah Wong. 2005. Comparative experiments on learning information extractors for proteins and their interactions. *Artificial Intelligence in Medicine (special issue on Summarization and Information Extraction from Medical Documents)*, 33(2):139–155.

Andrew Carlson, Justin Betteridge, Estevam R. Hruschka, and Tom M. Mitchell. 2009. Coupling semi-supervised learning of categories and relations. In *SemiSupLearn '09: Proceedings of the NAACL HLT 2009 Workshop on Semi-Supervised Learning for Natural Language Processing*, pages 1–9, Boulder, Colorado.

Michael Collins. 2002. Ranking algorithms for named-entity extraction: Boosting and the voted perceptron. In *Proc. of the 40th Annual Meeting of the Association for Computational Linguistics (ACL-2002)*, pages 489–496, Philadelphia, PA.

Nello Cristianini and John Shawe-Taylor. 2000. *An Introduction to Support Vector Machines and Other Kernel-based Learning Methods*. Cambridge University Press.

Claudio Giuliano, Alberto Lavelli, and Lorenza Romano. 2007. Relation extraction and the influence of automatic named-entity recognition. *ACM Trans. Speech Lang. Process.*, 5(1):1–26.

D. Jurafsky and J. H. Martin. 2008. *Speech and Language Processing: An Introduction to Natural Lan guage Processing, Computational Linguistics, and Speech Recognition*. Prentice Hall, Upper Saddle River, NJ.

Rohit J. Kate and Raymond J. Mooney. 2006. Using string-kernels for learning semantic parsers. In *Proc. of the 21st Intl. Conf. on Computational Linguistics and 44th Annual Meeting of the Association for Computational Linguistics (COLING/ACL-06)*, pages 913–920, Sydney, Australia, July.

Rohit J. Kate. 2008. A dependency-based word subsequence kernel. In *Proceedings of the Conference on Empirical Methods in Natural Language Processing (EMNLP 2008)*, pages 400–409, Waikiki,Honolulu,Hawaii, October.

Daphne Koller and Nir Friedman. 2009. *Probabilistic Graphical Models: Principles and Techniques*. The MIT Press, Cambridge, MA.

Huma Lodhi, Craig Saunders, John Shawe-Taylor, Nello Cristianini, and Chris Watkins. 2002. Text classification using string kernels. *Journal of Machine Learning Research*, 2:419–444.

Scott Miller, Heidi Fox, Lance A. Ramshaw, and Ralph M. Weischedel. 2000. A novel use of statistical parsing to extract information from text. In *Proc. of the Meeting of the N. American Association for Computational Linguistics*, pages 226–233, Seattle, Washington.

Alessandro Moschitti. 2009. Syntactic and semantic kernels for short text pair categorization. In *Proceedings of the 12th Conference of the European Chapter of the ACL (EACL 2009)*, pages 576–584, Athens,Greece, March.

John C. Platt. 1999. Probabilistic outputs for support vector machines and comparisons to regularized likelihood methods. In Alexander J. Smola, Peter Bartlett, Bernhard Schölkopf, and Dale Schuurmans, editors, *Advances in Large Margin Classifiers*, pages 185–208. MIT Press.

Vasin Punyakanok and Dan Roth. 2001. The use of classifiers in sequential inference. In *Advances in Neural Information Processing Systems 13*.

Longhua Qian, Guodong Zhou, Fang Kong, Qiaoming Zhu, and Peide Qian. 2008. Exploiting constituent dependencies for tree kernel-based semantic relation extraction. In *Proceedings of the 22nd International Conference on Computational Linguistics (Coling 2008)*, pages 697–704, Manchester, UK, August.

Sebastian Riedel, Hong-Woo Chun, Toshihisa Takagi, and Jun'ichi Tsujii. 2009. A Markov logic approach to bio-molecular event extraction. In *Proceedings of the BioNLP 2009 Workshop Companion Volume for Shared Task*, pages 41–49, Boulder, Colorado, June. Association for Computational Linguistics.

D. Roth and W. Yih. 2004. A linear programming formulation for global inference in natural language tasks. In *Proc. of 8th Conf. on Computational Natural Language Learning (CoNLL-2004)*, pages 1–8, Boston, MA.

D. Roth and W. Yih. 2007. Global inference for entity and relation identification via a linear programming formulation. In L. Getoor and B. Taskar, editors, *Introduction to Statistical Relational Learning*, pages 553–580. The MIT Press, Cambridge, MA.

Erik F. Tjong Kim Sang and Fien De Meulder. 2003. Introduction to the CoNLL-2003 shared task: Language-independent named entity recognition. In *Proc. of 7th Conf. on Computational Natural Language Learning (CoNLL-2003)*, Edmonton, Canada.

Erik F. Tjong Kim Sang. 2002. Introduction to the CoNLL-2002 shared task: Language-independent named entity recognition. In *Proceedings of CoNLL-2002*, pages 155–158. Taipei, Taiwan.

Min Zhang, Jie Zhang, Jian Su, and Guodong Zhou. 2006. A composite kernel to extract relations between entities with both flat and structured features. In *Proc. of the 21st Intl. Conf. on Computational Linguistics and 44th Annual Meeting of the Association for Computational Linguistics (COLING/ACL-06)*, Sydney, Australia, July.

Distributed Asynchronous Online Learning for Natural Language Processing

Kevin Gimpel Dipanjan Das Noah A. Smith
Language Technologies Institute
Carnegie Mellon Univeristy
Pittsburgh, PA 15213, USA
{kgimpel,dipanjan,nasmith}@cs.cmu.edu

Abstract

Recent speed-ups for training large-scale models like those found in statistical NLP exploit distributed computing (either on multicore or "cloud" architectures) and rapidly converging online learning algorithms. Here we aim to combine the two. We focus on distributed, "mini-batch" learners that make frequent updates *asynchronously* (Nedic et al., 2001; Langford et al., 2009). We generalize existing asynchronous algorithms and experiment extensively with structured prediction problems from NLP, including discriminative, unsupervised, and non-convex learning scenarios. Our results show asynchronous learning can provide substantial speedups compared to distributed and single-processor mini-batch algorithms with no signs of error arising from the approximate nature of the technique.

1 Introduction

Modern statistical NLP models are notoriously expensive to train, requiring the use of general-purpose or specialized numerical optimization algorithms (e.g., gradient and coordinate ascent algorithms and variations on them like L-BFGS and EM) that iterate over training data many times. Two developments have led to major improvements in training time for NLP models:

- **online** learning algorithms (LeCun et al., 1998; Crammer and Singer, 2003; Liang and Klein, 2009), which update the parameters of a model more frequently, processing only one or a small number of training examples, called a "mini-batch," between updates; and
- **distributed** computing, which divides training data among multiple CPUs for faster processing between updates (e.g., Clark and Curran, 2004).

Online algorithms offer fast convergence rates and scalability to large datasets, but distributed computing is a more natural fit for algorithms that require a lot of computation—e.g., processing a large batch of training examples—to be done between updates. Typically, distributed *online* learning has been done in a **synchronous** setting, meaning that a mini-batch of data is divided among multiple CPUs, and the model is updated when they have all completed processing (Finkel et al., 2008). Each mini-batch is processed only after the previous one has completed.

Synchronous frameworks are appealing in that they simulate the same algorithms that work on a single processor, but they have the drawback that the benefits of parallelism are only obtainable within one mini-batch iteration. Moreover, empirical evaluations suggest that online methods only converge faster than batch algorithms when using very small mini-batches (Liang and Klein, 2009). In this case, synchronous parallelization will not offer much benefit.

In this paper, we focus our attention on **asynchronous** algorithms that generalize those presented by Nedic et al. (2001) and Langford et al. (2009). In these algorithms, multiple mini-batches are processed simultaneously, each using potentially different and typically stale parameters. The key advantage of an asynchronous framework is that it allows processors to remain in near-constant use, preventing them from wasting cycles waiting for other processors to complete their portion of the current mini-batch. In this way, asynchronous algorithms allow more frequent parameter updates, which speeds convergence.

Our contributions are as follows:

- We describe a framework for distributed asynchronous optimization (§5) similar to those described by Nedic et al. (2001) and Langford et al. (2009), but permitting mini-batch learning. The prior work contains convergence results for asynchronous online stochastic gradient descent

Proceedings of the Fourteenth Conference on Computational Natural Language Learning, pages 213–222,
Uppsala, Sweden, 15-16 July 2010.

for convex functions (discussed in brief in §5.2).

- We report experiments on three structured NLP tasks, including one problem that matches the conditions for convergence (named entity recognition; NER) and two that depart from theoretical foundations, namely the use of asynchronous stepwise EM (Sato and Ishii, 2000; Cappé and Moulines, 2009; Liang and Klein, 2009) for both convex and non-convex optimization.
- We directly compare asynchronous algorithms with multiprocessor synchronous mini-batch algorithms (e.g., Finkel et al., 2008) and traditional batch algorithms.
- We experiment with adding artificial delays to simulate the effects of network or hardware traffic that could cause updates to be made with extremely stale parameters.
- Our experimental settings include both individual 4-processor machines as well as large clusters of commodity machines implementing the MapReduce programming model (Dean and Ghemawat, 2004). We also explore effects of mini-batch size.

Our main conclusion is that, when small mini-batches work well, asynchronous algorithms offer substantial speed-ups without introducing error. When large mini-batches work best, asynchronous learning does not hurt.

2 Optimization Setting

We consider the problem of optimizing a function $f : \mathbb{R}^d \rightarrow \mathbb{R}$ with respect to its argument, denoted $\boldsymbol{\theta} = \langle \theta_1, \theta_2, \ldots, \theta_d \rangle$. We assume that f is a sum of n convex functions (hence f is also convex):[1]

$$f(\boldsymbol{\theta}) = \textstyle\sum_{i=1}^{n} f_i(\boldsymbol{\theta}) \tag{1}$$

We initially focus our attention on functions that can be optimized using gradient or subgradient methods. Log-likelihood for a probabilistic model with fully observed training data (e.g., conditional random fields; Lafferty et al., 2001) is one example that frequently arises in NLP, where the $f_i(\boldsymbol{\theta})$ each correspond to an individual training example and the $\boldsymbol{\theta}$ are log-linear feature weights. Another example is large-margin learning for structured prediction (Taskar et al., 2005; Tsochantaridis et al., 2005), which can be solved by subgradient methods (Ratliff et al., 2006).

For concreteness, we discuss the architecture in terms of gradient-based optimization, using the following gradient descent update rule (for minimization problems):[2]

$$\boldsymbol{\theta}^{(t+1)} \leftarrow \boldsymbol{\theta}^{(t)} - \eta^{(t)} \boldsymbol{g}(\boldsymbol{\theta}^{(t)}) \tag{2}$$

where $\boldsymbol{\theta}^{(t)}$ is the parameter vector on the tth iteration, $\eta^{(t)}$ is the step size on the tth iteration, and $\boldsymbol{g} : \mathbb{R}^d \rightarrow \mathbb{R}^d$ is the vector function of first derivatives of f with respect to $\boldsymbol{\theta}$:

$$\boldsymbol{g}(\boldsymbol{\theta}) = \left\langle \frac{\partial f}{\partial \theta_1}(\boldsymbol{\theta}), \frac{\partial f}{\partial \theta_2}(\boldsymbol{\theta}), \ldots, \frac{\partial f}{\partial \theta_d}(\boldsymbol{\theta}) \right\rangle \tag{3}$$

We are interested in optimizing such functions using distributed computing, by which we mean to include any system containing multiple processors that can communicate in order to perform a single task. The set of processors can range from two cores on a single machine to a MapReduce cluster of thousands of machines.

Note our assumption that the computation required to optimize f with respect to $\boldsymbol{\theta}$ is, essentially, the gradient vector $\boldsymbol{g}(\boldsymbol{\theta}^{(t)})$, which serves as the descent direction. The key to distributing this computation is the fact that $\boldsymbol{g}(\boldsymbol{\theta}^{(t)}) = \sum_{i=1}^{n} \boldsymbol{g}_i(\boldsymbol{\theta}^{(t)})$, where $\boldsymbol{g}_i(\boldsymbol{\theta})$ denotes the gradient of $f_i(\boldsymbol{\theta})$ with respect to $\boldsymbol{\theta}$. We now discuss several ways to go about distributing such a problem, culminating in the asynchronous mini-batch setting.

3 Distributed Batch Optimization

Given p processors plus a master processor, the most straightforward way to optimize f is to partition the f_i so that for each $i \in \{1, 2, \ldots, n\}$, $\boldsymbol{g}_i$ is computed on exactly one "slave" processor. Let I_j denote the subset of examples assigned to the jth slave processor ($\bigcup_{j=1}^{p} I_j = \{1, \ldots, n\}$ and $j \neq j' \Rightarrow I_j \cap I_{j'} = \emptyset$). Processor j receives the examples in I_j along with the necessary portions of $\boldsymbol{\theta}^{(t)}$ for calculating $\boldsymbol{g}_{I_j}(\boldsymbol{\theta}^{(t)}) = \sum_{i \in I_j} \boldsymbol{g}_i(\boldsymbol{\theta}^{(t)})$. The result of this calculation is returned to the master processor, which calculates $\boldsymbol{g}(\boldsymbol{\theta}^{(t)}) = \sum_j \boldsymbol{g}_{I_j}(\boldsymbol{\theta}^{(t)})$ and executes Eq. 2 (or something more sophisticated that uses the same information) to obtain a new parameter vector.

It is natural to divide the data so that each processor is assigned approximately n/p of the training examples. Because of variance in the expense

[1]We use "convex" to mean convex-up when minimizing and convex-down, or concave, when maximizing.

[2]We use the term "gradient" for simplicity, but subgradients are sufficient throughout.

of calculating the different $\boldsymbol{g}_i$, and because of unpredictable variation among different processors' speed (e.g., variation among nodes in a cluster, or in demands made by other users), there can be variation in the observed runtime of different processors on their respective subsamples. Each iteration of calculating $\boldsymbol{g}$ will take as long as the *longest-running* among the processors, whatever the cause of that processor's slowness. In computing environments where the load on processors is beyond the control of the NLP researcher, this can be a major bottleneck.

Nonetheless, this simple approach is widely used in practice; approaches in which the gradient computation is distributed via MapReduce have recently been described in machine learning and NLP (Chu et al., 2006; Dyer et al., 2008; Wolfe et al., 2008). Mann et al. (2009) compare this framework to one in which each processor maintains a *separate* parameter vector which is updated independently of the others. At the end of learning, the parameter vectors are averaged or a vote is taken during prediction. A similar parameter-averaging approach was taken by Chiang et al. (2008) when parallelizing MIRA (Crammer et al., 2006). In this paper, we restrict our attention to distributed frameworks which maintain and update a single copy of the parameters $\boldsymbol{\theta}$. The use of multiple parameter vectors is essentially orthogonal to the framework we discuss here and we leave the integration of the two ideas for future exploration.

4 Distributed Synchronous Mini-Batch Optimization

Distributed computing can speed up batch algorithms, but we would like to transfer the well-known speed-ups offered by online and mini-batch algorithms to the distributed setting as well. The simplest way to implement mini-batch stochastic gradient descent (SGD) in a distributed computing environment is to divide each *mini-batch* (rather than the entire batch) among the processors that are available and to update the parameters once the gradient from the mini-batch has been computed. Finkel et al. (2008) used this approach to speed up training of a log-linear model for parsing. The interaction between the master processor and the distributed computing environment is nearly identical to the distributed batch optimization scenario. Where $M^{(t)}$ is the set of indices in the mini-batch processed on iteration t, the update is:

$$\boldsymbol{\theta}^{(t+1)} \leftarrow \boldsymbol{\theta}^{(t)} - \eta^{(t)} \textstyle\sum_{i \in M^{(t)}} \boldsymbol{g}_i(\boldsymbol{\theta}^{(t)}) \quad (4)$$

The distributed synchronous framework can provide speed-ups over a single-processor implementation of SGD, but inevitably some processors will end up waiting for others to finish processing. This is the same bottleneck faced by the batch version in §3. While the time for each mini-batch is shorter than the time for a full batch, mini-batch algorithms make far more updates and some processor cycles will be wasted in computing each one. Also, more mini-batches imply that more time will be lost due to per-mini-batch overhead (e.g., waiting for synchronization locks in shared-memory systems, or sending data and $\boldsymbol{\theta}$ to the processors in systems without shared memory).

5 Distributed Asynchronous Mini-Batch Optimization

An *asynchronous* framework may use multiple processors more efficiently and minimize idle time (Nedic et al., 2001; Langford et al., 2009). In this setting, the master sends $\boldsymbol{\theta}$ and a mini-batch M_k to each slave k. Once slave k finishes processing its mini-batch and returns $\boldsymbol{g}_{M_k}(\boldsymbol{\theta})$, the master immediately updates $\boldsymbol{\theta}$ and sends a new mini-batch and the new $\boldsymbol{\theta}$ to the now-available slave k. As a result, slaves stay occupied and never need to wait on others to finish. However, nearly all gradient components are computed using slightly stale parameters that do not take into account the most recent updates. Nedic et al. (2001) proved that convergence is still guaranteed under certain conditions, and Langford et al. (2009) obtained convergence rate results. We describe these results in more detail in §5.2.

The update takes the following form:

$$\boldsymbol{\theta}^{(t+1)} \leftarrow \boldsymbol{\theta}^{(t)} - \eta^{(t)} \textstyle\sum_{i \in M^{(\tau(t))}} \boldsymbol{g}_i(\boldsymbol{\theta}^{(\tau(t))}) \quad (5)$$

where $\tau(t) \leq t$ is the start time of the mini-batch used for the tth update. Since we started processing the mini-batch at time $\tau(t)$ (using parameters $\boldsymbol{\theta}^{(\tau(t))}$), we denote the mini-batch $M^{(\tau(t))}$. If $\tau(t) = t$, then Eq. 5 is identical to Eq. 4. That is, $t - \tau(t)$ captures the "staleness" of the parameters used to compute the gradient for the tth update.

Asynchronous frameworks do introduce error into the training procedure, but it is frequently the case in NLP problems that only a small fraction of parameters is needed for each mini-batch

Input: number of examples n, mini-batch size m, random seed r

```
θ_ℓ ← θ;
seedRandomNumberGenerator (r);
while converged (θ) = false do
    g ← 0;
    for j ← 1 to m do
        k ~ Uniform({1, ..., n});
        g ← g + g_k(θ_ℓ);
    end
    acquireLock (θ);
    θ ← updateParams (θ, g);
    θ_ℓ ← θ;
    releaseLock (θ);
end
```

Algorithm 1: Procedure followed by each thread for multi-core asynchronous mini-batch optimization. $\boldsymbol{\theta}$ is the single copy of the parameters shared by all threads. The convergence criterion is left unspecified here.

of training examples. For example, for simple word alignment models like IBM Model 1 (Brown et al., 1993), only parameters corresponding to words appearing in the particular subsample of sentence pairs are needed. The error introduced when making asynchronous updates should intuitively be less severe in these cases, where different mini-batches use small and mostly non-overlapping subsets of $\boldsymbol{\theta}$.

5.1 Implementation

The algorithm sketched above is general enough to be suitable for any distributed system, but when using a system with shared memory (e.g., a single multiprocessor machine) a more efficient implementation is possible. In particular, we can avoid the master/slave architecture and simply start p threads that each compute and execute updates independently, with a synchronization lock on $\boldsymbol{\theta}$. In our single-machine experiments below, we use Algorithm 1 for each thread. A different random seed (r) is passed to each thread so that they do not all process the same sequence of examples. At completion, the result is contained in $\boldsymbol{\theta}$.

5.2 Convergence Results

We now briefly summarize convergence results from Nedic et al. (2001) and Langford et al. (2009), which rely on the following assumptions: (i) The function f is convex. (ii) The gradients $\boldsymbol{g}_i$ are bounded, i.e., there exists $C > 0$ such that $\|\boldsymbol{g}_i(\boldsymbol{\theta}^{(t)})\| \leq C$. (iii) $\exists$ (unknown) $D > 0$ such that $t - \tau(t) < D$. (iv) The stepsizes $\eta^{(t)}$ satisfy certain standard conditions.

In addition, Nedic et al. require that all function components are used with the same asymptotic frequency (as $t \rightarrow \infty$). Their results are strongest when choosing function components in each mini-batch using a "cyclic" rule: select function f_i for the kth time only after all functions have been selected $k - 1$ times. For a fixed step size η, the sequence of function values $f(\boldsymbol{\theta}^{(t)})$ converges to a region of the optimum that depends on η, the maximum norm of any gradient vector, and the maximum delay for any mini-batch. For a decreasing step size, convergence is guaranteed to the optimum. When choosing components uniformly at random, convergence to the optimum is again guaranteed using a decreasing step size formula, but with slightly more stringent conditions on the step size.

Langford et al. (2009) present convergence rates via regret bounds, which are linear in D. The convergence rate of asynchronous stochastic gradient descent is $O(\sqrt{TD})$, where T is the total number of updates made. In addition to the situation in which function components are chosen uniformly at random, Langford et al. provide results for several other scenarios, including the case in which an adversary supplies the training examples in whatever ordering he chooses.

Below we experiment with optimization of both convex and non-convex functions, using fixed step sizes and decreasing step size formulas, and consider several values of D. Even when exploring regions of the experimental space that are not yet supported by theoretical results, asynchronous algorithms perform well empirically in all settings.

5.3 Gradients and Expectation-Maximization

The theory applies when using first-order methods to optimize convex functions. Though the function it is optimizing is not usually convex, the EM algorithm can be understood as a hillclimber that transforms the gradient to keep $\boldsymbol{\theta}$ feasible; it can also be understood as a coordinate ascent algorithm. Either way, the calculations during the E-step resemble $\boldsymbol{g}(\boldsymbol{\theta})$. Several online or mini-batch variants of the EM algorithm have been proposed, for example incremental EM (Neal and Hinton, 1998) and online EM (Sato and Ishii, 2000; Cappé and Moulines, 2009), and we follow Liang and Klein (2009) in referring to this latter algorithm as **stepwise EM**. Our experiments with asynchronous minibatch updates include a case where the log-likelihood f is convex and one where it is not.

	task	data	n	# params.	eval.	method	convex?
§6.1	named entity recognition (CRF; Lafferty et al., 2001)	CoNLL 2003 English (Tjong Kim Sang and De Meulder, 2003)	14,987 sents.	1.3M	F_1	SGD	yes
§6.2	word alignment (Model 1, both directions; Brown et al., 1993)	NAACL 2003 parallel text workshop (Mihalcea and Pedersen, 2003)	300K pairs	14.2M ×2 (E→F + F→E)	AER	EM	yes
S6.3	unsupervised POS (bigram HMM)	Penn Treebank §1–21 (Marcus et al., 1993)	41,825 sents.	2,043,226	(Johnson, 2007)	EM	no

Table 1: Our experiments consider three tasks.

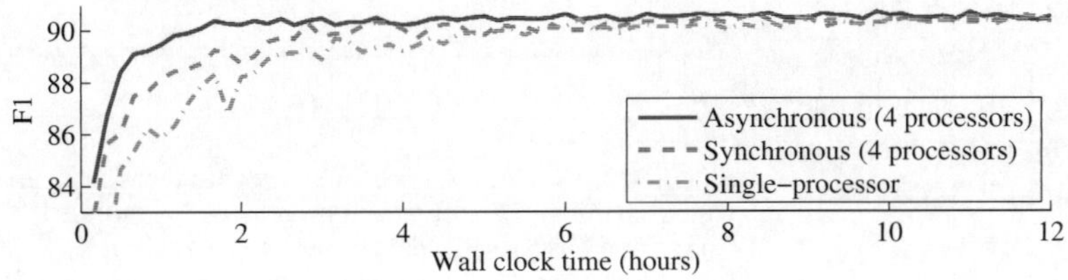

Figure 1: NER: Synchronous mini-batch SGD converges faster in F_1 than the single-processor version, and the asynchronous version converges faster still. All curves use a mini-batch size of 4.

6 Experiments

We performed experiments to measure speed-ups obtainable through distributed online optimization. Since we will be considering different optimization algorithms and computing environments, we will primarily be interested in the wall-clock time required to obtain particular levels of performance on metrics appropriate to each task. We consider three tasks, detailed in Table 1.

For experiments on a single node, we used a 64-bit machine with two 2.6GHz dual-core CPUs (i.e., 4 processors in all) with a total of 8GB of RAM. This was a dedicated machine that was not available for any other jobs. We also conducted experiments using a cluster architecture running Hadoop 0.20 (an implementation of MapReduce), consisting of 400 machines, each having 2 quad-core 1.86GHz CPUs with a total of 6GB of RAM.

6.1 Named Entity Recognition

Our NER CRF used a standard set of features, following Kazama and Torisawa (2007), along with token shape features like those in Collins (2002) and simple gazetteer features; a feature was included if and only it occurred at least once in training data (total 1.3M). We used a diagonal Gaussian prior with a variance of 1.0 for each weight.

We compared SGD on a single processor to distributed synchronous SGD and distributed asynchronous SGD. For all experiments, we used a fixed step size of 0.01 and chose each training example for each mini-batch uniformly at random from the full data set.[3] We report performance by plotting test-set accuracy against wall-time over 12 hours.[4]

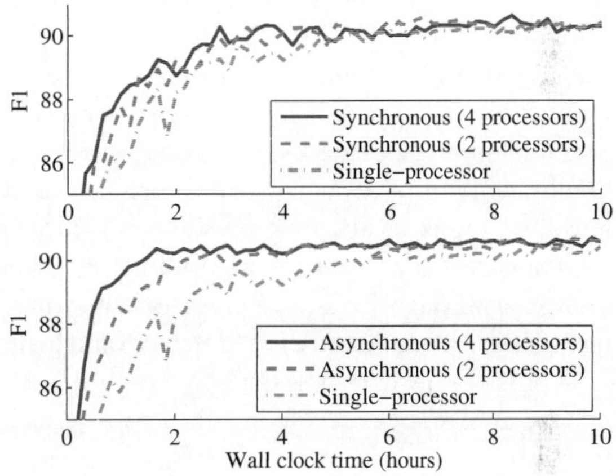

Figure 2: NER: (Top) Synchronous optimization improves very little when moving from 2 to 4 processors due to the need for load-balancing, leaving some processors idle for stretches of time. (Bottom) Asynchronous optimization does not require load balancing and therefore improves when moving from 2 to 4 processors because each processor is in near-constant use. All curves use a mini-batch size of 4 and the "Single-processor" curve is identical in the two plots.

Comparing Synchronous and Asynchronous Algorithms Figure 1 shows our primary result for the NER experiments. When using all four available processors, the asynchronous algorithm converges faster than the other two algorithms. Error due to stale parameters during gradient computation does not appear to cause any more varia-

[3]In preliminary experiments, we experimented with various fixed step sizes and decreasing step size schedules, and found a fixed step size to work best for all settings.

[4]Decoding was performed offline (so as not to affect measurments) with models sampled every ten minutes.

tion in performance than experienced by the synchronous mini-batch algorithm. Note that the distributed synchronous algorithm and the single-processor algorithm make identical sequences of parameter updates; the only difference is the amount of time between each update. Since we save models every ten minutes and not every ith update, the curves have different shapes. The sequence of updates for the asynchronous algorithm, on the other hand, actually depends on the vagaries of the computational environment. Nonetheless, the asynchronous algorithm using 4 processors has nearly converged after only 2 hours, while the single-processor algorithm requires 10–12 hours to reach the same F_1.

Varying the Number of Processors Figure 2 shows the improvement in convergence time by using 4 vs. 2 processors for the synchronous (top) and asynchronous (bottom) algorithms. The additional two processors help the asynchronous algorithm more than the synchronous one. This highlights the key advantage of asynchronous algorithms: it is easier to keep all processors in constant use. Synchronous algorithms might be improved through load-balancing; in our experiments here, we simply assigned m/p examples to each processor, where m is the mini-batch size and p is the number of processors. When $m = p$, as in the 4-processor curve in the upper plot of Figure 2, we assign a single example to each processor; this is optimal in the sense that no other scheduling strategy will process the mini-batch faster. Therefore, the fact that the 2-processor and 4-processor curves are so close suggests that the extra two processors are not being fully exploited, indicating that the optimal load balancing strategy for a small mini-batch still leaves processors under-used due to the synchronous nature of the updates.

The only bottleneck in the asynchronous algorithm is the synchronization lock during updating, required since there is only one copy of $\boldsymbol{\theta}$. For CRFs with a few million weights, the update is typically much faster than processing a mini-batch of examples; furthermore, when using small mini-batches, the update vector is typically sparse.[5] For all experimental results presented thus far, we used a mini-batch size of 4. We experimented with additional mini-batch sizes of 1 and 8, but there was very little difference in the resulting curves.

[5]In a standard implementation, the sparsity of the update will be nullified by regularization, but to improve efficiency in practice the regularization penalty can be accumulated and applied less frequently than every update.

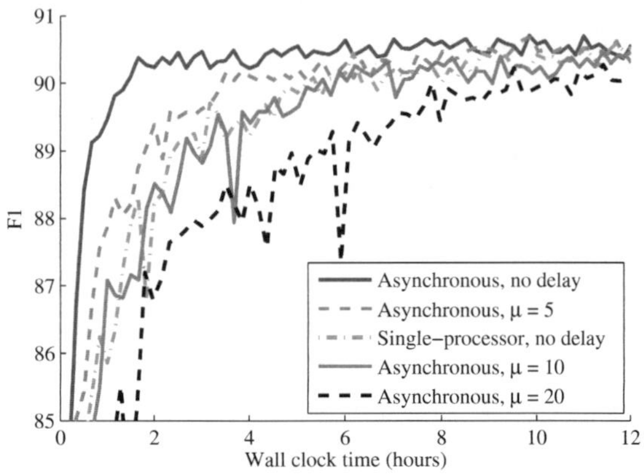

Figure 3: NER: Convergence curves when a delay is incurred with probability 0.25 after each mini-batch is processed. The delay durations (in seconds) are sampled from $\mathcal{N}(\mu, (\mu/5)^2)$, for several means μ. Each mini-batch (size = 4) takes less than a second to process, so if the delay is substantially longer than the time required to process a mini-batch, the single-node version converges faster. While curves with $\mu = 10$ and 20 appear less smooth than the others, they are still heading steadily toward convergence.

Artificial Delays We experimented with adding artificial delays to the algorithm to explore how much overhead would be tolerable before parallelized computation becomes irrelevant. Figure 3 shows results when each processor sleeps with 0.25 probability for a duration of time between computing the gradient on its mini-batch of data and updating the parameters. The delay length is chosen from a normal distribution with the means (in seconds) shown and $\sigma = \mu/5$ (truncated at zero). Since only one quarter of the mini-batches have an artificial delay, increasing μ increases the average parameter "staleness", letting us see how the asynchronous algorithm fares with extremely stale parameters.

The average time required to compute the gradient for a mini-batch of 4 is 0.62 seconds. When the average delay is 1.25 seconds ($\mu = 5$), twice the average time for a mini-batch, the asynchronous algorithm still converges faster than the single-node algorithm. In addition, even with substantial delays of 5–10 times the processing time for a mini-batch, the asynchronous algorithm does not fail but proceeds steadily toward convergence.

The practicality of using the asynchronous algorithm depends on the average duration for a mini-batch and the amount of expected additional overhead. We attempted to run these experiments on

	AER	Time (h:m)
Single machine:		
Asynch. stepwise EM	0.274	1:58
Synch. stepwise EM (4 proc.)	0.274	2:08
Synch. stepwise EM (1 proc.)	0.272	6:57
Batch EM	0.276	2:15
MapReduce:		
Asynch. stepwise EM	0.281	5:41
Synch. stepwise EM	0.273	27:03
Batch EM	0.276	8:35

Table 2: Alignment error rates and wall time after 20 iterations of EM for various settings. See text for details.

a large MapReduce cluster, but the overhead required for each MapReduce job was too large to make this viable (30–60 seconds).

6.2 Word Alignment

We trained IBM Model 1 in both directions. To align test data, we symmetrized both directional Viterbi alignments using the "grow-diag-final" heuristic (Koehn et al., 2003). We evaluated our models using alignment error rate (AER).

Experiments on a Single Machine We followed Liang and Klein (2009) in using synchronous (mini-batch) stepwise EM on a single processor for this task. We used the same learning rate formula ($\eta^{(t)} = (t+2)^{-q}$, with $0.5 < q \leq 1$). We also used asynchronous stepwise EM by using the same update rule, but gathered sufficient statistics on 4 processors of a single machine in parallel, analogous to our asynchronous method from §5. Whenever a processor was done gathering the expected counts for its mini-batch, it updated the sufficient statistics vector and began work on the next mini-batch.

We used the sparse update described by Liang and Klein, which allows each thread to make additive updates to the parameter vector and to separately-maintained normalization constants without needing to renormalize after each update. When probabilities are needed during inference, normalizers are divided out on-the-fly as needed.

We made 10 passes of asynchronous stepwise EM to measure its sensitivity to q and the mini-batch size m, using different values of these hyperparameters ($q \in \{0.5, 0.7, 1.0\}$; $m \in \{5000, 10000, 50000\}$), and selected values that maximized log-likelihood ($q = 0.7$, $m = 10000$).

Experiments on MapReduce We implemented the three techniques in a MapReduce framework. We implemented batch EM on MapReduce by converting each EM iteration into two MapReduce jobs: one for the E-step and one for the M-step.[6] For the E-step, we divided our data into 24 map tasks, and computed expected counts for the source-target parameters at each mapper. Next, we summed up the expected counts in one reduce task. For the M-step, we took the output from the E-step, and in one reduce task, normalized each source-target parameter by the total count for the source word.[7] To gather sufficient statistics for synchronous stepwise EM, we used 6 mappers and one reducer for a mini-batch of size 10000. For the asynchronous version, we ran four parallel asynchronous mini-batches, the sufficient statistics being gathered using MapReduce again for each mini-batch with 6 map tasks and one reducer.

Results Figure 4 shows log-likelihood for the English→French direction during the first 80 minutes of optimization. Similar trends were observed for the French→English direction as well as for convergence in AER. Table 2 shows the AER at the end of 20 iterations of EM for the same settings.[8] It takes around two hours to finish 20 iterations of batch EM on a single machine, while it takes more than 8 hours to do so on MapReduce. This is because of the extra overhead of transferring $\boldsymbol{\theta}$ from a master gateway machine to mappers, from mappers to reducers, and from reducers back to the master. Synchronous and asynchronous EM suffer as well.

From Figure 4, we see that synchronous and asynchronous stepwise EM converge at the same rate when each is given 4 processors. The main difference between this task and NER is the size of the mini-batch used, so we experimented with several values for the mini-batch size m. Figure 5 shows the results. As m decreases, a larger fraction of time is spent updating parameters; this slows observed convergence time even when using the sparse update rule. It can be seen that, though synchronous and asynchronous stepwise EM converge at the same rate with a large mini-batch size ($m = 10000$), asynchronous stepwise

[6] The M-step could have been performed without MapReduce by storing all the parameters in memory, but memory restrictions on the gateway node of our cluster prevented this.

[7] For the reducer in the M-step, the source served as the key, and the target appended by the parameter's expected count served as the value.

[8] Note that for wall time comparison, we sample models every five minutes. The time taken to write these models ranges from 30 seconds to a minute, thus artificially elongating the total time for all iterations.

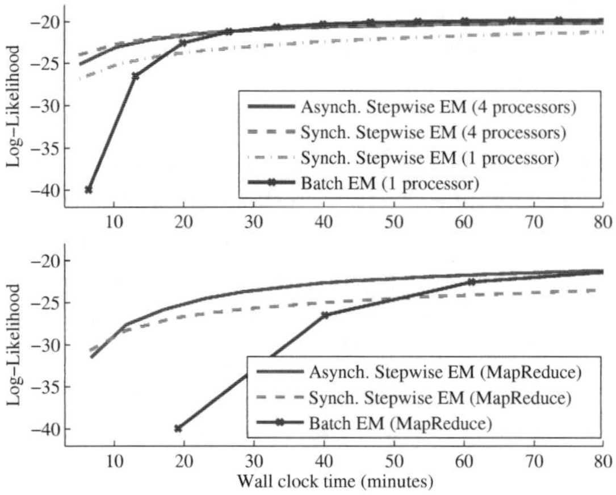

Figure 4: English→French log-likelihood vs. wall clock time in minutes on both a single machine (top) and on a large MapReduce cluster (bottom), shown on separate plots for clarity, though axis scales are identical. We show runs of each setting for the first 80 minutes, although EM was run for 20 passes through the data in all cases (Table 2). Fastest convergence is obtained by synchronous and asynchronous stepwise EM using 4 processors on a single node. While the algorithms converge more slowly on MapReduce due to overhead, the asynchronous algorithm converges the fastest. We observed similar trends for the French→English direction.

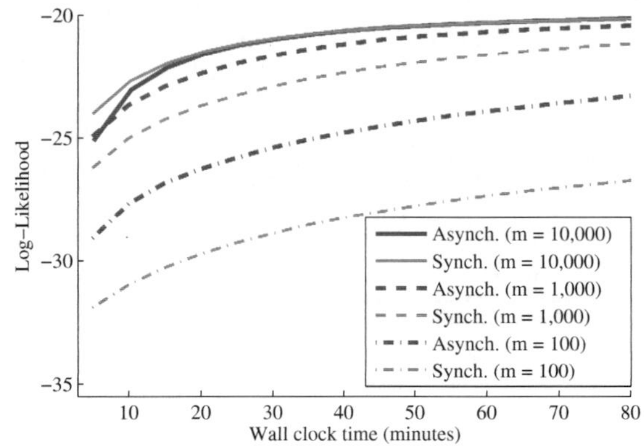

Figure 5: English→French log-likelihood vs. wall clock time in minutes for stepwise EM with 4 processors for various mini-batch sizes (m). The benefits of asynchronous updating increase as m decreases.

EM converges faster as m decreases. With large mini-batches, load-balancing becomes less important as there will be less variation in per-mini-batch observed runtime. These results suggest that asynchronous mini-batch algorithms will be most useful for learning problems in which small mini-batches work best. Fortunately, however, we do not see any problems stemming from approximation errors due to the use of asynchronous updates.

6.3 Unsupervised POS Tagging

Our unsupervised POS experiments use the same task and approach of Liang and Klein (2009) and so we fix hyperparameters for stepwise EM based on their findings (learning rate $\eta^{(t)} = (t+2)^{-0.7}$). The asynchronous algorithm uses the same learning rate formula as the single-processor algorithm. There is only a single t that is maintained and gets incremented whenever any thread updates the parameters. Liang and Klein used a mini-batch size of 3, but we instead use a mini-batch size of 4 to better suit our 4-processor synchronous and asynchronous architectures.

Like NER, we present results for unsupervised tagging experiments on a single machine only, i.e., not using a MapReduce cluster. For tasks like POS tagging that have been shown to work best with small mini-batches (Liang and Klein, 2009), we did not conduct experiments with MapReduce due to high overhead per mini-batch.

For initialization, we followed Liang and Klein by initializing each parameter as $\theta_i \propto e^{1+a_i}$, $a_i \sim \mathrm{Uniform}([0,1])$. We generated 5 random models using this procedure and used each to initialize each algorithm. We additionally used 2 random seeds for choosing the ordering of examples,[9] resulting in a total of 10 runs for each algorithm. We ran each for six hours, saving models every five minutes. After training completed, using each model we decoded the entire training data using posterior decoding and computed the log-likelihood. The results for 5 initial models and two example orderings are shown in Figure 6. We evaluated tagging performance using many-to-1 accuracy, which is obtained by mapping the HMM states to gold standard POS tags so as to maximize accuracy, where multiple states can be mapped to the same tag. This is the metric used by Liang and Klein (2009) and Johnson (2007), who report figures comparable to ours. The asynchronous algorithm converges much faster than the single-node algorithm, allowing a tagger to be trained from the Penn Treebank in less than two hours using a single machine. Furthermore, the 4-processor synchronous algorithm improves only marginally

[9] We ensured that the examples processed in the sequence of mini-batches were identical for the 1-processor and 4-processor versions of synchronous stepwise EM, but the asynchronous algorithm requires a different seed for each processor and, furthermore, the actual order of examples processed depends on wall times and cannot be controlled for. Nonetheless, we paired a distinct set of seeds for the asynchronous algorithm with each of the two seeds used for the synchronous algorithms.

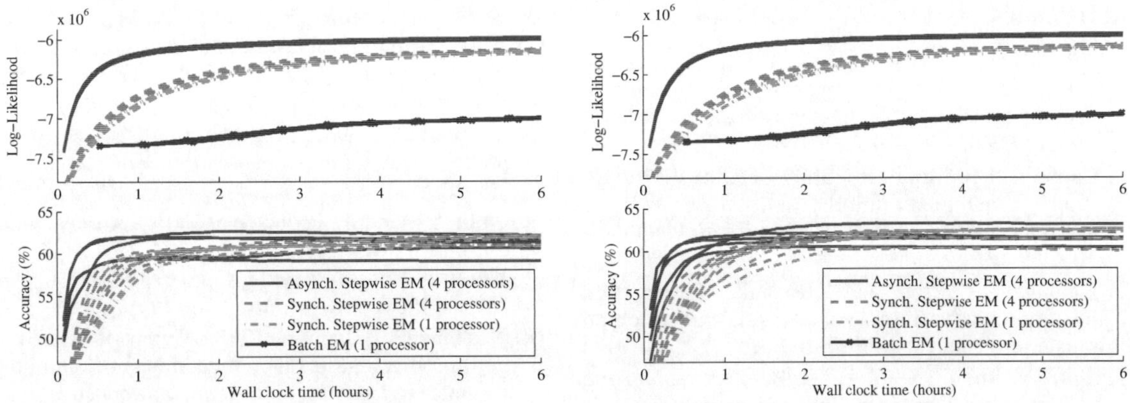

Figure 6: POS: Asynchronous stepwise EM converges faster in log-likelihood and accuracy than the synchronous versions. Curves are shown for each of 5 random initial models. One example ordering random seed is shown on the left, another on the right. The accuracy curves for batch EM do not appear because the highest accuracy reached is only 40.7% after six hours.

over the 1-processor baseline.

The accuracy of the asynchronous curves often decreases slightly after peaking. We can surmise from the log-likelihood plot that the drop in accuracy is not due to the optimization being led astray, but probably rather due to the complex relationship between likelihood and task-specific evaluation metrics in unsupervised learning (Merialdo, 1994). In fact, when we examined the results of synchronous stepwise EM between 6 and 12 hours of execution, we found similar drops in accuracy as likelihood continued to improve. From Figure 6, we conclude that the asynchronous algorithm has no harmful effect on learned model's accuracy beyond the choice to optimize log-likelihood.

While there are currently no theoretical convergence results for asynchronous optimization algorithms for non-convex functions, our results are encouraging for the prospects of establishing convergence results for this setting.

7 Discussion

Our best results were obtained by exploiting multiple processors on a single machine, while experiments using a MapReduce cluster were plagued by communication and framework overhead.

Since Moore's Law predicts a continual increase in the number of cores available on a single machine but not necessarily an increase in the speed of those cores, we believe that algorithms that can effectively exploit multiple processors on a single machine will be increasingly useful. Even today, applications in NLP involving rich-feature structured prediction, such as parsing and translation, typically use a large portion of memory for storing pre-computed data structures, such as lexicons, feature name mappings, and feature caches. Frequently these are large enough to prevent the multiple cores on a single machine from being used for multiple experiments, leaving some processors unused. However, using multiple threads in a single program allows these large data structures to be shared and allows the threads to make use of the additional processors.

We found the overhead incurred by the MapReduce programming model, as implemented in Hadoop 0.20, to be substantial. Nonetheless, we found that asynchronously running multiple MapReduce calls at the same time, rather than pooling all processors into a single MapReduce call, improves observed convergence with negligible effects on performance.

8 Conclusion

We have presented experiments using an asynchronous framework for distributed mini-batch optimization that show comparable performance of trained models in significantly less time than traditional techniques. Such algorithms keep processors in constant use and relieve the programmer from having to implement load-balancing schemes for each new problem encountered. We expect asynchronous learning algorithms to be broadly applicable to training NLP models.

Acknowledgments The authors thank Qin Gao, Garth Gibson, André Martins, Brendan O'Connor, Stephan Vogel, and the reviewers for insightful comments. This work was supported by awards from IBM, Google, computing resources from Yahoo, and NSF grants 0836431 and 0844507.

References

P. F. Brown, V. J. Della Pietra, S. A. Della Pietra, and R. L. Mercer. 1993. The mathematics of statistical machine translation: parameter estimation. *Computational Linguistics*, 19(2):263–311.

O. Cappé and E. Moulines. 2009. Online EM algorithm for latent data models. *Journal of the Royal Statistics Society: Series B (Statistical Methodology)*, 71.

D. Chiang, Y. Marton, and P. Resnik. 2008. Online large-margin training of syntactic and structural translation features. In *Proc. of EMNLP*.

C. Chu, S. Kim, Y. Lin, Y. Yu, G. Bradski, A. Ng, and K. Olukotun. 2006. Map-Reduce for machine learning on multicore. In *NIPS*.

S. Clark and J.R. Curran. 2004. Log-linear models for wide-coverage CCG parsing. In *Proc. of EMNLP*.

M. Collins. 2002. Ranking algorithms for named-entity extraction: Boosting and the voted perceptron. In *Proc. of ACL*.

K. Crammer and Y. Singer. 2003. Ultraconservative online algorithms for multiclass problems. *Journal of Machine Learning Research*, 3:951–991.

K. Crammer, O. Dekel, J. Keshet, S. Shalev-Shwartz, and Y. Singer. 2006. Online passive-aggressive algorithms. *Journal of Machine Learning Research*, 7:551–585.

J. Dean and S. Ghemawat. 2004. MapReduce: Simplified data processing on large clusters. In *Sixth Symposium on Operating System Design and Implementation*.

C. Dyer, A. Cordova, A. Mont, and J. Lin. 2008. Fast, easy, and cheap: Construction of statistical machine translation models with MapReduce. In *Proc. of the Third Workshop on Statistical Machine Translation*.

J. R. Finkel, A. Kleeman, and C. D. Manning. 2008. Efficient, feature-based, conditional random field parsing. In *Proc. of ACL*.

M. Johnson. 2007. Why doesn't EM find good HMM POS-taggers? In *Proc. of EMNLP-CoNLL*.

J. Kazama and K. Torisawa. 2007. A new perceptron algorithm for sequence labeling with non-local features. In *Proc. of EMNLP-CoNLL*.

P. Koehn, F. J. Och, and D. Marcu. 2003. Statistical phrase-based translation. In *Proc. of HLT-NAACL*.

J. Lafferty, A. McCallum, and F. Pereira. 2001. Conditional random fields: Probabilistic models for segmenting and labeling sequence data. In *Proc. of ICML*.

J. Langford, A. J. Smola, and M. Zinkevich. 2009. Slow learners are fast. In *NIPS*.

Y. LeCun, L. Bottou, Y. Bengio, and P. Haffner. 1998. Gradient-based learning applied to document recognition. *Proceedings of the IEEE*, 86(11):2278–2324.

P. Liang and D. Klein. 2009. Online EM for unsupervised models. In *Proc. of NAACL-HLT*.

G. Mann, R. McDonald, M. Mohri, N. Silberman, and D. Walker. 2009. Efficient large-scale distributed training of conditional maximum entropy models. In *NIPS*.

M. P. Marcus, B. Santorini, and M. A. Marcinkiewicz. 1993. Building a large annotated corpus of English: The Penn treebank. *Computational Linguistics*, 19:313–330.

B. Merialdo. 1994. Tagging English text with a probabilistic model. *Computational Linguistics*, 20(2):155–172.

R. Mihalcea and T. Pedersen. 2003. An evaluation exercise for word alignment. In *HLT-NAACL 2003 Workshop: Building and Using Parallel Texts: Data Driven Machine Translation and Beyond*.

R. Neal and G. E. Hinton. 1998. A view of the EM algorithm that justifies incremental, sparse, and other variants. In *Learning in Graphical Models*.

A. Nedic, D. P. Bertsekas, and V. S. Borkar. 2001. Distributed asynchronous incremental subgradient methods. In *Proc. of the March 2000 Haifa Workshop: Inherently Parallel Algorithms in Feasibility and Optimization and Their Applications*.

N. Ratliff, J. Bagnell, and M. Zinkevich. 2006. Subgradient methods for maximum margin structured learning. In *ICML Workshop on Learning in Structured Outputs Spaces*.

M. Sato and S. Ishii. 2000. On-line EM algorithm for the normalized Gaussian network. *Neural Computation*, 12(2).

B. Taskar, V. Chatalbashev, D. Koller, and C. Guestrin. 2005. Learning structured prediction models: A large margin approach. In *Proc. of ICML*.

E. F. Tjong Kim Sang and F. De Meulder. 2003. Introduction to the CoNLL-2003 shared task: Language-independent named entity recognition. In *Proc. of CoNLL*.

I. Tsochantaridis, T. Joachims, T. Hofmann, and Y. Altun. 2005. Large margin methods for structured and interdependent output variables. *Journal of Machine Learning Research*, 6:1453–1484.

J. Wolfe, A. Haghighi, and D. Klein. 2008. Fully distributed EM for very large datasets. In *Proc. of ICML*.

On Reverse Feature Engineering of Syntactic Tree Kernels

Daniele Pighin
FBK-irst, DISI, University of Trento
Via di Sommarive, 14
I-38123 Povo (TN) Italy
daniele.pighin@gmail.com

Alessandro Moschitti
DISI, University of Trento
Via di Sommarive, 14
I-38123 Povo (TN) Italy
moschitti@disi.unitn.it

Abstract

In this paper, we provide a theoretical framework for feature selection in tree kernel spaces based on gradient-vector components of kernel-based machines. We show that a huge number of features can be discarded without a significant decrease in accuracy. Our selection algorithm is as accurate as and much more efficient than those proposed in previous work. Comparative experiments on three interesting and very diverse classification tasks, i.e. Question Classification, Relation Extraction and Semantic Role Labeling, support our theoretical findings and demonstrate the algorithm performance.

1 Introduction

Kernel functions are very effective at modeling diverse linguistic phenomena by implicitly representing data in high dimensional spaces, e.g. (Cumby and Roth, 2003; Culotta and Sorensen, 2004; Kudo et al., 2005; Moschitti et al., 2008). However, the implicit nature of the kernel space causes two major drawbacks: (1) high computational costs for learning and classification, and (2) the impossibility to identify the most important features. A solution to both problems is the application of feature selection techniques.

In particular, the problem of feature selection in Tree Kernel (TK) spaces has already been addressed by previous work in NLP, e.g. (Kudo and Matsumoto, 2003; Suzuki and Isozaki, 2005). However, these approaches lack a theoretical characterization of the problem that could support and justify the design of more effective algorithms.

In (Pighin and Moschitti, 2009a) and (Pighin and Moschitti, 2009b) (P&M), we presented a heuristic framework for feature selection in kernel spaces that selects features based on the components of the weight vector, $\vec{w}$, optimized by Support Vector Machines (SVMs). This method appears to be very effective, as the model accuracy does not significantly decrease even when a large number of features are filtered out. Unfortunately, we could not provide theoretical or intuitive motivations to justify our proposed apporach.

In this paper, we present and empirically validate a theory which aims at filling the above-mentioned gaps. In particular we provide: (i) a proof of the equation for the exact computation of feature weights induced by TK functions (Collins and Duffy, 2002); (ii) a theoretical characterization of feature selection based on $\|\vec{w}\|$. We show that if feature selection does not sensibly reduces $\|\vec{w}\|$, the margin associated with $\vec{w}$ does not sensibly decrease as well. Consequently, the theoretical upperbound to the probability error does not sensibly increases; (iii) a proof that the convolutive nature of TK allows for filtering out an exponential number of features with a small $\|\vec{w}\|$ decrease. The combination of (ii) with (iii) suggests that an extremely aggressive feature selection can be applied. We describe a greedy algorithm that exploits these results. Compared to the one proposed in P&M, the new version of the algorithm has only one parameter (instead of 3), it is more efficient and can be *more easily* connected with the amount of gradient norm that is lost after feature selection.

In the remainder: Section 2 briefly reviews SVMs and TK functions; Section 3 describes the problem of selecting and projecting features from very high onto lower dimensional spaces, and provides the theoretical foundation to our approach; Section 4 presents a selection of related work; Section 5 describes our approach to tree fragment selection; Section 6 details the outcome of our experiments; finally, in Section 7 we draw our conclusions.

Proceedings of the Fourteenth Conference on Computational Natural Language Learning, pages 223–233,
Uppsala, Sweden, 15-16 July 2010. ©2010 Association for Computational Linguistics

2 Fragment Weights in TK Spaces

The critical step for feature selection in tree kernel spaces is the computation of the weights of features (*tree fragments*) in the kernel machines' gradient. The basic parameters are the fragment frequencies which are combined with a decay factor used to downscale the weight of large subtrees (Collins and Duffy, 2002). In this section, after introducing basic kernel concepts, we describe a theorem that establishes the correct weight[1] of features in the STK space.

2.1 Kernel Based-Machines

Typically, a kernel machine is a linear classifier whose decision function can be expressed as:

$$c(\vec{x}) = \vec{w} \cdot \vec{x} + b = \sum_{i=1}^{\ell} \alpha_i y_i \vec{x_i} \cdot \vec{x} + b \quad (1)$$

where $\vec{x} \in \Re^N$ is a classifying example and $\vec{w} \in \Re^N$ and $b \in \Re$ are the separating hyperplane's *gradient* and its *bias*, respectively. The gradient is a linear combination of ℓ training points $\vec{x_i} \in \Re^N$ multiplied by their labels $y_i \in \{-1, +1\}$ and their weights $\alpha_i \in \Re^+$. Different optimizers use different strategies to learn the gradient. For instance, an SVM learns to maximize the distance between positive and negative examples, i.e. the margin γ. Applying the so-called *kernel trick*, it is possible to replace the scalar product with a *kernel function* defined over pairs of *objects*, which can more efficiently compute it:

$$c(o) = \sum_{i=1}^{\ell} \alpha_i y_i k(o_i, o) + b,$$

where $k(o_i, o) = \phi(o_i) \cdot \phi(o)$, with the advantage that we do not need to provide an explicit mapping $\phi : \mathcal{O} \to \Re^N$ of our example objects $\mathcal{O}$ in a vector space. In the next section, we show a kernel directly working on syntactic trees.

2.2 Syntactic Tree Kernel (STK)

Tree Kernel (TK) functions are convolution kernels (Haussler, 1999) defined over pairs of trees. Different TKs are characterized by alternative fragment definitions, e.g. (Collins and Duffy, 2002; Kashima and Koyanagi, 2002; Moschitti, 2006). We will focus on the syntactic tree kernel described in (Collins and Duffy, 2002), which relies on a fragment definition that does not allow to break production rules (i.e. if any child of a node is included in a fragment, then also all the other children have to). As such, it is especially indicated for tasks involving constituency parsed texts.

Tree kernels compute the number of common substructures between two trees T_1 and T_2 without explicitly considering the whole feature (fragment) space. Let $\mathcal{F} = \{f_1, f_2, \ldots, f_{|\mathcal{F}|}\}$ be the set of tree fragments, i.e. the explicit representation for the components of the fragment space, and $\chi_i(n)$ be an indicator function[2], equal to 1 if the target f_i is rooted at node n and equal to 0 otherwise. A tree kernel function over T_1 and T_2 is defined as

$$TK(T_1, T_2) = \sum_{n_1 \in N_{T_1}} \sum_{n_2 \in N_{T_2}} \Delta(n_1, n_2), \quad (2)$$

where N_{T_1} and N_{T_2} are the sets of nodes in T_1 and T_2, respectively and

$$\Delta(n_1, n_2) = \sum_{i=1}^{|\mathcal{F}|} \chi_i(n_1) \chi_i(n_2). \quad (3)$$

The Δ function counts the number of common subtrees rooted in n_1 and n_2 and weighs them according to their size. It can be evaluated as follows (Collins and Duffy, 2002):

1. if the productions at n_1 and n_2 are different, then $\Delta(n_1, n_2) = 0$;
2. if the productions at n_1 and n_2 are the same, and n_1 and n_2 have only leaf children (i.e. they are pre-terminal symbols) then $\Delta(n_1, n_2) = \lambda$;
3. if the productions at n_1 and n_2 are the same, and n_1 and n_2 are not pre-terminals then

$$\Delta(n_1, n_2) = \lambda \prod_{j=1}^{l(n_1)} (1 + \Delta(c_{n_1}^j, c_{n_2}^j)), \quad (4)$$

where $l(n_1)$ is the number of children of n_1, c_n^j is the j-th child of node n and λ is a decay factor penalizing larger structures.

2.3 Tree Fragment Weights

Eq. 3 shows that Δ counts the shared fragments rooted in n_1 and n_2 in the form of scalar product, as evaluated by Eq. 2. However, when λ is used in Δ as in Eq. 4, it changes the weight of the product $\chi_i(n_1)\chi_i(n_2)$. As λ multiplies Δ in each recursion step, we may be induced to assume[3] that the

[1] In P&M we provided an approximation of the real weight.

[2] We will consider it as a weighting function.

[3] In (Collins and Duffy, 2002), there is a short note about the correct value weight of lambda for each product components (i.e. pairs of fragments). This is in line with the formulation we provide.

weight of a fragment is λ^d, where d is the depth of the fragment. On the contrary, we show the actual weight by providing the following:

Theorem 1. *Let T and f be a tree and one of its fragments, respectively, induced by STK. The weight of f accounted by STK is $\lambda^{\frac{s(f)}{2}}$, where $l_f(n)$ is the number of children of n in f and $s(f) = |\{n \in T : l_f(n) > 0\}|$ is the number of nodes that have active productions in the fragment, i.e. the* size *of the fragment.*

In other words, the exponent of λ is the number of fragment nodes that have at least one child (i.e. active productions), divided by 2.

Proof. The thesis can be proven by induction on the depth d of f. The base case is f of depth 1. Fragments of depth 1 are matched by step 2 of $\Delta(n_1, n_2)$ computation, which assigns a value $\lambda = \chi_i(n_1)\chi_i(n_2)$ independently of the number of children (where $f_i = f$). It follows that the weight of f is $\chi_i(n_1) = \chi_i(n_2) = \lambda^{1/2}$.

Suppose that the thesis is valid for depth d and let us consider a fragment f of depth $d+1$, rooted in r. Without loss of generality, we can assume that f is in the set of the fragments rooted in n_1 and n_2, as evaluated by Eq. 4. It follows that the production rules associated with n_1 and n_2 are identical to the production rule in r. Let us consider $M = \{i \in \{1, .., l(n_1)\} : l(c_r^i) > 0\}$, i.e. the set of child indices of r which have at least a child. Thus, for $j \in M$, c_r^j has a production shared by $c_{n_1}^j$ and $c_{n_2}^j$. Conversely, for $j \notin M$, there is no match and $\Delta(c_{n_1}^j, c_{n_2}^j) = 0$. Therefore, the product in Eq. 4 can be rewritten as $\lambda \prod_{j \in M} \Delta(c_{n_1}^j, c_{n_2}^j)$, where the term 1 in $(1 + \Delta(c_{n_1}^j, c_{n_2}^j))$ is not considered since it accounts for those cases where there are no common productions in the children, i.e. $c_{n1}^j \neq c_{n2}^j \forall j \in M$.

We can now substitute $\Delta(c_{n_1}^j, c_{n_2}^j)$ with the weight of the subtree t_j of f rooted in c_r^j (and extended until its leaves), which is $\lambda^{s(t_j)}$ by inductive hypothesis (since t_j has depth lower than d). Thus, the weight of f is $s(f) = \lambda \prod_{j \in M} \lambda^{s(t_j)} = \lambda^{1+\sum_{j \in M} s(t_j)}$, where $\sum_{j \in M} s(t_j)$ is the number of nodes in f's subtrees rooted in r's children and having at least one child; by adding 1, i.e. the root of f, we obtain $s(f)$. Finally, $\lambda^{s(f)} = \chi_i(n_1)\chi_i(n_2)$, which satisfies our thesis: $\chi_i(n_1) = \chi_i(n_2) = \lambda^{\frac{s(f)}{2}}$. □

2.4 Weights in Feature Vectors

In the light of this result, we can use the definition of a TK function to project a tree t onto a linear space by recognizing that t can be represented as a vector $\vec{x}_i = [x_i^{(1)}, \ldots, x_i^{(N)}]$ whose attributes are the counts of the occurrences for each fragment, weighed with respect to the decay factor λ.

For a normalized STK kernel, the value of the j-th attribute of the example $\vec{x}_i$ is therefore:

$$x_i^{(j)} = \frac{t_{i,j}\lambda^{\frac{s(f_j)}{2}}}{\|\vec{x}_i\|} = \frac{t_{i,j}\lambda^{\frac{s(f_j)}{2}}}{\sqrt{\sum_{k=1}^{N} t_{i,k}^2 \lambda^{s(f_k)}}} \quad (5)$$

where: $t_{i,j}$ is the number of occurrences of the fragment f_j, associated with the j-th dimension of the feature space, in the tree t_i. It follows that the components of $\vec{w}$ (see Eq. 1) can be rewritten as:

$$w^{(j)} = \sum_{i=1}^{\ell} \alpha_i y_i x_i^{(j)} = \sum_{i=1}^{\ell} \frac{\alpha_i y_i t_{i,j}\lambda^{\frac{s(f_j)}{2}}}{\sqrt{\sum_{k=1}^{N} t_{i,k}^2 \lambda^{s(f_k)}}} \quad (6)$$

3 Projecting Exponentially Large Spaces

In order to provide a theoretical background to our feature selection technique and to develop effective algorithms, we want to relate our approach to statistical learning and, in particular, support vector classification theory. Since we select features with respect to their weight $w^{(j)}$, we can use the following theorem that establishes a general bound for margin-based classifiers.

Theorem 2. *(Bartlett and Shawe-Taylor, 1998) Let $\mathcal{C} = \{\vec{x} \to \vec{w} \cdot \vec{x} : \|\vec{w}\| \leq 1, \|\vec{x}\| \leq R\}$ be the class of real-valued functions defined in a ball of radius R in $\Re^N$. Then there is a constant k such that $\forall c \in \mathcal{C}$ having a margin γ, i.e. $|\vec{w} \cdot \vec{x}| \geq \gamma, \forall \vec{x} \in \mathcal{X}$ (training set), the error of c is bounded by $b/\ell + \sqrt{\frac{k}{\ell}\left(\frac{R^2}{\gamma^2}\log^2\ell + \log\frac{1}{\delta}\right)}$ with a probability $1 - \delta$, where $\ell = |\mathcal{X}|$ and b is the number of examples with margin less than γ.*

In other words, if $\mathcal{X}$ is separated with a margin γ by a linear classifier, then the error has a bound depending on γ. Another conclusion is that a feature selection algorithm that wants to preserve the accuracy of the original space should not affect the margin.

Since we would like to exploit the availability of the initial gradient $\vec{w}$ derived by the application of SVMs, it makes sense to try to quantify the percentage of γ reduction after feature selection, which we indicate by ρ. We found out that γ is linked to the reduction of $||\vec{w}||$, as illustrated by the next lemma.

Lemma 1. *Let $\mathcal{X}$ be a set of points in a vector space and $\vec{w}$ be the gradient vector which separates them with a margin γ. If the selection decreases $||\vec{w}||$ of a ρ rate, then the resulting hyperplane separates $\mathcal{X}$ by a margin larger than $\gamma_{in} = \gamma - \rho R||\vec{w}||$.*

Proof. Let $\vec{w} = \vec{w}_{in} + \vec{w}_{out}$, where $\vec{w}_{in}$ and $\vec{w}_{out} \in \Re^N$ are constituted by the components of $\vec{w}$ that are selected in and out, respectively, and have zero values in the remaining positions. By hypothesis $|\vec{w} \cdot \vec{x}| \geq \gamma$; without loss of generality, we can consider just the case $\vec{w} \cdot \vec{x} \geq \gamma$, and write $\vec{w} \cdot \vec{x} = \vec{w}_{in} \cdot \vec{x} + \vec{w}_{out} \cdot \vec{x} \geq \gamma \Rightarrow \vec{w}_{in} \cdot \vec{x} \geq \gamma - \vec{w}_{out} \cdot \vec{x} \geq \gamma - |\vec{w}_{out} \cdot \vec{x}| \geq \gamma - ||\vec{w}_{out}|| \times ||\vec{x}||$, where the last inequality holds owing to Cauchy-Schwarz inequality. The margin associated with $\vec{w}_{in}$, i.e. γ_{in}, is therefore $\gamma - ||\vec{w}_{out}|| \times ||\vec{x}|| \geq \gamma - ||\vec{w}_{out}||R = \gamma - \rho R||\vec{w}||$. □

Remark 1. *The lemma suggests that, even in case of very aggressive feature selection, if a small percentage ρ of $||\vec{w}||$ is lost, the margin reduction is small. Consequently, through Theorem 2, we can conclude that the accuracy of the model is by and large preserved.*

Remark 2. *We prefer to show the lemma in the more general form, but if we use normalized $\vec{x}$ and classifiers with $||\vec{w}|| \leq 1$, then $\gamma_{in} = \gamma - ||\vec{w}||\rho > \gamma - \rho$.*

The last result that we present justifies our selection approach as it demonstrates that most of the gradient norm is concentrated in relatively few features, with respect to the huge space induced by tree kernels. The selection of these few features allows us to preserve most of the norm and the margin.

Lemma 2. *Let $\vec{w}$ be a linear separator of a set of points $\mathcal{X}$, where each $\vec{x}_i \in \mathcal{X}$ is an explicit vector representations of a tree t_i in the space induced by STK and let ν be the largest $s(t_i)$, i.e. the maximum tree size. Then, if we discard fragments of size greater than η, $||\vec{w}_{out}|| \leq \frac{\nu}{\gamma^2}\sqrt{\frac{(\lambda\nu)^\eta - (\lambda\nu)^\nu}{1-\lambda\nu}}$.*

Proof. By applying simple norm properties, $||\vec{w}_{out}|| = \left\|\sum_{i=1}^{\ell} \alpha_i y_i \vec{x}_{out_i}\right\| \leq \sum_{i=1}^{\ell} ||\alpha_i y_i \vec{x}_{out_i}|| = \sum_{i=1}^{\ell} \alpha_i ||\vec{x}_{out_i}||$. To evaluate the latter, we first re-organize the summation in Eq. 5 (with no normalization) such that $||\vec{x}_i||^2 = \sum_{k=1}^{\nu} \sum_{j:s(f_j)=k} t_{i,j}^2 \lambda^{s(f_j)}$. Since a fragment f_j can be at maximum rooted in ν nodes, then $t_{i,j} \leq \nu$. Therefore, by replacing the number of trees of size k with the upperbound ν^k, we have $||\vec{x}_i|| < \sqrt{\sum_{k=1}^{\nu} \nu^2 \lambda^k \nu^k} = \sqrt{\sum_{k=1}^{\nu} \nu^2 (\nu\lambda)^k} = \sqrt{\nu^2 \frac{1-\mu^\nu}{1-\mu}}$, where we applied geometric series summation. Now if we assume that our algorithm selects out (i.e. discards) fragments with size $s(f) > \eta$, $||\vec{x}_{out_i}|| < \sqrt{\nu^2 \frac{\mu^\eta - \mu^\nu}{1-\mu}}$. It follows that $||\vec{w}_{out}|| < \sum_{i=1}^{\ell} \alpha_i \sqrt{\nu^2 \frac{\mu^\eta - \mu^\nu}{1-\mu}}$. In case of hard-margin SVMs, we have $\sum_{i=1}^{\ell} \alpha_i = 1/\gamma^2$. Thus, $||\vec{w}_{out}|| < \frac{\nu}{\gamma^2}\sqrt{\frac{\mu^\eta - \mu^\nu}{1-\mu}} = \frac{\nu}{\gamma^2}\sqrt{\frac{(\lambda\nu)^\eta - (\lambda\nu)^\nu}{1-\lambda\nu}}$. □

Remark 3. *The lemma shows that for an enough large η and $\lambda < 1/\nu$, $||\vec{w}_{out}||$ can be very small, even though it includes an exponential number of features, i.e. all the subtrees whose size ranges from η to ν. Therefore, according to Lemma 1 and Theorem 2, we can discard an exponential number of features with a limited loss in accuracy.*

Remark 4. *Regarding the proposed norm bound, we observe that ν^k is a rough overestimation of the the real number of fragments having size k rooted in the nodes of the target tree t. This suggests that we don't really need $\lambda < 1/\nu$. Moreover, in case of soft-margin SVMs, we can bound α_i with the value of the trade-off parameter C.*

4 Previous Work

Initial work on feature selection for text, e.g. (Yang and Pedersen, 1997), has shown that it may improve the accuracy or, at least, improve efficiency while preserving accuracy. Our context for feature selection is different for several important reasons: (i) we focus on structured features with a syntactic nature, which show different behaviour from lexical ones, e.g. they tend to be more sparse; (ii) in the TK space, the a-priori weights are very skewed, and large fragments receive exponentially lower scores than small ones; (iii) there is high redundancy and inter-dependency between such features; (iv) we want to be able to observe the most relevant features automatically generated by TKs; and (v) the huge number of features makes it impossible to evaluate the weight of each feature individually.

Guyon and Elisseeff (2003) carries out a very informative survey of feature selection techniques. Non-filter approaches for SVMs and kernel machines are often concerned with polynomial and

Gaussian kernels, e.g. (Weston et al., 2001; Neumann et al., 2005). In (Kudo and Matsumoto, 2003), an extension of the PrefixSpan algorithm (Pei et al., 2001) is used to efficiently mine the features in a low degree polynomial kernel space. The authors discuss an approximation of their method that allows them to handle high degree polynomial kernels. Suzuki and Isozaki (2005) present an embedded approach to feature selection for convolution kernels based on χ^2-driven relevance assessment. With respect to their work, the main differences in the approach that we propose are that we want to exploit the SVM optimizer to select the most relevant features, and to be able to observe the relevant fragments.

Regarding work that may directly benefit from reverse kernel engineering is worthwhile mentioning: (Cancedda et al., 2003; Shen et al., 2003; Daumé III and Marcu, 2004; Giuglea and Moschitti, 2004; Toutanova et al., 2004; Kazama and Torisawa, 2005; Titov and Henderson, 2006; Kate and Mooney, 2006; Zhang et al., 2006; Bloehdorn et al., 2006; Bloehdorn and Moschitti, 2007; Moschitti and Zanzotto, 2007; Surdeanu et al., 2008; Moschitti, 2008; Moschitti and Quarteroni, 2008; Martins et al., 2009; Nguyen et al., 2009a)

5 Mining Fragments Efficiently

The high-level description of our feature selection technique is as follows: we start by learning an STK model and we greedily explore the support vectors in search for the most relevant fragments. We store them in an index, and then we decode (or linearize) all the trees in the dataset, i.e. we represent them as vectors in a linear space where only a very small subset of the fragments in the original space are accounted for. These vectors are then employed for learning and classification in the linear space.

To explore the fragment space defined by a set of support vectors, we adopt the greedy strategy described in Algorithm 5.1. Its arguments are a model M, and the *threshold factor* L. The greedy algorithm explores the fragment space in a small to large fashion. The first step is the generation of the all *base* fragments F encoded in each tree, i.e. the smallest possible fragments according to the definition of the kernel function. For STK, such fragments are all those consisting of a node and all its direct children (i.e. production rules of the grammar). We assess the cumulative relevance of each

Algorithm 5.1: GREEDY_MODEL_MINER(M, L)

```
B ← BASE_FRAGS(model)
B ← REL(BEST(B))
σ ← B/L
D_prev ← FILTER(B, σ)
UPDATE(D_prev)
while D_prev ≠ ∅
  do
    D_next ← ∅
    τ ← 1 /* widthfactor */
    W_prev ← D_prev
    while W_prev ≠ ∅
      do
        W_next ← ∅
        for each f ∈ W_prev
          do
            E_f ← EXPAND(f, τ)
            F ← FILTER(E_f, σ)
            if F ≠ ∅
              then
                W_next ← W_next ∪ {f}
                D_next ← D_next ∪ F
                UPDATE(F)
        τ ← τ + 1
        W_prev ← W_next
    D_prev ← D_next
return (result)
```

base fragment according to Eq. 6 and then use the relevance B of the heaviest fragment, i.e. the fragment with the highest relevance in absolute value, as a criterion to set our fragment mining threshold σ to B/L. We then apply the FILTER($\cdot$) operator which discards all the fragments whose cumulative score is less than σ. Then, the UPDATE($\cdot$) operator stores the ramaining fragments in the index.

The exploration of the kernel space is carried out via the process of fragment expansion, by which each fragment retained at the previous step is incrementally grown to span more levels of the tree and to include more nodes at each level. These two directions of growth are controlled by the outer and the inner *while* loops, respectively. Fragment expansion is realized by the EXPAND(f, n) operator, that grows the fragment f by including the children of n *expandable* nodes in the fragment. Expandable nodes are nodes which are leaves in f but that have children in the tree that originated f.

After each expansion, the FILTER($\cdot$) operator is invoked on the set of generated fragments. If the filtered set is empty, i.e. no fragments more relevant than σ have been found during the previous iteration, then the loop is terminated.

Unlike previous attempts, this algorithm relies on just one parameter, i.e. L. As it revolves around the weight of the most relevant fragment, it operates according to the norm-preservation principle described in the previous sections. In fact, if we call N the number of fragments mined for a given value of L, the norm after feature selection can be bounded by $\frac{B}{L}\sqrt{N} \leq \|w_{in}\| \leq B\sqrt{N}$.

The choice of B, i.e. the highest relevance of a base fragment, as an upper bound for fragment relevance is motivated as follows. In Eq. 6, we can identify a term $T_i = \alpha_i y_i / \|t_i\|$ that is the same for all the fragments in the tree t_i. For $0 < \lambda \leq 1$, if f_j is an expansion of f_k, then from our definition of fragment expansion it follows that $\lambda^{\frac{s(f_j)}{2}} < \lambda^{\frac{s(f_k)}{2}}$. It can also be observed that $t_{i,j} \leq t_{i,k}$. Indeed, if $t_{i,k}$ is a subset of $t_{i,j}$, then it will occur at least as many times as its expansion $t_{i,k}$, possibly occurring as a seed fragment for different expansions in other parts of the tree as well. Therefore, if $\mathcal{E}_f$ is the set of expansions of f, for every two fragments $f_{i,j}, f_{i,k}$ coming from the same tree t_i, we can conclude that $x_i^{(j)} < x_i^{(k)}\ \forall f_{i,j} \in \mathcal{E}_{f_{i,k}}$. In other words, for each tree in the model, base fragments are the most relevant, and we can assume that the relevance of the heaviest fragment is an upper bound for the relevance of any fragment [4].

6 Experiments

We ran a set of thorough experiments to support our claims with empirical evidence. We show our results on three very different benchmarks: Question Classification (QC) using TREC 10 data (Voorhees, 2001), Relation Extraction (RE) based on the newswire and broadcast news domain of the ACE 2004 English corpus (Doddington et al., 2004) and Semantic Role Labeling (SRL) on the CoNLL 2005 shared task data (Carreras and Màrquez, 2005). In the next sections we elaborate on the setup and outcome of each set of experiments. As a supervised learning framework we used SVM-Light-TK[5], which extends the SVM-Light optimizer (Joachims, 2000) with support for tree kernel functions.

Unless differently stated, all the classifiers are parametrized for optimal Precision and Recall on a development set, obtained by selecting one example in ten from the training set with the same positive-to-negative example ratio. The results that we show are obtained on the test sets by using all the available data for training. For multi-class scenarios, the classifiers are arranged in a one vs. all configuration, where each sentence is a positive example for one of the classes, and negative for the others. While binary classifiers are evaluated in terms of F_1 measure, for multi-class classifiers we show the final accuracy.

The next paragraphs describe the datasets used for the experiments.

Question Classification (QC) Given a question, the task consists in selecting the most appropriate expected answer type from a given set of possibilities. We adopted the question taxonomy known as *coarse grained*, which has been described in (Zhang and Lee, 2003) and (Li and Roth, 2006), consisting of six non overlapping classes: Abbreviations (ABBR), Descriptions (DESC, e.g. definitions or explanations), Entity (ENTY, e.g. animal, body or color), Human (HUM, e.g. group or individual), Location (LOC, e.g. cities or countries) and Numeric (NUM, e.g. amounts or dates).

The TREC 10 QA data set accounts for 6,000 questions. For each question, we generate the full parse of the sentence and use it to train our models. Automatic parses are obtained with the Stanford parser[6] (Klein and Manning, 2003), and we actually have only 5,953 sentences in our data set due to parsing issues. During preliminary experiments, we observed an uneven distribution of examples in the traditional training/test split (the same used in P&M). Therefore, we used a random selection to generate an unbiased split, with 5,468 sentences for training and 485 for testing. The resulting data set is available for download at `http://danielepighin.net/cms/research/QC_dataset.tgz`.

Relation Extraction (RE) The corpus consists of 348 documents, and contains seven relation classes defined over pairs of mentions: Physical, Person/Social, Employment/Membership/Subsidiary, Agent-Artifact, PER/ORG Affiliation, GPE Affiliation, and Discourse. There are 4,400 positive and 38,696 negative examples when the potential relations are generated using all the entity/mention pairs in the same sentence.

Documents are parsed using the Stanford Parser, where the nodes of the entities are enriched with information about the entity type. Overall, we used the setting and data defined in (Nguyen et al., 2009b).

[4] In principle, the weight of some fragment encoded in the model M may be greater than B. However, as an empirical justification, we report that in all our experiments we have never been able to observe such case. Thus, with a certain probability, we can assume that the highest weight will be obtained from the heaviest of the base fragments.

[5] `http://disi.unitn.it/~moschitt/Tree-Kernel.htm`

[6] `http://nlp.stanford.edu/software/lex-parser.shtml`

Semantic Role Labeling (SRL) SRL can be decomposed into two tasks: *boundary detection*, where the word sequences that are arguments of a predicate word w are identified, and *role classification*, where each argument is assigned the proper role. For these experiments we concentrated on this latter task and used exactly the same setup as P&M. We considered all the argument nodes of any of the six PropBank (Palmer et al., 2005) core roles[7] (i.e. A0, ..., A5) from all the available training sections, i.e. 2 through 21, for a total of 179,091 training instances. Similarly, we collected 9,277 test instances from the annotations of Section 23.

6.1 Model Comparison

To show the validity of Lemma 1 in practical scenarios, we compare the accuracy of our linearized models against vanilla STK classifiers. We designed two types of classifiers:

LIN, a *linearized STK model*, which uses the weights estimated by the learner in the STK space and linearized examples; in other words LIN uses $\vec{w}_{IN}$. It allows us to measure exactly the loss in accuracy with respect to the reduction of $||\vec{w}||$.

OPT, a linearized STK model that is *re-optimized in the linear space*, i.e. for which we retrained an SVM using the linearized training examples as input data. Since the LIN solution is part of the candidate solutions from which OPT is selected, we always expect higher accuracy from it.

Additionally, we compare selection based on gradient $\vec{w}$ (as detailed in Section 2.4) against to χ^2 selection, which evaluates the relevance of features, in a similar way to (Suzuki and Isozaki, 2005). The relevance of a fragment is calculated as

$$\chi^2 = \frac{N(yN - Mx)^2}{x(N-x)M(N-M)},$$

where N is the number of support vectors, M is the number of positive vectors (i.e. $\alpha_i > 0$), and x and y are the fractions of N and M where the fragment is instantiated, respectively. We specify the selection models by means of **Grad** for the former and **Chi** for the latter. For example, a model called *OPT/Grad* is a re-trained model using the features selected according the highest gradient weights, while *LIN/Chi* would be a linearized tree kernel model using χ^2 for feature selection.

[7]We do not consider adjuncts because we preferred the number of classes to be similar across the three benchmarks.

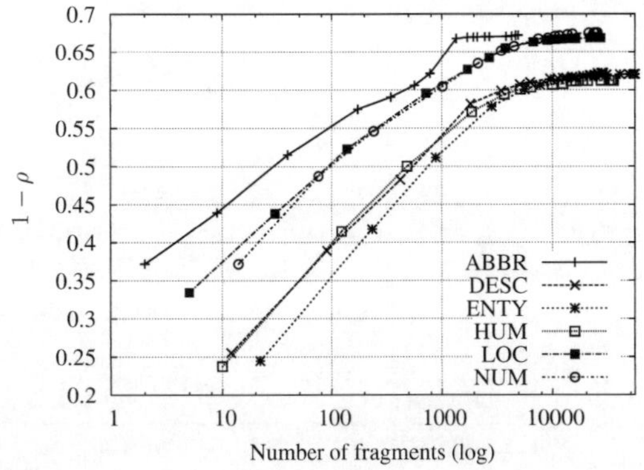

Figure 1: Percentage of gradient Norm, i.e. $1 - \rho$, according to the number of selected fragments, for different QC classifiers.

	STK		Linearized			
				LIN		OPT
	F_1	$\vert\vert\vec{w}\vert\vert$	Frags	F_1	$\vert\vert\vec{w}_{in}\vert\vert$	F_1
A	80.00	11.77	566	66.67	7.13	90.91
D	86.26	41.33	5161	81.87	25.10	83.72
E	76.86	51.71	5,702	73.03	31.06	75.56
H	84.92	43.61	5,232	80.47	26.20	77.08
L	81.69	38.73	1,732	78.87	24.27	82.89
N	92.31	37.65	1,015	85.07	24.53	87.07

Table 1: Per-class comparison between STK and the LIN/Grad and OPT/Grad models on the QC task. Each class is identified by its initial (e.g. A=ABBR). For each class, we considered a value of the threshold factor parameter L so as to retain at least 60% of the gradient norm after feature selection.

6.2 Results

The plots in Figure 1 show, for each class, the percentage of the gradient norm (i.e. $1 - \rho$, see Section 3) retained when including a different number of fragments. This graph empirically validates Lemma 2 since it clearly demonstrates that after 1,000-10,000 features the percentage of the norm reaches a plateau (around 60-65%). This means that after such threshold, which interestingly generalizes across all classifiers, a huge number of features is needed for a small increase of the norm. We recall that the maximum reachable norm is around 70% since we apriori filter out fragments of frequency lower than three.

Table 1 shows the F_1 of the binary question classifiers learned with STK, LIN/Grad and OPT/Grad models. It also shows the norm of the gradient before, $||\vec{w}||$, and after, $||\vec{w}_{in}||$, feature selec-

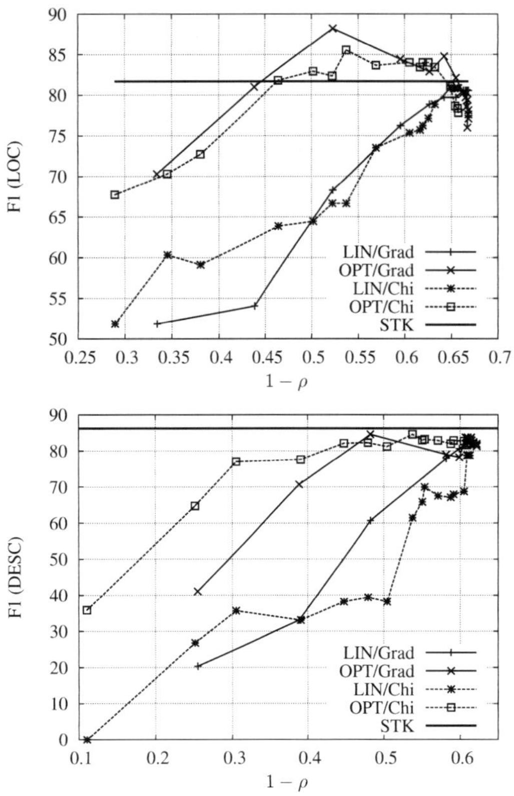

Figure 2: F1-measure of LOC and DESC wrt different $1 - \rho$ values.

tion along with the number of selected fragments, *Frags*. Instead of selecting an optimal number of fragments on a validation set, we investigated the 60% value suggested by the previous plot. Thus, for each category we selected the feature set reaching approximately 60% of $||\vec{w}||$. The table shows that the accuracy of the OPT/Grad model is in line with STK. In some cases, e.g. ABBR, the projected model is more accurate, i.e. 90.91 vs. 80.00, whereas in others, e.g. HUM, STK performs better, i.e. 84.92 vs. 77.08. It is interesting to see how the empirical results clearly complement the theoretical findings of the previous sections. For example, the LOC classifier uses only 1,732 of the $\sim 10^{12}$ features encoded by the corresponding STK model, but since only 40% of the norm of $\vec{w}$ is lost, classification accuracy is affected only marginally.

As mentioned above, the selected number of features is not optimal for every class. Figure 2 plots the accuracy of the LIN/Grad and OPT/Grad for different numbers of fragments on two classes [8]. These show that the former, with

[8]The other classes, which show similar behaviour, are omitted due to lack of space.

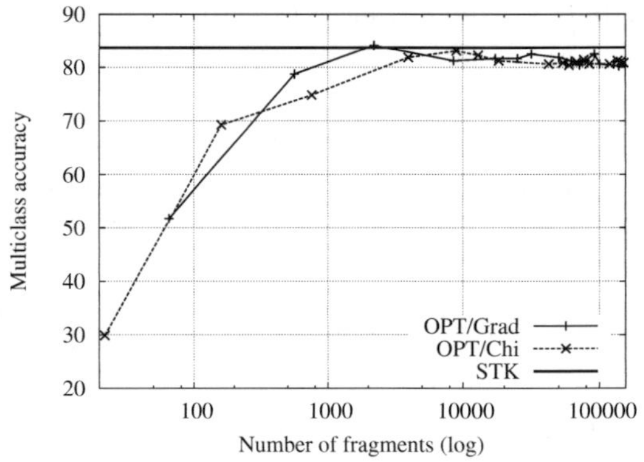

Figure 3: Multiclass accuracy obtained by including a growing number of fragments.

more than 60% of the norm, approaches STK whereas the latter requires less fragments. The plots also show the comparison against the same fragment mining algorithm and learning framework when using χ^2-based selection. This also provides similar good results, as far as the reduction of $||\vec{w}||$ is kept under control, i.e. as far as we select the components of the gradient that mostly affect its norm.

To concretely assess the benefits of our models for QC, Figure 3 plots the accuracy of OPT/Grad and OPT/Chi on the multiclass QC problem wrt the number of fragments employed. The results for the multi-class classifier are less biased by the binary Precision/Recall classifiers thus they are more stable and clearly show how, after selecting the optimal number of fragments (1,000-10,000 i.e. 60-65% of the norm), the accuracy of the OPT and CHI classifiers stabilize around levels of accuracy which are in line with STK.

	STK	OPT/Grad	
	F_1	F_1	Frags
QC	83.70	84.12	~2k
RE	67.53	66.31	~10k
SRL	87.56	88.17	~300k

Table 2: Multiclass classification accuracy on three benchmarks.

Finally, Table 2 shows the best results that we achieved on the three multi-class classification tasks, i.e. QC, RE[9] and SRL, and compares them against the STK [10]. For all the tasks OPT/Grad

[9]For RE, we show lower accuracy than in (Nguyen et al., 2009b) since, to have a closer comparison with STK, we do not combine structural features with manual designed features.

[10]We should point out that this models are only partially

produces the best results for all the tests, even though the difference with OPT/Chi is generally not statistically significant. Out of three tasks, OPT/Grad manages to slightly improve two of them, i.e. QC (84.12 vs. 83.7) and SRL (88.17 vs. 87.56), while STK is more accurate on RE, i.e. 67.53 vs. 66.31.

6.3 Comparison with P&M

The results on SRL can be compared against those that we presented in (Pighin and Moschitti, 2009a), where we measured an accuracy of 87.13 exactly on the same benchmark. As we can see in Table 2, our model improves the classification accuracy of about 1 point, i.e. 88.17. On the other hand, such comparison is not really fair since the algorithms rely on different parameter sets, and it is almost impossible to find matching configurations for the different versions of the algorithms that would result in exactly the same number of fragments. In a projected space with approximately 10^3 or 10^4 fragments, including a few hundred more features can produce noticeably different accuracy readings.

Generally speaking, the current model can achieve comparable accuracy with P&M while considering a smaller number of fragments. For example, in (Pighin and Moschitti, 2009b) the best model for the A1 binary classifier of the SRL benchmark was obtained by including 50,000 fragments, achieving an F_1 score of 89.04. With the new algorithm, using approximately half the fragments the accuracy of the linearized A1 classifier is 90.09. In P&M, the algorithm would only consider expansions of a fragment f where at most m nodes are expanded. Consequently, the set of mined fragments may include some small structures which can be less relevant than larger ones. Conversely, the new algorithm (see Alg. 5.1) may include larger but more relevant structures, thus accounting for a larger fraction of the gradient norm with a smaller number of fragments.

Concerning efficiency, the complexity of both mining algorithms is proportional to the number of fragments that they generate. Therefore, we can conclude that the new implementation is more efficient by considering that we can achieve the same accuracy with less fragments. As for the complexity of decoding, i.e. providing explicit vector representations of the input trees, in P&M, we used a very naive approach, i.e. the generation of all the fragments encoded in the tree and then look up each fragment in the index. This solution has exponential complexity with the number of nodes in the tree. Conversely, the new implementation has approximately linear complexity. The approach is based on the idea of an FST-like index, that we can *query* with a tree node. Every time the tree *matches* one of the fragments, the index increases the count of that fragment for the tree. The reduction in time complexity is made possible by encoding in the index the sequence of expansion operations that produced each indexed fragment, and by considering only those expansions at decoding time.

optimized, as we evaluated them by using the same threshold factor parameter L for all the classes. Better performances could be achieved by selecting an optimal value of L for individual classes when building the multi-class classifier.

7 Conclusions

Available feature selection frameworks for very high dimensional kernel families, such as tree kernels, suffer from the lack of a theory that could justify the very aggressive selection strategies necessary to cope with the exceptionally high dimensional feature space.

In this paper, we have provided a theoretical foundation in the context of margin classifiers by (i) linking the reduction of the gradient norm to the theoretical error bound and (ii) by proving that the norm is mostly concentrated in a relatively small number of features. The two properties suggest that we can apply an extremely aggressive feature selection by keeping the same accuracy. We described a very efficient algorithm to carry out such strategy in the fragment space. Our experiments empirically support our theoretical findings on three very different NLP tasks.

Acknowledgements

We would like to thank Truc-Vien T. Nguyen for providing us with the SVM learning and test files of the Relation Extraction dataset. Many thanks to the anonymous reviewers for their valuable suggestions.
This research has been partially supported by the EC project, EternalS: "Trustworthy Eternal Systems via Evolving Software, Data and Knowledge", project number FP7 247758.

References

P. Bartlett and J. Shawe-Taylor, 1998. *Advances in Kernel Methods — Support Vector Learning*, chapter Generalization Performance of Support Vector Machines and other Pattern Classifiers. MIT Press.

Stephan Bloehdorn and Alessandro Moschitti. 2007. Structure and semantics for expressive text kernels. In *In Proceedings of CIKM '07*.

Stephan Bloehdorn, Roberto Basili, Marco Cammisa, and Alessandro Moschitti. 2006. Semantic kernels for text classification based on topological measures of feature similarity. In *Proceedings of ICDM 06, Hong Kong, 2006*.

Nicola Cancedda, Eric Gaussier, Cyril Goutte, and Jean Michel Renders. 2003. Word sequence kernels. *Journal of Machine Learning Research*, 3:1059–1082.

Xavier Carreras and Lluís Màrquez. 2005. Introduction to the CoNLL-2005 Shared Task: Semantic Role Labeling. In *Proceedings of CoNLL'05*.

Michael Collins and Nigel Duffy. 2002. New Ranking Algorithms for Parsing and Tagging: Kernels over Discrete Structures, and the Voted Perceptron. In *Proceedings of ACL'02*.

Aron Culotta and Jeffrey Sorensen. 2004. Dependency Tree Kernels for Relation Extraction. In *Proceedings of ACL'04*.

Chad Cumby and Dan Roth. 2003. Kernel Methods for Relational Learning. In *Proceedings of ICML 2003*.

Hal Daumé III and Daniel Marcu. 2004. Np bracketing by maximum entropy tagging and SVM reranking. In *Proceedings of EMNLP'04*.

G. Doddington, A. Mitchell, M. Przybocki, L. Ramshaw, S. Strassel, and R. Weischedel. 2004. The Automatic Content Extraction (ACE) Program–Tasks, Data, and Evaluation. *Proceedings of LREC 2004*, pages 837–840.

Ana-Maria Giuglea and Alessandro Moschitti. 2004. Knowledge Discovering using FrameNet, VerbNet and PropBank. In *In Proceedings of the Workshop on Ontology and Knowledge Discovering at ECML 2004, Pisa, Italy*.

Isabelle Guyon and André Elisseeff. 2003. An introduction to variable and feature selection. *Journal of Machine Learning Research*, 3:1157–1182.

David Haussler. 1999. Convolution kernels on discrete structures. Technical report, Dept. of Computer Science, University of California at Santa Cruz.

T. Joachims. 2000. Estimating the generalization performance of a SVM efficiently. In *Proceedings of ICML'00*.

Hisashi Kashima and Teruo Koyanagi. 2002. Kernels for semi-structured data. In *Proceedings of ICML'02*.

Rohit J. Kate and Raymond J. Mooney. 2006. Using string-kernels for learning semantic parsers. In *Proceedings of the 21st ICCL and 44th Annual Meeting of the ACL*, pages 913–920, Sydney, Australia, July. Association for Computational Linguistics.

Jun'ichi Kazama and Kentaro Torisawa. 2005. Speeding up training with tree kernels for node relation labeling. In *Proceedings of HLT-EMNLP'05*.

Dan Klein and Christopher D. Manning. 2003. Accurate unlexicalized parsing. In *Proceedings of ACL'03*, pages 423–430.

Taku Kudo and Yuji Matsumoto. 2003. Fast methods for kernel-based text analysis. In *Proceedings of ACL'03*.

Taku Kudo, Jun Suzuki, and Hideki Isozaki. 2005. Boosting-based parse reranking with subtree features. In *Proceedings of ACL'05*.

Xin Li and Dan Roth. 2006. Learning question classifiers: the role of semantic information. *Natural Language Engineering*, 12(3):229–249.

André F. T. Martins, Noah A. Smith, Eric P. Xing, Pedro M. Q. Aguiar, and Mário A. T. Figueiredo. 2009. Nonextensive information theoretic kernels on measures. *J. Mach. Learn. Res.*, 10:935–975.

Alessandro Moschitti and Silvia Quarteroni. 2008. Kernels on linguistic structures for answer extraction. In *Proceedings of ACL-08: HLT, Short Papers*, Columbus, Ohio.

Alessandro Moschitti and Fabio Massimo Zanzotto. 2007. Fast and effective kernels for relational learning from texts. In Zoubin Ghahramani, editor, *Proceedings of the 24th Annual International Conference on Machine Learning (ICML 2007)*.

Alessandro Moschitti, Daniele Pighin, and Roberto Basili. 2008. Tree kernels for semantic role labeling. *Computational Linguistics*, 34(2):193–224.

Alessandro Moschitti. 2006. Efficient convolution kernels for dependency and constituent syntactic trees. In *Proceedings of ECML'06*, pages 318–329.

Alessandro Moschitti. 2008. Kernel methods, syntax and semantics for relational text categorization. In *Proceeding of CIKM '08*, NY, USA.

Julia Neumann, Christoph Schnorr, and Gabriele Steidl. 2005. Combined SVM-Based Feature Selection and Classification. *Machine Learning*, 61(1-3):129–150.

Truc-Vien T. Nguyen, Alessandro Moschitti, and Giuseppe Riccardi. 2009a. Convolution kernels on constituent, dependency and sequential structures for relation extraction. In *Proceedings of EMNLP*.

Truc-Vien T. Nguyen, Alessandro Moschitti, and Giuseppe Riccardi. 2009b. Convolution kernels on constituent, dependency and sequential structures for relation extraction. In *EMNLP '09: Proceedings of the 2009 Conference on Empirical Methods in Natural Language Processing*, pages 1378–1387, Morristown, NJ, USA. Association for Computational Linguistics.

Martha Palmer, Daniel Gildea, and Paul Kingsbury. 2005. The proposition bank: An annotated corpus of semantic roles. *Comput. Linguist.*, 31(1):71–106.

J. Pei, J. Han, Mortazavi B. Asl, H. Pinto, Q. Chen, U. Dayal, and M. C. Hsu. 2001. PrefixSpan Mining Sequential Patterns Efficiently by Prefix Projected Pattern Growth. In *Proceedings of ICDE'01*.

Daniele Pighin and Alessandro Moschitti. 2009a. Efficient linearization of tree kernel functions. In *Proceedings of CoNLL'09*.

Daniele Pighin and Alessandro Moschitti. 2009b. Reverse engineering of tree kernel feature spaces. In *Proceedings of EMNLP*, pages 111–120, Singapore, August. Association for Computational Linguistics.

Libin Shen, Anoop Sarkar, and Aravind k. Joshi. 2003. Using LTAG Based Features in Parse Reranking. In *Proceedings of EMNLP'06*.

Mihai Surdeanu, Massimiliano Ciaramita, and Hugo Zaragoza. 2008. Learning to rank answers on large online QA collections. In *Proceedings of ACL-08: HLT*, Columbus, Ohio.

Jun Suzuki and Hideki Isozaki. 2005. Sequence and Tree Kernels with Statistical Feature Mining. In *Proceedings of NIPS'05*.

Ivan Titov and James Henderson. 2006. Porting statistical parsers with data-defined kernels. In *Proceedings of CoNLL-X*.

Kristina Toutanova, Penka Markova, and Christopher Manning. 2004. The Leaf Path Projection View of Parse Trees: Exploring String Kernels for HPSG Parse Selection. In *Proceedings of EMNLP 2004*.

Ellen M. Voorhees. 2001. Overview of the trec 2001 question answering track. In *In Proceedings of the Tenth Text REtrieval Conference (TREC*, pages 42–51.

Jason Weston, Sayan Mukherjee, Olivier Chapelle, Massimiliano Pontil, Tomaso Poggio, and Vladimir Vapnik. 2001. Feature Selection for SVMs. In *Proceedings of NIPS'01*.

Yiming Yang and Jan O. Pedersen. 1997. A comparative study on feature selection in text categorization. In Douglas H. Fisher, editor, *Proceedings of ICML-97, 14th International Conference on Machine Learning*, pages 412–420, Nashville, US. Morgan Kaufmann Publishers, San Francisco, US.

Dell Zhang and Wee Sun Lee. 2003. Question classification using support vector machines. In *Proceedings of SIGIR'03*, pages 26–32.

Min Zhang, Jie Zhang, and Jian Su. 2006. Exploring Syntactic Features for Relation Extraction using a Convolution tree kernel. In *Proceedings of NAACL*.

Inspecting the Structural Biases of Dependency Parsing Algorithms *

Yoav Goldberg and **Michael Elhadad**
Ben Gurion University of the Negev
Department of Computer Science
POB 653 Be'er Sheva, 84105, Israel
yoavg|elhadad@cs.bgu.ac.il

Abstract

We propose the notion of a *structural bias* inherent in a parsing system with respect to the language it is aiming to parse. This structural bias characterizes the behaviour of a parsing system in terms of structures it tends to under- and over- produce. We propose a Boosting-based method for uncovering some of the structural bias inherent in parsing systems. We then apply our method to four English dependency parsers (an Arc-Eager and Arc-Standard transition-based parsers, and first- and second-order graph-based parsers). We show that all four parsers are biased with respect to the kind of annotation they are trained to parse. We present a detailed analysis of the biases that highlights specific differences and commonalities between the parsing systems, and improves our understanding of their strengths and weaknesses.

1 Introduction

Dependency Parsing, the task of inferring a dependency structure over an input sentence, has gained a lot of research attention in the last couple of years, due in part to to the two CoNLL shared tasks (Nivre et al., 2007; Buchholz and Marsi, 2006) in which various dependency parsing algorithms were compared on various data sets. As a result of this research effort, we have a choice of several robust, efficient and accurate parsing algorithms.

These different parsing systems achieve comparable scores, yet produce qualitatively different parses. Sagae and Lavie (2006) demonstrated that a simple combination scheme of the outputs of different parsers can obtain substantially improved accuracies. Nivre and McDonald (2008) explore a parser stacking approach in which the output of one parser is fed as an input to a different kind of parser. The stacking approach also produces more accurate parses.

However, while we know how to produce accurate parsers and how to blend and stack their outputs, little effort was directed toward understanding the behavior of different parsing systems in terms of structures they produce and errors they make. Question such as *which linguistic phenomena are hard for parser Y?* and *what kinds of errors are common for parser Z?*, as well as the more ambitious *which parsing approach is most suitable to parse language X?*, remain largely unanswered.

The current work aims to fill this gap by proposing a methodology to identify systematic biases in various parsing models and proposing and initial analysis of such biases.

McDonald and Nivre (2007) analyze the difference between graph-based and transition-based parsers (specifically the MALT and MST parsers) by comparing the different kinds of errors made by both parsers. They focus on single edge errors, and learn that MST is better for longer dependency arcs while MALT is better on short dependency arcs, that MALT is better than MST in predicting edges further from the root and vice-versa, that MALT has a slight advantage when predicting the parents of nouns and pronouns, and that MST is better at all other word categories. They also conclude that the greedy MALT Parser suffer from error propagation more than the globally optimized

* We would like to thank Reut Tsarfaty for comments and discussions that helped us improve this paper. This work is supported in part by the Lynn and William Frankel Center for Computer Science.

Proceedings of the Fourteenth Conference on Computational Natural Language Learning, pages 234–242,
Uppsala, Sweden, 15-16 July 2010.

MST Parser.

In what follows, we complement their work by suggesting a different methodology of analysis of parsers behaviour. Our methodology is based on the notion of *structural bias* of parsers, further explained in Section 2. Instead of comparing two parsing systems in terms of the errors they produce, our analysis compares the output of a parsing system with a collection of gold-parsed trees, and searches for common structures which are predicted by the parser more often than they appear in the gold-trees or vice-versa. These kinds of structures represent the bias of the parsing systems, and by analyzing them we can gain important insights into the strengths, weaknesses and inner working of the parser.

In Section 2.2 we propose a Boosting-based algorithm for uncovering these structural biases. Then, in Section 3 we go on to apply our analysis methodology to four parsing systems for English: two transition-based systems and two graph-based systems (Sections 4 and 5). The analysis shows that the different parsing systems indeed possess different biases. Furthermore, the analysis highlights the differences and commonalities among the different parsers, and sheds some more light on the specific behaviours of each system.

Recent work by Dickinson (2010), published concurrently with this one, aims to identify dependency errors in automatically parsed corpora by inspecting *grammatical rules* which appear in the automatically parsed corpora and do not fit well with the grammar learned from a manually annotated treebank. While Dickinson's main concern is with automatic identification of errors rather than characterizing parsers behaviour, we feel that his work shares many intuitions with this one: automatic parsers fail in predictable ways, those ways can be analyzed, and this analysis should be carried out on structures which are larger than single edges, and by inspecting trends rather than individual decisions.

2 Structural Bias

Language is a highly structured phenomena, and sentences exhibit structure on many levels. For example, in English sentences adjectives appear before nouns, subjects tend to appear before their verb, and syntactic trees show a tendency toward right-branching structures.[1]

Different combinations of languages and annotation strategies exhibit different *structural preferences*: under a specific combination of language and annotation strategy some structures are more frequent than others, some structures are illegal and some are very rare.

We argue that parsers also exhibit such structural preferences in the parses they produce. These preferences stem from various parser design decisions. Some of the preferences, such as *projectivity*, are due to explicit design decisions and lie at the core of some parsing algorithms. Other preferences are more implicit, and are due to specific interactions between the parsing mechanism, the feature function, the statistical mechanism and the training data.

Ideally, we would like the structural preferences of a parser trained on a given sample to reflect the general preferences of the language. However, as we demonstrate in Section 3, that it is usually not the case.

We propose the notion of *structural bias* for quantifying the differences in structural preferences between a parsing system and the language it is aiming to parse. The structural bias of a parser with respect to a language is composed of the structures that tend to occur more often in the parser's output than in the language, and vice-versa.

Structural biases are related to but different than common errors. *Parser X makes many PP attachment errors* is a claim about a common error. *Parser X tends to produce low attachment for PPs while the language tends to have high attachment* is a claim about structural bias, which is related to parser errors. *Parser X can never produce structure Y* is a claim about a structural preference of a parser, which may or may not be related to its error patterns.

Structural bias is a vast and vague concept. In order to give a more concrete definition, we pose the following question:

Assuming we are given two parses of the same sentence. Can we tell, by looking at the parses and without knowing the correct parse, which parser produced which parse?

Any predictor which can help in answering this question is an indicator of a structural bias.

[1]As noted by (Owen Rambow, 2010), there is little sense in talking about *the structure of a language* without referring to a specific annotation scheme. In what follow, we assume a fixed annotation strategy is chosen.

Definition: structural bias between sets of trees Given two sets of parse trees, A and B, over the same sentences, a *structural bias* between these sets is the collection of all predictors which can help us decide, for a tree t, whether it belongs to A or to B.

The structural bias between a parsing system and an annotated corpus is then the structural bias between the corpus and the output of the parser on the sentences in the corpus. Note that this definition adheres to the error *vs.* bias distinction given above.

Under this task-based definition, uncovering structural biases between two sets of trees amounts to finding good predictors for discriminating between parses coming from these two sets of trees. In what follows, we present a rich class of structural predictors, and an algorithm for efficiently searching this predictor class for good predictors.

2.1 Representing Structure

A dependency representation of sentences includes words and dependency relations between them (one word is the ROOT of the sentence, and each other word has a single word as its *parent*). Whenever possible, we would like to equate words with their part-of-speech tags, to facilitate generalization. However, in some cases the exact identity of the word may be of interest. When analyzing a language with a relatively fixed word order, such as English, we are also interested in the linear order between words. This includes the *direction* between a parent and its dependent (does the parent appear before or after the dependent in the sentence?), as well as the order among several dependents of the same parent. The *length* of a dependency relation (distance in words between the parent and dependent) may also be structurally interesting.[2]

In order to capture this kind of information, we take a *structural element* of a dependency tree to be any connected subtree, coupled with information about the incoming edge to the root of the subtree. Examples of such structural elements are given in Figure 1. This class of predictors is not complete – it does not directly encode, for instance, information about the number of siblings

[2]Relations can also be labeled, and labeling fit naturally in our representation. However, we find the commonly used set of edge labels for English to be lacking, and didn't include edge labels in the current analysis.

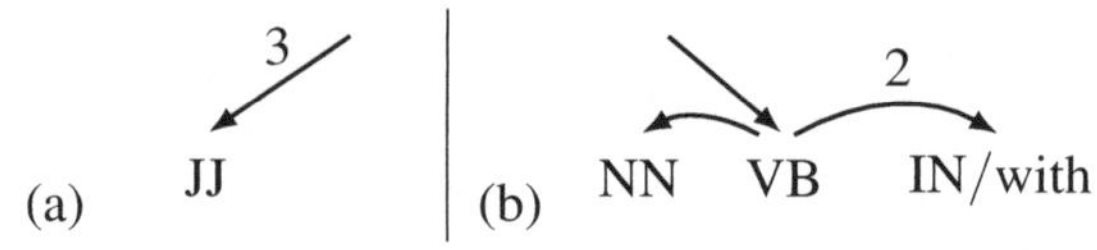

Figure 1: **Structural Elements Examples.** (a) is an adjective with a parent 3 words to its right. (b) is a verb whose parent is on the left, it has a noun dependent on its left, and a preposition dependent 2 words to its right. The lexical item of the preposition is *with*. The lexical items and distance to parent are optional, while all other information is required. There is also no information about other dependents a given word may have.

a node has or the location of the structure relative to the root of the tree. However, we feel it does capture a good deal of linguistic phenomena, and provide a fine balance between expressiveness and tractability.

The class of predictors we consider is the set of all *structural elements*. We seek to find structural elements which appear in many trees of set A but in few trees of set B, or vice versa.

2.2 Boosting Algorithm with Subtree Features

The number of possible predictors is exponential in the size of each tree, and an exhaustive search is impractical. Instead, we solve the search problem using a Boosting algorithm for tree classification using subtree features. The details of the algorithm and its efficient implementation are given in (Kudo and Matsumoto, 2004). We briefly describe the main idea behind the algorithm.

The Boosting algorithm with subtree features gets as input two parse sets with labeled, ordered trees. The output of the algorithm is a set of subtrees t_i and their weights w_i. These weighted subtrees define a linear classifier over trees $f(T) = \sum_{t_i \in T} w_i$, where $f(T) > 0$ for trees in set A and $f(T) < 0$ for trees in set B.

The algorithm works in rounds. Initially, all input trees are given a uniform weight. At each round, the algorithm seeks a subtree t with a *maximum gain*, that is the subtree that classifies correctly the subset of trees with the highest cumulative weight. Then, it re-weights the input trees, so that misclassified trees get higher weights. It continues to repeatedly seek maximum gain subtrees, taking into account the tree weights in the gain calculation, and re-weighting the trees after each iteration. The same subtree can be selected in different iterations.

Kudo and Matsumoto (2004) present an effec-

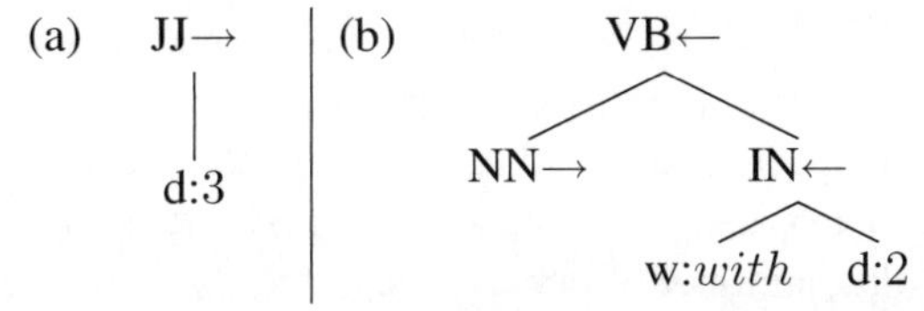

Figure 2: **Encoding Structural Elements as Ordered Trees**. These are the tree encodings of the structural elements in Figure 1. Direction to parent is encoded in the node name, while the optional lexical item and distance to parent are encoded as daughters.

tive branch-and-bound technique for efficiently searching for the maximum gain tree at each round. The reader is referred to their paper for the details.

Structural elements as subtrees The boosting algorithm works on labeled, ordered trees. Such trees are different than dependency trees in that they contain information about nodes, but not about edges. We use a simple transformation to encode dependency trees and structural elements as labeled, ordered trees. The transformation works by concatenating the edge-to-parent information to the node's label for mandatory information, and adding edge-to-parent information as a special child node for optional information. Figure 2 presents the tree-encoded versions of the structural elements in Figure 1. We treat the direction-to-parent and POS tag as required information, while the distance to parent and lexical item are optional.

2.3 Structural Bias Predictors

The output of the boosting algorithm is a set of weighted subtrees. These subtrees are good candidates for structural bias predictors. However, some of the subtrees may be a result of over-fitting the training data, while the weights are tuned to be used as part of a linear classifier. In our application, we disregard the boosting weights, and instead rank the predictors based on their number of occurrences in a validation set. We seek predictors which appear many times in one tree-set but few times in the other tree-set on both the training and the validation sets. Manual inspection of these predictors highlights the structural bias between the two sets. We demonstrate such an analysis for several English dependency parsers below.

In addition, the precision of the learned Boosting classifier on the validation set can serve as a metric for measuring the amount of structural bias between two sets of parses. A high classification accuracy means more structural bias between the two sets, while an accuracy of 50% or lower means that, at least under our class of predictors, the sets are structurally indistinguishable.

3 Biases in Dependency Parsers

3.1 Experimental Setup

In what follows, we analyze and compare the structural biases of 4 parsers, with respect to a dependency representation of English.

Syntactic representation The dependency treebank we use is a conversion of the English WSJ treebank (Marcus et al., 1993) to dependency structure using the procedure described in (Johansson and Nugues, 2007). We use the Mel'čuk encoding of coordination structure, in which the first conjunct is the head of the coordination structure, the coordinating conjunction depends on the head, and the second conjunct depend on the coordinating conjunction (Johansson, 2008).

Data Sections 15-18 were used for training the parsers[3]. The first 4,000 sentences from sections 10-11 were used to train the Boosting algorithm and find structural predictors candidates. Sections 4-7 were used as a validation set for ranking the structural predictors. In all experiments, we used the gold-standard POS tags. We binned the distance-to-parent values to 1,2,3,4-5,6-8 and 9+.

Parsers For graph-based parsers, we used the projective first-order (MST1) and second-order (MST2) variants of the freely available MST parser[4] (McDonald et al., 2005; McDonald and Pereira, 2006). For the transition-based parsers, we used the arc-eager (ARCE) variant of the freely available MALT parser[5] (Nivre et al., 2006), and our own implementation of an arc-standard parser (ARCS) as described in (Huang et al., 2009). The unlabeled attachment accuracies of the four parsers are presented in Table 1.

Procedure For each parser, we train a boosting classifier to distinguish between the gold-standard trees and the parses produced for them by the

[3]Most work on parsing English uses a much larger training set. We chose to use a smaller set for convenience. Training the parsers is much faster, and we can get ample test data without resorting to jackknifing techniques. As can be seen in Table 1, the resulting parsers are still accurate.

[4]http://sourceforge.net/projects/mstparser/

[5]http://maltparser.org/

MST1	MST2	ARCE	ARCS
88.8	89.8	87.6	87.4

Table 1: Unlabeled accuracies of the analyzed parsers

Parser	Train Accuracy	Val Accuracy
MST1	65.4	57.8
MST2	62.8	56.6
ARCE	69.2	65.3
ARCS	65.1	60.1

Table 2: Distinguishing parser output from gold-trees based on structural information

parser. We remove from the training and validation sets all the sentences which the parser got 100% correct. We then apply the models to the validation set. We rank the learned predictors based on their appearances in gold- and parser-produced trees in the train and validation sets, and inspect the highest ranking predictors.

Training the boosting algorithm was done using the `bact`[6] toolkit. We ran 400 iterations of boosting, resulting in between 100 and 250 distinct subtrees in each model. Of these, the top 40 to 60 ranked subtrees in each model were good indicators of structural bias. Our wrapping code is available online[7] in order to ease the application of the method to other parsers and languages.

3.2 Quantitative Analysis

We begin by comparing the accuracies of the boosting models trained to distinguish the parsing results of the various parsers from the English treebank. Table 2 lists the accuracies on both the training and validation sets.

The boosting method is effective in finding structural predictors. All parsers output is distinguishable from English trees based on structural information alone. The ArcEager variant of MALT is the most biased with respect to English. The transition-based parsers are more structurally biased than the graph-based ones.

We now turn to analyze the specific structural biases of the parsing systems. For each system we present some prominent structures which are *under-produced* by the system (these structures appear in the language more often than they are produce by the parser) and some structures which are *over-produced* by the system (these structures are produced by the parser more often than they appear in the language).[8] Specifically, we manually inspected the predictors where the ratio between language and parser was high, ranked by absolute number of occurrences.

4 Transition-based Parsers

We analyze two transition-based parsers (Nivre, 2008). The parsers differ in the transition systems they adopt. The ARCE system makes use of a transition system with four transitions: LEFT,RIGHT,SHIFT,REDUCE. The semantics of this transition system is described in (Nivre, 2004). The ARCS system adopts an alternative transition system, with three transitions: ATTACHL,ATTACHR,SHIFT. The semantics of the system is described in (Huang et al., 2009). The main difference between the systems is that the ARCE system makes attachments as early as possible, while the ARCS system should not attach a parent to its dependent until the dependent has acquired all its own dependents.

4.1 Biases of the Arc-Eager System

Over-produced structures The over-produced structures of ARCE with respect to English are overwhelmingly dominated by spurious ROOT attachments.

The structures ROOT→“ , ROOT→DT, ROOT→WP are produced almost 300 times by the parser, yet never appear in the language. The structures ROOT→” , ROOT→WRB , ROOT→JJ appear 14 times in the language and are produced hundreds of time by the parser. Another interesting case is ROOT $\xrightarrow[9+]{}$ NN , produced 180 times by the parser and appearing 7 times in the language. As indicated by the distance marking (9+), nouns are allowed to be heads of sentences, but then they usually appear close to the beginning, a fact which is not captured by the parsing system. Other, less clear-cut cases, are ROOT as the parent of IN, NN, NNS or NNP. Such structures do appear in the language, but are 2-5 times more common in the parser.

A different ROOT attachment bias is captured by

ROOT VBZ VBD and ROOT VBD VBD ,

[6] http://chasen.org/~taku/software/bact/

[7] http://www.cs.bgu.ac.il/~yoavg/software/

[8] One can think of over- and under- produced structures in terms of the *precision* and *recall* metrics: over-produced structures have low precision, while under-produced structures have low recall.

appearing 3 times in the language and produced over a 100 times by the parser.

It is well known that the ROOT attachment accuracies of transition-based systems is lower than that of graph-based system. Now we can refine this observation: the ARCE parsing system fails to capture the fact that some categories are more likely to be attached to ROOT than others. It also fails to capture the constraint that sentences usually have only one main verb.

Another related class of biases are captured by the structures →VBD $\underset{9+}{\rightleftarrows}$ VBD, →VBD $\underset{5-7}{\rightleftarrows}$ VBD and ROOT→VBZ→VBZ which are produced by the parser twice as many times as they appear in the language. When confronted with embedded sentences, the parser has a strong tendency of marking the first verb as the head of the second one.

The pattern $\underset{+9}{\rightleftarrows}$ IN suggests that the parser prefers high attachment for PPs. The pattern 9+ DT← NN captures the bias of the parser toward associating NPs with the preceding verb rather than the next one, even if this preceding verb is far away.

Under-produced structures We now turn to ARCE's under-produced structures. These include the structures IN/*that*← , MD← , VBD← (each 4 times more frequent in the language than in the parser) and VBP← (twice more frequent in the language). MD and *that* usually have their parents to the left. However, in some constructions this is not the case, and the parser has a hard time learning these constructions.

The structure →$→RB appearing 20 times in the language and 4 times in the parser, reflects a very specific construction ("$ 1.5 *up* from $ 1.2"). These constructions pop up as under-produced by all the parsers we analyze.

The structures $\underset{1}{\rightleftarrows}$ RB→IN and →RB→JJ appear twice as often in the language. These stem from constructions such as "not/RB unexpected/JJ", "backed away/RB from/IN", "pushed back/RB in/IN", and are hard for the parser.

Lastly, the structure JJ←NN←NNS←, deviates from the the "standard" NP construction, and is somewhat hard for the parser (39 times parser, 67 in language). However, we will see below that this same construction is even harder for other parsers.

4.2 Biases of the Arc-Standard System

Over-produced structures The over-produced structures of ARCS do not show the spurious ROOT attachment ambiguity of ARCE. They do include ROOT→IN, appearing twice as often in the parser output than in the language.

The patterns ROOT→VBZ$\underset{9+}{\rightleftarrows}$, , →VBP$\underset{9+}{\rightleftarrows}$, , →VBD$\underset{9+}{\rightleftarrows}$VBD and →VB→VBD all reflect the parser's tendency for right-branching structure, and its inability to capture the verb-hierarchy in the sentence correctly, with a clear preference for earlier verbs as parents of later verbs.

Similarly, $\underset{9+}{\rightleftarrows}$NNP and $\underset{9+}{\rightleftarrows}$NNS indicate a tendency to attach NPs to a parent on their left (as an object) rather than to their right (as a subject) even when the left candidate-parent is far away.

Finally, WRB ← MD → VB , produced 48 times by the parser and twice by the language, is the projective parser's way of annotating the correct non-projective structure in which the wh-adverb is dependent on the verb.

Under-produced structures of ARCS include two structures WRB ← VBN and WRB ← VB , which are usually part of non-projective structures, and are thus almost never produced by the projective parser.

Other under-produced structures include appositive NPs:

→IN NN , ,
(*e.g.*, "by Merill , the nation's largest firm , "), and

the structure → NN DT ← NN , which can stand for apposition ("a *journalist*, *the* first *journalist* to ...") or phrases such as "30 %/NN *a month*".

TO usually has its parent on its left. When this is not the case (when it is a part of a quantifier, such as "x *to* y %", or due to fronting: "Due *to* X, we did Y"), the parser is having a hard time to adapt and is under-producing this structure.

Similar to the other parsers, ARCS also under-produces NPs with the structure JJ←NN$\underset{1}{\rightleftarrows}$NN, and the structure →$→RB.

Finally, the parser under-produces the conjunctive structures →NN→CC→NN→IN and →IN→CC→IN.

5 Graph-based Parsers

We analyze the behaviour of two graph-based parsers (McDonald, 2006). Both parsers perform exhaustive search over all projective parse trees, using a dynamic programming algorithm. They differ in the factorizations they employ to make the search tractable. The first-order model employs a single-edge factorization, in which each edge is scored independently of all other edges. The second-order model employs a two-edge factorization, in which scores are assigned to pairs of adjacent edges rather than to a single edge at a time.

5.1 Biases of First-order MST Parser

Over-produced structures of MST1 include:

→IN NN NN   →IN NNP NN

→IN NNP NNS   →IN NN VBZ/D

where the parsers fails to capture the fact that prepositions only have one dependent.

Similarly, in the pattern: →CC NN NNS the parser fails to capture that only one phrase should attach to the coordinator, and the patterns

NN NN VBZ   NNS NNS VBP

highlight the parser's failing to capture that verbs have only one object.

In the structure ROOT WRB VBD , produced by the parser 15 times more than it appears in the language, the parser fails to capture the fact that verbs modified by wh-adverbs are not likely to head a sentence.

All of these over-produced structures are fine examples of cases where MST1 fails due to its edge-factorization assumption.

We now turn to analyzing the structures under-produced by MST1.

Under-produced structures The non-projective structures

WRB ← $\overset{1}{}$ VBN and WRB ← $\overset{1}{}$ VB

clearly cannot be produced by the projective parser, yet they appear over 100 times in the language.

The structure WRB←VBD←VBD which is represented in the language five times more than in the parser, complements the over-produced case in which a verb modified by a wh-adverb heads the sentence.

IN/*that*←, which was under-produced by ARCE is under-produced here also, but less so than in ARCE. →\$→RB is also under-produced by the parser.

The structure CC$\overset{\leftarrow}{_1}$, usually due to conjunctions such as *either*, *nor*, *but* is produced 29 times by the parser and appear 54 times in the language.

An interesting under-produced structure is →NN IN CC NN . This structure reflects the fact that the parser is having a hard time coordinating "heavy" NPs, where the head nouns are modified by PPs. This bias is probably a result of the "in-between pos-tag" feature, which lists all the pos-tags between the head and dependent. This feature was shown to be important to the parser's overall performance, but probably fails it in this case.

The construction $\overrightarrow{_{6-8}}$JJ, where the adjective functions as an adverb (*e.g.*, "he survived X *unscathed*" or "to impose Y *corporate-wise*") is also under-produced by the parser, as well as IN ← NN in which the preposition functions as a determiner/quantifier ("*at* least", "*between*", "more *than*").

Finally, MST1 is under-producing NPs with somewhat "irregular" structures: JJ←NN←NNS or JJ←NN←NNS ("*common stock* purchase *warrants*", "*cardiac bypass patients*"), or JJ←JJ← ("a *good many* short-sellers", "*West German* insurance giant")

5.2 Biases of Second-order MST Parser

Over-produced structures by MST2 are different than those of MST1. The less-extreme edge factorization of the second-order parser successfully prevents the structures where a verb has two objects or a preposition has two dependents.

One over-produced structure, NNS JJ NNP , , , produced 10 times by the parser and never in the language, is due to one very specific construction, "*bonds due Nov 30 , 1992 ,*" where the second comma should attach higher up the tree.

Another over-produced structure involves the internal structure of proper names: NNP NNP NNP NNP (the "correct" analysis more often makes the last NNP head of all the others).

More interesting are: $\xrightarrow[1]{}$CC→VBD and $\xrightarrow[1]{}$CC→NN→IN . These capture the parser's inability to capture the symmetry of coordinating conjunctions.

Under-produced structures of MST2 are overall very similar to the under-produced structures of MST1.

The structure CC$\xleftarrow[1]{}$ which is under-produced by MST1 is no longer under-produced by MST2. All the other under-produced structures of MST1 reappear here as well.

In addition, MST2 under-produces the structures ROOT→NNP→. (it tends not to trust NNPs as the head of sentences) and $\xrightarrow[6-8]{}$TO$\xrightarrow[1]{}VB$ (where the parser is having trouble attaching TO correctly to its parent when they are separated by a lot of sentential material).

6 Discussion

We showed that each of the four parsing systems is structurally biased with respect to the English training corpus in a noticeable way: we were able to learn a classifier that can tell, based on structural evidence, if a parse came from a parsing system or from the training corpus, with various success rates. More importantly, the classifier's models are interpretable. By analyzing the predictors induced by the classifier for each parsing system, we uncovered some of the biases of these systems.

Some of these biases (*e.g.*, that transition-based system have lower ROOT-attachment accuracies) were already known. Yet, our analysis refines this knowledge and demonstrates that in the Arc-Eager system a large part of this inaccuracy is not due to finding the incorrect root among valid ambiguous candidates, but rather due to many illegal root attachments, or due to illegal structures where a sentence is analyzed to have two main verbs. In contrast, the Arc-Standard system does not share this spurious root attachment behaviour, and its low root accuracies are due to incorrectly choosing among the valid candidates. A related bias of the Arc-Standard system is its tendency to choose earlier appearing verbs as parents of later occurring verbs.

Some constructions were hard for all the parsing models. For example, While not discussed in the analysis above, all parsers had biased structures containing discourse level punctuation elements (some commas, quotes and dashes) – we strongly believe parsing systems could benefit from special treatment of such markers.

The NP construction (JJ←NN←NNS←) appeared in the analyses of all the parsers, yet were easier for the transition-based parsers than for the graph-based ones. Other NP constructions (discussed above) were hard only for the graph-based parsers.

One specific construction involving the dollar sign and an adverb appeared in all the parsers, and may deserve a special treatment. Similarly, different parsers have different "soft spots" (*e.g.*, "backed away from", "not unexpected" for ARCE, "at least" for MST1, TO← for ARCS, etc.) which may also benefit from special treatments.

It is well known that the first-order edge-factorization of the MST1 parser is too strong. Our analysis reveals some specific cases where this assumptions indeed breaks down. These cases do not appear in the second-order factorization. Yet we show that the second-order model under-produces the same structures as the first-order model, and that both models have specific problems in dealing with coordination structures, specifically coordination of NPs containing PPs. We hypothesize that this bias is due to the "pos-in-between" features used in the MST Parser.

Regarding coordination, the analysis reveals that different parsers show different biases with respect to coordination structures.

7 Conclusions and Future Work

We presented the notion of *structural bias* – specific structures that are systematically over- or under- represented in one set of parse trees relative to another set of parse trees – and argue that different parsing systems exhibit different structural biases in the parses they produced due to various explicit and implicit decisions in parser design. We presented a method for uncovering some of this structural bias, and effectively used it to demonstrate that parsers are indeed biased with respect to the corpus they are trained on, and that different parsers show different biases. We then analyzed the biases of four dependency parsing systems with respect to an English treebank. We argue that by studying the structural biases of parsing systems we can gain a better understanding on where dependency parsers fail, and how they differ from each other. This understanding can in turn lead us toward designing better parsing systems.

We feel that the current study is just the tip of the iceberg with respect to the analysis of structural bias. Any parsing system for any language and annotation scheme can benefit from such analysis.

References

Sabine Buchholz and Erwin Marsi. 2006. CoNLL-X shared task on multilingual dependency parsing. In *Proc. of CoNLL*.

Markus Dickinson. 2010. Detecting errors in automatically-parsed dependency relations. In *Proc. of ACL*.

Liang Huang, Wenbin Jiang, and Qun Liu. 2009. Bilingually-constrained (monolingual) shift-reduce parsing. In *Proc of EMNLP*.

Richard Johansson and Pierre Nugues. 2007. Extended constituent-to-dependency conversion for english. In *Proc of NODALIDA*.

Richard Johansson. 2008. *Dependency-based Semantic Analysis of Natural-language Text*. Ph.D. thesis, Lund University.

Taku Kudo and Yuji Matsumoto. 2004. A Boosting Algorithm for Classification of Semi-Structured Text. In *Proceedings of EMNLP*.

Mitchell P. Marcus, Beatrice Santorini, and Mary Ann Marchinkiewicz. 1993. Building a large annotated corpus of English: The penn treebank. *Computational Linguistics*, 19:313–330.

Ryan McDonald and Joakim Nivre. 2007. Characterizing the errors of data-driven dependency parsing models. In *Proc. of EMNLP*.

Ryan McDonald and Fernando Pereira. 2006. Online learning of approximate dependency parsing algorithms. In *Proc of EACL*.

Ryan McDonald, Koby Crammer, and Fernando Pereira. 2005. Online large-margin training of dependency parsers. In *Proc of ACL*.

Ryan McDonald. 2006. *Discriminative Training and Spanning Tree Algorithms for Dependency Parsing*. Ph.D. thesis, University of Pennsylvania.

Joakim Nivre and Ryan McDonald. 2008. Integrating graph-based and transition-based dependency parsers. In *Proceedings of ACL*, pages 950–958.

Joakim Nivre, Johan Hall, and Jens Nillson. 2006. MaltParser: A data-driven parser-generator for dependency parsing. In *Proc. of LREC*.

Joakim Nivre, Johan Hall, Sandra Kübler, Ryan Mcdonald, Jens Nilsson, Sebastian Riedel, and Deniz Yuret. 2007. The CoNLL 2007 shared task on dependency parsing. In *Proc. of EMNLP-CoNLL*.

Joakim Nivre. 2004. Incrementality in deterministic dependency parsing. In *Incremental Parsing: Bringing Engineering and Cognition Together, ACL-Workshop*.

Joakim Nivre. 2008. Algorithms for deterministic incremental dependency parsing. *Computational Linguistics*, 34(4), December.

Owen Rambow. 2010. The Simple Truth about Dependency and Phrase Structure Representations: An Opinion Piece. In *Proceedings of NAACL*.

Kenji Sagae and Alon Lavie. 2006. Parser combination by reparsing. In *Proceedings of HLT-NAACL*, pages 129–133.

Author Index

Association for Computational Linguistics
209 N. Eighth Street
Stroudsburg, Pennsylvania 18360

CURRAN ASSOCIATES INC
proceedings.com